Pronunciation Guide

The diacritical marks used are standard for Indic transcription. Anyone can pronounce most of the words by following three basic rules:

1) Vowels are pronounced as in Latin and are long where so indicated, as in these examples:

a	bun	ā	barn
e	Ben	ē	bane
i	bin	ī	bean
o	bon	ō	bone
u	book	ū	boon
	ai	aisle	
	au	cow	

In Hindī and in some other North Indian languages *e* and *o* are inherently long but *ai* and *au* tend toward short *e* and *o*. The broad American *a*, as in *ban*, is not found (except in Sinhala, where it is transcribed as *ä* and *ä̈*), and readers who wish to avoid the clearest example of an American accent should be careful *not* to pronounce the first syllable of Pākistān like *pack*, nor Harijan like *Harry*.

2) A series of consonants called retroflex are pronounced with the

tongue touching the palate farther back than with the corresponding English consonants; these are written with a dot under them: *ṭ, ṭh, ḍ, ḍh, ṇ, ḷ, ṣ*. But in this book *ṣ* is generally written *sh*. The *ś* is intermediate between the *s* and the *sh*, merging with the former in the South and the latter in the North. The second most common American mispronunciation is of *t* and *d*, which are *not* pronounced as in English but are dental consonants, said with the tongue placed just behind the front teeth, and clearly contrasting with *ṭ* and *ḍ*. The *r* is always trilled in South Asia, and *ṛ* is pronounced something like *ḍ*. Tamil has an *ḻ* pronounced between *ḷ* and the English *r* (often popularly transcribed as *zh*). Persian and Urdū have *x, f, z, ḳ,* and *ġ*, the last two being rough gutteral sounds.

3) Consonants followed by *h* in transcription (except *sh*) are aspirated; that is, pronounced with a little puff of air. Therefore *th*, *ṭh* and *ph* should *not* be pronounced as in English but are aspirated forms of *t*, *ṭ*, and *p*.

Table 0–1 lists all the phonemes. In this book diacritical marks are generally left off names of countries and living people but are inserted in other South Asian terms and names, as otherwise many would be pronounced in an unrecognizable way. The names of some cities and states have become accepted in garbled English spelling, as Calcutta, Mysore, Colombo, Lahore, Assam, and we retain many of these. In this book South Asian terms are italicized only the first time employed; a glossary is combined with the index.

C. M.

Contents

Maps

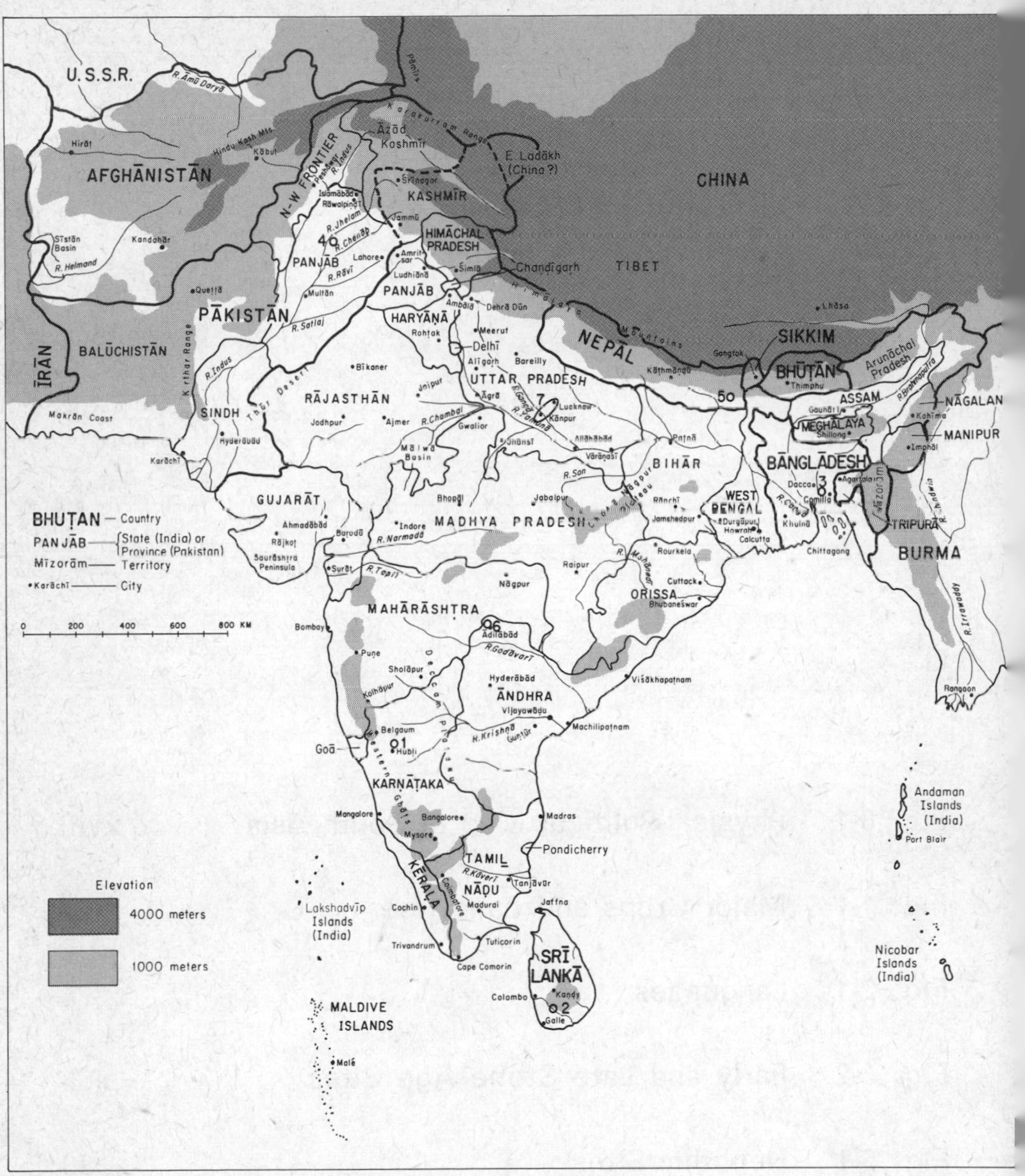

Fig. 0–1 Physical-Political Map of South Asia.

Table 0–1 South Asian Countries and States with Languages and Populations

Country	*Language*	*1971 Population (millions)*
India		548
Northern and Central States		
Uttar Pradesh	Hindī	88.4
Bihār	Hindī, some tribal	56.3
Madhya Pradesh	Hindī, some tribal	41.7
Haryāṇā (formerly part of Panjāb)	Hindī	10.0
Panjāb	Panjābī	13.5
Western States		
Rājasthān	Hindī	25.7
Gujarāt	Gujarātī	26.7
Mahārāshṭra	Marāṭhī	50.3
Eastern Plains States		
West Bengal	Bāngālī	44.4
Orissa	Uṛiyā, some tribal	21.9
Assam	Assamese	15.0
Southern States		
Āndhra Pradesh	Telugu	43.4
Tamil̠ Nāḍu (formerly Madras)	Tamil̠	41.1
Karṇāṭaka (formerly Mysore)	Kannaḍa	29.3
Kēraḷa	Malayāḷam	21.3
Himālayan States		
Jammū and Kashmīr	Kashmīrī, Ḍogrī	4.6
Himāchal Pradesh	Hindī, Pahāṛī	3.4
Eastern Hill States		
Tripurā	Tripurī, other tribal	1.6
Maṇipur	Maṇipurī, tribal	1.1
Meghālaya (formerly part of Assam)	Khāsi, Gāro	1.0
Nāgaland	Nāga languages	.5
Territories		
Arunāchal Pradesh (formerly N-E Frontier)	various tribal	.4
Mīzorām (formerly part of Assam)	Mīzo	.4
Delhī	Hindī	4.0
Chaṇḍīgaṛh	Panjābī	.3
Goā (formerly Portuguese)	Konkaṇī	.9
Pondicherry (formerly French)	Tamil̠	.5
Andaman and Nicobar Islands	various Indian, Hindī	.1
Lakshadvīp (Laccadive Islands)	Malayāḷam	.03
Pākistān	(1972)	64.9
Panjāb Province	Panjābī, Urdū	37.7
Sindh Province	Sindhī, Urdū	13.9
N-W Frontier Province, and Tribal Areas	Pashto	10.9
Balūchistān Province	Balūchī, Brāhūī	2.4
Bānglādesh	Bāngālī, some tribal	70
Afghānistān	Persian, Pashto, Uzbek, Turkoman	17
Srī Lankā (formerly Ceylon)	Sinhala, Tamil̠	12.7
Nepāl	Nepālī, various Himālayan	12
Bhūṭān	Lhoke, other Himālayan	1
Sikkim	Bhoṭiyā, Nepālī	.2
Maldive Islands	Maldivian	.1
Mauritius	various Indian, Creole	.8

Peoples of South Asia

1

The Land

The culture and civilization of the Indian subcontinent has been nurtured in the warm bosom of its plains, sheltered from the cold world of the north by the Himālayan massif, bathed and assuaged by its monsoon showers, and fed by its alluvial soils and forest-clad hills.

This world-island the ancients called Bhārata. Its philosophers knew the bounds of their world. Its northernmost kingdom was Kashmīr, and atop of the center of the world's land mass on Mount Meru sat Lord Śiva, spouting forth the Gangā (Ganges) waters from his head. The southernmost kingdom was Śrī Lankā (Ceylon), on a pearly island, while at the extremity of the peninsula at Cape Comorin the waters of three oceans mingled, guarded by a sacred Virgin. The south was the realm of Yama, God of Death. The easternmost region was Assam, and beyond it were tiger-infested hills occupied by aborigines, into which no plainsman would dare enter. But Sūrya the Sun commenced his daily sojourn from those regions. Beyond the westernmost plains in Panjāb were the hills inhabited by Afghāns and Turks who respected neither the men nor the gods of Bhārata. Encompassing this world-island on three sides were the oceans, where lived the Nāga water spirits.

This kindly land nurtured a kindly civilization which no ancient

traveler could have mistaken for the great civilizations surrounding it: Persia to the west, Central Asia to the north, Tibet on the high plateau, the world of China to the northeast, and the civilizations of Burma and further Southeast Asia on the east. These were all kept at bay by the two arms of the ocean stretching northward, which met and clasped the two mountainous arms extending from either end of the Himālayas southward to the coasts. In this hearth Indian culture fed upon itself, warm and protected.

Nevertheless from time to time outsiders were attracted to Bhārata, and they came in increasing numbers, first by land and then by sea. The passes from the west through Afghānistān and down to the Indus traverse precipitous and very arid terrain. Still, intruders entered and fanned out over the western plains of the subcontinent, bringing important cultural innovations: early and later stone tools, then agriculture, metallurgy, writing, stone masonry, and Islamic faith. And on the eastern side over the rough and forested hills came an important horticultural complex from Southeast Asia. Gradually the barrier of the ocean became a highway, beginning 4000 years ago and increasing in intensity with classical Indian civilization, the Arabs, the Portuguese, and the British, so that the whole perimeter of the peninsula experienced repeated cultural cross-fertilization.

This is not to say that South Asia has always received and never given. Indian civilization was extended to every coastal part of Southeast Asia, providing the basic civilizational underpinning on that subcontinent. Moreover with Buddhist expansionism Indian civilization pervaded Afghanistan and Central Asia, with elements affecting Tibet and China. It also contributed a number of features to the Arab world and to Europe, ranging from mathematical ideas and asceticism to textile techniques.

Yet the Indian subcontinent has remained, because of its geography, civilizationally distinct from Europe and the Arab world, and from China with which it has hardly anything in common. It is one of the half dozen major world culture areas.

Surface Features

The great tabular block which forms the Indian peninsula is geologically and paleontologically connected with East Africa. As continental masses were drifting, this Archaean block separated from Africa, leaving Madagascar on the side, and pushed up against the rest of Asia, resulting in the eruption of the Himālayas (pronounced Himā'layas). These mountains and their extensions form an extremely complex geological system; fringing them to the south in India and Nepāl are parallel lesser ranges, while to the west the lofty Karakurram and the Hindū Kash range extending into Afghanistan block off Pakistan from Central Asia. Lesser ranges extend southward through Balūchistān, the western lobe of Pākistān, to the sea. On the east

the Himālayas merge into the hill parts of Southeast Asia and southwestern China; a series of parallel north-south ranges effectively block off communication between eastern India and Burma. Hence Burma belongs to the Southeast Asia culture area.

The Himālayas seem to be still rising and expanding laterally. There are periodic earthquakes in Assam and elsewhere in this mountainous zone; major rivers have captured each other or changed direction of flow. Here and there are basins of surpassing beauty, such as the Vale of Kashmīr and the central valleys of Nepal and Bhūṭān. But for the people of the vast Indian plains, the Himālayas are more than a thing of beauty; they are the center of the cosmos.

Between the Himālayas and the peninsular block are alluvial soils extending in a great arc from the Arabian Sea to the Bay of Bengal, laid down by the riverine systems only in the last few million years. This alluvium measures 6500 feet deep in places, and the underlying rock is still being depressed as more is deposited. The runoff from the Himālayas coalesces in three vast systems: seven tributaries draining the western side and the Hindū Kash merge to form the Indus River; all those from the central Himālayas plus drainage from the central Indian uplands flow into the Gangā; waters from Tibet form the Brahmaputra which flows eastward for 600 miles before it finally breaks through the eastern Himālayas into Assam. Both the Indus and the Gangā carry an estimated million tons of suspended matter daily and the Brahmaputra brings even more. The wide plains of Bānglā (Bengal) were formed by the alluvium brought by the Gangā and the Brahmaputra, which today merge in a morass of waters in Bāngladesh. These three great riverine systems flow perennially, fed by the Himālayan snows. It is not surprising that the Indus plain nurtured South Asia's first civilization and that the Gangā plain gave rise to its classical phase.

A series of hills across central India naturally formed a barrier between the cultures of the northern arc of plains and those of the peninsula. The Vindhyās and other ranges extend from Gujarāt across Madhya Pradesh to western Orissa and southern Bihār, where the uplands are known as Choṭā Nāgpur. On the west, the Indus plain is separated from the peninsula by the Arāvalī Hills in the state of Rājasthān.

The best known geological feature of the peninsula is the Deccan Plateau, extending from the Vindhyās to the southern boundary of the state of Karṇāṭaka (formerly known as Mysore). On the western flank of this plateau is a chain of hills running all the way from Gujarāt to Cape Comorin at the tip of the peninsula; these are known as the Western Ghāṭs, and range in height from 3000 or 4000 feet in the north to peaks above 8000 feet in the south. Isolated by the Western Ghāṭs is a narrow but important coastal strip extending from Bombay to the Cape. A series of scattered hills in the state of Āndhra which rise to above 8000 feet in Orissa are called the

Eastern Ghāṭs. Southeast of the Deccan Plateau is the broad peneplain that forms the state of Tamil̠ Nāḍu. Separated by only 20 miles of shallows is the luxuriant isle of Sri Lanka, its high central hills being the end point of the Western Ghāṭs.

Since the great rocky block which forms the peninsula is tilted up on the western side, most of the rivers run into the Bay of Bengal. Four of these are major rivers which have produced alluvial plains and deltas, forming nucleii for culture zones within India: the Mahānadī for the plains of Orissa, the Godāvarī and the Krishṇā for the lowlands of Āndhra, and the Kāvēri for Tamil̠ Nāḍu. However, two large rivers, the Narmadā and the Taptī, flow eastward through the central Indian hills and cut through to the Arabian Sea in Gujarāt. Whereas the great rivers of the northern plains are perennial, these peninsular rivers are shallow and maturely graded, becoming almost dry in the hot season.

So intimately are the major culture zones within South Asia tied in with the major riverine systems and alluvial flatlands that the reader, even if he knew nothing of the cultural mosaic of South Asia, could easily spot on a map the location of the major cultural entities of the subcontinent; around and between them are the variegated populations of the uplands and the mountains.

Climate

Because of the Himālayan mountain arc the whole of South Asia is tropical, even though half of the subcontinent actually lies north of the Tropic of Cancer. The northern mountains block out the cold winds of Central Asia and keep South Asia all within the influence of the Indian Ocean. The monsoons, which are marked seasonal winds from the ocean, govern life to an extent not easily realized by people living in temperate climates. In the summer, beginning in June and lasting until September, the southwest monsoon blows from the southern Arabian Sea, watering the whole of the peninsula and the Gangā plains, and swinging up from the Bay of Bengal to the eastern Himālayas. Across the northern plains precipitation increases toward the east. In Pakistan at the city of Peshāwar on the western edge of the Indus plain, rainfall is 16 inches yearly; it is 20 in Panjāb state in India, 26 in Delhi, 39 in Allāhābād on the middle Gangā, 48 in Paṭnā in Bihār state, 62 in Calcutta, and 90 inches in eastern Bangladesh. The northern slopes of Assam get even more, and at Cirapūnjī in the little state of Meghālaya rainfall averages over 400 inches yearly! During the monsoons, cyclones frequently devastate the low-lying deltas around the Bay of Bengal, especially in Bangladesh, causing loss of life even to the extent of tens of thousands of people in a season.

The coastal strip from Bombay southward to the Cape receives abundant

rain, but inland in the Deccan Plateau annual rainfall is much less, averaging as little as 15 inches in places. The northwestern part of Sri Lanka is similarly in a rain shadow. But a second monsoon sweeps down from the Bay of Bengal in the late fall, blessing the eastern coasts of South India and Sri Lanka with rain for a second crop.

In Pakistan and Afghanistan precipitation decreases as one moves southward, so that only 5 to 10 inches falls in the lower Indus valley and in the Balūchistān hills. On the western side of the Indus, extending into the state of Rājasthān, is the Great Indian Desert, the Thār. Whatever monsoon winds would blow northward from the Arabian Sea tend to get deflected by a prevailing wind from southern Īrān, so that the whole of western South Asia tends to be arid.

In North India the hottest months are March to May, when foreign tourists stay home and the temperatures soar well above 100 degrees. Annoying dust storms envelop Rājasthān and Delhi. Even the rice fields of Bānglā become hard and cracked. But in winter it gets cool enough to use a couple blankets, and Kashmīr gets heavy snows. South India scarcely has any winter at all, and the dry months from January to June are hotter than the summer months. The British opened a number of hill resort towns, about 7000 feet high, in the Himālayas and in the southern Western Ghāṭs, to which the affluent can flee from the pre-monsoon heat. During the monsoon humidity is high, especially in the areas receiving almost continuous rains such as the eastern hilly zone, Kēraḷa, and Sri Lanka.

There are droughts or floods in some part of the subcontinent every year. The monsoon may come early or late or scarcely at all. Winds may flatten standing rice, or floods drown it out. Such vicissitudes must be considered as normal rather than abnormal in planning for food supplies. In past centuries they resulted in local famines, but the network of railroads constructed by the British alleviated these as a cause of death, so that when food shortages occur now a state or the whole country is affected. In 1971 a notable cyclone devastated the coast of Bangladesh, causing several hundred thousand deaths, and in 1973 floods drowned out many crop areas. In 1970-1972 in Afghanistan the most severe drought and famine known to its history produced numerous reported cases of human starvation, and half the animals of the country died, a severe blow to its economy. The country has no railroads and few roads, while administrative corruption impeded distribution of emergency food supplies. In 1972 South India and Pakistan got good rains, but all across western India from Rājasthān to Karṇāṭaka the drought was terrible, food was unavailable, and the Government ran out of buffer stocks. Performance of the whole economy dropped because of inflation, need to use foreign exchange to import food, and reduction of hydroelectric power which reduced electricity even in parts of India distant from the drought to a few hours a day. Life in South Asia is not so insulated from the environment as in Western countries.

In the United States there is a widespread but pernicious opinion that it is somehow unhealthy to live in the tropics. Such an opinion is no doubt fostered by an exaggerated idea of the noxious effects of insects, and by fear of cholera, smallpox, typhoid, and the like. Now there are few spasms of such diseases. If one is not overprotective he builds up resistance to the local intestinal microbes within a few weeks. It is a fact that British civil servants in India had a life expectancy as long as did their peers in England, and life expectancy in Sri Lanka today has approached that in European countries. Most people from Western countries, once they throw off superfluous dress items of North European origin such as socks, hose, shoes, coats, and ties, find they can easily become acclimated.

Soils and Crops

The same monotonous yellow-gray soil that clings to one's shoes on the Gangā plains extends westward as far as the Khyber Pass and eastward to the hills on the Burma border. These plains hold the greatest population because they are agriculturally the most responsive. The region called Panjāb (divided between India and Pakistan) is the breadbasket of South Asia because wheat is the main crop (Fig. 1–1). Canals built by the British opened up vast areas of the Panjāb to new settlement, and more canals have been built by the governments of Pakistan and India, utilizing the waters of the Indus which are divided between the two countries by treaty. This region, especially Panjāb state in India, has entered a new phase of prosperity because of doubled wheat yields since the mid-1960s. Wheat is the main crop as far east as middle Uttar Pradesh and is grown to some extent in Madhya Pradesh. In Sindh, the lower Indus region, rice is the main crop.

If the Panjāb is the breadbasket of South Asia, the eastern Gangā plains and Bānglā are the largest rice bowl. This region was probably forested in prehistoric times and was not heavily settled until the 1st millennium B.C. when iron tools became available. But these plains soon evolved a culture in tune with rice production, supported a dense population, and gave rise to India's first historic empires. River waters are available to flood the rice fields, but in Bānglā the monsoon rains are so abundant in most areas that natural flooding is sufficient. Except around the margins of the hills, these plains are all devoid of stones, and traditionally material culture has relied on the clayey soil and whatever vegetable matter grows in it. If stones are wanted, they have to be brought from the Himālayan foothills.

Other rice-growing alluvial regions are the coasts of Orissa and Āndhra, parts of Tamiḻ Nāḍu, the Sri Lanka lowlands, and the western coast along Kērala and coastal Karṇāṭaka; Āndhra is usually blessed with a surplus of

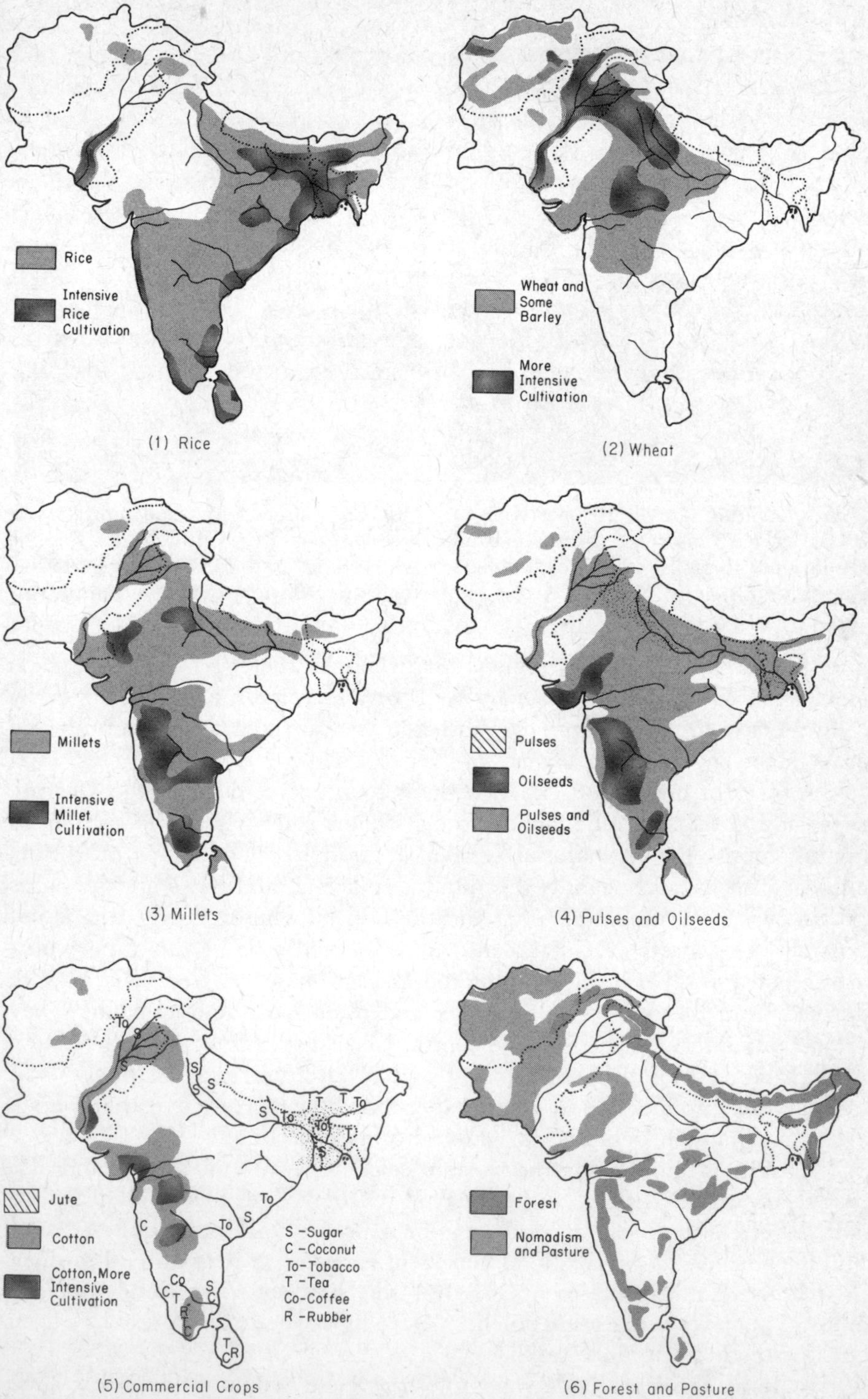
Rice
Intensive Rice Cultivation
(1) Rice
Wheat and Some Barley
More Intensive Cultivation
(2) Wheat
Millets
Intensive Millet Cultivation
(3) Millets
Pulses
Oilseeds
Pulses and Oilseeds
(4) Pulses and Oilseeds
Jute
Cotton
Cotton, More Intensive Cultivation
S -Sugar
C -Coconut
To-Tobacco
T -Tea
Co-Coffee
R -Rubber
(5) Commercial Crops
Forest
Nomadism and Pasture
(6) Forest and Pasture

FIG. 1–1 Major crops and land use.

Hand-pounding gravel for roads in a Bihār town. Stones are brought from Himālayan foothills to these stoneless Gangā plains.

Crushing oilseeds in stone mortar with wooden pestle in Tamil̲ Nāḍu. Sesame seed oil is used for cooking; residue, for cattle. On left is village temple.

rice. Rice is grown in other regions too, wherever there is land that can be terraced and irrigated, whether by wells or reservoirs in South India, or by the waters of the major drainage basins in central India. It is the preferred crop in the midmontane valleys of Nepal too.

A black or brown soil called regur is found over much of the Deccan, especially in the state of Mahārāshṭra. Its black color is not due entirely to humus, for its parent material is lava. It produces good crops of cotton, millets, oilseeds, and peanuts if rainfall is sufficient, and these are the crops grown over most of central India and the Deccan wherever irrigation is not possible. The coasts of Gujarāt also have alluvial soils of this type which are responsive. Over large parts of the Deccan, however, red soils prevail, derived from the old crystalline rock and often loose and gravelly. They are notably infertile. Much of the central Deccan in Karṇāṭaka and western Āndhra consists of this reddish soil and in addition gets relatively little rainfall, thus producing only one meager crop a year. Here and there, however, are loams in depressions which are more productive.

Laterite is found along the western coast, especially in Kēraḷa, and also in Orissa. Strictly defined, it is a clayey red or yellow rock which can be easily sliced when wet but hardens upon exposure to the atmosphere; most buildings in Kēraḷa are made of blocks of it. Because it is an end-product of weathering and contains up to 30% iron, it is not very useful for agriculture, but over wide areas in the Kēraḷa hills where the forest has been cut it is made to produce tapioca.

In India farmers divide land into wet land (irrigated) and dry land. The three main wet land crops are rice, sugar cane, and jute. Sugar cane

is a commercial crop increasing in importance everywhere, but jute is grown primarily in Bānglā, which produces the world's supply. Most people in South Asia who do not raise rice or wheat subsist on millets of various kinds, including *jvār*, *bajṛā*, *rāgi*, and *varaku*, which are grown over a wider area than either rice or wheat. Two commercial crops of great importance in South Asia are oilseeds—required in quantity for the vast population to cook with—and cotton, in which India is deficient because the whole population uses it. Gujarāt is first in production of oilseeds and along with Mahārāshṭra produces much of the cotton; it is also widely grown in Pakistan. Pulses are an important category of crop, for they provide much of India's protein; there are many kinds, called *grām*, such as black grām, green grām, and Bengal grām. These may be grown as a second crop on rice land or dry land. Other crops which generally require irrigation are bananas (grown in a hundred varieties), chilies, and tomatoes. But most of the vegetables and tubers grown in South Asia are not at all familiar to Americans, and almost all the fruits are different.

In the mountains potatoes and some "English vegetables" are grown. Kashmīr produces apples. Of great importance to the South Asian countries are the commercial or plantation crops, grown on "estates." Tea is the most important such crop, grown all around Assam and in northern Bangladesh, in the hills of South India, and in the Sri Linka highlands. Coffee, cardamom, and rubber are important estate crops in the Western Ghāṭs of South India.

Man and the Environment

Geographers have long known that tropical soils, on the whole, are not as fertile as some people might imagine when they see pictures of luxuriant forest cover. If the forest is cut down the humus is rapidly destroyed by bacterial action and by decomposition in the high temperatures. Heavy seasonal rains leach the soils. There is a continuing process of eluviation, whereby the soluble materials and fine particles get carried below the surface, sometimes forming a hardpan, leaving a gritty, sandy, or loamy surface soil. Humus can accumulate only if there is forest or heavy grass cover, or if farmers add organic fertilizer seasonally. Farmers know how to make good compost by digging a pit and throwing in dung, straw, ashes, and kitchen refuse, and when full, covering it up to let it ripen. Nowadays they also apply bone meal and inorganic fertilizers to the fields.

The best way to maintain the fertility of the soil is to terrace and flood it and plant crops such as rice. The rice-cultivating peasant way of life is finely attuned to the ecosystem, and there is a symbiotic relationship between man, the cattle, and the land. The cattle live off rice straw and provide all the motive power for agriculture: plowing, threshing, grinding

oilseeds, pulling carts, and sometimes irrigating. They also provide milk and leather, and yield bones for use as fertilizer. The reason why India has 190 million cattle and 60 million buffaloes is not so much that they are sacred but that they are economically essential. The rice-cultivating way of life has long supported a very heavy population without depleting the resources. Perhaps, in a way, it has been too successful, for it is precisely the parts of South Asia where this economy prevails that today suffer the stifling effects of overpopulation while at the same time the people are so inured to the ecological system they are very conservative.

Throughout the western side of South Asia an increasing population has to be supported on arid or semiarid terrain, and the expansion of agriculture and grazing is having undesirable consequences. The Thār desert in Rājasthān seems to be expanding, while peasants are increasingly pressured to cultivate and graze animals on the margins of it. Whether or not the climate is getting dryer is a matter of dispute, but certainly these activities are not helping to stabilize the desert. Every two or three years the Government of India has to rush fodder to Rājasthān for cattle suffering in drought. The increasing number of people and animals living off the meager vegetation in the hills of Afghanistan and Balūchistān has caused erosion to proceed at an enhanced rate, so that the rivers are laden with sediment. Especially destructive are the sheep and goats, which crop the grass very short. Though only a sixth of the people of Afghanistan are nomads, the demands for sheepskin and similar products are increasing.

With the introduction of large-scale canal irrigation in the Panjāb after the 1860s, the deposition of salty encrustation became a problem, especially after Independence when more canals were built so there was less water available for proper flushing. In the 1950s in Pakistani Panjāb tens of thousands of acres a year were being taken out of production until a program to restore the soils was undertaken with United Nations assistance. In Sindh increased irrigation raised the water table so that continuous evaporation leaves salts on the surface, which affect not only agriculture but cause the disintegration of the ruins of the protohistoric city of Mohenjo-dāṛo. The same problem has been encountered in the Helmānd Valley Project of Afghanistan and elsewhere, and can be alleviated only if sufficient water is available for flushing and drainage is good.

Deforestation has been proceeding in South Asia in spite of the efforts of the various governments to set aside forest preserves. In central India hundreds of square miles have become exposed and barren, the reddish or sandy soil eroded by gullies and now unfit for cultivation. Secondary forest growth in most of central India never develops satisfactorily. Tribal people in the hills all around Assam and also in central India have traditionally practiced migratory or slash-and-burn cultivation, but the government is trying to curtail this practice which is wasteful in terms of the national economy. India still has considerable areas classified as "forests,"

Rice fields in Tamil̲ Nāḍu. After fertilizing, plowing, leveling, and repairing field dividers, seedlings are transplanted by hand. Only men handle the plow; in this area transplanting is the woman's work, but the man supervises.

with some good wood along the Western Ghāṭs and in parts of Madhya Pradesh and Orissa, but much of the reserved area consists only of scrub forest which is of scant commercial use. In India lumber has become very expensive, and woods such as teak and rosewood are not sufficient for the demand. Firewood is also in short supply, forcing people to burn cow dung

Frying savories in a Rājasthān roadside cafe. For lack of firewood, cow dung cakes (in basket) are used as fuel.

which should be used on the fields; many cannot afford wood even for cremation.

The Himālayan regions still have considerable forests, but they have been greatly reduced in the last few decades. The northern rim of the Gangā plains, a somewhat swampy area called the *tarāī*, has been opened up for habitation by malaria eradication, providing a new frontier for settlement in the Nepal lowlands. But around the populated valleys of the Nepal middle altitudes almost all trees have been cut, and firewood has to be brought in from many miles. Early in this century tree cutting in the Śiwālik mountains, a sub-Himālayan range along northwestern India, resulted in unexpected erosion and a declined water table, which affected nearby farmers. The Pakistan government is counting on the forest reserves of Chitrāl, its northernmost reaches, for national development, but in fact the forests of that region have little remaining commercial potential. In India scientific afforestation efforts are proceeding, but it is impossible to effectively patrol all the forest preserves.

Though some Westerners imagine that South Asia is full of game, it should be pointed out that the land is, in fact, full of people, not wild

animals. The national symbol of Nepal is the rhinoceros, but the country has fewer than 80 of these beasts left. Sri Lanka has only some 500 elephants in its forests. The population of famous Bengal tiger has decreased from 40,000 to 2000 in a generation.

Physical-Cultural Regions

South Asia, in size and population, is roughly comparable to the subcontinent of Europe. It has about the same number of cultural and linguistic regions, though with a greater variety of marginal peoples. The European subcontinent has some 26 countries, each with its own language for the most part and its own cultural identity. The South Asian subcontinent has India with 21 states, Pakistan with four provinces, and six other countries.

The difference between a person from Kēraḷa on the southwest coast and a Panjābī is about the same order of difference as that between a southern Italian and a Norwegian. The east-west differences in South Asia are even greater than in Europe because climatic variation is greater; hence the Paṭhān of the western hills of Pakistan is culturally farther removed from a Nāga tribesman on the Burma border than is an Irishman from a Latvian.

Remarkable as the cultural diversity within India is, one should think it even more remarkable that it has achieved, through the historical accident of colonialism, a political unity. Some people think of the cultural plurality of India as somehow a primitive feature, without stopping to think that Western Europe with an equal number of major ethnic entities has not been able to achieve the political unity India has under its federal system. It is a unique achievement in the world's history that a dozen major linguistic-cultural entities, each having 20 to 50 or more million people, plus many lesser linguistic-cultural entities, should manage to coexist under one central government without one region coercing the others.

The major cultural regions have become the states of India, the provinces of Pakistan, and to some extent the smaller countries of the subcontinent. Before pursuing the following survey of regions the reader is urged to consult the physical-political map (Fig. 0–1), the table of political entities (Table 0–1), and the language map (Fig. 2–1).

The Western Frontier and the Indus Plains

The lofty but narrow Hindū Kash range strikes southwestward from the Himālayas into the heart of Afghanistan. To the north the terrain drains into the Uzbek and Turkmen Republics of the Soviet Union, with which northern Afghanistan has cultural affinities. Western Afghanistan is geo-

graphically and culturally an extension of eastern Iran. But the southeastern half of the country may be considered part of South Asia in that it is linked with the Indus plains through the Kābul River, the Khyber Pass, and other passes to the south, and its people are Pathāns such as also inhabit Pakistan's North-West Frontier Province. Central Afghanistan is forbiddingly rugged and the southwestern part is desert; all of it is sparsely populated, with agriculture in valleys here and there and most of the land given over to grazing sheep and other animals. Ancient towns such as Kābul and Kandahār live by trade on the roads connecting Iran with India.

Balūchistān, the western lobe of Pakistan, is even more arid and very sparsely populated. The two largest tribal groups are the Balūchīs and Brāhūīs, and geographically Balūchistān spills over into southern Afghanistan and western Iran. At the juncture of the three countries is the Sīstān basin with a salty lake. The coast of Balūchistān, called the Makrān, is quite inhospitable. After Alexander the Great had conquered the Indus plains he led part of his army back across the Makrān coast but lost half his men from lack of food and water.

The Paṭhāns are the most recent of a long series of peoples who infiltrated from these hills down to the plains and impinged upon South Asia. The main routes have always been through the Khyber, Gomāl, and Bolān passes. In the 4th and 3d millennia B.C., neolithic cultures began to diffuse onto the Pakistan plains, to be followed in succeeding millennia by the main intrusive elements that have affected South Asian history, such as the Āryans, Achaemenian Persians, Greeks, Bactrian Greeks, Śakas (Scythians), Hūṇas (Huns), and several waves of Central Asian, Persian, and Afghān Muslim peoples. Also through these passes Indian civilization, especially Buddhism, expanded briefly during the Mauryan and Gupta periods into Afghanistan and Central Asia. In spite of this, the Afghān and Balūchistān hills are zones of isolation and cultural stagnation, as far as the mainstream South Asian cultures are concerned.

The Panjāb ("five rivers"), the plain drained by the major tributaries to the Indus, is now cut by the India-Pakistan border. The Indian part comprises the states of Panjāb and Haryāṇā, while the Pakistan part comprises Panjāb Province. This has historically been a zone of fusion of diverse intrusive elements with preexisting Indian cultures. It was the geographical focus of the Vedic age and the prize for which Persians, Greeks, Afghāns, and others came down from Afghanistan and fanned out over the plains. It has historically been a prosperous area and a prize for conquest. Even today its irrigated soils provide the largest part of South Asia's wheat, and its people are thought of as energetic.

Successive lines of movement from the Panjāb can be traced down the Indus to the Sindh region, which is a partial cul-de-sac with some historic overflow into western Gujarāt. Sindh lives by the Indus; its rainfall in the south is only four inches yearly, yet the soils by the river are

swampy in large areas. The middle Indus plain was the seat of the subcontinent's first urban culture, after which the Gangā plains became the heartland of Indian civilization for the rest of history.

On the whole, the Indus region is culturally and geographically the most distinct of the major plains regions of South Asia. The region's proximity to Arab, Persian, and Afghān influences, plus its scanty rainfall and the necessity to focus strongly on the Indus river system, gives it a distinct identity within the South Asian world. From the viewpoint of geography alone, apart from religious differences, it is not surprising that the Indus drainage region separated from India, and it is unlikely that Pakistanis will ever wish to be identified as Indians.

The Himālayan Arc

The submontane alluvial basins of the Western Himālayas, such as the Swāt Valley, Kohistān, and the Vale of Kashmīr, though cultural cul-de-sacs, have been settled by peasant peoples from the plains. Above these in Chitrāl, Baltistān, Gilgit, and the famed valley of Hunza are an assortment of relatively isolated peoples, but even these have almost all become Muslims. Contact with the outside world is increasing, for Pakistan and China have recently constructed a road rising 15,400 feet over the Karakurram range from Gilgit into Tibet.

Ladākh, the eastern lobe of Kashmīr, is on the Tibetan plateau. The higher reaches of the Indian states of Himāchal Pradesh and Uttar Pradesh and of Nepal are within the orbit of Tibetan civilization, as are most of Sikkim and Bhutan. The midmontane valleys of Nepal have provided a refuge for a number of distinctive peoples who have benefited from both Indian and Tibetan civilization. Nepal and Sikkim opened to the outside world in the 1950s. Bhutan opened up only in the 1960s, and though a member of the United Nations, is still relatively unknown. All along the Himālayas are charming vales of surpassing beauty, cupped by lofty ranges, with never-failing streams gushing through to the plains below. Most of these vales have had an influx of refugee populations from the plains and are more or less drawn into Indian civilization. Along the tarāī at the foot of the hills the people are not much different from the Hindī-speakers of the Uttar Pradesh plains.

If one were to draw lines on a map separating the cultural realms of South Asia, the boldest line would have to be drawn around the perimeter of the Assam plain and along the eastern edge of Bānglā. Beyond this the people of the eastern hills are Mongoloid in appearance and have cultural affinities with the people of the Burma hills and farther upland Southeast Asia. They engage in hoe cultivation and are called tribal, though today many of them are not at all primitive. These hill regions are divided into

four small states: Nāgaland, Meghālaya, Maṇipur, and Tripurā, of which the latter two have some Hinduized plains populations. In addition there are two Territories: Arunāchal Pradesh, north of the Assam Valley which has been the most isolated until the 1960s, and Mīzorām, a hilly area extending southward from Assam.

The Northern and Eastern Plains

The imperceptible watershed between the Indus and the Gangā riverine systems runs through Haryāṇā and Rājasthān. The tongue of land between the Gangā and its major tributary, the Yamunā, is called the *Doāb* (two rivers), and this region, mostly in western Uttar Pradesh, has historically been a zone of cultural synthesis and conflict. This is where the Mahābhārata War of epic tradition was fought. It is only natural that the Mughals, the British, and the Indians established their successive capitals here at Delhi. At the end of the Doāb at the confluence of the rivers is the ancient and sacred city of Allāhābād.

Eastern Uttar Pradesh, beyond Allāhābād, together with northern Bihār form the middle Gangā plain, a vast and fertile rice-growing region with a featureless surface. Countless kingdoms have expanded from these plains, only to contract back into them, while peasants continued to be governed more by the rhythm of the monsoons than by kings. Today this region has lost its civilizational dynamism and is regarded as conservative, typified by the sacred city of Vārāṇasī (Banares). It is characterized by overpopulation, unemployment, and an excess of cattle.

A constriction in the Gangā plains is caused by the protrusion northward of the Choṭā Nāgpur plateau, east of which is the wide alluvial region of Bānglā (Bengal), where the waters of the Gangā and the Brahmaputra mix with lesser rivers and make their way southward to the sea. This stoneless and featureless plain 250 miles wide has produced a distinctive cultural identity of its own, but has nevertheless been influenced by the successive cultural waves that pulsed down the Gangā. The distinctiveness of Bānglā is symbolized in the Bāngālī language. Although the plain is divided between the Indian state of West Bengal and the nation of Bangladesh, the region is relatively homogeneous except that one is predominantly Hindu and the other Muslim. The urban complex of Calcutta dominates West Bengal. In all parts rice is cultivated, generally with natural monsoon flooding and perhaps with pump irrigation for a second or third crop. A truly dense population is supported, about 1300 per square mile, and the level of subsistence is very low. There are virtually no resources on this plain except what can be grown.

Attached to the Bānglā plain is the 400-mile-long Assam Valley, formed

Banks of the Gangā; a sādhu (holy man) at Banares.

Bangladesh in the monsoon. Fields flood naturally and boats move over them to transport grain.

by the Brahmaputra, which has a culture and ecology similar to those of Bānglā. To the southwest is the coast of Orissa, centered in the Mahānadī delta, which has developed its own linguistic and cultural identity.

Western and Central India

Rājasthān is India's only desert state. Peasants who try to eke out a living in the western parts have to have very large farms, and then are sometimes overwhelmed by dust or drought. This region has produced the Māṛwāṛīs, merchants who have found an easier way to earn a living than by scratching the sandy soil, and they have set up shops all over India. The eastern half of Rājasthān, east of the Arāvalī Hills, is part of a large basin called Mālwā where satisfactory agriculture is possible, though usually unirrigated. It is culturally an extension of the Hindī-speaking northern plains region.

Gujarāt appears on the map to consist of three parts, but it has a cultural unity because it is bounded by the desert on the north and by the Vindhyās and Western Ghāṭs on the east. Though in a sense it comprises a zone of isolation from the mainstream of Indian culture, it has ever been a transition area between India and lands to the west. Prehistoric and historic intrusions from Sindh have come overland, and the indentations of the coast combined with its proximity to the Near East have made Gujarāt the focus of Indian shipping for four millennia. Moreover it exports crops

and products in demand in the arid Near East, especially its woods, gems, oilseeds, and cotton. But while there are many Gujarātī capitalists who are both industrious and politically conservative, the majority of the people here too are peasants. An interesting physical feature of Gujarāt is the Rann of Kacch, an immense low-lying area which becomes a swamp in the rainy season. The central peninsula of Gujarāt is called Kāṭhiāwāṛ.

Mahārāshṭra occupies the northern Deccan Plateau, with a long eastward extension into central India and a coastal strip stretching southward from Bombay. Its boundary with Āndhra is a natural one, coinciding with the line where the black Deccan regur ends and the red soils begin. Most historic influences reaching South India diffused down the Deccan, and apart from the Western Ghāṭs most of it has not been heavily forested. Mahārāshṭra spawned the kingdom of the Marāṭhās which held out against the Muslim Mughal rulers of Delhi. But after the British founded Bombay and made it into India's greatest port, the region began to look coastward, and the whole of it is now stimulated by the industry and commerce generated by that city.

The state of Madhya Pradesh occupies the largest part of central India. North-south traffic is impeded by the Vindhyā and Śatpurā hills and by the valleys of the Narmadā and Taptī rivers. Most of the hills in Madhya Pradesh and southern Bihār are not over 2000 feet, but some relics rise to 3600 feet. The whole central Indian massif has been a zone of very slow penetration. Its outlines coincide with the central Indian tribal belt in general. The main tribal concentrations are in southern Bihār, western Orissa, and eastern Madhya Pradesh, especially the southward-projecting finger of the state called Bastar. But Hindī-speaking peoples from the northern plains have gradually penetrated central India, settling in the major riverine basins such as Mālwā on the west, the Bundelkhaṇḍ valley which is drained by the northward-flowing Son River, the long Narmadā Valley, and the Chattīsgaṛh basin on the upper Mahānadī. Besides Hindī-speakers, peasants from other linguistic groups have moved into the fringes of central India, coming from Gujarāt, Mahārāshṭra, Āndhra, Orissa, and Bānglā. This whole zone lacks a geographical or cultural epicenter.

The Southern Peninsula and the Islands

The four South Indian states are recognized as distinct because they speak Dravidian languages and are different from the North in kinship systems, food, and to some extent, dress, though they also have been drawn into Indian civilization. Āndhra is the largest, a Telugu-speaking state having as its epicenter the twin deltas of the Godāvarī and the Krishṇā which produce much rice. The northwestern part of the state, known as Telengāna, is on the Deccan Plateau and its reddish soils are not particu-

larly fertile; the main crops are millets, pulses, and oilseeds. The southwestern part of Āndhra is rather dry and poor.

Karṇāṭaka (formerly called Mysore) occupies the southwestern Deccan, and parts of it are rather dry, though in the south there is some irrigation. The boundary between Mahārāshṭra and Karṇāṭaka is not marked by any natural features and historically Marāṭhīs have been impinging on the Dravidian-speaking South here. The formation of linguistic states has probably stopped this. The coast of Karṇāṭaka is rice-growing and is geographically similar to Kēraḷa to the south. North of coastal Karṇāṭaka is the former Portuguese colony of Goā, now an Indian Territory.

Tamiḻ Nāḍu (formerly called Madras State) has Tamiḻ as its language and has well-defined natural boundaries. Its epicenter is the Kāvēri plain and delta, though there is rice cultivation elsewhere along the coasts. But rivers are mostly seasonal, and farmers rely upon "tanks" (reservoirs) and subsurface water for irrigation; in the unirrigated regions millets, pulses, and oilseeds are grown. The state is naturally flanked along the west by the Western Ghāṭs which here rise to 9000 feet, and on the northwest by the escarpment of the Deccan Plateau. Geographically and linguistically distinct, this region has asserted a political self-identity within India.

Kēraḷa, where Malayāḷam is spoken, has a number of unique features. A littoral originally covered with rain forest, it has been a zone of isolation accessible mostly through the Palghat Gap from Tamiḻ Nāḍu or around the southern end of the Western Ghāṭs. The narrow coastal strip produces rice and coconuts and supports an exceedingly dense population, while in the undulating interior people are forced to rely on tapioca which they can coax from the lateritic soil. Forests and tea and rubber estates occupy the upper altitudes. Though isolated by land, Kēraḷa has been open to sea traffic, and its interesting indigenous cultural features have been modified by Brāhmaṇ, Christian, and Muslim influences which came by sea. High population and a high literacy rate, combined with a low level of industrial productivity, have caused severe problems in this state.

Sri Lanka (known as Ceylon until 1972) has a distinctive culture history growing out of its location. The 72% who are Buddhists speak Sinhala, a language derived from North India, for when peripeninsular sea traffic developed in the mid-first millennium B.C., the island was something of a frontier. The northern part is settled by Tamiḻs culturally like those of South India. Geologically the island is an extension of India, with a southwest coast much like Kēraḷa, hills to over 6000 feet, and a somewhat dry northern zone. Sri Lanka, located at the juncture of traffic lanes in the Indian Ocean, has been affected by the waves of every culture phase blown along the coasts of South Asia.

The Andaman and Nicobar Islands, across the Bay of Bengal, form an Indian Territory. The Andamans are sizable islands, and since the aboriginal population is almost extinct, are being settled by immigrants

Salt for 100 million households. Sea water is evaporated in an old river channel.

from India. The islands have wooded hills and provide an important base for the Indian Navy.

The Maldive Islands, to the southwest of Sri Lanka, are coral atolls having no resources except fish and coconuts. The Maldives are now an independent country. The original settlers were apparently like the people of Sri Lanka, and they all became Muslims long ago.

Mauritius is closer to Madagascar than to India, but we include it with South Asia because the majority of its people are of Indian origin. The island is an independent country. Its dense population is supported by the export of sugar, grown on its soil of volcanic origin.

IMPORTANT SOURCES

Crane, Robert (ed.). *Regions and Regionalism in South Asian Studies: An Exploratory Study*. Durham, N.C., 1966. (A useful symposium.)

Eberhard, Wolfram. *Settlement and Social Change in Asia*. Hong Kong, 1967. (Has a useful section on settlements in Pakistan.)

Government of India. *Census of India, 1961. Census Atlas*, Part IX. New Delhi, 1970. (A hefty synthesis of census data with considerable information on economic geography.)

Karen, Pradyuma. *Nepal: A Cultural and Physical Geography*. Lexington, Ky., 1960.

Misra, S. D. *Rivers of India*. New Delhi, 1970.

Raychaudhuni, S. P. *Land and Soil*. New Delhi, 1966.

Robinson, Harry. *Monsoon Asia: A Geographical Survey*. New York, 1967.

Schwartzberg, Joseph. *Historical Atlas of India*. New York, in press. (An exhaustive compendium based on sources ranging from classical literature to census data.)

Spate, O. K. H. *India and Pakistan, A General and Regional Geography*, 2d ed. New York, 1957. (The standard work; includes a chapter on Sri Lanka.)

Spencer, J. E., and William L. Thomas. *Asia, East by South: A Cultural Geography*. New York, 1971. (A text, with a section on South Asia.)

Stamp, K. Dudley. *Asia: A Regional and Economic Geography*, 11th ed. New York, 1962. (The basic format is now outdated.)

Subbarao, B. *The Personality of India*, 2d ed. Baroda, 1958. (A geographically oriented archeological survey, useful though the archeological data is outdated.)

2

The Languages

No part of the world affords more opportunity for the study of anthropological linguistics than does South Asia. Here we have at least five distinct linguistic phyla, some of which comprise several linguistic families. There are about 20 major literary languages, each spoken by many millions of people, plus some 150 languages of lesser importance preserved largely in tribal areas. These languages also have several hundred dialects. But its linguistics differs from that of Africa, for instance, for in South Asia there are vast literary resources available for the study of language change; they give us knowledge of Indo-Āryan speech for over three millennia and Dravidian speech for over two millennia.

But the language picture is not chaotic, for the number of major literary languages is about the same as the number in Europe, and in fact 97% of the people of South Asia speak one of these major languages. Moreover, the superimposition of Indian civilization has tempered the diversity of these tongues.

The American who has not traveled outside his homeland which is characterized by mass culture can seldom appreciate the importance of language as a symbol of one's culture and as the vehicle of its transmission. It is imperative that the social scientist who wishes to pursue the study of

South Asia master at least one of the important languages in both its vernacular and literary varieties, or he will certainly misconstrue the opinions of the 2% English-knowing elite as representative of the whole population. Anthropologists in particular must be committed to the use of linguistics in coming to understand contemporary and past cultures as well as culture dynamics. In India, Pakistan, and Sri Lanka no issues since Independence have appeared on the surface more frequently or have produced more excitability or more letters to newspaper editors than language policies. Some of the sociological implications of these problems will be reviewed in Chapter 9, Sociolinguistics.

The Linguistic Map

The most important linguistic family in South Asia is the Indo-Āryan, which is part of the Indo-European phylum of languages. This group contains most of the major literary languages of North India and Pakistan, including Sanskrit. The second linguistic phylum is the Dravidian, comprised of four major literary languages of South India as well as about 18 other unwritten languages used in restricted areas. Dravidian languages are spoken by about 140 million people and are not genetically related to the Indo-European nor to any other linguistic group in the world. The third language category consists of Muṇḍa languages, of which there are over a dozen spoken in tribal areas of Orissa, southern Bihār, and neighboring regions. Some 8 million people speak these tongues, which are genetically connected with the Mon-Khmer (Austroasiatic) linguistic phylum of Southeast Asia. The fourth category comprises the Tibeto-Burmese family of Sino-Tibetan languages; these are spoken in the Himālayan belt and in the hill regions around Assam. The fifth linguistic phylum is represented by one existing lanugage, Burushaski, a linguistic relic preserved in the isolated valley of Gilgit in Pakistani Kashmīr. Andamanese, of the Andaman Islands in the Bay of Bengal, is also not related to any other linguistic group.

Since Independence the states of India have been redrawn, largely on linguistic considerations. There are 21 states; 6 are Hindī-speaking, 11 others are linguistic states, and 4 are eastern hill states whose languages are also increasing in prominence. Hindī is the official language of Uttar Pradesh, Madhya Pradesh, Bihār, Rājasthān, Haryāṇā, and Himāchal Pradesh, besides the territory of Delhi. Urdū is claimed as the distinct language of the majority of India's 62 million Muslims, but linguists consider this a variant of Hindī, with a script and some vocabulary derived from Persian and Arabic. The population of the Hindī-speaking states in 1971 was about 230 million; thus Hindī-Urdū ranks numerically as the fourth language in the world (after Mandarin, English, and Spanish), and though divided by several dialects is spoken by 42% of the people of India. Next in order

Railway station in northern Āndhra with sign in Hindī, English, Telugu, and Uṛiyā. In states with strong regional identity the order is: state language, Hindī, English.

within India are Bāngālī (West Bengal), Telugu (Āndhra) Marāṭhī (Mahārāshṭra), and Tamil̲ (Tamil̲, Nāḍu); each of these has over 40 million speakers. The other state languages are Gujarātī, Panjābī, Uṛiyā (Orissa), Assamese, Kashmīrī, Kannaḍa (Karṇāṭaka), and Malayāḷam (Kēraḷa). The languages of the eastern hill states are also becoming more widely used, though Assamese is a second language in some of these areas. In addition, Sindhī is recognized along the western border of India, and Sanskrit is recognized as one of the National Languages.

The state languages are recognized in the Constitution as National Languages, while Hindī is designated as the Official Language of the Central Government. English has temporary status as an adjunct Official Language, but in effect it remains dominant at higher administrative levels.

In Bangladesh Bāngālī is spoken everywhere except by some of the tribal people on the southeastern fringe. In Bangladesh and India there are 120 million Bāngālī speakers, so that this language ranks as sixth in the world (after Hindī and Russian).

In Pakistan the four provinces are defined linguistically. Panjābī is the vernacular everywhere in Panjāb, but Urdū is used for writing. Sindhī is the language of Sindh. Pashto prevails in the North-West Frontier Province, and Balūchī is the most important language of Balūchistān. In the northern Himālayan regions there are languages of the Dardic family of Indo-European speech, and also Burushaski in a limited region. One Dravidian language, Brāhūī, is spoken in a considerable part of eastern Balūchistān. The Pakistani government has declared Urdū as the official language, and except in Sindh, conducts schools in that language only. But Urdū is the mother tongue of only 7.5% of the people of Pakistan, and many of these are in the city of Karāchī. English is retained for many higher administrative purposes.

In Afghanistan, Pashto in several dialects is spoken by the Paṭhāns who populate the south and east. A dialect of Persian is the lingua franca throughout most of the rest of the country, and Persian provides the literary

FIG. 2–1 Languages.

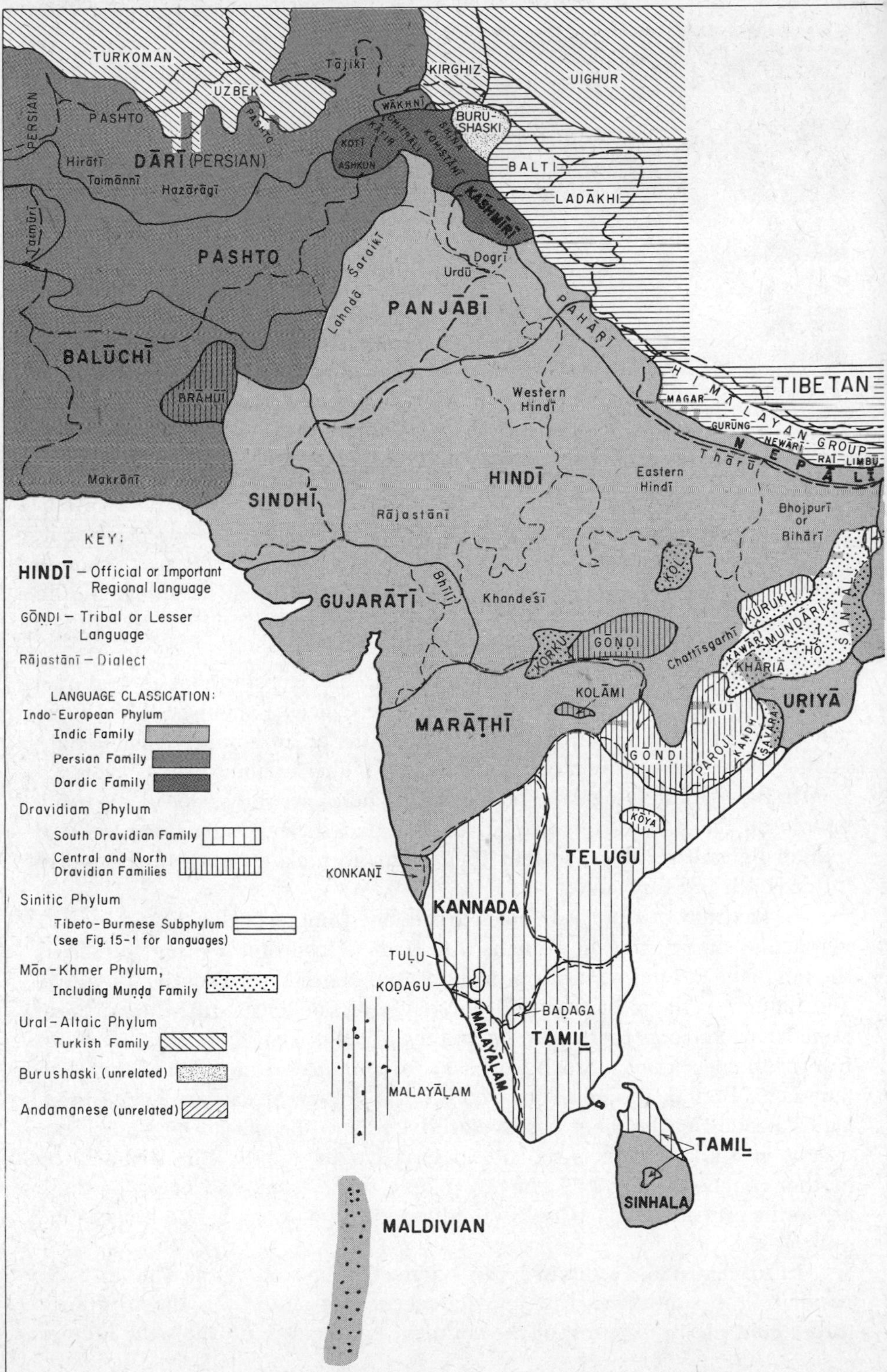

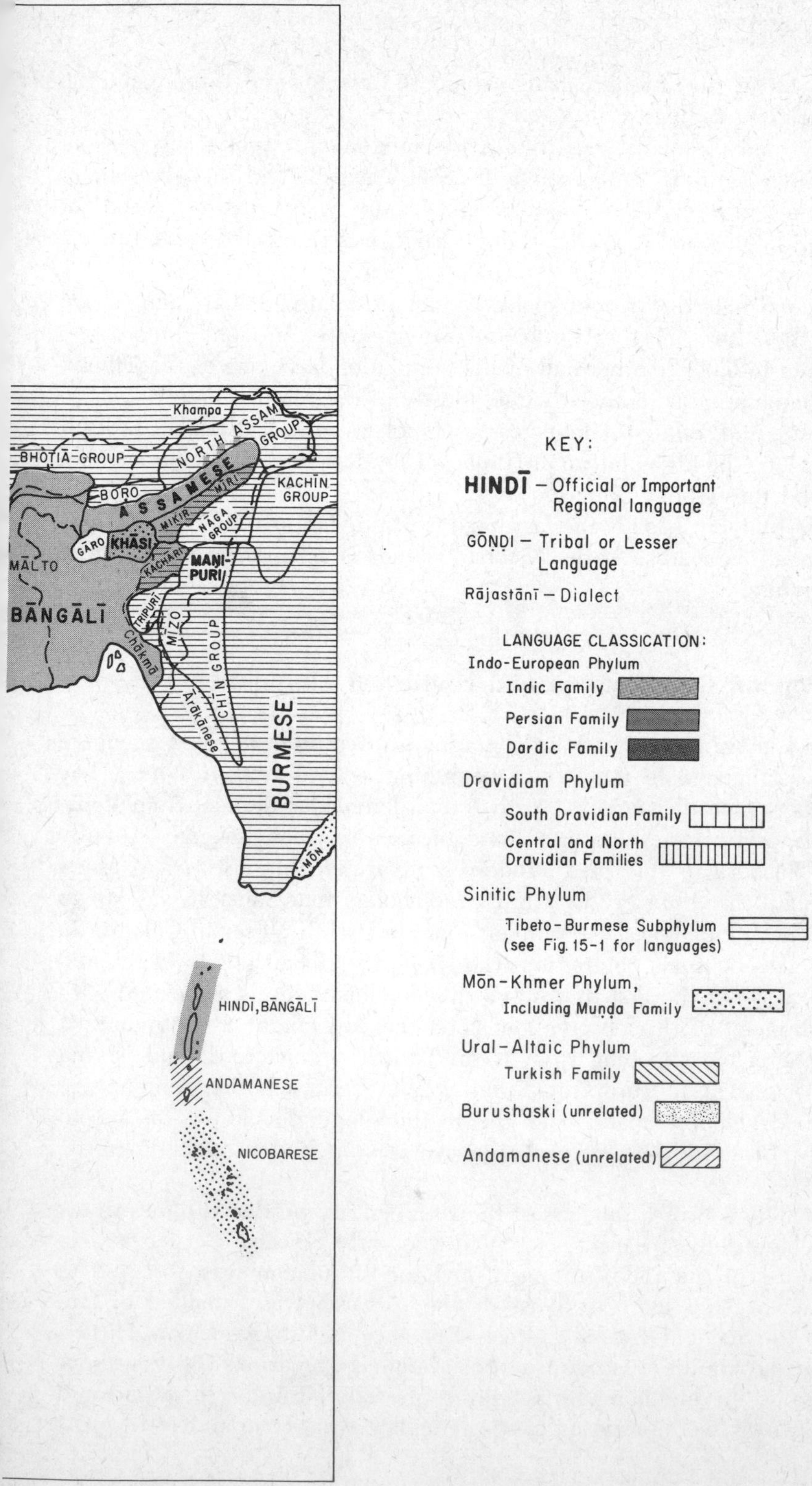
Khampa
NORTH ASSAM
GROUP
BHOTIĀ-GROUP
ASSAMESE
MIRI
KACHĪN GROUP
BORO
MIKIR
NĀGA GROUP
GĀRO
KHĀSI
KACHĀRI
MANI-PURI/
MĀLTO
BĀNGĀLĪ
TRIPURI
MIZO
Chakmā
CHIN GROUP
Ārākānese
BURMESE
MŌN
HINDĪ, BĀNGĀLĪ
ANDAMANESE
NICOBARESE
KEY:
HINDĪ – Official or Important Regional language
GŌṆḌI – Tribal or Lesser Language
Rājastānī – Dialect
LANGUAGE CLASSICATION:
Indo-European Phylum
Indic Family
Persian Family
Dardic Family
Dravidiam Phylum
South Dravidian Family
Central and North Dravidian Families
Sinitic Phylum
Tibeto-Burmese Subphylum (see Fig. 15-1 for languages)
Mōn-Khmer Phylum, Including Muṇḍa Family
Ural-Altaic Phylum
Turkish Family
Burushaski (unrelated)
Andamanese (unrelated)

standard. Along the southern fringe there is Balūchī, and throughout the north, Turkic languages are spoken.

In Sri Lanka, Sinhala, and Indo-Āryan language, is spoken by the majority, though Tamil̲ is the language of 28%. The policy of the government is to strengthen Sinhala, and both it and Tamil̲ are increasingly used for official and intellectual purposes, though English is supported by the urban elite.

In Nepal half the people speak Nepālī or related Pahāṛī and Thārū dialects; these are mostly Hindus whose ancestors brought Indo-Āryan speech from India. The other half of the population have one of the Tibeto-Burmese languages as mother tongue, mostly in the midmontane valleys.

Tibetan and related languages are spoken in the Ladākh part of Kashmīr, along the high plateau of Himāchal Pradesh and Nepal, in northern Sikkim, and throughout Bhutan.

In the Maldive Islands the language is Maldivian, a relative of Sinhala in Sri Lanka. Nicobarese of the Nicobar Islands is a language of the Mon-Khmer phylum.

Indo-European Comparative and Historical Linguistics

Indian grammarians and lexicographers attempted the first scientific analysis of language in the world, beginning several centuries B.C. They tried to show that all words in North Indian languages derived from Vedic or early Sanskrit forms, though some of their etymologies are patently incorrect because of this bias. Modern comparative linguistics had as its starting point the discovery by European scholars that Sanskrit was kin to most European languages. Sir William Jones, a British officer in Calcutta in the latter 18th century, pointed out the similarity of Sanskrit to Greek and Latin. He was not the first to observe this, but his name is associated with the development of this observation. Soon the concept of a continuum of related languages stretching from Iceland to Sri Lanka took hold, giving rise to the term Indo-European. From this, modern scientific comparative linguistics developed apace, and the methodology developed for reconstructing ancient Indo-European languages was applied to other linguistic phyla.

German and British scholars of the 19th century produced tomes showing the relationship of Sanskrit and Vedic to early classical Persian and to other families of the Indo-European phylum. Lithuanian was observed to be in some respects close to Sanskrit, and research was extended to languages of the Slavic, Germanic, Greek, Romance, Celtic, Armenian, Hittite, and Tocharian families of Indo-European languages. Various theories about the spread of "Āryan" nomadic people from eastern Europe in the 3d and 2d millennia B.C. were proposed to accommodate what comparative linguists

hypothesized of patterns of grammatical, lexical, and phonetic change by which these languages diversified.

The earliest family of Indo-European speech to penetrate South Asia was the Dardic, appearing some time in the 2d millennium B.C. Dardic must have been current in Panjāb and perhaps in the whole of the Indus valley because modern languages there show traces of Dardic speech. Today Dardic languages are relegated to the Himālayas and their foothills in the far north of Pakistan and in Kashmīr. The most characteristic language of this family is Kohistānī, spoken by the virile people of Kohistān in upper Pakistan. Related speech is Khuwār and Kāfir, the latter extending westward into northeastern Afghanistan. Kashmīrī is spoken in only the central part of Kashmīr and is at base a Dardic-type language, though it has been largely influenced by the more recently evolved Hindī-type languages.

The second family of Indo-European speech to appear in South Asia was the Indo-Āryan, in the latter 2d millennium B.C. The four Vedas, most sacred of the Hindu scriptures, are written in an old form of Sanskrit called Vedic. This is somewhat close to the language of the Avesta, the ancient Persian Zoroastrian text. The Vedas have been preserved in oral form since the latter half of the 2d millennium B.C. and thus are among the oldest records in Indo-European speech. They were transmitted virtually unchanged until a phonetic alphabet was developed in the 7th or 6th century B.C., after which they were written down.

The cultural equipment of these nomads can be discerned from the vocabulary items cognate in the various Indo-European language groups, such as words for boat, wheel, copper, cow, and king. The original "Āryan" nomads did not know iron, and were neither urbanized nor literate. After diffusing through Persia they trickled over into the Indus plains where they may or may not have destroyed the Indus Civilization, which withered away about 1300 B.C. Early Vedic literature provides us with an unparalleled view of nomadic society over three millennia ago. The Vedic hymns are cosmic in outlook but magical in function. The fusion of these Indo-Āryan speakers with the indigenous inhabitants of the plains, plus the stimulus of the Persian Achaemenian empire, caused the floresence of the foundations of classical Indian civilization beginning in the 7th to 4th centuries B.C.

The third family of Indo-European speech is the Īrānian or Persian. Pashto, the language of the Paṭhāns, is a member of this family; it is spoken by some 8 million people in the North-West Frontier Province of Pakistan and also by the Afghāns of the southeastern half of Afghanistan. Most of the rest of Afghanistan is within the orbit of Persian speech, and some 20,000 Pakistanis claim Persian as their language. Balūchī is also a Persian-type language; it is not an offshoot of East Persian dialects, but is genetically a western Īrānian language which apparently diffused into Balūchistān only in late medieval centuries, where it has encroached on the Dravidian relic Brāhūī.

The Indo-Āryan Languages

The *Linguistic Survey of India*, produced by G. A. Grierson over the first quarter of this century, divides the Indo-Āryan family of languages into the "inner" languages and the "outer" ones. Some contemporary linguists criticize this scheme as being an invalid simplification in the light of modern linguistic research, but it will help the reader perceive the overall pattern. The outer languages have evolved from old vernaculars and now surround the Gangā plains and the heartland of North India where Hindī-type speech has evolved. In the east the outer group consists of Bāngālī, Assamese, and Uṛiyā (of Orissa). These are contiguous and therefore have much in common, being linked with Hindī by the Bihārī transition dialects. On the southwest is Marāṭhī (of Mahārāshṭra) and Konkaṇī (of Goā), a southward protrusion of Indo-Āryan speech. On the west are Sindhi and Lahndā, a western Panjābī transition dialect. Sinhala of Sri Lanka and its offshoot Maldivian of the Maldive Islands must also be classified in the outer group.

The inner group of languages includes Hindī with its several dialects, Nepālī, Panjābī, Gujarātī, and Bhīlī (a tribal language in Gujarāt). All the forms of speech that employ standard Hindī in writing are to be considered dialects of Hindī, such as Western Hindī, Eastern Hindī, Western and Central Pahāṛī (in the sub-Himālayan belt), and Rājasthānī. These all have about the same vocabulary, but their patterns of phonetic shifts differ and they employ different grammatical indicators. Some linguists would also classify Panjābī as a dialect of Hindī. Urdū is nothing but standard Hindī written with a different script and with some foreign vocabulary. Because these two symbolize two religious systems, they are popularly thought of as two different languages.

All the modern Indo-Āryan languages evolved from old vernacular

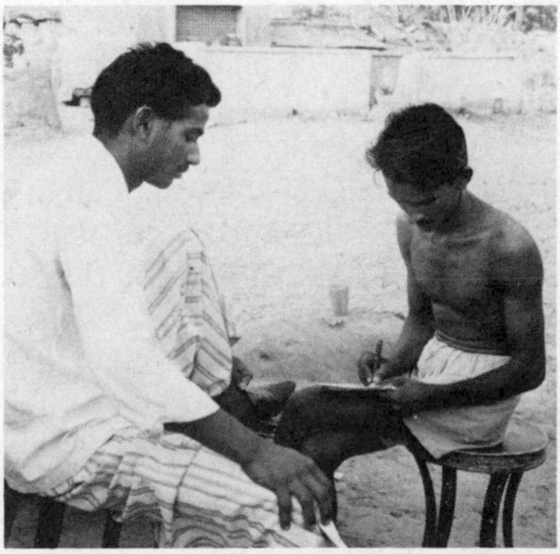

A Rājasthānī employs a letter writer, a scene becoming rarer as literacy increases. Standard Hindī, the written form in this area, is divergent from the Rājasthānī dialect.

forms called Prākrits, and not directly from Vedic or Sanskrit as some Indians believe. The Prākrits were sometimes used as literary media, and through them linguists can trace the development and diversification of Indo-Āryan speech. The basic lexical material of all these languages is remarkably similar. They all shade into each other, each language held together by its literary standard but consisting of a gradation of dialects. But there are differences in the patterned phonetic shifts and in grammatical indicators such as verbal suffixes. The eastern languages, for instance, have lost gender distinctions, others have lost the dual number, and all have been affected by the Dravidian, Muṇḍa, or Tibetan languages they presumably displaced. A form of Prākrit called Pāli became the vehicle of the sacred literature of orthodox Buddhism and was particularly preserved for that purpose in Sri Lanka, though Sinhala evolved from a basic core of western Prākrit. A special literary dialect called Buddhist Hybrid Sanskrit was used for medieval works of Northern Buddhism.

Sanskrit itself apparently developed from an early vernacular speech of the Panjāb region, with accretions of other dialects, and became formalized with the increasing elaboration of Brāhmaṇ rituals several centuries before Christ. It experienced a florescence during the 4th to 7th centuries A.D. and developed into one of the most intellectualized languages in the world. Because of the huge store of Sanskrit vocabulary in philosophy, theology, science, astronomy, law, medicine, grammar, architecture, and other learned pursuits, and because of the metaphysical power attributed to Sanskrit speech by most Hindus, all the other vernaculars borrowed heavily from its vocabulary. This was often true even though the borrowed Sanskrit words were cognates of words already existing in the other Indo-Āryan languages. It was even drawn upon by South Indian languages, and became the lingua franca of the educated. Because of its role in transmitting Indian civilization, the emulation of formal Hindu behavior and ideals has been called "Sanskritization." The role of this language has been analogous to that of Latin in medieval Europe. However, it declined during Muslim rule and was further displaced by English and the rising literary vernaculars; today only some learned priests and scholars can converse in Sanskrit, but its literary heritage is immense.

Dravidian Comparative and Historical Linguistics

Dravidian linguistics is a newer study, but invaluable for understanding the roots of South Asian culture. Attempts have been made to show genetic connection between Dravidian languages and Sumerian, Somali, Pelasgian, or languages of the Caucasus group. Such studies show that in all probability Dravidian languages did derive from prehistoric and protohistoric forms of speech in lands to the west of India, particularly Iran, but since

five or more millennia must have intervened since their separation, the evidence is not precise enough to convince rigorous comparative linguists of proved genetic connection with any specific known language of the Near East.

Dravidian languages may be divided into southern, central, and northern groups. The southern group contains Tamiḻ, Kannaḍa, and Malayāḷam, with Telugu having separated from the others early in the 1st millennium B.C. Tamiḻ has been a literary language since about 200 B.C. Old Tamiḻ bifurcated into Tamiḻ and Malayāḷam around the 9th century A.D. as the latter adopted a Sanskritized script and vocabulary. Kannaḍa has written records dating back to the 5th century A.D., and Old Kannaḍa has a number of resemblances to Tamiḻ. A fifth important southern Dravidian language, Tuḷu, is spoken by a million people on the southwestern coast of Karṇāṭaka, but it has scarcely any literature. There are three languages of the southern Dravidian group spoken in the Nīlagiri Mountains: Toḍa and Koṭa by tribal people, and Badaga.

The central Dravidian languages include Gōṇḍi and its several dialects spoken in southern Madhya Pradesh and the northern fringe of Āndhra. It is now fragmented by the onslaught of Hindī and Marāṭhī. Also related are Kolāmi, Parji, Kui, and other tribal languages of southern and eastern central India. These may have split off from the southern Dravidian languages over 3000 years ago.

The northern Dravidian group includes Kurukh, spoken by close to a million tribal people in and around western Orissa, and Malto, found as far north as eastern Bihār and overlooking the eastern Gangā plains. There is evidence that Dravidian speech was diffusing northeastward in this part of India, at the expense of Muṇḍa languages, until the southward penetration of Hindī into Madhya Pradesh accelerated in recent decades. These tribal languages have now adopted a quantity of Indo-Āryan vocabulary.

The most aberrant of the Dravidian languages is Brāhūī, spoken by some 400,000 tribesmen in the Balūchistān hills just west of the lower Indus plains, though some Brāhūīs are scattered along the eastern edge of Iran. It is estimated to have separated from other Dravidian languages over 5000 years ago. Brāhūī has only some 200 vocabulary items that are Dravidian, but these are words for parts of the body, domestic things, local environment, pronouns, first numerals, and basic verbs—the lexical material which is most conservative in any language. The phonology has been influenced by Balūchī and Sindhī, but the grammatical system has preserved a sturdy existence over the millennia.

Dravidian elements seem to have crept into all the languages in western India, especially Konkaṇī and Marāṭhī, and also Gujarātī and Sindhī. Doubtless Dravidian languages were once spoken in the Panjāb, according to the postulated metamorphosis of proto-Indo-Āryan. The possibility of the migration of Brāhūī from South India to Balūchistān seems ruled out on

linguistic grounds. The probability is strong that Dravidian speech was once current in the whole Indus region and western India, and indeed, is the most likely candidate as the type of language of the Indus Civilization, perhaps diffusing to Gujarāt and southward with the spread of that civilization and its aftermath.

Muṇḍa Languages

More than a dozen of these languages, spoken by some eight million people in the uplands of east-central India, are now under pressure from Hindī, Bāngālī, and Uṛiyā as the speakers are becoming detribalized. Santālī, with perhaps 3.5 million speakers, is the best known of these, and other important ones are Muṇḍārī, Ho, Savara, Bhūmij, Kūrku, and Khāṛiā. Khāsi, spoken in eastern Meghālaya on the other side of the Bānglā plains, also belongs within this language phylum, but is more distantly related. These languages are agglutinative, with suffix piled on suffix. English parts of speech are not very applicable to an analysis of them.

There is little doubt that the existence of these languages in India reflects an early cultural diffusion from Southeast Asia into India and that they were formerly much more widespread in eastern India than they are today. There is a related linguistic substratum in the languages of the sub-Himālayan regions from Bhutan and Sikkim and eastern Nepal, as far west as Himāchal Pradesh, where traces of it are found in Kanaurī spoken around Śimlā. The Muṇḍa languages are related to Mon, spoken today by half a million people in southern Burma but in former times much more widespread, and to Khmer (Cambodian). Mon-Khmer forms of speech were used across mainland Southeast Asia before the penetration of Burmese, Thai, Shan, Lao, and other Chinese-type languages. Nicobarese of the Nicobar Islands, an Indian Territory in the Bay of Bengal, is also related, and must have diffused there by sea.

It is probable that Muṇḍa languages penetrated South Asia together with other items of cultural equipment from Southeast Asia. A whole prehistoric horticultural complex with Southeast Asian cultigens and tool types reached India by the 2d and 1st millennia B.C. The question is discussed more fully in the contexts of prehistoric archeology and the cultures of the tribal people of eastern India.

Sino-Tibetan Languages

About two thirds of the distinct languages of South Asia belong to the Sino-Tibetan linguistic phylum, and are found in the valleys of the eastern Himālayas, on the Tibetan plateau, and in the four hill states and two

Territories around Assam, as well as in the Chittagong Hills of Bangladesh. The linguistic diversity, of course, is due to the rugged terrain.

The Thai language family is represented in South Asia by only one language, Khāmti, a dialect of Shan spoken in a limited region south and east of the Brahmaputra River in Assam. When the Thais filtered southward from South China into Thailand and Laos, their close kin the Shans diffused across northern Burma, and a branch of them, the Āhoms, penetrated the Assam Valley and dominated it during the 16th and 17th centuries. The name Assam comes from Āhom. There is little trace of this Shan influence today except in the presence of Khāmti, which is in the process of becoming an inflected and agglutinative language, though originally built on a monosyllabic base typical of Sinitic languages.

The vastly varied Tibeto-Burmese family of languages may be divided into three subfamilies: the Tibeto-Burmese group, the Burmese-type languages, and the North Assamese languages. The first includes Balti, spoken over a sizable area around the Indus headwaters, while Ladākhi is a dialect of Tibetan spoken in the barren heights of Ladākh claimed by both India and China. Sharpa and Kāgate of Nepal, Lhoke of Bhutan, and Lepcha of Sikkim are all related to Tibetan, though there is little standard Tibetan spoken south of the Himālayan watershed. The languages of the midmontane valleys are also related, though Muṇḍa features have been noted in some of them. The chief Tibeto-Burmese languages of Nepal are Newārī, Gurūng, Limbū, and Magarī. Newārī was the state language of the kingdom centered at Kāṭhmāṇḍū until the 18th century, and had a literature. All these languages in Nepal are now in retreat before Nepālī, brought in from the plains by the Gorkhā invasion and now the only official language of the country. In the western Himālayas also, with the intrusion of military personnel along new roads, the Himālayan languages may not be able to hold their own.

The North Assamese group consists of Abor, Mīri, Mishmi, and other tongues spoken by the 450,000 people of the newly created Territory of Arunāchal Pradesh north of the Assam Valley. These languages were not written until the 1960s, and most people who wish to communicate more widely learn Assamese.

South of the Assam Valley the Burmese-related languages are divided into a number of groups. The westernmost one is known as the Boḍo group, of which Gāro is the principal language. Gāro is spoken in western Meghālaya and shares that state with Khāsi, the Muṇḍa language. Languages related to Gāro include Boḍo, Rangdānia, Mikir, Kāchārī, and Tripurī, spoken around the Shillong Plateau and southward towards Tripurā.

The linguistic picture in the regions flanking Burma is really quite complex. Nāgaland seems to have linguistic diversity as great as in any comparable part of the world; the settlements on every ridge have a dialect nearly unintelligible to people on opposite ridges! Linguistic change is

known to have been rapid because of the fiercely maintained social isolation of each group and the original monosyllabic nature of the languages. But Nāgas have now given up their fierce ways, many speak English and Assamese, and their languages are written in the Roman script. Some of the languages of the Nāga group are Āngāmi, Sema, Āo, and Lhota.

Another big group of languages has been termed by Grierson the Kuki-Chīn group. Historically the most important of these has been Meithei, spoken in the state of Maṇipur by 700,000 people. In addition there are some 40 other languages spoken by the Mīzos in the Territory of Mīzorām and neighboring regions; these are actually dialects of the Chīn languages of the western Burma hills. There are also speakers of Kachīn dialects in and around the state of Maṇipur. Farther south, in the Chittagong Hills of Bangladesh, one finds tongues such as Marma, Morung, and others that are essentially dialects of Ārākānese, which is spoken in the Ārākān strip of southwestern Burma.

Other Languages

Burushaski remains as a relic of some pre-Indo-European speech, and is now confined to part of Gilgit and the long narrow Hunza Valley in the northern extremity of Āzād Kashmīr in Pakistan. It is not known to be related to any other language.

Undoubtedly there were other linguistic groups in South Asia that have become extinct. Even such isolated tribal groups as the Kāḍar in the Kēraḷa hills now speak Dravidian languages, but must have once spoken something else if Dravidian speech diffused from Pakistan southward into the peninsula.

On the Andaman Islands in the Bay of Bengal, Andamanese is spoken by a handful of aboriginals who have managed to survive. It was formerly divisible into about 10 dialects, coinciding with sept divisions. So long have those islanders been isolated from the mainland that their language is not known to be related to any other. It reflects the extraordinary simplicity of the indigenous culture, reportedly lacking words for abstract ideas such as joy, happiness, friendship, or beauty. There are only four colors, and numerals go only up to four. Even the four numerals mean respectively: one or very few, more, still more, and whole or most numerous. The language is agglutinative.

Then there are the languages of European origin. English is claimed as mother tongue by the Anglo-Indians of mixed descent. It is claimed as a second language by 2.5% of the people of India, but many of these cannot speak it effectively. Only 2% of Pakistanis claim to know it, and 1% in Bangladesh. Many foreign visitors to India who spend their time in large cities overestimate the percentage of English-knowing people. English is

retained in the higher administrative levels in India, Pakistan, Sri Lanka, and Bangladesh for prestige and because people get used to expressing certain kinds of Western ideas in it. In India it is also an important force holding the country together.

Other foreign powers have left their languages as legacies. French is understood in Pondicherry on the coast south of Madras. Portuguese is known by many in Goū, and Dutch was spoken by some people of mixed descent in Sri Lanka. More important are Persian and Arabic, known by many Muslims. Persian is still studied as the vehicle of sophisticated thought of Muslim civilization. There is little interest in other major languages of the world, such as are studied in schools in Western countries.

Script

The phonology of Indo-Aryan languages was analyzed so early that the first phonetic script (not counting the ideographic writing of the Indus Civilization) was already well adapted to Indian speech. This was the Brāhmī script, which diffused throughout South Asia by at least the 3d century B.C. Another script used at the same time in northwestern India, the Kharoshṭhī, was also well adapted and was clearly derived from a Semitic alphabet. Brāhmī too seems to have evolved from Semitic scripts, but its exact antecedent cannot be traced.

The Brāhmī script and indeed all modern scripts stemming from it represent vowels as marks attached to consonantal symbols, perhaps because early Semitic scripts were deficient in vowels. The scripts of all Indian languages (except those which use adaptations of the Roman or Arabic) are derived ultimately from the Brāhmī. In fact, phonetic scripts of all other parts of Asia are also derived from India, such as modern Burmese and Thai and many writing systems formerly used in Indonesia, Malaysia, Cambodia, Viet Nam, the Philippines, and even the Caroline Islands. The Tibetan script is of Indian origin, and this in turn inspired the creation of the Korean syllabic system.

So well did these unknown early scholars organize the script that they arranged the letters in the same order as they appear in the columns of the accompanying chart (with the exception of the non-Sanskrit letters). Vowel symbols, unless occurring initially in a word, are simply strokes added to the consonant. This orthographic system represented contrasting phonemes better than that of any other classical civilization.

The stages by which Brāhmī script evolved into the scripts of languages transmitting Hindu and Buddhist civilizations can be traced in the abundant stone inscriptions; in the North the letters came to be hung from a line, while in the South they were written in rounded form so that the iron stylus would not split the palm leaves. Most of these languages have letters for the Sanskrit phonemes shown in Table 2–1, though aspirated

TABLE 2–1 Phonemes Represented by South Asian Scripts

Short Vowels	Long Vowels	Dipthongs
a	ā	ai, (ăi)
i	ī	au
u	ū	
(e)	e, (ē)	
(o)	o, (ō)	
ṛ		
ḷ		

Consonants

	gutteral	palatal	retroflex	dental	labial
Unvoiced	k, [ḳ]	c	ṭ	t	p
Unvoiced aspirate	kh, [x]	ch	ṭh	th	ph, [f]
Voiced	g, [g̣]	j, [z]	ḍ, ṛ	d	b
Voiced aspirate	gh	jh	ḍh, ṛh	dh	bh
Nasal	ṅ	ñ, (n̲)	ṇ	n	m
Semivowels		y	r, (r̲, ḷ, l̲)	l	v
Sibilants		ś	ṣ	s	
		Aspiration: h, ḥ			

The Sanskrit orthography essentially represents the phonemes not shown in parentheses or brackets, and was arranged in the above categories by the ancient linguists. Phonemes in parentheses are characteristically represented in Dravidian scripts. Consonants in brackets are of Persian origin and are represented in the scripts on the western side of South Asia, in Urdū, and some of them in Hindī. For pronunciation, see Pronunciation Guide following the Preface.

phonemes in Dravidian languages are found mostly in borrowed words while in Sinhala they tend to become unaspirated. But the Tamil̲ script has no symbols for aspirated phonemes, neither does it distinguish voiced from unvoiced consonants.

Arabic script gave rise to the Persian, which in turn evolved into the scripts used for Urdū, Sindhī, Pashto, Kashmīrī, and Balūchī, and these are written from right to left. The Roman (English) script has been adapted by missionaries to some tribal languages such as Mīzo and the Nāga tongues. It is quite unlikely that the Roman script will replace the indigenous South Asian scripts, which are valued for their antiquity and distinctiveness, and in any case the Roman script does not have enough symbols. Efficiency studies have shown that the South Asian scripts can be written as rapidly as the Roman script.

South Asia as a Linguistic Area

The three major linguistic phyla in South Asia have to some extent merged by borrowing phonemes, morphemes, and syntactical forms from each other. The situation is analogous to the effect of the inclusion in the Indo-European geographical region of Europe of such languages as Hun-

FIG. 2–2 Samples of South Asian scripts*

The following are approximate translations of the sentence: "You are now reading a sentence written in (Hindī) script."

Hindī	अब आप हिन्दी लिपि में लिखा एक वाक्य पढ़ रहे हैं। Ab āp Hindī lipi mẽ likhā ek vākya paṛh rahe haĩ.
Urdū	اب آپ اردو رسم الخط میں ایک جملہ پڑھ رہے ہیں۔ Ab āp Urdū rasm-ul-ḳhat mẽ ēk jumlā paṛh rahē haĩ.
Sanskrit	संस्कृतलिप्या निबद्धं वाक्यं भवान् अधुना पठति। Saṁskṛta lipyā nibaddham vākyam bhavān adhunā paṭhati.
Kāshmīrī	ونیہ چھوِ تِوھیہ کیشرِ لِپِس اندر لیوکھمُت اکھ جملعہ پران - वञ' छिवि' तोह्य का'शरि लिपी अन्दर ल्यूखमुत अख जुम'ला परान. Vañ' chivi toh'i Kāśiri lipī andar lyūkhmut akh jumili parān.
Sindhī	توهين هاڻي سنڌيءَ ۾ لکيل جملو پڙهي رهيا آهيو. तव्हीं हाणे सिंधीअ में लिख्यलु जुम्लो पढ़ी रह्या आह्यो. Tavhĩ hāne Sindhīa mẽ likhyalu jumlo paṛhī rahyā āhyo.
Pashto	ته اوس په پښتو حرفونو کښې ليکلې يوه فقره لولې Tə os pa paxto ḥarfuno kxe likəle yawa fiqra lwale.
Panjābī	ਤੁਸੀਂ ਹੁਣ ਪੰਜਾਬੀ ਲਿਪੀ ਵਿਚ ਲਿਖਿਆ ਇਕ ਵਾਕ ਪੜ੍ਹ ਰਹੇ ਹੋ। Tusĩ huṇ Pañjābī lipī vic likhiyā ik vāk paṛh ræ ho.
Nepālī	नेपाली अच्छेरहरूमा लेखेको वाक्य पढ़दै हुनुहुन्छ Nepālī accherharūmā lekheko bākya paṛhdai huruhuncha.
Gujarātī	ગુજરાતી લિપિમાં અત્યારે તમે વાકય વાંપો છો। Gujarātī lipimā̃ atyāre tame vākya vā̃co cho.
Marāṭhī	तुम्ही आता मराठी लिपीत लिहिलेले एक वाक्य वाचीत आहात. Tumhī ātā Marāṭhī lipīt lihilelē ek vākya vācīt āhāt.
Bāngālī	এখন আপনারা বাংলা অক্ষরে লেখা একটি বাক্য পড়ছেন। Ekhan āpnārā Bāṅglā akṣarē lēkhā ekṭi bākya paṛchēn.
Assamese	আপুনি এতিয়া অসমীয়া লিপিত লিখা বাক্য এটা পঢ়ি আছে। Āpūni etiyā Ahomīyā lipit likhā vākya eṭa paḍhi āse.
Uṛiyā	ତୁମେ ବର୍ତ୍ତମାନ ଓଡ଼ିଆରେ ଲେଖା ଏକ ବାକ୍ୟ ପଢୁଛ। Tumhe bartamān Uṛiyāre lekhā ēko bākya paṛucha.

Sinhala	ඔබ දැන් සිංහලඅකුරෙන් ලියා තිබෙන වාක්‍යයක් කියවනවා.	Oba dän Siṁhala-akuren liyā tibena vāsagamak kiyavanavā.
Telugu	మీరు ఇప్పుడు తెలుగులో వ్రాయబడిన వాక్యమును చదువుచున్నారు	Mīru ippuḍu Telugulō vrayabaḍina vākyamunu caduvucunnāru.
Kannaḍa	ನೀವು ಈಗ ಕನ್ನಡ ಬರವಣಿಗೆಯ ಒಂದು ವಾಕ್ಯವನ್ನು ಓದುತ್ತಿದ್ದೀರಿ.	Nīvu īga Kannaḍa baravaṇigeya ondu vākyavannu ōduttiddīri.
Tamiḻ	தமிழ் எழுத்தில் எழுதியுள்ள வாக்கியத்தை இப்பொழுது படித்துக்கொண்டிருக்கிறீர்கள்.	Tamiḻ eḻuttil eḻutiyuḷḷa vākkiyattai ippoḻutu paḍittukkoṇḍirukkiṟīrkaḷ.
Malayāḷam	നിങ്ങൾ ഇപ്പോൾ മലയാള ലിപിയിൽ എഴുതിയ ഒരു വാചകമാണ് വായിക്കുന്നതു്.	Niṅṅaḷ ippōḷ Malayāḷa lipiyil eḻutiya oru vācakamāṇu vāyikkunnatu.
Tibetan	ཁྱོད་ཀྱིས་ད་ལྟ་བོད་སྐད་དུ་བྲིས་པའི་ཚིག་བརྗོད་ཅིག་ཀློག་གི་འདུག །	Khyod-kyis-da-lta-bod-skad-du-bris-pa'i-tshig-brjod-cig-klog-gi-'dug.
Lepcha	ᰝᰨ ᰀᰜᰵ ᰊᰪ ᰟᰨᰵ ᰕᰪᰰ ᰞᰨᰭ ᰓᰬᰮ	Hó álaṅ do róṅ yuk thok bám.
Marma	ယခု ကိုယ်တော်သည် မြန်မာ စကား ဖတ်နေသည်။	Ya khụ ko daw thi myan ma za ga: pha' nei thi.
Mīzo		Mizo ṭawngin thuchâng khat tunah hean i chhiar a ni.

* All the languages in the above list from Hindī through Sinhala are of the Indo-Āryan linguistic family, except that Kashmīrī has a Dardic base and Pashto is related to Persian. Telugu, Kannaḍa, Tamiḻ, and Malayāḷam are Dravidian, and Sinhala has some Tamiḻ admixture.

Scripts used for Urdū, Kashmīrī, Sindhī, and Pashto are Arabic derived. All other scripts are derived from Brāhmī, such as was used in the Aśokan inscriptions and in Śrī Lankā in the 3d century B.C. as the following example from a cave entrance:

Upaśaka-Nagamitaha bariyaya upaśika-Śilaya leṇe śagaśa
The cave of the female lay-devotee Śilā, wife of the
lay-devotee Nagamitta, [is given] to the Sangha [brotherhood].

All these Indic scripts are phonetic, with vowel marks attached to consonants. Most languages evolved unique scripts from Brāhmī, but Devanāgarī is the script used for Sanskrit, Hindī, Nepālī, Marāṭhī, and by Hindus speaking Kāshmīrī and Sindhī.

The Tibetan sample is Classical Tibetan.

Lepcha is one of the languages spoken in the country of Sikkim.

Marma is spoken by the Buddhist Marma "tribe" in the Chittagong Hills of Bangladesh; its script is Burmese script, which was derived from South India.

Mīzo is spoken by Mīzos in the Indian Territory of Mīzorām, south of Assam; missionaries introduced the Roman script.

Languages of the Muṇḍa linguistic group are not represented here because they are seldom written; when they are, scripts of neighboring regional languages are used.

garian, Finnish, Turkish, and Basque, which in some ways are now closer to their geographical neighbors than to their genetically related languages far away. Because isolated Dravidian languages are found as far north as Bihār and even in Balūchistān in Pakistan, it may be assumed that Indo-Āryan displaced and absorbed Dravidian speech in northwestern, western, and central India. It has displaced Muṇḍa speech in eastern India. Of the three linguistic groups, the influence of Muṇḍa on the other two is least, though numerous words in North Indian languages have been etymologically traced to Muṇḍa: the name of the Gangā (Ganges) River is derived from Muṇḍa.

Indo-Āryan and Dravidian have each contributed an important series of phonemes to the South Asian linguistic pool. Retroflex phonemes, produced by curling the tongue toward the back of the palate, seem originally to have been Dravidian, as languages of that phylum have the fullest set. They are not found in Indo-European languages to the west, nor even in Persian, though Vedic has them. Their frequency and contrastive importance decrease as one moves eastward down the Gangā. They are also found in Muṇḍa languages, though one such language lacks them, suggesting that they are a borrowed feature for Muṇḍa. Even Burushaski in northern Kashmīr has retroflex phonemes. The Indo-Āryan linguistic group has contributed aspirate phonemes, consonants pronounced while expelling a puff of air, a feature shared with other Indo-European languages. Most Dravidian languages have borrowed these to some extent, though in Tamil̠ they are either missing or not contrastive, and are not represented in the Tamil̠ script. Sinhala, though Indo-Āryan in origin, has also shown a tendency to lose this set of phonemes.

M. B. Emeneau has pointed out the syntactical influence of Dravidian on Indo-Āryan and Muṇḍa, best exemplified by a feature of most Indian languages: a string of phrases ending in nonfinite verbs closed or completed by a finite verb. Another trait common to all three language groups is a type of construction based on nominalized or adjectivized forms of verbs, followed by postpositions (the equivalent of prepositions). This may be from Muṇḍa or Dravidian. The prevalence of echo words in these languages is perhaps of Dravidian origin. Languages in eastern and central India belonging to all three groups have a set of classifier morphemes used with numerals, a feature borrowed from Indo-Āryan. Both Muṇḍa and Dravidian have a gender system distinguishing animate from inanimate nouns.

The extent to which the lexical inventory of Indo-Āryan languages, even of Sanskrit, contains a large percentage of Dravidian and other non-Indo-European morphemes has been demonstrated only in the last few decades, somewhat to the dismay of Sanskritists who had come to acquire some of the Brāhmaṇical reverence for the "purity" of that language and had studied the etymologies of the ancient grammarian Pāṇini. These borrowings include not only the names of flora and fauna, but morphemes connoting many common objects and actions.

Diffusion of the Prākrits had considerable lexical impact on languages surrounding the Indian heartland. More popularly recognized is the infusion of Sanskrit vocabulary on non-Indo-Āryan languages in southern and eastern India and throughout Southeast Asia (betrayed by so many place names of Sanskrit origin such as Jāva, Singapore, and Cambodia). Dictionaries of modern Telugu and Malayāḷam show that half the lexical items in those tongues are from Sanskrit or the Prākrits and that the borrowed vocabulary consists of semantemes of intellectual connotation. The situation is analogous to the heavy overlay of Latin and also of Greek vocabulary on the Anglo-Saxon base of English. In late medieval times, Malayāḷam, for instance, was sometimes written in a style in which the majority of words were Sanskrit, strung together with Dravidian suffixes and syntax; each such Sanskrit word was likened to a gem in a necklace. Since the decline of Sanskrit learning, this practice has become modified. Tamil̲ has fewer words of Sanskrit origin, and within the last decade its literary style has been largely purged of the words thought to be of northern origin.

Sanskrit forms were borrowed in large numbers by other Indo-Āryan languages. Bāngālī obviously developed from an early eastern Prākrit, but in medieval literature many classical Sanskrit words were borrowed which partially displaced forms which were cognate in Bāngālī; hence some Bāngālīs thought that their language was the best of the vernaculars because it appeared to them to have been derived directly from Sanskrit. The affected literary styles of these languages are now giving way to new and more vigorous prose. There is no doubt that the greatest traditional linguistic binder of South Asia has been the Sanskrit vocabulary common to all languages, which represented ideas of philosophy, theology, science, and all intellectual pursuits.

The influence of Persian and, to a lesser extent, Arabic vocabulary has extended through all the major South Asian languages because of the centuries of Mughal rule. Such words are more noticeable in the languages of Pakistan. Urdū is distinguished from standard Hindī, aside from its script, chiefly in the substitution of Persian words for Indian. All the other Indian languages have borrowed practically the same set of West Asian vocabulary.

The tendency of all South Asian languages to borrow the same inventory of foreign vocabulary is also apparent in their reaction to European languages. A legacy of Portuguese is a set of words (including those for table and key) found throughout the subcontinent. The impact of English has been much greater. Not only has a similar list of English vocabulary been borrowed by all the major languages, but unusual meanings of some words, which baffle the tourist, cut across languages; for example, "rooms" for a hotel, "hotel" for a restaurant, "pleasure" (pleasure car) for automobile, "service" for salaried employment, and "line" meaning geographical direction. Government clerk-types are especially habituated to sprinkling every sentence with many English words.

It is apparently no great strain for an individual to be bilingual in two

juxtaposed languages. John Gumperz studied a village on the border of northern Karṇāṭaka where 70% of the people spoke Kannaḍa, while there was also some Marāṭhī and Deccani Hindī (Urdū). Even though Kannaḍa is Dravidian and Marāṭhī Indo-Āryan and remained "lexically distinct in almost every respect," he found that syntax had so merged that a person could "translate from one to the other by a simple process of word for word or morph for morph substitution. . . . He can switch from one language to the other by merely substituting one item in a pair for the other without having to learn any new grammatical rules other than the ones he already controls."[1] There is a linguistic deep structure which pervades the subcontinent and even cuts across linguistic phyla. This is analogous to the fundamental cultural features which pervade the subcontinent, though expressed in different regional cultures.

REFERENCES AND NOTES

[1] John Gumperz, "Communication in Multilingual Societies," in Stephen Tyler (ed.), *Cognitive Anthropology* (New York, 1967).

IMPORTANT SOURCES

Basham, A. L. *The Wonder That Was India.* New York, 1954. (Chap. IX is an excellent survey of language and literature.)

Buhler, G. *Indian Paleography.* Bombay, 1904.

Burling, Robbins. *Man's Many Voices.* New York, 1970. (An introduction to anthropological linguistics with examples drawn from Gāro and other Indian languages.)

Burrow, T. *The Sanṣkrit Language.* London, 1964.

Dani, A. H. *Indian Paleography.* Oxford, 1963. (A synthesis of data on script development, but with some misleading chronology.)

Dr. R. P. Sethu Pillai Silver Jubilee Commemorative Volume. Madras, 1961. (Contains short but useful articles on Dravidian historical linguistics by Kamil Zvelebil and M. Andronov.)

Emeneau, M. B. "India as a Linguistic Area," in Dell Hymes (ed.), *Language in Culture and Society.* New York, 1964.

Ferguson, Charles, and John Gumperz (eds.). *Linguistic Diversity in South Asia, International Journal of American Linguistics,* XXVI, No. 3 (1960). (An important collection of articles on comparative linguistics and contemporary language problems.)

Government of India. *Census of India, 1961.* New Delhi, 1970. (There is a volume on language data for each state and territory and one for all India.)

Government of Pakistan. *Census Report of Tribal Agencies.* Karachi, 1961.

Grierson, G. A. *Linguistic Survey of India.* Calcutta, 1927. (Contains samples of most Indo-Āryan languages; Vol. I:1 is a provocative monograph.)

Gumperz, John. "Speech Variation and the Study of Indian Civilization," in Dell Hymes (ed.), *Language in Culture and Society.* New York, 1964.

Keith, A. B. *History of Sanskrit Literature.* Oxford, 1928.

3

The Races

Why does some ancient Indian literature rave at the beauty of a woman whose face is round like the moon, with teeth like two strings of glistening pearls? Why does classical Indian art exaggerate full lips and large eyes? Why don't college girls cut and curl their hair? And why is fair skin color so much valued in South Asia? The answers lie in the ways in which the cultures and the physical characteristics of the people have interacted. Ideas of physical beauty are not arrived at independently of racial characteristics; they may in fact be determined by the physical traits of the dominating ethnic element.

It is the ancient Tamiḻ literature that praises the moon face, and in fact it is toward the south and east that people's faces are sometimes broader, with chins weakly developed in comparison with, for example, the people of Afghanistan. Moreover their dark complexion is complemented by teeth which seem large, white, and sparkling. Almost all South Asian art portrays women with eyes which seemingly fill the upper face because people of the subcontinent generally have darker skin around the eyes than over the

rest of the face, so the eyeballs seem large and contrastive. The full lips of temple sculpture, when gracefully curved, are regarded as sensuous; they are more common in South Asia than in Europe. But miniature paintings of the Mughal and Rājpūt schools idealize the aquiline nose, betraying their Iranian and Near Eastern ideals. The population in general has black hair which is less whispy than that of Europeans; it may be straight or wavy. It is quite becoming for college girls to preserve their long jet-black hair, gathered in a braid down to the waist. The Mediterranean-type skeletons and flexible joints of Indian people must have helped along the development of the Bharatanāṭyam form of dancing with its endless subtleties of body movement and of Yoga with its contorted postures.

There is a great range of skin color in South Asia. Some people are light, like Italians; others are light to medium brown, dark brown, very dark, blackish brown, and grayish brown, while in the eastern hills the Mongoloid people have a yellowish tinge. In general, darkness increases from Kashmīr to Tamil Nāḍu and to a less noticeable extent from Balūchistān to Bāngla. People of the central Indian tribal belt are often darker than the dominant castes of surrounding peoples, but many of the tribals of the hills around Assam are lighter than the Bāngālīs. Paṭhāns in Pakistan tend to be light, as do some Kashmīrīs, Panjābīs, and other people of northwestern India. But on the other hand some Panjābīs and many Sindhīs are medium or dark brown.

Because lighter color is associated with higher castes and with people claiming pedigrees, usually pointing north and west, light skin is recognized as desirable. Untouchables and other low castes are generally dark, but not uniformly. Parents are always joyful at the birth of a light or "tumeric-colored" baby, but express disappointment if the child is "black." A menial servant may be unhesitatingly identified as a "black fellow"—and black has not become synonymous with beautiful in South Asia.

The complexion of the bride is important in marriage negotiations; if she is light she may get a more highly qualified husband, but if she is dark her parents may have to give a larger dowry. Newspapers carry notices of eligible singles in the classified advertisement section, generally placed by parents, which often specify that a "fair" girl is desired. People of Indian origin do not generally mix with Negroes or Melanesians, whether in Guyana, Trinidad, Fiji, East Africa, or American university campuses, but remain ethnically and socially separate. But the majority in South Asia are medium or dark brown and not as interested in complexion as the elite who advertise in English newspapers. Dark pigmentation is by itself hardly ever the cause of discrimination against an individual, except as part of a complex of social indicators such as low caste or menial occupation. In the workaday world a person who is black is not thereby disadvantaged.

Racial Classification

A person from South Asia, when walking on the sidewalks of New York or London, is almost always recognizable as a South Asian, for the partial geographical isolation of the subcontinent has bred a physiological type as well as a distinctive pattern of culture. But South Asians cannot easily be lumped with any of the major racial categories popularly enumerated. They are not quite Caucasoid, Negroid, Mongoloid, nor Australoid. South Asia falls in the middle of these four and its people naturally have biological affinity with all four, though perhaps the Caucasoid and Australoid elements predominate. The concept of geographical races is perhaps more useful, but this too is full of difficulties because of the social compartmentalization within India and South Asia generally.

The classification attempts of scholars of the British period, four of which are summarized below, lacked historical depth because of paucity of archeological skeletons. They also failed to follow specific traits through several generations and neglected factors of environment and adaptation. In the last two decades many articles on racial traits have appeared in Indian anthropological journals, but almost no work of this type has been forthcoming from Pakistan or the other countries, no doubt because these countries lack the long traditional penchant of Hindu scholarship to classify things and engage in introspection. Our post-World War II data, therefore, is mostly confined to India.

Herbert Risley is the best known early physical anthropologist of South Asia, whose observations on racial categories, based on many measurements, were published in the *Census of India, 1901*, and later in his book *The People of India*. Risley classified the people of British India and the princely states into seven types. But we should stress that his use of linguistic terms for racial types is *not* acceptable today even though one might hear them so used in India. The physical types Risley identified were:

1) Turko-Īrānian. These are characterized by broad heads, fair complexion, plentiful hair, very long noses, and dark but occasionally gray eyes. Brāhūīs, Paṭhāns, and some other peoples of the North-West Frontier Province of Pakistan fall in this group, all of whom came from the Īrānian side.

2) Indo-Āryan. These are distinguished from group 1 by longer heads, the tallest stature in India, and fine but not especially long noses. They are quite fair, and include especially the upper and middle classes of the Panjāb, Kashmīr, and Rājasthān.

3) Scytho-Dravidian. This group features especially broad heads, less abundant hair, and medium stature. They have spread down the western side of India from Gujarāt to Coorg in Karṇāṭaka.

4) Āryo-Dravidian. The characteristic head form is long with a tendency to medium, the nose ranges from medium to broad, and stature is less than that found in groups 1 and 2. Their skin color ranges from wheat-colored to very dark. This group includes the populations of Uttar Pradesh and Bihār and merges into Mongoloid peoples in the northeast. To some extent this type is also characteristic of Haryāṇā, Rājasthān, and Sri Lanka. Their origin is ascribed to the mixture of Indo-Āryan and Dravidian types.

5) Mongolo-Dravidian. These are distinguished from the Āryo-Dravidian by their broader heads and darker complexion. Hair is fairly plentiful, and the nose is medium with a tendency to be broad. This is the Bāngālī type.

6) Mongoloid. These have broad heads, less than average stature, somewhat flat faces, oblique eyelids, and scanty facial hair. Their complexion has a yellowish tinge and may also be dark. They inhabit the Himālayan regions including Nepal, Assam, and Burma.

7) Dravidian. Typically these have long heads, broad noses with the root usually depressed, and somewhat short statures. Their hair is sometimes wavy or curly, and complexion is dark or very dark. They form the bulk of the population of the peninsula from the edge of the Gangā plain to Sri Lanka.

These seven categories are here listed not so much because this system finds favor today, but because it reflects certain biases long current among professional anthropologists and even today met with in popular parlance. Most striking is the confusion of linguistic categories and races, an attitude bred by traditional Hindu literature. The sacred Vedas, presumably composed by folk of "Āryan" descent, refer to the Dāsas, a word which means "slaves" in classical Sanskrit. Dāsas are described as dark, ill-favored, bull-lipped, snub-nosed, and of hostile speech. They lived in forts or towns and were the indigenous people against whom the presumably noble and intrusive "Āryans" waged war. This distinction was popularly extended to produce an apparent dichotomy in the population of all of South Asia: all those who spoke Indo-Āryan languages and followed Brāhmaṇical ritual were "Āryans," but the outcaste groups and those speaking Dravidian or Muṇḍa languages were considered to be Dāsas, who were eventually dominated and civilized by the Āryans. Only since Risley's time has it been realized that the earliest urban people of India probably spoke Dravidian languages and had gracile features, whereas the Āryans were originally nomadic and became urbanized or civilized only after entering the Indian area. The words "Āryan" and "Dravidian" today are reserved as *linguistic* terms; they are not to be used in discussing races.

Risley thought that the nasal index (ratio of breadth to length) was the most significant diagnostic measurement for correlating physical type with caste and social hierarchy. He listed all his average caste measurements on the basis of nose form and in fact did show a fair correlation between broad noses and low social status. But it was pointed out long ago that the

nasal index and head form of many Tamiḻs and Telugus is not far removed from those of peoples of the Gangā plains, whereas the tribal peoples of central India do often have broad noses and a degree of longheadedness. Because Risley lived in Bānglā and was insufficiently acquainted with peninsular India, he lumped all the peoples of the peninsula except some on the western side as "Dravidians" and assumed that the degree of mixture with "Āryans" and other intruders could be determined by measuring noses, head form, and skin color.

The above scheme also assumes that broadheadedness, such as extends from Gujarāt to Karṇāṭaka is the result of the intrusion of "Scythians" (called Śakas in Indian history), Kushāṇas, Hūṇas, Turks, and others from Central Asia. The broad or medium heads of Bāngālīs, Risley explained, resulted from mixture with Mongoloid immigrants to the plains. But Indian anthropologists have of late become wary of explanations of racial variation which rest entirely on theories of immigration. Notwithstanding these criticisms, Risley for the first time observed the population of South Asia in a broad, sweeping view, made a plethora of measurements, and laid the groundwork for evolving a scientific classification of the physical characteristics of the people.

More Anthropometry

A more satisfactory classification was worked out by von Eickstedt in the twenties and thirties. He proposed a threefold grouping of Veddids, Melanids, and Indids. Veddids (named after the hunter Väddās of Sri Lanka who are about extinct now) he subdivided into a) Gondids, such as the tribal people of central India, with medium to short stature, dark brown skin, and rather broad noses, and b) Malids, characterized by the tiny tribal minorities of Kēraḷa having short stature, curly hair, and black-brown color. Melanids he divided into a) South Melanids, consisting of the bulk of the dark-colored population of the peninsula, and b) North Melanids, such as the Santāls of tribal South Bihār. Indids included a) Gracile Indids, the Bāngālīs, and b) North Indids, the light brown people of North India and Pakistan. He recognized a "Mediterranean" racial element, influenced in India by "Paleomongolid" and "Orientalid" strains, in addition to the broadheaded "Alpine" and "Dinaric" tendencies in the western part of the subcontinent.

The *Census of India, 1931* included a volume by B. S. Guha which tabulated anthropometric figures for 2511 subjects from all over undivided India measured by Guha himself. He summarized the existing knowledge of physical types and published a map drawn according to cephalic index (ratio of breadth to length of the head). He reclassified the peoples of undivided India in six categories.

I. Negrito
II. Proto-Australoid
III. Mongoloid
  A. Palco-Mongoloid
    1. Longheaded
    2. Broadheaded
  B. Tibeto-Mongoloid
IV. Mediterranean
  A. Paleo-Mediterranean
  B. Mediterranean
  C. Oriental type
V. Western Brachycephalic type
  A. Alpinoid
  B. Dinaric
  C. Armenoid
VI. Nordic

The existence of a Negrito substratum was postulated on the basis of frizzly hair having been observed on a handful of individuals of the Kāḍar and Iruḷar, numerically insignificant tribes of the Kēraḷa hills. The Proto-Australoid of this system is the same as what is sometimes called Australoid or Pre-Dravidian; the Väddās of Sri Lanka are the epitomy of this category. Guha characterized the Āngāmi Nāgas (of Nāgaland) as longheaded Mongoloids, and Bhūṭānese as broadheaded ones, whereas the people of the western Himālayas are mixed Tibetan and Indian in origin. He listed Telugu Brāhmaṇs as characteristic of the basal Mediterranean type, Eickstedt's Melanid; they are rather short in stature, longheaded but with smallish head size, black hair, and dark or tawny skin. Nagar Brāhmaṇs of Gujarāt epitomized another Mediterranean type; the backs of their heads tend to be flat. A superimposed "Alpine" strain was said to be responsible for the physical characteristics of the Dardic-speaking peoples. The broadheadedness of the Balūchīs and many castes of Gujarāt, Mahārāshṭra, Karṇāṭaka, and even of Bānglā, was said to have been brought by other intruding people from the west. Guha's Nordic type is what Risley called the Indo-Āryan—the long and narrowheaded, tall and sturdy people found in and around the Panjāb.

D. N. Majumdar, the best known of the last generation of Indian anthropologists, measured the heads and other features of 3017 people in Uttar Pradesh and showed that the population of that state was largely homogeneous, but to the extent that variant types could be classified he called them 1) Proto-Australoid, a longheaded, broad-nosed type represented by the tribal minorities on the southern fringe of the state and by the servile castes, 2) Indo-Mediterranean, the longheaded and fine-nosed type represented by upper castes and pedigreed Muslims, 3) Mongoloid, the medium-headed types having medium to short noses, represented by the

Thārūs of the low Himālayan slopes, and 4) Alpine, a slight strain of broad-headed, olive-complexioned people in the northern part of the state.

All these classification systems are now more or less questioned. Yet this brief review may have helped the reader to appreciate the racial mosaic that is South Asia together with its unifying features, and mentally to compare it with Europe which is comparable in size and population.

Racial History

A number of Indian anthropologists have said there is not sufficient evidence to postulate a Negrito substratum in the population because frizzly hair has been seen on only a handful of individuals and might be the result of Negro admixture. J. H. Hutton, however, alleged that there were indeed Melanesian traits submerged in the populations of the Nāga hills toward the Burma border and also in the Nicobar Islands. The suspicion still persists that South Asia had a prehistoric population that formed a continuum with early population types in Africa on the one hand and with the Negritos of Southeast Asia on the other, remnants of which persist in the Andaman Islands and the interiors of Malaysia, New Guinea, the Philippines, and Taiwan. Melanesian characteristics have been spotted in Viet Nam as recently as the last century, and frizzly hair was noted in southwest China by medieval Chinese writers. The question cannot be further elucidated without analysis of more prehistoric skeletal material. There has been some bias against identification of Negro or Negrito traits in the population of India.

The terms most commonly used today by those who hazard classification of the substratum of the population of South Asia are Australoid, Proto-Australoid, and Pre-Dravidian; those who reject the Negrito hypothesis think the Proto-Australoids are the earliest identifiable population type. The Väddās of Sri Lanka, the Cencu hunting tribe of Āndhra, and to a lesser extent, low castes through peninsular India are said to preserve Proto-Australoid characteristics. Carleton Coon's analysis, however, of the morphology of the Väddās and also of skeletal material from Sri Lanka suggests that their racial affinity, as in the rest of the people of South Asia, is more Caucasoid than anything else, but with Negroid and Australoid overtones. Australoids have more pronounced supraorbital ridges, a considerably greater nasal index, greater stature, thicker cranial bones, and heavier mandibles than do Väddās or other partially Australoid peoples of India. Other features in the substrata of Indian population are tendency to prognathism (protrusion of the lower face), firmly set teeth, tendency for the chin to be weakly developed, long and narrow head, smallish and not vertical forehead, broad nose with the root depressed, thick but not everted

lips, dark brown color, tendency to wavy or curly hair, scanty facial hair, and relatively low frequency of balding and graying. Some of these traits are found in Negroid, Mongoloid, and Southeast Asian populations as well as among Australian aborigines. An experienced observer will be struck by similarities of body motions between Australian aborigines and Indians.

The extent of Mongoloid influence in the subcontinent has also been debated on the basis of anthropometric data. Risley showed that cephalic index increases as one moves down the Gangā from Panjāb to Bānglā, while nasal index also increases. Bāngālīs are not as broadheaded as Balūchīs or Gujarātīs, however, and most fall within the middling range. Guha dispelled the idea that this head shape in the eastern Gangā region was entirely due to the admixture of a Mongoloid racial element by pointing to Assam tribes that were essentially Mongoloid but were also longheaded and had either narrow or middling noses. It is obvious, though, that admixture of Mongoloids has taken place along the hilly fringes of Bangladesh and in the whole Brahmaputra valley of Assam where the people are clearly Hinduized Mongoloids. Then too, at least some of the ancestry of the Muṇḍa-speaking peoples of central India must be traced to the Burma side; there are measurable Mongoloid features among the tribes of Choṭā Nāgpur. Traits considered Mongoloid are also found farther south in the peninsula, as the frequency of shovel-shaped incisors and the lumbar blue spot on babies.

It is generally agreed that the majority of Indians and Pakistanis exhibit physical traits which are essentially Mediterranean Caucasoid, and have narrow heads, thin bones, supple joints, and angular noses and chins. Alpine-Armenoid Caucasoid strains have been invoked to explain why the Balūchīs have the broadest heads in India or Pakistan. This is an evident influence from Iran. But whether the broadheadedness of Karṇāṭaka can be historically traced northward to Iran is questionable because there is less of it in Mahārāshṭra. Those who rely on migration theories to explain all regional racial differences also trace the flattened occiput of Bāngālīs to "Alpine" or "Armenoid" immigration from the west which appeared in the India region before the latest wave of Indo-European speech, perhaps coincidental with the "outer" band of Indo-European languages. Bāngālī high castes have a tendency to longheadedness, a trait which increases toward Panjāb and is said to be the result of the more recent of the "Āryan" or "Nordic" invasions.

A more relevant view is that of Stanley Garn, who classified the Indian Geographical Race as one of nine world geographical races, which also has within it many breeding populations, distinguished as regional peoples, tribes, and castes. The Indian physical type developed in the warm bosom of the subcontinent while yet maintaining gene flow with other races to the west and also to the east. Garn suggests that both disease selection

and nutrition selection have been particularly intense in South Asia within the last century.

Indian anthropologists have recently turned more to the study of multilineal evolution and local adaptation rather than reconstruction of mass invasions and migrations. Many kinds of physical traits are now under study, such as body chemistry, palm and finger prints, blood pressure of Himālayan peoples, length of ear lobes, hairiness of the ears, and the hairiness of certain finger joints. The Anthropological Survey of India has recently collected anthropometric and serological data on 80,000 people from all districts of the country, which after tabulation will provide a firmer basis for study of racial variation and evolution.

Skeletons

There are no datable early prehistoric skeletons found in South Asia, but a few have been recovered from neolithic (preurban cultivating) levels and early archeological sites. We can summarize what they suggest about racial types.

From the well-known neolithic site of Brāhmagiri in Karṇāṭaka there were skeletons having a dominant "Australoid" element, and there was another more robust type, medium statured with a somewhat broad head and very broad nose.[1] From the same state at the site of Piklihāl were unearthed skeletons with either long or medium heads, narrow noses, prognathism, and rounded occiput.[2] From pot-burials at the site of Ādicanallūr on the southern coast of Tamil̲ Nāḍu there were a half dozen skeletons that have been studied in some detail, though they are not earlier than the Christian era. They are said to be predominantly "Australoid" but not of the most primitive type, with much "Mediterranean" admixture and also an "Armenoid" strain.[3] The same could be stated of the existing populations in these regions and of tribal peninsular India.

An Iron Age site in Raigir, Āndhra, yielded the skulls of six persons. Some have heavy supraorbital ridges; in general the forehead is low and the degree of its inclination ranges from a bulbous projection to a very pronounced slope. The size of the frontal eminences is just as variable. The occipital region is quite curved. Some of the skulls are very narrow and some are very broad, and both A and B blood types are represented. In general the skeletons are "Mediterranean" but it is apparent that we cannot assume that Iron Age people of the peninsula were homogeneous.[4]

The important neolithic site of Nevāsā in Mahārāshṭra produced a set of skeletons like those of Piklihāl. They have a tendency to prognathism, and the males have rather noticeable supraorbital ridges. The forehead is not very high and is notably inclined. Frontal eminences are large. Noses

are medium to broad and moderately depressed at the root. All these features are common to the tribal people living today in eastern Gujarāt, Mahārāshṭra, and western Madhya Pradesh. A further skeleton from an "Indo-Roman" level at Nevāsā is more typically Mediterranean, having a greater stature and a quite narrow skull. K. Kennedy suggests that a Mediterranean population became established on the western side of the subcontinent during neolithic times, while an earlier "Mediterranean-Proto-Australoid" type was dominant in the Indian heartland and central parts.

The largest collection of skeletons has come from the Indus Civilization sites, and those from Harappā have been statistically studied. The skeletons from Cemetery R-37 at Harappā, contemporary with the civilization, are on the whole like those of the Nevāsā specimens. They have similar frontal bones, shallow to medium depression of the nasal root, moderate development of the mastoid process, longheadedness, and in the males noticeable supraorbital ridges and muscular robusticity of the vault. The Indian archeologists who studied these preferred to avoid using terms having geographical connotations, but the specimens fit the categories of Proto-Australoid, Mediterranean, and Proto-Nordic.[5]

At Mohenjo-dāṛo, the largest Indus Civilization city, a series of skeletons found near the end of the city's florescent period has been classified according to the older terminology. Four were defined as Proto-Australoid, six as Mediterranean, four as Alpine, and one as Mongoloid. At Lothal, the chief site of that civilization in Gujarāt, there was a longheaded and rugged Proto-Nordic type, a mediumheaded Mediterranean type, and also broadheaded specimens. At Harappā in Cemetery H, however, which is post-Indus in culture, there are more broadheaded specimens which do not so closely resemble those of Nevāsā. This may be considered as rather skimpy evidence of genes flowing from western Asia gradually modifying the relatively aboriginal population of the western side of the subcontinent.

There is not much evidence the people in the Gangā plains were ever very different than they are now. From Kauśāmbī, an ancient city near Allāhābād, five crania have been found which are datable to roughly the time of Christ. The people were relatively tall with medium heads and broad noses. The foreheads had either medium or low height and receded somewhat. The occiput was more or less rounded on all specimens. Development of the supraorbital ridges ranged from slight in females to medium in males. The lower jaw was strong, the chin prominent, and the bones of the extremities robust.[6] The people living in the region today have generally the same features.

If anything can be summarized, it is that the populations of most regions were mixed and that practically all measurements fall within the normal range of variation found in some segments of the populations of India and Pakistan today. Only a few diagnostic traits have been included in this anthropometric data, and there are not many skeletons. But it is worth

noting that a fair number of specimens do show features which have been described as primitive or Proto-Australoid and that the later specimens to the west do suggest intrusive physical types. But the evidence does not support the supposition that massive immigration anywhere accounted for any rapid alteration of the racial composition, contrary to some popular assumptions about history.

The Andamanese

The people of the Andamans were isolated for so long before their discovery that they are of considerable anthropological interest. The people of Great Andaman Island, who are now virtually extinct or absorbed, once numbered about 5000 and were slightly mixed with Burmese immigrants. On Little Andaman a few score Onges still exist in a fairly isolated state. A third group of Andamanese called Jarawa have also remained isolated as they have a reputation for summarily disposing of all comers. Having no resistance to the diseases spread during the colonial period, many died of syphilis and influenza, while at one time half of them died of measles.

Measuring under 5 feet, the Onges fall into the pygmy category. They have sometimes been classified as Negritos, but over two thirds of those tested by Guha have blood type A and very few have O, whereas Philippine Negritos and African Bushmen have more O blood. Onges do not have the sickle cell trait found in Africa and somewhat in India, but they do have the typically Negroid Rhesus gene R_0. Onges have peppercorn hair and very little body hair except in the pubic region, and even there it is scanty. Both men and women have noticeable steatopygia (protruding fatty buttocks) and their ears are smallish. Their skin is dark but not black, and it is different from that of Bushmen because it is silky smooth, not wrinkled and folded. As with Malaysian Semangs and Philippine Aetas, their crania are high-vaulted, with relatively vertical foreheads of low to moderate height, and their faces are broad. Their noses are short and moderately broad.

P. Gupta's study of nine Onge skeletons showed that though their cranial index is relatively high, in fact they are smallheaded, with cranial capacity ranging only between 1100 and 1200 cubic centimeters, which is near the bottom of the range of variation of modern man's brain size. Their cheek bones are more or less prominent, the nasal root is usually broad, and orbits are high. Both alveolar and facial prognathism are evident in all the specimens studied. An interesting feature is that there is evidence of side-to-side movement of the mandible in chewing. Incisor teeth are shovel-shaped, and all the teeth are worn from grinding rough food. Differences between males and females are not pronounced. The long bones are small and slender and show some indications of primitiveness.

The people of Nicobar Islands to the south are essentially Malay in culture as well as in physical type, but it may be that the Nicobarese absorbed an earlier Negrito population. They have a very high percentage of O blood (86%), lack sickle cells, and have shovel-shaped incisor teeth.

The interesting traits of the Onges, preserved probably since the rising sea cut off the Andaman Islands, may indeed have been characteristic of a Negrito or Negrillo population stretching all the way across the Old World tropical belt. On the other hand, it must be understood that these islands were inhabited by small breeding populations whose genetic composition was therefore somewhat susceptible to change.

Bāngālī Physical Types and Castes

Is there a racial basis for caste distinctions? Rather than tackle this question for all South Asia, let us select one region: Bānglā. D. N. Majumdar made anthropometric surveys in Uttar Pradesh and Gujarāt, and subsequently drew upon his experience to make a survey of the Bāngālī people. Since he did this just before Partition of India and Pakistan his results apply to both parts of the Banglā plains.

In the anthropometric survey of Uttar Pradesh, sitting height was found to best discriminate between tribal and nontribal people. In Bānglā also there is good correlation between caste and sitting height. Tribal groups such as the Māhāto of Midnapur, the Goālā, Mājhī, and Santāl in the eastern extremity of West Bengal have sitting height means ranging from 790 to 813 centimeters. At the other end of the scale, the higher castes such as Baidyā, Baiśyā, Kāyastha, Brāhmaṇ, and "Kshatriya," in that order, have mean values ranging from 869 to 872 centimeters. Bāngālī Muslims occupy an intermediate position, but fall closer to the tribal than to the high caste range. This suggests that Bāngālī Muslim converts (now in Bangladesh) were largely of low or outcaste origin and that their genealogies tracing Arab descent are mostly fanciful. By contrast, the Muslims of Uttar Pradesh and most of western India tend to be tall and relatively fair with few Proto-Australoid features; their genealogies pointing westward may rest on better evidence. The Namaśūdras are a large and low-status Hindu group who also have a low sitting height; they were so stigmatized in medieval times that they adopted Buddhism.

Stature also tends to correlate with caste, for measurements of tribal groups cluster and are separate from those for nontribal castes. In regard to forehead breadth, low or outcaste groups such as Namaśūdra, Bāgdī, and Telī yield measurements that cluster and contrast with those for Hindu high castes.

Table 3–1, plotting cephalic and nasal indices, supports the picture we have from sitting height and stature measurements; there is a clustering

TABLE 3–1 Nasal and Cephalic Indices of Bāngālī Castes and Tribes (adapted from Majumdar and Rao 1960, by permission of Asia Publishing House, Inc.).

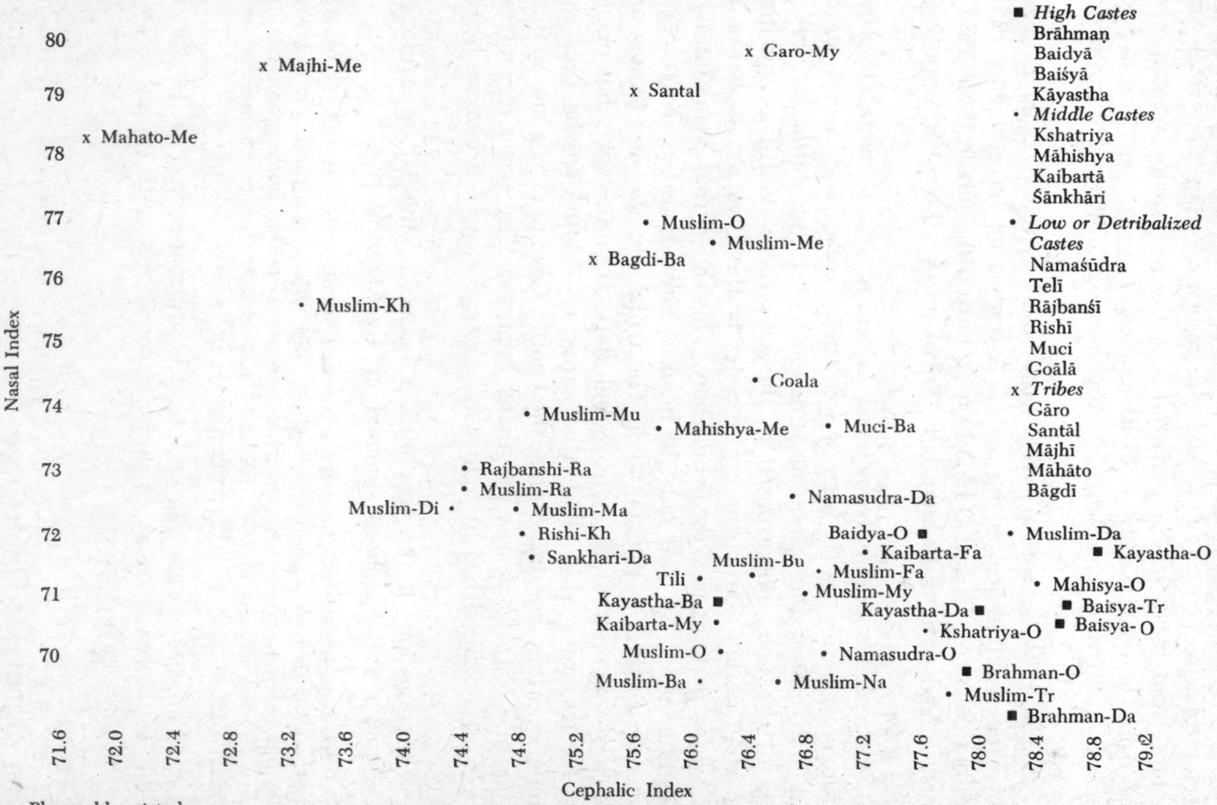

Places abbreviated:

Barisāl	Dacca	Faridābād	Maldā	Murshidābād	Nadiā	Rangpur
Burdwān	Dinājpur	Khulnā	Medinipur	Mymensingh	(others)	Tripurā

of groups of castes. Brāhmaṇs, Baiśyās (merchants), Kāyasthas (scribes), and Baidyās (doctors) are practically indistinguishable from each other. Tribal groups are more homogeneous and far outside the clusters of high and intermediate castes, but outcaste groups overlap the tribal groups. Muslims from the northern parts fall into the low caste clusters, whereas those from the coastal districts of Bangladesh have narrower noses because of a little admixture with Arabs, Portuguese, and others who intruded from the sea.

Considerable statistical work with blood types of Bāngālīs has not shown much difference among castes. A few castes have slightly different distributions of A, B, and O blood types, but on the whole these are not so clearly linked with caste hierarchy. Tribal groups, however, appear statistically different.

Skin color is popularly believed in South Asia to correlate with the hierarchy of castes, partly because low castes are exposed to the sun more than high castes. But when measurements of pigmentation are taken on parts of the body not exposed to the sun, there is still a gradation of increasing darkness from the upper castes to the lower, as shown in Table 3–2, which pertains to West Bengal only. This shows that Namaśūdras, agricultural laborers, have not only the blackest individuals but also the greatest range of variation in pigmentation. The tribal Muṇḍas and Oraons in the hilly western corner of the state, though dark, are much more homogeneous. The Riāngs are a Mongoloid tribe native to Tripurā in the hills east of Bāngla, and they are darker than the central Chinese. Poḍs are an outcaste group, and Māhishyas were originally boatmen. The castes of professional people are distinguished by lighter average color, with Brāhmaṇs being the lightest.

The question of the relationship between physical appearance and traditional castes has been summed up by Majumdar:

> Whatever arguments may be advanced against the usefulness of Anthropometry as a tool to explain the existing, and almost accepted, social hierarchy, it has been demonstrated on more than one occasion that anthropometric findings do support the scheme of social precedence, and that the correspondence between physical pattern and social stratification is not merely fortuitous.[7]

But the range of variation of each trait is so great within each caste that it would be foolhardy to try to pinpoint someone's caste simply by looking over his biological features.

Other Genotypic Differences

D. N. Majumdar, starting shortly after World War II, gave impetus through his extensive surveys to the study of blood types. There are now data on the ABO types covering most population categories in India, but

TABLE 3–2 Skin Color of Bāngālī Castes and Tribes (adapted from A. K. Mitra 1964)

Skin Color	*Lushan's Scale*	*Radhiyā Brāhmaṇs (Calcutta)*	*Radhiyā Kāyasthas (Calcutta)*	*Bancajā Vaidhyās (Khulnā, Jessore)*	*Suvarṇavanik Baniyās (Calcutta)*	*Māhishyas (Howrah)*	*Radhiyā Vaidyās (Calcutta)*	*Poḍs (24 Parganās)*	*Namaśūdras (Khulnā)*	*Muṇḍas (tribe)*	*Oraons (tribe)*	*Riāngs (Tripurā tribe)*	*Central Chinese*
	9	—	1.0	7.2	1.2	—	—	—					
Very fair	10	—	3.0	1.6	1.6	—	0.8	—					
	11	6.0	1.0	7.2	4.8	0.8	1.6	—					7.6
	12	—	10.0	17.6	6.8	0.8	3.2	—					9.6
	13	18.0	12.0	7.2	7.6	4.0	4.0	—					16.5
Light	14	38.0	26.0	21.6	22.4	23.2	7.2	2.0	0.4				14.5
	15	26.0	29.0	19.2	29.2	21.6	16.0	10.0	—			0.95	—
	16	—	—	—	1.2	—	10.4	6.0	—			8.57	24.2
	17	12.0	17.0	9.6	9.6	20.0	28.0	16.0	5.6			24.76	4.7
	18		—	—	0.8	—	1.6	16.0	2.4			3.81	9.6
	19		—	—	—	—	—	—	—			—	6.7
Medium brown	20		—	—	—	—	—	—	0.4			0.95	3.9
	21		—	—	0.4	—	0.8	—	1.2			6.67	0.9
	22		—	2.4	9.2	12.0	10.4	2.0	4.4			40.95	1.8
	23		1.0	5.6	5.2	15.2	14.4	32.0	39.2		0.4	10.48	
	24			—		0.8	1.6	—	16.4		—	—	
	25			—		—		—	12.8	1.2	2.4	2.86	
Dark brown	26			—		—		2.0	2.8	1.6	—		
	27			0.8		0.8		14.0	5.6	16.0	36.8		
	28					—			0.4	18.8	21.6		
	29					—			0.4	60.4	38.8		
	30					0.8			5.2	1.6			
Very dark	31								—	0.4			
	32								2.0				
Reddish brown	33								0.4				
Blackish brown	34								0.4				
Grayish brown	35												

work on other blood types such as the subgroups of A and the MN types has not progressed to the extent that useful maps can be made of their distribution.[8]

Type O is present in 30% to 32% of the population. It is slightly higher in Uttar Pradesh than in central India, and higher yet toward Balūchistān (47%). It is also higher among people whose ancestry is part Arab or European. The Great Andamanese and Onges have the lowest incidence of Type O (10% and 15% respectively), while their neighbors, the Nicobarese, who came from around Malaya, have the highest (86%).

India generally has a low incidence of Type A. It is high among the tribes of the eastern hills, as it is among East Asians generally. Whereas it is high among Australian aborigines and Polynesians, it is generally low (12% to 20%) among the low castes of north and peninsular India. It is surprisingly high among some of the small tribes of the South (37% to 62%). Type A may be low among the major population groups because it is selected against by smallpox.

Type B has provoked the most discussion, for it is higher in India even than in East Asia and Southeast Asia, though slightly less than in Central Asia. Its incidence ranges from 25% to 35% across North India, with pockets in Uttar Pradesh and southern Bānglā having 40% and in Bihār 50%. It falls off in western and southern India, however. It is interesting that there is a high incidence of B among depressed castes such as Ḍoms and Camārs (40% to 55%) except that it is not particularly high among the tribals of central India and even falls to 10% among the tribals of western Madhya Pradesh and eastern Gujarāt. It is also low in the eastern hills, falling to 10% among some Nāgas. Perhaps this genotype had a center of dispersal on the Indian plains, some environmental factors selecting for it that were not operative in the mountainous periphery.

Another trait that has an interesting distribution is the inability to taste PTC (phenylthiocarbamide), which has been mapped, based on surveys by S. R. Das and others. It is highest in the central Indian tribal belt (40% to 50%), rivaled elsewhere only by the Australian aborigines (50%) and New Guinea pygmies. It is lower in Malaysia (16%), Western Europe (25%), and among Negroes (6%). Among the central Indian tribes it is very high among the Parojas of Orissa (54%), Ḍankās of Gujarāt (56%), and others, but much lower among the small Kēraḷa tribes. The fact that the percentage of nontasters is high among the low caste peasants of central and eastern India suggests that these people are largely detribalized castes; it is high among the low Kolīs of Mahārāshṭra (38%) and Bāngālī Rājbanśīs and Muslims (40%). The adaptive function of this trait is not known. Here we have another trait supporting observations inferentially made by earlier anthropologists about the racial affinities of the substrata of South Asian populations.

Color blindness in India is quite variable, ranging from under 1% to 10% among males of various castes and geographical regions. In a large heterogeneous sample, 3.75% of males tested were affected by one of the types of red or green color blindness. This sex-linked trait is considerably higher in Europe than in India, and also high in China. The incidence in Japan is similar to that in India, but it is lower among Negroes (2.25%) and Melanesians.

The differential within India is interesting. In general, its incidence is lowest among tribals (1% or 2%), a little more among low castes (2% to 3%), and more still among intermediate and higher castes (3% to 7%). There are exceptions, but this pattern holds for the South as well as the North, and even the Assam region. It is highest in Panjāb.

A Sikh albino in a bus in Panjāb. He shields his eyes from the sun and writes a postcard at close range.

Color blindness is more common in parts of the world where agriculture or settled life has been established earliest because selection against this disability operates more efficiently in hunting or gathering societies. In the latter, confusion of dark reds and browns, light reds and greens, purples and blues, might be disadvantageous to survival. This probably explains why color blindness is higher among high castes and settled people than among tribal populations. Roberts and Tanner have shown that this trait is quite variable in India, whereas in Africa the population is much more homogeneous in this regard. In India, aside from the differential evolution of the peasant way of life, further factors are immigration of Caucasoids from the Near East and the genetic compartmentalization of society by castes. Further research is necessary to discover the mutation rates of this trait and to trace it through several generations.

Malaria-Related Traits

Since parts of South Asia have been, and still are, highly malarial, the several polymorphisms that have developed in response to this disease in Africa and the Mediterranean basin are also found in South Asia. Frank Livingston has synthesized the data on abnormal hemoglobins in this connection. South Asia has hemoglobin S (the sickle cell trait), better known for its occurrence in Africa, hemoglobins D, E, K, and rarer ones such as J, L, N, and Q. In addition there is G6Pd (glucose-6-phosphate dehydrogenase) deficiency and thalassemia, all of which apparently have some survival value in malarial environments.

The sickle cell trait is found mostly in the central Indian tribal belt, in neighboring low castes, and in western India where it is particularly high among low castes in Mahārāshṭra such as Mahārs and Telīs, and the five "tribal" minorities of Gujarāt. It affects 10% to 15% among some Gōṇḍ groups in central India, rising to 40% among the Mahrā (Mahārs) of Bastār in southern Madhya Pradesh; this is equilibrium, since persons homozygous for the trait generally die in infancy of anemia while those who are heterozygous resist malaria.

In the central Indian tribal belt, slash-and-burn cultivation has been common, a practice that provides swampy pools for the anopheles mosquito to breed in, while at the same time there are few cattle for the mosquitos to feed on. Central India and the tarāī on the northern edge of the Gangā plains have been in the past as malarious as any part of the world, but the tarāī was not much populated until malaria eradication. The small tribes of the Kēraḷa hills also have the sickle cell trait.

This gene may have appeared in India from the Near East because it has a distribution around the Mediterranean as well as in Africa and has been spotted in Iraq and Kuwait. It has an occasional incidence in Pakistan and among the Sikhs. In India it is much lower among the peasant populations than among tribals and slightly higher in the South than in the North. But the Andaman Islanders were too isolated to receive this gene. Interestingly, higher castes have little of the sickle cell trait, and urban populations practically none.

Hemoglobin E is found heavily represented in Southeast Asia, especially Thailand. It does not occur in India except in Assam, the eastern hills, and to a very slight extent, Bānglā. Strangely, it is found among the Väddās or mixed Väddās-Tamiḻs of Sri Lanka. Since this trait diffused rather recently throughout Southeast Asia, an explanation for its occurrence in Sri Lanka might be that it was brought there directly from Southeast Asia and proved advantageous because there was so little of the sickle cell trait.

Thalassemia, which impairs synthesis of hemoglobin and causes early death to those homozygous for the trait, also affords some protection against

malaria to those who are heterozygous. It is found in Mahārāshṭra, Tamil̲ Nāḍu, and Kēraḷa; other regions have not been sufficiently studied for this trait. It probably diffused into South Asia from the Mediterranean regions.

The G6Pd deficiency is a sex-linked trait that produces an allergic-like response to the fava bean, and is especially noted around the Mediterranean where this bean is eaten. Shown to be related to malarial environments, this deficiency has been found in western India, the southern tribes, and to a lesser extent, the peasant populations of Āndhra and the Gangā plains, but its incidence is less than in malarial parts of Africa or Southeast Asia. The abnormal hemoglobin D is found in the North and K is around Madras.

Since a number of these traits, such as the sickle cell and thalassemia, are deleterious except as they provide resistance to malaria, it is likely that their incidence will decrease as this disease is eradicated. Sri Lanka was the object of an intensive eradication campaign by the World Health Organization, which succeeded to the extent that the island's population growth rate doubled as a result of this and other health improvements. In the 1960s huge campaigns in India led to the periodic spraying with DDT of every house over vast regions, with considerable success, but in the early seventies it seems that malaria was on the increase again, enhancing the adaptive function of these abnormal hemoglobins and other adaptive polymorphisms.

Adaptation

Most of the earlier studies by physical anthropologists concentrated on specific traits presumed to have been brought by invading hordes such as Scythians, Mongoloids, or Āryans. Guha went to the trouble of distinguishing four kinds of longheaded invaders, besides Australoids, and three kinds of broadheaded folk, all supposed to have come from the west. But neither the history nor the archeology of the subcontinent speaks to us about invading hordes—only trickles. Doubtless, a trickle can spread over a continent after some time, but the linguistic, dynastic, and cultural indicators of the past give no evidence that intrusive elements at any given time were very numerous when compared with the indigenous population.

The newer view is that South Asia may be considered an evolutionary field. Just as the partial isolation of the subcontinent bred a distinct cultural pattern, so it defined a type of person almost always recognizable as South Asian. One need not feel compelled to look far afield for the origins of such features as "Mediterranean" or gracile skeletal types, skin pigmentation, suppleness of joints, hemoglobin variants, or even head forms, which might prove to be adaptive to the climate and culture of South Asia. On the other hand, long-isolated minor breeding populations such as the tribes of Nāgaland, Assam, and central India have certainly grown to be distinct in minor

specific traits. Together with the great range of geographical features and the tendency toward segmentation of society, these have helped to keep the population of the subcontinent polytypic for most traits.

D. K. Sen, after having graphically plotted and studied by states the distribution of ABO blood types and reviewed other genotypic and phenotypic characteristics, was able to show that there are really no clusterings at all showing major immigrant groups in the heavily populated plains regions of India. Even Majumdar found this true as regards blood types in Bānglā. Sen concludes that the population of Uttar Pradesh, now numbering 90 million, is really homogeneous except for the Bhoṭiyā of Tibetan affinity in the Himālayas; he holds the same for Gujarāt except for the tribes on its southeast. He finds no clusterings among Bihār tribals coincident with Muṇḍa and Dravidian linguistic families, and points out that in Mahārāshṭra there is more variation of blood type among three Brāhmaṇ castes than among some castes of diverse social strata. Kēraḷa is more heterogeneous since the state includes ethnic groups ranging from the minuscule hill tribes to Syrian Christians and Muslims with some Arab ancestry, but even there nothing can be proved about immigration by the study of one trait by itself.

Of course, this emphasis on the homogeneity of the major plains populations and the decreased emphasis on the history of immigration falls in line with contemporary social and political attitudes, when countries are building up their identity and caste is in official disfavor. Yet, it is a necessary corrective to the research of the past which stressed differences rather than similarities.

As the adaptive functions of the various genotypic differences become more clear the general trends within South Asia as an evolutionary field will become more apparent. The adaptive functions of the abnormal hemoglobins and color blindness have already been partly perceived, and now differences in blood types are beginning to appear significant for survival. Chakravartti and Vogel have shown, for instance, that people having blood type A are more susceptible to attacks of smallpox and are also more likely to die of the disease than persons having O or B blood. The reason is that the smallpox virus contains an A-like antigen, so the antibodies effective against the disease may attack the red blood cells of persons having A and AB blood, but persons having O or B blood have anti-A antibodies. Fatality from smallpox has been higher in South Asia than anywhere else in the world. In 1963 in India there were about 65,000 attacks and 19,500 deaths from it, and in the same year in Pakistan there were over 5500 deaths, but by the seventies it was much better controlled. Since this disease selects against blood type A, this may be one reason why B numbers so high, especially among low castes. Another line of recent research has led to the suggestion that both A and B blood have some survival value in that certain white blood cells are more effective in fighting infection by animal parasites than in persons having O blood.

Genetic adaptation to diet has been little studied. Since South Asians have had a long tradition of consuming cow's milk, are they better able to digest this than are East Asians who have never drunk it? Since Indians in the South have not traditionally eaten wheat, might the reason why they say it makes them sick be that some of them have an allergic reaction against it as do some Japanese? What are the cumulative effects of dietary deficiencies such as riboflavin, calcium, and proteins, or of the high incidence of goiter in the Himālayan regions? What of the surprising low caloric intake—as little as 1000 calories a day—on which adult male farmers sometimes seem to be able to manage? Demographers would like to know answers to such questions.

REFERENCES AND NOTES*

[1] Sarkar.

[2] Kailash C. Mohotra, "Further Observations on the Human Skeletal Remains from Neolithic Piklihal," *The Anthropologist* XIV, No. 2 (1967).

[3] S. Zuckerman, *The Adichanallur Skulls.* Bull. Madras Gov't. Museum, 1930.

[4] Kennedy.

[5] P. Gupta, P. C. Datta, and A. Basu, *Human Skeletal Remains from Harappa.* Memoirs of the Anthro. Survey of India, No. 9, Calcutta, 1962.

[6] P. Gupta, P. C. Datta, and A. Basu, "The Human Remains of the Syenaciti of the Purusamedha and Other Trenches from the Historical Site at Kausambi," *J. Indian Asiatic Soc.* I, No. 2 (1966).

[7] Majumdar and Rao, p. 101.

[8] See Majumdar, pp. 107–116; P. N. Bhattacharjee, "Blood Group Investigation in the Abor Tribe," *Bull. Dept. Anthro.* III, No. 1 (1958); P. N. Bhattacharjee and N. Kumar, "A Blood Group Genetic Survey in the Dudh Kharias of Ranchi District," *Human Heredity* XIX (1969); S. R. Das and others, "Blood Groups, ABH Secretions, Sickle-cell, P.T.C. Taste, and Colour Blindness in the Mahar of Nagpur," *J. Royal Anthro. Inst.* XCI, Part 2 (1961); H. Kumar, "ABO Blood Groups and Sickle-cell Trait Distributions in Malwa, Western Madhya Pradesh," *J. Indian Anthro. Soc.* I, No. 2 (1966); H. Kumar and D. P. Mukherjee, "A Genetic Survey among the Desi Bhumji of Chota Nagpur in Bihar," *The Anthropologist*, Special Volume, 1968; and S. S. Sarkar, "Blood Groups from the Andaman and Nicobar Islands," *Bull. Dept. Anthro.* I, No. 1 (1952).

* In the *References and Notes*, at the end of each chapter, where only an author's name is given, please see *Important Sources* below for full reference data.

IMPORTANT SOURCES

Bose, H. K. *Fifty Years of Science in India: Progress of Anthropology and Archaeology.* Calcutta, 1963.

Chakravartti, M. R., and F. Vogel. "Relation between Incidence of Small-Pox and the ABO System of Blood Groups," *J. Indian Anthro. Soc.* VI, No. 2 (1966).

Chatterjee, B. K., and G. D. Kumar. *Comparative Study and Racial Analysis of the Human Remains of the Indus Valley Civilization*. Calcutta, n.d.

Coon, Carleton. *The Origin of Races*. New York, 1962.

Das, S. R. "Application of Phenylthiocarbamide Taste Character in the Study of Racial Variation," *J. Indian Anthro. Soc.* I, No. 1 (1966).

Garn, Stanley. *Human Races*. Springfield, Ill., 1965.

Guha, B. S. *Census of India, 1931* I, Part III. (A synthesis of anthropometric data, and still provocative.)

———. "A Comparative Study of the Somatic Traits of the Onges of Little Andaman," *Bull. Dept. Anthro.* III, No. 2 (1954).

Gupta, Pabitra, and others. "A Study on Onge Skeletons from Little Andaman (Parts 1 and 2)," *Bull. Dept. Anthro.* IX, No. 1 (1960).

Hutton, J. H. *Census of India, 1931 Report* I, Part I (A sweeping view—outdated but provocative.)

Kennedy, Kenneth A. R. "Megalithic Calvariae from Raigir, Andhra Pradesh," *The Anthropologist* VIII, Nos. 1 and 2 (1961).

———, and K. C. Malhotra. *Human Skeletal Remains from Chalcolithic and Indo-Roman Levels from Nevasa*. Pune, 1966. (Includes a useful summary of skeletal material from several sites.)

Livingston, Frank. *Abnormal Hemoglobins in Human Populations*. Chicago, 1967.

Majumdar, D. N. *Races and Cultures of India*. Bombay, 1961. (The most comprehensive synthesis of data on races, but apparently hastily put together.)

———, and C. Radhakrishna Rao. *Race Elements in Bengal: A Quantitative Survey*. Bombay, 1960. (Pertains to both parts of Bānglā, chart is from p. 100.)

Mitra, A. K. "Racial Stratification in the Caste Hierarchy of Bengal," *The Anthropologist* XI, Nos. 1 and 2 (1964). (Chart is from Table 3.)

Negi, R. S. "The Incidence of the Sickle-Cell Trait in Bastar," *Man in India* LXIV (1964).

Risley, Herbert. *The People of India*, 2d ed. London, 1915. (The first comprehensive study of South Asian races; his measurements are useful but his terminology is outdated, as are many of his interpretations.)

Roberts, D. F., and R. E. S. Tanner. "Some Problems of Colorblindness: A Discussion of East African Data from Indian and African Samples," *J. Indian Anthro. Soc.* II, No. 1 (1967).

Sarkar, S. S. "Human Skeletal Remains from Brahmagiri," *Bull. Dept. Anthro.* 1960.

Sen, D. K. "The Racial Composition of Bengalis," in T. N. Madan and Gopala Sarana (eds.), *Indian Anthropology*. Bombay, 1962.

———. "Racial Studies in India: Recent Trends," *J. Indian Anthro. Soc.* II, No. 1 (1967).

von Eickstedt, Egon. "The History of Anthropological Research in India," in L. A. Krishna Iyer, *The Travancore Tribes and Castes* II. Trivandrum, 1939. (An attempt at racial classification.)

4

Prehistory

This chapter is about the dead rather than the living. Yet dead men tell tales, at least to the archeologist. The origins of South Asian patterns of culture are not to be understood merely by referring to classical or primary levels of civilization; one must go back to the Neolithic (earliest agricultural) and beyond that to the late hunting period. The distribution of even the very earliest and crudest stone tool types shows the beginnings of regionalism and interaction with geographic realities.

Archeologists in India have now agreed upon a set of terms for the three main phases of stone tool techniques in the subcontinent, calling them Early, Middle, and Late Stone Ages. These are roughly equivalent to what might elsewhere be termed Paleolithic, Upper Paleolithic, and Mesolithic. South Asian archeologists feel it is better to use terms which do not connote European prehistoric phases, particularly because there is nothing like European Upper Paleolithic in this part of the world. Though these three phases are easily distinguished by typology and stratigraphy, at a few sites there are transitional stages. Man, therefore, probably continuously inhabited South Asia for the past half million years.

Scarcely any human skeletal material earlier than the 3d millennium B.C. has come to light in South Asia, though bones of many other mammals

of the Middle Pleistocene (Ice Age) have been found in the Narmadā Valley and central India. One can only hope that some day an Indian or Pakistani scientist will discover a fossil to link the early hominids of Africa and the Near East with those of Jāva and China.

Early Stone Age: Hand Axes

Hand axes (Fig. 4–1) are the most distinctive cultural creation we know of produced by *Homo erectus* (Pithecanthropus). These tools were not real axes, for they were not hafted. They have been found over much of central and South India and to some extent in the Panjāb. Characteristically, they are accompanied by cleavers, as well as sundry flakes, cores (from which flakes were knocked), and pebble tools (pebbles made into tools by knocking off a few flakes). We can suppose that this primitive tool complex spread from Africa and the Near East into India, though Pakistan and Iran are something of a gap in our knowledge. We can visualize *Homo erectus* folk, having reached Panjāb, being enticed ever southward over the savanna and mixed woodland zones of the Deccan, avoiding such dank forested regions as Kērala. No hand axes have been found in the Himālayan regions nor in the Gangā plains, which must have been heavily forested and therefore unfavorable; they are also absent from Assam and the Burma side.

The hand ax industry may be dated to the Middle Pleistocene and perhaps lasted up to 200,000 years ago, and probably much later in the case of South Asia. Everywhere from Gujarāt to Orissa where rivers have made

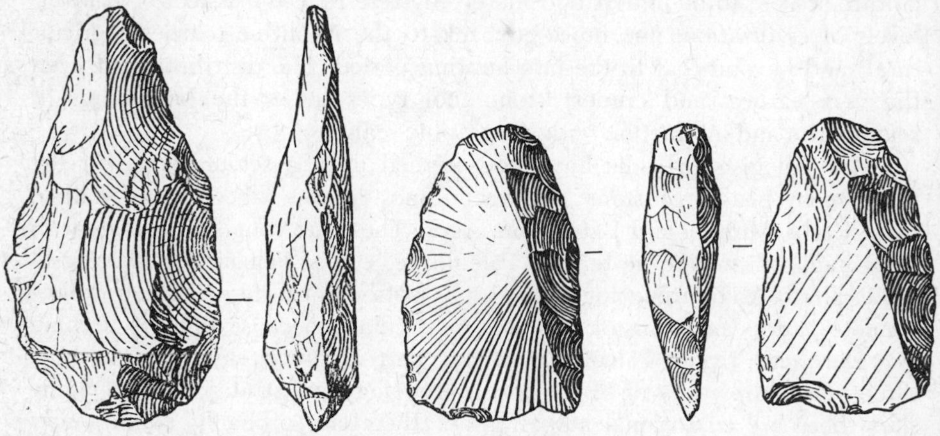

1 2

FIG. 4–1 Early Stone Age tools from Giddalūr, Āndhra, 1/3 size: 1) hand ax; 2) cleaver.

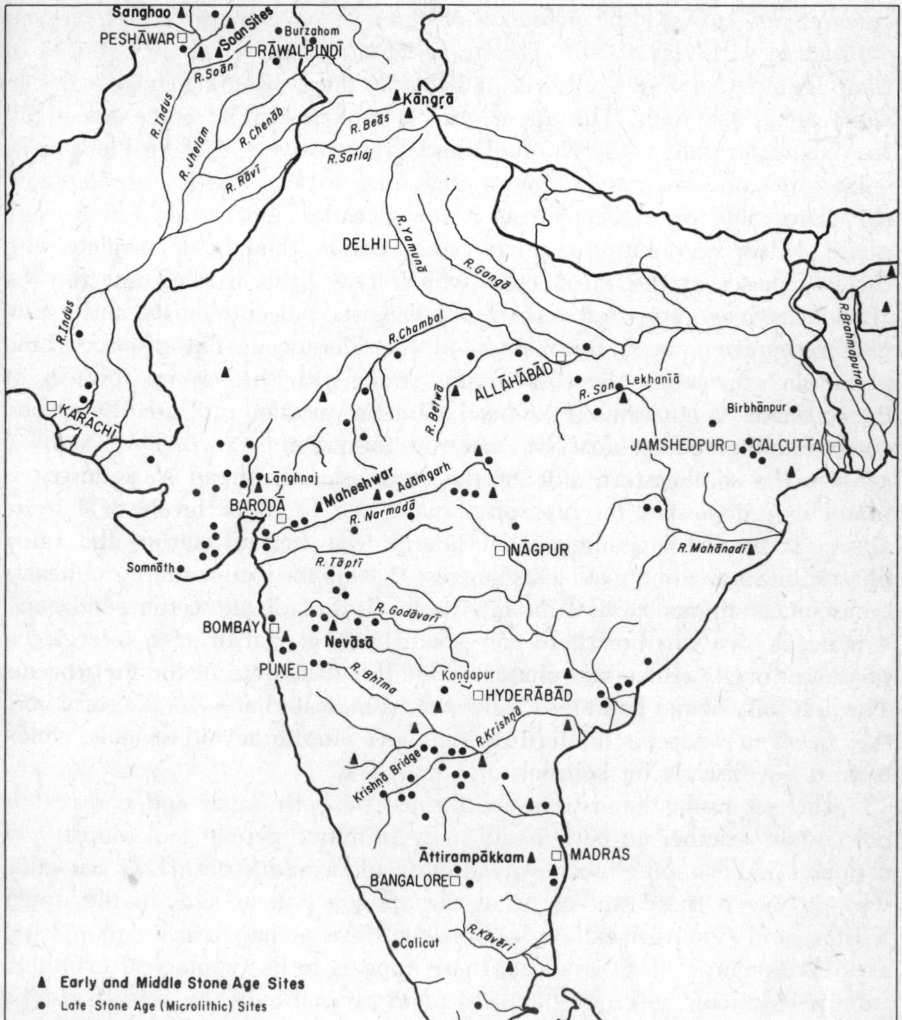

FIG. 4–2 Early and Late Stone Age sites.

cuttings one can see the evidence of three or so climatic cycles, gravels alternating with clay or silt. The gravels indicate the beginning phases of river aggradation, and the lower and middle ones, often cemented, contain Early Stone Age tools. The upper gravels contain Middle Stone Age tools. In Mahārāshṭra along the Narmadā and Pravarā rivers, Middle Pleistocene animal remains have been found including extinct species of elephant, rhinoceros, and ox. Archeologists a few decades ago assumed that each phase of river aggradation implied a rainy period, thought to correlate with the icy phases of the Pleistocene which have been worked out for the Himālayas. Now, however, Indian archeologists, paleontologists, and geologists recognize a need for restudy of the Pleistocene chronology of the peninsula, correlating the fossiliferous strata with the several terraces of the Narmadā, fluctuations of sea level, climatic variation indicated by seabed core sampling, pollen analysis, and soil formation.

On the southeastern side of the peninsula, the hand ax industry is found in redeposited laterite, often with one or more levels of laterite above. It has been assumed that laterite was formed during the rainy phases, but now some geologists suggest that its formation simply indicates monsoon conditions. Even if the laterite levels do indicate wetter conditions, it is not known whether these correspond with glacial or with interglacial phases, or even with stadial phases within the glaciations of the Pleistocene. The antiquity of the hand axes, however, is indicated at several sites where they occur in redeposited laterite lying above laterite devoid of tools, which in turn lies directly on bedrock.

The peninsular hand axes are formed on both flakes and cores. It is not certain whether an earlier and more primitive pebble tool industry of choppers and chopping tools evolved into hand ax industries. H. D. Sankalia, who pioneered these studies, is of the opinion that at sites in the upper Krishṇā and Godāvarī valleys, pebble tools are perhaps earlier than hand axes. At Kamārpol in Orissa also, there appears to be typological evolution from pebble tools, to crude hand axes and bifacial tools, to Acheulian-type hand axes. There is little evidence of this at sites in Āndhra and Tamiḻ Nāḍu, however. Archeologists have dug numerous sites on the Deccan Plateau, such as Maheśwāṛ which has a typical sequence. There are three gravel layers, each capped with silt, and the topsoil is the black regur characteristic of the northern Deccan. The lower gravel has a few Abbevillian-type crude hand axes with large concave flake scars. The second gravel contains more refined hand axes and cleavers. The third gravel has tools made by the relatively advanced Levallois technique which may be classified as Middle Stone Age artifacts. It seems paleolithic man came down the peninsula east of the Western Ghāṭs, avoiding the more heavily forested parts of central India and also the sea coast.

A typical sequence farther east was uncovered at Kurnool, Āndhra. Here the lowest laterite has no tools, but above it was soil originating in a

drier phase which has the usual hand axes and cleavers; their creators apparently lived in the open plains. Next was a wet phase, during which the rivers probably became aggraded, and the resulting gravels contain late Early Stone Age tools. Following was another dry phase associated with Middle Stone Age tools. The final deposit, fine gravels laid down during the last wet phase, contains Late Stone Age microliths (tiny tools). At the site of Āttirampākkam near Madras, all three phases of the Stone Age tools were also found, this time capped by a layer with tools of the Neolithic period.

Early Stone Age: Soan

The Himālayan slopes, as ever, seem to have harbored a relic culture even in the Middle Pleistocene. On the Soan River, a tributary of the upper Indus in Pakistan, de Terra and Paterson studied a crude tool industry in the 1930s, which has since been found elsewhere in the western Himālayas on the Beās, Bangangā, and Satlaj rivers. These Soan tools are crude choppers and chopping tools with some roughly pointed implements, mostly made on pebbles but with a few flakes. In the Panjāb they are found mixed with hand axes.

Even a pre-Soan industry was identified by de Terra and Paterson, consisting of a few crude flakes, but possibly these are not even artifacts. The Soan chronology is suggested by the geology of the lower ranges of the western Himālayan complex. Beds originally dated to the early Pleistocene have recently been classified by Indian scientists, on the basis of pollen analysis, as having originated earlier in the Pliocene. Above these beds is a boulder conglomerate. River terraces 1 and 2 (the highest and the oldest) are devoid of tools. Terraces 3, 4, and 5 have tools, and the last was of post-Pleistocene origin. From the dating of these terraces it seems that the Soan pebble tool industry originated in the lower Middle and Middle Pleistocene, preceding and contemporary with the hand axes of western and peninsular India.

It has been pointed out that typologically the Soan tools belong with the chopping tool tradition of the Middle Pleistocene of East Asia, including the Early Anyathian of Burma, the Tampanian of Malaya, and the tools of Peking Man in China, as well as those of Jāva. Hand axes are missing in this part of the world; some tools in Jāva that approach hand ax shape are regarded by Movius as simply pointed bifacial choppers. If this is so, then the western edge of the forested Gangā plain marked the limit of eastward diffusion of the hand ax folk. Movius studied the paleolithic tools in upper Burma on river terraces analogous with those of northwest India. Terraces 1 and 2 had tools which he classified as Early Anyathian, terraces 3 and 4 as Late Anyathian, and terrace 5 as neolithic. The early tools included hand adzes, double-sided choppers, and other types all made of fossil wood!

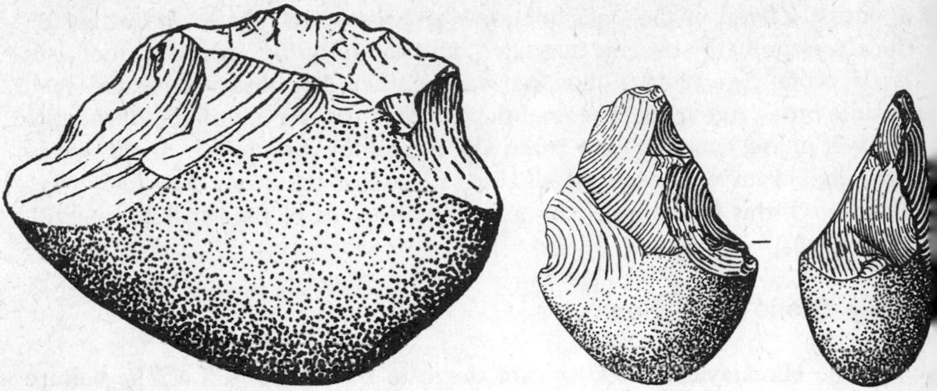

1 2

FIG. 4–3 Early Stone Age pebble tools: 1) Soan, 1/2 size; 2) Giddalūr, Āndhra, 1/3 size.

These are possibly related to the Soan tools, but not to the hand ax and cleaver complex. Recently pebble tools have come to light in three sites in Assam, so perhaps the geographical gap between the Soan and East Asian tools will be closed in, though Nepal is still a void in our knowledge.

Indian scholars have questioned the theory of two distinct paleolithic traditions because pebble tools are found with hand axes and cleavers in several places in India, and in the Panjāb they comprise more than half the artifacts. Moreover, pebble tools were used very late, even with microliths of the Late Stone Age, and in Kāngṛā in the Himālayan foothills they have been found associated with polished stone tools of neolithic cultivators. They were scrapers made on split pebbles or thick pebble flakes like Middle Pleistocene tools. In the Tājik Republic of the Soviet Union they have also been found with microliths and polished stone axes. In spite of the tenacious persistence of such old traits in the Himālayan zone, it seems that the Soan is really a very early and primitive stone tool tradition, and one can only hope that some day fossils of its makers will be discovered.

Middle Stone Age

In the western Himālayan foothills on river terraces of the Soan, Beās, and Bangangā, there is a more highly developed class of tools apparently evolved from the Soan, consisting of a variety of worked pebble nodules. It is regarded as Late Soan because there are no hand axes or cleavers, but chopping tools and a variety of other worked pebble nodules. Found on the fourth and fifth river terraces, it is chronologically classified with the Middle Stone Age.

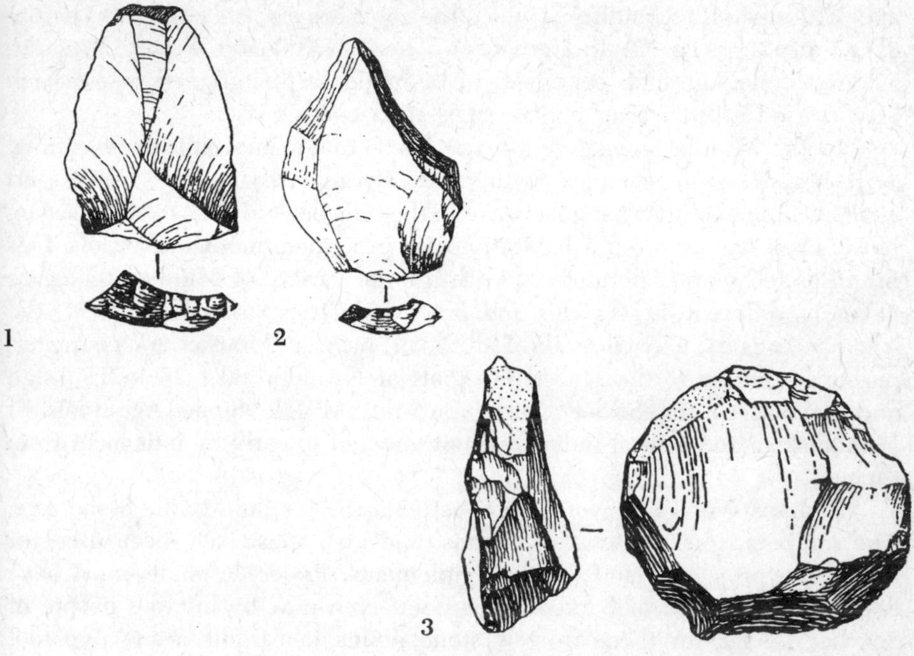

FIG. 4–4 Middle Stone Age tools, 1/2 size: 1) and 2) flake tools, Panjāb; 3) Late Soan.

Elsewhere in South Asia, the hand ax and cleaver industries gave way to predominantly flake tools, which occur generally in upper gravels or later phases of river aggradation. The flakes are made into a variety of tools, such as scrapers, borers, burins, points, and tortoise cores. In most regions these tools are clearly differentiated from Early Stone Age artifacts because they are made on jasper, chert, agate, chalcedony, or other fine-grained stone. Some of them are made from cores with prepared platforms. They may be dated to the late Pleistocene or early Recent.

These implements were first identified by H. D. Sankalia at Nevāsā in Mahārāshṭra and since have been found in many other sites in the Deccan and throughout central, southern, and western India, mostly wherever Early Stone Age tools are found. At a few sites there are suggestions that the one evolved into the other, especially on the Narmadā where study of fauna shows only a gradual ecological change. In western Rājasthān, tools were discovered on the edge of the Thār desert in the only existing gravel level. Associated were small finely worked hand axes and cleavers, suggesting continuity from the Early Stone Age, as well as points said to be produced by pressure flaking, a technique which does not occur elsewhere before the Late Stone Age. In the Panjāb, where the hand ax and Soan Early Stone Age traditions merged, both flake and pebble tools occur, with some appear-

ance of Levallois techniques in which the cores are carefully prepared before flakes are knocked off. In Karṇāṭaka, Tamiḻ Nāḍu, and western Gujarāt, Middle Stone Age tools continued to be made on fine-grained quartz such as was used in the earlier period, suggesting continuity.

In the Middle Stone Age we see, then, that man's culture diversified as it became more complex, with gradually intensifying regionalism and intrusive influences. At Sanghao Cave in the hills beyond Peshāwar, Pakistan, A. H. Dani has explored a habitation site in a steep mountain valley. This promises to be an important site with a large variety of Middle Stone Age flakes in different strata. This and other industries toward the west, the Allchins suggest, as well as the Late Soan, have a "Mousterian" character, perhaps pointing to the Mousterian tools of Neanderthal man in Tājikstān and beyond in the Soviet Union. But the Middle Stone Age tools of Mahārāshṭra and central India were not affected so early by influences from the west.

Perhaps Wood Age would be a better name for the Middle Stone Age. The scrapers, concave scrapers, burins, and awls must have been used for fashioning projectiles and wooden implements. Projectile points must have been made of wood or bamboo as is done even now by hunting people of Southeast Asia, for there are few stone points in Middle Stone Age tool collections. Probably leather and bark were also worked. The smaller size of these tools suggests that they were used with much more care and delicacy than Early Stone Age tools. This was the time of the Upper Paleolithic in Europe, with its famous cave art. There is nothing of the sort in South Asia, and by comparison with European Upper Paleolithic stone tools, these seem inordinately crude.

Late Stone Age: The South

The characteristic tools of the Late Stone Age are microliths, little stone flakes more or less the size of one's thumbnail. Such tools are widely distributed from Kacch (the western lobe of Gujarāt) across central India to Choṭā Nāgpur (the plateau of south Bihār) and throughout the peninsula and Sri Lanka. It is notable that no microliths have been found in Assam, Nepal, or east of the Gangā and Bānglā plains. It seems these heavily forested regions were as much a barrier to Late Stone Age folk as they had been from man's earliest occupation of South Asia.

The Late Stone Age, also called the Indian Mesolithic, seems to have appeared rather abruptly. One would think that microliths came with intrusive influences from the west, but Pakistan is a hiatus in our knowledge. Dating, too, is on a shaky basis; probably microliths were used in the 5th millennium B.C., but we don't know how much earlier. Several stages of Late Stone Age tools have been excavated at some sites, and it is now clear

that such tiny tools continued to be manufactured after the introduction of pottery, cultivation, and even after the introduction of metals. In the western parts of South Asia, where hunting first gave way to village and then to early urban life, microlithic tool traditions were gradually modified so that blades and knives more suitable for sedentary peoples were produced.

On the southeastern coast of Tamil̲ Nāḍu, opposite Sri Lanka, there is a somewhat distinctive microlithic industry found in a dozen sites on fossil dunes. There are many types of flakes showing signs of use, some short blades, backed blades, and a few discoids, lunates and other geometric stones, transverse arrowheads, and unique almond-shaped bifacial points produced by pressure flaking, besides a few quartz hammer stones. These fossil sand dunes are 20 to 30 feet above sea level, and on the basis of raised beaches, Zeuner has dated this industry to about 4000 B.C., leaving open the possibility of even greater antiquity because a few implements are on a 50-foot beach level. Undoubtedly the makers of these microliths were hunters and fishers living off the lagoons perpetually made and unmade by the shifting sands of the straits. Fishing and fowling in these lagoons have been carried on down to the present. Early Tamil̲ literature of the 2d century A.D. describes the huts of fishers on the sand dunes of that same coast; one may still see them.

In Sri Lanka there is a similar microlithic industry, also with pressure-flaked points. In the southern part of the island at Bandarawela, an excavation produced several thousand finished tools, in addition to waste material. Here also there were geometric stones, especially lunates, together with transverse arrowheads, awls, and burins, mostly made on quartz. Microliths of quartz have also been excavated in caves in the interior of Sri Lanka associated with stone hammers and pounders and bone tools. In upper levels, pottery appears, with microliths continuing into the Iron Age, whereupon the stone industry declines in quality. Neither the antiquity of this culture nor the possibility of the island's having been attached to India in the past several thousand years has been established.

Now for the first time we have evidence of man's occupation of the verdant coastal strip between Bombay and Cape Comorin. At Kōl̲ikkōḍu (Calicut) in northern Kēraḷa, a factory site where quartz microliths were made was found near a former pond. The Late Stone Age in southern Karṇāṭaka was geographically transitional, with tools typologically like those farther north but made on quartz as were those of Sri Lanka and Tamil̲ Nāḍu. In all these southern sites, quartz was preferred even though it cannot be controlled easily, either because of tradition derived from the Middle Stone Age, or because it was discovered that if quartz is heated before being struck, it will shatter easily. This method has been recorded for the Andaman Islanders, who thereby easily produce sharp-edged tools suitable even for shaving.

An interesting example of the relentless dictates of geographical fea-

tures on transportation patterns was uncovered by the Allchins excavating in northern Karṇāṭaka. Near the bank of the Krishṇā River they uncovered a microlithic factory site near a place where the river had been forded during every habitation phase from the Late Stone Age up to the railroad era. A bridge now spans the river at that point. The tools here, in contrast with those farther south, were made of agate or other fine-grained stones, and consisted of flakes, blades, simple points, some truncated blades, concave scrapers, burins, lunates, primary and secondary guide flakes, and hammer stones. The Late Stone Age population of Karṇāṭaka has given rise to the present population. Such purely geometric microliths lie below strata containing neolithic-chalcolithic artifacts (polished stone tools and copper), which may be dated here from about 1800 B.C. In this part of India, the mesolithic merges with the beginning of cattle keeping and agriculture, and even the appearance of copper did not make microlithic tools obsolete.

Late Stone Age: Central and Western India

Fortunately, we now have a number of sites showing stages in the evolution of the culture of the Late Stone Age, in central India ranging from Gujarāt and Mahārāshṭra to West Bengal (see the map, Fig. 4–2). Over two dozen sites have been located in southern Uttar Pradesh, mostly situated on knolls or slopes with streams flowing nearby. Some of these show four stages of the Late Stone Age. The first has rather crude nongeometric microliths, whereas in the second the tools are more geometric, more standardized. In the third, handmade pottery appears with an even greater percentage of tools with geometric shapes. In the last stage, microliths become diminutive. The earliest pottery is coarse and gray and sometimes ochre-washed, but in the fourth stage it is better fired, thinner, with an ochre or reddish slip. This sequence has been especially well established at the site of Lekhāniā, a rock shelter where there are drawings of hunting scenes which may or may not be contemporary with the microlithic tools. Possibly climate change helped propel this culture change, for there is evidence of increasing aridity in the last two stages. Sites in eastern central India seem to have been settled after the last wet phase when the climate had become more dry and the vegetation less thick. At Birbhānpur on the Dāmodar River in West Bengal a Late Stone Age site extends over a square mile!

In western India, Late Stone Age people occupied a variety of ecological niches. Just north of Bombay a site was found on low hillocks or rocky ground. Since this was formerly an island inundated with tidal creeks and mangrove swamps, the people must have fished as well as hunted. In Gujarāt numerous microlithic sites have been discovered by archeologists from Indian universities. Many are on promontories overlooking rivers or

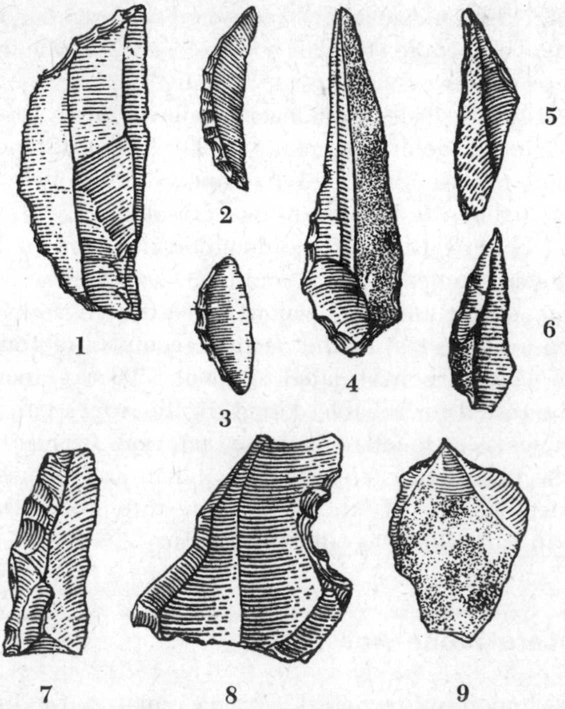

FIG. 4–5 Microliths from Birbhānpur, Dāmodar Valley, West Bengal, actual size: 1), 2), 3) lunates; 4), 5), 6) points; 7) blade; 8) concave scraper; 9) borer.

on top of old sand dunes. Zeuner, who studied the geochronology of these dunes, suggests that the tools date from a time when the climate was getting wetter, the dunes becoming fixed, and the hollows between them becoming seasonal ponds.

At Lānghnāj in Gujarāt also culture change is thought to be associated with climate change. With the onset of a wet phase, the microliths of Period I appeared. There were many associated animal bones, including a shoulder blade of a rhinoceros which had for some reason been scored around a hollow in it. (Rhinoceroses formerly roamed all over the peninsula, but now they are extinct except on the Himālayan lower slopes.) No doubt the animals at Lānghnāj came to drink in the ponds which had also attracted the Late Stone Age people. Here at last we have human burials, the bodies highly flexed and the knees drawn up to the chins. The skulls of the people were longheaded and prognathous. Buried with one man was a dog. Period II of Lānghnāj seems to have been associated with drier climate, and here we have crude pottery and a doughnut-shaped polished stone, probably a mace head or perhaps a digging stick weight. The people now seem to have practiced cultivation. Period III, with wetter climate, lasted

into the Iron Age, for an iron arrowhead was discovered together with more refined pottery. The people still had not given up use of microliths, though their quality was poorer now.

A provocative site called Ādamgaṛh Hill on the Narmadā was excavated by R. V. Joshi, yielding as many as 25,000 Late Stone Age artifacts. The tools include the usual microlithic scrapers, borers, awls, burins, blades, and cores; but at this site, thought to be Late Stone Age, there were many animal bones including those of the domestic dog, Indian humped cattle, water buffalo, goat, domestic sheep, and pig. Perhaps this site suggests that Late Stone Age people took to keeping domesticated animals before they had cultivation and the rest of the neolithic complex of traits. Shells from the excavation were carbon-14 dated to about 5500 B.C., though more samples need to be tested for reliable dating. In the upper part of the excavation, glass bangles were found, and above that, iron. It is certain that within a few years the persistent explorations of Indian archeologists will pay off with a congruent picture of late hunting life throughout the country and the transition to cattle keeping and cultivation.

Life in the Late Stone Age

The most important technical advance enjoyed by Late Stone Age hunters must have been the bow and arrow, inferred from the presence of transverse arrowheads. Now species of game formerly inaccessible could be secured. A variety of compound tools made with microliths also helped, such as spears studded with lunate-shaped microlithic flakes. As with mesolithic peoples everywhere, a variety of traps, nets, pitfalls, and techniques for fishing and fowling must have been invented. The bones of wild animals excavated at Lānghnāj, Gujarāt, include ten large species: Indian wolf, one-horned rhinoceros, wild boar, spotted deer, hog deer, swamp deer, black buck, nilgai, mongoose, and cattle (possibly domesticated), in addition to bones of smaller animals such as squirrels, rats, tortoises, and fish, which also must have been used for food. The bones had been charred over an open fire.

There is no doubt that during this period many implements of wood were fashioned. The concave stone scrapers were used to smooth arrow shafts, for the concavities are small in diameter. Microliths were made into composite tools, hafted and held in place with gum or resin. A stick was split at the end to hold a geometric microlith used for cutting and scraping. As the stone became blunt through use, it was flaked again and gradually became smaller, resulting in the small tool called a thumbnail microlith. Bifacial projectile points are only found in a few microlithic collections, the best ones being in the far South and Sri Lanka. Probably their scarcity is explained in that bamboo and wood arrow points were used, as is true in

hunting groups in Southeast Asia today. Bone must have been much used, and evidence of this is increasing, for bone points and awls have recently been found in half a dozen Late Stone Age sites. Hunting dogs, found in burials in Lānghnāj, Gujarāt, and in Burzahom, Kashmīr, are also characteristic of the mesolithic way of life.

Fishing must have been important in the subsistence of such Late Stone Age people as occupied the islands of Bombay, the north Kēraḷa coast, and the dunes along the southeast Tamiḻ Nāḍu coast. The location of settlements by bodies of water in such places as the Krishṇā Bridge suggests the manufacture of devices to cross water, no doubt similar to the large and small coracles, rafts, and canoes still in use in many remote parts of South Asia. Almost certainly mats and baskets would have been fashioned. There would have been some trade, or perhaps diffusion from tribe to tribe, of raw material for manufacturing stone tools. Dentalium shells at Lānghnāj came from the ocean at least 60 miles away.

Hunting scenes drawn with hematite and other pigments on the walls of caves and rock shelters give us an idea of what was most important in the lives of these Late Stone Age people. The drawings are difficult to date, but in a few rock shelters in eastern Gujarāt and in southern Uttar Pradesh, hematite lumps which had been rubbed by use were found associated with microliths. In Raisen District in the central plateau, four rock shelters show animals singly or in rows, some in outline, others filled in or dotted. Bison, boar, rhinoceros, stag, elephant, leopard, and other animals not easily identifiable are portrayed, and in other sites there are antelopes, wild pigs, monkeys, and humped cattle. Dogs are shown with the hunters who carry both spears and bows. Some scenes show men in combat or spearing one another. The drawings are comparatively crude; men are represented as simple stick figures. Yet there is life, movement, and vitality. Several drawings have scenes of rows of stick-figure men, hand in hand, dancing as before a hunt—in one case 13 men are thus represented. The same motif has been found on potsherds from chalcolithic sites of Nāvḍāṭolī and Daimābād in Mahārāshṭra. Ritual dances performed before hunting are still in vogue among some central Indian tribal people and even among a few low castes. The Boyas, for instance, an agricultural caste living in little conical huts, hold hands and dance before setting out on ritual hunting parties.

The Väddās of central Sri Lanka, observed early in this century, were an example of a people whose way of life was essentially that of mesolithic hunters, though they were able to acquire iron arrowheads. These arrowheads were used as multipurpose tools, for skinning and for cutting sticks. Hunting was central to their world view, symbolized in their cherishing of their longbows and making miniature bows and arrows for toddlers. They highly valued their hunting dogs, practically considering them as family members. For containers they had gourds, and to produce fire they struck

A Väddā in eastern Sri Lanka stringing his bow, about 1910. (From *The Veddas* by C. G. Seligmann and Brenda Seligmann. By permission of Cambridge University Press, New York.)

stones. They preferred to live in rock shelters, one of which they occupied at the time it was excavated half a century ago! In a communal cave each extended family occupied one part of it and was jealous of its territory. The life of the Väddās, as described by C. G. Seligmann, helps us to understand many traits of villagers and especially of more recently detribalized low castes which have relics of a late hunting stage of culture. Details of Väddā ritual dances and shamanism and their exogamous clans with cross-cousin marriage suggest that similar traits of peninsular Indian village life originated in the Late Stone Age.

We can also infer that population increased during the Late Stone Age. The many thousands of microliths uncovered at some sites indicate occupation by more than a single family or small band. Certainly at Birbhānpur, where tools extended over a square mile, as at a number of sites covering over an acre, we have to visualize many people living together, even though those tools might have been laid down over a number of generations. Cooperative effort in hunting is depicted in the rock shelter drawings, while the skeletons at Lānghnāj show signs of blows, breaks, and splits in the skulls, the effect of blunt weapons. Increased interaction of contiguous clans or tribes would have led to organized combat and the absorption of lesser tribes by stronger ones.

South Asian religious ideas were also germinating. Seventeen burials were uncovered at Lekhāniā in and near rock shelters; all had been placed extended in graves with microlithic tools and cores thrown in. Most had the head to the west, but one head pointed north and one south. Some of the graves contained ochre and weathered lateritic nodules. The burials at Langhnāj were flexed, oriented either east–west or west–east. In some cases, bones were missing, indicating secondary burials. Such practices continued into the Indian Iron Age. If we can extrapolate from Väddās and other modern hunting-gathering peoples of South and Southeast Asia, we can suppose that the Late Stone Age gave rise to such concepts as the soul, mana, rebirth, certain kinds of pollution, recognition of sacred spots, shamanism and trance, performance of vows, and the feeling of empathy with living things, all of which later became elaborated in formal philosophical systems of the classical civilization.

Stone Age Regionalism and Diffusion

Because South Asia has such marked geographical regions, there were differences in tool traditions even in the Early and Middle Stone Ages. By the Late Stone Age, these differences already forecast most of the geographical and cultural regions of the subcontinent as recognized today by language and state boundaries. The quartz tools of southern Tamiḻ Nāḍu and Sri Lanka show some independent development. Those of Karṇāṭaka are

an intermediate group, their forms reflecting the microliths of the central and northern Deccan. The abundance of tools in the Godāvarī and Krishṇā valleys suggests a nucleus in Āndhra. But those of Orissa and Choṭā Nāgpur, even now a transition zone suffering isolation, are poorly developed. The industries of southern Uttar Pradesh are reported to be similar to those of Mālwā (western Madhya Pradesh). No microliths are reported from the Panjāb. Kashmīr has a different industry, consisting of a variety of bone points, awls, needles, and harpoons, perhaps technically neolithic, but the people were largely dependent upon hunting. And judging from the neolithic stone tools and cultigens in Assam, it would appear that during this period, as before, its connections lay primarily with the east.

In western India, however, Late Stone Age tools are found extending through a number of climatic phases, perhaps indicating considerable antiquity. In Gujarāt and western central India, pottery, and probably cattle keeping and agriculture also, made their appearance earlier than elsewhere. In these parts the microlithic tradition lost its Middle Stone Age character earlier than in the South, at the same time developing an emphasis on blades, so that by the time of the Indus Civilization, true microliths had ceased to be made in western South Asia.

It is difficult to prove much about diffusion of microlithic tool types from western countries. A site is reported near Karāchī, but it must be a late one because pottery is associated. A few sites are reported from the northern part of Pakistan, but the tools are not well known. From Kili Ghul Muhammad, a site in Balūchistān, Fairservis describes a prepottery neolithic level containing chert and jasper blades and bone points. This deposit is below a neolithic level containing crude pottery dated about 3700 B.C., but the excavated area was so small that it does not shed much light on the origin of the Indian Mesolithic.

Bridgit Allchin in *The Stone-tipped Arrow* has imaginatively compared Late Stone Age hunters of Africa, South Asia, Indonesia, and Australia. She concludes that the resemblance between late hunting cultures in India and sub-Saharan Africa in particular is very marked, and suggests a common origin. She also points out that the nature and range of Late Stone Age tools in Africa and India are closer to the Natufian and Zarzian culture complexes of the Near East than to European or other mesolithic traditions. The Zarzian microlithic industry of northeastern Iran included lunates, triangles, borers, and similar artifacts made on jasper and chert, and existed earlier than 10,000 B.C. The stone tools at Jarmo, also similar, are dated to the 7th millennium B.C. and are said to resemble the late microliths collected near Karāchī. The earliest dates for the mesolithic phase so far obtained in India are 5500 B.C. at Ādamgaṛh Hill in Gujarāt, and roughly 4000 B.C. for microlithic industries in Tamil̠ Nāḍu.

Bridget Allchin finds that the personalities of the cultures of the existing hunting peoples across the Old World tropical belt, such as the African

pygmies, Bushmen, Väddās, Andamanese, Semang, and Australians are so different that where any choice is open to them, they almost always react differently. Yet their hunting life is determined largely by environment, so that a number of features often go together and can be thought of as characterizing the mesolithic, notably techniques of making small stone tools, the bow and arrow, the dog, and methods of crossing water. In both Africa and India these cultures in prehistoric times preferred areas of intermediate rainfall, though in modern times they have differentiated even more because hunting people have been relegated to unfavorable habitats.

The question of cultural evolution in India as against diffusion from Africa is not one that can be definitively answered with the present archeological data. Since stone working techniques in Australia were independently developed, the same could conceivably have been true of India; however the Indian traditions seem closer to the African. There are microlithic industries in the Horn of Africa, Yemen, and Saudi Arabia. Most innovations occurred more definitively and earlier in western India. There is no doubt that at the end of the Pleistocene and then in the early Recent, climate was more favorable in the regions bridging India and Africa. Indeed, we can go further and suggest that Dravidian languages seem to be connected with linguistic strains to the west of India, but have been isolated in South Asia so long that their specific antecedents to the west cannot be identified (as would be expected of linguistic groups which diverged six or more millennia ago). The evidence of physical anthropology in Chapter 3 also tenuously suggests early links between India and Africa. We can be sure, however, that the late hunters of South Asia were sufficiently isolated by the semideserts to the west and the rain forests to the east that they developed a cultural individuality unique to South Asia, the effects of which are with us today.

IMPORTANT SOURCES

General works on South Asian archeology are listed in Chapter 5; the following deal with Early, Middle, and Late Stone Ages.

Himālayas

de Terra, H., and T. T. Paterson. *Studies on the Ice Age in India and Associated Human Cultures*. Washington, D.C., 1939.

Graziosi, P. *Prehistoric Research in Northwestern Punjab*. Leiden, 1964.

Gupta, S. P. "The Mountainous Neolithic Cultures of Central Asia and Northern India," *The Anthropologist* XIV (1967).

Lal, B. B. "Paleoliths from the Beas and Banganga Valleys, Panjab," *Ancient India* XII (1956).

Movius, Hallam. *The Stone Age of Burma*. Transactions of the American Philosophical Society, New Series XXXII (1943).

Pakistan

Paterson, T. T. *Soan*. Karachi, 1962; see also a review, H. D. Sankalia, *The Anthropologist* XIV (1967).
Dani, A. H. "Sanghao Excavation: The First Season, 1963," *Ancient Pakistan* I (1964).
Fairservis, W. A. *Excavations in the Quetta Valley*. New York, 1956.

Western India

Karve-Corvinus, G., and K. A. R. Kennedy. "Preliminary Report on Langhnaj, 1963," *Bull. Deccan College and Research Inst.* XXIV (1964).
Malik, S. C. *Stone Age Industries in Bombay and Satara Districts*. Baroda, n.d.
Misra, V. N. "Paleolithic Culture of Western Rajputana," *Bull. Deccan College and Research Inst.* XXI (1960) and XXIV (1963).
Todd, K. R. U. "The Microlithic Industries of Bombay," *Ancient India* VI (1950).
Zeuner, F. E. *Stone Age and Pleistocene Chronology in Gujarat*. Puṇe, 1960.

Central India

Joshi, R. V. "Narmada Pleistocene Deposits at Maheshwar," *J. Paleontological Soc. of India* II (1958).
———. *Pleistocene Studies in the Malaprabha Basin*. Puṇe, 1961
———. "Stone Industries of the Damoh Area, Madhya Pradesh," *Ancient India* XII (1961).
Khatri, A. P. "Rock Paintings of Adamgarh (Central India) and their Age," *Anthropos* LIX (1964).
Sankalia, H. D. *From History to Prehistory at Nevasa*. Puṇe, 1960.
———. *Godavari Paleolithic Industries*. Puṇe, 1952.

Eastern India

Lal, B. B. "Birbhanpur, a Microlithic Site in the Damodar Valley," *Ancient India* XV (1958).
Mohapatra, G. C. *The Stone Age Cultures of Orissa*. Puṇe, 1962.

South India and Sri Lanka

Allchin, B. "The Late Stone Age of Ceylon," *J. Royal Anthro. Inst.* LXXXVIII (1958).
Allchin, F. R., and B. Allchin. "The Archaeology of a River Crossing," in T. N. Madan and Gopala Sarana, *Indian Anthropology*. New York, 1962.
Nagaraja Rao, M. S. *The Stone Age Hill Dwellers of Tekkalakota*. Puṇe, 1965.
Soundara Rajan, K. V. "Stone Age Industries near Giddalur, District Kurnool," *Ancient India* VIII (1952).
Zeuner, F. E., and B. Allchin. "The Microlithic Sites of the Tinnevelly District, Madras State," *Ancient India* XII (1956).

5

The Rise of Village and Urban Life

The rise of early complex cultures in South Asia was due to the interfertilization of four great streams of early cultivating peoples: the western neolithic which gave rise to the Indus Civilization, the peninsular neolithic, the eastern neolithic, and the "Āryan" intrusion. Of these four, Hindu tradition and mythology gives precedence to the last, but we now know that settled village life and even urbanization preceded it, and that this intrusion served rather as a catalyst than as the basis for civilization. It supplied a certain dynamic quality so that the cultural features of the Indus and Gangā plains and the peninsula were incorporated and formalized into an overarching system.

The neolithic way of life was economically dependent upon hoe cultivation and domestication of animals; the people made pottery, textiles, and polished stone tools. The development of a settled village way of life was of great importance in the evolution of more complex social patterns. In spite of considerable archeological searching, there is no evidence that a hunting economy gave way to neolithic economy in South Asia earlier than the mid-4th millennium B.C. when it appeared in the western hills of Pakistan. The neolithic did not take root in the rest of India, according to present evidence, before 2300 B.C.

Why does cultivation of plants appear so late in South Asia? It began in the Near East before 8000 B.C., and recent evidence from Thailand indicates that horticulture there began as early as 20,000 B.C. There is no evidence of an independently evolved neolithic "revolution" in South Asia. The arid wastes of the eastern Īrānian plateau and of Afghanistan were an effective impediment to diffusion, while on the eastern side the tangled wooded hills were an equally effective barrier. We await the perspicacity of Indian and Pakistani archeologists to cast some light on these problems. If indeed South Asia was a great gulf dividing the two areas of the world having the earliest incipient cultivation, then this would show in relief the geographical impediments on both east and west that caused South Asia to develop as such a distinctive culture region of the world.

Early Village Life in Afghanistan and Pakistan

The spread of the neolithic way of life across Iran and into South Asia was a slow movement. It did not appear in eastern Iran before 4000 B.C., it seems. But to the north near the Caspian Sea at Belt Cave, there is a neolithic level with pottery dated 6500 B.C. Undoubtedly the route of diffusion eastward was an arc to the north following the Āmū Daryā (Oxus) rather than over the arid wastes of eastern Iran. In northern Afghanistan at Ghar-ī-Mār near the Āmū Daryā, there is a neolithic level dated about 5000 B.C., and below it an even earlier neolithic level, but without pottery. The role of Afghanistan in filtering prehistoric innovations into South Asia has been elucidated by Louis Dupree after years of research in that country.

Village life appeared in Balūchistān shortly after. A date of 3700 B.C. is ascribed to an early neolithic level at Kili Ghul Muhammad near Queṭṭā. Sheep, goats, and oxen were tended, and the tools included stone blades, grinding stones, and bone awls. These early villagers lived in huts of mud bricks or hard-packed clay. Wheel-made pottery and copper appeared soon after the onset of the neolithic, while settled village communities proliferated over the Balūchistān hills.[1]

By the beginning of the 3d millennium B.C., influences from central Iran had finally begun to penetrate Afghanistan directly across the Sīstān basin. An important site is Muṇḍigāk in southeastern Afghanistan, excavated by the French under J-M Casal. Here even the lowest level included a needle and a copper blade as well as wheel-made pottery. A crude figurine of a humped bull was a preview of what was coming to be important to people in this part of the world. This culture phase spread through Balūchistān, but not onto the Indus plains. Muṇḍigāk II was a period of some stagnation, but again in Level III there was a proliferation of cultural variety and imported elements coupled with the extension of these village settlements into southern Balūchistān and the Indus plains. Now we have bronze, stone

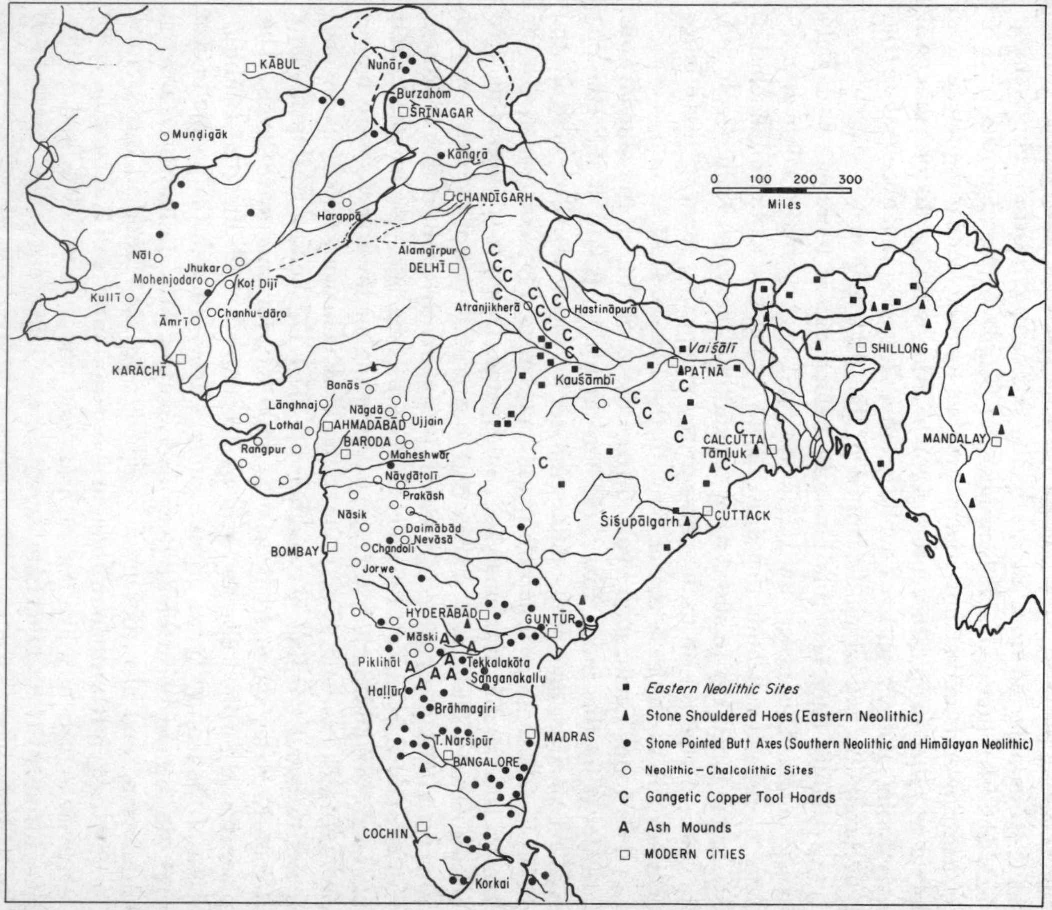

FIG. 5–1 Neolithic sites.

seals, the shaft-hole ax, and clay female figurines. At the site of Dāmb Sadāt in northern Balūchistān this level is dated from about 2500 B.C.

There were two other neolithic cultures in the Balūchistān uplands. One was characterized by a polychrome ceramic industry called Nāl ware, which also appears to have had its roots on the Iran side. Beads of lapis lazuli were imported from the north, and this culture boasted copper stamp seals and clay humped bull figurines. Nāl people persisted in the kind of agriculture and animal husbandry suitable to their semiarid plateau and left it to other people to venture into the fringes of the Indus plain. Nāl polychrome pottery with its white painted loops is not ancestral to the polychrome pottery which developed in the Indus region.

A slightly later neolithic phase in Balūchistān is represented at Kullī in the south. This lasted until 1900 B.C. and was therefore contemporary with the urban civilization that arose on the plains, but southern Balūchistān is a region too stingy to afford many agricultural blessings. Kullī people did, however, participate in trade crosscurrents connecting them with the cities on the plain to the east as well as with the Persian Gulf.

The Indus Civilization evolved from the neolithic on the alluvial soils laid down by the Indus River. (Indian archeologists call it the Harappā civilization after one of its cities; the term "Indus" is used here in the archeological sense as a culture phase, not a region.) What evidence of its origins is available was analyzed by George Dales as representing two culture phases. The first is represented at Āmrī, a series of mounds covering 20 acres in Sindh excavated by Casal. It apparently derived from northern Balūchistān. Early levels included copper, bronze, fine parallel-sided chert blades, bolas, and buried storage jars. In a higher lever there were houses of mud bricks as well as of stone, some of which were raised up on platforms to avoid flooding. At another site, Koṭ Dijī, east of Mohenjo-dāṛo, carbon-14 dates range from 2600 to 2100 B.C. for successive levels. This place was a fortified city and remained occupied until after the establishment of the mature Indus urban centers nearby. Though the people of Koṭ Dijī still did not burn bricks, they made pottery with designs like those on Indus ware, and also the curious terracotta "cakes" found in Indus cities. Farther east in Rājasthān in India at the important site of Kālibangan lower levels yielded pottery like that of Āmrī, and above these levels is the fully-blown Indus Civilization. Late Āmrī and Koṭ Dijī were at the threshold of civilization.

The real contribution of these preurban villagers is that they pioneered the use of the fertile alluvial soils of the Indus plains. Whether they relied on natural seasonal flooding or a network of channels, the land must have had adequate flushing and draining to prevent accumulation of alkali salts. They did build long embankments and erect their dwellings on high platforms. Their mastery of the desert alluvium and water is paralleled by the Ubaid of Mesopotamia, the Amratian of Egypt, and the Moche of coastal

Peru. In these four parts of the world, early domination of a similar environment led to proliferation of population, urbanization, and impressive civilizations.

The Himālayan Neolithic

A distinctive neolithic complex has been identified in the Kāngṛā valley in Himāchal Pradesh. Besides polished stone axes, it has scrapers of split pebbles and thick pebble flakes, so it is likely that it evolved from the mesolithic Upper Soan culture. It is not dated, but has affinity with neolithic cultures of Central Asia, such as that found in the Turkmen Republic from about 6000 B.C. and the Gissar complex of the Tājik Republic from about 3000 B.C. The latter includes a range of tools from polished stone axes, stone querns, and microliths, to scrapers seemingly evolved from chopping tools. People lived in huts, paved with stones, and kept animals.

On the alluvial plains of Kashmīr near Śrīnagar is another site, Burzahom, which also has affinity with neolithic complexes north of the Himālayas. There is a pit dwelling with hearths and post holes. Artifacts include a good variety of points, harpoons, and needles of bone, polished stone tools, and pottery; no grindstones or stone blades were unearthed. The earliest date ascertained is 2375 B.C., but in a subsequent level dated 1400 B.C. dogs had been buried with corpses, and one person had had his skull trepanned during life. There was a single copper arrowhead. A still later level is remarkable because of the erection of massive megalithic boulders in a partial circle. This Kashmīr neolithic may have affinity with the Mongolian, Chinese, and even the Japanese neolithic, as well as with Central Asia; essentially it was transitional from hunting to a sedentary way of life. It had no visible influence on the Indus Civilization with which it was contemporary. These finds are of interest because they reflect a way of life that gave rise to the indigenous Himālayan cultures of India and Nepal, which have in recent centuries been affected by the expansion of Indian and Tibetan civilization.[2]

The Peninsular Neolithic

In the Allchins' survey of Indian archeology, *The Birth of Indian Civilization*, they identify three phases of the peninsular neolithic. The first was based on cattle keeping, perhaps supplemented by some cultivation, and this subsistence method spread through the Deccan contemporary with the Indus Civilization. Probably its antecedents were the early neolithic cultures of Balūchistān. In Gujarāt in the site of Lānghnāj people lived in wattle and daub houses; they used neolithic ground tools as well as Late

Stone Age ones. Copper appeared here early in the neolithic. A comparable level at Nāvḍāṭolī on the middle Narmadā has been dated 2300 B.C., while 2000 B.C. has been assigned to a similar phase at Eran in Mālwā. At some sites pigs were kept along with cattle. The route down the Deccan followed by earlier Stone Age culture phases was now the natural route of diffusion of cattle keeping, which found the mixed savanna and deciduous forest favorable.

Strange-looking ash mounds are scattered over northern and central Karṇāṭaka. F. R. Allchin excavated some of these, notably at Utnūr, and found them to be ashes of cow dung, datable from 2000 B.C. Where the cattle were penned at night, dung accumulated to several feet in depth and was periodically burned by the cattle keepers in fertility rituals. The pen at Utnūr might have enclosed 600 cattle, while others were made to contain twice that number. Surely this was a way of life to be envied by mesolithic hunters.

The cattle keepers lived in flimsy huts constructed outside the cattle stockades. From the beginning they had pottery, but at first it was handmade and unburnished. Later they produced burnished and ochre-washed pots, turntable-made wares, and finally about the time copper was introduced, wheel-made pottery. Outside the stockades they dropped blade tools as well as microliths and characteristic neolithic tools such as ground and pecked stone axes, querns, pestles, rubbers, and hammer stones. The cattle included the two types now kept in peninsular India: the heavier sturdy ones useful for plowing and presumably at that time for meat, and the lightly built animals maintained now for their milk. There were no signs of agriculture or other domestic animals except a few scattered bones of sheep. Though pottery styles suggest this culture came by way of Mahārāshṭra and Gujarāt, it became specialized to the relatively dry parts of the Deccan.

Such dung mounds continued to be fired from 2000 to 750 B.C. in peninsular India. These ritual fires had the function of warding off disease and ensuring reproduction of the cattle; there were similar practices in prehistoric Europe. Modern pastoral castes such as Āhīrs throughout North India and Āyar in the South are widely distributed, and undoubtedly descended from such prehistoric cattle keepers. Some of the tribal groups such as Bhīls also seem to have been keepers of cattle in scrub forests.

Many cultural elements found in India today seem to have had their origin with preagricultural and early agricultural cattle keepers. A huge corpus of mythology revolves around the pastoral tradition, with folk heroes, deities, and attendant rituals. Best known is the Krishṇa cycle of stories, partly set in Gujarāt. Cattle stealing is a recurring theme in the literature—and it even occurs several times in the earliest Vedas. The bull is a common fertility symbol commonly linked with Śaivite Hinduism. In the South there are such events as bull wrestling of the southern Tamil̠ country, bull

FIG. 5–2 Stone blades from Māski, a chalcolithic site in Karṇāṭaka. Such tools were commonly used in the Indus Civilization.

racing of Karṇāṭaka and Tuḷuva, and the *māṭṭu-pongal* festival at which cattle are honored. The early emphasis on the bull merged in Hinduism with the emphasis on the cow which grew up after the Āryans introduced valuation of dairy products.

A second phase of the peninsular neolithic may be dated 1800 to 1500 B.C. This is in evidence at many sites in Karṇāṭaka such as Piklihāl, Brāhmagiri, Tekkalakōṭa, Haḷḷūr, T. Narsipur, and Śanganakallu. There are clear evidences of influence from the north at this time, obviously radiating from the Indus Civilization, such as tall vessels perforated all over (perhaps for cooking by steaming), spouts, terracotta objects, small pieces of copper, and even bronze. There is no evidence of metallurgy; the culture was essentially neolithic. The basis of the economy was still cattle keeping, especially of the humped variety, but sheep were raised, and varieties of grām (pulses)

and millets were grown. This phase is represented in Tekkalakōṭa I, which had utensils of handmade pottery and huge jars presumably for storing grain. Urns in which children were buried were shaped like pregnant women, with breasts and globular bellies, and were buried under or near the floors of their little circular huts. It is probable that the concept of rebirth was part of the belief system and was pre-Āryan. The adult dead were exposed, and after desiccation were interred with the head to the south.

A third phase of the Deccan neolithic-chalcolithic is represented at Tekkalakōṭa, excavated by Nagaraja Rao. Corpses were buried with the head to the north, and wheel-turned Black and Red Ware was produced for funerary purposes. Houses were both round and rectangular. Copper, by this time smelted in the Deccan itself, was fashioned into bangles, fish hooks, and axes; gold ornaments had come into fashion. Even yet microliths were used, set in handles with gum, along with neolithic ground stone tools. Of course many traits of this third neolithic phase can be traced to the post-Indus cultures of western India. A similar neolithic complex appeared in Tamil̠ Nāḍu about 1000 B.C., but not in coastal Kērala or the deltas of Āndhra.

This kind of subsistence economy, dependent upon millets, pulses, oilseeds, and cotton, has remained the basis of village life in the unirrigable lands of the Deccan until today. But during the 1st millennium B.C. iron appeared in the South, and the lowlands were gradually utilized for irrigated rice cultivation. Urban life, state systems, and civilization did not appear in the South before about the 4th and 3d centuries B.C.

The Eastern Neolithic

The appearance of an array of cultivated plants from Southeast Asia has had an impact on South Asia that demands our attention. Moreover, the tribal people of eastern central India and the hills around Assam owe their distinctive cultural features largely to Southeast Asia influence. First came the Muṇḍa languages, which jumped across the Bānglā plain to central India; then came the Burmese-type languages found everywhere in the hills east of Bānglā and Assam.

Ground or polished pointed-butt stone axes have been found in Assam, at many places in central India, in the Deccan, and as far as the tip of the peninsula. Recently they have been found associated with the Himālayan neolithic, and even in Pakistan, though they are not generally characteristic of sites in western South Asia. Similar pointed-butt axes, polished or pecked, are found in Burma, Laos, Viet Nam, Yunnan, Szechwan, and North China. Mortimer Wheeler has pointed out that the major exploitation of this tool type has been on Indian soil, even though it might have originated to the

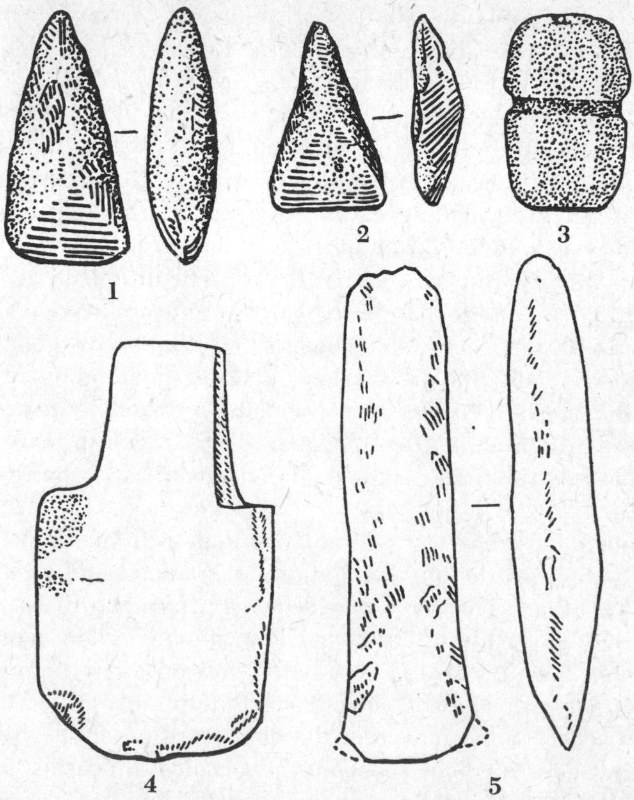

FIG. 5–3 Neolithic stone tools: 1) polished pointed-butt ax, Brāhmagiri, Karṇāṭaka; 2) polished adze, Brāhmagiri; 3) polished hammer-stone, Bihār, all 1/4 size; 4) shouldered stone hoe, Bānglā; 5) bar-chisels, Bihār, both 1/2 size.

east. Specimens from Southeast Asia have more rounded butts than do the Indian ones. The lower date of their manufacture in India is not known, but the neolithic culture represented by these artifacts is not associated with copper in Assam. Pointed-butt axes were used in South India until the arrival of iron.

Another tool type which presumably came into India from the east is the hoe or adze with sawed shoulders. Such are found in Assam, southern Bihār, Orissa, and Āndhra, with a few specimens in west central India; they are absent from the Deccan, western India, and the territory north of the Gangā. Shouldered hoes are found in North and Southeast China, Burma, Thailand, Cambodia, and Viet Nam. It is probable that this tool type originated in China, and if it was copied from a copper prototype as some suggest, its origin would be of chalcolithic date. A. H. Dani, who has made a detailed study of the eastern neolithic, thinks metal was necessary to saw

the stone. With patience, however, the job might have been done with agate blades or with fiber and abrasives. No metal has been found associated with these tools in Assam.

The neolithic assemblage in Assam also includes quantities of pottery impressed with striated or cord-wrapped beaters. Such pottery is characteristic of the neolithic of Thailand and Malaysia. Related wares have been found in preurban levels in excavations in the South along the Tamiḻ-Nāḍu and Kērala coasts and in Sri Lanka.

We have hardly any idea when these horticultural influences began to affect South Asia. There has been scarcely any archeology in the Assam region or in Burma. Some archeologists feel that it was not until the 2d millennium B.C. and that it was long delayed in jumping over the then-inhospitable forests between Burma and India, reaching central India only as the lower Gangā plains were cleared. It was a true primary horticultural economy; in central Indian sites it directly overlies prepottery microlithic tools.

We have here a clear cultural continuum from India into China's Yunnan Province on the one hand and into Thailand and the Malay Peninsula on the other. The recent evidence of horticulture in northwestern Thailand dating as early as 20,000 B.C. is startling. Certain legumes, at least, seem to have been cultivated very early, and probably pepper, areca nut, bottle gourd, and a kind of cucumber.[3] But this neolithic complex might not have reached India until after the domestication of the banana.

The cultigens of chief economic importance appearing in India from Southeast Asia include first the banana with its hundred varieties, coconut, sugar cane, yam, areca nut, betel leaf (chewed with the nut), and pepper, all of which reached South Asia by the time of Christ. The sago palm (which has an edible pith), certain legumes, and ginger also appeared. By early medieval times cloves and nutmeg had been brought from Indonesia. Rice might also have come from Southeast Asia. Quite probably the chicken was domesticated there, and also the water buffalo (no other part of the world would contend for the invention of such an ungainly beast!). This repertory of important plants and animals blended into the Indian scene as one of the mainstreams of neolithic culture giving rise to Indian civilization.

The origin of rice cultivation is obscure. Dry (unirrigated) rice is grown by shifting cultivation in the hilly flanks of Southeast Asia, the eastern Indian hills, and central India. Rice appeared by 2000 B.C. in the Indus Civilization sites in Gujarāt, and elsewhere in India, but not in the Indus plain at that time. The site of Paṇḍurājārdhibī in the plains of West Bengal suggests that irrigated rice was grown there by 1000 B.C., and soon after spread down the whole eastern side of India. In Southeast Asia and to some extent in India the water buffalo is adapted to cultivation of paddy (unhusked rice).

Ethnographic data well support the intrusion of the eastern neolithic

from Southeast Asia. In addition to the evidence from languages (Khāsi is a Muṇḍa language remaining in the eastern hills in Meghālaya), many cultural traits of the eastern and central Indian tribal peoples have been shown to have affinity with Southeast Asia. These include use of adolescent dormitories, exposing the dead in booths or erecting funerary megaliths, headhunting procedures, and other religious, social, and kinship features.

The Indus (Harappā) Civilization

Nobody knew before the 1930s that a widespread primary civilization stretched out over most of Pakistan and parts of western India. No ancient Hindu books explicitly refer to it. Yet this urban complex must now be ranked third among the primary civilizations of the world, after Sumer and Egypt; its mature period is dated 2400 to 1750 B.C., and it petered out about 1300 B.C. One thing, however, has become increasingly clear within the last two decades: though it died, it rose again, a new metamorphosis. Its antique cultural patterns were caught up into the mushrooming classical civilization beginning in the 6th century B.C.

The three star sites of this civilization are Harappā, in the southern Pakistani part of the Panjāb, Mohenjo-dāṛo, nearly 400 miles to the south in Sindh, and Kālibangān in northwestern Rājasthān. While poking around a Buddhist *stūpa* (semispherical monument containing relics of Buddhist saints) atop the mound at Mohenjo-dāṛo, British archeologists discovered the different civilization whose ruins lay beneath it. Sir John Marshall excavated the site, discovering it to be three miles around, and published his report in 1931. Later E. Mackay excavated there and at nearby Chanhu-dāṛo. In 1940 M. S. Vats brought out his report of the site of Harappā. After World War II Sir Mortimer Wheeler probed further at Mohenjo-dāṛo and published a number of works on the nature of the civilization. We have also had contributions from Piggott, Fairservis, Gordon, Casal, Dales, Raikes, Lal, and the Pakistan Department of Archeology. Indian archeologists were pleased to discover that Indus-type cities flourished in Gujarāt: Lothal and Rangpur have been described by S. R. Rao, and the large sites of Sūrkoṭāḍā and Deśalpur are now being excavated. They were elated to discover Kālibangan, a site in Rājasthān rivaling Mohenjo-dāṛo, excavated by B. B. Lal and B. K. Thapar but not yet fully published.

Seals used by businessmen of the Indus cities found their way to Mesopotamia, but contrary to earlier opinion, none of these is earlier than King Sargon, confirming the recent carbon-14 runs giving 1400 or 1300 B.C. as the beginning date of the maturing civilization. The basic *ideas* leading to the development of script, bronze, cargo boats, massive granaries, and perhaps civic government, priesthood, and temples must have diffused somehow from Mesopotamia. While sea contact has often been invoked as

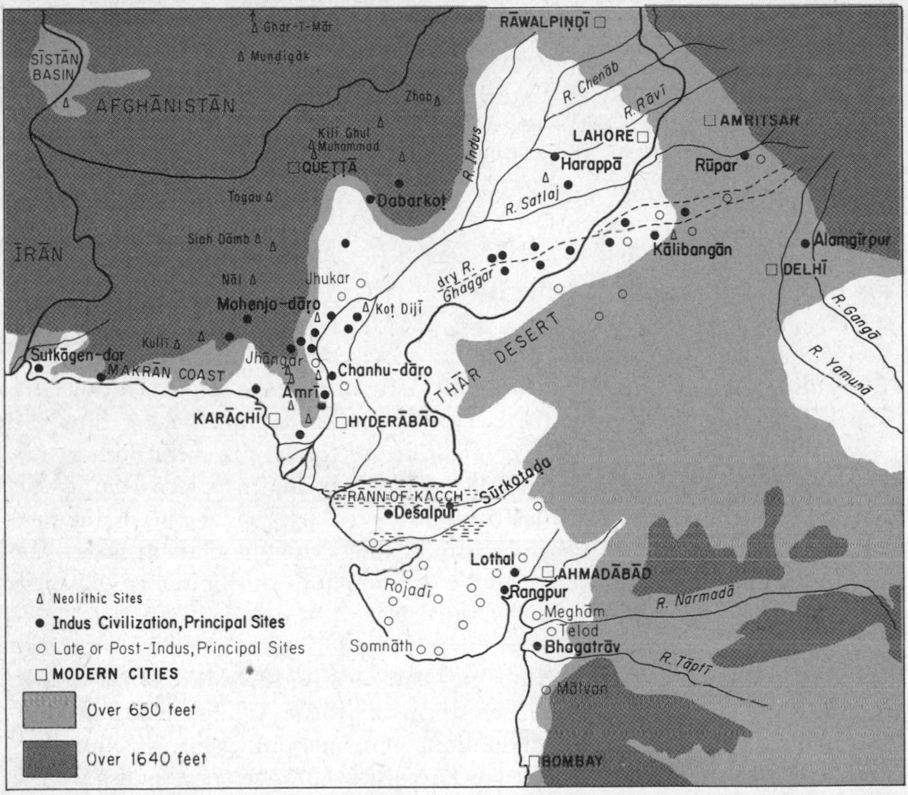

FIG. 5–4 Indus Civilization sites.

the cause of this civilization springing up, clearly it is not a copy of Sumerian Civilization. Recently an important site toward the eastern edge of Iran, named Tepe Yāhyā, has been excavated by Lamberg-Karlovsky. Tepe Yāhyā flourished at this time and was clearly an extension of Mesopotamian Civilization, with cuneiform script; details await publication. Yet the Indus Civilization was not transplanted from anywhere, but the ideas filtering in from the west took root in this new environment and the civilization evolved locally out of the Āmrī protourban culture.

No other primary civilization covered such a vast area. From its westernmost outpost of Sutkāgen-dor near the border of Iran to Alamgīrpur near Delhi, a distance of 1000 miles, the civilization was uniform. In Panjāb, the site of Rūpar on the Satlaj River is 700 miles north of Bhagatrāv, an Indus outpost south of the Narmadā River, and Indian archeologists claim to have recently found evidence of it even further south in Mahārāshṭra.

Many questions are unanswered. Was cultural uniformity over this wide area due to purposeful colonization from the lower Indus? To an aggressive militaristic state? To the dispersal of dominant castes? Or to

pressure for conformity exerted by guilds and a high level of commercial activity and trade? Since the script cannot be read, these questions cannot be answered. The civilization seems to have exploded northeastward up the now-dry Sarasvatī and Ghaggar streams, where 35 sites have been found, then across the Indus-Gangā divide. It also spread southeastward down a branch of the Indus which flowed into the huge Rann of Kacch swamp in western Gujarāt. Sea traffic must have caused the founding of Lothāl and Rangpur, urban outposts at the head of the Gulf of Cambay (in Gujarāt) as well as port towns near the mouth of the Narmadā.

An Indus Burgher's Morning Stroll

Now let us suppose a burgher living in one of the great Indus towns takes an early morning walk. Donning a loose-hanging cotton garment, he comes down from the upper room of his solid brick house and passes through the downstairs into the courtyard. To one side is a huge storage jar, and beyond it the bathroom. The women folk have been working since dawn and have drawn water from the nearby brick-lined circular well so that he can take his bath upon returning from his morning walk and defecation in the fields. Some of his neighbors have built privies which drain into the street sewers, but our householder does not have this convenience. He and his family so love to take pouring baths in their little brick-paved bathrooms that he has had to add a second one for his household. The town is dusty and the days hot, but water is always there not far down in the well.

Our gentleman passes from his courtyard into a narrow alley winding past his neighbors' houses to the main street of the ward. Hey! Which of those neighbor rascals was responsible for throwing aside these bricks covering the drain? Why, the city government has just now completed that brick-lined drain to carry off household water down the edge of the street to the main sewer system. Our man, passing down the street, makes a right-angle turn into the main thoroughfare, a straightaway 45 feet wide, which is already busy this sunshiny morning with ox carts coming and going. Some are bringing freshly threshed grain to the government granary on the other side of town. Interlaced among the cart trains are goats, sheep, and humped cattle being taken out to pasture, while chickens scratch in the dust on the side.

The burgher decides to take a walk over to the citadel built on a high separate mound to the west; it gives him a sense of security to see the rectangular bastions and guard rooms atop the great wall, which after all, is 40 feet thick and faced with burned bricks. The priests and nobility in the citadel are safe from any onslaught of tribespeople from the western hills as well as from the rampaging floods of the Indus which can destroy

(*Above*) Mohenjo-dāṛo: "Low Lane."

(*Below*) Mohenjo-dāṛo: the great tank or bath on the citadel, 39 feet long, with steps at both ends, flanked by 8 small bathing rooms; doubtless a prelude to the ablutions of Hindu tradition. (Both photographs from *The Indus Civilization* by Sir Mortimer Wheeler. By permission of Cambridge University Press, New York.)

less well-protected towns. By the time he climbs up the citadel to the great tank, our townsman can see the green fields stretching far out, heavy with crops of wheat, barley, pulses, sesame, and cotton, fringed here and there by date palms. Out in the river there are picturesque boats with high upturned ends, standards flying, the pilots wielding steering oars. Some boats have cabins amidship for important passengers. Those coming from the north, he knows, bear wood from the mountains and jade from beyond them, or lapis lazuli and tin from the Persian side. Others coming from the south have skirted the perilous ocean, bringing from ports on the Narmadā and the Gulf of Cambay various woods, copper, lead, silver, ivory, and semiprecious stones.

The burgher, coming down from the citadel into the town itself, passes through streets where artisans are already at their morning's work. The smith is making a flat ax from bronze he has prepared himself. In the potter's workshop a boy is kneading clay while his father paints geometric and animal designs on large plates and bowls yet to be fired. Lapidaries are busy on their working platforms, and in the ivory carver's house a man is completing a set of gamesmen. Yonder someone is polishing a set of graded stone weights for merchants' scales. Bundles of goods, tied up and affixed with clay sealings, are being taken to warehouses.

Our burgher, having walked three miles around the city, decides he had better dally no more, but return to his waiting wife and his bath. His musings are disturbed by no books of history; the uniformity of his sedate way of life has been unchallenged for hundreds of miles in each direction. As far as he knows, things would be the same for his children and for his descendants indefinitely.

Problems of the Indus Civilization

Such citizens could not have known that their writing system would be forgotten, perhaps never to be deciphered. All major sites of the civilization have yielded little rectangular or oval seals, typically made of baked steatite and 1¼ inches long, which were used to stamp clay sealings on knotted cords of baled goods. A line or two of writing is engraved and below is an animal or other symbol. The humped bull, elephant, rhinoceros, antelope, crocodile, unicorn-like beast, and odd composite creatures are common. Many of the seals are miniature masterpieces of naturalistic engraving.

Though 2500 seals have been found, the script remains enigmatic. It consists of some 300 separate symbols plus some modifying marks. Some appear to be fish, chair, trident, leaf, town wall, crab, bird, or spear point. These ideographs occur on a few ivory pieces and potsherds, but there is no written document. Only one seal has as many as three lines of writing,

which do read from right to left. Since such short inscriptions have little grammatical structure and probably consist mostly of names of owners or guilds, a bilingual inscription may be necessary for decipherment. Scholars from England, India, Sri Lanka, and Russia have tackled it, usually reading it as early Indo-European or early Dravidian. Recently Danish and Finnish scholars have claimed decipherment, reading it as proto-Dravidian. The direction of their work is intuitively sensible, and has been supplemented by the Indian scholar, Iravatham Mahadevan,[4] but precise proof to satisfy professional linguists is still lacking.

It is doubtful if the language will prove to be an Indo-Āryan one because probably Āryans had not even penetrated Iran by 2400 B.C., much less the Indus region, and in any case they were nomadic and militaristic tribesmen not likely to have quickly built up an urban civilization. But Dravidian speech not only has a local remnant in Brāhūī but also seems to have influenced the formation of Sanskrit, Sindhī, Gujarātī, and certainly Marāṭhī. Scholars do not know of the former extent of Burushaski nor whether there were other language families.

Another problem is the effect of Sumerian and Old Babylonian civilizations on the Indus region. Evidence remains elusive, though a few Indus seals reached the Persian Gulf and Mesopotamia. S. N. Kramer suggests that Tilmun (Dilmun) and maybe Meluhha and Magan mentioned in Mesopotamian cuneiform records as overseas places, refer to the Indus region. Magan may be the Makrān coast of Balūchistān. From these places the Mesopotamians imported ebony and other woods, ivory, gold, gems, copper, and pearls[5]; these are all available from Gujarāt or its hinterland. The woods of the northern Western Ghāṭs must have been especially coveted. Perhaps the sea trade for which the Gujarātīs have been renowned even in the earliest historical records is a tradition going back to this protohistoric period.

The most discussed problem is why this civilization disintegrated about 1750 B.C. Wheeler in 1953 noted groups of skeletons in the upper levels of Mohenjo-dāṛo and suggested that it had been destroyed, perhaps by invading Āryans. Dales and Raikes think that floods brought about the city's demise; they think the coast was uplifted causing flooding of the Indus plains. Evidence of floods is abundant, but it seems that the citadel and city itself, built up on 50-foot mounds, would have escaped the severest floods. Another suggestion is that the burning of so many millions if bricks demanded fuel, denuding the land of its tamarisk tree cover and causing dust to blow and the water table to be lowered. Then again, irrigation might have entailed the accumulation of alkali deposits, rendering the land useless; indeed, this is the most serious problem facing irrigation in Pakistan today. Climate change has also been cited; desiccation did not destroy the cities along the Indus, but the Sarasvatī to the northeast did dry up, mortally affecting the two dozen Indus settlements along it.

Mohenjo-dāṛo: seals of steatite with the Indus script, three-quarters size. "Unicorn" and "offering stand" are common motifs.

Mohenjo-dāṛo: terracotta female figurine, three-quarters size. On such figurines multiple necklaces, wide belt, and fan-shaped headdress are common adornment.

We do not know if Mohenjo-dāṛo finally fell because of social or political anarchy. But there was an internal weakening before the final demise. Buildings of the last phase were built in haphazard and shoddy manner, encroaching on older, well-planned streets and sewers as if civic discipline had become lax. Small houses were built up on the citadel around the granary, while arts and crafts suffered decline. But the skeletons of some 38 persons were left lying in the corners of the last levels of the Indus Civilization; a few show evidence of violence, apparently killed as they huddled together. Wheeler's suggestion that internal decay invited violent invaders, probably "Āryans," stands as the most plausible explanation we have.

If culture change poses problems, refusal of people to adopt more efficient and available techniques is an even more pertinent concern of anthropologists. Indus ox carts, drawn by two yoked oxen, were cumbersome things with heavy solid wooden wheel discs. The wheels were permanently affixed to the axle which was able to revolve under the cart, so that when the cart turned a corner one wheel had to skid. Toy models of such carts turned up in several Indus sites (and toy carts of mud are favorite toys of Pakistani boys today). A far more efficient vehicle with light spoked wheels that revolved independently of the axle was introduced in the 1st millennium B.C., from which developed the several varieties of carts in use in India today. But in Sindh one can still see the lumbering skidding Indus-type carts—and they travel right over the mound at Mohenjo-dāṛo! Even the axle length is still the same as it was 4000 years ago. That the Sindhī peasant still uses a cart with a revolving axle three millennia after a more efficient type appeared is a testimonial to the impact of the Indus culture in particular and to the selective conservatism of the South Asian peasant in general.

Peasant Cultures of Western India and the Deccan

After about 2000 B.C. the peasant peoples of western India and the Deccan achieved a means of subsistence so suitably adapted to the environment it has essentially persisted to the present. Technologically they were chalcolithic (using copper with stone tools). In Panjāb wheat cultivation continued; Indus pottery shapes and designs persisted more or less (indeed vessels of pink fabric with black designs reminiscent of those made 4000 years ago can be bought on the streets of Panjāb towns today); and life in the clustered villages must have been similar to that in isolated regions today. There is some archeological evidence that the aftermath of the Indus civilization penetrated the Gangā valley.

In Gujarāt the cities of Indus-type which had been transplanted there—

particularly Sūrkoṭāḍā, Deśalpur, Rangpur,and Lothal–passed their florescent peak as those in the Indus plains did. Gujarāt was then cut off from the Indus region, it seems, and a stage of the Indus Civilization sometimes called "degenerate" appeared in the Saurāshṭra part of Gujarāt. Town planning and drainage systems ceased to be regulated, and a huge brick-lined tank (reservoir) at Lothal was abandoned. Pottery became coarser. This phase lasted some centuries, 1800 to 1500 B.C. in Lothal, while in Rangpur it is represented by 12 feet of accumulated debris. Truly though, it was not degenerate but was adapting to local environmental conditions. Population increased, and over 50 sites of this culture have been spotted in and around the Saurāshṭra peninsula.

One reason for the evolution of this new culture phase in Gujarāt must have been the adoption of rice as the staple food, while wheat remained the mainstay in Sindh and Panjāb. Beginning in 2000 B.C., rice cultivation spread from Gujarāt southward, supplementing the millets and pulses that grow easily on the Deccan. About the same time presumably, rice cultivation took hold in the Gangā region, and subsequently became an important factor differentiating it from Panjāb. It is time, as Wheeler points out in his 1966 survey, to concede the importance of dietary customs in the study of culture dynamics.

A separate culture flourished throughout the 2d millennium B.C. in the Mālwā regions, astride the border of Rājasthān and Madhya Pradesh, called the Banās culture. Since copper ore was locally available it produced and exported copper, probably providing that which was exported by sea from Gujarāt. The pottery included the Black and Red Ware.

In Gujarāt after the Indus Civilization had faded and writing had been forgotten, a new culture arose, characterized by Lustrous Red Ware and lasting from 1500 to 1000 B.C. The reservoir at Lothal was again put to use. But houses had no drainage systems nor brick-paved floors as in the preceding civilization, and were built only of mud bricks and lime mortar. But this Lustrous Red Ware culture derived from the Indus Civilization, for pottery shapes and metal tools remained almost the same. There were terracotta figurines, shell bangles, and carnelian beads which provide links with both preceding and succeeding cultures. From these levels Black and Red Ware was also unearthed, suggesting links with Rājasthān to the north. This pottery (interestingly enough, reminiscent of the black-topped ware of predynastic Egypt) later spread all over western and peninsular India with the Iron Age.

Farther south, in Mahārāshṭra, at Nāvḍāṭolī on the middle Narmadā, an offshot of the Lustrous Red Ware culture has been dated to the middle of the 2d millennium B.C. The peasants built rectangular houses of wooden posts and bamboo screens together with circular storage bins such as are used today. They cultivated rice, wheat, pulses, cotton, and oilseeds, and

Tamiḻ potter and children. Wheel is twirled with pole; clay on left is from reservoir bottom.

Potter and wife place pots and clay idols among coconut husks in kiln for firing. Full kiln is covered with straw and mud plaster and fired from below. Pots have a red wash but are undecorated.

tended cattle, sheep, goats, and pigs. Though there were some copper tools, the people relied mainly on the long stone blades such as were used in the Indus Civilization, and even used microliths.

Important excavations have been conducted inland from Bombay at Maheśwāṛ, Prakāsh, Nāsik, Jorwe, Nevāsā, and elsewhere. At Prakāsh a mound of habitation debris 57 feet high had accumulated. The early level, datable to 1500 B.C., had copper and wheel-turned pottery, a painted terra-

cotta bull, a toy cart wheel, and beads of carnelian, shell, and paste. The succeeding level had Lustrous Red Ware showing influence from Gujarāt. From Nevāsā and Candolī we know that people lived in wattle and daub houses built on wooden frames and slept on mud-plastered floors spread over sand or gravel. They used copper flat axes, chisels, spearheads, fish-hooks, and dagger blades, yet retained the older ribbon-like stone blades. Cotton and flax were spun and the usual animals herded. The high phase of this culture extended from 1450 to 1050 B.C., after which there is somewhat of a gap until the 6th century or so B.C. when the new civilization in the Gangā began to have an impact on this part of India.

These post-Indus cultures were enriched by some influences of the Indus Civilization which have persisted to the present as characteristic of western and peninsular India. These influences included village planning with streets at right angles (in contrast with the generally amorphous settlement pattern of the Gangā and eastern plains) and the proclivity to larger villages which naturally took on some urban functions. Another influence is navigation and sea trade, for such port towns in Gujarāt as Prabhāspatān, Broach, and Nagarā (Cambay) doubtless provided continuity for Gujarātī capitalists and sea traders—though there are still some archeological gaps. Scratch marks on peninsular Indian pottery resemble those on Indus pottery and were probably ownership symbols, though there was no script. Many gem types are similar. Plow cultivation, the ox cart, the potter's wheel, metals, some of the deities, and probably Dravidian speech diffused southward in the aftermath of the Indus Civilization, merging with the earlier Deccan neolithic cultures.

The Āryans

Swarming hordes of Āryans, tall, fair-skinned, and noble, some astride sleek horses, drove over the Khyber and Bolān passes into the fertile plains of the Panjāb, chanting Vedic hymns as they advanced, flooding India with the warmth and light of their intellectual prowess as they defeated the black and barbaric local tribes: this is the popular image of India's Pilgrims. Unfortunately, the Āryans were neither literate nor touched by urbanization when they began filtering in, presumably between 1500 and 1000 B.C. The chief evidence of them is linguistic: Dardic, Indic, and Persian-type languages successively appeared. There is scant firm historical evidence supporting the myth about Āryans until the literary records beginning with the Persian Achaemenian occupation of the Panjāb and Sindh in the 6th century B.C. The *Rig Veda*, oldest of the four Vedas, was composed well before 1000 B.C., but it contains no reference to invasion of Āryans nor to any particular regard for the west. Yet its authors must have been distant

cousins of speakers of Indo-European languages which spread through Europe, Central Asia, the Near East, and Persia.

As early as 2200 B.C. the military aristocracy of the Hatti (Hittites) crossed the Caucasus and by 1800 had formed a confederacy and penetrated Turkey. At the same time the Mitanni came south of the Caucasus and by the 15th century B.C. occupied the Zagros Mountains of western Persia. After 1800 B.C., a related people, Kassites, invaded Mesopotamia, ruling there until 1171 B.C., after which they became absorbed. In western Anatolia the Luwian language appeared and developed into classical Lycean, while the Achaeans penetrated Greece from the north, uniting the Greek mainland under the kings of Mycenae by the 14th century B.C. Some of them, the Ahhiyawa, took to trading by sea with Crete and the coast of Syria. Yet other related people, Dorians, invaded Greece in the 13th century B.C. Another great branch of Indo-European speakers apparently rounded the Caspian Sea, penetrated Bactria and touched western China, crossed the Syr Daryā and Āmū Daryā rivers into Iran, and diffused into Afghanistan and the Panjāb plains.

Everywhere the Indo-European speakers formed a military aristocracy, an exclusive caste, which dominated but later was absorbed by the more urbane people whom they conquered. The king or chief (*rājā* in Sanskrit, related to *rex* in Latin) was not divine, nor was he originally a priest, but a war leader. This military aristocracy can be seen as but one of the long succession of invasions spilling out in all directions from the nomadic heartland of Eurasia. Their nomadic origin is betrayed by cognate words in differing Indo-European languages for cows and milk products; they also had copper, textiles, horses, boats, and wheeled vehicles.

Their military success was possible because they had horses, to which they gave due credit. To the Kassites, the horse was a divine symbol. A Mitanni account of horse training uses the words *aika-wartanna* for "one turn," obviously close to Sanskrit *eka vartana*, while terms for three, five, seven, and nine turns are similar in these two languages. The *Rig Veda* refers to a divine horse, and to the *aśvamedha* (horse sacrifice), which was the most important ritual supporting the kingship of the Āryans in India. The Kassites had the light spoked-wheel chariot by the 16th century. At some point Āryans must have introduced such vehicles into the Indus region in place of the disc-wheeled carts of the Indus plains.

The Āryan gods in early South Asia have parallels among Indo-European speakers to the west. Kassites worshiped Shuraish, the same as the Hindu sun god Sūrya. Their Marutash was the Indian Marut, and their Buraish, the Greek Goreas. Mithra, Varuṇa, Indra, and Nasatya, introduced into Persia and India, have parallels among Mitanni gods. The Persian wind god Vahyu became the Sanskrit Vāyu.

Archeological evidence is just beginning to jell. At Sīyālk in central Iran a level thought to have Āryan associations is dated 1200 to 1000 B.C.

'he horse must have been important, for horse bits and bells were put in ,raves, the war chariot was known, and winged horses were painted on ottery. People worshiped the sun disc. They buried their dead in cemeeries outside the town according to Āryan practice, not beneath house loors as their predecessors had done. Into graves they put jewelry, bronze nklets, and a type of animal-headed pin thought to be associated with Āryans. They were a broadheaded folk. Their northerly origin is suggested n their habit of building up graves of brick and stone to resemble gabled ouses.

By the time of the classical Persian civilization beginning in the 6th entury B.C., many of these traits had become formalized in the Zoroastrian eligion, which became official with the Achaemenian empire. This may be alled the first world empire, stretching from the Aegean to the Indus and rom Egypt to Bactria. Among parallels with Vedic religion in the Panjāb were the *Avesta*, fire and sun worship, an initiated priestly class, a ritual drink (*soma*), and a similar cosmic outlook and philosophical predilection. Avestan hymns in language and content are close to the Vedas.

Most Indian archeologists are agreed that the spirit of the Indus Civilization is quite different from that of the early Āryans as represented in the Vedas. The Allchins feel that the cultures in the Indus valley which succeeded the Indus Civilization—the Jhukar and the Jhāngar at Chanhudāṛo, and the Cemetery-H from Harappā itself—show evidence of intrusions from Iran and Afghanistan and therefore almost certainly imply the appearance of Āryans. The Jhukar culture represents the advent of agricultural tribes from Balūchistān whose material equipment was unmistakably similar to Bronze Age remains in Iran and also in Turkmenistān; the Jhāngar culture is thought to be suggestive of the steppe tribes of Russia. Perhaps some group of invading Indo-Aryan speakers did indeed cause the final demise of the Indus cities, for Vedic hymns praise Indra, the Āryan war god, as destroyer of 90 forts. There are later references to *pur* (walled cities or forts) as well as to citadels of stone and maybe of mud bricks. These passages, in hymns transmitted orally at first, suggest that the "Āryans" did indeed encounter urbanization in the land they came to dominate.

Beyond this we have to rely upon the epics. How long did it take before Indo-Āryan speech covered Sindh? What about Gujarāt and Mahārāshṭra? Since in Gujarāt the "degenerate Indus" and Lustrous Red Ware phases seem to have evolved directly from the Indus over a period of five centuries, and there is no evidence of mass invasion, perhaps people speaking Dravidian languages were responsible for the Deccan chalcolithic, which lasted up to 1000 B.C. A Dravidian substratum seems to underlie Marāṭhī and perhaps also Gujarātī. The *Mahābhārata*, the all-inclusive Hindu epic, speaks of people from the Panjāb and the Doāb moving down into Sindh while others, primarily associated with the Krishṇa myth, moved into Gujarāt. It may not have been until the epic period, 900 to 500 B.C., when iron

was in use, that the fusion of "Āryans" and indigenous cultures in the Panjāb became strong enough to expand southward. By the middle of the millennium, though, Indo-Āryan speech dominated all of western India including Gujarāt.

Peasant Cultures of the Gangā Plains

The late Indus towns of Rūpar in Panjāb and Alamgīrpur near Delhi faded into oblivion in the 18th or 17th century B.C., but shortly another culture developed in South Bihār and the middle Gangā plain. This is characterized by Ochre Colored Ware, which is a porous pottery made on a slow turntable, underfired, with rough incised designs. Some of the shapes, such as bowls and dish-on-stand, recall Indus forms, but in general this appears to have developed independently.

Ochre Colored Ware is associated with an interesting complement of copper tools. Hoards of them, sometimes hundreds, have been recovered from some 40 sites in the upper and middle Gangā and Choṭā Nagpur. There are flat axes with splayed edges, shouldered axes, bar celts or chisels, rings, harpoon heads, spearheads, swords with tanged hilt and midrib, and anthropomorphic objects with flared legs and incurved arms. At Alamgīrpur this level overlies the Indus level, but is unconnected with it. It may be roughly dated to 1500 B.C. and certainly preceded the onset of the Iron Age, which was under way by 1000 B.C. in North India.

There is some evidence that this culture moved westward up the Gangā from a focal point in Choṭā Nāgpur; it might have accompanied the diffusion of Muṇḍa-type languages and such tribes as the Asuras who did spread up the Gangā region. Muṇḍa languages might have been current in the whole Gangā valley because this linguistic element apparently underlies the pronominalized languages of the sub-Himālayan peoples. Even the word *Gangā* is of Muṇḍa origin. This was the florescence of the eastern neolithic and the Mon-Khmer linguistic element, both of which were intrusions from Southeast Asia. But copper and bronze, derived from the west, must have been crucial in the utilization of the wooded plains environment.

Near Delhi at the site of Atranjikheṛā, an Ochre Colored Ware level has above it a horizon with Black and Red Ware, dated as early as 1200 B.C., but still without iron. This is a nice pottery, made on a wheel, and it may be related to the earlier Black and Red Ware of the Banās culture of Rājasthān. Black and Red Ware appears at many other sites in western India; at Eran in Madhya Pradesh it is dated 1270 to 1040 B.C. and is the final phase of the chalcolithic. It might be that both these types of ware represent pre-Āryan cultures.

A somewhat different Gangā chalcolithic culture has recently come to light in an excavation at Paṇḍurājārdhibī in western West Bengal. The

tools here include stone blades and ground stone axes besides copper objects. Black and Red Ware and channel-spouted bowls suggest affinity with the west. A carbon-14 date of 1012 ± 120 B.C. is the earliest date so far for the occupation of the eastern plains by a settled rice-growing people.[6]

The Iron Age in North India

Two decades ago scholars were convinced that iron did not appear in the India region until the invasion of the Panjāb by Darius and the Achaemenian Persians in the late 6th century B.C. Now 1000 B.C. is accepted as the date of the arrival of iron technology. But very recently Rājasthān archeologists asserted that they had found it datable to the 12th century B.C., associated with Black and Red Ware. Iron diffused into India without any significant time lag after it appeared at Sīyālk in Iran where implements of this metal were interred with the presumably Āryan equestrian nobility.

A question that has been much debated is whether the *Rig Vedic* Āryans knew iron. Now there is no doubt that during the later Vedic period it was used; it is called *ayas*, etymologically related to English *iron*. This word also occurs in the *Rig Veda*, where it might mean iron or might refer to copper or bronze, as does the related Latin word *aes*. The only other metal mentioned in the *Rig Veda* is gold, but later Vedas speak of tin, lead, and silver. Perhaps some *Rig Veda* hymns were not composed until 1200 or 1000 B.C., by which time iron was known. In any case, some intrusive Indo-European speakers, if not the earliest ones, introduced this metal into South Asia.

A great deal of cultural information is provided by the later Vedic literature. Crops grown included wheat, barley, millets, and rice. The plow had been introduced. A priestly class had by now emerged, and kingship had become more structured. Rituals and philosophies were being formulated as indigenous animistic beliefs were rising to the surface and being absorbed into the Vedic ethereal outlook; a newly synthesized world view was appearing.

This incipient civilization was continually moving eastward. Though the Panjāb was home to the *Rig Veda*, the later Vedic literature was more eclectic in geographical knowledge as well as in content. The *Brāhmaṇas*, lengthy elaborations on the Vedic poems, were set in the upper Gangā. The Doāb, the tongue of land between the Gangā and the Yamunā, was the site of the *Mahābhārata*, the epic (and mostly mythical) war. By the 6th century B.C., great tracts of land in Uttar Pradesh had been cleared, and we hear of such kingdoms as Kosala and Kāśī; by the time of Buddha, Magadha in Bihār had grown into India's first real empire. The clearing of so much heavy forest must have been due to the introduction of iron tools, while the

plow made possible the first intensive cultivation of the alluvial Gangā plain. Iron reached Bānglā by 700 B.C.

From the Panjāb to the middle of the Doāb, the Iron Age is associated at all important archeological sites with a ceramic called Painted Gray Ware; this is not found in Gujarāt or in the middle Gangā. At Atranjikheṛā it overlies the chalcolithic Black and Red Ware level. Five subphases are distinguished, but even the first has iron. A middle subphase is carbon-14-dated 1025 ± 125 B.C. Now at last stone blades became obsolete, for we have iron knives as well as shaft-hole axes, kitchen tongs, and fishhooks. Iron Age people at Atranjikheṛā had houses with wooden posts supporting thatched roofs and floors thickly plastered with mud. They had individual semioval domestic hearths as well as large circular pits which presumably served as communal hearths.

A place known to millions of Indians is Hastināpura, 60 miles north of Delhi, where there is a mound 60 feet high excavated in 1950–1952 by B. B. Lal. Hastināpura is referred to in Sanskrit literature, such as the *Mahābhārata* and the *Purāṇas* (mythical histories), and in early Jain and Buddhist literature. It was the capital of the Kaurava (Kuru) king who fought the Mahābhārata War on a plain not far from Delhi. The original war, of which practically nothing is really known, was perhaps fought between 950 and 800 B.C. The recounting of this war evolved into an exceedingly vast epic, later written in 18 volumes, which somehow ingested into the story all the known kingdoms and important folk heroes of ancient India, plus other religiohistorical and didactic content.

At Hastināpura the lowest level is chalcolithic containing some Ochre Colored Ware, followed by a slight break. Period II is Iron Age, with Painted Gray Ware, piles of iron slag, glass bangles, copper, weights, bone ornaments, gamesmen and dice, and terracotta animal figurines. Cattle and buffaloes must have been important, for their bones are abundant. People also kept horses, sheep, pigs, and raised rice. A similar complex has been unearthed at other sites connected with the Mahābhārata War such as Mathurā, Ahicchatrā, Kurukshetra (where the war was fought), and Bārnawā, and came to an end only about 540 B.C. After a hiatus we have Period III which belongs to the true historical period. Iron Age construction at Hastināpura is not impressive but at Ahicchatrā, capital of the North Pañcālā kings, huge ramparts 3.5 miles around were found to enclose the city. Here then is the earliest evidence of urban life in the Gangā plains.

The Iron Age in the Peninsula

Somehow creativity in the cultures of Gujarāt and the western Deccan tapered off in the five centuries before the beginning of the historical period in the 6th century B.C.; there is a partial archeological gap at most sites. Yet

life must have gone on, for Black and Red Ware characteristic of the Iron Age florescence was derived from earlier chalcolithic cultures. When B. K. Thapar excavated the site of Prakāsh, he found 15 feet of deposit with Black and Red Ware below historic material, and R. N. Mehta while excavating Nagarā near Cambay found even more. Prābhaspatān (Somnāth) in Saurāshṭra was an important port during the Iron Age, as it was during the chalcolithic high phase; the same is true of sites at the Narmadā mouth.

It is likely that seafaring traditions persisted at these Gujarāt ports, for the epics and purāṇas refer to rich tribes on the coast which had an abundance of pearls, coral, precious stones, coins, and blankets, which they are said to have given as tribute to the heroes of the Mahābhārata War. Bharukaccha (modern Broach) and Śuppāraka (Sopārā) were ports in Gujarāt whose merchants are referred to in the very earliest levels of Buddhist literature. There is reason to believe that even earlier in the 10th century B.C. King Solomon imported goods from India. After a three-year voyage his ships returned with peacocks, precious stones, gold, silver, lead, and copper. Later the Assyrians traded in the Arabian Sea, and when the Persians came to the fore, they also coveted the profits of this sea trade. When Alexander the Great supplanted Persian influence in the Indus region, he in turn built two ports at that river's mouth to garner profits from this sea trade. Yet the archeological evidence is that the Deccan as a whole had to await the full force of the northern Iron Age culture before attaining a new period of florescence. Probably the epic myths of Krishṇa and his tribe, the Yādavas, and related peoples moving from the Panjāb-Delhi region in a southerly direction may be thought of as associated with the diffusion of iron and Indo-Āryan speech to Gujarāt and the northern Deccan.

An important transition in cultural evolution was the establishment of rice-growing peasant cultures on the deltas of Orissa and Āndhra and the coasts of Tamil̲ Nāḍu and Kēraḷa. This has not been exactly traced archeologically, but there were settled villages in northern Tamil̲ Nāḍu by 1000 B.C. and in a rice-growing delta on the extreme southern coast by 750 B.C. The most important tool type in these regions was the neolithic pointed-butt polished ax.

The Iron Age in South India began about the middle of the last millennium B.C., and perhaps somewhat earlier on the Deccan for there is a date for the iron-using culture at Haḷḷūr, Karṇāṭaka, of 1000 B.C. We may picture Dravidian-speaking warlike tribes venerating their iron arrowheads and with their horses, moving down the Deccan and fanning out over the coastal plains. The same Black and Red Ware we observed in Gujarāt became distinctively characteristic of the Iron Age in the far South and in Sri Lanka, notably as a funerary ware.

Megalithic (huge stone) monuments are found all over the peninsula from Mahārāshṭra southward and in Sri Lanka, raising a number of unanswered questions. They are invariably associated with iron and with Black

Iron Age megalithic burial, Brāhmagiri, Karnāṭaka. Cist contained 62 pots. After exposure, bones were inserted through porthole and the cist sealed by a door slab. Three adjacent cists containing pottery were built later.

Walls of Kauśāmbī and earthen rampart with thick brick veneer, dating from about the time of Buddha.

and Red Ware. They occur in many varieties: cists built of rough granite slabs with or without a circle of boulders, pit burials often including granite slab or laterite blocks, dolmens, menhirs, alignments of granite slabs, and grids of standing stones. Kēraḷa has several special forms of these spectacular relics such as laterite capstones over burials, multiple inward-leaning laterite blocks, and caves cut in laterite containing sarcophagi. Urn burials occur throughout the South, having been encountered in most large villages in southern Tamil̠ Nāḍu, while there are also burials in legged sarcophagi. These all belong to the Iron Age complex. Generally corpses were exposed, the urns or cists having been used for secondary burials. At Māski in Karṇāṭaka, Wheeler showed that above the megalithic level was a level with artifacts of Roman inspiration. In parts of the South megaliths were erected in the historic period, and in isolated valleys, perhaps well after the time of Christ.

The original stimulus leading to this megalithic development may be traced back to western India and Pakistan. There are a few such structures scattered in Uttar Pradesh, Rājasthān, and around Karāchī. Cairn burials in Balūchistān contain iron weapons and are probably datable to the earlier part of the millennium. Some of the southern burial cists have curious round apertures in the slab walls. Such "portholes" also occur in the Near East and in Europe, though dated in those regions to the 3d and early 2d millennia B.C.

There are also megalithic monuments in Assam and the tribal belt of eastern India. The Khāsis of Meghālaya construct benches of stone slabs and erect menhirs in funerary rites, and similar practices have been noted among present-day Muṇḍa-speaking tribal groups. Rather than being related to the Deccan megalithic tradition, these seem to be part of the eastern neolithic.

Each of the four major Dravidian languages covers a wide area and has distinct boundaries. Probably the wide diffusion of these, plus Tuḷu and Gōṇḍi, occurred during the Iron Age. By the 3d century B.C. state systems were coalescing and the civilization of North India had begun to make an impact, across the Deccan in the case of Āndhra and by sea in the case of Tamil̠ Nāḍu. Tamil̠ literature of the first three centuries A.D. tells of the wars, the gods, and the loves of the Tamil̠ chiefs, for a considerable quantity of it has been preserved unadulterated to the present day.

A New Civilization

By the 6th century B.C. in the middle Gangā region sociopolitical organization based on tribal structure was giving way to state systems. The legacy of the Indus Civilization was an ovum fertilized in the Panjāb by the Āryan-speaking intruders and then transplanted for gestation to the

womb of the Gangā heartland, where after some centuries it brought forth a new creature.

At the end of the epic period a new capital was erected at Kauśāmbī, near modern Allāhābād, and from it ruled the kingdom Vatsa. The walls of Kauśāmbī were 4 miles around and 40 feet high; inside were well-built brick houses and a Buddhist monastery. Down the Gangā to the east the kingdom of Kosala appeared, and to the southwest in Mālwā, Avanti; these are mentioned in early Buddhist and Jain texts. North of the Gangā in Bihār, Vaiśālī became the capital of the Licchavis, a tribal republic which had incorporated indigenous peoples of the sub-Himālayan region. Excavation shows that Vaiśālī goes back to the 6th century B.C.

These incipient states coalesced in the kingdom of Magadha. One of its capitals was Rājghāṭ which underlies modern Vārāṇasī (Banaras) and was founded before 500 B.C. Another urban complex arose at Rājagṛha (Rājgir) beyond Paṭnā in Bihār; its walls have been traced for 25 miles. In the 5th century B.C., the kings of Magadha built a new capital called Pātaliputra, modern Paṭnā. This imposing city was nine miles long, fortified by a great ditch and timber palisades. It had parks, groves, and tanks with fish; its architecture and sculpture were of Persian inspiration.

The growing cultural unity of North India under Magadha and the Nandas and later under the Mauryan state is typified by the wide distribution of Northern Black Pottery, a beautiful hard fabric with a distinctive glossy finish. It was traded as a luxury item from the Panjāb to Bangla and down to Gujarāt. Coins took the form of silver bars punched with curious symbols, thousands of which have been found, even in the far South and Sri Lanka.

Meanwhile in the Northwest, Persian influence was strong. Cyrus, founder of the Achaemenian empire, invaded the upper Indus region and Darius annexed it about 518 B.C. They called it Gandhāra and considered it the richest satrapy of the Persian empire. Its capital, Pushkalāvatī (Chārsaddā), was located in the Peshāwar plain. By 500 B.C. the new city of Takshaśilā, which the Indo-Greeks called Taxila, was founded on an elevated plain not far from Rāwalpiṇḍī and Islāmābād, the modern capital Pakistan is building. Taxila, excavated by Sir John Marshall, was really an imposing city, laid out in a grid. It was a commercial center, and its universities were reputed as the best in the subcontinent.

Both the Brāhmī and the Kharoshṭhī forms of script came into use, inspired from the west and adapted to Indian phonology; Brāhmī was employed by the Mauryas and thus gave rise to all the scripts used in South and Southeast Asia before Islam appeared. The Persian empire must be acknowledged as the source of many other features of this early historical civilization: silver coins, stone sculpture, royal roads, architectural patterns, and perhaps even the idea of empire itself. Yet it was the Gangā plains that in the 6th and 5th centuries B.C. gave rise to formal Brāhmaṇism, Buddhism,

and Jainism, each with its philosophy, corpus of scripture, and religious specialists. True civilization had again burst forth, and this time it was in a position to provide an overarching set of ideals for the whole of South Asia.

Society at the Time of Buddha

Narendra Wagle's anthropological study, *Society at the Time of Buddha*, based on early Pāli Buddhist texts, shows that by 500 or 300 B.C., a complex social structure had arisen in the North Indian heartland, with enhanced population and interaction between peasant and urban life. People (using Pāli terms) commonly distinguished a hamlet or village (*gāma*), a kin group with the name of a village, a town or market (*nigama*), a city or fort (*pura, nagara*), a large city (*mahānagara*), a sociocultural region (*janapada*), and an extended kin group (or tribe). It is clear that while kin groups ("tribes") such as the Śākyas ruled around the periphery, the important kingdoms such as Magadha were territorially defined.

Wagle has inferred much about kinship and marriage from these texts. There were several recognized kinds of marriage. The house was distinguished from the household, the family (*kula*), the agnatic group (*ñāti*), and the bilineal group (*ñātaka*). Affines were not included among kin, and women had low status unless protected. Brāhmaṇs especially had mythological lineages (*gotta*). The common householder (*gahapati*) was subordinate to the village administrative chief (*gamaṇi*) who represented the governor or king.

The king addressed Brāhmaṇs in a formal manner, and they in turn addressed him using terms of divinity, but Buddha, being outside the political system, did not address the king with servility. Brāhmaṇs and Kshatriyas contended for superior social status. It was only in theory that there were four classes of people (*vaṇṇas*) and eight assemblies. People could also be divided into groups (*jātis*) based on occupation, trade, sect, region, or marrying group. There were a large number of occupational specialists: painter, barber, potter, smith, needlemaker; and professionals: doctor, scribe, accountant, money changer; and people in the king's service: elephant trainer, jailer, park keeper, estate manager, territorial governor—besides numerous categories of entertainers and many kinds of traders.

These occupational groups might have been largely hereditary, but neither the alignment of these along a rigid hierarchy nor their distinction by rules of eating had yet appeared. Such aspects of caste developed during the Brāhmaṇical resurgence in medieval times. Otherwise, society at the time of Buddha had the basic pattern it retains today, though in recent centuries overlaid with Islamic ideals and now with 20th-century equalitarianism.

REFERENCES AND NOTES

[1] See the summary and bibliography in Dales.

[2] Archeological sites in India are described in articles in *Ancient India* or the excavation results are summarized in *Indian Archaeology—A Review*.

[3] Chester Gorman, "Hoabhinian Transformations in Early Southeast Asia" (manuscript); see also reports by Solheim and Gorman in issues of *Asian Perspectives* (Hawaii).

[4] Recent opinions of 11 authors on this subject are in *J. of Tamil Studies* II, No. 1, Special Number on the Decipherment of the Mohenjodaro Script (Madras, 1970).

[5] S. N. Kramer, "Dilmun, Quest for Paradise," *Antiquity* XXXVIII (1963); see also W. F. Leemans, *Foreign Trade in the Old Babylonian Period* (Leiden, 1960).

[6] B. Allchin and R. Allchin, p. 338.

IMPORTANT SOURCES

General

Allchin, Bridget. *The Stone Tipped Arrow*. London, 1966. (A comparison of the mesolithic from Africa to Australia.)

———, and Raymond Allchin. *The Birth of Indian Civilization*. Baltimore, 1968. (A thorough summary of South Asian prehistory; the best single source.)

Gordon, D. H. *The Prehistoric Background of Indian Culture*. Bombay, 1958. (An attempted synthesis of western neolithic sites.)

Misra, V. E., and M. S. Mate (eds.). *Indian Prehistory: 1964*. Pune, 1964. (A useful symposium on accomplishments and problems in Indian prehistoric archeology.)

Piggott, Stuart. *Prehistoric India*. London, 1950. (The standard summary for the 1950s.)

Sankalia, H. D. *Prehistory and Protohistory in India and Pakistan*. Bombay, 1962. (A survey of the main sites.)

Subbarao, B. *The Personality of India*, 2d ed. Baroda, 1958.

Wheeler, Sir Mortimer. *The Civilization of the Indus Valley and Beyond*. New York, 1966.

———. *Early India and Pakistan*. London, 1959. (The standard summary for the 1960s.)

Western Neolithic and Indus Civilization

Casal, J.-M. *Fouilles d'Amri*, 2 vols. Paris, 1964.

———. *Fouilles de Mundigak*, 2 vols. Paris, 1961.

Dales, George. "Afghanistan, Baluchistan and the Indus Valley," in Robert Erich (ed.), *Chronologies in Old World Archaeology*. Chicago, 1965. (A synthesis of carbon-14 data.)

Dupree, Louis. *Prehistoric Research in Afghanistan*. Philadelphia, 1973.

Fairservis, W. A. *Excavations in the Quetta Valley*. New York, 1956.

Mackay, E. J. H. *Chanhu-daro Excavations.* New Haven, Conn., 1943.
Marshall, Sir John. *Mohenjo-daro and the Indus Civilization,* 3 vols. London, 1931.
Raikes, R. L. "The Prehistoric Climate of the Indus and Baluchistan," *American Anthropologist,* 1961.
Rao, S. R., and others. "Excavations at Rangpur," *Ancient India,* 1962–1963.
Vats, M. S. *Excavations at Harappa,* 2 vols. Delhi, 1941.
Wheeler, Sir Mortimer. *The Indus Civilization,* 3d ed. Cambridge, England, 1968. (The standard work.)

Neolithic

Allchin, F. R. *Neolithic Cattle-Keepers of South India.* Cambridge, England, 1963.
———. *Piklihal Excavations.* Hyderabad, 1961.
Dani, A. H. *Prehistoric and Protohistoric of Eastern India.* Calcutta, 1960.
Krishnaswami, V. D. "The Neolithic Pattern of India," *Ancient India,* 1960.
Nagaraja Rao, M. S. *Stone Age Hill Dwellers of Tekkalakota.* Puṇe, 1965.

Chalcolithic

Deo, S. B., and Z. D. Ansari. *Chacolithic Chandoli.* Puṇe, 1965.
Lamberg-Karlovsky, C. C. "Archaeology and Metallurgical Technology in Prehistoric Afghanistan, India and Pakistan," *American Anthropologist* 69, 1967.
Sankalia, H. D., B. Subbarao, and S. B. Deo. *Excavations at Maheshwar and Navdatoli.* Puṇe, 1958.
———, and others. *Excavations at Nasik and Jorwe.* Puṇe, 1955.
Thapar, B. K. "Maski 1954," *Ancient India,* 1957.
———. "Prakash 1955," *Ancient India,* 1964–1965.
Wheeler, Sir Mortimer. "Brahmagiri and Chandravalli," *Ancient India,* 1947–1948.

Āryans and Iron Age

Banerjee, N. R. *Iron Age in India.* Delhi, 1965.
Dani, A. H. *Indian Paleography.* Oxford, 1963.
Lal, B. B. "Excavations at Hastinapura," *Ancient India,* 1954–1955.
Majumdar, R. C. (ed.). *The History and Culture of the Indian People.* Vol. I, *The Vedic Age.* Bombay, 1965.
Marshall, Sir John. *A Guide to Taxila.* Cambridge, England, 1960.
Wagle, Narendra. *Society of the Time of Buddha.* New York, 1967.

Periodicals

Ancient Ceylon, Colombo.
Ancient India, New Delhi.
Ancient Pakistan, Peshāwar.
Indian Archaeology—A Review, New Delhi.
Pakistan Archaeology, Karāchī.
Spolia Zeylanica, Colombo.

6

South Asia as a Culture Area

At a symposium on "Regions and Regionalism in South Asian Studies," one participant was a geographer, Wilbur Zelinsky, who had not been trained in South Asian studies. After hearing the papers presented, he felt constrained to remark that he had

> . . . a debt to discharge, payment to be made for an opulent educational experience and for a sharp sense of what previously had been only dimly perceived: the immense cultural variety of India and the great difficulties and rewards of sorting out the facts spacially and of explaining and interpreting them meaningfully. . . . Perhaps nowhere else have subnational culture areas so obstreperously intruded themselves into the affairs of nations. . . . All in all, a strong case can be made out for South Asia as the laboratory *par excellence* for study and experimentation in cultural differences, spatial and otherwise. And students of other areas might well watch it with hope and envy as they await the outcome of Indian researches.[1]

It is this colorful mosaic of diversity in South Asia that makes it so fascinating for the scholar and the tourist alike. To the complexities of geographical and cultural regions are added the diversification of society by innumerable castes and many religions, plus the accommodation of the traditional and the modern.

Yet somehow South Asia has achieved a personality of its own. In this chapter we want to see how this occurred. What have been the processes and forces which enabled the overarching pattern of civilization to catch up into its net all the regional and social diversities? Is there a pool of symbols distinguishing South Asia from other major regions of the world? For the social scientist interested in the processes of culture, South Asia is peculiarly suited for study because it has such *cultural diversity* combined with such known *time depth*; it has thus been in a position to generate contributions to the development of anthropological theory. But if anyone wishes to take part in any discussion of anthropological theory involving South Asia, he simply must know its history.

The Concept of the Great and Little Traditions

Cultural anthropologists working in South Asia before World War II, who were very few indeed, followed the lead of the profession and concentrated on tribal peoples. The Government of British India commissioned the collection of a vast quantity of data on villages and castes of different regions, but this work was usually supervised by administrators rather than anthropologists.

After the war anthropologists in Western countries turned to more intensive study of peasant populations. Robert Redfield who worked in Mexico stressed the nature of the "little community," the structured, integrated, and partially self-sufficient community. Most "little communities" are peasant villages, and these were explained as different from the "folk society" in that they have links with urban regions and the wider civilization, the greater community. Peasants in the Old World use the plow (which distinguishes them from hoe cultivators). Another definition of peasants is cultivators who consume half or more of what they raise, and by this definition half the world's people are peasants, mostly living in "little communities" tied to wider civilizations.

In the 1950s anthropologists working in South Asia, following this lead, began to produce a spate of village studies such as "The Indian Village" by Irawati Karve, *India's Villages* of the *Economic Weekly, Indian Village* by S. C. Dube, and *Village India* edited by McKim Marriott. The latter was a landmark in showing the kinds of links villages have with the wider civilization. It became clear that the social structure of a peasant village is complemented by intense interaction with the rest of the culture region, so much so that in one case it was suggested in Marriott's book that a village might cease to become a significant unit of investigation. In the 1950s village studies appeared representing a number of parts of India and Sri Lanka, with many more in the 1960s, including some from Nepal. A few ethnographers went to Afghanistan in the late 1960s. Unfortunately only

one book and a few articles have been produced describing plains villages in Pakistan, and Bangladesh is also poorly represented. Bhutan, the Maldives, and a few peasant regions in India are still virgin territories for aspiring anthropologists who wish to conduct village studies—though India has become quite sensitive to foreign social science inquiries.

Social anthropologists working in parts of the world where communities and tribes were relatively isolated from one another and where there was no written history, such as sub-Saharan Africa, often took an ahistorical approach, eschewing questions of origins and preferring to study minutely the interrelationships of kinship, social stratification, religion, and social aspects of economics. These attempts to ascertain the fundamental *structural* principles of societies proved fruitful in the development of theoretical positions. But the increased study of peasant villages embedded in vast civilizational regions demanded that the findings of social anthropology be combined with knowledge of history, thus leading to the emphasis on *process* which characterized much of the research of the 1960s. While British anthropologists have pursued a rather precise and structured *social* anthropology, Americans have preferred a broader *cultural* anthropology.

It was pointed out by Oscar Lewis after he had studied an Amerind village in Mexico and a village near Delhi dominated by Jāṭ cultivators that there could be fundamental dissimilarities of cultural and social patterns in peasant villages in different parts of the world:

> One conclusion to be drawn from these facts is that separate institutions or aspects of culture develop at different rates, within limits, in accord with particular historical circumstances. It is this factor which creates serious difficulties in the construction of holistic societal or cultural typologies which are not historically and regionally defined. This would also help exlain how Tepoztlan and Rampur can be so similar in terms of economics and so different in terms of social organization.[2]

Lewis showed that his Mexican village was more homogeneous and that it appeared to be a better centralized and organized community than his North Indian village whose population was fragmented in many ways by kinship, caste, and factions. Social relations were atomistic in the former, but the Indian villagers were much more convivial and their role behavior was expectable in terms of caste and kinship. The Mexican village indeed had trade connections with a city, but the North Indian village was part of a dense rural network of kinship ties involving over 400 villages, besides being embedded in Indian civilization in many other ways. Though these two villages had comparable economic levels, they were so different because they were part of very different *great traditions*—civilizational-cultural patterns and traditions accepted over a wide area. Moreover the ways the great traditions impinged on the two villages were very different.

The primary civilizations of the Old World—Sumer, Egypt, Indus, and Shang China—evolved into early classical civilizations which coalesced into

four secondary-level premodern civilizations: Medieval Europe, the Near East (Arab Civilization), South Asia (Indian Civilization), and East Asia (Chinese Civilization), plus a number of hangers-on along the peripheries. Each of these four had an elaborate tradition, formalized in its texts, which validated and put into historical context the distinctive script, music, architecture, social ideal, and world view. Each was a superstructure supported by a peasant economy. Such a great tradition is *little traditions* which have coalesced and become elaborated and formalized. As it spreads over a wide area, it has a tendency to absorb and validate specific elements of the little traditions it encompasses, or it drives them under as people grope for leverage enabling them to participate in the prestige of a widespread cultural system. The unification of Europe by the Roman-Christian-Latin assimilative force was analogous to the unifying effect of Indian Civilization.

Indian Civilization has, however, produced several specific great traditions, each expressed in the symbolism of a world-view system: Brāhmaṇical Hinduism, Jainism, Theravāda Buddhism, Tibetan Buddhism, and Sikhism. Those borrowed from outside include Zoroastrianism, Islam, and Christianity. Each is supported by a mythological "history," a set of texts, a language, an architecture, and an ideal social system. Each was propagated by an elite who used it to elevate themselves and thus made it a model for imitation on a wide scale. Each was at some time in its history supported by a state system. Each, in short, represented a form of civilization overarching peasant villages.

It has become increasingly clear that the image of a peasant village as unchanging millennium after millennium is misleading. True, subsistence technology may seem to be static—though over a period of generations it is not. There is a constant dynamism and flux of persons and social groups, and therefore of models and ideals, albeit within certain firmly established institutional patterns. Civilization in South Asia has built within it the mechanisms for promoting continuous change within these patterns, most clearly shown in the study of caste hierarchy and of religions.

Sanskritization and Modernization

The dynamics of the relationship between the peasant village and the predominant Great Tradition (capitalized in referring to a particular one) in the case of India has been analyzed by M. N. Srinivas. He wrote three books and a number of articles which have popularized the word "Sanskritization." By this term Srinivas means the process by which castes in India tend to imitate higher castes. Since Brāhmaṇ castes are at the top of the ritual chain in traditional Hindu society, it has been Sanskrit or Sanskritized languages, worship of mainstream deities, ablutions, and the whole pool of symbols particularly associated with the Sanskrit texts and features of the

life of Brāhmaṇs, that have been emulated. It is these Sanskritic elements which are conceived of as giving Brāhmaṇs their prestige. Sanskritization, as a process of acculturation, has covered not only an entire subcontinent and produced a major world culture area, but has also diffused vertically downward to the villagers of the middle and low castes, at the same time clothing their folkways with respectability and esoteric significance.

Were it not for this, the cultural fragmentation of South Asia today might be analogous to that of sub-Saharan Africa; indeed, the tribal groups of central India and the Assam region are considered as tribals even though most of them live in settled villages precisely because they have not been much affected until recently by Sanskritization. Their social structures and value systems, in addition to their religious patterns, have been outside the mainstream currents of Indian civilization. The process of Sanskritizing the tribes is still going on, and study of this throws much light on how Hindu civilization spread over the subcontinent.

Srinivas has since broadened his definition of Sanskritization to include different kinds of ideal images or models, not just Brāhmaṇs, a concept explained in his book *Social Change in Modern India*. His original thesis was based on the study of the Koḍagu (in Coorg, southern Karṇāṭaka), and his examples of the role of Brāhmaṇs in Sanskritization also came from that limited region. Now he and Milton Singer have drawn attention to the fact that within formal Hinduism there are three, and possibly four, classes of castes referred to in Hindu texts. Besides the *Brāhmaṇ* model, there is the *Kshatriya* model, which has been the ideal of Rājpūts and a host of essentially peasant castes and even tribals. The Kshatriya category originally comprised warriors or landed aristocracy descended from warriors. The third class of this ideal system is *Vaiśyas*, generally merchants or townspeople, occasionally taken as a model by villagers. Even the fourth class, *Śūdras*, can be considered as such a model; though originally a peasant or serf type, it is now sometimes claimed by outcaste and tribal groups.

Whereas the Brāhmaṇ model emphasizes religion and ritual, especially ritual purity, the other three stress different kinds of status determinants. Each model provides culture heroes together with a partially distinctive mythology and a pool of symbols, and dictates rituals and genealogical patterns. Because the Sanskrit texts recognize this kind of segmentation of the population, this whole process has been called Sanskritization. The relative prestige of the four categories differs from region to region, as do the life styles and literary traditions thought to be associated with them. This fourfold system, called the *varṇa* system, as a description of the actual social order is mostly imaginary, for it is truncated in eastern India and never really existed in the South. Yet diverse castes did emulate the cultural models implicit in the words Brāhmaṇ, Kshatriya, or Vaiśya, so these have been among the means whereby little traditions were assimiliated into the Great Tradition.

The Sanskrit language developed as a literary vehicle in late Vedic times and experienced a revival during the 4th to 7th centuries A.D. when Hindu civilization reached its apogee in North India, so it was the primary medium of communication in the expansion of the Hindu Great Tradition. The Jain religion also used Sanskrit for its literature. But the Prākrits (vernaculars) were the linguistic media of civilizational diffusion in the centuries before and after Christ, when merchants were carrying Indian civilization to peripheral regions; it would be technically correct to refer to this process as Prākritization. Orthodox Buddhism (Theravāda) was transmitted in the Pāli language, which continued to be used in Sri Lanka, Burma, and Thailand. Mahāyāna Buddhist texts were written in a dialect called Buddhist Hybrid Sanskrit, and later in Classical Tibetan. And in recent centuries the Sikh Great Tradition has been elaborated, using Panjābī with a special script.

The Islamic Great Tradition was brought originally in Arabic, stimulated by Persian, and developed its South Asian form in Urdū. It has provided a quite divergent set of culture heroes, rituals, symbols, texts, and social ideals. The Portuguese brought yet another distinct ideal culture-type, the Roman Catholic, which was adopted by coastal fisher folk and others who had pressing reasons to emulate the Portuguese.

A new direction of acculturation has been set in motion within the last two centuries, the model being the secular and urbane way of life initiated during the days of British rule and continued now by the English-educated elite. English has replaced Sanskrit as the language required of the truly initiated. This has often been termed Westernization, for among the educated the culture heroes tend to be industrialists, scientists, and even English literary figures. At the village level there is no doubt an increasing tendency to secularism, with political heroes often receiving greater acclaim than religious ones, while at all levels acquistion of manufactured goods is symbolic of the new mood.

But the terms Sanskritization or Westernization should not be construed as implying simple straight-line trends of acculturation. Ishwaran objects to both these terms because it is not just Sanskrit rituals which people wish to emulate, but any form associated with prestige, power, and wealth. Westernization is perhaps not the best term for the altogether Indian style of secularism and socialism that is evolving. Ishwaran suggests that in Śivapur, a village in Karṇāṭaka, neither Sanskritization nor Westernization is taking place, but that society is stable and that though there may be superficial changes and shifts of groups within institutions, yet the basic institutions of family, religion, landholding, and caste represent core values which have not preceptibly changed.

Another view is that held by A. Aiyappan, who came back to study a village in Kēraḷa four decades after his initial research. So great was the change he entitled his book *Social Revolution in a Kerala Village*. He refers

especially to individualism as an ideal that began during British rule and is now strengthened as the village is brought into the ambit of urbanization. Inevitably, any of the great historical trends of acculturation in South Asia has proceeded at a very uneven rate, given the geographical diversity and social cleavages characteristic of the subcontinent.

In the remainder of this chapter we shall survey in historical sequence the main currents of the great traditions that have provided a measure of cultural unity to South Asia.

Early Hindu Civilization

A sweeping survey of Hindu literature from the Vedas to the purāṇas, epics, and medieval devotional literature shows quite clearly how the original Vedic religion became vastly modified as Brāhmaṇism became institutionalized and diffused over the subcontinent. The *Rig Veda* with its 1028 hymns is the earliest (composed somewhere between 1500 to 1000 B.C.) and most "Āryan" of these texts, and it contains little that we generally associate with Hinduism. It mentions no temples or idols nor much of fertility symbolism. Asceticism was scarcely an ideal, and Brāhmaṇs had not become a powerful class. Practices pertaining to pollution, purification, and water ablutions are hardly evident, and there was no pollution by touch. There was no belief in the key Hindu concepts of rebirth, *karma*, and *dharma*. There was no Śiva or Krishṇa; deities were largely personified natural elements analogous to those of other Indo-European peoples.

The last of the four Vedas, the *Atharva Veda*, begins to show the absorption of indigenous ideas into the developing system; it is a work of excorcists' spells and incantations interpreted in the light of the earlier Vedas. The next set of texts, the *Brāhmaṇas*, shows the religious structure symbolizing the growing complexity of social stratification. By now a formal priesthood was necessary because sacrifices were required to bend the will of the gods. Brāhmaṇs thus became intermediaries between gods and men, the privileged eaters of the oblations. Lesser priests did the invoking, chanting, and execution of sacrifices. The incipient urbanization of the middle Gangā region required an institutionalized priesthood.

At the end of the Vedic period, about 600 B.C., the *Upanishads* were written. These consist of philosophical speculations, meeting the needs of enhanced intellectual sophistication. Sacrifices were important, but it was accepted that they led to new births, for the doctrine of transmigration had come to the surface. Ideas inherent in pre-Āryan civilization and in prehistoric animism were beginning to bend and shape and recast what might have appeared to be a rigid priestly elite. In the *Upanishads* knowledge and self-realization were expounded as the new urban society demanded a systematic world view. The universal soul-force came to be recognized as

Brahmā; residing in the human soul, it was known as Ātman, the Self. Assorted theories of creation were posited based on cosmic sacrifice or cosmic sexual union, the nature of such elements as fire and water, atomic particles, or the developing self-consciousness of the Purusha (Primeval Man). The *Upanishads* have served to this day as a seed bin of philosophical ideas. Though these ideas take the form of intellectual probings, they in fact reflect assimilation of diverse and inherently Indian ideas as the formal Hindu Great Tradition continued to spread. This eclecticism, indeed, is the reason why original Brāhmaṇism survived at all.

By the 5th century B.C., Brāhmaṇical orthodoxy could no longer contain the wide range of world views and symbolic systems prevalent over all the North. Other religious systems jelled, of which Buddhism and Jainism have persisted to the present; in these two, asceticism rose from beneath to become respectable. In all three religions, gnosis, or at least the search for the Real, superseded reliance on rituals and sacrifices as described in the *Brāhmaṇas*. As with the contemporary Hundred Schools of philosophy in China, there were different and competing systems synthesizing all the tidbits derived from prehistoric peoples over a vast region.

But formation of religions was just one of the synthesizing processes. Another was the growth of the state. King Bimbisāra of Magadha, a contemporary of Gautama Buddha and the first important political name in Indian history, is known to have built roads, established an administrative system, appointed the jurisdiction of village headmen, and initiated a taxation system. He was murdered about 490 B.C., and his successor, Ajātaśatru, incorporated for the first time part of the Bānglā plains, the Śākya kingdom, and others toward the Himālayas, as well as Kāśī (Banaras). After 413 B.C. another dynasty initiated by Śiśunāga ruled for half a century, and was succeeded by the Nandas who ruled all the Gangā region until 321 B.C. For this reason the soldiers of Alexander the Great prevailed upon their general not to cross into the Gangā plains, but rather to go down the Indus. Indian civilization had become so established that Alexander's invasion made almost no impact on the culture of South Asia, and he is not even remembered in its history (except as the mythical Śaivite warrior deity Skanda). But the successor Greek kingdoms in Bactria, Persia, and Afghanistan did have impact on stone sculpture styles of Gandhāra, for example, and there are textual records of dialogues between Greek and Buddhist philosophers.

The Mauryan empire (322–185 B.C.), founded by Candragupta Maurya, moved westward in the wake of the Greeks, so that from his famed capital of Pāṭilaputra (Paṭnā) he extended sway into the Panjāb, Sindh, and even Afghanistan. Now Indian civilization with its peculiar stamp of the Gangā plains became the synthesizing system even for the semidesert regions to the west. The South was not spared, for the Mauryas ruled the Deccan, exploiting the gold mines of Karṇāṭaka. Candragupta's son, Aśoka, the most famous king of all South Asian history, ruled the Mauryan empire stretching

from Kandahār in Afghanistan to the deltas of Bānglā, and from the foot of the Himālayas to Karṇāṭaka. Only the three Tamiḻ states of the far South, Cōḻa, Pāṇḍiya, and Kēraḷa, remained independent.

It would be misleading to explain the spread of the ideal culture model only in terms of the function of religious symbolism and social mobility; South Asia joined the ranks of classical civilized culture regions of the world precisely at the time it experienced forceful political unification. A third factor, after religion and the state, was trade. From literary sources we know that there were land routes and sea routes reaching all parts of South Asia (except the hills of the Assam region). Sea trade was a royal monopoly. Pearls, gems, and textiles were imported from the Tamiḻ kingdoms and Sri

Karlā, inland from Bombay, 1st century B.C. Donor couple caused elaborate pillared hall and stūpa to be excavated out of mountain rock. The relaxed stance, public caressing, and minimal clothing contrast with ideals of elite Indian behavior in recent centuries.

Lanka, and Indian civilization was beginning to impinge on lower Burma and the rest of Southeast Asia. Products were imported from the Himālayas and Afghanistan.

Culture historians of South Asia often attribute to it an unbalanced religiosity, probably because all pre-Mauryan texts except religious ones have been lost. The elaborate Sanskrit grammar system devised by Pāṇini at the university town of Takshaśilā in the 4th century B.C. in fact was based on several preceding systems. A book providing a valuable corrective to the yoga-image of ancient India is the *Arthaśāstra*, purported to have been written by Kauṭilya, a minister of Candragupta Maurya, but amended in later centuries. It sets forth Mauryan polity in great detail. There are such chapters as "The Institution of Spies," "Duty toward the Harem," "Construction of Forts," "The Superintendent of Liquor," "Division of Inheritance," and "Sexual Intercourse with Immature Girls." Whereas the *Laws of Manu* and other Brāhmaṇical texts stressed dharma (good conduct), the *Arthaśāstra* supported the totalitarianism of the Mauryan state and advocated "law and order." It makes interesting reading.

Jainism

This religion is practiced today by some 3 million persons, mostly of merchant castes in Gujarāt and Bombay. Jainism claims as its chief historical personage Mahāvīra, born about 540 B.C. and a contemporary of Gautama Buddha. Mahāvīra left his princely home in Vaiśālī at the age of 30 to be an ascetic. He abjured all appurtenances of the world, even all his clothes, and expired in old age of self-starvation. The sect he founded grew little in the Gangā region, but in Mauryan times it spread across central India and picked up support in the South. It was strong in Karṇāṭaka until the 10th century, and even now is important there.

Jainism never succumbed to the theism of Vedantic Hinduism or Mahāyāna Buddhism, but has remained essentially atheistic, denying even any act of original creation. Its philosophy grew to be most abstruse and subtle in the discussion of space, time, and matter. Space, for example, is of three types. The universe is composed of atoms, but neither atoms nor moments of time have measurable dimensions except as they relate to each other (a sort of theory of relativity). Any number of atoms can occupy the dimensional space of an atom. There is a plurality of souls, which pervade all bodies, and on the awareness that souls are finite depend bondage and release, joy and sorrow, and transmigration itself.

A righteous man is one who considers the happiness of all souls, particularly by not destroying life; hence the Jains avoid killing living things, even insects. Jain monks would have others harvest vegetables for them. They thought that the annihilation of karma (effects of one's deeds which

adhere to his soul) could be achieved through asceticism, the goal being to escape the succession of rebirths so that the soul would ascend in blissful vacuity above the universe.

Jainism had some state support but not sufficient to propel it into position as a culture model capable of gaining mass converts on a wide scale. Candragupta Maurya may have become a Jain, retiring to Karṇāṭaka in old age. A king from Orissa, Khāravela, conquered large parts of India in the 1st century B.C. and was a patron of Jainism. About this time the religion split into two sects, one of which took to wearing white clothes while the other refused to succumb to the pressures of decorum and maintained that being space-clad (naked) was essential to the freeing of the soul from its burden of karma.

This faith was historically important because its monks preserved rare texts in monasteries and because it led to the creation of a sizable body of literature in Prākrit and Sanskrit. Yet it remained a faith of the ascetics, becoming a Great Tradition only among restricted groups, principally in Gujarāt and Karṇāṭaka. It did not enfold enough popular deities and symbols, and was not flexible enough.

Theravāda Buddhism

A very clear example of the kinds of modification any overarching system must undergo as it interacts with local religious elements is provided by the history of Buddhism in South Asia. Theravāda (also called Hīnayāna, Orthodox, or Southern) Buddhism was too esoteric; it completely disappeared in India and Pakistan. Yet in Sri Lanka it did become modified and thus remained as a vital Great Tradition. The difference lies in the capacity of the system for almost unlimited compromise with little tradition elements and practices, so that it becomes a meaningful pool of symbols for common folk.

The historical myth of Theravāda Buddhism has as its core the life and teachings of Gautama, called Buddha because he became "enlightened." Born a prince of the Śākya tribe on the border of modern Nepal, he became disenchanted with the effete life and harem at the age of 29, and left his patrimony. He began to practice extreme asceticism in an effort to understand life. After some years he quit this method and thought it better to sit under a sort of fig tree called a *pīpal* or *bodhi* until he understood the riddle of life with all its sorrow. Though tempted by evil personified as Māra, he did achieve enlightenment, whereupon he went about preaching. His life ended, it is said, at the age of 80, about 475 B.C. His enlightenment enabled him to rise above the mundane world and escape from the endless chain of rebirths; therefore he did not die, but had a "final blowing out," whereupon he achieved the state of final nothingness or bliss, *nirvāṇa*.

The Four Noble Truths are the essence of Buddha's enlightenment: 1) all life is sorrowful, 2) sorrow is due to having desire, 3) sorrow can only be overcome by conquering desire, and 4) the means to conquer desire are moral conduct, discipline, and meditation. Moral conduct is outlined as the Eightfold Path with such principles as Right Views, Right Speech, and Right Conduct. One should strive to achieve enlightenment to be released from earthly rebirths.

There are no supreme or lesser gods, but the force of karma pervades the universe. There is no separable part of the living individual called the soul, but at death life passes on like a flame from candle to candle, though no actual substance is transferred. Nothing is eternal, since all things are in a constant state of flux and therefore transient. It is useless to crave for permanence.

This nontheistic sect was one of many competing in pre-Mauryan India, practiced mostly by ascetics or religious specialists. Its ultimate diffusion is due in large measure to King Aśoka who took over the Mauryan throne about 270 B.C. Buddhist accounts tell how he fought a bloody war to incorporate Orissa, then became converted, renounced war and hunting, and spent the rest of his career providing moral leadership and propagating dharma (righteousness) throughout his kingdom. He sent missionaries to distant regions such as Macedonia, Egypt, Southeast Asia, Sri Lanka, and many parts of India, who arrived at their posts supported by the prestige of the Mauryan state. Aśoka also set up inscribed stones (in Brāhmī script) ranging from Afghanistan to the Deccan encouraging his subjects to follow dharma, exercise self-control, compassion, and justice, and not to take animal life.

According to tradition, three successive Councils canonized a body of scripture. Written in the Pāli language, it comprises a small library and incorporates a lot of folktale under such guises as accounts of the "former lives" of the Buddha, as narrated in the *Jātakas*. Theravāda Buddhism was essentially the property of the fellowship of monks, and indeed, monasteries ranging from Central Asia to Southeast Asia interchanged monks and ideas. The monasteries developed standardized methods of studying philosophy and some of them became great educational institutions. The architectural form of the *stūpa* originated as a simple burial mound but grew to be a large hemispherical structure enclosing relics of the dead, particularly Buddha's bone fragments or a hair. The sculpting on the stūpa complex at Sānchī in central India is truly wonderful, while the limestone slabs finely sculpted for the monasteries and stūpas at Amarāvatī in Āndhra from 200 B.C. to 200 A.D. show Buddhist art at its best. The stūpa in Sri Lanka grew to monstrous proportions, while in Burma and Thailand the form acquired a pointed spire.

The brotherhood of monks formed a closed—and celibate—fraternity, belaboring complex metaphysical philosophies far beyond the interests of

Sānchī: Stūpa I, 2d and 1st centuries B.C. The devout would circumambulate inside the railing. Lively panels on gateways depict scenes from the life of Buddha; sculptures and railings were conceived in wood, though executed in stone.

the laity. Nontheistic, early Buddhism could not ingest local deities or spirits, nor even prayers. Its vast geographical spread was not equaled by its vertical depth. It phased out in South India in the 6th to 8th centuries A.D. What remained of it in North India was modified into Mahāyāna Buddhism. Orthodox Buddhism, at first almost a tool of the imperial Mauryas, did vastly strengthen the cultural unity of South Asia because of contacts among the monasteries, and its effects were many; for instance, its institutionalized reverence for all living things was a factor in the persistence of this principle in modern India, Sri Lanka, and Nepal. The personality of Gautama Buddha, mythical or historical, has been South Asia's most important export.

Processes of Acculturation: the Example of Early Sri Lanka

The history of this island provides us with the best opportunity to see how outlying regions were drawn into the ambit of Indian civilization. Far from the innovative epicenter, all contact was by sea and therefore we can more easily trace it. Sri Lanka also has an admirable collection of epigraphs, including over 1000 cave inscriptions in Brāhmī script written between 250 B.C. and 100 A.D. There is also considerable literature, including the

Mahāvamsa, a chronicle of the 5th century A.D. containing material from the 3d century B.C.

The legends in the chronicles view the indigenous inhabitants of the island, called *yakkhas*, as practically subhuman. Who they were, whether people like Väddās or Dravidian-speakers, is not known (though the Sinhala language has considerable Dravidian content). Yet these legends say the yakkhas had towns, a king, rice, and spinning. There is archeological evidence of an Iron Age culture and megalithic burials, as well as of prehistoric complex irrigation works. The chronicles also refer to Nāga "kingdoms" in the island in the 5th or 4th century B.C. which engaged in sea trade. How have all these (excepting the Tamiḻs in the north of the island) been absorbed into the Sinhala people and acquired the Buddhist religion and the Sinhala language which is derived from a northwest Indian Prākrit?

It is probable that sea trade linked Sri Lanka with the coasts of Gujarāt and Sindh even before Mauryan times. Gem stones, pearls, ebony, and cinnamon were exported going back to prehistoric times. The Chinese traveler Hsüan-tsang, who visited the island in the 7th century A.D., was told there that the earliest settlers were merchants who came for pearls and gems. The first city founded by intrusive settlers, according to the chronicles, was Tambapaṇṇi, near the pearling beds on the north of the island. Not only Sri Lanka but the whole periphery of peninsular India was opened up to Indian civilization first by sea traders. Indeed, we must see this as the first wedge in opening up all of Southeast Asia to Indianization.

The Great Tradition of the Sinhalas is derived from North India, first Hindu influence from the western side, then Buddhist accretions in which the east was idealized. Language, religions, nomenclature, mythology, dynastic genealogies—all were intrusive. Trading settlements sparked the contact, but here again we see that the Great Tradition came to be accepted largely because it was used by the state for civilizational consolidation and for moral justification of its authority.

The tremendous pressure of this intrusive ideal culture model on the indigenous people of Sri Lanka can be seen in the *Mahāvamsa* myth of Vijaya, acclaimed as the first king of the island, who came from North India. Though Vijaya is certainly not a historical figure, myths surrounding him do represent what went on in early Sri Lanka. Vijaya encountered a *yakkhiṇī* (female yakkha) queen, caught her, called her "slave," and made her subjects feed his men. To entice Vijaya she became a lovely maiden and made a bed at the foot of a tree, adorned with a canopy. Then the king

took her to him as his spouse and lay with her blissfully on that bed; and all his men encamped around the tent. As the night went on he heard the sounds of music and singing, and asked the yakkhiṇī, who was lying near him, "What means this noise?" And the yakkhiṇī thought: "I will bestow kingship on my lord and all the yakkhas must be slain, for else the yakkhas will slay me, for

it was through me that men [humans] have taken up their dwelling [in Sri Lanka]. And she said to the prince: "Here there is a yakkha-city called Sirīsavatthu. Even today do thou destroy the yakkhas, for afterwards it will no longer be possible." Since he listened to her and did even as she said he slew all the yakkhas and he himself put on the garments of the yakkha-king and bestowed the other raiment on one and another of his followers.[3]

This myth legitimizes both the slaying of the unacculturated indigenous peoples and the ruling of their remnants, and any ethical lapse is ascribed to the self-preserving duplicity of their queen. This suggests, moreover, that yakkhas were not really human in any case! Such was the ethnocentrism of emerging states.

Another principal process is what the venerable historian of South India, K. Nilakanta Sastri, has called dynastic drift. By this he means that the names of dynasties and also their genealogies were derived from dynasties prominent in the epics, most of which were originally located in the Panjāb or generally in the Northwest. For the historian, the chief problem here is that it is impossible to determine to what extent there were actual migrations of branch dynasties and to what extent existing dynasties simply adopted the nomenclature and mythology of the epic culture heroes. The anthropologist, however, is not so interested in that as in the function of myth.

The *Mahāvamsa* is the myth of the Sinhalese people. The last half of it is the kind of myth that is sometimes called history because it is meant to be true. But true or not, it is a symbol of the cultural unity of the people because it ascribes to them a common origin.

The whole political history of Sri Lanka follows the pattern of dynastic drift. The early Nāga dynasties were probably named after, if not descended from, prehistoric mercantile clans in western India (later confused with mythical Nāga water spirits and serpent deities). The original story showed that Vijaya came from western India (subverted in a later level of myth to eastern India). He stopped at the Gujarāt ports of Bharukaccha and Sopāra, landed in northern Sri Lanka with his generals, religious functionaries, and clan, and founded the city of Tambapaṇṇi. This hero thus provides a link in the chain of dynastic drift. Through him subsequent kings traced their ancestry back to northwestern India where Vijaya was said to have been born to a princess who had intercourse with a lion. The lion was the royal symbol of the Persians, adopted by them from the Assyrians, and this totemic symbol spilled over into Panjāb and thence to Sindh and Gujarāt, and to Sri Lanka. In the Sinhala myth the lion is an actual totemic symbol, ancestor of the royal line and of the people. All the people of the island caught up in this intrusive culture-type and political system called themselves Sinhaḷas after *sinha* (lion). The word became Sīhaḷa, garbled by Europeans as Ceylon. The name Śrī Lankā, now chosen for the island, is derived from a different Indian myth. In the Hindu epic *Rāmāyaṇa*, Rāma

rescues Sītā from an island (*lankā*), and when this myth expanded over India, the island was imputed to be this one. *Śrī* means prosperous and sacred.

The people of the island, including even the Väddās, came to speak the intrusive Prākrit language that eventually became Sinhala. Only the Tamils of the north and east remained separate, and some of them descended from later historical invasions. Hindu astrology, worship of the *linga* (male sex symbol), the cult of Śiva (whom the Greeks called Hercules), the cult of Skanda (probably Alexander), the Brāhmī script, the totemic lion symbol, Brāhmaṇism, Jainism—all these intrusive elements essentially derived from northwestern India became the Great Tradition of pre-Buddhist Sri Lanka. A line of Paṇḍu princes, seven of whom ruled the island, are also said to have come from northwestern India and founded different cities. Their name is obviously linked with the Pāṇḍyas of *Mahābhārata* fame. Further, the Pāṇḍiya kingdom of Tamil Nāḍu seems to have originated about the same time parallel with or as a branch of these Sri Lanka Paṇḍu princes. This is another example of dynastic drift.

When Aśoka Maurya adopted Buddhism and the epicenter of Indian civilization moved eastward to Bihār, the Sri Lanka monarchs had to engineer new links. Not being able to claim Mauryan descent, they did whatever else they could to vicariously benefit from Mauryan prestige. The Sri Lanka king sent envoys to Aśoka, according to the *Mahāvamsa*; they returned to Sri Lanka with Aśoka's authority to reconsecrate the king as a Buddhist. The king, Tissa, took the name Devānampiya, which was one of Aśoka's titles and means "beloved of the lord." Aśoka sent to Sri Lanka Mahinda, a monk sometimes said to have been his own son. He also sent by ship a branch of the Bodhi tree under which Buddha had sat. Its arrival and acceptance is described with great detail; it still grows in Anurādhapura, the most venerated of all Buddhist symbols in Sri Lanka. Devānampiya Tissa imitated Aśoka in other ways: personifying dharma, supporting monks, donating rock-cut caves to ascetics, and building stūpas. The Sinhalas then gradually modified their legends until they made Vijaya appear to have come by ship from the Bānglā side, as had the Bodhi branch, and on this was superimposed the whole body of Buddhist myth derived from eastern India.

We must mention one more process leading to the acceptance of the new religion: mutual support of monarchs and religious professionals. Kings subsidized the priests and monks; they in turn supported the king's claims of right to rule—a powerful combination, which indeed has been behind every one of the great traditions that have taken root in South Asia. Vijaya is said to have brought Brāhmaṇ chaplains with him. The pre-Buddhist Sinhala capital of Anurādhapura was laid out with quarters for monks of half a dozen sects, while the king's chaplains were Brāhmaṇs. After Buddhism became official, kings built monasteries and stūpas, gave rice-

feeds, and supported festivals. The monks, in turn, eulogized their exemplary righteous leadership and memorialized their deeds in chronicles. Duṭṭhagāmaṇi (1st century A.D.) had a long, war-filled career, but he also contributed vast sums to build the stūpa at Anurādhapura and dedicated it with appropriate festivities. When he died, the chronicler wrote "He who, holding the righteous life to be the greatest good, does works of merit, passes, covering over much that perchance is evil-doing [alluding to war], into heaven as into his own house."[4]

Theravāda Buddhism in Sri Lanka thus began a long adjustment with indigenous religious practices and ultimately accommodated shamanism, spirit propitiation, and Hindu deities, which are not today regarded as contradictory by most Buddhist laymen. From this island also Theravāda Buddhist monks transmitted the formal system to Burma, Thailand, and Cambodia.

Mahāyāna Buddhism

In the first two centuries A.D., Buddhism in the North underwent a fundamental modification and became known as Mahāyāna ("great vehicle") Buddhism, while the religion of Sri Lanka was contemptuously referred to as the "lesser vehicle." Buddhism in the North now became widespread from Afghanistan to the Chittagong Hills beyond Bānglā precisely because it had become assimilative and flexible. Before this no icons were made of Buddha, but the deep-seated proclivity of South Asian peoples to worship both icons and saintly persons came to the surface. The fusion resulted in the belief in *bodhisattvas*, beings on the way to becoming Buddhas. Bodhisattvas at first grew out of the *Jātaka* tales, narratives of the "previous lives of the Buddha," but in time innumerable other deities were thought of as on the way to achieving full enlightenment. Some of them were at the point of attaining Nirvāṇa, but refrained from crossing the threshold in order to help other living beings. In this way there came to be room for an infinite number of benevolent deities, all striving for the welfare of man. Buddhists could now pray and believe in the transfer of merit from deities to men. A model had been found for incorporation of deities and practices of the little traditions.

Meanwhile intellectual Buddhism in the monasteries evolved schools of the most subtle philosophies. For example, Nāgārjuna, who lived in Āndhra in the 1st century A.D., convoluted his philosophy of *māyā* (illusion) until it became nihilism: all events are transitory, impermanent, and unreal; rational theories and logic, and even life itself, are unreal; the only reality is the Void itself, Nirvāṇa, which is indeed the primeval Buddha. But there were other schools of philosophy, too, such as Yogācāra, which taught that higher levels of meditation could be achieved by yogic practices.

A further modification of this Great Tradition occurred in Bānglā, Orissa, and Bihār with the evolution of Tantra Buddhism from the 7th century. The chief divinities were females, spouses of the bodhisattvas (analogous to the stress on female goddesses in the modern Hinduism of Bānglā). Sexual union was thought to symbolize creation; hence individuals could attain power by performing coitus as a religious rite. At times of tantric orgies, all norms of behavior were reversed; devotees killed animals, ate meat, and drank liquor. They repeatedly chanted the phrase, *ōm maṇi padme hūm*, which is symbolic at different levels. Ōm is a sacred syllable and the rest means "the jewel in the lotus" which may be considered as suggestive of coitus between a bodhisattva and his *tārā* (consort). Such ritual reversal of norms of behavior is not uncommon in South Asian religions, and has the function of highlighting the standard norms. The Buddhist Great Tradition in this form was modified by localisms almost beyond recognition.

Meanwhile in Sindh, the Panjāb, and Afghanistan, influences from the west trickled in. Greco-Bactrian kings became part Buddhist and part Hindu. In the 1st century A.D. the Śakas (Scythians) invaded and penetrated the Gangā plain. The disturbances of the Yüeh-chih and Parthians coming from Central Asia caused the Pahlava kings of Persia to penetrate India's western frontier. The next invaders were the Kushāṇas, who ruled as far as the Doāb. Their most famous king, Kanishka, ascended in 78 A.D. (the beginning of the Śaka era, now official in India), and was a strong patron of Buddhism. Other Śakas ruled in Gujarāt. In the 5th century the Hūṇas, or White Huns, swept in from the west, ruthlessly destroyed all the venerable Buddhist monasteries, ruled the western regions for a generation, and then became generally absorbed.

Mahāyāna Buddhism with its bodhisattvas and icons was an amenable faith to the Kushāṇas and Śakas, through whose influence it diffused into Afghanistan, eastern Iran, Bactria, all Central Asia, and to Khotān in the Tārīm Basin north of Tibet. It reached China in the 1st century A.D., and in the 5th century swept that country, to penetrate Japan two centuries later. The Pāla kings of Bānglā, ruling from the 8th to 10th centuries, caused eastern forms of Buddhism to be propagated in the valleys of Nepal, whence it was carried to Tibet. The time had finally come for the people of that high plateau to be brought within the fold of one of the world's great traditions. The animistic deities of the Himālayan Bon religion were absorbed into Buddhism, Sanskrit Buddhist texts were translated, a script derived from India was adapted to Tibetan, and the monastic state system of Lāmaism evolved.

Most lay people, it seems, paid less attention to the distinctives of Buddhism by the 4th and 5th centuries, especially in the west where the monasteries were destroyed by the Hūṇas. In the east, monasteries such as Nālandā (near Paṭnā) remained influential until the 10th century. Nālandā

Visit of Indra to Buddha, 2d century A.D. Gandhāra school of Buddhist art (northern Pakistan) was patronized by the Kushāṇas and betrays Greek influence. Flames around cave mouth are kindled by Buddha's radiance, and animals are at peace in his presence. Umbrella denotes royalty of Indra. Harpist is on left, while heavenly beings cast flowers in homage to Buddha. (From *The Buddhist Art of Gandhara* by Sir John Marshall. By permission of Cambridge University Press, New York.)

Part of great monastic university near trade city of Takshaśilā (Taxila) in northern Panjāb (Pakistan), 2d century A.D. Scholars' cubicles surround courtyard.

was a great university drawing thousands of students, some from Southeast Asia and China. It was supported by the revenues of a number of neighboring villages which had been donated to it over the years. But monasteries had become wealthy and isolated from the peasant society while they increasingly came to profit from investment in trade and commerce. For peasant villagers, Mahāyāna Buddhism, with its pantheon essentially derived from indigenous Hindu-type deities and its texts in a form of Sanskrit, was scarcely distinguishable from the revised Sanskritic Hinduism that began to flourish at the time of the Gupta empire. In Bangladesh Tantra Buddhism retained some strength at the Maināmati monastery until the 13th century, after conversion to Islam had begun. But the demise of Theravāda Buddhism in the land of its birth was partly due to the exclusiveness of the institution of the brotherhood of monks. Buddhism simply lacked a caste-based hereditary priesthood such as Brāhmaṇs; the moral suasion of the monks, once state support was lost, could not compete with the model for caste mobility provided by Brāhmaṇism.

Classical Indian Civilization

During the hegemony of the Gupta dynasty (319 to about 550 A.D.) and the good king Harsha (606 to 647 A.D.) in North India, Indian Civilization took its classical form. Most social norms, schools of philosophy, and all the arts came to be subsumed under what we call Hinduism. This Great Tradition came to be the ideal, the model, from Afghanistan to Assam. In the peninsula, too, where it was carried by Brāhmaṇs, it began making headway, to flourish with creativity in late medieval centuries. The Khmers (Cambodians) and several other dynasties of Southeast Asia also supported and were supported by Brāhmaṇism.

It was the uncanny assimilative power of Indian Civilization rather

than the force of any single state system that caused this vast region to be brought together. For the most part, there was a multitude of competing states ranging from the Kābul River to the Mekong Delta; Indian Civilization diffused over this area in spite of the weakness of the Indian political system in those centuries.

King Candragupta in 319 A.D. founded the Gupta dynasty. By the time of his grandson, Candragupta II, Pāṭilaputra had once again become the capital, and all the Gangā plain and parts of Nepal had been incorporated, as well as Mālwā, Saurāshṭra, and the lower Indus. The princes of Rājasthān, the Panjāb, Assam, and lower Bānglā were tributary. The northern Deccan was also tributary for a time, while the Guptas overran Āndhra and briefly penetrated Kāñcipuram in the Tamil̲ country. But after the 5th century only the middle Gangā region remained under the control of the successors of the Guptas who resided in Kānyakubja (Kanauj), while the Pushyabhūtis ruled north of Delhi, another Gupta line in Mālwā, the Maitrakas in Saurāshṭra, and lesser kingdoms in Bānglā and Assam. Three great states competed for the South: Cālukyas in Karṇāṭaka, Pallavas in northern Tamil̲ Nāḍu and Āndhra, and Pāṇḍiyas in the far South. King Harsha once again briefly incorporated most of the North but never penetrated the South.

The important generalization to be made is that the expansion of Indian Civilization over the subcontinent and beyond did not require a single political system as was the case in China. Only during the Mauryan and Gupta periods was there substantial political integration. The expansion of Indian Civilization was due to its own genius, to the increasing tempo of land and sea trade, and to the interaction between Brāhmaṇs and kings in the individual states. These states were linked together by the principle of dynastic drift, however, and by mythology such as that derived from the *Mahābhārata*, whereby the weaker ones vicariously enjoyed the prestige of the stronger ones.

Trade was quite vigorous. The earliest shipping, hence cultural export, came from Gujarāt ports, and by Mauryan times included the east coast. By early medieval centuries ships holding 500 or more people crossed the open ocean and professional pilots knew the nuances of currents and monsoons. In the first two centuries A.D. scores of Roman ships yearly visited Kēraḷa, taking pepper and cotton textiles for gold and wine, but this dwindled to nothing by the 3d century. A Jewish colony was established in Kēraḷa—though we do not know exactly when—and Christianity was brought to its coasts. Tradition says the Apostle Thomas brought it; at least some Thomas and other missionaries brought the faith there in the early centuries A.D., where it has survived as a Great Tradition.

We have a description in Tamil̲ literature of a port in the Cōl̲a kingdom, of about the 2d century. Goods were piled high in the streets, and there were large warehouses. Foreigners lived in different sections of the town (Kāvērippaṭṭinam) speaking different languages. Busy and efficient customs agents

stamped the king's tiger seal on all goods for which duty had been paid. A lighthouse accessible by a tall ladder beckoned to bypassing ships. Horses were imported from North India and gems from Sri Lanka. Tamiḻ epics of the 7th century A.D. say nutmegs, cloves, and other spices were imported from Indonesia by ships sailing directly across the Bay of Bengal.

Legend has it that a party from Gujarāt became the first Indians to settle on Jāva, while there is also some evidence that Śakas reached that island. In medieval centuries, traders from Orissa settled in southern Burma, Jāva, and even affected the Philippines. Such ports as Tāmraliptī in Bānglā and Maśulipaṭām in Āndhra engaged in constant sea trade, while the Tamiḻ Cōḻas were the most active in Southeast Asia in the 7th to 10th centuries A.D. The Indian Ocean became veritably an Indian lake—a vital factor in the formation of South Asia as a major world culture area and in the transplantation of Indian themes to Southeast Asia.

Guilds of artisans and merchants were powerful political and economic forces, and also preserved certain occupations as prerogatives of certain castes. Guilds maintained their legal autonomy, which was respected by the government. Financiers loaned money to shippers at set rates of interest, which was higher for shippers not of the usual trading castes under the assumption that they were poorer risks. Buddhists and Jains were involved with commerce more than Brāhmaṇs because they were not so conscious of maintaining ritual purity and caste status. (In medieval centuries Brāhmaṇs developed the idea that crossing the sea polluted them because they would have to associate with ritually impure people, follow new customs, eat strange food, and suffer without the sanctifying power of India's sacred spots and Gangā water.) From the 3d century A.D. on, Jain and Buddhist influence weakened, but a class of Hindu financiers called *śreshṭhins* developed, the modern Śeṭhs of the North and Ceṭṭis of the South.

These medieval centuries were the period of real Sanskritization. The Vedas were so far removed that they were highly sanctified but had little effect on the main currents of Hinduism. Parallel with the role of Latin in culturally unifying Europe, Sanskrit became the medium of communication among the educated in diverse linguistic regions. Never understood by the masses, Sanskrit was exploited by Brāhmaṇs as a symbol of their distinct high status, much as English is by the elite in South Asia today. It became one of the richest languages to develop in the classical world, with a vocabulary estimated at 250,000 words. Not only did Indians have a remarkable interest in linguistics, which was an essential part of the education curriculum, but Sanskrit had to serve as a vehicle to cope with ideas ranging from astronomy, mathematics, and abstruse cosmogony to law, drama, epics, and devotional literature. In medieval dramatic works, men were made to speak Sanskrit while women and menials conversed in the lowly Prākrits. Enriched by Sanskrit, the Prākrits evolved into the modern Indo-Āryan languages of South Asia.

The Indian attitude toward science was characterized by a compulsion to classify, which is the beginning of science everywhere. Yet there were uncanny accomplishments. The astronomer Āryabhaṭa in 499 A.D. knew that the earth was a sphere, rotated on its axis, and eclipsed the moon. He also calculated pi as 3.1416 and computed the year at 365.3586805 days. The decimal system and zero had already been invented, and the Indian system of numeral notation was later borrowed by the Arabs and transmitted to Europe, where it was referred to as "Arabic" numerals, replacing the cumbersome Roman system. Astronomy had its practical application in navigation and astrology, popular in India then as now. In technology, processes of making steel were invented as well as techniques for producing the very finest cotton textiles. Both these areas of technology were later drawn on by Arab civilization and hence transmitted to Europe.

The reader by now will have understood that Indian civilization was not all asceticism and introspection. It can as well be thought of as heavy on moneymaking and sex. In fact, it tolerated a wider range of emotional experiences, a greater variety of personality types, and more diverse subculture fragments than does our own civilization. Even in one's lifetime there were differing and even contradictory goals. The four aims of life were *dharma* (righteousness, merit, the law), *artha* (wealth, political power), *kāma* (love, pleasure, sensual gratification), and *moksha* (salvation, release from rebirth). According to the ideal, an individual went through several stages in his life. First he would be a free child, then a young man practicing discipline and austerity as a student, then a householder making his fortune. Finally he would detach himself for religious pursuits and might in old age become a hermit.

The *Kāma Sūtra*, though it has a reputation today as a handbook on the erotic arts, also sets forth ideals about kāma (pleasure) in general. The following excerpt from Chapter IV portrays the ideal life of the man who has successfully passed into the householder stage.

A Day in the Life of a Citizen

Having thus acquired learning, a man, with wealth that he may have gained by gift [as a Brāhman], conquest [as a Kshatriya], purchase, deposit [as a Vaiśya] or inheritance from his ancestors, should become a householder, and pass the life of a citizen. He should take a house in a city, or large village, or in the vicinity of good men, or in a place which is the resort of many persons. This abode should be situated near some water, and divided into different compartments for different purposes. It should be surrounded by a garden, and also contain two rooms, an outer and an inner one. The inner room should be occupied by the females, while the outer room, balmy with rich perfumes, should contain a bed, soft, agreeable to the sight, covered with a clean white cloth, low in the middle part, having garlands and bunches of flowers upon it, and a canopy above it, and two pillows, one at the top, another at the bottom. There

Kāṭhmāṇḍū, Nepal: scene of a noble and a courtesan on a balcony of the palace.

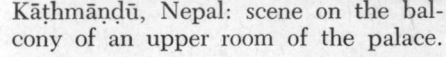

Kāṭhmāṇḍū, Nepal: scene on the balcony of an upper room of the palace.

should be also a sort of couch besides, and at the head of this a sort of stool, on which should be placed the fragrant ointments for the night, as flowers, pots containing collyrium and other fragrant substances, things used for perfuming the mouth, and the bark of the common citron tree. Near the couch, on the ground, there should be a pot for spitting, a box containing perfume, some books, and some garlands of the yellow amaranth flowers. Not far from the couch, and on the ground there should be a round seat, a toy cart, and a board for playing with dice; outside the outer room there should be cages of birds, and a separate place for spinning, carving and such like diversions. In the garden there should be a whirling swing and a common swing, as also a bower of creepers covered with flowers, in which a raised parterre should be made for sitting.

Now the householder, having got up in the morning and performed his necessary duties [elimination and ablutions], should wash his teeth, apply a limited quantity of ointments and perfumes to his body, put some ornaments on his person and collyrium on his eyelids and below his eyes, color his lips with alacktaka and look at himself in the glass. Having then eaten betel leaves, with other things that give fragrance to the mouth, he should perform his usual business. He should bathe daily, anoint his body with oil every other day, apply a lathering substance to his body every three days, get his head (including face) shaved every four days and the other parts of his body every five or ten days. All these things should be done without fail, and the sweat of the armpits should also be removed. Meals should be taken in the forenoon, in the afternoon, and again at night, according to Charayana. After breakfast, parrots and other birds should be taught to speak, and the fighting

of cocks, quails, and rams should follow. A limited time should be devoted to diversions with [art instructors, rich compatriots, and buffoons—standard character types of Sanskrit drama], and then should be taken the midday sleep. After this the householder, having put on his clothes and ornaments, should, during the afternoon, converse with his friends. In the evening there should be singing, and after that the householder, along with his friends, should await in his room, previously decorated and perfumed, the arrival of the woman that may be attached to him, or he may send a female messenger for her or go to her himself. After her arrival at his house, he and his friends should welcome her and entertain her with a loving and agreeable conversation. Thus ends the duties of the day.

When men of the same age, disposition and talents, fond of the same diversions and with the same degree of education, sit together in company with public women . . . the subjects of discourse are to be the completion of verses half composed by others, and the testing of the knowledge of one another in various arts. . . . Men and women should drink in one another's houses . . . spending nights playing with dice, going out on moonlight nights, keeping the festive day in honour of spring, plucking the sprouts and fruits of the mango trees, picnicking in the forests when the trees get their new foliage. These and similar other amusements should always be carried on by citizens.

Thus a citizen living in his town or village, respected by all, should call on the persons of his own caste who may be worth knowing. He should converse in company and gratify his friends by his society, and obliging others by his assistance in various matters, he should cause them to assist one another in the same way.

The Hindu Resurgence

Malinowski's view of the function of oral tradition and epic literature in welding together a people is well supported by Hindu literature. The two great epics, *Mahābhārata* and *Rāmāyaṇa*, achieved their final form in Sanskrit by the Gupta period, and in medieval centuries appeared as rescensions in other languages in India as well as in Indonesia. The *Mahābhārata* came to be an epic of the whole Indian people, incorporating a plethora of little traditions into the Hindu Great Tradition. Its final version comprises 18 volumes and 88,000 verses—by far the longest epic in the world. It incorporates the names of all significant kingdoms, cities, sacred places, and folk heroes from the whole of Bhārata (Hindu name for the subcontinent). Wherever people gathered in the evenings to hear it sung, ways could be found to somehow link local tradition with it. This epic, still alive and popular, has been a major instrument in the welding of Hindus of South Asia into a "we, the people." From it has come the name Bhārata, official name for India in Indian languages.

The *Harivamśa*, an appendix of the *Mahābhārata*, is a genealogy which provides mythical links for all the important Hindu dynasties. This was important, for to maintain legitimate status, most kings had their genealogies drawn up by Brāhmaṇs back to the culture heroes and kings of the great epic. The *Bhagavad Gītā*, a dialogue in the great epic between the warrior

Arjuna and the mythical king-deity Krishṇa, has been called the Hindu New Testament. It expresses the main themes of Hindu ethics: that one should do his duty according to one's station in life and that he should worship with devotion the Lord, Krishṇa in this case.

The *Rāmāyaṇa* is an epic about the abduction of Sītā and how her consort Rāma found her. Rāma was undoubtedly a king of the dim past, but now, like other important culture heroes of the epics, he is a widely revered deity. Another great body of literature is the Purāṇas, of which there are said to be 18 major and 18 minor ones; most temples also have their own purāṇas providing mythical links to the broader traditions and epics. These incorporate even more of the popular theism than do the epics, and are even less useful than the *Mahābhārata* for purposes of historical research. The style of some was an affected archaism.

With this limitless capacity for ingestion, the Hinduism represented in the early texts underwent vast changes in ritual and worship. The icon emerged as the center of formal worship. Cruder images had, of course, been reverenced from prehistoric times, but now stone sculpture techniques had been perfected. Along with the stone icon the ritual of *pūjā*, the service performed to the image, was assimilated into formal Hinduism (more fully discussed in the following chapter). Accompanying the increased reliance on flowers and fruits offered for pūjā was a decline of sacrifices. The Vedic horse sacrifice was not performed after the 7th century A.D., while the Vedic sacrificial altar had long since been forgotten. Local forms of sacrifice, however, were absorbed into Hinduism, such as the goat offerings in Bānglā to bloodthirsty Kālī, goddess of death and destruction. Goats and chickens everywhere were offered as people came to fulfill their vows. Some forms of sacrifice did not find meaning within the system, and continued to be considered as tribal: buffalo sacrifice among the Toḍas of the Nīlagiri Hills of the South as well as of some indigenous Nepal people, cow sacrifice of some of the central Indian tribes, *mithān* (an indigenous bovid) rites of Assam and Arunāchal Pradesh, and the human sacrifice of the Khoṇḍs of Orissa. These were not acceptable to Brāhmaṇs.

The city temple came to be a complex social institution, which was also the center of cultural and sometimes economic life. Temples grew especially prominent throughout the South and in Orissa, and to some extent in central and western India. Ideally, a temple was located at the geographical epicenter of the town, beside a tank (reservoir). Its construction provided employment to the best of architects and sculptors and the daily routine gave scope for musicians, florists, dancing girls, cooks, and accountants. They maintained schools for the study of Sanskrit and local texts, and sometimes even hospitals. The annual festival and other fairs would draw huge crowds from the countryside. Some of them supported hundreds of priests. Temples were patronized by kings or merchants, and some of them came to be controlled by merchant guilds. With accruing endowments of land and

cash the temple was often able to acquire a store of gems for adornments of its deities. It would sometimes be the biggest landlord, and in addition served as banker, lending money at 12% interest. Temples in the South especially have left us masses of stone inscriptions and have preserved ancient texts in palm-leaf manuscripts. K. A. Nilakanta Sastri writes:

> It is no exaggeration to say that the temple gathered round itself all that was best in the arts of civilized existence and regulated them with the humaneness born of the spirit of *dharma*. As an agency of social well-being the medieval Indian temple has few parallels.[5]

Temples were built according to a carefully prescribed sacred architecture, whose evolution has been traced by art historians. The temples of the Guptas must have been unpretentious and of perishable materials. Wooden temples became highly elaborate in Kashmīr, Nepal, and Kēraḷa, where such are still in use. A few small stone structures appeared from the 5th century in western India, and by the 10th century highly elaborate stone ones were built.

There were five regional schools of temple architecture, but none of these appeared on the Indus or Gangā plains, perhaps because of lack of stone and also because Islam appeared there when Hindu culture was achieving its florescence in the peninsula. In some places, as at Mathurā and Kanauj, Muslims destroyed temples and looted the jewels.

A western temple style, found in Gujarāt and Rājasthān, is epitomized by the great Jain temple atop Mount Ābū. The central Indian style is best represented by the complex of soaring towers at Khajurāho, once a capital city but now deserted. The third temple style is found in Orissa; best-known are the complex structures at Purī, Konārak, and Bhubaneśwar. These have numerous relief panels depicting sexual orgies such as were practiced in Tantra worship. The fourth architectural school arose in Karṇāṭaka, where the chief dynasties patronized a temple style with a star-shaped floor plan. Among these temples, Haḷebīḍu and Bēlūr are particularly known for their exquisite reliefs completely surrounding the temples, depicting the wars and loves, the kings and courtesans, the gods and godlings of the time—a fit anthropological study in stone.

The fifth temple style arose as a distinctive one in Tamil̲ Nāḍu, noted especially for the soaring towers over the gates as high as 200 feet, said by villagers to warm their hearts when viewed from afar. The temple at Śrīrangam on the Kāvēri River has an enclosure over a quarter of a square mile and an inner shrine enclosed by six successively built walls, each financed by a king who tried to outdo his predecessor. The great temple at Madurai is among the most opulent, with two sanctums and a sacred tank, pillared halls, sanctuaries for lesser deities and scores of lingas, sacred trees, rows of classrooms and offices, halls for the sale of flowers, and other items for *pūjā* (worship ritual)—all enclosed by a great outer wall pierced by

(Top) Haḷebīḍu, Karṇāṭaka: sculptured friezes around temple narrate epic tales. (*Bottom*) Mīnākshi temple, Madurai, Tamil̲ Nāḍu. Sculpted towers rise above walls, and pillared hall surrounds Golden Lotus Tank, used for ablutions. Temple complex is focus of concentric main streets of the city.

four gateways, each surmounted by a soaring tower writhing with a multitude of richly painted stucco scenes from the purāṇas and the epics.

In countless villages stone temples of lesser note were erected, patronized by local landowners, merchants, and peasants. The larger ones attracted Brāhmaṇs while the others were served by local priestly castes. But still there remained in each village half a dozen or several dozen lesser shrines, the deity sometimes enclosed in a small cubicle but more often exposed to the weather. These local gods were considered incarnations of the gods of the mainstream Hindu pantheon—another way in which the Great Tradition and the little traditions interacted to provide a measure of cultural unity to South Asia.

Florescence of the South

The principle of dynastic drift operated in the three dynasties competing for the South in early medieval centuries. The Cālukyas apparently took their name from the Seleucids, successors of Alexander the Great in the Near East; by the 7th century the Cālukyas ruled from Gujarāt to Karṇāṭaka. Contemporary with them was the Pallavas, whose name might have been derived from the Pahlava dynasty of Persia; Pallavas had their capital on the coast south of Madras. The Pāṇḍiyas ruled southern Tamil̲ Nāḍu, and as we have noted, their name is doubtless linked with the Paṇḍu princes of Sri Lanka and with the Paṇḍavas of the Mahābhārata War. Whether or not based on fact, these links with prestige dynastic names of the Northwest validated the right of these kings to rule and ensured a measure of ideological conformity within South Asia. The kings hired Brāhmaṇs to produce appropriate genealogies going back to epic heroes, and in return the monarchs patronized temples and monasteries, endowed them with lands, and lent prestige to the Sanskritization of the South.

The Sanskritization of the South is personified by the sage Agastya, who was supposed to have served as chaplain to the Pāṇḍiya kings, brought 18 families of Brāhmaṇs from Gujarāt, and written the first Tamil̲ grammar (after the style of the Sanskrit grammarian Pāṇini). These legends appeared only after the 7th century and had the function of validating growing Brāhmaṇ influence in society in this region. A similar process occurred on the whole of the west coast, from Goā through Kēraḷa. Here Brāhmaṇs came to control much of the land and supported their right to it by the myth of Paraśurama, a hero who is supposed to have slain the Kshatriyas, made the coastal land appear from the sea, and given it to Brāhmaṇs to settle on. Brāhmaṇs persuaded the Pallava monarchs around Madras to turn from Jainism to Hinduism, then rewarded those monarchs by proclaiming them to be divine. The Cōḻas in their expansion made vast contributions to Brāhmaṇs and to the great temples.

From the 10th to the 14th centuries, while the Gangā plains were in the doldrums of history, the far South and Gujarāt maintained lively overseas trade and considerable kingdoms arose on the Deccan. In the 11th and 12th centuries the Tamiḻ Cōḻa kingdom expanded from the fertile Kāvēri plains to incorporate most of South India and Sri Lanka and even the Maldive Islands, sent three emissaries to the Chinese court, and successfully invaded the Sri Vijaya kingdom in Indonesia. It maintained a highly developed system of village governance and a stable prosperous society.

The Sanskritic Great Tradition which had become implanted in the South merged with indigenous cultural elements so that philosophy, literature, music, architecture, and other learned pursuits moved beyond what had been achieved in the northern heartland. For instance, the Vedānta philosophy, the basis of orthodox Hindu scholarship even now, originated with Śankara, a Brāhmaṇ from Kēraḷa who traveled all over India in the 9th century disputing with Buddhists and founding an order of monks. He brought a revival to Hinduism by asserting that salvation could come through knowledge of the Vedas. A Tamiḻ Brāhmaṇ who had immense influence in the North was Rāmānuja who taught in the temple of Śrīrangam about 1100 A.D. He intellectually assented to Vedānta philosophy but believed that the worshiper should have such intense devotion for Lord Vishṇu that he would abandon himself and trust implicitely in His grace. A philosopher from Karṇāṭaka, Madhva, synthesized with devotional Hinduism certain elements from the Christian church which had flourished on the Kēraḷa coast from the early centuries of the Christian era. Another religious revolutionary from Karṇāṭaka was Basava, founder of the Lingāyat sect which rejected the Vedas and all forms of Brāhmaṇism, but stressed the worship of Śiva, symbolized by the linga which Lingāyats hang on themselves. This was the forerunner of the anti-Brāhmaṇ movements which have pervaded the South in the past few decades, for Brāhmaṇs, though only 3% of the population, had become domineering.

The devotional Hinduism which swept South Asia in late medieval centuries took form largely in the South. Peripatetic poet-saints produced a large volume of devotional literature of heart-moving power, and the philosophy of Rāmānuja provided an aura of Sanskritization to this adoration of the lords. This devotionalism, called the *bhakti* movement, swept all India, and was paralleled by the Muslim devotional Sūfī sects.

Other accomplishments cannot all be enumerated. South Indian music reached a stage of perfection equaled in few parts of the world. Bharatanāṭyam dancing evolved in the temples. Vast quantities of literature in the four southern languages complemented what was produced in Sanskrit. But permanent political unification could not be achieved. The last great kingdom of the South, Vijayanagara, from its center on the Deccan did indeed incorporate Āndhra, Orissa, and most of Tamiḻ Nāḍu. Arabs reported that in the 15th century it had an army of over a million men and garnered

wealth from 300 ports in the kingdom. It was able to support the apogee of dancing, temple architecture, and Tamil̲ and Telugu literature. But this was the last empire that could patronize such Hindu institutions, for even Vijayanagara was not able to halt the pervasive effects of Islam and the Delhi Sultanate. On the Deccan itself there were several rival Muslim kingdoms. Nor was it able to stop the encroachments of the Portuguese along the coasts. With its demise, Hindu civilization ceased to be creative.

Integration of the North

From the time of Harsha (7th century A.D.) to the establishment of the Muslim Delhi Sultanate in 1211 the North was fragmented with competing kingdoms. In Bānglā the Buddhist Pālas were succeeded after the 9th century by the Hindu Senas. Meanwhile, in the west the Pratihāras were dominant, and succeeded in repulsing the Arabs who had managed to get a foothold in lower Sindh in the 8th century. But the Rāshṭrakūṭas from the northern Deccan drove the Pratihāras from the Gangā plains.

Kashmīr appeared in history in the 7th century when it came to control the northern Panjāb and repulsed the Arabs who were trying to move up the Indus. Thereafter the Kashmīrī monarchs retired to their beautiful vale, which they developed by constructing impressive irrigation works for agriculture. Brāhmaṇism flourished there, and a unique school of Śaivism known as Trika arose, based on Vedānta and on the doctrine of māyā (illusion), to which was added the Buddhist idea of sudden enlightenment.

Nepal sits astride Tibetan and Indian civilizations. In the mountainous north the indigenous Bon religion was assimilated into Tibetan Buddhism, but in the foothills there has been a continual Hinduizing pressure. In the 9th century the Kāṭhmāṇḍū region broke away from Tibet, though it remained Buddhist; by the 11th century, an urban civilization flourished there, a creation of the Tibeto-Burmese-speaking Newārs. Other valleys continued to be dominated by related peoples as the Gurūngs, Magars, and Tāmāngs, while Pahāṛī-speaking Hindus gradually infiltrated from the plains. In 1768 the Gorkhās came from the south and invaded Kāṭhmaṇḍū and began to unify Nepal under their Hindu dynasty. Other small kingdoms in the Himālayan valleys and foothills, such as Kumāon, Kullū, and Jammū were similarly drawn into the web of Hindu civilization by invaders from the plains.

Assam, called Kāmarūpa, began to integrate elements of Indian civilization in early medieval centuries, but it was always on the tail end of the diffusion of innovation, since the Brahmaputra valley is but a tail-like extension of the Bānglā alluvial plains. The people of the main valley, though assimilated into Hinduism and following cultural models essentially derived from Bānglā, betray in their physical features the original Mongoloid popu-

lation of the region. Kāmarūpa was conquered from the east in 1253 by the Āhoms, a people related to the Shans and Thais, and from their name we get the word Assam. Their effect was transitory. People north, east, and south of the Brahmaputra plain were not assimilated into Indian civilization, so they have always been regarded as "tribal." They refused to emulate Brāhmaṇs or Kshatriyas as models of caste mobility, recognized neither the Vedas nor Hindu social and legal norms, and did not adopt Indo-Āryan speech. They were brought into a relationship with the South Asia culture region only by the British administration, Christian missionaries, and the Indian government.

Orissa, called Uṭkalā, generally remained politically independent because of its geographical isolation, though it was affected by the civilization of Bānglā when the Pālas were strong. Tantric practices long persisted there, both in Hinduism and in Buddhism. Brāhmaṇical Hinduism was strengthened by the construction of the famous temples of Orissa by royal patronage.

In later medieval centuries, a number of other kingdoms which arose to oppose the ever-growing Arab and Turk intrusive forces included the Cāhamāṇas of Rājasthān, the Candellas of Bundelkhaṇḍ (who built the Khajurāho temple with its famous sculptures), and the aggressive Solankīs in Gujarāt. The last great Hindu empire, that of the Marāṭhās, originated in the 17th and 18th centuries when Śivājī, hero of the Marāṭhās, unified the Deccan and pushed northward. This brave attempt to forestall further Mughal expansion and Muslim influence, though providing the chief myth uniting Mahārāshṭra today, did not last long enough to patronize a new revival of Hindu civilization.

In western India during the period of Muslim rule, a variant model within the Hindu Great Tradition came to be emulated. This was the Kshatriya (warrior) image rather than Brāhmaṇism. A series of composite castes appeared in gradually extending arcs eastward and southward. Gūjaras, Jāṭs, Rājpūts, and Āhīrs all claimed Kshatriya rather than Brāhmaṇ status, while Brāhmaṇs, especially in the Panjāb and the western Gangā plains, were becoming less aloof from the rest of society and were so numerous that many had taken to cultivation. Rājpūts mysteriously appeared about the 10th century, and their clans expanded from Rājasthān and Gujarāt in all directions. They were provided with genealogies tracing them back to mythical epic Solar or Lunar races, legitimizing their claims to Kshatriya status. The tendency for assimilation of castes into the Rājpūt and other Kshatriya categories is still a strong one and now operates among central Indian tribal peoples. This is but a variant of the dynastic drift process which linked southern dynasties to the epic traditions.

Political organization was a kind of feudalism in that there was a hierarchy of feudatories and subfeudatories under the king; these were assigned the income of villages and lands. The feudatories were required to supply military forces when needed by the king, and in return they were

allowed to use bombastic titles. Villages were ideally grouped into clusters of 12 or 16 and were supposed to be administered in units of 84. A third or a sixth of the crop was paid by the peasant as land tax to the feudatory, and he also had to provide free labor. Crown lands were retained by the king himself for his own revenue. Villages had assemblies or committees (*pancāyats*) in which village headmen (*ṭhākurs*) played a prominent part. Brāhmaṇs supported the royal mythology as well as the genealogies of the Kshatriya clans, and were awarded lands. They gave religious sanction to the formal caste structure and to the social and economic cleavages characterizing Indian society.

On the whole, late medieval North India had passed its creative period and the social order had become oppressive, especially in the Panjāb and Gangā plains. Such evidence as there is suggests that prosperity declined after the 14th century. Interminable short-lived dynasties and Rājpūt lineages ruled, but failed to patronize culturally unifying institutions. The stage was set for a new integrative force.

Integration under Islam

Now a wholly new Great Tradition came to test the digestive power of Hinduism and Indian Civilization. The result was a siege of indigestion which has lasted a thousand years and is still sour with India-Pakistan rivalry. Yet Islamic rule renewed the political integration of South Asia, while its administrative procedures, certain of the arts, and the Persian language added a new vitality to the history of the cultural integration of South Asia.

From the year 1000 a Turkish chief, Mahmūd of Ghaznī in Afghanistan, began to make annual raids into the Panjāb plains. He looted temples ranging from Saurāshṭra to the middle Gangā while the Rājpūt clans continued to fight each other. In the late 12th century, Afghān armies appeared, descending via the Gomāl Pass to Sindh and penetrating the Panjāb. In the early 13th century, a Sultanate was established at Delhi which saw a succession of rulers and courtiers of Afghān, Turk, and Persian origin, and which later gave rise to independent Muslim dynasties in many parts of the North. Though they could not control the peninsula, they raided in the South, even as far as Madurai, to obtain booty and solicit tribute. Vijayanagara, the Pāṇḍiyas, and several lesser Hindu kingdoms remained independent. In 1398 the Mongols raided under the leadership of Tīmūr, a Turk from Central Asia, and a succession of other rulers occupied Delhi for another century. Bānglā, to which Islam had first come by Arab and other Muslim traders along the coast, had its own sultan and remained prosperous as it monopolized trade between North India and Ming China.

The Mughals founded their dynasty in the 16th century. The most

illustrious ruler of that line, Akbar, began in 1556 to annex Gujarāt, Bānglā, Kashmīr, Orissa, and parts of the northern Deccan. His rule was the heyday of the Mughals. Akbar developed his own synchretistic religion, a fusion of Hinduism and Islam which really revolved around himself, but it failed to succeed him. The 17th century saw the rule of Jahāngīr and Shāh Jahān (who built the Tāj Mahal). The last great Mughal ruler, Aurangzib, was followed by a succession of lesser lights who dissipated the strength of the empire, while the Persians under Nādir Shāh came down and sacked Delhi in 1739. The British unsuspectingly began to victimize them when in 1757 they occupied Bānglā, and within 80 years these strange intruders came to incorporate the whole subcontinent within their sphere of influence.

The five centuries of Muslim rule from Delhi saw the conversion to Islam of most people in the Indus and western Panjāb plains and the western Himālayas, the majority in Kashmīr, a significant percentage in the Gangā plains, the Deccan, and the west coast, and most of the people of eastern Bānglā (Bangladesh). A quarter of the population of South Asia took up this alien tradition which in its imported state was at odds with the traditional Indian views of the meaning of life, and moreover was an exclusive creed. It is interesting that the regions where the greatest numbers turned to Islam, Panjāb and Bānglā, were precisely the regions where Buddhism lasted longest and was never thoroughly replaced by Brāhmaṇism.

There were many practical advantages in accepting Islam. Conversions during the early period of Mughal rule were abetted by the traditional Muslim head-tax on non-Muslims, but because of the importunity of the Rājpūt chiefs whose loyalty was essential to Mughal rule, this tax was abolished. The Mughal army was a source of conversions. Those who pretended to know something of the arts—literature, architecture, gardening—as well as law or philosophy had to be thoroughly familiar with the Arab and Persians traditions on which they were based.

For those who desired it the Islamic tradition had a highly developed philosophy of man's relationship with Allah, as well as of the state, the social order, law, and even history. It was able to draw upon the scholarship of Egypt and the whole Islamic world. Yet the basic credo propounded by this new elite was a very simple one, easily assented to for practical rewards. But though it was an exclusive creed, in the context of South Asia it accommodated itself to such indigenous features as caste and saint worship. While the bhakti cults pervaded the peninsula and Bānglā, Sūfī mysticism, derived in part from Persia, provided a parallel emotional outlet for Muslims; Hindu vernacular devotional literature was paralleled by tremendously emotive Persian poetry.

The Mughals contributed little to the unification of South Asia by their economic policies, which were characterized chiefly by excessive taxation, or by their communication networks, but they built a few roads and canals. Their administrative structure, however, was more organized than

Amber Palace near Jaipur, Rājasthān, 17th century. Pillared hall is in Hindu style, while elaborate doorway is of Persian inspiration, exemplifying fusion of cultural traditions under the Mughals and the Rājpūt kings.

that of the Hindu kingdoms, and the British built upon it. During the Mughal regime the Persian language was the medium of polite speech, as well as the vehicle of administration and law. Hindus took to this far more readily than they did to Arabic. The effect of Persian on the formation of Urdū and Hindustānī, and hence of Hindī, has been an important boon to the unification of North India and also of Pakistan.

The best-known legacies of the Mughals were the symbols of their own vainglory; they preferred to revel in the delights of their formal gardens and reflecting pools rather than dig canals. And the fact that their most lavish expenditures were on their own tombs is symbolic of where their hearts were; they remained a ruling elite minority. Yet it is these works of architecture, the miniature paintings, Persian dress styles, and associated

manners that are thought of as the best of premodern civilization in India and Pakistan.

The Mughals reestablished the idea of unity from Kandahār in Afghanistan to Chittagong near Burma, else the British would have had a very different history in South Asia. By vaunting the symbols of the alien Mughal veneer, the even more alien British were able to gloss over the regional cultural differences in forging together British India; these symbols included the palatial neo-Mughal architecture, the Red Fort and Delhi, and the veneration of emperor which in 1858 was transferred to Queen Victoria herself.

A New Overarching System

Since the thrust of this book is anthropological, we cannot trace all the historical processes that have changed the face of South Asia in the last two or three centuries. Contemporary rural and urban change is discussed in Chapters 16 and 17 as well as in the profiles in the accompanying volume. Numerous historians have dealt with the history of British India and independent India, Pakistan, and Sri Lanka (American historians of South Asia particularly so because they could more easily handle sources in English).

But one thing is sure. The changes initiated with the British and still in process are not simply the grafting of a new great tradition on an old great tradition. A new mood has overtaken the land, which is not leaving unchallenged a single institution of Hindu, Muslim, Buddhist, or Christian society. Faith in the great traditions has explicitly begun to transmute to faith in modernization. The historian Percival Spear refers to the "magic cloak of Persian culture" of the Mughal society which disintegrated as the British appeared:

> But then, instead of a new cultural cloak for a few at the top, came an injection (in the form of the education policy) of new ideas into the ideological life-blood of Indian society. Thereafter the gradual transformation of Indian society, as it prepared antibodies against some forms of the western virus and modified itself under the influence of other forms, provided the inner meaning of the modern Indian history.[6]

The Portuguese, envious of the profits of Arab sea trade, established themselves in Goā in 1510 and were to rule that territory for four and a half centuries, using it to administer their enclaves in Gujarāt and Sri Lanka and as a base for their trade empire in Southeast Asia. They made a permanent imprint on India; items of material culture they introduced are still in vogue, as lock designs, carpenter tools, and furniture. Such converts as they won to Catholicism, especially fisher folk along the coasts, were attracted by their naval superiority over the Arabs, while through undue pressure they persuaded a section of the native Christian church in Kēraḷa to merge with

the Roman Church. Imbued with Counter-Reformation zeal, they preached an all-or-nothing dogma, introduced the Inquisition, and forbade Hindu temples in Goā. Thus the Great Tradition of Iberian Catholicism was not acceptable as a model for South Asia, though the land was ready for a new one.

The Dutch challenged the Portuguese, and though they ruled Sri Lanka for a century, they had little impact on India. The French, developing a late interest in India, jumped into the fray and almost came to dominate the peninsula. They were defeated by the British in Karṇāṭaka about 1800, and their cultural contribution to South Asia was nil except in Pondicherry, an enclave they retained in Tamil̠ Nāḍu.

The locus of power in the subcontinent began to drift from the heartland to the coasts. The East India Company established commercial activities in Madras in 1640, Bombay in 1674, and Calcutta in 1690, in each case founding a city where none had existed. Nibbling at the fringe, the British traders were beyond the range of Mughal authority. Little did the effete rulers of Delhi realize that the heartland would no longer serve to hold their civilization together. The centrifugal trend continued with the founding of many other port cities, such as Karāchī, Cochin, Colombo, and Chittagong—geographical symptoms of what was beginning to happen to the culture of South Asia. These port cities remained the centers of innovation even after the demise of colonialism. Though political power has today accumulated in Delhi, that city has not yet matched the cultural dynamism of Calcutta and Bombay, and it will be some time before the new Pakistan capital inland at Islāmābād can outpace the influence of Karāchī. The skin of South Asia had been punctured in a score of places, and at each point the inoculation had produced an important local reaction which diffused deep into the corpus, ultimately to converge in the heartland of modern India and Pakistan.

From the 1750s the English expanded from Bānglā until by 1836 they had come to control all the Gangā plains up to the Panjāb, plus Assam, the coastal tracts of Orissa and Āndhra, most of the South, Sri Lanka, and large parts of Mahārāshṭra and Gujarāt. In 1843 the *amīrs* of Sindh, unable to cooperate among themselves, were overthrown, and after fierce wars with the Sikhs, a devotional sect turned militaristic, the British added the Panjāb. The remaining independent mahārājās were powerless to prevent British usurpation of their foreign and military affairs, though they retained a figment of internal administrative autonomy. The most important of these were Hyderābād, Mysore, Travancore (southern Kēraḷa), Kashmīr, and Balūchistān, in addition to a host of greater or lesser Rājpūt lineages in Rājasthān and parts of Gujarāt. Since the Paṭhāns were provocative, the British defeated them and installed a new ruler in Kābul. Yet they had to wage further Afghān wars, for the clans of those arid hills were too jealous of their own prerogatives and their leaders too confident in their individual

personalities to be much acculturated from British India. The British sent a vain expedition to Lhasa, Tibet, in 1904. Upper Burma was annexed in 1886, but before Independence, in recognition of the different personality of Burma, it was detached from British India and given a separate administration. The British inevitably found the natural boundaries of the South Asian culture area.

The New Faith

The list of institutions and devices by which the British administration began to unite South Asia and guide it toward the new faith in modernization is a long one. The railroads, planned in the 1850s, had by 1900 provided a fine mesh covering almost all the subcontinent. They made British and later Indian factory goods available everywhere so that people in remotest villages began using matches, mill cloth, paper, and kerosene, while they also averted local famines and facilitated frequent travel. A close network of roads, telegraph service which villagers could afford, and a well-organized postal system were credits to the British rule. The government public works programs repaired the decrepit Mughal canals in the North and deepened the medieval irrigation reservoirs dotting the South. Massive irrigation schemes along the tributaries of the Indus sparked the economic development of the Panjāb. Bridge construction and harbor works facilitated communication, while hydroelectric power became available in more and more towns. Thus the whole population of the subcontinent became aware of the materials of modernization.

But finding themselves unable to make much change in the structure of society or basic cultural institutions, the British took the tack that their administration was not to interfere in these matters. True enough, a few practices so wounded the sensibility of the British that they were suppressed—among them *satī* (widow-burning), *ṭhagī* (thuggee, fanatical organized looting), the headhunting of the Nāgas, the interminable feuding of the Paṭhān clans, and the occasional human sacrifice of some central Indian tribes. Missionaries were allowed a free hand, but in two centuries of dedicated labor won only 2% of the population to Christianity in all its forms.

A set of institutions based on European models was introduced; these at first duplicated the services of, and then superseded, indigenous institutions. One of these was the legal system. Village and caste legal procedures had in medieval centuries been partly superseded by Mughal law based on the Qur'ān, and this was now capped by the alien British legal system. The lower courts in the British system compromised their respect for individual rights to accommodate traditional caste, marriage, and inheritance rules, but the higher courts, with judges educated in English judicial prac-

Madras University. In this colonial port city the British established a new institution, the secular university, with buildings in neo-Mughal style with Hindu motifs (right). A building constructed since Independence is in international style (left).

tice, did provide a unifying force and presaged the trend to individualism. Another institution was the Civil Service. Far more highly organized than Hindu or Mughal government, it cut across all regional cultural values because it was conducted in English. The administrative system, which provided careers to hundreds of thousands of officers and clerks, was one of the most important legacies the independent South Asian countries inherited from British rule. The unification of South Asia by this means had as a by-product, however, the intensification of caste divisions within several of the provinces, for the British found it expedient to draw Brāhmaṇs, Kāyasthas, and other traditional leaders into the administration in disproportionate numbers. A third institution was the banking system, which gradually displaced indigenous banking and moneylending institutions. A common currency, a common economic policy, and the protection of accumulated capital and investments anywhere in British India were other major unifying factors inherited by independent South Asian countries.

But above all, it was the cutting edge of the new education that probed

deepest into the traditional value system. The decision to have English as the medium of instruction at the high school and college levels, while intended to produce a cadre of civil servants amenable to British ideas, had in fact the effect of disseminating widely the best of English literature. The idealism about individual rights, democratic procedures, and the equalitarian society were in conflict with what the college-educated class observed of the presence of the British in India, and were directly responsible for the formation of the Congress Party before 1900, the Gandhian movement, and the rapidity of achieving Independence. It also led to the establishment of several socioreligious movements, such as the Brāhmo Samāj and the Rāmakrishṇa Mission in Bānglā, the Ārya Samāj of Panjāb, and the Theosophical Society of Madras, which attempted to recast Hindu values to be respectable in the light of Western ideals.

The assumption that India and Pakistan are almost changeless has been one that ignored the effect of the new educated class, the English-speaking elite. Schools and colleges abounded, established not only by the British government and mission societies but by private individuals. It was not the peasants, but the groups exercising leadership in traditional society that went in for education—Brāhmaṇs, Ṭhākurs, Kāyasthas, Vaidyās, Baniyās, Pārsīs. For them an English education provided a means to continue to exercise respectable leadership and maintain their position in the changing social hierarchy. They became the civil servants, teachers, lawyers, businessmen, and clerks. Yet, this

> new class felt a chill vacuum at the vital point of religious experience. This was filled by the new sentiment of political nationalism. Freedom was an interesting idea but patriotism was a warm emotion. In this way Indian nationalism was superimposed upon Bengali and Marathi regionalism by a new class.[7]

After Independence the new South Asian countries flashed around the world symbols of their traditional cultural heritage: for India the lion-capital of Aśoka, the Buddhist Wheel on its flag, the extension into international politics of the ancient nonviolence principle, Gandhian moral power, and the determination to replace English with the national languages; for Pakistan, the crescent, the Muslim foundation for statehood and the social order, and fraternity with Muslim countries on international issues; for Sri Lanka, the Temple of the Tooth, Buddhist holidays, and Sinhala; for Nepal, the Hindu monarchy and the temples of Kāṭhmāṇḍū.

But these symbols of the ancient civilizations of the countries were chosen in reaction against foreign rule and more particularly, were intended to focus on the distinctions of each South Asian country as apart from its neighbors. The real symbols chosen by Nehru and his contemporaries and propagated for internal consumption are those of the new faith, the relief that modernization will bring the good life; this is the "Great Tradition" of the English-educated elite. The symbols of this faith advertised by govern-

ments include: dams (beautified with carefully-tended gardens), industrial production (proudly announced by the export of electric fans or sewing machines), agricultural productivity (accompanied by continual statements about immanent self-sufficiency), and social welfare (with slogans such as "socialist pattern of society"). Indeed, this faith may now be stronger among the elite of South Asia than those of some Western countries.

REFERENCES AND NOTES

[1] Wilbur Zelinsky, "India (or non-India) Seen from Afar: On the Mutual Relevance of Varied Cultural Geographies," in Crane, pp. 139–141.
[2] Oscar Lewis, "Peasant Culture in India and Mexico: A Comparative Analysis," in Marriott.
[3] *Mahāvamsa* vii, pp. 19–36 (see Geiger).
[4] *Mahāvamsa* xxxii, p. 84 (see Geiger).
[5] Nilakanta Sastri (1958), p. 315.
[6] Spear (1965), p. 14.
[7] Spear (1965), p. 166.

IMPORTANT SOURCES

Processes of Cultural Assimilation

Aiyappan, A. *Social Revolution in a Kerala Village: A Study in Culture Change.* New York, 1965.
Cohn, Bernard, *India: The Social Anthropology of a Civilization.* New York, 1971.
Crane, Robert (ed.). *Regions and Regionalism in South Asian Studies: An Exploratory Study.* Durham, N.C., 1966.
Dube, S. C. *Indian Village.* London, 1955.
Economic Weekly. India's Villages. West Bengal Government Press, 1955.
Ishwaran, K. *Shivapur: A South Indian Village.* London, 1968.
Karve, Iravate. "The Indian Village," *Bull. of the Deccan College and Research Inst.* xviii (Jan. 1957).
Marriott, McKim (ed.). *Village India.* Chicago, 1955.
Singer, Milton, and Bernard Cohn (eds.). *Structure and Change in Indian Society.* Chicago, 1968. (Note especially the Preface, and Bernard Cohn, "The Study of Indian Society and Culture.")
Srinivas, M. N. *Caste in Modern India and Other Essays.* Bombay, 1962.
———. *Religion and Society among the Coorgs of South India.* London, 1952.
———. *Social Change in Modern India.* Berkeley, Calif., 1967.

Traditional Culture and Civilization

Basham, A. L. *The Wonder That Was India.* New York, 1959. (This excellent work is the standard introduction to pre-Muslim Indian civilization.)
The Cambridge History of India, 6 vols. Cambridge, from 1922.
Gokhale, B. G. *Ancient India: History and Culture.* New York, 1952.
Majumdar, R. C. (ed.). *The History and Culture of the Indian People.* Bombay,

1950s. (This compendium in eight tomes, though occasionally written in an old style of history, is invaluable because it is comprehensive.)
Nilakanta Sastri, K. A. *History of India*. Madras, 1950. (Authoritative, based on literary sources.)
———. *A History of South India*. Madras, 1958.
Pillay, K. K. *A Social History of the Tamils*. Madras, 1961.
Ray, H. C. (ed.). *History of Ceylon*, 3 vols. Colombo, 1959.
Saletore, R. N. *Life in the Gupta Age*. Bombay, 1943.
Sen-Gupta, N. C. *Evolution of Ancient Indian Law*. Calcutta, 1953.
Tarn, W. W. *The Greeks in Bactria and India*, 2d ed. Cambridge, England, 1951.
Thapar, Romila. *A History of India, Part I*. Baltimore, 1966. (A thorough and readable summary.)

Culture and Civilization of Muslim and British Periods

Abdulla, Ahmed. *The Historical Background of Pakistan and Its People*. Karachi, 1973.
Brown, W. Norman. *The United States and India, Pakistan, Bangladesh*, 3d ed. Cambridge, Mass., 1972. (By a foremost Indologist.)
Chand, Tara. *Influence of Islam on Indian Culture*. Allahabad, 1954.
Griffiths, Sir Percival. *The British Impact on India*. New York, 1952.
Hutchins, Francis. *The Illusion of Permanence*. Princeton, N.J., 1967. (A study of the British presence in India.)
Mujeeb, M. *The Indian Muslims*. London, 1967. (Comprehensive and pertaining to the Pakistan region also.)
Sharma, S. R. *The Crescent in India: A Study in Medieval History*, rev. ed. Bombay, 1954.
Spear, Percival. *A History of India, Part II*. Baltimore, 1965. (The most readable summary.)
———. *India, A Modern History*. Ann Arbor, Mich., 1961.

Texts in Translation

Burton, Richard (trans.). *Kāma Sūtra*. New York, 1962.
Cowell, E. B., and others (trans.). *The Jākata*, 2d ed., 6 vols. Cambridge, England, 1957.
de Bary, Theodore (ed.). *Sources of Indian Tradition*. New York, 1958. (This useful work contains translated excerpts, with notes, of important texts from the Vedas to Gandhi.)
Geiger, Wilhelm (trans.). *The Mahāvamsa*. London, 1964.
Griffith, R. T. H. (trans.). *The Rig Veda*, 3d ed., 2 vols. Banares, 1963.
Hume, R. A. (trans.). *Thirteen Principal Upanishads*. Oxford, 1921.
Kangle, R. P. (trans.). *The Kauṭilīya Arthaśāstra*. Bombay, 1963.
Narasimhan, Chakravarthi (trans.). *The Mahābhārata: An English Version Based on Selected Verses*. New York, 1965.

7

Religion

The visitor from the West set down in a village in South Asia will soon begin to wonder if all that he has read about formal Buddhism, Hinduism, or Islam bears any relationship at all to what he sees around him. Yet it does. One boggles at the mosaic, both vertical and horizontal. Yet, withal, there is a unity. And if the visitor is an anthropologist, he will find no better laboratory in the world than South Asia to study religion and world view—whether he be interested in structure and change, the folk-formal continuum, ritual and symbolism, or ethnopsychology.

India had the following adherents of religions, estimated on a midyear population in 1973 of 575 million:[1]

487,000,000	Hindus
64,000,000	Muslims
15,000,000	Christians (half Roman Catholics)
12,000,000	Sikhs
4,000,000	Buddhists
2,700,000	Jains
130,000	Pārsīs (Zoroastrians)
105,000	atheists
20,000	Jews

	Tribals claiming a tribal religion in the 1961 census:
191,000	Ho (Bihār)
175,000	Gāro (Meghālaya)
174,000	Khāsi (Meghālaya)
91,000	Santāl (mostly in Bihār)
52,000	Nāga (Nāgaland)
34,000	Konyak (Nāgaland)
21,000	Mikir (Assam)

Pakistan had about 69 million people in 1973, with the following estimated adherents of religions:[2]

67,000,000	Muslims
810,000	Christians
660,000	"Scheduled Caste" Hindus
265,000	other Hindus
6,000	Pārsīs
2,000	Buddhists

Bangladesh had roughly 73 million people in 1973, with the following adherents of religions:[3]

61,000,000	Muslims
5,400,000	"Scheduled Caste" Hindus
5,200,000	other Hindus
533,000	Buddhists (in Chittagong Hills)
285,000	Christians

Sri Lanka had about 13.4 million people in 1973, with the following adherents of religions:[4]

8,800,000	Buddhists
2,500,000	Hindus
1,150,000	Christians (85% Roman Catholic)
875,000	Muslims

Afghanistan had perhaps 17 million people in 1973, and practically 100% are Muslims.

Nepal had about 12 million people in 1973. It is difficult to determine the adherents of religions. The majority, including almost all those on the southern lowlands, are Hindus, while in the central valleys there is a mixture of tribal religions, Buddhism, and Hinduism, with Tibetan Buddhism on the higher slopes.

Bhutan, with fewer than a million people, is almost all Tibetan Buddhist. Sikkim has Buddhism in the north and Hinduism in the south.

The Maldive Islands, with a population of 100,000, is entirely Muslim.

In Mauritius the people of Indian origin, who form the majority, are 73% Hindu and 23% Muslim.

South Asia as a whole is Hindu at the center but Muslim and Buddhist at the fringes. The only place outside South Asia where Hinduism is practiced today is the island of Bāli in Indonesia, a relic of Indian culture transplanted to Southeast Asia. Of course, Hindus have emigrated from India to such places as East and South Africa, Malaysia, Singapore, Burma, Fiji, Guyana, and Trinidad.

Though British India was partitioned to accommodate the wishes of South Asian Muslims for a Muslim homeland, one should note that 11.2% of the people of India are Muslims, while over 14% of the people of Bangladesh are Hindus. The most populous Muslim country in the world is Indonesia, and the next three in order of numbers of Muslims are Pakistan, India, and Bangladesh, followed by the major countries of the Near East.

It should be understood at the outset that the image many Westerners have of South Asia and especially of India, that it is a land where most people are inclined to be mystical and ascetic, is wrong. South Asians can as easily be characterized as reveling in all of life—its color, sensuality, and wealth. But the subject of religion and world view is an exceedingly complex one, and in this chapter we can only briefly survey some of its structure, symbolism, and change. Whereas Indologists have extensively studied religion as represented in literature, we are more interested here in actual behavior and its underlying meaning.

Philosophical Synthesizing Mechanisms

All the philosophical concepts of indigenous Indian religions had their roots in prehistory and were universalized; that is, were validated and given wider meaning by the great traditions. The roots of the abstruse philosophical concepts can be seen in a half million villages—in worship and festivals, agricultural and pastoral fertility beliefs, tribal mythology, ancestor worship, or ways of coping with anxiety and fear of the unknown. It is true that Hinduism is so diverse it defies definition. But with the development of secondary-level civilization, philosophical integrative mechanisms necessarily appeared, and by medieval times these had become highly complex and esoteric systems. From the pool of prehistoric religious elements there arose three indigenous classical religions: Hinduism, Buddhism, and Jainism. But the genius of all these was their facility to accommodate a vast range of diverse and contradictory elements. For instance, in Hinduism there are six formal schools of classical philosophy ranging from atheism to yoga to devotionalism, in addition to more recent systems, all somehow conceived of as the same religion as the cults of literally hundreds of millions of deities in Indian villages.

The concept of rebirth (reincarnation or transmigration), that every living thing has an essence somehow reborn from a previous existence,

is accepted at the formal level by all three indigenous religions. This notion certainly originated in misty prehistoric times, for archeologists have found from Pakistan to Assam ancient burials in urns under or near houses; sometimes bones were interred in womb-like pots resembling pregnant women with distended bellies and breasts molded on. This belief is doubtless a geographical continuum of notions found farther east, such as the two souls doctrine in China and Southeast Asia, the Australian aboriginal idea of fertilization of the womb by a reborn soul, and the concept of mana (embodied power) in Oceania. Though not part of the Āryan religion and not found in the Vedas, the notion of rebirth was taken for granted by the time the *Upanishads* were written. Bubbling to the surface from below, it was incorporated into formal philosophies of Brāhmaṇism as well as Buddhism and Jainism between the 6th and 1st centuries B.C. Coincidentally, this doctrine surfaced in Greece about the same time and found its way into philosophical treatises. Since early Buddhism had a nontheistic world view it developed an ambivalent attitude toward rebirth, but the idea could not be discarded, and became accepted as doctrine in Mahāyāna Buddhism.

The greatest single historic device for synthesizing all living things, all people, and all cults into one coherent and orderly cosmic system was this concept of rebirth, called *samsāra*. Man saw himself as part of the world of all living things and derived from other living things; he was not specially created by divine fiat to dominate all the rest. Samsāra predated but served the same function as our concept of biological evolution.

Not only man, plants, and animals are linked by rebirths, but also the gods and all the spirits and ghosts; all are but emanations or spiritual incarnations of other beings. The gods are not in a separate and distant world; one can identify with them because they might have formerly lived as men. As tribal society gave way to state systems, the cult deities and legendary heroes of diverse cultural systems could be drawn into the net of the evolving Great Tradition. Now all particularized beliefs could be universalized.

Given the doctrine of samsāra, polytheism is not irrational. Any number of greater or lesser deities, as well as spirits, ghosts of the dead, and demons, are but aspects of others. The millions of gods of later Hinduism can be theologically reduced by merging until one realizes there are but three gods: Brahmā, Vishṇu, and Śiva, and even these may be reduced to Brāhmaṇ, the World Soul. Not only deities peculiar to families, villages, or regions but also semidivine culture heroes of folklore or epics can be conceived of as incarnations or emanations of one of the major Hindu deities found in textual sources.

In Mahāyāna Buddhism diverse deities of essentially Hindu origin came to be regarded as bodhisattvas, on the way to being incarnated as a Buddha. Similarly, the deities of the Bon religion indigenous to Tibet were incorporated into Tibetan Lamaistic Buddhism. Even in Theravāda Bud-

dhism, supposed to be orthodox, early saints or heroes were regarded in Pāli literature as the "previous lives" of Gautama Buddha. In modern Sri Lanka deities of local origin are regarded simply as "helpers" of Buddha.

Formal Islam, of course, rejects the whole idea of samsāra, but one might suspect that even this intrusive religion has been affected by it. There is widespread veneration of *pīrs* (Muslim saints) and of ghosts of the dead. It is believed that in every generation a few are born who are holy, who become pīrs or *faqīrs* (tomb caretakers or mendicants), and their tombs become shrines. Even the Christian doctrines of the incarnation and resurrection of Christ are not difficult to comprehend in the light of samsāra.

This belief, having become idealized in formal indigenous religions because of its integrative function, came to determine behavior. Nonviolence, *ahimsā*, came to be an ideal in both Jainism and Buddhism, especially among those elite enough to be able to practice it. The highest virtue in Jainism came to be avoidance of injuring any living thing, and in Buddhism, too, both hunting and slaughter were regarded as great sins. In Hinduism, protection of certain animals, such as the cow and monkey, came to be Brāhmaṇically rationalized in that these might be reborn souls of humans.

The doctrine of ahimsā was seldom applied at the level of the state, however, for kings adhering to all three indigenous religions considered it their normal function, indeed their duty, to be militaristic and aggressive, so that the history of South Asia has been as bloody as that of Europe or China. The major exception was king Aśoka. More recently Gandhi lifted the concept of ahimsā out of its religious matrix and gave it a new social meaning, determining to wear out the British by continued passive resistance. After Independence the governments of both India and Sri Lanka tried to project an international image of nonviolence by their policies of not becoming actively aligned with any superpowers, a convenient moralistic rationalization of hard political necessities. But Pakistan never held out such an ideal, for ahimsā is not part of Islam. Since India has militarily confronted both China and Pakistan, its international ahimsā image has been tarnished.

Formal Hindu Philosophy and the Social Ideal

By propounding belief in rebirth, those at the apex of the social structure have been able to reinforce their position because it has provided a forceful theory integrating and explaining the caste hierarchy. The idea that one's birth is determined by one's actions in a previous life has certainly been emphasized in the Brāhmaṇical texts and even in the Hindu law books, to support the hierarchy of castes and the position of Brāhmaṇs at

the top. Even the inferior treatment accorded women could be rationalized in this way. Doing one's duty according to one's station in life has been a cornerstone of traditional Hindu ethics; it has ever been used to keep the servile castes in place.

The logical development of the doctrine of samsāra has led to two more key concepts: *karma* and *dharma.* These two words are so basic to Indian thought that they cannot be reduced to simple definitions. Karma is the accumulation of the effects of one's actions, which adhere to the soul; it may be merit, or it may be evil karma. It is also fate, the cause of whatever happens. Sacred people and objects have a great deal of good karma. This is related to the idea that holy temples or deities, or pure castes have about them a field of sanctity, whereas ritual impurity is an expression of evil karma. Good karma is doubtless ultimately related to the concept of mana. Jains thought of karma as a concrete substance adhering to the soul. Both they and the Buddhists thought that its accumulation was automatic and subject to a natural law and that one could not obtain release from the perpetual cycle of rebirths until the weight of karma had been shed. These nontheistic philosophers saw no need for a divine agency to enforce the moral order. In Hinduism also, one cannot escape the law of karma, which determines not only the social level into which one is born but also the level of his prosperity or failure in life. Some philosophers saw it as the weighing in the balance of the good and evil one has done, as did ancient Egyptians. Others of the Yoga school thought karma could be turned to one's advantage by knowledge and by physical self-control. But in bhakti (devotional Hinduism) this doctrine came into conflict with the idea that the Lord was merciful and gracious. Rāmānuja said that through devotion, God could change one's karma, and for this reason late medieval devotional Hinduism with its emphasis on grace had wide popular appeal. In the Brāhmaṇical scheme of things, karma appears as a wonderfully logical concept that explains suffering, differential social status, and samsāra; it has also been used as a tool for the preservation of orthodoxy and control of society.

Dharma is all that is good, righteous, or charitable. It is also what is legally right or dutiful. In the Sanskrit texts, doing dharma is the first and primary aim of man in this life. The king was the supreme exemplar of dharma. But dharma differs according to context, like situational ethics. One's karma is accumulated in the context of what is dharma for him in a particular life and in a particular time or circumstance. For the Brāhmaṇ, dharma is maintaining ritual purity or reciting the Vedas, but that would be blasphemy for the untouchable. Dharma is generally ahimsā, but the warrior cannot be nonviolent. In the *Bhagavad Gītā* the archer hero Arjuna did not want to fight because he and his troops were arrayed against their own kinsmen. But Lord Krishṇa assumed the form of a charioteer and conducted a dialogue with Arjuna while driving his chariot. He told Arjuna

that he had to fight and that Kshatriyas (warriors) were blessed for having the opportunity to engage in such a battle as the Mahābhārata War. Krishṇa said:

> For, to one who is born death is certain and certain is birth to one who has died. Therefore in connection with a thing that is inevitable you should not grieve.
>
> But if you do not fight this battle which is enjoined by dharma, then you will have given up your own dharma as well as glory, and you will incur sin.
>
> Either, being slain, you will attain heaven; or being victorious, you will enjoy [i.e., rule] the earth. Therefore arise, O son of Kuntī, intent on battle.
>
> Therefore, without attachment, always do the work that has to be done, for a man doing his work without attachment attains to the highest goal.
>
> These worlds would fall into ruin if I did not do my work. I would then be the creator of chaos and would destroy these people.[5]

So the gods, as well as men, do their dharma. The beggar on the street, when he asks for alms, calls out "dharma, dharma," here meaning alms. The giving of alms is expectable and right and produces good karma for the giver. But it is also the beggar's dharma to ask for alms.

Even within a single life there are several stages, so that a person's dharma would be different as a celibate young student than as a householder or as an ascetic who in old age renounced the cares of the world. Also, according to the Brāhmaṇical texts the three major aims of life—dharma, artha (worldly gain), and kāma (pleasure)—were all valid. To these three was added a fourth, moksha, the afterlife or heaven. Moksha may be interpreted in a variety of ways—as bliss, nothingness, release, self-realization, or as a concrete heaven with maidens, green grass, and plump cows. But attainment of moksha however one defines it is dependent upon his dharma.

Hindu Villagers' Philosophical Views

How well are such doctrines as dharma, karma, samsāra, and moksha understood or believed in villages, or expressed in the behavior of the people? Of course there is a wide range of ideals among caste and ethnic groups, even within a village. But in general people hardly ever talk about rebirth in mundane conversations, and obviously attainment of moksha is not a serious goal in daily activities. It is here that the anthropologist and the Indologist need to find a common meeting ground.

Ethnographic work among high caste people suggests that the doctrines of karma and samsāra are verbally maintained by high castes to support their social position. G. M. Carstairs reports that among Brāhmaṇs whom he interviewed in Rājasthān, most were eager to impart their religious views, but only 16 of 36 were at all assiduous in attempting to practice them. They said that the aim of life is liberation from karma and from the need to be successively reborn. Moksha comes when one has purged his nature

of all that is terrestrial and carnal so that his soul can become one with *paramātmā*, the spirit of the universe. But of more immediate concern is performance of the multitudinous rituals of bathing or defecation, and getting the help of a good *gurū* (religious teacher). These Brāhmaṇs in Rājasthān denounced the deities of the low caste villagers. Some who were actually trying to advance in holiness by meditation, bodily control, and rituals were envisaging a time when others would turn to them for leadership and guidance.

In a village near Delhi, Oscar Lewis says Brāhmaṇs tend to stress that sin is disbelief in God and acts contrary to dharma, and that one is reborn from life to life according to karma until the soul ultimately attains release and reaches God. But Brāhmaṇs are not powerful here. Jāṭs, a high agriculturalist caste, dominate the village because they own the land and do not have to rely upon the sanctifying effect of Brāhmaṇical ritual for status. Usually they are bold enough to deny reincarnation, karma, moksha, and any afterlife. They emphasize life on earth and consider murder, causing pain, stealing, and lying as important sins. Their status is based on landholding, and they do not need to support it by piety. But Brāhmaṇs revile the "disbelief" of the Jāṭs, who in fact have not lost all belief but have been influenced by a reformist brand of Hinduism, the Ārya Samāj.

Middle caste people, if asked, generally assent to these doctrines, but they have no effect on their present lives. Kathleen Gough writes that in a Kēraḷa village the Nāyar, a formerly warlike caste, legitimize their status by the karma theory, and in this they are supported by Brāhmaṇs who are in the orthodox hierarchy a step above them. S. C. Dube says of a village in western Āndhra that people believe that "the course of our present life is largely predestined on the basis of our acts in the past life, but by acting 'rightly' in this life we can materially influence the course of our life after death."[6] But he makes no observation implying that this belief affects behavior. Gerald Berreman, writing about Pahāṛī Hindus of the Uttar Pradesh Himālayas says that the idea of life after death, especially the time between death and reincarnation, is a vague and confused one to villagers. "Many have no systematic conception of what occurs, and others hold firmly to mutually contradictory views." They all say they believe that acts in this life determine the nature of the next life and even make a joke that "when we Pahāṛīs die we are reborn on the plains as donkeys." Some suggest Americans eat meat and lead wicked lives so are probably reborn as low caste Indians. Yet this verbally expressed belief "does not lead Pahāṛīs to give up animal sacrifice, nor would it prevent them from behaving like other wicked Americans were they to be reborn in America."[7]

Low caste people do not much emphasize the relationship between dharma, karma, samsāra, and caste, even though in some cases they might give verbal assent to these doctrines. Pauline Kolenda reports that among sweepers in an Uttar Pradesh village only important things in life, such as

time of death, length of life, identity of spouse, illness, and children, form an individual's karma. They refuse to admit that low caste persons such as themselves have been less virtuous in past lives than those who rank immediately above them; indeed, some refuse to admit any ranking among men. They explain their status in terms of myths or historical accidents which ignore the doctrine of karma. Their goal is not moksha or a better next life, but prevention of suffering in this life. For this reason, they are more concerned with spirits and shamans than with textual theology or the high gods.

In a village in Tamil̲ Nāḍu studied by the author, scarcely anyone would say directly that he believes in rebirth. The village has no Brāhmaṇs, but several middling and Harijan (untouchable) castes. The village astrologer, who is not a Brāhmaṇ but had studied with Brāhmaṇs, estimates that fewer than 10% of the people believe in rebirth, and he himself is evasive on the matter. The only person in the village who is firm in this belief is an older man, a college graduate, whose family had formerly owned much land, but now he is poor and is attempting to reassert his hereditary status by implying that people in castes beneath his had sinned in previous lives. The village priest, of a non-Brāhmaṇ priestly caste, said: "People never think about rebirth. They only eat today. As for Brāhmaṇs, people do regard them as high, but their beliefs have not come here." When questioned whether the Paḷḷar (a Harijan caste) were low because of sins in this or a previous life, he replied, "People treat them that way. But the Nāḍar [wealthiest caste in the village] sin more than the Paḷḷar; they kill, steal, and drink." The Paḷḷar, when asked about rebirth, state, "Big people say it is so," or more commonly flatly deny it.

The dilemma of morality for low caste people is that so often goodness is defined in terms of ritual and purity rather than direct action. If one is born into a caste that steals or eats meat or works leather, one cannot help doing so even though the "big people" regard these as sinful acts. One has to conform, for conformity to one's born status is also a moral ideal. One gains merit by following dharma according to his position, but for the low caste person this may mean doing what is evil or polluting. If a low caste person is asked whether he is inferior, he is likely to respond with an evasive answer, such as, "People say so." But he hardly ever talks about the doctrines of karma and samsāra; neither does hope of being reborn at a higher level seem to motivate his daily life.

Tribal people being assimilated into Hinduism are also not quick to swallow these doctrines. C. von Fürer-Haimendorf, in his study of morals and merit among tribal people, compares the beliefs of some in Nepal with the beliefs of the Chetrīs (Kshatriyas), the intrusive and dominant Hindu population. Some of the tribal people believe in a sequence of lives. Some also set great store on the acquisition of social merit which raises a person's status in this life. But "in none of the tribal societies did we encounter the

ea that moral choices affect a person's fate in a future existence."[8] On ie other hand, the Chetrīs are motivated at least to some degree by aims ther than material success and social ambition, and think that merit quired by prayers, rituals, pilgrimages, alms giving, and support of rāhmaṇs and temples does affect life beyond death. Many Chetrīs believe an actual heaven, where those who have acquired a great store of merit re reborn to enjoy the company of gods and celestial maidens. One's merit ets used up in time, even in heaven, and one is subject again to the law f rebirth. The functional implications of belief in karma and rebirth are pparent in the Chetrīs' immediately critical attitude to any deviation from ie narrow path of orthodox behavior on the part of caste members.

On the whole, peasants in South Asia appear to be satisfied and find ieir lives fulfilling because of the intense human relations, even though ey often acknowledge that they are poor and are aware of exploitation. uffering is an inevitable part of life, and must be so accepted in a culture iat formed when half one's children died before maturity and food supplies eriodically became critically low. Revolutionary leaders have had only potty success in mobilizing peasants. An evangelical missionary, newly rrived and preaching on the corner of a village street, asked the crowd iat had gathered, "Would you like to have joy? Would you like to have nner peace and satisfaction?" He knew not how to proceed with his sermon vhen the men replied, "Oh, we have satisfaction and happiness here."

atalism

Ethnographers differ in their evaluation of the extent of fatalism in outh Asian villages. Unwillingness to change is sometimes interpreted as esignation to fate—the will of Allah or the law of karma. But Hindu, Buddhist, and Muslim villagers act as if they believe fate or karma can be nitigated by devotion to god(s), rituals, magic, or vows. Even the control of a person by godlings, ghosts, *jins* (spirits revered by Muslims), a possessing spirit, or the evil eye, can be altered by human effort. The attitude of fatalism makes its appearance usually when people have tried to solve a problem and find that neither actions nor propitiations have changed natters—or as rural development specialists discover, when an outsider suggests people change things which they know from experience cannot or should not be changed.

The practice of astrology may be interpreted as resignation to fate. But though it is widespread and universally used in matching Hindu couples for betrothal, it is doubtful that most people implicitly believe in the tyranny of the celestial bodies over the individual. The astrologist is employed by the parents of people about to be betrothed to see if their horoscopes match, which he does by referring to tables in his books. But he is seldom pressed

for many specific details of the forecast, which is generally forgotten aft the wedding. The function of horoscopy here is as the first of a series rituals symbolizing the finality of marriage, and the astrologist is an imparti outsider who can play an advisory role at a crucial time. The astrologi also can tell people, by consulting his tables, auspicious times to begin journey, start a project, or erect a building; this is widely practiced. B rather than resigning themselves to an inevitable fate, people use the predictions to avoid evil consequences. They thereby have some contr over their own fortunes, while at the same time if something goes wron they can always attribute it to some oversight in the prediction rather tha to a mistake in their own judgment.

In Sri Lanka Buddhism, the individual is recognized as entirely r sponsible for himself, since at the philosophical level this religion is no theistic. Theoretically neither good works, nor mystical pursuits, nor ritua nor devotion can change one's state, and there is no savior, no prayer, an no predestination. Salvation can only be achieved through meditation. It widely believed, however, that suffering and misfortune can be removed b magic or propitiation of spirits. There is a hierarchy of spirits and deiti popularly believed to be responsive to rituals and requests.

In Himālayan Buddhism there is the belief that by lengthy and intensiv meditation one can alter his situation and ameliorate the effects of ev karma. Repetitive prayers and incantations also alter things. Hence praye are written on paper and made to revolve in cylindrical prayer whee turned by hand or by water power, or are written on fluttering prayer flag Divination from the smoke of fires, bird calls, or dreams may be used t avoid the effects of fate, while direct appeals to the deities through peopl in trance provide further aid in decision making.

Some scholars, such as K. W. Kapp, have applied the Weberian thesi of the relationship of the Protestant ethic to economic development, er larged upon it, and have suggested that modernization in India is impede by certain characteristics of its culture such as fatalism, reliance on magi and astrology, belief in cyclical time (Hindus believe that the present age i a degenerating one), and the tendency to mysticism and contemplation, a of which have resulted in a feeling of helplessness. But Milton Singe responds to this that we cannot "deduce realistic consequences from basi beliefs, values, or motives postulated in isolation from concrete social an cultural contexts." He refers to successful businessmen who possess all th character traits of the capitalistic spirit while also believing in karma an rebirth. Interpreters of Hinduism in temples have pointed out that "belie in karma did not prevent a Hindu householder from the performance o his worldly duties or even, in the case of merchants, from the pursuit an accumulation of wealth." They have pointed to "past achievements o Hindus in building empires, trade, and cities as counter-evidence to th notion that Hinduism was excessively other-worldly in its effects."[9] Bu

·lief in fate is important to mental health, for if a farmer loses his crop, a erchant his fortune, or a woman her health, they can invoke fate, and they ın similarly invoke it for a good crop, a profit windfall, or a pregnancy. he universe is not perceived as chaotic, but operates by natural laws.

atalism in Islam

The dichotomy between man and god—and thus the question of pre- stination by divine will—has been raised much more frequently in Islam an in the indigenous Indian religions. Allah is viewed as a distinct per- nality having a will. Hence in Pakistan villages one very frequently hears ention of the will of Allah. But the will is not unbendable, for prayers ould be said to Him five times daily, goat sacrifices are to be made at ecified festivals, and the ghosts of the pīrs (saints) are to be revered at eir tombs.

Muslim philosophers have eloquently wrestled with the question of ee will. A 17th-century Sunnī writer, 'Abdul Haqq, stated that to say all uman motions and actions are compulsory is to deny virtue. Creation is om God and action is of men. "The problem of divine power and ordina- on and the problem of man's choice" become known to one by the study f the Sharī'at (Qur'ānic law). "One must believe in both. In this matter ith in the middle way is necessary. . . . One has to act. The real truth f the matter is that which is with God."[10]

As Islam became superimposed over Buddhism and Hinduism, resig- ation to the will of Allah replaced to some extent, but was not more harsh han, belief in karma. Mysticism and devotionalism of Sūfī Islam negated he importance of involvement in things of the world, somewhat comparable o the bhakti cults in Hinduism, while at the same time devotional worship f the pīrs was an expression of the real belief that they could alter men's ircumstances. The five-times-daily prayers are more a matter of piety than means of succor.

Activism, in fact, was advocated by Iqbāl who wrote in the early 20th entury and is now regarded as Pakistan's national poet. Belief in finite time, e said, led to conceiving human action as temporal and perishable. But if ime is eternal, human action has lasting importance. He wrote of the Self:

> Subject, object, means, and causes—
> All these are the forms which it assumes for the purposes of action.
> The Self rises, kindles, falls, glows, and breathes,
> Burns, shines, walks, and flies.
> The spaciousness of time is its arena,
> Heaven is a billow of the dust on its road.
> From rose-planting the world abounds in roses;
> Night is born of its sleep, day springs from its taking.[11]

Dawn in a Pakistani Panjāb village. While others sleep, old man gets up to pray on prayer platform.

Honigmann describes the Paṭhāns of the North-West Frontier Province of Pakistan as oriented to achievement, success, proving oneself, and future goals. They also have a low frustration threshold and are dogmatic. In fact the tribal people of Balūchistān, and the people of Afghanistan, as well as to some extent Panjābīs, are thought to have these characteristics of personality. There is a certain self-assertion and compulsion, but this does not particularly lead to innovation. It is, of course, the males who are expected to exhibit self-assertion, which is part of their concept of honor. These personality traits decrease as one moves eastward through India to Bānglā. Villagers in Pakistan tend to think of things as either good or bad, dichotomies are clearer, and philosophies less relativistic than in India. These qualities are reflected in the international images of Pakistan and India. They explain the universal verbal allegiance to the principles of Islam in Pakistan villages and cities, and the frequent references to Allah, the scriptures, and Islamic principles. But rather than being bound by fate, people of the Panjāb—Muslims and Sikhs—are known for their vigor and entrepreneurship, and their region has had the fastest economic growth rate in South Asia.

Hindu Deities

Since deities are projected on the basis of values of human society, it is not surprising to find in South Asian religions several levels of deities whose hierarchy is analogous to the hierarchy of castes.

The apparent chaos of the Hindu pantheon is not an impediment to faith, since "the 330 million gods" can be progressively reduced to one or even to none. All deities, indeed all souls, are but emanations of the World Soul, Brahman, and thus deities are not at all mutually exclusive. Beals reports for a small village in Karṇāṭaka: "There is no sharp line of demarcation between gods, men, and animals." All are part of the single unity described as God, Brahman, or Paramahātmā (Supreme Great Soul). "God is all-inclusive as well as all-powerful and all-knowing." In the Sānkhya school of classical philosophy, which was an essentially atheistic school, even Brahman is reduced to self-consciousness or intelligence, as opposed to matter.

The high gods are those whose rituals are performed by Brāhmaṇs and who are mentioned in the Sanskrit texts. Some of them are of Vedic origin, such as Indra (originally a war god), Varuṇa (god of water), Vāyu (wind), Sūrya (sun), Candra (moon), Agni (fire), and Yama (death). These gods are referred to in Brāhmaṇical liturgy but seldom have temples or devotees and are scarcely ever represented as icons.

Most popular gods can be subsumed either under Vishṇu or Śiva. There is a bifurcation in Hinduism in that most gods are considered as incarnations or emanations of one or the other. People whose chief deities are linked with Vishṇu are called Vaishṇavites, and with Śiva, Śaivites. Each of these categories is exceedingly diffuse and can hardly be called a sect, but fertility symbols are more fundamentally Śaivite. The distinction between the two is more important to Brāhmaṇs and other high castes—who generally belong to one or the other—than to low castes. But even in a large temple whose chief deity is a Vaishṇavite one, for example, there may be small Śaivite deities or a Śivalinga.

Many of the gods originated as heroes of the epics, warriors, or kings, who in course of time became deified. Some of these common to Hinduism everywhere are the Vaishṇavite Rāma, Krishṇa, Balārama, and Vāsudeva, and the Śaivite Śiva, Subrahmanya, and Skanda. Brahmā is thought of in literature as a creative power but is not a popularly represented deity. All these have consorts or wives such as Lakshmī, wife of Vishṇu and goddess of fortune, or Sarasvatī, wife of Brahmā and patroness of learning. Rāma, hero of the epic *Rāmāyaṇa* and originally a tribal king in the Gangā area, sought for his consort Sītā. Krishṇa in his role as a youthful flute player attracted the cowgirls, of whom his favorite was Rādhā, with whom he sported. Some Hindu deities are derived from saints or Brāhmaṇs, such as Agastya and Paraśurāma, Brāhmaṇical heroes of the South, or Buddha, who is considered an incarnation of Vishṇu.

Some of the pan-Hindu deities are derived from animals. Gaṇeśa is the delightful and benevolent elephant-headed patron of business, whose image is kept in a little shrine inside shops. Hanuman is the monkey helper of Rāma. Other animals, such as the bull, peacock, or rat, are invariably linked

Mural in a Kēraḷa temple, late medieval. Krishṇa, in the form of an adorable youth, hung the clothes of the gopī cow-girls in a tree while they were bathing in the river.

The monkey-god Hanuman. In his hands are a mace and Sri Lanka, whither he went in the epic *Rāmāyaṇa* to vanquish a demon king and rescue Rāma's consort Sītā. During pūjā, a priest strews flowers, lights incense, and rings bell.

with particular deities who ride on them. The incarnations of Vishṇu include a fish, tortoise, boar, and man-lion. Some of these are doubtless derived from prehistoric totemic cults, and it is likely that most of the animals ridden by gods represent indigenous tribes or peoples defeated in early times, whose totems then became the vehicles for the hero-gods of the victorious people.

Another category of deities is the female aspect of strength and procreation, *śaktī*. These originated with the "mother goddess" cults represented by protohistoric terracotta figurines. Female goddesses take many forms, such as the benevolent Pārvatī, wife of Śiva, or the Gaurī, beloved of women because she is the deification of marriage. More ominous is Kālī, the bloodthirsty war goddess who stands on a corpse and wears a garland of skulls, demanding multiple goat sacrifices. Durgā is a mother aspect. These are pan-Hindu deities, but they have hundreds of thousands of emanations or aspects in the female deities in villages. Throughout the South every village has its protective mother-goddess. In Bānglā female deities are

very commonly venerated but in western India it is mostly the women who worship them, which is doubtless an expression of the more rigid patriarchy on the western side of South Asia.

There are many important regional deities. Śivājī, for instance, was the 18th-century founder of the Marāṭhā empire, and his likeness is now represented in temples throughout the Marāṭhī country, but he is not regarded as a deity in the Sanskrit literature. Aiyanār is a god who protects the Tamil countryside. Manasā is a goddess in Bānglā who protects from snakebites.

Sexual symbolism takes many forms, and male-female principles are symbolized by gods and their consorts. The most common procreative symbol is the linga, the phallus, which is an upright cylindrical stone often set in a *yonī*, the vagina symbol. Some temples have dozens of them, even hundreds, flanking the temple courtyard. The linga complements the warrior aspect of Śiva's personality, and its veneration goes back to the Indus Civilization.

But in half a million predominantly Hindu villages people may pay more attention to local godlings and spirits than to the pan-Hindu deities. A village may have several, or even several score, spots considered sacred, marked with a boulder or a post or a mud pyramid sometimes whitewashed. A godling may be some warrior hero of the village little tradition, the village boundary deity, or the local version of the smallpox goddess. Or a sacred spot may be the place where someone died under unusual circumstances or had a vision. McKim Marriott found that in a village in the Doāb in the Gangā plains there were 90 deities. These, he said, could be divided into three levels. Of them 30 were recognizable as gods of the great pantheon, whereas 60 had not been integrated into the Sanskritic tradition. Of these 60 a dozen were regional deities mentioned in Hindī literature, having important cults and temples. Nearly half the deities in the village were not mentioned in any literature, though some were known in other villages nearby. Surprisingly, even among Brāhmaṇs, gods mentioned in Sanskrit literature comprised only 45% of the deities they worshiped. And among low castes only 15% of their deities were Sanskritic ones. This shows the extent to which Sanskritization is an ongoing process, even in the heartland of classical Hinduism.

The multiplicity of deities does not bother most villagers; thoughtful ones often volunteer the opinion that they are all the same anyway. They are a chain whose links are rebirth. But Hindu society, being a truly pluralistic society, provides scope in this manner for expression of differences of region, locality, caste, occupation, clan, or family; individuals also become devotees of particular deities. Each segment of society, therefore, expresses its uniqueness in the deities it venerates, and the deities deify the legends or traditions supporting the individuality of each region, village, caste, or lineage.

Demons, Ghosts, and Spirits

Nāgas seem to have originally been a trading people on the coast of Sindh or Gujarāt who had cities and palaces and who traded in gems—if we can interpolate from the legendary literature—but they were enemies of the "Āryans." By the process of dynastic drift there came to be a Nāga kingdom in early Sri Lanka, another in Rājasthān, and yet another in the middle Gangā region. The name somehow came to be applied to the Nāgas of Nāgaland who in fact had no historic connection with any of these. Nāgas transmuted to water deities mentioned in early Buddhist literature as living in the ocean and on islands. These then became confused with snakes, also called *nāgas.* In the courtyard of a village temple there may be dozens of nāga stone images, cobras with hoods spread, set up under trees and occasionally anointed with oil. The nāga is a sexual image because the snake is reminiscent of the phallus. It is also a general fertility symbol because in mythology nāgas are associated with water. Women wishing to become pregnant may circumambulate a hundred times a sacred tree having nāga images under it. Nāgas are represented in folktales as heroic deities, perhaps with a jewel, which symbolized wealth and wisdom, set in the forehead. The snake in general, and especially the cobra, is also a symbol of evil power, and should be placated by calling it "good snake" when encountered on a path. The cobra is sculpted as Vishṇu's couch, and the skin hood around its neck which expands when it gets excited forms a canopy over the reclining deity. The same imagery has been transferred to statues of Buddha. If one asks half a dozen villagers what nāgas symbolize, one will get as many answers, and all will be right.

Ghosts (souls of the dead) will become malevolent *bhūtas* which wander about and harm people unless funeral ceremonies are properly performed. Brāhmaṇs and other orthodox Hindus perform the *śrāddha* ceremony for 10 days after death, offering up rice balls for the ghost to eat, and libations of water. After that time the ghost is reborn or takes on a "subtle body" to enter the afterlife. Śrāddha is performed on the anniversary of death for several years. In ancient times this ceremony had the function of preserving family unity as relatives participated. Throughout India today the eldest son should light the funeral pyre (hence the pressure on women to bear sons), or at least another male relative should do so. Veneration of ancestors also preserved cultural continuity, as it did in China. Some people who have clans, such as Rājpūts, venerate a clan ancestor. Doubtless, ancestor worship made an important contribution to the development of the doctrine of karma and rebirth.

Bhūtas are particularly harmful to relatives of the dead, a belief which encourages performance of the śrāddha ceremony. In Bānglā, bhūtas of Brāhmaṇs live in fig trees and break the necks of those why try to climb

up without doing obeisance. Bhūtas of lower caste people are black and tall and wander about the fields looking for women to possess. In Karṇāṭaka, hero stones abound, raised in honor of those who died in battle or by violence. Among Hindus anyone who dies in an unusual way is likely to become a bhūta, and may be buried instead of cremated. Ghosts are angered if their bodies' deaths are brought about by childbirth, murder, suicide, smallpox, or mauling by a tiger. One dying with an unfulfilled wish, or an unmarried woman, or a man who never had sexual experience may become a miserable and malevolent bhūta. Instances have been noted of causing a corpse to be married to a tree or of paying some unfortunate fellow to have intercourse with a female corpse.

Dube, in writing about a village near Hyderābād in Āndhra, says about 40 ghosts were feared. Some had been tamed, but people avoided a large hillock inhabited by the ghost of a woman who died in childbirth. A woman who killed herself jumping into a well became a ghost and was driven from the village, but came back. The worst ghost was that of an agriculturalist of the Reḍḍi caste, who dwelt in the east side of the village. People hesitated to go "to his place" at midday, dusk, or late at night. A young Muslim who died without sexual experience left a ghost who molested many young women.

Almost everywhere it is important for pregnant women to avoid inauspicious things or the haunts of ghosts. Kashmīr Brāhmaṇ women, for instance, should not see an eclipse or a malformed child and should not frequent old trees, creeks, graves, or cremation grounds where ghosts might hang out.

Innumerable crude stones set up by the wayside or under trees are cared for by non-Brāhmaṇ priests, who anoint and garland them. An unusual boulder, a rocky knoll, a large tree, or a crossing of two paths is likely to be the residence of some godling, ghost, or spirit.

Muslims also fear jins and revere ghosts. They everywhere use amulets as charms, and illness is believed to be due to evil forces. In Bangladesh when people are possessed by jins, they may quiver and shake. The jin "mixes with the blood" and the person so affected may have special power. People may call the *mullā* (prayer leader) to exorcise it.

A pīr, or Muslim saint, upon death becomes a benevolent ghost, worshipped with an annual ceremony which may be the most important of the year to sectarian members. They may collect money for it in a mammoth pot placed on the street corner and surrounded with colored paper flags. In Pakistan an annual procession to a tomb may be led by a troupe of drummers and prancing male dancers festooned with colorful pantaloons and tinkling anklets, while the faithful come in train carrying banners and large decorations. A saint's reputation may grow after death; the author once saw a Muslim grave 30 feet long, designed to show how great and tall was the saint!

The Evil Eye

Fear of the evil eye is ubiquitous among people of all religions in South Asia. Essentially, this is a fear of jealousy, a nagging suspicion that someone was envious and therefore set about to do one in. It ranges throughout the Near East and up to Spain. Some people in India and Pakistan believe that every eye is potentially able to cast an evil spell, while others suspect only certain persons, perhaps old women. Some think the caster of the evil eye can be found out because of repeated occurrences, but others are not so sure. In general this does not lead to witch hunts. One who is sick and suspects an evil eye as the cause thinks he may be cured if a friend follows local curative practices, such as waving salt or red chilies or a lime over the afflicted one. Though conscious fear of the evil eye is phasing out among the urbane and the educated, some associated practices still remain.

All over South Asia, babies may be seen with spots of lampblack on their temples or cheeks to give the appearance of being disfigured so nobody will be too envious of the nice plump and smiling baby. Perhaps the black spot applied on the forehead originally had the same function (though people now say it is for beauty), or it might have distracted anyone who tried to put a spell on a person by looking into his eye. The Bhīls, a large Gujarātī-speaking tribe, put lampblack on their ear lobes as well as on the forehead; the Nāyakās, another Gujarāt tribe, wear a bead necklace or leather cord to avert the evil eye.

Visitors to South Asia, especially to India, have sometimes commented that eating there is not a time for convivial talk. High caste people prefer to eat in their homes, which are protected from evil and polluting influences, and outsiders are not allowed in the kitchens. Common laborers can be seen having their lunch, individually squatting down facing a wall or at least facing away from the gang, gulping their rice. Tribal people in Gujarāt may sit in different corners of the house to eat. At feasts village people do sit in rows, but generally eat quickly without chattering much. The idea is to have as few people as possible see one's food and to have it exposed to strangers as little as possible. Many people who no longer believe in the evil eye nevertheless feel more comfortable if they dine in private.

A housewife in Pakistan gets up in the morning to churn the milk; fearing that someone might be envious of the large pot full of creamy buffalo milk and affect it so that her family gets sick, she ties a black ribbon to the churn. Her son goes to Peshāwar to try his luck at driving a motor ricksha; since it is enviably painted with floral designs in 10 colors, he disfigures it by tying a black ribbon to the windshield wiper. A man in Bangladesh, having recently built a house, puts a potsherd painted with

white spots on the thatch above the doorway. The same Muslim farmer in Bangladesh, or one in Karṇāṭaka, seeing he has a luxuriant crop coming and fearing some envious person will cause it to be diseased, places a pot upside down on a stake driven into the field and paints white dots over the upturned black bottom of the pot. A farmer in the Gangā plain owns a nice cow that is about to freshen; he ties colored strings around her horns and legs to distract any evil influence so she will not get sick.

In a village in Rājasthān, according to Minturn and Hitchcock, people believe that a handsome baby, or any handsome person, is especially susceptible. Rājpūt mothers in the village are warned not to dress their children too well or too often. One must not praise a child by saying that it is pretty or exceptionally strong or healthy. In such a situation, an American visitor complimenting or praising a child would cause panic rather than pride. Among these Rājpūts even during birth ceremonies the baby remains wrapped up, so no visitor makes an attempt to see it.

In Hinduism there is a parallel between such malevolent forces as the evil eye and evil spirits, and untouchables, who are not only ritually impure but are surrounded by impurity. But the high gods are benign and are served with pure foods by pure Brāhmaṇs. In the Rājasthān village mentioned above, mothers believe that one who has at some time eaten feces is likely to have the evil eye, so they are careful to keep feces away from their babies' faces; this highlights the analogy between impurity, ritual impurity, and malevolent power.

It is also likely that the lack of freely expressed personal compliments,

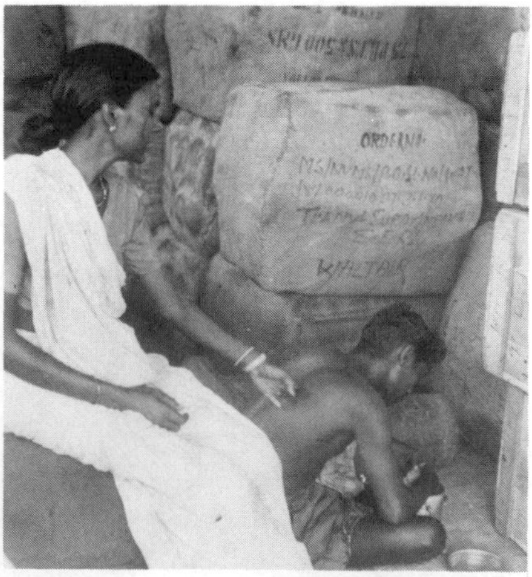

A railway coolie in Āndhra eats facing a corner, a habit originating with need to protect food from evil eyes. Wife warns him picture is being taken.

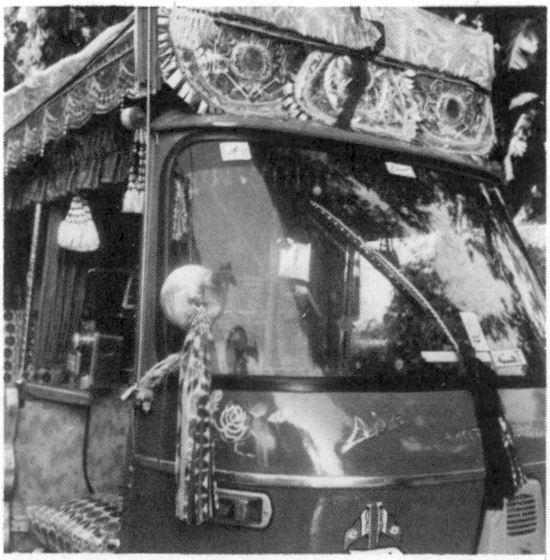

Gaily painted motor ricksha in Peshāwar, Pakistan. Muslim driver tied black ribbons on to avert evil eye.

which some American visitors to South Asia wonder at, is due partly to a deep-seated fear of the consequences of such compliments. But this is also functional, for it religiously reinforces the belief that if people, especially children, are complimented much they will become proud.

Religious Practitioners: Priests

The gods of Hindu literature reside in idols in the inner sanctums of temples. They have about them, to use Edward Harper's phrase, a field of purity. Only Brāhmaṇs can enter the inner sanctum, for they are likewise pure. Flanking the doorway of the temple to a high god will be two guardian godlings in stone or wood, commissioned to keep out of the pure temple all malevolent spirits. Around the temple courtyard is a wall, and until the 1930s untouchables could not come within it, for they carry around themselves a field of impurity. According to traditional standards people who worship in temples of major deities should be of clean caste, ritually purified before they enter. Brāhmaṇ priests, who serve the gods, are the most pure people by birth and must continually perform ablutions to remove from themselves any taint of impurity. Brāhmaṇs should not touch a plow lest they injure Mother Earth and impugn themselves by killing living creatures. They generally will not do manual work. In South India, Brāhmaṇs, who form 3% or 4% of the population, have traditionally remained quite dis tinct from non-Brāhmaṇs, but in Uttar Pradesh where they are numerous, or in Haryāṇā where they are less powerful than landowning cultivating castes, they do sometimes engage in manual work. Brāhmaṇs who do not serve as priests today often become educated, work as clerks, enter professions, or open restaurants. Besides those who serve as priests, others are gurūs (teachers), *purohitas* (family chaplains), or astrologers.

The chief duty of the temple priest is to perform pūjā, the morning and evening service to the icon in the inner sanctum of the temple. The priest washes his Lord, perfumes, dresses, and garlands Him, and offers up foods considered to be pure such as bananas, coconuts, or milk. Lamps are lit and incense is wafted. Devotees pass by in a row, and in Śaivite temples they are given some cow dung ash, which they smear on their foreheads, and are sprinkled with a little "Gangā water." These priests also serve the lesser gods in the temple and preside at the annual festival of the temple deity.

The word *pūjā* is of Dravidian origin and the offering of fruits and flowers was not part of Vedic religion. In fact, most of the priestly practices of Brāhmaṇs, as also their ablutions to maintain ritual purity, were assimilated into Hinduism from pre-Āryan practices. Brāhmaṇs do not serve as priests for low castes or tribals, and indeed many village shrines and temples are served by non-Brāhmaṇ priestly castes or part-time priests.

Brāhman priest completes pūjā in Karṇāṭaka temple; having dressed the god, he opened curtain. Forehead mark shows priest is a Vaishṇavite.

Warrior godling in a fort in Rājasthān. A passing devotee burns incense.

Gods of untouchables are served by certain of themselves who act as priests. A man may dream that a deity resides in a stone of a certain size and shape on a hill and wishes him to serve it. The man will search for the stone, and finding it, bring it to his village and construct a small shrine. He will then serve as priest there, and possibly his son after him. The pūjā ceremony is performed on all icons, but on the lesser ones it may be only weekly or yearly, and may not involve dressing the deity. Brāhmaṇs and high caste or orthodox Hindus often also have worship at home, before a shrine or picture at which the man (or in South India women or children) may do daily pūjā after the morning bath. In such a case a person acts as his own priest.

Brāhmaṇs who are attached to certain families perform rituals for them, especially those marking the several stages of life. They are called upon to name children, initiate boys of high castes with the sacred thread ceremony (those who wear it are known as twice-born), conduct puberty ceremonies for girls, and perform funerary rites. Marriage is the most important ceremony. In one conducted by a Brāhmaṇ he will tend the ritual fire, pouring *ghī* (liquid clarified butter) over it while the couple circumambulates, and will chant Sanskrit *mantras* (sacred and powerful verses).

Not all Brāhmaṇs serve as priests, indeed the majority of Brāhmaṇ castes are not priestly. But those who are priests are traditionally supported within a complex economic system of exchange of goods and services which has been termed the *jajmānī* system, wherein landowners and people of means provide goods for services rendered. Such families will have Brāhmaṇ purohitas or chaplains attached to them who will provide any needed services in return for a yearly quantum of grain and other provisions. Brāhmaṇs attached to temples are supported by the income from the temple lands. In times past kings and chiefs were served by purohitas who had a political function in legitimizing the authority of their clients by fabricating genealogies, reading horoscopes, and performing little-understood rituals shrouded in mystique. In return Brāhmaṇs were given lands and grants (sometimes recorded on copper plates), and were settled in villages in the king's territory. In this way Brāhmaṇs came to own a large percentage of the cultivated land in parts of India. In village life the real basis of Brāhmaṇ authority has been economic more than ritual.

One gains merit by giving pure foods or nonpollutable gifts such as land, money, or cows to Brāhmaṇs. The subject of the cow is an intriguing one to Westerners, and there have been several factors causing the elevated status of this animal. In Āryan society milk products were important so their use—such as the pouring of ghī over fire and milk over icons—became widespread in Brāhmaṇical ritual. Cows came to be valued by Brāhmaṇs for these products and for curds, which vegetarians eat for protein. These products are thought to be pure and "cooling," in the sense of a hot-cold medicinal dichotomy. In the Indus Civilization and in Śaivite cults it is the

bull that is valued. The cow and bull are fundamental to Indian peasant economy, the bull plowing, irrigating, drawing carts, threshing, and so on, and the cow providing valued products. The cow came to be the unit of currency, the most important type of movable property, in early historic times. Hence because of its intrinsic and symbolic value the giving of a cow to a Brāhmaṇ came to be regarded as a meritorious act. This attitude has been reinforced by the application of the principle of ahimsā, so that the killing of cows was particularly sinful. Only very low caste Hindus eat beef, and in a number of Indian states cow slaughter is forbidden. Some pious businessmen have established old cow homes. But India has many cattle because they are economically necessary and most of the cows one sees in city streets eating stray leaves and straw belong to people. With monetization the giving of cows to Brāhmaṇs as payment has ceased.

Hindu society has charged Brāhmaṇs with preservation of the Great Tradition. They cannot innovate. Their elaborate rituals are prescribed; their prayers and mantras are recited from memory. The most important qualification of a Brāhmaṇ priest is his purity, not his spirituality. By maintaining orthodoxy he ensures continuity of the social order. By performing rituals and servicing the gods he ensures continuity of the cosmic order.

Other Religious Practitioners

Low castes and untouchables are generally not served by Brāhmaṇs, who wish to avoid the effect of their pollution; these groups have their own priests, as do many of the intermediate castes and tribals. To many villagers the non-Brāhmaṇ priests are the only priests they need, for these service village godlings and the scores of village shrines with short pūjā ceremonies; they anoint crude sacred stones with oil and drape them with garlands and conduct the annual ceremonies. There are also caste priests who perform puberty, marriage, and funerary ceremonies. Such people may live by farming or labor.

The barber is an important figure in India and Pakistan. He handles such ritually unclean things as hair and fingernail parings and may also perform minor surgery. His wife serves as midwife. In Muslim regions the barber performs the important circumcision ceremony. In the South barbers serve as funeral priests and thus have lower ritual status than in the North where they do not. But barbers may also have power because they say mantras to heal people and cure snakebite. In some areas other occupational groups such as washermen and goldsmiths have priestly functions.

Astrologers may be Brāhmaṇs or non-Brāhmaṇs, as the client chooses. They read horoscopes before marriage and pick auspicious times to initiate important events. If a journey is to be commenced, a well dug, a store

A chapel in Gujarāt maintained by merchant families who follow a certain gurū. He may come once a year and sit on the dais; his picture is garlanded. Sect members come daily or weekly to meditate.

A group of sādhus and pilgrims camp overnight under a tree in a temple courtyard in Jammū. They are en route to an annual festival in the Himālayas of Kashmīr; they hail from five states. In such a circumstance caste is irrelevant.

opened, a car remodeled, or a foundation laid for a house or modern factory, work must commence on a lucky day and time lest the project come to naught.

The gurū has been an important figure in Hindu society. Many Hindu families are followers of a particular gurū, forming in effect a sect. The gurū's picture hangs on the wall. A well-known gurū may have a widespread clientele of people who hardly ever see him but acknowledge him as their spiritual preceptor, or he may make annual visits. In the past, gurūs were teachers of the young. A boy was educated by being attached to a particular gurū, serving him in his house in return for instruction, or the gurū would visit the boy at home while making regular rounds. The proliferation of public education has reduced the function of gurūs as educators, though as spiritual preceptors they still play an important role.

Hindu *sādhus* are numerous, as anyone knows who has been to India. There are some 5 million of them, mostly wandering about as holy beggars, identifiable by their ochre-colored robes. The anthropologist Agehananda Bharati, an Austrian who joined an Indian order of monks, has vividly described them from the inside in *The Ochre Robe*; he asserts that 90% of them are not sincere, but pretend piety to earn a living. Still, many Indians feel a compunction to put something into the begging bowl, for this is dharma. Some sādhus are men who have raised families but have followed the traditional injunction that in later life one should renounce carnal attachments and turn to spiritual things. Jain holy mendicants wear

white robes and cover their mouths with gauze to avoid inhaling insects. They are particularly supported by Baniyās (merchants), whose way of life is moneymaking and who should be tempered by dharma.

Buddhist monks form a brotherhood, the *sangha*, and this is one of the three central "jewels" of the faith, the other two being Buddha and dharma. Buddhism was originally a religion of monks, initiated by donning the ochre robe, shaving their heads, taking vows of poverty, celibacy, and ahimsā, and avoiding beds, garlands, jewelry, dancing, and singing. Though Theravāda monks were to own nothing but their begging bowls, after Buddhism became established as a religion of states, they began to receive property in the name of their monasteries and came to be quite prosperous during the apogee of Buddhism in India. In Sri Lanka today monks enjoy deference and are given privileges by the government, such as reserved compartments in trains; they also exert considerable political and moral influence on the Sri Lanka government.

South Asian culture is characterized by the polarization of what we may call the formal and the informal: Brāhmaṇs versus sādhus, ritual versus spirituality, establishment versus nonestablishment, wealth versus asceticism. Inevitably, the antiritual, antiestablishment social elements in time come to evolve their own rituals and establishments, exemplified by sādhu orders and the Buddhist clergy.

Shamans

A shaman—devotee of a deity who can draw upon and utilize his power—has authority based not on orthodoxy or piety as does the Brāhmaṇ priest, but on his spiritual capacity. Such are more important to most villagers than are Brāhmaṇs. The shaman has direct contact with the particular deity he represents, speaks as his mouthpiece, acts as his agent, and manifests his power. Anyone may become a shaman—sex or caste makes little difference. Sometimes older women become shamans to regain usefulness and prestige. Some shamans acquire their power at one stroke, while others undergo a long period of training including continence, bathing in sacred rivers, and uttering incantations. Shamans may also serve as exorcists, oracles, healers, or priests at local shrines. They may lose self-control as they are possessed by their deities and attain a state of trance, but this never occurs involuntarily.

Gerald Berreman has described shamans in the Pahāṛī-speaking region in the foothills of northern Uttar Pradesh. To become a shaman, one must compete with other such practitioners and acquire a reputation, which depends on competence to achieve the appropriate psychological state and represent the particular deity in a convincing manner. When a client comes, the shaman begins a ceremony in honor of the deity, singing and drumming,

until gradually the deity takes possession of him and he begins to twitch or dance. When the spirit is in control, he diagnoses the problem of the client and gives appropriate advice, which usually includes a recommendation that he hold a ceremony to worship the offended deity. But if the cause of the trouble is a ghost rather than a deity, the shaman will identify what ghost it is so the client will know what kind of exorcist will be appropriate. In the North Indian plains the shaman himself will consult the deity, acting as intermediary and making known its demands.

A shaman in Tamil̠ Nāḍu is the chief devotee of one of the village godlings, and acts for it. Though at other times a common villager, at the annual festival of that deity, he will dance in the street before its temple, attain a state of "possession" while swirling a bunch of *nīm* (margosa) leaves, and flit about uncontrollably inside a circle of onlookers. Others who have made vows to that deity or especially revere it may dance with him. After regaining self-control, he will bless some of the onlookers by putting sandal paste on their foreheads. They can then, or at a later time in his house, tell the shaman their problems. Often he will prescribe that a vow be taken, which means that the client promises to perform some ceremony after his need is met. If he is sick, the shaman may tell him to vow to raise a goat and sacrifice it to the same deity at the following year's festival. (If he does not get well in the meantime, he is absolved from the vow.) Or it may be a vow to sacrifice a chicken, or have clay images of the god made for the next year's festival, or ceremoniously go with musicians to carry a pot of milk to the high god in an important nearby temple whose chief deity is an aspect or incarnation of the shaman's deity, or to vow to fire-walk (if it is the fire god speaking through the shaman). When the shaman speaks he may turn up his eyes so that pupils are hidden, or speak with an unnatural voice, or quiver.

In such a Tamil̠ village, besides those serving as shamans at the annual festivals of the various deities, there are others who are able to attain the state of trance weekly, or twice weekly on the special days of their patron deity. Such shamans have reputations as being able to handle certain kinds of problems. One may have a specialty in helping barren women, for instance, and on every Thursday afternoon he will be visited by 50 people including 20 barren women from surrounding villages. After doing pūjā to his patron deity he will call them one by one and read their prognosis in ashes in a winnowing fan on his lap. He may occasionally go into a trance, and the barren women may also lose self-conscious control, weaving around and wailing for a time. He may instruct them to do certain things, such as to keep visiting him regularly for a number of months. He may earn his living at this work.

Shamans use a great variety of techniques to convince people of their ability to get the deity's help. In Himāchal Pradesh he may inhale cedar

smoke and thus purify himself. A Muṇḍa tribal shaman may consult grains of rice laid out on leaves. A shaman in the South may throw down 10 cowrie shells as if they were dice and read them. The kinds of problems people have are similar everywhere, and the majority have to do with illness. People ask: "Where is my lost buffalo?" "I have dug a dry well; where can I dig with success?" "Who stole my areca nuts?" "How can my cow be cured?" "How can I get my wife back?" "How can I get rid of insects in the cattle shed?" "What should I do to get a job?" "Will you cure my girl of fever?" Since a shaman is a master of practical psychology he often gives an evasive answer without seeming to. Or he asks that a vow be fulfilled some time after the need is met, or defers giving a reply until a ceremony is performed, by which time the problem might resolve itself.

Yet most villagers will visit a shaman or healer in case of illness or snakebite before they will visit a government hospital, going there only if all else fails. Of course some feel that certain shamans are frauds, but practically none doubt that there are villagers who can draw on the power of a deity. Brāhmaṇs do not approve of shamanism, saying spirit dancing and fire-walking are frauds—and with good reason, for the whole matter is beyond their control. But for most villagers these manifestations of the power of local deities is the fundamental reason they believe in them, they say. Because of this they give generously to support the shrines and for the annual festivals. It is the power of the local village deities, thus manifest, that solves their problems.

Himālayan Buddhist Religious Practitioners

In Northern Buddhism the priests are *lāmas* whose training is in the tradition of Tibetan civilization. Though there are different sects, the monastery at Lhāsa grew to be dominant, and its Dalai Lāma was in effect head of the state system until in 1959 the current one had to flee Tibet. As the Chinese invaders shelled the chief monastery at Lhāsa, he disguised himself, fled out a rear entrance, and reached India after a 10-day trip surreptitiously helped along by the local peasantry. Now he and his ministers maintain a Tibetan government in exile in the Himālayan town of Dharmaśālā. Little is known of the condition of Buddhism in Tibet since the Chinese marched in and annexed the region. But the monasteries in Bhutan, Sikkim, the higher ranges of Nepal, and parts of India such as Ladākh and the northern regions of Himāchal Pradesh and Kumāon, are still strongly dominant institutions, and a high percentage of men become monks. The social hierarchy of lāmas provides a strong model for emulation because monasteries own considerable land and monks in general are an exploiting class. Social mobility by imitation of Lāmaistic practices is analogous to

Sanskritization in India. Also, like Brāhmaṇs, lāmas acquire their status by learning orthodoxy and not by inspiration. Lāmaism is supported by a huge body of scripture, liturgy, theology, and the political interconnection of the monasteries.

Lāmaism from Tibet was brought to Sikkim by the Bhoṭiyās (Tibetans) in the 17th century, and the Lepchas of that tiny country have been caught up in the Mahāyāna Great Tradition. Lāmaism brought to the Lepchas a long list of sins, the worst of which is killing animals (though conveniently leeches and mosquitos are said to have no souls!), which also supports the local hierarchy because only lāmas can avoid most of the deeds called sins.

Geoffrey Gorer's study of the Lepchas shows that Buddhism was superimposed on an indigenous religion which he called Mun, and that had been superimposed on a still earlier cult of "people of Mayel." The latter is primarily a grain fertility cult, and its rituals contain elements quite at variance with Lepcha behavior, such as discrimination against women for menstruation and insistence on virginity of some of the celebrants. This earlier cult has now been merged into Mun. Mun, in some ways similar to the pre-Buddhist Tibetan Bon religion, has in Sikkim been raised to the level of an organized religion by copious validating mythology and theology. Mun shamans serve as priests too, and must be present at the rites of passage of every Lepcha.

Gorer recounts the feelings of a Mun priest-shaman at a biannual ceremony attended by many sacrifices at which a large vessel gets spirit-possessed and the power of the deity comes on the priest.

> The day before the sacrifices I start feeling ill; I feel heavy and pressed down and cannot bear any noise; I tremble constantly and am covered with sweat. I pray to the gods to let me off and I offer them incense in preparation for them to wait for the true sacrifices. The next day the ceremony is held inside a house and many people are present. I sit down cross-legged in front of the offerings. I feel as though a heavy burden were pressing over my shoulders and as if my flesh were being poked with sticks—zinga—zinga—zinga—zinga—; suddenly a sort of darkness comes over my eyes, it is as if I was in a dream so that I know, see, and remember nothing; I put on the flower necklace [which nobody else can wear] and walk outside in the courtyard. When I return everybody is hushed, even the children. I blow into each person's face and on the offerings; then I scatter [millet beer] and prophesy in a loud and audible voice the things which are going to take place in the following half-year. After the prophecy I recover consciousness but not till the cock-crow the next day do I feel all right again.[12]

The Mun priest-shamans and the lāmas are not exclusive. "In by far the greater number of ceremonies for private individuals, Mun and lāmas perform simultaneously contradictory rites for identical ends, with Mun usually in the 'kitchen' and the lāmas in the 'parlor'." Though its relationship here is different, shamanism is as fundamental to Himālayan Buddhism as it is to village Hinduism.

Muslim Religious Practitioners

Islamic doctrine states that a priest as intermediary between Allah and man is not necessary, and neither are hoary and elaborate rituals such as Brāhmaṇs practice. But the *ulamā*, a scholar of Islamic scriptures, and the *maulvī*, a religious teacher, are respected because they answer theological and legal questions. In a village the religious functionary is the mullā, a lesser teacher, or the *imām*, leader of congregational prayers. Such a person in effect serves as priest; he manages the mosque, delivers Friday sermons, leads the congregation in prayers, officiates at Ramazān (Ramaḍān) and other special days, and tenders ethical advice. He operates the mosque school and teaches Arabic so people can read the Qur'ān, and interprets Muslim law. He or his wife may also teach Arabic to the girls. The imām also serves the family, for instance by validating a marriage by asking the groom's guardian three times if he accepts the bride, or by reciting the Qur'ān near the corpse at a funeral.

Pakistan ex-President Ayub Khan talking with ulamā (scholars) of various schools of thought who have come "to felicitate him on giving a workable and democratic Constitution suited to the genius of the people and in consonance with the ideology of Islam."

Imāms have traditionally held considerable influence over political and cultural affairs at the local level in Pakistan and Bangladesh, but within this century their influence has waned. One reason is that the type of education they impart is deemed less relevant for these times. Moreover, their sermons generally stress the punitive aspects of Islam and their tone is reactionary. Like the Brāhmaṇ, the imām has a place in the traditional jajmānī system of economic reciprocity, receiving a portion of the produce, say one fifteenth, in addition to fees from his students and remuneration for special services.

South Asian people's deep-seated need for personified spiritual power is satisfied in Islam by veneration of pīrs. A pīr is a saint who because of his holiness is intermediary between the Creator and man, and is a spiritual teacher; "pīr" is from Persian and means "guide." A pīr can grant wishes, and by a prayer or touch can remove difficulties. He can perform miracles, and may be exempt from some ordinary Islamic mores. He thus combines some of the functions of shamans, sādhus, and gurus for Hindus. A few such holy people are born in every generation, and anyone who manifests these qualities can become a pīr regardless of caste or class, though it is true that most often pīrs are Sayyids (a fictitious lineage claiming descent from the Prophet). Descendants of pīrs tend to form distinct endogamous lineages.

The arrival of a pīr in a Panjābī village in Pakistan has been described by Zekiya Eglar. The pīr comes once a year, though some families have their own pīrs whom they consult whenever they feel a need. When it is known that the pīr will visit the village, men and boys whitewash the mosque, clean the yard in front, and plant bushes along the path leading to the mosque. They stretch paper streamers across the compound and set a big armchair and table on the veranda of the mosque. In the late afternoon when the pīr and his retinue approach, they are met at the edge of the village and escorted to the house of one of the pīr's disciples. The guests are provided with fruits, raisins, and sweets. The leftovers are distributed in the village, for they have contracted edification by association with the pīr and bring blessings when eaten. Then the pīr goes to the mosque.

> In the courtyard, where mats are spread for them, and outside the walls of the mosque, the men crowd; among them are men from neighboring villages. Women and children sit crowded together on the roofs of the houses overlooking the mosque. One of the men who came with the *pir* beautifully chants religious songs in which are described the life and death of the Prophet. Then the *pir* explains to the people the meaning of various aspects of religion. He usually speaks forcefully and effectively so that the people are deeply stirred. Some of the men in the mosque sob; the women weep. The sermon and the chanting last well into the night. The children, feeling miserable, fall asleep on the cots outside, but their mothers are too much moved to attend to them.
>
> On the following morning breakfast is prepared for the *pir* by a family other than the one which entertained him for the evening, for it is a great privilege to

do so. After breakfast, people call on the *pir* and bring him presents of money, grain, or cotton blankets. Then the *pir* and his followers leave the village.[13]

Almost every village has the tomb of some pīr. At the anniversary of the death of a pīr a celebration is organized which serves to preserve the fellowship of his descendants and disciples who bring gifts for the caretaker of the tomb. A feast is provided by the descendants of the pīr. People directly beseech the ghost of a pīr, which in effect becomes a deity. Indeed, the countryside is dotted with tombs which have become shrines.

There are many sects in Islam. Most South Asian Muslims are Sunnīs, who claim to be orthodox, but some also are adherents of the other main school, Shī'ā, centered in Iran. Within these there are sects such as the Isma'īlī, which began in Sindh in the 10th century and now is an urban Shī'ā sect under the leadership of the Āga Khān. The Qadiyānī sect was founded in 1889 by a scholar who claimed that he had new revelations. The followers of each pīr form a sect, and some of these have become large movements.

In many villages there are devotees of a pīr or other worthy who live at his tomb and care for it. They live by charity in many cases. There are many other religious practices not enjoined in the Muslim scriptures. Mullās upon request provide charms, often little silver cylinders tied around the neck, arm, or leg of the afflicted person. In Pakistan and Bangladesh as well as in India this is common, but whereas Muslims insert scraps of paper with verses from the Qur'ān in the charms, Hindu healers insert magic diagrams. Or a black string may be tied onto the patient, accompanied by recitation of Muslim or Hindu mantras, as the case may be. The mullā may be called upon to dispel jins which cause fainting spells or bring misfortune to young women, and may function similar to a Hindu exorcist or healer. There are also Muslims who serve as shamans and attain a state of trance. Belief in the evil eye is widespread, and its effect can be dissipated by a verse from the Qur'ān.

Festivals and Calendars

In every village there are numerous calendrical festivals, one for each deity important in the village. But not all will be celebrated by all the people in the village. Let us note the inventory of festivals in four villages in different parts of India.

A village near Delhi studied by Lewis has 20 festivals; six are annual festivals of deities, three for change of seasons, two for purification, and one each for fertility, tying on of charms, a local ghost, and honoring husbands, children, and ancestors; two other major festivals are Divālī, associated with lamps and cattle here, and Holī, when bonfires are lit and social roles reversed; in addition there is a monthly celebration of the moonless night.

In a village 100 miles to the east on the Gangā plains, Marriott found 19 annual festivals. Of these 15 are mentioned in at least some Sanskrit text and four are not. Some are nearly India-wide such as Divālī, Holī, Daśahra, and Śiv Rātrī (Śiva's Night); others such as those in honor of cattle, leftover food, and regional deities are celebrated only in the Hindī region or even in a small part of Uttar Pradesh; yet others are peculiar to this village such as those honoring a well godling and a local ghost. While the majority of festivals are linked with the Great Tradition they all incorporate some indigenous practices and "explanations."

In a village in the Himālayan zone of Uttar Pradesh, Berreman found only 12 festivals. Three of them are not connected with wider traditions. Of the remaining nine, two are given only lip service while another is celebrated differently than on the plains. Two festivals celebrated throughout North India, Holī and Daśahra, are ignored here.

A village in western Āndhra studied by Dube has 23 annual festivals celebrated by Hindus, plus seven Muslim ones. Of the Hindu festivals, three are unique to this village and the rest either regional or widespread. Seven of these are limited to Brāhmaṇs and other high castes in the village, while such people participate with noticeable lack of enthusiasm in festivals of village godlings. Hindu festivals are held according to phases of the moon as dictated by astrologers, but Muslim celebrations are held according to the Muslim calendar.

At such times a village comes to life. Paper streamers and extra lights are hung; people take off from work and prepare feasts. A deity annually honored will be taken from the temple, or a separate icon of him will be taken and carried around the village in a highly decorated palanquin or in a temple cart. In villages the expenses of such festivals are raised by levying a tax on every household, but larger temples have land endowments. Major temples draw thousands, even hundreds of thousands of people for their annual festivals. Even for lesser periodic festivals, a family may come to a large temple, do pūjā, then spread out leaves for eating in the temple courtyard and enjoy a family picnic. At shrines high in the Himālayas or in other mountains thousands of people worship at the annual festivals, having endured a difficult trek preceded by days of purificatory rites. (In the companion volume Obeyesekere describes a pilgrimage in Sri Lanka.) People from small and poor villages will attempt to participate in such pilgrimages on occasion; nowadays they may go by train or chartered bus.

The agricultural and festival cycles provide all the chronology necessary for most peasants, who in premodern times often did not know their own ages. The continuity of all life, the endless chain of rebirths—these obviated the need for any specific creation date or any fixed point in history, so the chronological approach to history was notably weak in Indian civilization. If a visitor at a temple encounters a local peasant and asks when the structure was built, he is likely to reply, "Oh, it was built in *that* time." Yet the

Annual festival to Māri Amman, smallpox goddess, in a Tamil̲ Nāḍu village. Brāhmaṇs boycott this one. Barbers shave devotees who have taken certain vows. Garlanded man carries fire pot to fulfill vow and dances uncontrollably as instrumentalists play wildly.

Garlanded woman has taken vow. Her widowed mother prays to deity to come upon daughter, herself becoming uncontrollably possessed and falling down.

A leper woman with deformed mouth and holding baby in her arms takes fire as priest pours on ghī; usually people fulfill vows after "healing," but she participates every year. Others sacrifice goats in fulfillment of vows.

Indian religions developed the most fantastic cosmogonies in the premodern world.

Time in the *Rig Veda* consisted of a succession of days and nights, months, seasons, and years, as in many villages today. By the time of the *Atharva Veda*, as W. Norman Brown points out, some hymns showed time as creator, rolling on unceasingly and containing within itself all that the universe contains. By the time of the Purāṇas scholars had invented a concept of time involving three levels of cycles. A year of Brahmā consists of 360 "days" called *kalpas*, and one kalpa is 4.32 billion of our years! It is divided into 14 secondary cycles. On a third level it is divided into 1000 cycles, each of which consists of four *yugas*, or ages, which endure respectively 4800, 3600, 2400, and 1200 "years of the gods." Each year of the gods is 360 human years! In each kalpa there is degeneration, as can be seen by the decreasing length of the yugas within it. We now live in the Kali Yuga, the last of the four, supposed to have begun in 3102 B.C. which is believed to be the year of the Mahābhārata War. At the end of the Kali Yuga, society and religion will become chaotic and the world will be destroyed, to be succeeded by a new cycle.

Jainism elevated the concept of time to an even more fantastic plane. Time is a monstrous wheel with 12 spokes, six of which descend while six ascend. A full cycle takes two nonillion (2 followed by 30 zeros) *eras*! We are now moving downward and are in the fifth part of a lesser cycle of eras. By the end of the sixth part of this lesser cycle, 39,000 years hence, man will be reduced to a foot and a half in stature and will have a maximum life span of 16 years. Only after the upward swing is under way, 80,000 years from now, can one hope to achieve salvation.[14]

Buddhism, also imbued with the concept of endless rebirths, produced a fantastic scheme of time too; yet it had something approaching the idea of history in the chronicles of Sri Lanka. This was because the religion had a specific founder whose death marked the beginning of a new era. This date was said to be 544 B.C. (actually it was about 478 B.C.).

With Islam a new ready-made calendar was introduced which Muslims everywhere adopted. The era begins with Muhammad, and because Muslims were interested in lineage and in the development of their faith, their scholars had a more precise chronological view of history. Muslims consciously reject the indigenous Indian cosmologies and the associated myths. The Muslim calendar enabled all Muslims to celebrate Muslim festivals simultaneously, but it has a major defect in that the year does not quite coincide with the solar year, so it is not coordinated with the agricultural cycle.

Peasants in South Asia, except for Muslims, all know that we are in the Kali Yuga, which is why there are so many troubles and salvation is almost impossible to achieve. A surprising number of villagers also know the day and the month—often according to the regional Hindu calendars. In

Bānglā, Orissa, Tamiḻ Nāḍu, and Kērala a solar calendar with 29 to 32 days is used, though it differs in each region because of differences in latitude. A luni-solar calendar of 12 months has been in use from late Vedic times and is now employed for Brāhmaṇical purposes. Use of the days of the week—the same that we have—was introduced only in the 5th century A.D., traceable back to Babylonian astrology. Hindu and Jain kings kept track of years within an era, usually beginning with a dynasty or a reign, hence the absence of a fixed point for Indian history as a whole. Whereas villagers formerly knew only the annual cycle and had a vague idea of yugas, secular education has broadened their concept of time, so that children now have to learn history and state their ages. Many people have to know both the regional calendar as given by the astrologers, which determines festivals, and the calendar introduced by the British.

Hindu and Muslim Ritual

The stated function of ritual in Brāhmaṇical texts is as a means of salvation. In Vedic times sacrifice was the preeminent ritual, and the prototype of all sacrifices was that of Purusha, a sort of giant primeval male principle, reincarnated by priests on Vedic altars. Then there was the horse sacrifice, a regal ritual of kings and warriors. There was also the sacrifice of *soma* (related to the ancient Persian *haoma*); A. L. Basham thinks this was not an intoxicating drink, but was perhaps made from hemp like *bhāng* taken in India today or hashish used in the Near East.

By the time of the *Brāhmaṇas*, rituals had become unbelievably detailed and from our point of view, arid. For example, to collect *dharba* grass used in sacrifice, one must first draw a line around it with a sickle while thrice reciting a specified formula, brush the grass from top to bottom with the sickle while uttering a different formula, cut the grass with a single stroke while uttering a different verse, and place it aside while intoning yet a fourth. The bunch should be of a certain thickness, and so on. But all these details were specified differently by different teachers.[15]

All such ritual was thrown out by the heterodox cults: Buddhism, Jainism, and Ājīvikism, which naturally evolved their own rituals as they became established. The Sanskritic renaissance which superseded these religions assimilated into formal Hinduism many rituals of pre-Āryan or presumably Dravidian origin, such as pūjā and ritual washings; it is these which preoccupy Brāhmaṇs today.

Nineteenth-century ethnographers recorded in great detail the ritual practices of the various castes and tribes of India. Thurston's voluminous *Tribes and Castes of Southern India*, Iyer's *The Mysore Tribes and Castes*, Risley's *Tribes and Castes of Bengal*, Russell and Hirlal's *The Tribes and Castes of the Central Provinces of India*, Crooke's *Tribes and Castes of the*

Funeral of a woman of Nāḍar caste in Tamil̲ Nāḍu. (*Left*) One woman holds head of corpse while others huddle and mourn and man blows conch shells. (*Right*) Corpse is tied in bier for taking to caste burial ground.

North-West Provinces and Oudh, and similar series recorded the life cycle and festival rituals of hundreds of groups. For the funerary ceremony of a caste, for instance, we are given details of washing and decking the corpse, method of transporting the corpse to cremation or burial ground, details of lighting the funeral pyre, number of times the bier was circumambulated, number of days before gathering the ashes, method of disposal of ashes, number of days of death pollution and accompanying restrictions, times and participants of śrāddha offerings, conclusion of mourning ceremonies, effect of the ghost if it becomes malevolent, restrictions on marriage after

A Hindu cremation in Nepal; only the feet remain.

Last rites performed in a Muslim mortuary in Rājasthān.

death of a spouse, inheritance ceremonies, and much, much more. This kind of ethnography is behind us, yet such rituals highlighted distinctions of caste and region that were vitally important and still are.

Muslim rituals, though not approaching in detail those of Brāhmaṇs, are as elaborate as the rites of other village Hindus. We cite here, for contrast with the above, Dube's account for a Muslim funeral ceremony in a village near Hyderābād. The toes of the corpse are tied together, salt is placed on the stomach to prevent its swelling, and the body is covered with a new cloth. A communal wooden box is borrowed to carry the corpse to the grave. Before putting the corpse in the box, it is covered with three more cloths (or five in the case of a woman), camphor powder is sprinkled on the forehead, eyes, palms, and legs, and perfume is applied. Four relatives or friends carry the box to the mosque, repeating as they go, "There is no God but Allah." Prayers are said, and the procession winds along to the Muslim graveyard. Portions of the Qur'ān are read, and all throw some earth into the grave, still reciting verses. They step back from the grave 40 paces and return again invoking Allah's blessings on the deceased. After returning home the family must make no fire on the hearth for two days, but are supplied food by relatives. On the third and tenth days, prayers are said in the mosque and flowers put on the grave; this is repeated on the 14th day and a feast is served. It is repeated again on the anniversary.

The data on rituals are truly unmanageable; besides the regional and caste compilations of the last century, there are District Gazetteers, ethnographies, and nearly 400 village studies incorporated into the 1500-volume 1961 census. There are details of daily and occasional rites, several categories of life cycle ceremonies, and calendrical rituals. If these categories are multiplied by the numbers of castes or lineages, geographic regions, and religions, the details are overwhelming.

The Meaning of Ritual

Such collections of ritual practices have two chief faults: they make the acts appear more important than the sociological relations they really symbolize, and they appear as permanent characteristics of discrete and fixed caste entities rather than as indicators of culture dynamics.

An obvious function of the ritual of higher castes is to indicate their leisure; Brāhmaṇs should be leisured landowners or professionals. It takes perhaps two hours for a Brāhmaṇ to complete his full morning ablutions and worship; then he eats, and comes to the office by 10 or preferably 11 A.M.—hence government offices open rather late. A farmer or artisan must begin work early.

A second function of Brāhmaṇical ritual is to maintain status by the purity-pollution syndrome. Brāhmaṇs are pure by birth and can remove acquired impurities by ablutions so they can serve the gods, but low caste

people cannot remove the impurity acquired by karma even if they take the time for sanctifying rites. Naturally this comes to be overlooked in the case of those castes which are able to succeed in rising in the ritual hierarchy because of power or money; their imitation of Brāhmaṇical ritual is part of the process of Sanskritization.

A third function is to support status by invoking the past. Shamans are spiritual and sādhus are holy but Brāhmaṇs are orthodox. In Buddhism, too, shamans are spiritual and monks are supposed to be pious, but in effect they derive their power from orthodoxy by their initiation, vows, and ritual worship. "Antiquity and continuance are the foundations of legitimacy," writes Lévi-Strauss. Ritual produces mythical history, and thus joins the past with the present. "Diachrony, in some sort mastered, collaborates with synchrony."[16]

Victor Turner sees a dialectical process in which ritual becomes symbolic of the structure of society, so that the more highly structured it is, the more the levels and segments must be distinguished by ritual. The opposing process is the negation of the social meaning of ritual and thereby the negation of such structured society.

The negation of ritual can in itself become a ritual. Marriott cites the example of the Holī festival in a village in Uttar Pradesh. In this festival in honor of Krishṇa, held during the full moon in March, almost every customary practice is the negation of usual practices. Wealthy Brāhmaṇ and Jāṭ farmers have their shins beaten with staves by women, and tolerate it. The village landlord has his head anointed with a gallon of diesel fuel, while the foreign anthropologist is doused by a woman throwing a pail of buffalo urine. All the other festivals of the village reinforce the proper social and cosmic structure, but Holī balances world destruction with world renewal. World pollution is followed by world purification.[17]

Carstairs refers to the bhakti (devotional) worship of a Hindu sect in Rājasthān in which the disciples of a particular gurū join in increasingly intense worship until they pair off in sexual union. Their devotion to each other fulfills the masculinity and femininity of each partner and also symbolizes the sexual union of Krishṇa with his consort Rādhā. The deity makes himself manifest in the "male and female semen" at the culmination of the ceremony. Such practices were common in both the Buddhist and Hindu Tantric cults of Bānglā. In the 16th century, Caitanya, himself considered an incarnation of Vishṇu, renewed this type of extreme devotionalism in Bānglā and supported it with religious literature. The ritual was not simply sensuous, but was a way of reaching God, a culmination of a protracted series of liturgical actions and recitation of mantras. Turner views these rites as the antithesis of marriage, since the female partner had to be the wife of another. It is also the antithesis of property ownership, since there was no giving and receiving, and one partner did not belong to another.

The full dialectic cycle can be seen in the development of Buddhism.

Fire-walking in Tamiḻ Nāḍu. Spectators worship as devotee walks over red-hot coals unharmed. He has been purified and has sufficient faith, it is believed.

Gautama Buddha gave up a princely inheritance to become an ascetic and eventually achieved enlightenment by meditation rather than by ritual. The religion he founded was originally the antithesis of Brāhmaṇical ritual, but later came to compete with it. Now the Buddhist Lāmas of the Bhoṭiyās and Lepchas in the Himālayas have made meditation into a ritual; they also have their ritual language (Classical Tibetan) and scriptures, chants, and a corpus of orthodox procedures.

Mahatma Gandhi renounced ritual of another kind. He gave up his career as an England-trained lawyer, divested himself of the symbols of English elite society such as English table manners and dress, and refused

to own property. Daily he used a spinning wheel and dressed only in handwoven cloth. Now the Congress Party, which has ruled India since Independence, has on its flag the symbol of the spinning wheel, and wearing of handwoven cloth has become a ritual for its members.

Thus, South Asia is known for its rigid religious and social institutions as well as for heterodoxy. Brāhmaṇs are honored for their ritual and ascetics for their avoidance of it. The orthodox are honored because they keep caste and sādhus because they break it. Maulvīs are respected for their liturgy and pīrs because they bypass it.

Syncretism: Muslim, Hindu, and Sikh

It would be incorrect to say that Islam in South Asia is a veneer; it is a cultural system to which adherents are solidly committed. Yet there are naturally relics of pre-Muslim beliefs and practices. We have already referred to veneration of pīrs whose role is analogous to that of gurūs, worship of ghosts, the role of the mullā in tying on amulets to dispel sickness, and the use of phrases from the Qur'ān as if they were mantras. To dispel the evil eye, people in Pakistan paint such verses on their buses and trucks. Muslims deny that they have caste, but they do have endogamous lineages and occupational hereditary groups which are tantamount to caste, only they are hierarchically arranged according to Islamic rather than Hindu values. Even the religious tolerance characteristic of South Asia and bred originally in the heterogeneity of Hinduism, may be observed in that there is more variation in Islam than in the Near East, and it is more mellow. Honigmann reports for a Sindhī village that on the whole people are not pious, piety being a quality associated with pīrs. They do not show antagonism to other religions such as Christianity, but reject non-Sindhīs even if they are Muslims from Panjāb or refugees from India. In religious dogma Sindhīs are no more rigid than Hindus.

The syncretistic nature of Hinduism has produced expectable results. Across North India a number of pīrs are venerated by Hindus, such as Ādhām (Adam) pīr and Zāhir (apparent) pīr. The latter was a Hindu deity associated with a serpent cult before he became a pīr; he is worshiped in the Panjāb and especially in the Himālayan Kāngṛā region. Lewis reports than in a village near Delhi a pīr, called Guga, is considered to be brother to a snake and is worshiped with the snake at the time of the year when snakes are dangerous. On the day of worship

> . . . the women of the household take the black soot from their iron griddles and draw figures on the wall representing a snake and a man on horseback. An earthen lamp is lit and placed before the drawing. Some oil and *ghi* are poured over a hot ember to make it flare up and burn. Everyone says, "Guga has

appeared." Then the worshipers fold hands and pray, "O Guga *pir*, please don't appear to us during the coming year." There used to be a Muslim fakir in Rampur who received the food offered to Guga.[18]

The Muharram festival, in honor of Muhammad's grandson who died in battle, is one of mourning and repair of graves, followed on the 10th day by feasts of rice and sweets. Across North India Hindus as well as Muslims may be found celebrating this festival. Muslims also take part in Hindu festivals, as in the frivolity of Holī when colored water is dashed on everyone in sight, but they do not engage in ceremonies in which the deities are actually worshiped.

The millennium of adjustment of Hinduism and Islam has left many scars, but like a married couple, each has been influenced by the other more than it cares to admit. Bhakti devotional Hinduism arose parallel with Sūfī mysticism in Islam and blended with great Muslim mystic sects that appeared from Persia in the 12th to 15th centuries. Both relied on the same sorts of mystic leadership, and both inspired composition of moving devotional poetry.

Since the Mughals could rule only with the support of the Rājpūt rājās, the emperor Akbar initiated discussion among the Sunnī ulamā, Sūfī *shaikhs*, and Hindu *paṇḍits* (scholars, teachers), also inviting Pārsīs (Zoroastrians), Jains, and Catholic priests from Goā. Ultimately he prohibited cow slaughter, celebrated Hindu festivals, and had Sanskrit texts translated. Akbar's grandson went even further, claiming that the Qur'ān is mostly allegorical, that both Hinduism and Islam reduce pantheism to a unitary God, that Brahmā is the same as Adam, and that the Vedas and *Upanishads* are really contemplative exercises of pure monotheism. These syncretistic attempts did not take root, for orthodox Sunnīs reaffirmed the Sharī'at (legal and social system) as the real foundation of Islam: the two religions have remained distinct at the formal level.

But in the 16th century, a new movement, Sikhism, arose in the Panjāb, the geographical meeting ground of the two religions. Though originally a syncretistic devotional sect (see Chap. 10), it became an army, combatted Muslims, then formed a state. Because Sikhs are more sympathetic with Hindus than with Muslims, since Independence they have hardened rather than softened Hindu-Muslim animosity.

In the little Kāṭhmāṇḍū Valley of Nepal, the Newārs were originally Mahāyāna Buddhists, and with that faith they built a colorful little civilization, justly famous for its architecture and other arts. Since the establishment of the Gorkhā rule in 1768, Hinduism has become more prestigious, and the religions have become inextricably mixed. Some Newārs are Buddhist and some Hindu, yet this distinction is not important among themselves. One way to distinguish them is to see which family calls Brāhmaṇ priests and which calls Buddhist priests, but even this is not a reli-

able indicator, as Colin Rosser points out, for families of the same caste may call both, or both may even be called by the same family to perform different rituals.[19] Newār monks have, on analogy with Brāhmaṇs, ceased to be celibate and have become a distinct and hereditary priestly caste. In village shrines Buddhas and Hindu deities are juxtaposed and worshiped with little distinction. Most Newārs in their hearts are Buddhist, but the structure of Buddhism has become dormant because of the Hindu monarchy and the pervasive immigrant Hindu Chetrīs.

In Sri Lanka where Buddhism has been supported by the state for 2200 years, a great many Hindu deities have provided a pantheon for Theravāda Buddhism, though it is supposed to have no deities. The highly popular Śaivite deity at Kataragama, a shrine where people fulfill vows, is considered as a "protector of religion," while other deities are "helpers of Buddha." A *vihāra* (Buddhist monastery) in a Sinhala village (the same one described in *South Asia: Seven Community Profiles*) has an image of Buddha flanked by guardians, gatekeepers, the Sinhala lion, and multi-colored paintings of four Hindu deities, two Brahmās, and a future incarnation of Buddha.

In cases such as these, the fused religions have been juxtaposed for centuries. Similarly the early Christianity of Kēraḷa adopted much from Hinduism, both rites and doctrine (Chap. 11), while in Karṇāṭaka Hinduism, Lingāyatism, and Jainism coexist harmoniously because there are few really important differences in world view or social ideal among them. An example of two juxtaposed religions not syncretizing, however, is provided by Sikkim. Having adopted Tibetan Lāmaism as their formal religion, the Lepchas are resisting acculturation by the recent Hindu immigrants from Nepal, even though these now comprise the majority in Sikkim. Tibetan Buddhism is a much more visible model for the Lepchas because it is more colorful than the Hinduism of the immigrants, who have few Brāhmaṇs and do not engage in elaborate rites. The Lāmas and monasteries remain economically and politically such a strong institution integrating Lepchas and Bhoṭiyās that they totally reject Hinduism. The Japanese anthropologist, Chie Nakane, in two months of fieldwork did not find any instance of crossing ethnic boundaries. She saw only one case of marriage between a Nepālī and a Lepcha, and that was outside Sikkim.[20]

From the history of syncretism among South Asian religions, one might expect that after some generations, when the initial antagonism is worn off, the Mun spirituality and Lāmaistic orthodoxy of the Lepchas would be enriched by Brāhmaṇism too. But this may never happen. The traditional world of South Asia is changing so that we cannot predict the interaction of religions based on processes normal to traditional South Asia. Instead, both Hindus and Buddhists are being drawn into a new and stronger set of overarching ideals, a new formal pattern: modernization. Even the high valleys of the Himālayas are not exempt.

Secularism

Since Independence there have been shifts in the structure and function of religions in South Asia. In part these result from the new political forces, and in part may reflect an actual slight decline in religiosity as the old great traditions are gradually eroded by modernization.

In a village in western Uttar Pradesh reported on by Minturn and Hitchcock, for instance, the Rājpūts call their priests less often than before. One reason is that the Ārya Samāj, a reformist Hindu movement, has been preaching here against the employment of priests and against all Brāhmaṇical rituals. In fact, priests would have little to do were it not for the conservatism of the women. The men have given up some of the rituals necessary to maintain ritual purity, but the women in this village will bathe and wash their hair if they inadvertently come in direct contact with an untouchable. Often in South Asia it is the women who insist on the rituals being performed, especially in northwestern India and in Pakistan where women have less contact with the wider world and are less educated. Men may be pious, but women are religiously conservative. Men can find emotional outlets in many new kinds of movements, especially in politics, which are not very open to female participation at the village level.

In a village near Delhi farmers of the Jāṭ caste questioned the existence of heaven and hell because nobody had seen them, and furthermore suggested that karma operates only in this life. They cited an argument of the Ārya Samāj that Mātā (mother) worship is useless: "If you put food on Mātā's shrine, a dog comes along and eats it. He also makes water there. Mātā can't stop him. If she had any power, she could kill that dog, but she does not." One Jāṭ said, "Our ancestors were stupid, and we are getting educated. We're learning that all such beliefs are false."[22] In this part of India Jāṭs and Rājpūts have traditionally been attracted by wealth and landowning as avenues to prestige, the Kshatriya model rather than the Brahmaṇical. But in this village the assent even Brāhmaṇs verbally give to traditional doctrines seems to be only minimally supported by actions.

Muslim villagers in Bangladesh universally give overt allegiance to Islam. So pervasive is the ethos of the faith that it is virtually impossible for Muslim Bāngālī villagers to deny the existence of Allah or the inspiration of the Qur'ān. They are really incredulous that people elsewhere in the world might deny the existence of God. But if the anthropologist asks them whether some might give lip service to Islam without having faith in the heart, the answer is a stunning silence. Even more clearly, attendance at the mosque is a little less regular and children are sent to public school now more often than to the mosque school. Also, the authority of the imām or mullā has suffered a definite decline. Of course, these changes may not in themselves indicate any loss of piety, for morning prayers are now avail-

able for some people on the radio, while the public schools and the village council administration have naturally usurped some of the authority formerly enjoyed by the mullā.

The sociological functions of religion are shifting from the village to the culture region, part of the new political awareness and the search of each region for its cultural identity. Obeyesekere points this out for a Sinhala village in Sri Lanka. He finds that faith is not particularly decreasing, but that the Buddhist festivals and rituals that formerly were vital to preservation of the social order within the hamlet or the village are now partly submerged in the practice of Buddhism as a symbol of Sinhala nationalism. People who participate in a pilgrimage to a high mountain shrine all mix together irrespective of caste or village in a spirit of the new equalitarianism, fortifying their consciousness as Sinhalas as well as Buddhists.

Some of the regional manifestations of Hinduism have increased in importance in recent decades. The Śivājī cult in Mahārāshṭra and the indigenous Murugan mountain deity cult of Tamil̠ Nāḍu have their political overtones, while Sikhs have succeeded in the demand for splitting the old Panjāb so they could have a predominantly Sikh state. Hinduism is widely used by the monarchy in Nepal to weld the country together and enhance the veneration of the king, even though many of the people are to some extent Buddhists. On a national scale the Jana Sangh is a political party centered in the heartland of North India which subscribes to Hinduism as part of Indian ethnic and national self-identity, while the Muslim League aims to provide the same function for Muslims all over India.

In India there were only two states in which a sizable number of people registered themselves as irreligious or atheistic in the 1961 census. Most of those so registering were in Tamil̠ Nāḍu (34,382) with adjacent Pondicherry (320), and Nāgaland (44,167) with some spillover in Assam (415). It is significant that in both regions this is part of an effort to establish regional identity. In the case of Tamil̠ Nāḍu the anti-Brāhmaṇ, anti-Sanskrit, and anti-Āryan sentiment has found expression in the DMK party which came to power in the state in the 1967 elections on the basis on Tamil̠ chauvanism. The theoretical position of this party is irreligious, though some of its members support worship of non-Brāhmaṇ indigenous Tamil̠ gods. But while electioneering, it does not preach atheism. After winning control of the state government it issued an order that pictures of deities on the walls of government offices should be removed, but the order raised such a protest it was later modified. Yet the existence of this party has made it possible for some people to openly say they are atheists, whereas in no other predominantly Hindu state in India did more than 100 people dare to claim atheism.

In the case of Nāgaland people clearly and totally reject Hinduism and Islam. Many are Christians (mostly Baptist), some adhere to the tribal

religions, and some are atheists or do not claim any religion. Their demands for creation of a separate Nāgaland had the purpose of stemming the tide of Hindu Assamese influence, for they have never been Hindu nor part of Indian Civilization. Some wish to go further and sever all relations with India; hence an underground government persists.

Pakistan was founded with the aim of achieving Muslim political self-identity, and it has officially been a Muslim state. So strong is this ethos that Hindus and Sikhs almost all felt they could not remain in Pakistan and fled to India in 1948. An equal number of Muslims left India for Pakistan, but in fact five times as many Muslims chose to stay in India. Hindu-Muslim animosity has been strongest in the heartland of North India, from which Muslims once ruled the subcontinent and now find themselves outdistanced.

India is a secular state. This was one of the firmest ideals of Nehru, and in spite of occasional religious strife in certain towns, the Government of India has made real efforts to bring Muslims and other minorities into the administration at all levels and constitutionally to guarantee personal freedom of religion. One of the first pronouncements of the new Bangladesh government is that it would be a secular state. The East Pakistan government was officially Muslim and in the 1960s harassed several million Hindus, as well as Christian and Buddhist tribals, into fleeing to neighboring parts of India. After Bangladesh achieved independence, all the refugees who had fled to India in 1971, including the Hindus, returned and were received as brother Bāngālīs by their covillagers. Religious differences were not the fundamental reason for the 1971 Bangladesh war, nor for the 1965 India-Pakistan war. It is doubtful that religious wars, as such, will ever again be fought in South Asia.

The symbolic functions of religion are being recast in the context of the altered village power structure, new ways to cope with the unknown, modern medicine, wider communications (so that people are less dependent upon local cults), and nationalism. As a symbol of regional identity, language is superseding religion. The educated tend to intellectualize their faith rather than express it in ritual. And village priests say there is a slight perceptible decrease in interest in religious activities and in donations. But then, this can also be expressed in religious terms. Is it not the Kali Yuga with inherent religious degeneration, awaiting revival in the next age?

REFERENCES AND NOTES

1 These estimates were obtained by projecting figures in *Census of India, 1971* according to the growth rate for the total population. In the case of the tribal religions, only a fraction of each tribe claimed to follow them; 1971 figures for tribals are not yet available.

[2] These estimates are projected from *Population Census of Pakistan, 1961.* No information on religion was gathered in the 1972 census.

[3] These estimates are projected from *Population Census of Pakistan, 1961,* and do not reflect possible dislocations from the 1971 war.

[4] These figures are projected from *Ceylon, Department of Census, 1971.*

[5] de Bary, pp. 284–288. The stanzas do not form one connected passage.

[6] Dube, p. 90.

[7] Berreman, pp. 84–85.

[8] Fürer-Haimendorf (1966), p. 168.

[9] Milton Singer, review article of Kapp, presented to American Sociological Assn., Los Angeles, August, 1963.

[10] 'Abdul Haqq, *The Perfection of Faith,* in de Bary, p. 399.

[11] Iqbāl, *The Secrets of the Self,* trans. R. A. Nicholson, in de Bary, p. 753.

[12] Gorer, pp. 220–221.

[13] Eglar, pp. 72–73.

[14] Brown, "Time is a Noose"; Basham, pp. 272, 290.

[15] From *Baudhāyana Śrauta Sutra,* in de Bary, pp. 24–25.

[16] Claude Lévi-Strauss, *The Savage Mind* (Chicago, 1962), pp. 216, 236.

[17] McKim Marriott, "The Feast of Love," in Singer.

[18] Lewis, p. 112.

[19] Colin Rosser, "Social Mobility in the Newar Caste System," in Fürer-Haimendorf (1966).

[20] Chie Nakane, "A Plural Society in Sikkim," in Fürer-Haimendorf (1966).

[21] Lewis, pp. 201–202, 249–259.

IMPORTANT SOURCES

General

Basham, A. L. *The Wonder That Was India.* New York, 1954. (Chap. VII discusses pre-Muslim religions.)

Bharati, Agehananda. *The Ochre Robe.* Seattle, Wash., 1961. (An anecodotal study of Hindu monks by an Austrian who became one.)

Brown, W. Norman. *Man in the Universe: Some Continuities in Indian Thought.* Berkeley, Calif., 1966. (Contains four stimulating essays based on Sanskrit sources.)

de Bary, William (ed.). *Sources of Indian Tradition.* New York, 1958. (Original sources in translation.)

Dumont, Louis. "World Renunciation in Indian Religions," in *Contributions to Indian Sociology* IV (1960).

Fürer-Haimendorf, C. von (ed.). *Caste and Kin in Nepal, India and Ceylon: Anthropological Studies in Hindu-Buddhist Contact Zones.* New York, 1966.

———. *Morals and Merit: A Study of Values and Social Controls in South Asian Societies.* Chicago, 1967. (Data based on tribal and Himālayan people.)

Ghurye, G. S. *Gods and Men.* Bombay, 1962. (Musings of a prolific Indian anthropologist.)

Harper, Edward (ed.). *Religion in South Asia.* Seattle, Wash., 1964. (An important volume, especially Harper's own article on ritual pollution.)

Maloney, Clarence (ed.). *The Evil Eye.* New York, 1974. (Includes a section on South Asia.)

Moore, Charles (ed.). *The Indian Mind: Essentials of Indian Philosophy and Culture*. Hawaii, 1967.
Singh, Gopal. *The Religion of the Sikhs*. New York, 1970.
Smith, Donald (ed.). *South Asian Religion and Politics*. Princeton, N.J., 1966.

Hinduism

Bhardwaj, Surinder. *Hindu Places of Pilgrimage in India*. Berkeley, Calif., 1973.
Diehl, Carl. *Church and Shrine*. Uppsala, 1965. (Christianity and Hinduism in Tamil̲ Nāḍu.)
———. *Instrument and Purpose: Studies in Rites and Rituals in South India*. Lund, 1956.
Dubois, Abbe J. A., and Henry Beauchamp. *Hindu Manners, Customs, and Ceremonies*. Oxford, 1906. (Fascinating observations of a missionary in Karṇāṭaka about 1800.)
Kapp, K. William. *Hindu Culture, Economic Development and Economic Planning in India*. New York, 1963. (The author believes that the Hindu outlook impedes economic development.)
Keith, A. B. *The Religion and Philosophy of the Vedas and Upaniṣads*. Cambridge, Mass., 1925.
Nilakanta Sastri, K. A. *Development of Religion in South India*. Bombay, 1963.
Renou, L. *Religions in Ancient India*. London, 1953.
Singer, Milton (ed.). *Krishna: Myths, Rites, and Attitudes*. Chicago, 1966. (A valuable collection of articles on one cult.)
Stevenson, Mrs. Sinclair. *The Rites of the Twice-Born*. Oxford, 1920.
Weber, Max. *The Religion of India*. Glencoe, Ill., 1958.

Buddhism

Conze, E. *Buddhism, its Essence and Development*, 2d ed. Oxford, 1953.
Gombrich. *Precept and Practice: Traditional Buddhism in the Rural Highlands of Ceylon*. Oxford, 1971.
Obeyesekere, G. "The Structure of Sinhalese Ritual," *Ceylon J. Historical and Social Studies* I (1958).
Rhy Davids, T. W. *Buddhism, its History and Literature*, 2d ed. London, 1926.
Spiro, Melford. *Burmese Supernaturalism*. Englewood Cliffs, N.J., 1967.

Islam

Eglar, Zekiya. *A Punjabi Village in Pakistan*. New York, 1960.
Fraser-Tytler, W. K. *Afghanistan*. London, 1967.
Ikram, S. M. *Muslim Civilization in India*. New York, 1963.
Maron, Stanley (ed.). *Pakistan: Society and Culture*. New Haven, Conn., 1957.
Mujeeb, M. *The Indian Muslims*. Montreal, 1967.

Village Religion

Berreman, Gerald. *Hindus of the Himalayas*. Berkeley, Calif., 1963.
Carstairs, G. Morris. *The Twice-Born: A Study of a Community of High-Caste Hindus*. Bloomington, Ind., 1967.
Crooke, William. *Religion and Folklore of Northern India*. London, 1926. (This study has retained its value over the decades.)

Dube, S. C. *Indian Village*. London, 1955.
Gorer, Geoffrey. *Himalayan Village: An Account of the Lepchas of Sikkim*. New York, 1967 (originally published 1938).
Harper, Edward. "Shamanism in South India," *Southwestern J. Anthrop.* XIII (1957).
Lewis, Oscar. *Village Life in Northern India*. New York, 1958. (A good source on festivals and beliefs of a village near Delhi.)
Mathur, K. S. *Caste and Ritual in a Malwa Village*. New York, 1964.
Minturn, Leigh, and John Hitchcock. *The Rājpūts of Khālapūr, India*. New York, 1966.
Whitehead, Henry. *Village Gods of South India*. Calcutta, 1916.

8

Society: Caste and Village

Everybody knows that caste, like the "sacred cow," is one of the curiosities of fabulous India. Hence it has been studied and studied some more. Already by the time the English withdrew from South Asia there were reported to be 5000 published works on the subject, and a plethora more have been added in the past quarter century.

The subject is so vastly complex and unwieldy that it can only be hoped that this chapter will stimulate the reader to pursue it in more detailed sources. Practically any statement made about caste may be valid for one region but not for another, for one village but not for its neighbor, for an urban setting but not for its suburb, for one religious group but not for some other sect, for one individual but not for his brother.

Basic patterns of segmental social organization find ingenious ways of expression in "modern" and urban contexts; the criteria of segmentation may change. Dismayed that caste is not disappearing, some educated people decry it as a "social evil"—much as African politicians view "tribalism"—and ascribe to it various ills of their countries. Some Indians have become reticent about the subject, or tell foreigners that the Constitution of India has "abolished" it. (But it has not; only the practice of untouchability has been "abolished" and caste discrimination in public places forbidden.)

Pakistanis are wont to deny that caste prevails in their country, for it is contrary to the Islamic ideal of brotherhood. If educated Pakistanis admit that their country has "almost caste-like" social structure, it is relegated as a surviving relic of Hindu civilization. Such attitudes, however, are found mostly among the English-educated elite and some urban segments of the population. Most who decry it continue to marry off their daughters within their own castes.

These attitudes are due in part to widespread misconceptions about caste. Within India there is the misconception that it originated with the Brāhmaṇical varṇa hierarchical system: Brāhmaṇs, Kshatriyas, Vaiśyas, Śūdras, and untouchables. This gave rise to the idea common in Western countries that caste is primarily an expression of religious values, but recent scholarship shows that change in caste ranking and ritual status generally follows change in power and wealth. Another misconception is that caste is the single criterion of social status, that it is an omnibus explanation of hierarchy and interaction. In truth there are many criteria, and the status of a family or an individual may not be that attributed to the caste. Another idea prevalent in Western countries is that caste is symptomatic of a stagnant and unchanging social mosaic. British ethnographers and administrators of the 19th century, as well as the courts, found it simpler to deal with social units presumed to be discrete and stable than to deal with social dynamics. Finally, it is not always recognized that all aspects of caste are found elsewhere in the world, though it is true that they have become more institutionalized in South Asia.

What Is Caste?

The word "caste" is derived from the Portuguese *casta*, meaning breed, race, or kind. A caste society is one that is segmented, with the segments hierarchically arranged and endogamous (in-marrying). A caste is quite distinct from a tribe, which tends to occupy a compact territory and is a complete cultural system. In any given village the 5, 20, or even 40 castes within it make up the cultural system; in a linguistic region there will be a number of hundreds of castes.

All the criteria we may devise to distinguish and define castes fail us in some situations. Occupation is often listed first, but it certainly does not explain caste divisions among farmers and laborers, while even among artisans there are many who do not follow caste occupations. Kinship or lineage is also sometimes mentioned, but most castes are far larger than a kin group and many contain clans. Muslims, and Hindus too, invent lineages which tend to support rather than determine caste distinctions. Endogamy is, of course, fundamental to caste, but in numberless villages it is tolerable for a man to take a concubine from a lower caste or a widower a second wife from an unusual source. It is primarily the first marriage which should

be strictly endogamous. Another acceptable violation of endogamy is in the form of hypergamy (in which the bride marries up). Rājpūts of the North-west took brides regularly from lower segments of their caste and lower castes, while hypergamy was highly institutionalized in the Kulīn system of Bānglā and in the Brāhmaṇ-Nāyar alliance system of Kēraḷa. In Nepal even among Hindus endogamy is violated in that an individual can at times leave his caste and marry into a higher category; it is also possible in Nepal for one to purchase entry into a higher caste if he can validate his claim economically and ritually. And there is continual flux of castes, caste fragments, and caste clusters.

Early students of India, and even now some historians, refer to "the four castes" meaning the four varṇas of Sanskrit literature. But since this definition is not based on field research, anthropologists generally reject it. By caste we mean *jāti* or *jāt*, a word found in most South Asian languages. It is a suitably vague word meaning a particular people, a caste or tribe, but the fundamental assumptions are that one's jāti is derived from birth and that the group is endogamous. In daily social intercourse it is enough to know that a person is a Baniyā (merchant), Rājpūt, or Kēraḷa Catholic. These act as subcultural entities and have their mythologies. But there are endogamous groups within them, which are also named. So is the jāti the Baniyā, Rājpūt, or Kēraḷa Catholic, or is it the minimal endogamous group? British and French social anthropologists and some Indians such as G. S. Ghurye refer to the larger group as the caste and the endogamous groups within it as subcastes. The justification for this is that in a given village there is most often only one category of Baniyā, Rājpūt, and so on. Many American anthropologists and some Indians such as I. Karve refer to the minimal endogamous group as the jāti and the named larger category as the jāti-cluster or caste-cluster. We will use the latter definition in this book.

A further complication arises because people might marry within their jāti within a range of 30 miles but not 100 miles. Even within an endogamous jāti there may be lineages identified by their place of origin or other criteria, whose relationships with each other vary. If a jāti is divided into two or more sects we would refer to each as a jāti.

Another level of complexity commonly arises when one encounters a system of clans, defined as exogamous (out-marrying), as among some Telugus and Rājpūts. A different distinction observed by Brāhmaṇs and numerous other Hindu castes is the *gotra.* A gotra may be thought of as like a lineage except that it is a ritual or mythical one, going back to some holy personage. Gotras are strictly *exogamous.* But Muslims have lineage-based categories which are preferentially *endogamous* so cannot be called clans, but function much like castes. In parts of North India and Pakistan a caste or lineage may be divided into *birādarīs* (brotherhoods, to which the word is etymolotically related) consisting of the males from a village or group of villages who claim a common male ancestor.

What is clear, however, is that caste or caste-like lineage is so funda-

mental to social organization in South Asia that it prevails in all parts except some tribal populations, and is found in all the main religions. Caste is strongest in the Hindu regions, supported by Brāhmaṇism and orthodox philosophy. It is highly complex in the peninsula, supported by elaborate purity and pollution symbols. It is also complex in the Gangā plains, but probably less fluid, and supported by especially precise food gradations. It tends to become lineage-based towards the west. Segmentation is a little less complex in Bānglā and still simpler in Assam and the Himālayan foothills. A range of castes paralleling that of adjacent Hindus is found among Sikhs in Panjāb, Jains in western India, and Lingāyats in Karṇāṭaka. Non-Hindu central Indian tribes each function as a caste when among Hindus. Some Buddhist and other non-Hindu ethnic groups in Nepal fall into the wider Hindu caste hierarchy (an example is provided in Caplan's chapter in the companion volume). In Buddhist Sri Lanka caste is not quite so complex as in India but is nevertheless fully institutionalized.

The religions of foreign origin have adjusted to this social pattern. When Hindus and Muslims live in the same region Hindu castes tend to have their Muslim counterparts. Though contrary to original Islam, caste is now tacitly supported by this religion to the extent that highest status is accorded to those lineages with mythological genealogies traceable back to the Prophet or his relatives, Muslim conquerors, or pīrs. Where Christianity has been long established, as in Kēraḷa, it has developed caste-like sectarian groups. Elsewhere converts to Christianity sometimes retain their caste identity, especially if they were untouchables, or else tend to divide up into denominations which are de facto castes, or geographical segments. The Jews of Cochin, in Kēraḷa, have caste-groups, each with its synagogue. Such minorities as Pārsīs, Anglo-Indians, and Europeans, though not divided into castes, find a place within the wider social system because each functions as an essentially endogamous cultural entity—and in each case they seem to be willing to play the role.

Only among tribal people do we not find social segmentation along caste lines. The jumble of peoples in the four ministates and two Territories surrounding Assam are divided ethnically rather than hierarchically. The tribes of central India are becoming assimilated as distinct castes. In western Pakistan among Paṭhāns lineage-based distinctions of tribal origin are the important social segments, while there are also elements of caste. In Balūchistān among the Balūchīs and Brāhūīs, and in the tribes of Afghanistan, social organization is not caste-like, though there might be minority populations performing occupational roles.

Caste-like structures have been described from a number of parts of the world. Most commonly cited is that of premodern Japan, especially of the Tokugawa period; not only were there hierarchical hereditary occupational groups, but an outcaste-like category lived in satellite hamlets. Both Shintoism and Buddhism stressed physical and spiritual purity such as lower

castes could not possibly attain. J. H. Hutton points out that in Burma there were seven distinct classes of outcastes performing degraded or unclean occupations. The Jews of Palestine at the time of Christ maintained elaborate purity and pollution distinctions which symbolized hierarchy as defined by the orthodox. Both in Somalia and in Rwanda (until the recent social revolution) there were tribes that had hierarchically coalesced and had different economic functions. And the relations between Whites and Blacks in the old United States South are sometimes described as caste-like; the refusal of the one to dine with or wear clothes of the other implied a tinge of the idea of ritual pollution.

Bernard Barber points out that the Hindu stratification ideology was not so different from that of medieval Europe in which divinely appointed "Estates"—nobility, clergy, freemen, and serfs—"collaborated entirely harmoniously for His greater glory and for the benefit of all mankind." He also suggests why the 19th century view of caste so closely followed the Hindu textual ideal and why it was deemed to be such an odd institution:

> By stressing the absolute differences between Indian stratification and that of the West, by describing a condition of radical inequality and complete lack of mobility in India, Westerners could, in the light of their own values, be asserting a moral superiority to the Indians which helped justify their imperialistic policy in India. Colonialism could be justified as a means of bringing better ways to an immoral stratification system. Thus the moral self-satisfaction of outsiders to India may have combined with native upper-class ideologies in perpetuating a distorted conception of the caste system.[1]

Origins of Caste

The chief candidates that have been suggested as being at the original basis of the caste system are 1) the varṇa scheme, 2) color or race, 3) Brāhmaṇical manipulation of society, 4) occupation or guilds, 5) kinship, ancestor worship, and modes of descent, 6) conquest, 7) tribalism, 8) totemism and particularistic deities, 9) purity-pollution distinctions, 10) political alignment and patronage locally and regionally, and 11) landownership and wealth. Various of these have been put forward as the original criterion of caste. In truth, they are all important.

Rather than try to discover a simplistic cause of the development of the institution of caste, it is better to acknowledge that all traditional civilizations have had social segmentation and stratification. It was inevitable in all premodern urban societies, and the criteria and symbols of this in South Asia are generally the same as are found elsewhere, only more elaborate. We should acknowledge that society in South Asia has been segmented since the earliest known times, that these segments gradually became more hierarchically arranged in medieval centuries, and that the pattern extended to all religious groups.

The four categories later called varṇas are said in the *Rig Veda* to have been created respectively from the head, arms, legs, and feet of Purusha. But the hymn in which this occurs is a late one, and the fourth varṇa, the Śūdras, originally had no status in the Āryan system. In late Vedic times the four-varṇa model developed. The *Mahābhārata* specifies that Brāhmaṇs are for learning, Kshatriyas for fighting and ruling, Vaiśyas for tending cattle, farming, and trading, and the Śūdras for serving all the others. Those outside this system, the polluted and the outcasted, formed a fifth category. The varṇas should *not* be called castes; A. L. Basham calls them classes.

The *Rig Veda* does not apply the word varṇa to these classes, but only to Āryans as contrasted with Dāsas, indigenous people thought of as slaves or inferiors. Those who considered themselves to be "Āryans" in the Vedic period were lighter in color than Dāsas, who were described as dark, flat-nosed, and despicable. From then to the present there has been a rough correlation between high caste status and light color, and likewise a gradation of color from the northwest toward the south and east. But this correlation is so inexact that it could never have been the cause of endogamy nor the criterion of purity-pollution, and therefore was not the cause of the evolution of caste.

The classical explanation in India, derived from the Sanskrit texts, is that castes proliferated from the four varṇas through miscegenation. It is true that bastards and children of irregular marriages or of widows sometimes band together to form new endogamous castes. It is also true that individuals or whole kin groups who violate important norms are outcast or excommunicated, forming new castes. Innumerable castes in their traditional "histories" claim original high caste status and explain their fall as due to some such cause. But this fission process, though it certainly exists, cannot be considered by social scientists as fundamentally the reason for the evolution of the modern caste structure. Indeed, the varṇa system has always been more an ideal than an actual system, and all five categories are not found everywhere; in the South there are essentially three, and in Bānglā the system is also truncated. But as a partially imposed system in which different castes were placed in one of the five slots, it had the advantage, as Srinivas points out, of providing a simple and clear scheme applicable over a very wide area—a common social language conducive to unity and a sense of familiarity even when it does not rest on facts.

To ascribe the origins of caste to Brāhmaṇical manipulation, as some anti-Brāhmaṇ political elements in India do, assumes the varṇa model to have been more real than it was. It also does not explain why caste, essentially, is found in Buddhist society in Sri Lanka, Christian Catholic society in Kēraḷa, or Muslim society in Pakistan.

An omnibus explanation of caste commonly stated, especially by Westerners whose observation is superficial, is that it arose essentially through

occupational specialization. Many caste names, it is true, are occupational names, particularly for artisans such as smiths or carpenters, or village serving specialists such as washermen, barbers, cobblers, winnowers, or potters. It is assumed that in a stable society these will naturally tend to be hereditary. If one looks at ideal society of the Mauryan period and after as described in the *Arthaśāstra*, it appears that divisions within it were mostly occupational. But the purpose of this work was to portray principles of polity—statecraft and generation of revenue for the king—and it paid no attention to society within the village nor to its religious underpinnings. Medieval guilds were exclusive, restricted apprenticeship, and functioned as fraternities, apparently giving rise to numerous artisan and trading castes.

But such explanations do not explain why cultivators, the majority in any village, are divided up into numerous castes. Nor does it explain why there are hundreds of Brāhmaṇ castes, or even endogamous jātis within particular occupational specialties. The conquest theory may be invoked to explain why Rājpūts in and around Rājasthān evolved as a distinct caste-cluster, or the more prestigious Muslim lineages, or at an earlier level the Gūjars of Pakistan and Gujarāt. But none of these historical explanations comes to grips with the critical question of the *structure* of society in South Asia.

We can, however, observe something of the social segmentation that existed in India before the evolution of the fully developed, Brāhmaṇ-sanctioned system of medieval centuries, for this early social segmentation was the raw material from which a more complex social pattern evolved. The Tamiḻ literature of almost 2000 years ago describes society before Brāhmaṇical influence became strong. There were in the far South many distinct groups in which membership was evidently obtained by birth. Some were associated with particular types of terrain, such as Paratavar (coasts), Malavar (mountains), and Maravar (deserts). Others were essentially tribes or minor dynasties, geographically delimited and under chiefs, such as Kaḍambar, Aruvāḷar, Oliyar, and Vēḷir. Yet others were occupational, such as Āyar (cowherds); there were goldsmiths, carpenters, saltmakers, and Brāhmaṇs. The evolution of some of these can be traced up to modern times, such as Paratavar (discussed below), Vēḷir who became a widespread agricultural caste, and Kaḍambar who developed into an important medieval dynasty in Karṇāṭaka.

Whereas these Tamiḻ sources tell us so little about purity-pollution that we cannot be sure it was important as a symbol of the separation of the castes, we do know from other literature that at least in North India it goes back much before the Brāhmaṇical Hinduism of the Gupta period. The *Laws of Manu*, compiled over several centuries up to 300 A.D., states that a Brāhmaṇ who touches a Caṇḍāla (an early name for untouchables), one outcasted, or a menstruating woman must purify himself by bathing. The Buddhist works of the same time refer to numerous occupational castes,

while also sometimes referring to the ranked varṇas, with Kshatriyas placed above Brāhmaṇs. They refer to Caṇḍālas as people one does not eat with nor even look at. The *Mahāvamsa* describes the royal city of Anurādhapura in Sri Lanka of the 4th century B.C. and states that the Caṇḍālas, who swept, bore the dead, and watched cemeteries, had a separate village outside the city near the cemetery.

The evolution of the caste structure is to be seen as a composite process that made possible the integration of diverse cultural elements into the ever-widening civilizational system. With the increasing cultural amalgamation the various social segments jelled into an increasingly formal hierarchical system. In general this occurred in North India in the 1st millennium B.C., in South India in the 1st millennium A.D., and in peripheral regions such as Assam and Nepal even later.

The social processes attendant upon the growing civilizational complexity were not unique to South Asia. The chief ones were: 1) Tribes were becoming peasantized. At first they tended to remain distinct on the basis of language, totemism, kinship, ancestor worship, or location, but ultimately they became Hinduized castes. 2) Urbanization appeared, with its concomitant specialization of labor and hereditary occupational groups which gradually became hierarchical with the growth of the urban class structure. 3) A state system was evolving with its royalty, greater and lesser feudatories, and warriors, who required the presence of service groups and serfs; successive conquest groups became new ethnic entities. Indian kings traditionally had the power to elevate or degrade particular castes, thus overriding the karma principle. 4) The maturing Indian religions were rationalizing and stabilizing the social order by rituals and philosophies. Social segments distinguished by a variety of criteria were forced into the implicitly hierarchical Brāhmaṇical five-tier varṇa system, whose chief categories were paralleled later in the Muslim hierarchical system.

We now turn to some of the specific features of caste, and at the conclusion of the chapter review some opinions on the fundamental nature of its structure.

Purity and Pollution

An exceedingly pervasive feature of South Asian life is the concept of *ritual* purity and pollution. It bears only slight relationship to physical or hygienic purity and pollution. This is one of the most distinctive traits of South Asian society, and is pre-Āryan in origin, if we can interpolate from the plethora of bathing rooms, drains, and wells of the Indus Civilization and the terminology of Dravidian languages. Pollution may be acquired by something in daily life, in which case it can be dispelled with a purifying ritual, or it may be acquired at birth as a result of bad karma. It is because

of the latter that the lowest castes are literally not to be touched, while high castes are born with an inherent purity which has to be maintained by avoiding the pollutants, by frequent ablutions and purifying ceremonies, and by worship of the pure and high gods. When villagers are asked to rank local castes they will do so according to the ritual purity-pollution continuum which is extremely subtle and involves a large number of rank indicators. Not only castes but also families, individuals, geographical regions, even animals, plants, and objects are ranked by their degree of polluting or purifying power. Thus this is generally not the *cause* of ranking of but the *expression* of it.

Among the pollutants are any body secretions such as spittle or blood, dung, urine, hair, leather, dirty clothes, a corpse, or street dirt. Pollution and unhygienic objects are inextricably linked.

Anybody who handles these things, such as a sweeper, barber, washerman, or leatherworker, carries the effects of them, and obviously is in a position where he has to because of evil karma; therefore even a person of Leatherworker caste (capitalized to refer to a particular caste) who does not work leather is untouchable for he was born as such and eats with other Leatherworkers. A cripple or a hungry person may harm one by a glance of his evil eye, which is also a form of pollution. Pollution and evil are inextricably linked.

Some objects transmit pollution more than others. There is a hierarchy of vessels: gold (which does not transmit pollution), brass (given at weddings), copper, iron, and clay. There is a hierarchy of textiles: silk does not transmit pollution whereas cotton does. There is a hierarchy of grains: rice, wheat, the large millets, rāgi. Foods fried in oil or enriched by ghī do not transmit pollution but foods cooked in water do. Pollution and poverty are inextricably linked.

Acts contrary to Brāhmaṇical behavior cause pollution, such as eating meat or especially beef, killing things, drinking liquor, or crossing the sea. Pollution and unorthodox behavior are inextricably linked.

A woman's low status relative to a man is expressed in her polluting state during menstruation or after childbirth. A person of any caste should not pollute himself by taking drinking water from the hand of a person of lower caste. Pollution and relatively low status are inextricably linked.

Some of these, especially menstrual and death pollution, are found in tribal societies. High in the Pakistan Himālayas, in Chitrāl, are the Kāfirs, or "pagans," who refused conversion to Islam and fled from the plains about the 10th century. They practice a polytheistic religion of presumably prehistoric indigenous elements mixed with practices derived from the very early Dardic-speaking stratum of Āryan influence. The Kāfirs have many ideas about ritual pollution. Hens are impure. Sacrificial goats are to be killed by young male virgins who are considered pure. Shamans are to be assisted by such boys. Of special concern is the segregation of menstruating

women. For six days a month as well as during the whole term of pregnancy, women are secluded in a special house. Food given them must be uncooked, as cooked food is capable of defilement. It is left on a stone outside the door so the carrier will not become defiled. If it becomes necessary for another woman to enter the special house, as in the case of childbirth, she must leave all her clothes outside and enter naked, even in freezing weather, as clothes carry defilement. This periodic ritual symbolizes the general inferiority of women to men. Women cannot enter religious sanctuaries at all.[2]

The menstruation tabu has evolved from prehistoric practices such as these into Brāhmaṇical ritual. In Karṇāṭaka the Havik Brāhmaṇs, described by Edward Harper, believe a menstruating woman is impure and literally untouchable for three days a month. She cannot come inside the kitchen or sleeping rooms but stays on the veranda or visits the verandas of other houses. She does not change clothes, comb her hair, nor wear the red forehead mark. After three nights she may bathe but remains partially impure. The following day, after another bath, she may rejoin the family. While secluded she uses a special blanket, cup, and water vessel which must be purified with water and a little cow dung after her seclusion. A small child may stay with its mother if it is naked, for it is the cloth that transmits pollution. During these days the housework is done by a kinswoman or by the husband himself.

The woman cannot take her first purificatory bath in the family bathing place except among very modern families; she is obliged to go out to the village tank or lake. There she also washes her menstrual cloth, a particularly defiling item. If a Brāhmaṇ contracts pollution by touching a menstruating woman, he must be purified by an elaborate ceremony including eating *pañcagavya*, the five products of the cow (milk, ghī, curds, dung, and urine), and a priest should be called to do pūjā to the new sacred thread which he must put on. If in the meantime he touches a second Brāhmaṇ, the latter need only bathe and changes his clothes. If the second touches a third, only change of clothes is required. The third person can touch a fourth without transmitting defilement.

Havik Brāhmaṇs recognize three degrees of purity: *maḍi* (ritually pure), *mailige* (normal ritual status), and *muṭṭuceṭṭu* (ritually impure). They must try to finish any polluting work, such as carrying manure to the garden or contacting an untouchable servant, before the morning bath; only after their ablutions can they eat and go to the temple.

> To become maḍi a person must have a complete bath, including pouring water over the hair, and the water should be drawn from a pure source by a Brahmin who is not in muṭṭucheṭṭu. If cotton clothing is worn it must have been washed by someone in maḍi, and to remain in a state of maḍi the wearer must not touch any cloth which is not maḍi. To illustrate with a male example: A man bathes in his *panche*, a piece of cloth wrapped around his waist. He then changes

to another panche while bathing so that he can remove and wash the one he has been wearing. While wet both panches are maḍi. He dries himself using the panche he has just washed (to use a dry towel which is not maḍi would remove his own maḍi), rewashes the panche he has just used as a towel, and then leaves the bathing area to go to the clothesline in the attic of the house. Maḍi clothes are generally dried and kept here to insure that no one not in a state of maḍi accidentally touches them. He then changes to the panche he had washed the previous day and hangs up to dry that which he has just washed and is wearing.

A person who is in dry "cotton maḍi" becomes mailige as soon as he is touched by anyone else in the house who is not in maḍi (a child is most likely to be involved in such an accident), if he touches a piece of cloth that is not maḍi, or if he steps into the public road in front of his house. For this reason, most Brahmins wear silk while in maḍi as it, like wet cotton, does not readily transmit pollution. Silk does not lose maḍi when the person wearing it eats, whereas dry cotton does. Also a Brahmin wearing silk (or wet cotton maḍi) does not lose his state of ritual purity when touched by another Brahmin in mailige, or by touching a piece of cloth in the house, or by stepping into the road. However, he does become mailige if he touches someone of a different caste or someone in his own caste who is muṭṭucheṭṭu, or eats, sleeps, urinates, or defecates. Silk retains its maḍi, without being washed, for one week. . . .

If a man in cotton maḍi speaks to a person of another caste, or to a menstruating woman, he becomes mailige. All but the most orthoprax agree that he can, however, talk to them through a third person. If he is alone he may pick up a stick and talk to it, and thus, speaking in the third person, indirectly converse. There is a great deal of variation concerning this custom, and few people consistently practice it. A man in maḍi going to a temple to do puja and finding a lower-caste man blocking his way may first clear his throat to get the other person to move aside; if this is not adequate, he may use the third person and say "He is in my way."[3]

The Hindu gods are to be worshiped by those who are ritually pure. Worship consists in part of services performed, as in pūjā. Those who perform pūjā must have similar services performed for them, and there must be a chain of peoples of increasing levels of pollution so that those who service the deities are socially removed as far as possible from those who perform ritually defiling services for other people. The Vedas are pure and cannot be recited by women or low caste people. Temples are sacred and have around them a field of purity which should not be violated by unclean people such as untouchables. High caste people also have a field of purity so should not be touched or even approached by the unclean. The degree of purity acquired at birth cannot be raised because one lives with his family and kin; hence it is useless for an untouchable to study the Vedas.

The Untouchables

India has some 90 million untouchables. The largest occupational category is leatherworkers, called Camārs in the Gangā plains where they comprise a large segment of the population. There are many untouchable

castes and every caste knows of castes beneath it. Everywhere, even in Muslims regions, Hindus employed to sweep streets are untouchables, and they also perform much of the hired agricultural labor. The status of washermen is variable but usually not quite untouchable.

J. H. Hutton, who administered the 1931 census and therefore became acquainted with innumerable caste practices, has described some of them in *Caste in India.* Until recent years distance pollution was a widespread phenomenon in the South. Hutton quotes Aiyappan in regard to distance pollution in Kēraḷa, where it achieved its most elaborate development. There a Nambūtiri Brāhmaṇ could not be approached closer than 7 feet by a Nāyar, 23 feet by an Īḻavan, 64 feet by a Ceruman, and 74 to 124 feet by a Nāyaḍi (a low untouchable). Also, Nāyaḍis could not use a long bridge over the Ponnāni River lest they pollute it, but had to go miles around. If a Nāyaḍi touched water in which high caste men were bathing, the water lost its purifying power as long as the Nāyaḍi was in contact with it in sight of the bathers. Among the untouchables there was a considerable hierarchy; around Tirunelvēli in Tamiḻ Nāḍu there was a caste of *unseeables*; they were washermen who washed the clothes of the untouchables and therefore were doubly polluting. They had to do their work between midnight and daybreak. (Washermen are susceptible to pollution because they wash menstrual cloths, or if not that, at least clothes possibly polluted with semen or saliva.)

While distance pollution is scarcely observed today in the towns, and in tea stalls at bus stands untouchables may not be noticed as such, untouchability is maintained in villages in most parts of South Asia. In Tamiḻ Nāḍu in coffee shops there is a separate set of cups for untouchable laborers and yet another set for the Leatherworkers. These people squat on the floor near the door and rinse out their own cups. In Uttaṛ Pradesh the clothes of some Washermen are washed by another caste who are untouchable for the Washermen. Foreigners are outside the Hindu system so are technically polluting; a Brāhmaṇ host may provide tea but not drink it with his foreign guests. But their status is ambivalent, for sometimes they are invited to stay in Brāhmaṇ homes. Helen Ullrich states that while staying in a village in Karṇāṭaka if she suddenly turned a corner where an untouchable was standing he would jump back, not to avoid collision but to avoid polluting *her*—but then, she was staying in a Havik Brāhmaṇ's house.[4]

The British attempted to define who the untouchables were for legislative purposes, and finally listed those who were literally untouchable for clean castes. In the 1931 census Hutton referred to them by the term Exterior Castes. Gandhi, after considerable thought, decided to call them Harijans, meaning God's people, and that term is widely understood among themselves now. The Government of India has listed them on a schedule (list) so they can be easily identified, and thus refers to them by the

innocuous term Scheduled Castes. The Pakistan government likewise distinguishes, for census purposes, Scheduled Castes from other Hindus.

In the 1930s legislation was promulgated forcing temples to open their doors to all untouchables, but most continued to worship from afar, outside the walls. At the same time there were movements for change. Christian missionaries had some success among them, and in Mahārāshṭra a large group, the Mahārs, adopted Buddhism. In Kēraḷa groups of them, sometimes under Christian leadership, marched down Brāhmaṇ streets where no untouchable had set foot before. The increased use of public conveyances and public eating places has done much to break down untouchability where people don't know each other, and the Constitution of India forbids (but does not in fact prevent) its practice. Recent developments are discussed in Chapter 16.

Bodily Functions

The visitor to South Asia will fail to understand the reasons behind many particular items of behavior unless he is aware of the pervasiveness of the concepts of ritual pollution and purity. In urban centers, and even in villages, the reasons may have been long forgotten but the behavior continues. For an Indian sanitation is more than avoidance of physical dirt; it is a means of keeping himself physically and spiritually pure.

Saliva, as a bodily excretion, is impure. Hence, food is never eaten by taking a bite from the whole, as we eat bread. Instead a fragment of *capātī* (baked unleavened pancake of wheat) is broken off, dipped in curry, and eaten. This is a basic rule of etiquette in all parts of South Asia, and applicable to modern foods such as bread or cake. Fruits are preferably cut up before eating. People of orthodox behavior—not only Brāhmaṇs but others such as Chetrīs of Nepal—drink without touching to their mouths the cup or glass, but will pour the water in (a skill which must be learned!). In some places such as Āndhra and Kēraḷa people may eat rice by rolling it into a ball in the palm of the hand and throwing it into the open mouth so as not to contaminate the uneaten food with saliva from the hand—a habit some Christians also persist in. The toothbrush is abhorred (except among the urban elite) since it is contaminated and then returned to the mouth the next day, and moreover it may be made with animal (pig!) bristles. People brush their teeth with a particular type of astringent twig, purchased in bundles in the market or picked from the tree, and used only once. More commonly, villagers clean their teeth in the morning with the finger and kitchen ashes, which are considered purifying. The habit of smoking *bīṛīs* (tobacco rolled in leaves) is widespread; in conservative areas such as the Bihār plains people smoke through the fingers without touching the bīṛī to the lips.

Woman of orthodox Hindu Newārī family in Nepal during menstrual period. While ritually polluted, she uses her own vessels and utensils and does no housework.

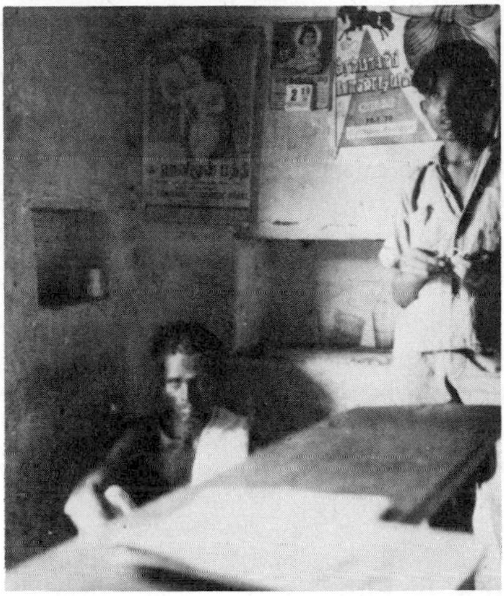

Coffee shop in Tamil̲ village. Clean castes sit at bench and are served coffee. Pa̤l̤lar (laboring) Harijans use glasses in center niche; lower Sweeper Harijans, those in left niche. Harijans squat on floor and rinse out own glasses. Low castes use separate vessels in village eating places in most parts of South Asia.

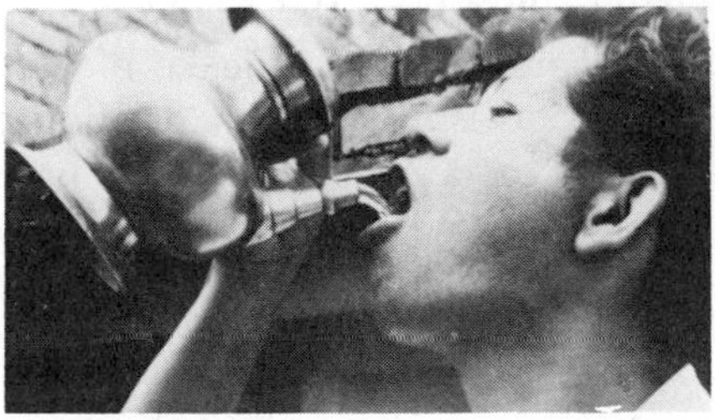

Orthodox Newārī brothers in Nepal avoid polluting themselves with saliva; neither cigaret nor drinking vessel touches the lips.

Though manufactured plates have come into vogue (porcelain in Pakistan while in India metal trays are often preferred for a meal), some people prefer not to reuse plates. In the South a proper meal, at home or in a restaurant, is eaten on a banana leaf. The diner sprinkles the leaf with a little water before the rice is served which cleanses it ritually more than actually, and eats with the fingers, never a spoon. After eating, the diner carries his own leaf to the garbage unless there are boys or people of distinctly lower status available to pick it up. In the North too some people eat on leaves; curries can be bought in leaf cups pinned with sticks. And

across the North at train stations one buys tea in a cheap throw-away clay cup which can be smashed on the tracks.

One must never eat with the left hand anywhere in South Asia—another fundamental rule of dining etiquette. But it may be used in preparing or even serving food; thus avoidance is ritual rather than from fear of germs. The left hand has lower status than the right because it is used for cleansing with water after defecation. Hands may or may not be washed before a meal by common folk. Some people are more careful to wash their feet than their hands as their feet are polluted by street dirt and sandals; at railway stations one can see people washing their feet before eating. Orthodox Hindus complete their washings and prayers, and only then do they eat their breakfast. Brāhmaṇs do not cook in pottery vessels, which are in any case porous and difficult to cleanse. Brass vessels can be rubbed with ashes to purify and polish them.

Nasal discharge, as a bodily secretion, is polluting, so should be blown on the ground where it will dry up; the foreign habit of blowing into a handkerchief carried around all day and used repeatedly on the face, is incomprehensible. Blood is polluting, hence the low status of the barber-surgeon; some Brāhmaṇs even avoided red or orange vegetables, or turmeric. Semen is polluting, hence the necessity of a morning bath, which all respectable Indians take by pouring water from a bucket.

When urinating a man should squat down, lest he be defiled by splashing. All elimination and cleansing functions should be performed outside the main part of the house. The foreign habit of locating expensively appointed bathing and toilet facilities in the center of the house, rather like a sanctum sanctorum, is viewed with incredulity. Traditionally one goes to a field to defecate, carrying a brass vessel of water to be applied with the left hand after defecation, or one finds a pond or stream. If a house has a latrine, it is in the farthest corner of the compound and consists of a hole in the ground, now sometimes leading to a septic tank. The Western sit-down toilet is viewed as unsanitary. The use of toilet paper is also a disgusting practice, since water is the only suitable cleansing agent.

The Abbe Dubois, describing Karṇāṭaka Brāhmaṇs about 1800, gives three pages of rules for defecation. A Brāhmaṇ must go out to the field with his brass vessel, put his triple cord over his left ear, stoop as low as possible, not look at the sun or moon or fire or another Brāhmaṇ or any sacred object, chew nothing, hold nothing on his head, and keep perfect silence. He must finish quickly, not look behind his heels, wash himself with the water mixed with a proper kind of earth using his left hand, then wash his hands five times with earth and water beginning with the left hand, and wash his genitalia with water and potter's earth. He must wash his face in a particular way, and rinse out his mouth eight times, spitting out on the left side. He must think on Vishṇu three times and swallow a little water while doing so. He then takes his morning bath, worships, and eats.

The breath is impure. Since fire is Agni, one should not blow on a fire but use a fan. This rule cannot always be followed; some blow on household fires but not on wedding or cremation fires. Others blow across the palm of the hand or through a bamboo tube, which purifies the breath.

Hair and fingernail parings are impure, and the barber cuts both. Tonsure of babies is a ritual which removes impurities contracted in the womb and at childbirth. One commonly shaves the head as part of purification after the death of a close relative, and fulfillment of some vows require shaving the head (though sādhus and people preparing for a pilgrimage let their hair grow long). Buddhist monks also keep their heads shaved.

The pollutability of women is manifest periodically by menstruation and the afterbirth, both of which require a time of purification. Yalman points out that in Sri Lanka women have to handle paddy, the purest of grains, with great care. They may not reap, and they are not allowed on the threshing floor (which is also sanctified) lest they cause a decline in the harvest.

Sexual intercourse pollutes women more than men. Whereas men can wash the genitalia, women are polluted internally by the semen. A man can thus have intercourse with a woman of lower status than himself, which accounts for hypergamy, since she is to be polluted more than he. Thus in villages untouchable women are available to men of higher castes for a small fee, though of course the men purify themselves afterwards. But a man will not eat food cooked by a woman of caste lower than himself; if he did he would be polluted internally.

In South Asia the handshake is not practiced, as it is an easy means of defilement. Likewise the gregarious backslap is not appreciated. People may jostle together in crowds, but those who are careful to maintain the purity of high caste will keep aloof if possible. A Hindu or Buddhist greets one by folding his palms together (originally a posture of worship). On the other hand, friends of the same sex enjoy much more bodily contact than in the West.

The pervasive use of water in rituals is common to all the religions, and has been mentioned as one of the most characteristic features of South Asian culture. All temples are built by tanks, rivers, or beaches, or at least have water in them somewhere. The morning bath is a ritual as well as a sanitary and cooling practice. (The foreign habit of sitting *in* one's own bathwater in a tub is viewed as quite defiling.) People sprinkle the street in front of houses and shops, which not only settles the dust but makes the premises appear invitingly clean. Ablutions are required to remove all forms of pollution—menstruation, contact with an untouchable, and such—while washing in the sacred water beside a temple or bathing in the Gangā is especially efficacious.

More purifying than water is oil, particularly in the form of ghī.

Many people regard an oil rubdown once a week as necessary too; they believe it not only cleanses, but cools the body.

More purifying yet is cow dung. In the morning women swab their house floors with a cow dung wash, which makes a suitable floor covering over the mud, and many women even spread it over tile or cement floors and sprinkle it on the street outside. As a paste it is often put on sores (it does contain acid), and is matted into the hair of sādhus. Brāhmaṇs can expiate many kinds of defilement by drinking the mixture of the five products of the cow. But leather, even of the cow, is polluting; hence sandals should always be left outside the doors of houses and temples.

Now there is no doubt that practices pertaining to ritual purity and pollution have become much weakened in recent decades. Educated people often wear sandals or shoes in the house, and menstrual pollution is widely ignored. Some apartments built in cities today have sit-down toilets. Pollution by untouchables is increasingly ignored in cities and even in smaller towns. Yet many South Asian practices, such as not biting off bread, not using toilet paper, not greeting with a handshake, and bathing regularly in the morning, can only be understood in the wider context.

Purifying Pollutants

There is a principle in the hierarchy of individuals, castes, saints, or gods that a pollutant of one rank may be purifying or edifying for the lower rank. The dung of a cow, which has high ritual rank, is an example. All feces are normally polluting, and stepping in it traditionally required a bath. Yet dung of the cow is used with water to remove all kinds of ritual pollution, as well as to pave house floors.

The lower parts of the body, especially the feet, are less pure than the upper. A devotee, a supplicant, or an employee may grasp his superior's feet to gain merit and express a relationship. Hence the footprints of deities of successive religions (Buddha, Adam for Muslims, and St. Thomas for Catholics) are said to be seen in Adam's Peak in Sri Lanka. In villages there are often crude outlines of feet said to represent the deity.

Hair, bones, or fingernails of Buddha were placed in early stūpas; normally such disjecta are defiling, but Buddha's are edifying. Before it became acceptable to make images of Buddha about the 1st century A.D., sculptors represented him by two footprints or a curl of hair. Because hair keeps growing, it symbolizes qualities other parts of the body lack.

It is common in Indian homes for a wife to eat a morsel or a grain from the plate of her husband after he finishes, though normally garbage left on a plate is a pollutant. A mother may ask her children to each take a morsel from the plate or leaf of a prestigious guest in the house, such as a sādhu, gurū, or American.

Semen has an ambivalent status like hair and fingernails. As a bodily excretion it is polluting so people should bathe in the morning. But it also has power and in a sense edifies the woman who receives it because the donor is of higher status. Blood, milk, and semen are thought to be related. Yalman reports that highland Buddhists in Sri Lanka believe blood distills into semen in the testicles when they become "heated" during intercourse, and milk is produced when the blood is "heated" in the breasts; both are white liquids. It requires 80 drops of blood to make a drop of semen. Father's and mother's semen mix in the uterus, forming a ball which grows and gets sustenance from the mother as well as from the semen of subsequent intercourse.

Young men throughout South Asia have a fear of semen loss because they are taught that it drains strength, whether from nocturnal emission, masturbation, or intercourse. Ascetics conserve theirs, and thus achieve great psychic and spiritual force. Practice of yoga helps control and utilize the semen thought to be in the spinal column and head. Carstairs says that of 36 Rājpūt informants in a Rājasthān village, 25 believed they suffered from spermatorrhea or had counteracted it by various measures, and the same was true for 6 of 9 Muslim informants. They all believed that semen is stored in a reservoir in the head, with a capacity of 20 *tolas* (6.8 ounces), and that he who possesses a good store of rich, viscous semen becomes a superman. "He glows with radiant health." Semen can be spoiled by eating wrong things, especially foods classified as "hot" in Indian medicine, and it can also be spoiled by bad deeds. Pus is identified as spoiled semen, as is any purulent body discharge, and venereal disease is caused in part by its deterioration.[5] Again we find bad karma and physical pollution inextricably linked. In spite of these ideas, Indians do boast of sexual prowess, even such "clean" people as Brāhmaṇs and Rājpūts.

The attitudes to milk and its products are analogous to this. Though a secretion, milk is auspicious and is poured over nāga icons. Cow's milk should not be polluted by adding water (a point seemingly overlooked by the milkman). Ghī is pure, and so are cream and other viscous substances such as egg-whites, oils, and honey. These "pure" and expensive items can generally be afforded only by the purer and higher castes, which highlights the sociological function of all this.

Muslims and Ritual Purity

Muslims observe many of these principles, though they are not so closely linked with definitive status categories as among Hindus. Sweeping streets and carrying off feces is thought to be so polluting that both in Pakistan and Bangladesh this is often done by Hindu untouchables. While Pakistan still has half a million untouchables, many more have gone to India

Smoking hukkā in a Pakistani Panjāb village. The Paṭvārī (village accountant) sits on cot, a prestigious place. Carpenter and Musallī (left) smoke together; discrimination against sweepers and laboring Musallīs has faded out in many areas.

and become Christians or Muslim converts, so in many villages people have to sweep up in front of their own houses. But the leatherworker is not polluting. Sandals are left outside houses and mosques, but it is a practical more than a religious matter. A fine test of pollutability is who smokes the *hukkā* (water pipe), and it varies from place to place. Often men of several farming castes (or lineages) will pass it among themselves. A landowner may smoke it but will draw the smoke through the hand and not touch the spout to his lips. Sometimes people put a cloth over the spout. Older people especially will not smoke with Muslim menials such as Musallīs.

Maintenance of personal purity is upheld not only by practices common to all South Asia but by some derived from the Near East with Islam. For instance, all Muslim males wash the genitals after urinating—or rather, they are supposed to. All mosques have a place to wash, and when the men come to say their morning prayers, they wash their hands, face, and feet, or sometimes take a bath. The morning bath is common in Pakistan as well as in India, but unless one goes to the mosque, it need not be taken so early in the morning as among Hindus of high caste who neither worship nor eat breakfast without bathing. Moreover, it gets warmer later in the morning. Women bathe in a secluded place behind the house. Before a wedding ceremony the bride and groom each undergo elaborate ceremonial bathing.

All Muslims should have their underarm hair shaved by the barber (whose occupation is hereditary). A distinctive Muslim practice is shaving off the pubic hair, which each person does himself or herself. The principle

of the purifying pollutants has to some extent carried over into Islam. A hair said to be that of Muhammad was kept in the important mosque in Śrīnagar, Kashmīr. When it disappeared in 1959 Muslims accused Hindus of stealing it, but after a couple months the Government of India claimed "the hair" had been found, and replaced it in the mosque. Muslims believe the pig and the dog to be especially unclean animals. They consider Māṛwāṛīs, Hindu traders who were numerous in Sindh, to be unclean because they are reported to eat carrion, prohibited by Islamic law.

Foods and Ranking

In the Brāhmaṇical food hierarchy ghī ranks highest; it purifies whatever it is poured on. Milk products, high-status grains, pulses, and vegetables are preferred foods. Brāhmaṇs in recent years have come to eat eggs (sometimes unfertilized, called "vegetarian eggs"). Most middle caste Hindus will eat goat meat ("mutton") and fish; chickens are a little less clean because they scavenge for food, while pigs are kept only by untouchables. Probably 90% of Indians are not, in fact, vegetarians, though the tendency has been for this Brāhmaṇical value to creep down the caste hierarchy. But one can never know how many high caste people succumb to the temptation to taste meat when away from home! Most villagers eat little or no meat however, except at special feasts, and generally even eggs are beyond their reach. Castes such as Rājpūts who emulate the Kshatriya rather than the Brāhmaṇ model may relish meat in general as strength-giving.

Beef is the most abhorrent of foods for Hindus. Killing an animal for food is itself sinful, and in the case of the cow, intolerable. Several states have laws prohibiting cow slaughter. Even castes which gave up beef eating 30 years ago may still be considered polluting by it, and tribals such as the Gōṇḍs, Savaras, or Hos as long as they eat beef can scarcely be considered Hindus. But numerous untouchable castes still eat it, and with gusto. They say it gives them strength to do hard work, and they might grinningly point out the large piles of beef apportioned to the various families in an untouchable hamlet when an ox is slaughtered in someone's front yard.

There is much regional variation as regards foods and ranking. Some middle castes in the South eat certain rats, considered a mark of an impure caste in the North. In Rājasthān fish are not eaten but in Bānglā it is a staple because it is what the terrain produces. The people on the western side of India may vent their disdain for Bāngālīs by referring to them as "those nasty fish eaters." In Sri Lanka where pollution sentiment is strong even Buddhists avoid beef. In Nepal as in neighboring Indian states, cow slaughter is banned. The Nepālī-speakers mostly avoid beef, and the Magars, a numerous Hinduized indigenous people, also avoid cow or buffalo meat,

but some other groups eat buffaloes. The Limbūs in the East will eat any meat. The Gurūng, a Tibetan-like people who employ both Lāmas and Brāhmaṇs, abjure mutton and domestic pig.

Most abhorrent to Muslims, of course, is the pig. They commonly serve "mutton" in their restaurants, and one can know in India that a Brāhmaṇ restaurant will be vegetarian and a Muslim one will serve mutton. Muslims do eat beef in Pakistan and some parts of India, but where local sentiment is strong or cow slaughter is prohibited they may not. The Qur'ān also prohibits the consumption of alcoholic beverages, but in Pakistan the matter is rationalized by interpreting the prohibition to apply to particularly strong beverages. Muslims and Christians in Kēraḷa can readily get beef, but in many other places Christians do without it; they usually reject village pork, which untouchables produce.

There is a classification of foods according to medicinal criteria into hot and cold (which Spanish-speakers in America also follow). "Cool" foods are healthy but "hot" ones produce strong urine. This is not a question of chilies (which are "hot" in this sense, however). Naturally this too is involved in ranking. Where rice is the staple, high castes consider millets such as jvār, rāgi, and kambu as inferior and somewhat "heating." (Foreigners have a hard time tasting these because they are never served in restaurants nor to guests, not even by poor people.) Alcoholic beverages are considered heating and are not taken by the orthodox—hence India's attempts, now mostly given up, to enforce prohibition, a Gandhian ideal. Toddy-tappers are low in the caste hierarchy. Other hot foods are some oils, unrefined sugar, meats, and pungent spices. Cool foods include the valued grains, milk, butter, sugar, vegetables like the cucumber, and most fruits (except papaya). Carstairs points out that the cool foods are generally more expensive and prestigious, whereas the hot ones are the staples of the low caste majority.

The kitchen is the most protected part of the house. Brāhmaṇs and even many middle castes refuse to let people except their kin in the kitchen. If the anthropologist does succeed in entering the kitchen of an orthodox house, it would have to be purified afterwards.

Hindu caste ranking across North India (but not so much in the South, Gujarāt, or Bānglā) is symbolized most precisely by the giving and receiving of three categories of foods: raw, *pakkā*, and *kaccā*. Raw food, such as grain, does not conduct much pollution and can be received by high castes from low castes (except sometimes untouchables). Pakkā food is superior because it is purified with the addition of a little ghī, or cooked entirely in oil. Kaccā food is the coarse daily fare of the majority, generally boiled, without ghī, and perhaps hot (medicinally). Brāhmaṇs will accept pakkā food from a certain range of castes beneath them, but will eat kaccā food only if prepared at home. Brāhmaṇ-operated restaurants in India are the best, and can be patronized by anybody, but the orthodox will not eat in

non-Brāhmaṇ restaurants. Who can take water from the hands of whom is also everywhere a very important criterion of caste ranking, and in villages each main bloc of castes is likely to have its own well.

In his monumental *History of the Dharmaśāstra*, P. V. Kane points out that food occupied more space in traditional Hindu law than any other subject except marriage.

Caste Ranking

In an attempt to establish caste ranking within a village in Uttar Pradesh, McKim Marriott asked people to shuffle cards with caste names and compared the results with his detailed observations of food transactions. In the accompanying table (Table 8–1) rank by opinion is shown to correlate quite well with food transactions. There are 24 castes in the village, and the numbers under each kind of food (plus garbage and feces) indicate in how many instances, in transactions with the other 23 castes, a particular caste can show superiority over the others by giving it food, minus the number of instances it acknowledges inferiority by receiving food and not being able to give the same kind. Under the "raw food" column the first 22 castes can all exchange whole grains and such among themselves. They can also give it to the two lowest castes, but not take it from their hands; thus, these two—Hunters and Sweepers—are below the Leatherworkers and all the rest of the 22 castes.

Transactions of pakkā food are more finely discriminatory. Each caste from Brāhmaṇs down to Watermen can invite all the first 11 castes for feasts; even Brāhmaṇs can come because the food is purified with ghī. Each of these can dominate 13 castes below those of this bloc by giving them pakkā food but refusing to eat the same from their hands, for even ghī doesn't purify to this extent. The kaccā food category is even more discriminating. Brāhmaṇs can take it only from the hands of other Brāhmaṇs, while 22 castes beneath them are in a position to take it from Brāhmaṇs who will not, in turn, take it from their hands. The same is true for 15 of the castes below Jāṭs. As for garbage, willingness to remove it from a person of another caste, if it cannot be reciprocated, shows inferiority. Marriott writes for this particular village:

> A wealthy person of low caste who wishes to demonstrate his power is not forbidden to feast high-caste persons, so long as he hires high-caste caterers to cook and serve, and does not attempt to feed the guests with his own hand; but in no such case which I investigated were the high-caste invitees pleased to attend (and thereby to accept even indirect, financial dominance) unless they were assured that some member of the host's caste would acknowledge that caste's inferiority unambiguously on the same occasion by gathering up the garbage-laden plates of the high-caste diners.[6]

TABLE 8–1 Caste Ranking in an Uttar Pradesh Village (adapted from Marriott in Singer and Cohn 1968, by permission of Aldine Publishing Company)

Caste	*No. of Families*	*Rank by Opinion*	*Rank by Food Transaction*	*Raw Food*	*Pakkā Food*	*Kaccā Food*	*Garbage*	*Feces*	*Total*
Sanādhya Brāhmaṇ	43	1	1	2	13	22	22	1	60
Jāṭ—cultivator	15	2	5	2	13	15	19	1	50
Bārahsenī—merchant	1	3	2	2	13	14	18	1	48
Kulaśreṣṭha—scribe	2	4	3	2	13	14	18	1	48
Maiṭhil—carpenter	8	5	4	2	13	14	18	1	48
Jogī—devotee	3	6	6	2	13	14	10	1	40
Phulmālī—gardener	1	7	7	2	13	14	10	1	40
Kāchī—cultivator	3	8	8	2	13	14	10	1	40
Baghele—goatherd	6	9	9	2	13	14	10	1	40
Ṭhākur—barber	6	10	10	2	13	4	4	1	24
Turai—waterman	4	11	11	2	13	−1	4	1	19
Gola—potter	12	12	12	2	−6	−6	−10	1	−19
Darzī—tailor	1	13	13	2	−6	−6	−10	1	−19
Kaṛhera—cottoncarder	5	14	14	2	−6	−6	−10	1	−19
Kolī—weaver	6	15	15	2	−6	−6	−10	1	−19
Khaṭīk—cultivator	9	16	16	2	−11	−6	−10	1	−24
Faqīr—devotee (Muslim)	11	17	17	2	−9	−9	−10	1	−25
Mirāsī—singer (Muslim)	1	18	18	2	−9	−9	−10	1	−25
Telī—oilman (Muslim)	1	19	19	2	−9	−9	−10	1	−25
Maṇihar—bangleman (Muslim)	1	20	20	2	−9	−9	−10	1	−25
Mathuriyā—washerman	6	21	22	2	−14	−14	−10	1	−35
Jāṭav—leatherworker	16	22	21	2	−14	−14	−10	1	−35
Kanjar—hunter	1	23	23	−22	−22	−22	−11	0	−77
Bhangī—sweeper	4	24	24	−22	−22	−22	−22	−22	−110
	No. of ranks			2	6	9	8	3	12

The Bhangīs (Sweepers) go about early in the morning and remove the night soil from the houses of all other castes, but will not do so for the Kanjar (Hunters), who have to remove their own.

Ranking by food transaction, then, can be used in this region more accurately than other diagnostic criteria for ranking castes according to traditional Hindu hierarchy. The chief anomaly in this case is that of the Carpenters, who for long have claimed to be a sort of Brāhmaṇ group and have succeeded in raising their ritual status above what people suppose they merit in other respects.

This list shows that the castes can be lumped together into blocs. The kaccā food column shows that below Brāhmaṇs and Jāṭs the next seven castes form a bloc. Below these, five Hindu artisan castes form another bloc. The four Muslim castes will feast each other as well as remove each other's garbage. The Washermen and Leatherworkers form another bloc, for both work with polluting items. The two lowest castes are untouchable, but Bhangīs are the lowest because they do scavenging work which Hunters do not. The total number of ranks or blocs significant in kaccā food transactions is 9, but the number of ranks or blocs significant in all five categories of transactions combined is 12.

But granted that the purity-pollution complex is a fine indicator of rank, we now have to consider to what extent this correlates with ranking by other kinds of criteria, such as power, authority, wealth, employment, erudition, caste size, or the varṇa system. That an individual is not always treated in accordance with his ritual rank is obvious in the case of the missionary or foreign visitor. Though technically outside the caste system and therefore unclean, villagers will often put such a person near the top of the anthropologist's list of rank by opinion. Other examples can be cited: adherents of the Lingāyat sect reject most Brāhmaṇical symbols (except vegetarianism) and neither observe menstrual pollution nor untouchability, yet they are ranked just below Brāhmaṇs. (See Ishwaran's chapter in *South Asia: Seven Community Profiles.*)

In a village there may, in fact, be two apexes in the pyramid of caste hierarchy, one based on ritual status and the other on political and economic power. The latter is the Kshatriya model followed by many of the important landowning castes; chief exemplars of this today are the Rājpūts who as princes and landowners are emulated in Rājasthān and throughout western and central India. They value power, wealth, valor, and worldly achievements; they like meat and liquor, and enjoy sex. They may balance this with some behavior defined as pious by Brāhmaṇs, and employ Brāhmaṇs. For many villagers this model is more meaningful and more attainable than the Brāhmaṇical. For instance, Jāṭ farmers, a large and prosperous caste-cluster, frankly say in places that they are higher in status than Brāhmaṇs. This is not a new feature, for even Pāli Buddhist literature ranked Kshatriyas above Brāhmaṇs. In the South there is, or was, a division of castes into

right-hand and left-hand castes. The right-hand ones were those who sought power and wealth, including many of the cultivators whose aim was essentially landowning. The left-hand ones were those who sought prestige through piety and observance of Brāhmaṇical rules, which included carpenters and stonemasons. The anomaly of the carpenters in Table 8–1 is explained this way. Power and wealth as the ultimate determinants of caste ranking have been obscured by Sanskrit literature, which was written by those whose prestige was based on piety.

A village having two such apexes to the caste pyramid has been described by D. N. Majumdar. In this village, near Lucknow in Uttar Pradesh, there were 123 families (Table 8–2). Majumdar classified Brāhmaṇs and Ṭhākurs, a numerous landowning caste, as together comprising the "high castes." A middle bloc consisted of 9 castes with 37 families, and a third bloc consisted of 4 unclean castes with 59 families. Castes of the intermediate bloc might claim to be Kshatriyas, Vaiśyas, or Śūdras, but it matters little. Ṭhākurs once held virtual monopoly over lands in this village and dominated it thoroughly, but deferred to Brāhmaṇ ritual superiority in food matters and in seating arrangements. Since the Ṭhākurs have been deprived of their land monopoly with abolition of the large estates, they have been seeking for new ways to maintain their old status, and this cannot be achieved through Brāhmaṇical emulation. These recent developments have resulted in increasingly acute intercaste rivalries, and also in a stronger intervillage axis of Ṭhākurs.

A much simpler pattern prevails in some Himālayan regions. Berreman

TABLE 8–2 Castes in a Village near Lucknow, U.P. (adapted from Majumdar 1958)

Castes and Traditional Occupations	*Families*
High castes	
Brāhmaṇ	3
Ṭhākur—headman, landowner	22
Intermediate castes	
Ahīr—cowherd, tenant	18
Kurmī—farmer	1
Gadariā—goatherd, farmer	4
Lohār—blacksmith	1
Barhāi—carpenter	3
Kumār—potter	5
Nāī—barber	3
Kathik—dancer	1
Kalwār—merchant	1
Unclean castes	
Pāsī—servant, laborer	21
Dhobī—washerman	7
Camār—leatherworker, laborer	29
Bhaksor—basket maker	2
	123

TABLE 8–3 Castes in a Pahāṛī Village in the Himālayas, U.P. (from Berreman 1963)

High Castes	*Households*
Brāhmaṇ	1
Rājpūt	37
Low Castes (Ḍoms)	
Lohār—blacksmith	2
Nāī—barber	1
Bāgjī—drummer, tailor	4
	45

has described a Hindu village in the Pahāṛī-speaking parts of upper Uttar Pradesh. Here there are only five castes (Table 8–3); 90% of the population consists of 37 Rājpūt families and one Brāhmaṇ family, while 10% of the population is comprised of Ḍoms, generally untouchables, with seven families divided into three castes. The gulf between the two blocs is quite wide. In this village the Rājpūts and Brāhmaṇs own 94% of the arable land and almost all the useful animals, so they require the services of the Ḍoms. The untouchability of the Ḍoms as contrasted with the clean state of the two high castes expresses the degree of economic dependence. The village council and its president told the Ḍoms, "If you want land, you will have to leave this village to get it." Within each of the two blocs there is a considerable degree of permissiveness in extramarital sexual relations. A further expression of the hierarchy is seen in that low caste women are often available to high caste men, but a low caste man would approach a high caste woman only if he felt he could avoid a severe beating, or even death.

Among the Ḍoms in this Pahāṛī village no caste would admit to being the lowest. They would point to Shoemakers as the lowest, but Shoemakers would in turn say that Sweepers of the plains or beef-eating Muslims or Christians are lower than themselves. One villager said, "Englishmen and Muslims are untouchable because they have an alien religion and eat beef, yet we too are treated as untouchables. This is not proper. We should be accorded higher status."[7] In this small village there has not yet been perceptible change in the caste structure, nor have the Ḍoms found ways to avail themselves of the educational incentives and other benefits extended by the government to Scheduled Castes.

The Economic System and Status

The economic expression of the caste structure, the traditional contractual exchange of goods and services, is termed by anthropologists the *jajmānī* system. This was first described by the Wisers for a village near

Āgrā in the 1930s and has since been found to operate in its essentials all over South Asia. A *jajmān* in Hindī is a person for whom a Brāhmaṇ performs rituals, often an owner of some land or a person of substance. He will be served by all the other occupational specialists in the village too, who will also exchange goods and services among themselves according to traditional formulae and under unwritten contract. This has been supplanted by money economy in large part, but still partially operates in most villages.

For instance, a Carpenter family will have a relationship with a certain number of farming families, agreeing to provide them with wooden plows and other implements as needed, and repair them, in return for a stipulated portion of the harvest. But if the farmer wants the Carpenter to do some fancy work or make something unusual he will have to make an agreement to pay in cash. A Potter will provide pots to a newly married couple and replace small and medium ones as needed, but large pots will have to be purchased. In Pakistan winnowing is a lowly job, and there is a caste of Winnowers who work day and night at harvest time to get the job done. They are paid one twentieth or so of the harvest, taken equally from the portions of the landlord and the tenant. Barbers cut hair, shave, cut fingernails, perform minor surgery, and in some areas perform rituals and serve as messengers on ceremonial occasions, all for traditionally specified yearly compensation. But Mandelbaum writes that he knows of Barbers that demanded payment in cash if a young man wanted a haircut in the city style. Even the method of work is traditional; the writer while living in a village was served by the Barber traditionally assigned to that house, and since there was no produce to give he paid the usual amount of a quarter rupee for a haircut. But when the Barber was asked to use hand clippers instead of scissors and comb, he demanded half a rupee!

Certain client families are practically inherited by a specialist. But in some areas the families of a Barber or Potter caste, for instance, will divide up the village geographically. Certain specialists—particularly Watchmen, Sweepers, Accountants, and Brāhmaṇs or others who serve in temples—serve the whole village and receive compensation from all. The members of an occupational caste may boycott a client, and may be supported by other occupational specialists. The strength of the system comes home to a foreigner if he takes a house in a village. He will likely be mysteriously approached by one Sweeper, one Washerman, one Gardener, and so on, and he will find it very difficult if not impossible to fire one and replace him with another. While it may be said that this system was exploitative and produced class inequalities, it may also be argued that in some respects the landowners are exploited by the specialists, and the latter certainly enjoy a measure of security, subject of course to the prosperity of the village as a whole.

There is a continual flux of castes so that successive families and castes

become landowners, then are threatened by intrusive peoples or groups who manage to improve their economic clout. The history of western South Asia is frought with successive peoples who came to dominate the land, such as Gūjaras, Jāṭs, Rājpūts, Khāns, and Ṭhākurs while in Mahārāshṭra the Marāṭhās and in Kēraḷa the Nāyars have in recent centuries increased their power. In the South Brāhmaṇs came to own much of the land, though they comprise only 3% of the population; only a few of them were priestly Brāhmaṇs. Most Hindu landowning groups except for Brāhmaṇs tend to emulate the Kshatriya model. But though there is some lag, ritual status in time tends to follow the power structure.

In the central highlands of Sri Lanka the dominant Sinhala caste-cluster is the Goyigamas, who are agriculturalists. Below them are a bloc of artisan castes, who in turn are served by the lowest and unclean castes. Yalman recounts how in a particular village a family of Blacksmiths came to own most of the land, and the poorer among the Goyigamas had to work the Blacksmiths' lands as sharecroppers. The relationship between the two caste groups was a difficult one:

> The contradictions inherent in such a situation always gave rise to subtle problems of etiquette. The high-caste laborers naturally found it difficult to treat the Blacksmiths as they would other low castes. In Sinhalese villages, it is customary for the low castes to crouch or stand while the high castes are seated. If the high-caste person is on a chair, then the low-caste person may sit on a mat. Hingappu [a Blacksmith] would often come to visit me. Sometimes a few of his workers would also be in my hut, sitting on chairs and gossiping as usual. The arrival of Hingappu would give rise to some embarrassment. The workers had to get out of their chairs, to show some sign of deference to their landlord, yet they had to pretend to me and to each other that they were not getting up for a low-caste man, but only wanted to stretch their legs. It was always possible to create further confusion by my insisting on getting a camp chair and offering it to Hingappu. The camp chair was considered of higher status than an ordinary chair, and this time Hingappu would be embarrassed to show his superiority.[8]

Caste Mobility

A widespread misconception about caste is that the system is a static and unchanging social mosaic. Bernard Cohn points out that this view is due in part to the collection and recording of data by the British colonial government:

> A caste was a "thing," an entity, which was concrete and measurable; above all it had definable characteristics—endogamy, commensality rules, fixed occupations, common ritual practices. . . . What was recorded could be collated so that the Lohars, or the Ahirs, or the Mahishyas, or the Okkiligas could be pigeonholed and one could then go on to the next group to be described. This way of thinking about a particular caste was useful to the administrator, because it gave the illusion of knowing a people, and he did not have to differentiate too much among individual Indians.[9]

It was deemed necessary for the government to categorize castes, for the whole body of British law could not be superimposed on Indian villages without giving some consideration to the village councils and caste councils (panchāyats) and the voluminous traditional laws written in the *Dharmaśāstras*. Legislation regarding land tenure, inheritance rights, or untouchability demanded quantitative data which was provided by the decennial censuses.

The matter of recording caste names became an increasing problem for the colonial government because each time a census was about to be taken, a greater number of petitions would be submitted requesting acknowledgment of higher status. Some wanted to be known by a more prestigious name, or wanted a name such as Rājpūt attached to their caste name, or desired that the occupational connotation be dropped, or wanted to be disassociated from a branch of the caste in an inferior direction. Many thousands of these were submitted to the government, coming to a climax with the 1931 census, which was the last to attempt a listing of castes. Though the officials conscientiously tried to sort out the requests, the problem became unmanageable. Moreover people with Western values said that by listing castes the government was perpetuating the whole institution. The Census of India today lists Scheduled Castes, Tribes, languages, and religions, but not castes.

Caste has built within it the mechanisms for fluidity—at least more so than is popularly believed in the West. It is precisely because the society is a plural one (cultural rather than just racial plurality) that change can and does occur in its parts, for a particular segment can strike out in a new direction more easily than a segment in a mass society with the melting-pot ideal. Though there is general correlation between high caste and worldly achievement, there are individuals and families who especially succeed in acquiring wealth, power, important jobs, or special recognition. If several related families thus succeed, the whole caste will enjoy increased deference, and after some lag, the ritual status will tend to follow the achieved status.

A caste may try to rise within the orthodox system, or bypass it. If the former route is chosen it has to creep up in the purity-pollution complex and the jajmānī system—as the aforementioned Carpenters—and generally sustain such claims with respectable prosperity. The price to be paid includes piety, performance of purity rituals, vegetarianism, and in many areas forbidding widows to marry. Rājpūts established their power by landowning but were within the Hindu system because they deferred to Brāhmaṇs in some matters. In Pakistan a birādarī that has high status must own land or have other wealth, and the most important symbolic price to be paid is seclusion of women.

In India kin and caste groups have attempted to achieve status by bypassing the whole Hindu hierarchy, perhaps by becoming Muslims, Chris-

tians, or Buddhists. But untouchables who do so and who remain in their villages generally find that their position does not really improve. They lack resources to invest or buy an education, are separated by a great gulf from the others, and lack confidence in their ability to succeed at a different level. But in modern South Asia there are many new avenues to achievement which bypass the old Hindu and Muslim hierarchies. Christians often achieve considerable respect, not because they have become Christian, but because they tend to go in for higher education and thereby get respectable jobs. New avenues abound in industry and politics. But in conservative regions such as Sindh, north Bihār, Bangladesh, or the Āndhra deltas there are fewer new avenues to achievement than in dynamic regions such as western Mahārāshṭra or Panjāb.

One can see the fallacy of the view that society is ossified by tracing the history of one caste over the centuries, following a few castes through the decennial censuses, or observing contemporary political activity. We cite two examples.

Fishermen Become Descendants of Noah

We can trace summarily the history of the Paravar caste of coastal Tamil̲ Nāḍu over 2000 years. Originally fishers, some rose in status through trade and Brāhmaṇism, while others later broke off and bypassed the system by joining Buddhism, Islam, or Catholicism, and modernization has provided yet other means of status mobility.

Some Tamil̲ Śangam literature (first three centuries) represents the Paravar as simple fisher folk living in miserable huts on the sands where stinking fish are laid out to dry. The children have unoiled hair and adorn themselves with green leaves. They are a rustic and happy lot. But other works refer to branches of the caste-group as traders, monopolizing the pearl fishery, selling shell bangles and fish, and importing gems, horses, and sandalwood. They lived on the Kāvēri River mouth in a port city with high-storied houses, great warehouses, and a tall lighthouse. They developed a political relationship with the Pāṇḍiyan king and ran his pearl industry. To support this new-found status they latched onto the Hindu Great Tradition and took the caste name Paravar (short for Paratavar), "people of Bhārata," ancestor of the Mahābhārata heroes. They invented a myth that they came from Ayodhyā in the North, were of the race of Varuṇa, and at the end of the last kalpa when the earth was deluged they escaped in an ark which landed on the southern Tamil̲ coast. They adopted the major Brāhmaṇical deities and later claimed Kshatriya rank. But part of the caste remained as poor fishers.

By the 7th century a new direction of acculturation got under way with the trade of Buddhist merchants along the east, who frequented the coasts between Bānglā and Sri Lanka. The bankers and moneylenders from

the North were called *śreshṭhins*, and after them these Tamiḻ coastal merchants called themselves Ceṭṭis, the forerunners of the modern Ceṭṭi caste-cluster of moneylenders and merchants who are today Hindus and have long since broken off any caste connection with the lowly fisher folk. Meanwhile some of the Paravar farther south had their own "kings" and capital city, supported by trade with Buddhist and Hindu kingdoms in Southeast Asia.

A third direction of acculturation set in when Muslims began to dominate the Indian Ocean. Some of the Paravar became Muslims or their women married Muslim traders. These built a new port (Kāyal, which Marco Polo visited) and devised a new genealogy going back to Noah, a sufficiently venerable ship's pilot, which goes like this: Adam and Eve were in Sri Lanka, the Garden of Eden, and when they were expelled they came over to the Tamiḻ coast of India (local Muslims point out the tomb of Abel at Rāmēśvaram which has unfortunately been corrupted by the construction of a large Hindu temple). There was a world flood (an account superseding the Hindu flood account), and Noah escaped in a wooden ship, so this Muslim caste is now called in Tamiḻ "People of the Wooden Ship." "Proof" of these events is that even in Kashmīr Muslims use wooden ships. Later, says the caste "history," Solomon visited India by ship, gave his name to the city of Cidambaram (!), and imported gold and peacocks to Palestine.

The original Paravars, therefore, had split into Hindu, Buddhist, and Muslims castes, while some continued their lowly fishing trade. With the Portuguese came a new Great Tradition. The Paravar perceived them to be stronger than the Arabs and in 1532 sent a deputation to Goā to request aid to fend off further Muslim encroachment. The Portuguese obliged, with the proviso that they be baptized by the Vicar-General of the Bishop, who also bestowed on them prominent Portuguese names. Then Francis Xavier visited them and won many more to the Catholic faith. All the fisher Paravar have been Catholics ever since. The original deities are essentially incarnated as Catholic saints, and a suitable mythology has been devised.

Today none of the four great traditions provides sufficient prestige, so the Paravar are embarking on a fifth direction of acculturation. Though retaining their pseudo-Portuguese heritage, these fishermen are now adopting secular criteria of status, such as houses of cement with tile roofs, motorized fishing boats, and educated children. Thus the Paravar fishers who did not become Ceṭṭis or Muslims are still in processes of caste mobility, fission, and fusion.

Saltmakers Become Rājpūts

How the Noniyās, a saltmaking caste of eastern Uttar Pradesh, have become Rājpūts has been described by William Rowe. Whereas elderly villagers claim that in their childhood Noniyās were "almost untouchable,"

they now are recognized as Cauhāns, a well-known Rājpūt lineage, and can be ranked 9th or 10th in the anthropologists list of 24 local castes.

Their rise in ritual status generally followed their economic advancement. After the 1850s some of them took up occupations other than salt-making such as earth digging, road construction contracting, and brick making. Some acquired money thereby, and within the caste emerged a small elite who began to contract laborers and marry wives from more distant villages. About 1900 these elite formed the Rājpūt Advancement Society which by 1935 claimed to represent the caste everywhere. In places where the Noniyās continued to follow demeaning occupations this society grew more slowly.

To support their claim to Rājpūt status (considered Kshatriya, whereas they had been Śūdras) a new mythology was devised as follows: The real origin of the caste was in the Delhi region (the western direction is the prestigious one). The last Hindu king of Delhi, a Cauhān who lived in the 12th century, was defeated by Muslims under Muhammad Ghūrī. The Cauhāns were so heroic in defending themselves that the new Muslim ruler demeaned them by forcing them to move eastward and make salt for a living. In their flight before the Muslim armies the Cauhāns removed their sacred threads to conceal their twice-born status. Over the centuries the Cauhāns have forgotten their origin and their right to wear the sacred thread, and now it is time to claim the rightful Kshatriya status.

A caste history published by the Advancement Society traces the genealogical links with various Rājpūt clans who fled eastward before the invading Muslims and states:

> Research and diligent work have shown that Loniya [Noniyā] is not the name of any caste, but it is only a trade name. When the origin of the "Loniyas" was traced, it was found that they were Rajputs in the beginning, but because they assumed the occupation of making and sale of salt, they became known as "Loniyas." *Lon* means salt. . . . With the passing of time, and having forgotten their ancestral work they have also forgotten their origin and began to be called by local names. However, there is no doubt but that these persons are in fact Rajput descendants. The sun of their fate is hidden under the shade of clouds. They are crushed by their work, and because of mean-minded persons, they are unable to earn their just profits. They are without hope of performing their duty (dharma). Seeing this state of the Rajputs, I pray to the Aryan people that not everything has been broken or perished. Let us forget that which has happened and save the Rajputs in the present. There is our hope, and it is our main duty, also.[10]

In line with these claims, the Noniyās conducted a mass ceremony to don the sacred thread, but the effort at that time was unsuccessful. Later they began to put it on an individual basis. Priests now appear willing to perform ceremonies for the affluent families among them who are able to give adequate remuneration. Within the last few years high caste opposition

So the fantasy of the Noniyās calling themselves Cauhān Rājpūts has begun to fade.

But at the same time there is an increasing change of values about the criteria of caste status, and there is loss of interest among the younger generation about the symbols of ritual status. Rowe reports that the very oldest Noniyās do not wear the sacred thread, a very considerable number of the middle generation do, and a decreasing number of the younger generation wear it. Among the reasons for the latter are the activity of the Ārya Samāj which opposes caste orthodoxy of the type Noniyās emulated, educational incentives for Scheduled Castes for which they are not eligible if they are Rājpūts, and the expense of Sanskritic rituals. Nonetheless it is agreed that they have indeed succeeded in rising somewhat in the caste hierarchy.

Endogamy among the Noniyās has remained unshaken, both in this upward movement and in the contemporary tendency to accept class rather than caste values. The history of this caste also exemplifies a tendency found everywhere among low castes and tribals: that at the very time upper castes are moving in new directions (modernization) they are moving toward the old orthodoxy.

Muslim Castes and Lineages

Islam says that every Muslim is brother to every other Muslim. But already before Islam reached India, it began adapting to hierarchical patterns in Persia. Persian scholars inherited the Āryan three-class ideal, and even as Muslims they wrote that each class should keep its own place, especially nobility, priests, soldiers, and the tribal people who had no priests. Islam was further fragmented because it was brought eastward by Arabs, Turks, Tājiks, and Afghāns, each original ethnic element tending to form hereditary lineages. In addition there were adherants of Shī'ā and Sunnī divisions and the sects within them. All these were distinguished from Muslims whose ancestors were converted in India.

Muslims in India generally have a range of castes parallel with that of the Hindus they live among, while in Pakistan the hierarchy is not quite so clearly marked for the middle groups at least. Muslims of Uttar Pradesh have been described by Ghaus Ansari. The most honorable category is called Ashrāf—and this is true in India generally. They claim foreign ancestry. Highest among the Ashrāf are the Sayyids, who claim descent from the Prophet himself through his daughter Fātima. They are divided into numerous lineages going back to Hasan, Husain, or various Sayyid saints, and these lineages are preferentially endogamous. A symbol of their status is their prohibition against helping any Sayyid in the name of charity.

The second category of Ashrāf is the Shaikhs, also claiming descent from Arabs. Among these the Ansārī claim descent from those Arabians who gave aid and shelter to Muhammad and his friends. Other Shaikhs include the Siddīqīs, Alvīs, and Fārūkīs (lineage names used today as last or family names), who claim descent from those who accompanied Muhammad when he migrated from Mecca to Medina. The third category of Ashrāf consists of Mughals, and the fourth of Paṭhāns, who are about equal in status. Mughals are supposed to be descended from invaders from Central Asia such as Uzbeks, Tājiks, Turkomens, and Qizilbāsh. Paṭhāns claim descent from Afghān royalty and are divided into Yūsufzāī, Lōdī, Ghourī, Kakār, and many others, some of whom have tribal territories in the North-West Frontier Province and in eastern Afghanistan. Many lineages are divided into sects, which also tend to be endogamous.

Artisan castes cannot easily claim foreign origin and are considered as converts from Hinduism; they are thought to retain many Hindu practices. Some of them in Uttar Pradesh are Julāhā (Weaver), Kumhār (Potter), Nāī (Barber, who also circumcises), Dhobī (Washerman, who is not unclean), Telī (Oilpresser), and Faqīr (holy man or tomb keeper or beggar); also Marriage Broker, Fireworks Maker, Jester, Waterman, Innkeeper, and Herdsman.

There are also Muslim castes that are essentially untouchable. The Bhangīs (Sweepers) traditionally could not enter mosques, and to this day are generally not seen eating or smoking with people of clean caste. But among Muslims untouchable status is determined more by occupation than by inherited ritual pollution.

Obviously the whole genealogical structure of the Ashrāf is largely fabricated, though it is true that many upper class Muslims have a little Arab or Persian ancestry. Ashrāf status is essentially a style of life and requires a suitable level of prosperity, such as comes with landowning. It is a common joke among Muslims that a Butcher can rise to Shaikh one year and to Sayyid the next. Uttar Pradesh Weavers, who are quite numerous, have started a social uplift movement and have begun to claim Shaikh descent. The most important symbol of Ashrāf status that an aspiring lineage or caste can adopt is *pardā* (seclusion of women), which is why this practice is found primarily in cities and among landowners in northern India and in Pakistan. Another symbol of higher status is securing the services of a respectable maulvī.

The term *caste* is often applied to these Muslim groups, and in fact they may use the Urdū word *zāt*, equivalent of jāti. But this is officially in disfavor in Pakistan, and in general Muslims do not wish to acknowledge that they have castes. The Ashrāf category has been compared with the twice-born among Hindus, those who can wear the sacred thread. Obviously such manifestations of caste mobility as getting the services of a respectable religious specialist, protecting women, and manufacturing genealogies have

parallels in the Brāhmaṇical caste hierarchy. Yet the system is more flexible than the Hindu caste structure, and endogamy is not so rigid. Mandelbaum points out that "village Muslims are strongly on guard against individual pollution, as in menstruation and childbirth, but their views of corporate, permanent pollution are more diffuse and are officially disclaimed."[11] Muslim groups in a village (except possibly untouchables) interdine freely, worship in the same mosque, and participate in ceremonies together.

Lineages or mythical lineages are divided into birādarīs consisting of a limited range of male kin. These tend to be endogamous among the Ashrāf, who have within them even smaller marriage circles to preserve purity of lineage. Marriage of close relatives is permitted (contrary to marriage rules for Hindus in North India). But marriage outside the birādarī or zāt is also fairly common if necessary to get a spouse, especially among groups of equivalent status. Hypergamy is also practiced; Muslim Rājpūts and landowners in general do sometimes take wives from among the castes beholden to them. Caste ranking is more difficult to determine than among Hindus, for there are few compunctions about the ritual purity of foods.

In Pakistan villages the jajmānī system is quite strong, clearly dividing landowners, tenants, artisans, and menials. In a Pakistani Panjāb village described by Zekiye Eglar there is a predominant bloc of landowning and tenant castes or lineages supported by a smaller bloc of occupational castes, such as Barber, Baker, Cobbler, Carpenter, Potter, Blacksmith, Weaver, Tailor, Bard, and Laborer. These serve the landed farmers according to traditional contract. Intermarriage among these service castes is common, though the occupations tend to be hereditary. In this village there are essentially two blocs of castes. Even in Swāt, the narrow northernmost Indus plains, the Paṭhān landowners have jajmānī-like relations with such occupational groups.

In Bangladesh the social segmentation among Muslims is not elaborate; many of them take the title Śekh (Shaikh) and are evidently descendants of converts from low Buddhist or Hindu cultivators. In contrast with Bangladesh and Pakistan, there are relatively few Muslim cultivators in North India, while most are occupational specialists or live in towns. In South India Muslims generally live in towns and prefer to live by trading, so in most places they have little function in traditional rural caste interaction. Muslim peoples are further discussed in Chapter 13 and in two of the village profiles in the companion volume.

Layout of a Tamil̲ Village

Though it might seem to the visitor that anyone could identify a village in South Asia, there are in fact several definitions. A village might be thought of as a geographical cluster of houses and huts, but then there

might be satellite hamlets for untouchables. It might be a settlement whose lands are essentially owned by descendants of an ancestral founder, with the necessary occupational specialists brought in. It might be the settlement having a common panchāyat (council), or thought of as a community by the residents. It might be the revenue village. And the census takers regard any settlement of less than 5000 people, with a few exceptions, as a village. In areas such as Bānglā and Kēraḷa where houses or homesteads are dispersed the village must be sociologically rather than geographically defined.

A village layout, particularly in the larger compact villages of western and South India and Pakistan is a geographical expression of the social order. The following example of a village in the Tanjāvūr rice-growing region of Tamiḻ Nāḍu has been described by the Indian sociologist André Béteille. It has 1389 persons in 349 families, divided into 41 castes. Béteille has ranked these (Table 8–4); they fall into three blocs as is usual in South India: Brāhmaṇ, non-Brāhmaṇ, and Harijan (Scheduled Castes). The terms Kshatriya, Vaiśya, and Śūdra might appear in some of the myths, but they are hardly relevant. Brāhmaṇs simplify things for themselves by regarding all the non-Brāhmaṇs (which does not include the Harijans) as Śūdras.

This village is not a typical one because it has an unusually large component of Brāhmaṇs; the majority of villages here, in fact, have none. But this example is instructive because we can see the large range of Brāhmaṇ castes, and the hierarchical difference between the temple priests and Smārtha Brāhmaṇs, who are orthodox Śaivites and own land. A historical tendency in the South has been for a small Brāhmaṇ minority to acquire much of the land, thereby becoming distinct from the rest of the clean castes and generating a three-class system. This accounts for the anti-Brāhmaṇ sentiment that pervades much of politics in the South in modern times.

The artisans, as usual, form a compact group of castes and rank below the main cultivator castes, the Veḷḷāḷar. And below the artisans is a group of castes following polluting occupations, such as toddy-tappers, barbers, and washerman, but they are not untouchable. The Harijans are divided into four castes. The Paḷḷar are the most numerous caste in the village and are not occupational specialists but agricultural laborers. (It is from the Paraiyar caste that we get the English word pariah.) Scavengers and cobblers are the lowest, for they remove garbage and offal.

Following now the schematic map (Fig. 8–1), we see that the village has three nucleii which coincide with the three blocs of castes. The Brāhmaṇ street, called the *agrahāram*, is nearest the main road which has frequent bus service. Behind it is the non-Brāhmaṇ section with an extension called Eastern Street, in which the non-Brāhmaṇ castes are more or less mixed. Separated by a paddy field and a coconut grove is a satellite hamlet where

TABLE 8–4 Castes in a Village in Tamil Nāḍu (from Béteille 1965)

Caste and Occupation	*Households*
Brāhmaṇs	
Smārthas, Telugu-speaking	
Kōṇasimadrāvaḍa	7
Vēlanāḍu	4
Mūlakanāḍu	10
Smārthas, Tamil-speaking	
Brihacharṇam	
Malanāṭṭu	9
Kandramaṇikya	5
Vaḍama: Cōladēśa	3
Astaśahāśram	1
Śrī Vaiṣṇava, Tamil-speaking	
Vaḍakalai	55
Tenkalai	2
Temple priests	
Bhaṭṭacār (Tenkalai)	1
Gurukkaḷ	1
Non-Brāhmaṇs	
Cultivating castes	
Kaḷḷar	34
Ambalakkārar	3
Muttiriyar	6
Akamudiyar	6
Cōliya Veḷḷāḷar	49
Karaikkaṭṭu Veḷḷāḷar	1
Koḍikkal Veḷḷāḷar	4
Gauṇḍa or Konga Veḷḷāḷar	4
Nāyanār	1
Mudaliyār—capitalists	3
Low cultivating castes	
Paḍayācci	27
Mūppanār	5
Oḍaiyar	3
Nāyakar	2
Other specialized castes	
Taṭṭan—goldsmiths	5
Taccan—carpenters	1
Kuśavan—potters	2
Paṇḍāram—priests for local gods	4
Mēlakkaran—musicians	3
Kōṇar—cattle herders	5
Nāḍar—palm tree tappers	1
Ambaṭṭan—barbers	3
Vaṇṇan—washermen	1
Non-Tamil castes	
Marāṭha, Marāṭhī-speaking	1
Reḍḍiyār, Telugu-speaking	1
Nāyaḍu, Telugu-speaking	1
Ādi-Drāviḍas (Harijans or Untouchables)	
Paḷḷar—laborers	82
Paraiyar—drummers, laborers	5
Toṭṭiyar—scavengers	1
Cakkiliyar—cobblers, scavengers	3
	365

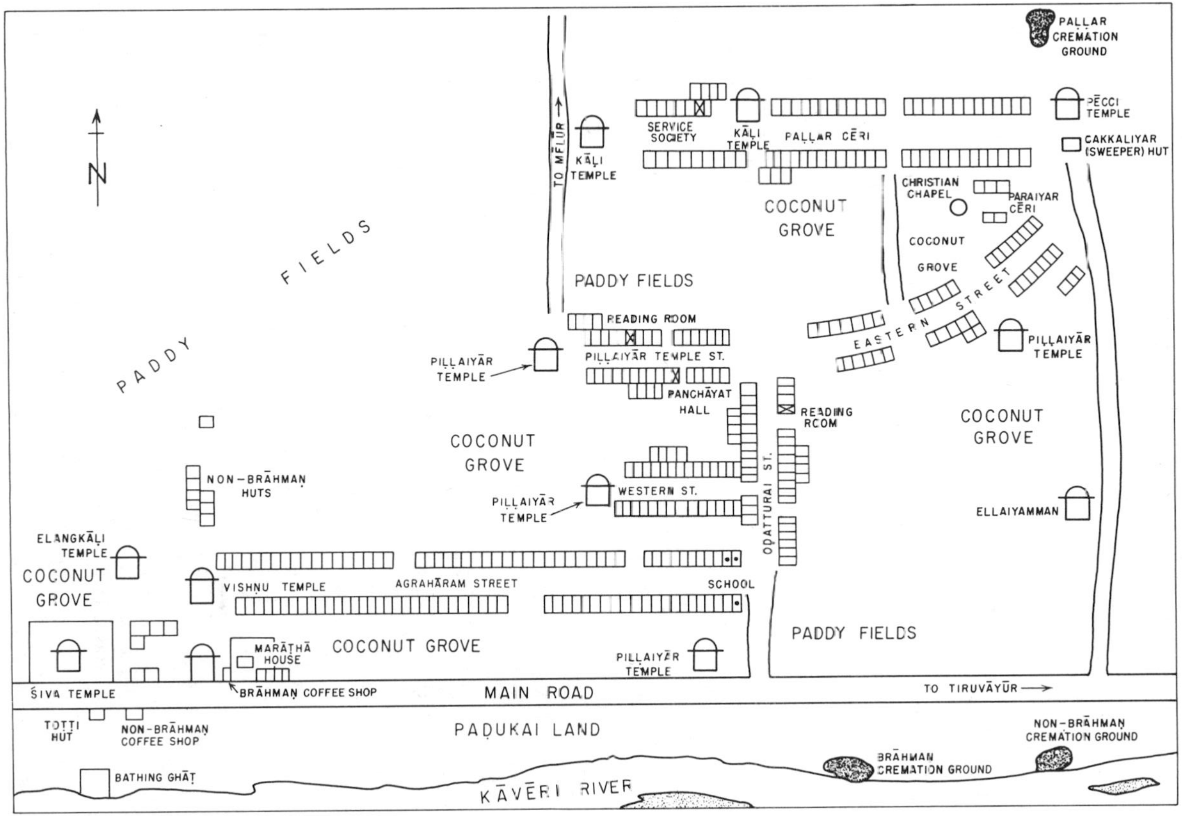

FIG. 8–1 Settlement plan of Śrīpuram village (not to scale) (after Béteille 1965).

Ādi-Drāviḍas (Harijans) live. Though only one is shown on this scheme, in fact the village has five other satellite hamlets farther removed.

All the houses in the agrahāram are pakkā (built of masonry and tiles); the houses in the non-Brāhmaṇ section are pakkā or of mud; all the huts in the satellite hamlet are made of mud with thatched roofs, and most have but one room. The economic pattern is clear. Brāhmaṇs were landowners brought here by medieval kings; non-Brāhmaṇs became their tenants, managers, artisans, or were small landholders or laborers; Harijans were, and still are, laborers. All are linked by a jajmānī-like system in which a portion of the harvest is given by landowners for services rendered.

No non-Brāhmaṇ has ever lived in this agrahāram, for it is not only a physical unit, it is a community and a way of life, says Béteille. If meat-eaters lived there the odors and waste would be offensive to the Brāhmaṇs.

Harijans were formerly not allowed in the agrahāram street, and even now do not go there, but remove garbage from the rear, for every Brāhmaṇ house and compound has a rear door. Brāhmaṇs may go into the non-Brāhmaṇ section of the village if they have business there but most have never seen the inside of the Harijan settlement. Indeed, the Harijans believe that if a Brāhmaṇ ever did come into their quarter it would bring sterility and misfortune, and they would then have to smash all their cooking vessels. But one or two Brāhmaṇs today do visit it with impunity. The drawing shows that the Brāhmaṇ, non-Brāhmaṇ, and Harijan settlements all have separate paths leading in from the highway.

The temples of the Brāhmaṇs clustered around the western end of the agrahāram are farthest removed from the residences of the other castes; they are the temples of the high gods. The temples in the non-Brāhmaṇ quarter contain icons of important village deities, and are served by the Paṇḍārams, non-Brāhmaṇ priests, though Brāhmaṇs may attend some of them on special occasions. The temples in the Harijan quarter have deities that are of low status, or demons to be feared, and are never attended by Brāhmaṇs. But there is one temple which is used by all castes, the shrine of Ellaiyamman, who is the village boundary deity. But the Harijans worship it without going inside. A Christian chapel is located near the Harijan hamlet because most of the Christians are ex-untouchables, especially Paraiyar here; naturally Brāhmaṇs would never patronize this chapel.

Near the Brāhmaṇ temples on the western side of the village is the *ghāṭ*, the steps on the river bank on which Brāhmaṇs perform their ablutions in the morning before worship. As far as possible downstream is the Brāhmaṇ cremation ground. Downstream from that is the non-Brāhmaṇ cremation ground. But the Harijans may not cremate nor bury near the river (the Kāvēri, a sacred one) but must use a field on the far side of the Harijan settlement.

The school is at the east end of the agrahāram on the path to the non-Brāhmaṇ quarter, a suitable location, for all may attend school without

coming into the agrahāram street, while Brāhmaṇ children do not have to go into other parts of the village. Brāhmaṇ and non-Brāhmaṇ coffee shops have appeared on the main road because of frequent bus service, and these have attracted some middle caste rowdies who have their houses near the western end of the agrahāram, which Brāhmaṇs do not appreciate. Also nearby, but not in the agrahāram, is a large house built by a Marāṭhā landlord brought here by a king.

But Brāhmaṇs here as elsewhere have taken to Western education and entered professions, and do not rely only on landowning today for status or wealth. Many have migrated to cities, perhaps leaving some family members to care for what lands they retain in the village. The jajmānī relations have become relaxed as more people work for daily wages. Correspondingly, the Veḷḷāḷar have come in recent years to economically dominate the village. Land reform legislation has assisted the breakup of the Brāhmaṇ-owned estates, and it is the Veḷḷāḷar, traditionally expert cultivators, who have been willing to pay careful attention to the farms and employ new methods. This power shift from Brāhmaṇs to Veḷḷāḷas is apparent in the political process, for voting power is now in the hands of the dominant non-Brāhmaṇ agricultural castes throughout the state.

The village layout shows this shift of power in two respects. The panchāyat hall used to be in the agrahāram when the panchāyat was dominated by Brahmaṇs, but now it is in the non-Brāhmaṇ quarter, and the council is dominated by the Veḷḷāḷar. Moreover, there are two reading rooms in the village, operated by political parties, and both are in the non-Brāhmaṇ quarter.

But the Harijans have acquired neither economic nor political power. Even if some of them get educated most continue to live by daily wages for field labor or menial services. Their satellite hamlet looks much as it did decades ago.

The Village as a Social Unit

Our extended discussion of caste may leave the impression that there are few social functions left to the village. In fact, the two are complementary. The caste structure can be described as a series of vertical links, while the network of villages provides a series of horizontal links.

People travel often, a fact noted with surprise by some visitors to South Asia. Train and bus service is frequent and the vehicles are usually full. Thousands of weekly markets are operated by village and town authorities, and there are specialized periodic markets for cattle and cotton. People crowd the buses or go in ox cart trains to temple festivals. Large parties go to weddings and life cycle rites. In the North, however, women travel much less than men and are most often escorted. When two strangers begin

to talk, as in a train, the first question asked is likely to be "What is your village?" One's caste need not always be asked (but is usually ascertained if a stranger spends some time in a village). At casual meetings as on trains it is enough to place a stranger in general perspective or in a bloc of castes, which can usually be done on the basis of quality of dress and jewelry, dialect, mannerisms, and general demeanor, or occasionally on specific items worn. One's full name commonly reveals his caste or lineage. In most groups there is no family name exactly as it is found in the West, but a person is called by his given name to which is appended a caste or lineage or clan name. In Kēraḷa people may also add their house name. In the South one may also precede his name with the initials of his father's and grandfather's names. A woman is known by her given name and her caste name is the same as her husband's; in the case of Muslims she likely belongs to the same birādarī as her husband. There are situations and areas in which people append their village or town name to their given name, as in the case of some musicians.

But people in cities will freely state "their village" a generation or two after having moved from it. In the North men are likely to leave their wives in their village while gone to work for years away from their homes. Even those who have fully moved to cities return to their village at times of weddings of kin, and sometimes retain some interest in landownership there.

The solidarity of a village is enhanced by many common physical facilities: grazing ground, threshing floor, tanks (reservoirs), roads, wells, great shade trees, waste lands, some temples. The worship of the village boundary deity, where it exists, clearly symbolizes the village as a unit. In the South especially there are village-wide religious holidays in which the chief village deities are worshiped, which are more important than the special days of the high gods. In the Gangā plains a village is quite clearly delineated by the principle of village exogamy, and moreover the occupation-based jajmānī relations within it provide most of the necessary services and provide for economic exchange. In some areas village lands are inherited by descendants of the founder, and in the old days a *zamīndār* often owned a whole village or a group of villages. And there are people who serve the whole village, especially the Watchman, and now also schoolteachers.

Any important celebration or ceremony is enjoyed by all in the village. Even Muslims take part in the horseplay of the Holī festival, but will generally not worship the Hindu deities. A wedding or other life cycle ceremony provides an opportunity for guests to come to a village, and such a guest may judge the whole village according to his treatment by one caste or in one ceremony. Marriages in particular provide an occasion for all subtle—and sometimes dormant—social relationships to be expressed. Alan Beals says that for a small village in Karṇāṭaka:

> The village as a whole must sanction any marriage that takes place between Gopalpur and any other villages, and the village as a whole undertakes the responsibility of ensuring that people from other villages get value received when they arrange a marriage in Gopalpur.[12]

At a wedding the participants and guests have to publicly observe who gives what kind of food to whom, who can sit in the same line and eat with whom, who is expected to give a certain kind of gift or a gift of certain value in return for a gift previously received, and who can command the patronage of whom—all these come out in the open on such occasions.

Within a village, caste ranking is likely to be subtly different than in neighboring villages. An example is given by Adrian Mayer of a village in western Madhya Pradesh of a Rājpūt and a Farmer on their way to a wedding party in a neighboring village. In their own village these two could not eat sitting in the same line, but in the other village it was customary for these two castes to eat together. "We shall also eat in one line; and it will not be a matter for our Ramkheri caste councils, because it is the custom of that village."[13]

In a Mahārāshṭra village described by Henry Orenstein a marriage in a self-respecting Marāṭhā or Rājpūt family (for these two castes are the predominant landowning groups) nearly always has a full complement of specialists so that such a marriage is essentially a village-wide affair. A Brāhmaṇ makes a horoscope before the marriage is decided upon. A Barber shaves the groom a few days before the ceremony (if the groom is from the village). The Barber also delivers invitations to all in the village who are to attend the ceremony. The Goldsmith cleans the household deities, accompanied by a procession to and from his house. A Water Carrier meets the incoming party and pours water at their feet to counteract evil influences. A Rope Maker stops the party to ensure good luck. A Washerman performs a ceremony on the night before the wedding and the Washerman's wife "cleanses" the bride and groom with turmeric.

The Goldsmith, on the following day, puts jewelry on the couple. A Washerman spreads a cloth as they walk to the marriage canopy so their feet do not touch the ground. The Barber holds the reins as the groom goes on horseback to the Hanuman temple to change his clothing. A Leatherworker had provided him with shoes just for this occasion. A Washerman or his wife prepares a magic design on the ground. The village Brāhmaṇ performs the ceremony (or in some cases non-Brāhmaṇ priests or Goldsmiths). The Water Carrier brings water for ritual washing during the ceremony. Afterwards the couple sit on a platform surrounded by a full complement of pots made by the Potter. The Potter and a Water Carrier help prepare the feast for all. The Watchman and Scavenger serve the visitors as long as they are in the village. Before going the couple might visit an ascetic at one of the temples to receive his blessings, and also worship at two local temples served by devotee-musicians. A non-Brāhmaṇ priest

draws the magic design for this, and a Muslim sacrifices an animal if this is desired. All these specialists are paid in grain yearly or twice yearly, and on such ceremonial occasions receive tips. With the feast to enjoy and the money circulating, the village is in a festive mood.[14]

An institution promoting cohesion within the village is the council, the panchāyat. The Government of India, harking back to an ancient tradition that a village was governed by a council of five, has instituted village-level government under panchāyats throughout the country. Nepal has followed suit, and in Pakistan and Bangladesh (instituted by the Pakistan government) there are also local councils. Panchāyats may be captured by dominant castes, though they are supposed to have representatives elected from all major groups. The shift of the panchāyat from the Brāhmaṇ to the Veḷḷāḷar part of the village in the Tamiḻ village described by Béteille is an example. Mandelbaum points out that an elder in the panchāyat must tread a narrow line between what is good for the village and what is to the advantage of his own kin and castemen. The functioning of this institution will be discussed in Chapter 16.

Factions and Leadership in the Village

The intense interpersonal relations which prevail in South Asia combined with the fragmentation of society into so many special interest groups produces a dynamism which keeps things rather lively in most villages.

In studying a village near Delhi, Lewis found 12 factions: 6 among the 79 Jāṭ families, 2 among the 21 Camār (Leatherworker) families, 2 among the 10 Bhangī (Sweeper) families, and others which were intercaste disputes. People within a faction tended to favor each other at times of ceremonies, visited each other more, and showed hostility to other factions at appropriate times. The causes of factions were quarrels over the inheritance of land, house sites, irrigation rights, sexual offenses, adoption of sons, and claims of caste status. Even cousins and brothers can form opposing factions if a quarrel over land inheritance has to be taken to court. But in most other kinds of quarrels members of a kin group generally provide each other with moral support.

The factions within the Paṭṭīdār caste in a village in Gujarāt are described by David Pocock.[15] A common cause of factions here was disputes over marriage payments. Since the Paṭṭīdārs practice hypergamy they command enormous dowries (money and gifts that come with the bride). Each Paṭṭīdār faction tends to carry along with it the lower caste people who are dependent or with whom there are jajmānī relations. One family, inheriting a little ancestral land, decided it would build a pump and sell water to its neighbors. Certain persons opposed the effort, fearing that this family would be able to unduly extend its influence, and tried to halt con-

struction of the pump by physical force. But it was set up, and that family, using the connections it established by the sale of water, began to sell oil products too. Ultimately it came to manage a distribution agency for selling gasoline to the other water pumps in the village and the interests of this family came to be regarded as a little family empire.

Factions within a caste may be mitigated by caste panchāyats. Some castes have these and some do not; some are part of wider caste societies and take part in caste "uplift" projects or become politically and economically active. But most caste panchāyats today primarily punish deviance from caste norms of behavior and settle disputes within it. Typical cases heard by Goswamy in a study of caste panchāyats in a Bihār village were marriage to other than the betrothed, failure to repay a loan borrowed from a widow, youths teasing women in a field, and failure to return borrowed ornaments. The caste panchāyat fines the guilty or declares a social boycott, and may outcaste a person. If an accused flouts the decision, action can be taken against his whole family. The accused can be admitted back to full caste status after retribution and a set period of time has elapsed, ceremonially reinstated when an elder serves him *śarbat* (sherbet). Such decisions are invariably unanimous, arrived at after discussion with unrestrained emotion. Membership in the panchāyat in this case was essentially hereditary, which is not always the case, but prominent families are generally represented. Meetings are open to any caste members, who may also contribute their opinions. Caste laws are unwritten, and decisions vary with the circumstances.[16]

The new statutory village panchāyats have become stronger at the expense of informal village panchāyats and caste panchāyats, which have no formal relationship with the wider legal and political system. Prominent families or landowners in a village are generally able to get the laborers and occupational specialists attached to them to vote as directed in panchāyat elections. Such people maintain a network of contacts throughout the village and among other villages to rally support in any crisis. The power structure of the village can often affect the results of court cases by influencing witnesses, or can cause information to be withheld or falsified when police come to investigate criminal cases or disputes.

An instance of this kind was observed by the author. Two brothers had a dispute over land inheritance, and one struck the other in the street with a sickle, cutting his ear and neck. The victim happened to work as cook in the largest landowning home in the village, whose household head was also the panchāyat president. The landowner supported his employee in the dispute, and in fact believed his claim was just. After the fight a son of the landowner gave the attacker a good kick and dispatched him from the village forthwith, so that he could not return for some days. The landowner saw that his employee was taken by taxi to the government hospital, and that night called in all who had been witnesses, one by one, and

instructed them exactly what to say when the police would come on the following day. The police were happy to be able to write a consistent report in their records. No villager questioned the propriety of the landowner in this both because of their economic relations with him and because of his position as panchāyat president.

The modern democratic political structure has opened up a new arena for the operation of factions and castes. It has not produced a casteless society as some had hoped, but rather has provided new avenues for the various social segments to vent their interests. A vivid example of the political process in a Pakistan village is provided in *South Asia: Seven Community Profiles.*

Views on the Structure of South Asian Society

At this point it may be premature to ask the reader (not having read about kinship in Chapters 10 through 15, nor the chapters on rural and urban change) to come to any conclusions about the fundamental nature of South Asian society. But certain questions have been so extensively debated it is necessary to summarize them.

Anthropologists and sociologists all seem to be agreed that the principle of segmentation is fundamental to South Asian society, and that it is a truly plural society—even if they disagree on 1) the basis of segmentation, 2) the degree of segmentation, 3) the fluidity of the segmentation, and 4) the nature of the superstructure incorporating the segments.

This author takes the position that there is consistency and logic in the ways in which the various segments—however defined—were brought into relationship with each other in Hindu Indian civilization, that these principles operate to some extent in non-Hindu systems such as the Muslim, and also may explain certain phenomena in elite or urban society. The methodology of the *structural* anthropological approach could be invoked to demonstrate in detail how: 1) in the realm of religion a plurality of deities and cults is linked into one hierarchical system and rationalized by the logic of multiple "aspects," samsāra or rebirth; 2) in the realm of the state a plurality of kingdoms and feudatories is linked into one system by the lesser ones vicariously invoking the authority and prestige of the stronger ones and by the principle of dynastic drift; 3) in the realm of society the diverse cultural and ethnic entities are linked into a hierarchical system as castes; 4) in the realm of history and mythology a multitude of local legends are linked to regional ones which are in turn linked to India-wide epics of gigantic proportions; 5) in the realm of economics multiple specialists and specialist groups are not economically atomistic but linked by jajmānī-like hierarchical structures at both the village and traditional state levels; and 6) in the realm of language the various forms of speech (among Hindus) are linked

by the fiction that most of them derived directly from Sanskrit while the rest drew their sustenance from it.

In this vast system the principle is that the lesser gods, states, languages, or castes retain the *right to exist* within distinct cultural or subcultural entities provided they are *validated* by being linked with the stronger. *Hierarchy*, therefore, is inherent. If indeed this is a system, it must have boundaries. Even the untouchables are within the system because of their placement *in*, not outside of, the clean-unclean spectrum. "Tribal" people, however, are outside the boundary of the system. So are dropouts such as sādhus.

David Mandelbaum in his exhaustive *Society in India* stresses the *adaptive* nature of this system—its capacity to absorb alien groups who yet retain their identity and then become contestants for rank and thereby support the whole system: "Structure and process, concord and conflict are viewed in the same general perspective. Stability and change, norm and deviance can be examined together. There need be no treatment of social control apart from social conformity."[17] Milton Singer has also stressed the fluidity and adaptive nature of Indian society and has demonstrated that traditional values and institutions can be quite easily maintained in modernizing segments of the society. Berreman, in fact, refers to caste as a *process*.

The concept of social stratification has become a central one for sociology. As Mandelbaum points out, "We are dealing with *the* classic instance of stratification as a frame and focus for a civilization." But differences of opinion appear when social scientists set out to demonstrate that one or another variable is fundamental to the stratification. Moreover sociologists and sometimes social anthropologists in their attempt to understand the *social* system may never get to the total *cultural* system nor to the subcultural entities that comprise it. André Béteille writes, "In India I think most social anthropologists have been dominated in their work by the implicit idea that the caste structure was *the* 'total social structure' of traditional Hindu society and have used it as a framework for ordering every kind of fact."[18]

A work that has stirred considerable recent controversy is Louis Dumont's *Homo Hierarchicus.* Dumont agrees with E. R. Leach that caste is not merely a cultural phenomenon of South Asia or of Hinduism but that it is a structural phenomenon, and inequality is inherent within it. But Dumont, as a French social anthropologist, goes beyond this to the isolation of a structural principle, namely hierarchy. He says that modern man is virtually incapable of fully recognizing hierarchy. Dumont rejects the "social stratification" position common to many sociologists because its proponents all have equalitarianism as a fundamental life value. The concept of social stratification blocks all understanding of hierarchy. Focus needs to be

moved from the separate castes to the principle that produces the structure, he says.

Whereas some early observers of the Indian scene developed the idea that a caste's rank derives from the characteristics of its way of life, the *attributional* theory, Dumont approves Marriott's advance on this in stressing *interaction*. But he believes one should go further, and stresses that interaction cannot be viewed apart from overall ideological orientation. This view of the ordered whole, in which each is assigned his place, is fundamentally *religious*, or if one prefers, a matter of *ultimate values*.[19] And whereas hierarchy is indeed universal, caste in the sense that it is a fundamental religious value supported by ritual purity and pollution is not found elsewhere in the world. The logical conclusion of his view is that in Pakistan in the Swāt Valley dominated by Paṭhāns the social structure must not be caste because it is not based on caste ideology (as he defines it) but on division of labor and on a system of patronage and clientele.

But Béteille, an Indian, takes issue with this, saying that Muslim rule, for instance, created and legitimized not only new structures of power but also new bases of status which were partly independent of caste such as zamīndārs and *jagīrdārs* (holders of land on condition of service) and many other categories, which sometimes coincided with caste and sometimes cut across it. British rule eliminated some of these categories and added others. Moreover Brāhmaṇs wielded material power at every level of Indian history, and there have been numerous Brāhmaṇ landowning groups and Brāhmaṇ kings and dynasties. He points out that focusing on purity and pollution has caused the neglect of the study of language as symbolic of social segmentation and stratification (see the following chapter). Three related arguments Béteille makes are that there is danger in Dumont's assimilating almost everything into what one regards as the dominant structure, that this does not account for ideological elements which have emerged in the past century, and that it is difficult to accept that Hindus themselves today have a very consistent view of the fundamental properties of their own society.

A different debate among scholars has centered on whether South Asian society should be viewed in Marxist terms, as antithesis between the bourgeoisie and the proletariat, or at least as characterized primarily by conflict and exploitation, or whether the structure is harmonious. Most recent anthropologist writers do not seem to find that the Marxist premise is real in the light of their extended residence in South Asia villages. Dumont rejects it on the grounds that the imputed social dialectic requires dissolution of the society, which is not happening, that the caste system should be seen as less "exploitative" than democratic society, and that if modern man does not see it this way, it is because he no longer conceives of justice as other than equality. However a number of writers, such as Gould in his

urbanization studies, do stress the transition from a *caste* to a *class* society, particularly in urban areas and in the modernizing context. In a class society there may indeed be exploitation but the inequalities are not based so much on ascriptive criteria as on a combination of acquired power and wealth. But Béteille, though he agrees that there has been too much emphasis on caste, refuses to generalize that it is being replaced by class, or that caste conflicts are simply distorted expressions of class conflicts, for such arguments reintroduce the concept of the total social structure.

Another item of disagreement is the effect of the South Asian religious or world view system on economic development and modernization. This debate goes back to Max Weber, who said that the effects of the caste system on the economy are completely negative, that it is "completely traditionalistic and anti-rational in its effects."[20] But as early as 1908 Bouglé in his study of Indian society had opined, "the caste system in no way stopped the economic life of the Hindus," and went on to quote the Indian judge and reformer Ranade that "what is particularly instructive about the economic life of India is that it does not seem to realize a single one of the 'postulates' of western classical political economics."[21] Anthropologists such as Singer and Cohn have pointed out the inherent capacity for change, but many Indian government officials are wedded to the ideology that casteism must be stamped out before real "development" can take place.

Scholars do seem agreed, however, that old forms are manifesting themselves in new ways these days and that caste, or forms derived from it, operates in politics, business, and other modern areas, while hierarchy is a pervasive feature extending all the way from the family to the government bureaucracy. They also seem agreed that there is more fusion of social segments than fission now, and in fact the middle castes in an Indian or Pakistani village may interact in a quite equalitarian manner in certain situations. S. G. Ghurye perceived years ago that consolidation of castes in the Bombay area produced super organizations which tended to become

Post office in a Pakistan town. Employees are ranked in bureaucratic hierarchy; peon is employed to run errands and move papers from desk to desk.

militant. Another point all scholars seem agreed on is that purity-pollution consciousness is deceasing, and in some contexts, especially in cities, is not functioning at all. But Ghurye reminds his countrymen that they should not suppose that the demise of that particular symbolic system will necessarily make it easy to uproot caste or that people will thereby adopt a socialist ideology.

Perhaps most of the disagreements among observers have their roots in the cultures of the observes. Srinivas has been frank enough to print E. R. Leach's question that had Srinivas not been a Brāhmaṇ, would he have developed the concept of Sanskritization and stressed emulation of Brāhmaṇs? Another Indian colleague said that this concept arose because Srinivas was a South Indian and that he could not locate Sanskritization in Bānglā. Dumont has not only pointed out the ethnocentricism of the equalitarian ideal among scholars, but also reminds us that "the modern mind believes in change and is quite ready to exaggerate its extent," from which he proceeds to state that there has been change *in* the society and not *of* the society.[22] But it would seem that most urban and English-knowing South Asians live in a milieu that demands an ideology different from this.

REFERENCES AND NOTES

1 Bernard Barber, "Social Mobility in Hindu India," in Silverberg, pp. 26–27.
2 Fosco Maraini, *Where Four Worlds Meet* (London, 1959), Chap. 9.
3 Harper, pp. 152–155.
4 Helen Ullrich, personal communication.
5 Carstairs, pp. 84–85.
6 Marriott (1968), p. 145.
7 Berreman (1963), pp. 221, 245.
8 Nur Yalman, *Under the Bo Tree* (Berkeley, Calif., 1967), pp. 70–71.
9 Bernard Cohn, "Notes on the History of the Study of Indian Society and Culture," in Singer and Cohn, p. 15.
10 William Rowe, "The New Cauhāns: A Caste Mobility Movement in North India," in Silverberg, pp. 73–74.
11 Mandelbaum, p. 547.
12 Alan Beals, *Gopalpur: A South Indian Village* (New York, 1964), p. 28.
13 Mayer, p. 49.
14 Henry Orenstein, *Gaon: Conflict and Cohesion in an Indian Village* (Princeton, N.J., 1965), pp. 219–222.
15 David Pocock, "The Basis of Faction in Gujarat," in Firth.
16 B. B. Goswamy, "Working of a Caste Panchayat in Bihar," *Bull. Anthro. Survey of India* XII, Nos. 3 and 4 (1963).
17 Mandelbaum, p. 660.
18 Béteille (1969), p. 86.
19 Dumont (1970), pp. 106–107.

[20] Max Weber, *The Religion of India: The Sociology of Hinduism and Buddhism*, trans. Gerth and Martindale (New York, 1958).

[21] Célestin Bouglé. *Essays on the Caste System*, trans. D. Pocock (Cambridge, England, 1971) (original French edition 1908).

[22] Dumont (1970), p. 210.

IMPORTANT SOURCES

Ansari, Ghaus. *Muslim Caste in Uttar Pradesh*. Lucknow, 1960.

Bailey, F. G. *Tribe, Caste, and Nation*. Manchester, 1960.

Berreman, Gerald. "Caste as a Social Process," *Southwestern J. Anthro.* XXIII, No. 4 (1967).

———. *Hindus of the Himalayas*. Berkeley, Calif., 1963.

Béteille, André. *Caste, Class, and Power: Changing Patterns of Stratification in a Tanjore Village*. Berkeley, Calif., 1965.

———. *Castes Old and New: Essays in Social Structure and Social Stratification*. Bombay, 1969. (Includes especially useful essays on closed and open stratification, the referents of caste, and the backward classes.)

Carstairs, G. Morris. *The Twice-Born*. Bloomington, Ind., 1967. (A study of the psychology and personality of high caste Hindus.)

Cohn, Bernard. *India: The Social Anthropology of a Civilization*. New York, 1971. (A diachronic view.)

de Reuck, Anthony, and Julie Knight (eds.). *Caste and Race: Cooperative Approaches*. Boston, 1967. (A useful symposium chaired by G. Myrdal.)

Dubois, Abbe J. A., and Henry Beauchamp. *Hindu Manners, Customs and Ceremonies*. Oxford, 1906. (The detailed and delightful observations of a French missionary in Karṇāṭaka about 1800.)

Dumont, Louis (ed., with others). *Contributions to Indian Sociology*. Paris, 1957-1966. (Subsequently edited by T. N. Madan; contains debate on many substantive topics.)

———, *Homo Hierarchicus*. Chicago, 1970 (original French edition 1966). (A view of Hindu caste as a coherent system, and an important work.)

Eglar, Zeikye. *A Punjabi Village in Pakistan*. New York, 1960.

Firth, Raymond, and others. "Factions in Indian and Overseas Indian Societies," *British J. Sociology* VIII, No. 4 (1957).

Ghurye, G. S. *Caste, Class and Occupation*. Bombay, 1961.

Harper, Edward. "Ritual Pollution, Caste, and Religion," in Edward Harper (ed.) *Religion in South Asia*. Seattle, Wash., 1964. (An important synthesis of the several kinds of ritual purity and pollution.)

Hutton, J. H. *Caste in India*, 4th ed. Oxford, 1963. (A classic first published in 1946; many details but not much synthesis.)

Kane, P. R. *History of the Dharmaśāstra*, 5 vols. Pūṇe, from 1930. (A lifetime work on Hindu law and the social order.)

Karve, Irawati. *Hindu Society: an Interpretation*. Pūṇe, 1961. (A view by a well-known anthropologist who also knows history.)

Leach, E. R. (ed.). *Aspects of Caste in South India, Ceylon and North West Pakistan*. Cambridge, England, 1960.

Mahar, Michael (ed.) *The Untouchables in Contemporary India*. Tucson, Ariz., 1972. (Contains 17 essays.)

Maloney, Clarence. "The Paratavar: Two Thousand Years of Culture Dynamics of a Tamil Caste," *Man in India*, Nov. 1969.

Mandelbaum, David. *Society in India*, vols. I and II. Berkeley, Calif., 1970 (Comprehensive; draws from most scholars in the field.)

Majumdar, D. N. *Caste and Communication in an Indian Village*. Bombay, 1958. (A study of a village near Lucknow.)

Marriott, McKim. *Caste Ranking and Community Structure in Five Regions of India and Pakistan*. Puṇe, 1960.

———. "Caste Ranking and Food Transactions: a Matrix Analysis," in Singer and Cohn.

Mayer, Adrian. *Caste and Kinship in Central India*. Berkeley, Calif., 1960. (A descriptive study of a village in Mālwā.)

Raza, Muhammad Rafique. *Two Pakistani Villages: A Study in Social Stratification*. Lahore, 1969.

Schwartz, Barton (ed.). *Caste in Overseas Indian Communities*. San Francisco, 1967. (Indians in Mauritius, Guyana, Trinidad, Surinam, Fiji, South Africa, and East Africa.)

Silverberg, James (ed.). *Social Mobility in the Caste System in India*. Paris, 1968.

Singer, Milton, and Bernard Cohn. *Structure and Change in Indian Society*. Chicago, 1968. (A symposium of 20 contributions by South Asian anthropologists.)

Srinivas, M. N. *Caste in Modern India and Other Essays*. Bombay, 1962.

———. *Social Change in Modern India*. Berkeley, Calif., 1967.

Wiser, William. *The Hindu Jajmani System*. Lucknow, 1958 (originally published 1936).

9

Sociolinguistics

Until the 1960s most Westerners who dabbled in the languages of South Asia approached them from the viewpoint of classical studies—as did South Asian people themselves—or else were content to learn the standard written form of one of the modern languages. But as more intensive fieldwork came to be done social scientists perceived that after they had studied a language a long time and thought they knew it, they could still only communicate in restricted situations. Such experiences make real the message of the sociolinguists: there is no single indicator of social interaction that can be observed in as controlled a manner, and yet is so subtle and accurate, as language. This kind of approach to the languages of South Asia is new in American and the few Indian universities where it exists, and has not yet begun in the other South Asian countries.

All of us use different linguistic forms in different social situations, and when we do we engage in what the linguists call code-switching. In technologically advanced societies there are a large number of specialized linguistic codes that can communicate very economically and very precisely among peers in professional or technical areas. Such codes are based on standard dialects, and people can switch back and forth without much conscious effort, while outsiders are likely to think of the speech as gobbledy-

gook. In South Asia too there are such professional speech forms, while there are also the Sanskritized, Persianized, or ultra-Tamiḻized gobbledygooks, as A. K. Ramanujan calls them, and often they are meant to communicate some sociological characteristic of the speaker as much as content. And then we have the Anglicized gobbledygook vaunted by government clerk types.

In Chapter 3 we observed, in our survey of South Asian languages, that this part of the world has about the same number of major literary languages as does Europe, and in both regions there are numerous geographical dialects. But South Asia has more social dialects because of the complexities of caste, multiplicity of great traditions, antiquity of literature, sacred languages, plus the demands of contemporary educational institutions and modern rapid communication.

Traditional Attitudes toward Language

Traditional Indian society, as in most parts of the world, attributed metaphysical power to certain speech forms. Sanskrit in both its Vedic and classical forms has been thought to have the most magical power. The hymns of the *Rig Veda*, as pointed out by W. Norman Brown, "as recited by the trained priest have such power, because they consist of the right sounds in the right combinations, uttered in the right sequence and with the right intonation; and when they are so recited and accompanied by the right manual acts, they are irresistible."[1] The elements, demons, and gods are subject to their power. Still more, at the time of creation "the gods or the supreme god formulated the idea and then uttered the names of creatures, whereupon those creatures came into existence." Sound or speech was personified as Vāc, a goddess.

Brāhmaṇs were entrusted with control of the cosmic power of sound. The Brāhmaṇ class was created from the mouth of the Primeval Being, whereas other classes came from his arms, thighs, and feet. It was access to this form of power that enabled Brāhmaṇs to command great respect, for even kings and warriors could not thus control cosmic forces. The Vedas were transmitted orally for a number of centuries before they were written down, and they were transmitted unchanged because they were the key to such power.

Brāhmaṇs were taught from the age of eight to quote the Vedas. Memorizing even one of the four Vedas was expected to take eight years. The scriptures were sometimes recited backwards, or with alternate syllables transposed, to avoid errors. Some Brāhmaṇs made their living by reciting the Vedas at ceremonies, while others emphasized analysis and the intellectual approach. A *śāstri* was one who was devoted to such learning as grammar,

rhetoric, poetry, logic, and philosophy, and was trained in a school in the town.

This emphasis on the cosmic power of speech combined with the early Indian predilection for classifying things led to very early linguistic analysis, so that by the Mauryan period the Brāhmī alphabet had been perfected, with a symbol for every contrasting phoneme. Several systems of Sanskrit grammar were in vogue before the Mauryan period. The one that ultimately became standard is attributed to Pāṇini, and is basic to the study of Sanskrit to this day. In the area of linguistic analysis, ancient Indian civilization accomplished something not duplicated elsewhere in the world until modern times.

Because of this fixation on Vedic and Sanskrit, the study of etymologies aimed at tracing all morphemes in Sanskrit and other languages back to original Vedic roots. The Prākrits were considered by learned scholars as bastard forms of speech. Even non-Indo-Āryan languages were studied under the same aura of Sanskrit reverence. Tamiḻ grammars were prepared in the early centuries of this era, but because scholars developed no theory of language families due to their reverence for Sanskrit as the mother of all speech, analysis of Tamiḻ grammar was forced into the mold of Sanskrit, with results even more incongruous than the superimposition of the Latin grammatical system on diverse types of European languages.

Reliance on the magical power of certain utterances is still widespread and has not been limited to Sanskrit nor to Hinduism. Tibetan Buddhists are famous for their prayer wheels which contain scraps of paper with sacred writing. A prayer is said or a power exerted each time the wheel revolves, so to derive more power from prayer wheels, they may be propelled by windmills or water wheels.

Muslims also have ascribed magic powers to words. Phrases from the Qur'ān are written on paper which is inserted in amulets to prevent disease, or are written on buildings and vehicles for their protective power. The Qur'ān itself is eternal. According to tradition everyone who knows how to read at least a little of the Qur'ān (in Arabic) will have a high place in heaven, and the more one can read the higher the place he will enjoy. The original Arabic has to be learned by rote, even though the reciters do not understand much or any of its meaning.

Village Hindus can be heard at night praying repetitiously, "Rām, Rām, Rām, . . ." or saying over and over the name of a deity in whose honor a pilgrimage is performed. The name itself has some of the power of the person it represents. On another plane, a wife in most parts of India today will not say the name of her husband for fear that to do so would shorten his life span. The Vedas themselves are really mantras, sacred or magical phrases; in most villages certain individuals can repeat mantras or incantations in the local language or as nonsense syllables when called upon in an emergency.

The writer recollects a case of an old man bitten by a cobra because e had thoughtlessly inserted his arm into a bamboo drainage pipe. The ctim, though he happened to be a Christian, was taken to the local antra-sayer who worked over him for half an hour with no success. Finally ne poor fellow was put on the back of a bicycle and taken four miles to ne government hospital, but by then he was too far gone and expired before e could be treated. The people had more faith in the power of words than the government hospital—and in spite of such failures, they cite repeated istances of the efficacy of mantras.

anguage Change and Civilization

The role of Sanskrit in Hindu South Asia was analogous to that of atin in medieval Europe; it not only welded the civilizational area but erved as a distinctive symbol of learning and elite status. Like Latin, anskrit had about it a mysterious aura so that common folk viewed with we those privileged few who could handle it and thereby wield power. very great tradition or major religion in South Asia has had a venerated nguage which could economically communicate its thought system: anskrit for Hinduism and Jainism, Pāli for Theravāda Buddhism; Buddhist Iybrid Sanskrit and Classical Tibetan for Mahāyāna Buddhism; Arabic, ersian, and Urdū for Islam; Panjābī written in a special script for Sikhs; yriac for Jews; and English for those whose elite status is defined in nodern terms.

In Europe the distinct civilized culture units, such as the Italian, rench, and German, emerged precisely as these languages replaced the acerdotal and ancient Latin language and came to be used in formal situaions and for intellectual pursuits. In Europe social leveling, and therefore inguistic leveling, proceeded faster than in South Asia. The process of the mergence of the regional languages is occurring in South Asia much as it lid in Europe, but later. The structure of society in medieval centuries lemanded the retention of Sanskrit in formal situations. Development of the egional languages was further hindered by the heavy hand of Persian during he Mughal regime and by English during and after the British period. The history of the modern world seems to show that a civilization which is ital and not based on antique or alien values is necessarily expressed in he language that is the mother tongue of the majority.

Geographically, most of the regional languages in Europe had a focus or epicenter, a city which set the standard and led the way in use of the anguage in formal situations. In South Asia this did not happen because he Mughal administration was in Persian while the Mughal feudatories did not coincide with culture regions within South Asia. Yet a broad-based

language did begin to develop, Hindustānī, or Hindī-Urdū, but its maturation was cut short when the British introduced English as the prestige language and caused new urban foci to develop on the coasts which eclipsed for a time the Hindustānī-speaking heartland. Since these new coastal cities were essentially British creations and were administered in English, their growth prevented the respective regional languages from developing as media to transmit the full vitality of civilization.

Some of the regional languages did have a long literary heritage and continued to be widely used during the colonial period, particularly for religious and other traditional subjects. However, they generally continued to borrow heavily from Sanskrit, or from Persian and Arabic in the case of languages of Muslims. Even in the 19th century the written forms of Dravidian languages, especially Malayāḷam and Telugu, included as many Sanskrit words as possible. In Bāngālī local Indo-Āryan words were ignored in favor of cognates borrowed from Sanskrit. Urdū too continued to borrow heavily from Persian. These formal styles of the regional languages were unintelligible to most villagers and could not be vehicles of regional cultural rejuvenation.

But language change is a dialectic process. The superimposition of English, though temporarily preventing the development of prestigious regional languages, nonetheless injected vitality into them. Formal speech, following the lead of English, has become less flowery, more direct, and more concise. Whereas much of the best traditional literature was in the form of poetry, a lucid prose style has developed under the influence of English. The regional languages have all borrowed English punctuation symbols. The old formal dialects required years of study, for the borrowed Sanskrit vocabulary was difficult, the texts were handwritten, and when they were read, the syllables were vocalized. There was no skimming, and it was expected that the reader would already half know the text he was reading. With the introduction of printing, a simpler prose style developed. As Ramanujan points out, when reading is freed from the necessity of articulation, hundreds of pages can be read effortlessly. The language comes to be regarded more as a vehicle than as an object in itself. Moreover, whole new genres of literature appeared with these developments. Novels, for instance, appeared in South Asian languages only after the model of English literature. Daily newspapers provided another new use for indigenous languages.

These styles affected the formal spoken varieties of the languages and contributed to linguistic leveling and the reduction of the distance between the formal and the informal modes of speech. During the British period, then, the regional languages acquired the capability of acting as vehicles of modern communication, though their full florescence still awaits the decline of English as a privileged alternative.

Geographical, Standard, and Literary Dialects

A dialect may be defined as an intelligible variant of a language—*not* a language spoken by a small number of people. By this definition the large variety of geographically and socially defined dialects can be grouped into a few major languages, especially in the case of languages around the periphery of the South Asian geographic heartland.

But the traveler proceeding from west to east across Pakistan and North India will encounter various speech forms which the speakers will claim as Panjābī, Sindhī, Rājasthānī, Urdū, Hindī, Bihārī, Bāngālī, and Assamese, and all will shade into one another. He will be hard put to draw a linguistic boundary between any two adjacent villages on the basis of spoken language. The speech at one end of the Hindī spectrum is unintelligible to a speaker at the other end without mediating factors such as similar education, kinsmen, or visiting between those areas; sometimes in this broad belt one or two hundred miles of distance is sufficient for unintelligibility. Here, then, the criterion of mutual intelligibility is not very satisfactory for determing linguistic boundaries, though at the extremes of the spectrum such languages as Sindhī and Bāngālī are better defined than those in the middle.

A better definition in this case is that all the varieties which share a common superimposed variety, such as a literary standard having substantial similarity of phonology and grammar, form one language. If a peasant wishes his son to become literate, and means literate in standard Hindī, then his speech can be considered a dialect of Hindī. Standard Hindī is taught in schools in six states. On the other hand, mutually intelligible variants having different literary standards may be considered as different languages. The most obvious example is Hindī and Urdū, which are the same except for script and some borrowed vocabulary.

Panjābī is linguistically quite close to Hindī, and might be considered a dialect. As Burling suggests, the "deep structure" (in the terminology of generative linguistics) is almost identical and the difference can be seen as the result of different rules leading to the "surface structure." It is thus easy for Panjābī speakers to borrow Hindī forms so that Panjābī can be almost indefinitely merged with Hindī. Yet Panjābī speakers in Delhi, for example, usually cling to a few distinguishing markers of Panjābī. "The markers must be seen as an attempt to cling to something special. They are signs that the speaker means to be speaking another 'language' however slightly it may differ from Hindī."[2] Panjābīs in Pakistan find it easy to learn Urdū, and it is the only language used in their schools. Because of the idealization of Urdū in Muslim tradition, Panjābī in Pakistan, though the mother tongue of 66% of all Pakistanis, has made no progress in developing into a literary language and has only now been recognized as a second language in

Electioneering banners in Karāchī, 1971. The democratic process requires the use of regional languages at the expense of English. Signs are in Urdū, Sindhī, and Gujarātī, but none in English. A crisp style has evolved for mass communication.

Panjāb Province. By contrast, in the new Indian state of Panjāb the Panjābī language is an important ethnic marker, with a considerable literature, and is written by Sikhs in their Gurmukhī script which is supported by religious tradition. Across much of North India and Pakistan, therefore, languages are demarcated on sociological rather than purely linguistic grounds.

Languages around the periphery of this heartland are better demarcated by geography. Bāngālī is separated by a constriction in the Gangā plains, and Assamese by another in the Brahmaputra plain. Nepālī, Uṛiyā,

Lottery tickets from three states on sale in a Panjāb market town. Writing above booth is Panjābī, but English lends prestige and credibility.

Gujarātī, and Kashmīrī are set off geographically, and now politically too. Sindhī is isolated by the Thār desert and a slight constriction in the Indus plain; it is the only language in Pakistan besides Urdū to develop a significant literature and be used in schools. It was declared the official language of Sindh Province in 1972, setting off riots in Karāchī.

The Dravidian languages are quite well demarcated from each other so that a linguistic boundary can be drawn between adjacent villages; they diverged from each other earlier than many of the languages of the North diverged from proto-Indo-Āryan. The regional dialects are beginning to merge somewhat into standard colloquials, which however are not written. The written dialects of these languages, used also in schools and on the radio, vary greatly from the standard informal dialects. The formal dialects tend to be antique, with a different set of verbal endings.

An impediment to the spread of literacy in South Asia is that often the literary style is not comprehensible without several years of schooling. To read Hindī, Marāṭhī or Bāngālī one must master the common standard dialect that has emerged, and in addition must master a dose of Sanskrit vocabulary, its quantity depending on the material to be read. In the South the written forms not only are quite divergent from the spoken standard, but tend to reincorporate old Dravidian forms and in some cases Sanskrit. In some areas the spoken languages are not used in schools at all, notably Pashto in northwestern Pakistan, which gives way to Urdū for all formal purposes. In Nepal Tibetan-type languages are spoken widely but everybody studies only Nepālī in school. Tribal people of central India are largely illiterate because they have to learn another language to learn to read at all.

Switching between two dialects or linguistic codes is a widespread ability in South Asia, and their use depends upon the social circumstances. The American who studies only a formal dialect of one of these languages will discover that he can hardly understand anything said in a village when he first goes there. He might make himself understood, and he might understand people talking to him when they use a semiformal dialect. But for a foreigner to understand two grandmothers conversing is exceedingly difficult, and the foreigner's conversation in the village is likely to always be stilted. Hence in some American universities South Asian languages are now taught beginning with a common informal dialect and progressing to the formal or high dialect.

Social Dialects: Kannaḍa

Because Kannaḍa has been studied sociologically by several scholars such as William Bright, A. K. Ramanujan, William McCormack, Helen Ullrich, and John Gumperz, we still cite it as an example. In the four southern states and Mahārāshṭra there is generally a three-way linguistic

division which also coincides with the three blocs of castes: Brāhmaṇ, non-Brāhmaṇ, and Harijan. Dialect differences among castes within these blocs are slight, though they have been demonstrated even for castes living in the same hamlet.

Kannaḍa has three main geographical dialects focused on the three largest cities: Dhāwār in the north, Bangalore in the southeast, and Mangalore on the south of the coastal strip; the first is influenced by Marāṭhī, the second by Tamiḻ, and the third by Tuḷu, but the boundaries of Kannaḍa are quite clear. In addition there is the formal literary dialect, which requires several years of schooling for a villager to use fluently; the gulf separating this from the standard colloquial that is beginning to form is wide. An educated person is expected to be able to code-switch from his village or caste dialect to the standard colloquial and to the formal dialect.

The Brāhmaṇ, non-Brāhmaṇ, and Harijan social dialects are separated by linguistic differences which are generally trivial as regards the basic linguistic core or deep structure, but they are social markers. In lexical inventory non-Brāhmaṇ and Harijan speech are not very different except for a few forms of address and kinship nouns, but they do differ in phonemics, with marked shifts of pronunciation of verbal suffixes. But Brāhmaṇs use many Sanskrit or alleged Sanskrit words; their speech is innovative primarily in vocabulary and reaches out for Sanskrit lexical material, and now for English also. This is partly due to the introduction of new abstract concepts through education, but it is also motivated by the linguistic "flight of the elite." Such new vocabulary is imitated to some extent by non-Brāhmaṇ speakers.

In phonology Brāhmaṇs contrast *ś*, *ṣ*, and *s*, aspirated and nonaspirated stops, and nasalized and nonnasalized vowels; under the influence of English they also contrast *f* and *p*. These sets are not usually contrastive in the Kannaḍa of uneducated villagers. Phonemic change in the Brāhmaṇ dialect may be restrained by literacy. Generally non-Brāhmaṇ and Harijan speech is responsive to the demands of efficiency and the general patterns of phonetic shifts occurring within the language. Even phonemically the non-Brāhmaṇ speech may imitate the Brāhmaṇ, as in the case of the word for milk. In old Kannaḍa this was *pāl*, but in medieval Kannaḍa had become *hāl*. Brāhmaṇs now pronounce it *hālu*, and the initial consonant has become partially voiced. But non-Brāhmaṇs do not notice this as contrastive and pronounce the word as *ālu*, perhaps by a misimitation of the Brāhmaṇ dialect. As William Bright suggests, the upper class now appears to originate sound change on the phonetic level, whereas the middle and lower classes, imitating this inaccurately, produce change on the phonemic level. The interaction between upper class lexical innovation and middle class phonemic innovation and economy keeps the language dynamic. Bright gives the following examples of three social dialects in the Dhārwār region:[3]

English	*Formal*	*Colloquial Brāhmaṇ*	*Colloquial non-Brāhmaṇ*
ame	hesaru	hesru	yesru
nan	manuṣya	manṣya	mansa
riend	snēhita	snēyta	sinēyta
loesn't do	māḍuvudilla	māḍolla	maḍalla
n a cart	banḍiyalli	banḍīli	bandyāgī

Statistically analyzed samples of Brāhmaṇ and non-Brāhmaṇ speech of Dhārwār show Brāhmaṇ speech to be more dramatic in description and o use lexical items that are less predictable, whereas non-Brāhmaṇ speech eveals greater concern with descriptive details, dress and physical appearance of the subjects to be commented on, and on the whole, is more estrictive with somewhat predictable lexicon. Differences in education and eading habits are partly responsible for this.

The formal dialect of Kannaḍâ, which is used for writing and speechnaking, is not the colloquial speech of any region nor of any social group. Words are not abbreviated as in colloquial dialects, and inflectional suffixes are used without deleting syllables. Efforts to make this the standard colloquial are not likely to succeed. Brāhmaṇ colloquial also will not become he standard, both because Brāhmaṇs are a small minority and because of eeling against them. The Harijan dialect lacks prestige. Consequently a common oral standard, to the extent that it is evolving, is that of the major agricultural and artisan castes.

The reader can appreciate the difficulty a foreigner encounters in learnng South Asian languages. Alan Beals, who has studied several villages in Karṇāṭaka, writes how he learned Kannaḍa:

> Counting the year and a half spent in Bangalore and six months in Gopalpur, t took me two years to begin to be able to converse.
>
> In this learning process, regular language lessons seemed of little value and I came to regret the time that I had spent studying Kanarese grammar. The grammar that I learned was that of Sanskrit and Latin and had little relevance to the way in which people actually formed sentences. The final breakthrough seemed to be due to two things: isolation from persons who could speak English and the transcribing of field notes in Kanarese. If I had to do it over again, I would go alone to a place where nobody spoke English and I would arrange for the constant companionship of an uneducated young man between the ages of nine and fifteen.[4]

Beals did well to begin to converse after two years; often it takes twice that long if one learns a formal or standard dialect and then has to start over again with a colloquial dialect. Few foreigners in South Asia develop the ability to code-switch among colloquial, standard, and formal dialects of a language.

Language and Social Change: Bāngālī

Bāngālī, with 70 million speakers in Bangladesh and 48 million in India ranks population-wise as the sixth language of the world. There are several regional dialects of Bāngālī, a standard urban colloquial, and a Sanskritized literary variety called Sādhu Bhāshā. These have interacted congruently with social change in Bānglā.

Sādhu Bhāshā was formely used by paṇḍits (Hindu scholarly teachers) for whom Sanskrit learning was an end in itself. They also had lurking in their minds some idea of the metaphysical relationship between a word and what it represented. For subjects of intellectual content, it was felt, as Edward Dimmock says, that a language of "spiritual adequacy" was imperative. Paṇḍits disliked the Persian and Arabic vocabulary that had crept into colloquial Bāngālī via Urdū. Their Sādhu Bhāshā drew so heavily upon Sanskrit, replacing even cognates, that many Bāngālīs thought their language was derived directly from Sanskrit, which is not the case.

But this cumbersome dialect could hardly be used for popular literature or for writings of social protest, and was too elaborate for use in trade and commerce. It was the changes set in motion by the appearance of Europeans that led eventually to development of a standard urban colloquial dialect. As Calcutta grew into an administrative and commercial city, a proletarian prose became accepted. Rabindranath Tagore especially gave impetus to the use of the standard urban colloquial in literature (he won the Nobel Prize in 1913), while increased literacy was also an important factor.

Bāngālī villagers in West Bengal today need learn, besides their regional dialect, only the Calcutta standard, which is taught in schools. The displacement of the Sādhu Bhāshā underlines the transfer of attention from Sanskrit learning to the dynamic urban processes of Calcutta. In this city caste began to lose its rigid hierarchical nature earlier than in most parts of India, with consequent linguistic leveling. Dimmock says there has been a slight merging of the two literary varieties of Bāngālī.

In Bangladesh there are four main geographical dialects, the most unique being that of the Chittagong area in the southeastern corner. In addition there is the even more aberrant Bāngālī of the Chākmā tribal people, who are Buddhists. The four main dialects differ more in morphology than in syntax or phonology. The Bāngālī of Bangladesh has about 2500 words of Persian or Arabic origin. Muslims differentiate themselves by pronouncing these words closer to the Arabic or Persian originals than Hindus can, for they are accustomed to reciting the Qur'ān and using Muslim names.

The Calcutta standard colloquial was lightly superimposed on eastern Bānglā before Partition. After the formation of Pakistan, however, there was some reversal of this trend; people were not so quick to hide rural or

regional origins behind the cloak of Calcutta Bāngālī. Fewer people criticized poor use of the standard, and university students, speaking among themselves, lapsed into region dialects without embarrassment.[5] Here again language accurately reflected political and cultural change.

Pakistan declared Urdū as the official language of the country and when that precipitated riots in its eastern wing, acknowledged Bāngālī as a second official language. Former President Ayub Khan suggested on a visit to East Pakistan that people should write Bāngālī in Urdū script to better distinguish themselves from Indian Bāngālīs, but that suggestion was not taken up. Rather in the late 1960s people became more devoted to their language as a symbol of their identity, and merchants put up signboards without any English as insurance against pro-Bāngālī student rioters. Since the 1971 war Urdū has been banished from the classroom, the remaining Urdū signboards have been painted over, and Bāngālī is to be used at all levels of government and in universities too. Whether the Calcutta dialect becomes the standard remains to be seen, but technical Bāngālī vocabulary is being developed by consultation between universities in both countries.

Language and Social Change: Hindī-Urdū

Hindī-Urdū is numerically the fourth language in the world. Pakistanis consider Urdū to be a separate language, however, and in fact it is evolving in that direction. The evolution of modern Hindī-Urdū as described by John Gumperz is a direct outcome of social and historical trends operating in the heartland of South Asia. When Mughals ruled from Delhi, a common *bāzār* (market) dialect, Hindustānī, began to develop in the empire. Written with a script derived from Arabic and influenced by borrowings from Persian and Arabic, it became Urdū. It developed a modern style in the second quarter of the 19th century after the consolidation of British rule and was used for administrative purposes at some levels, taught in schools, and popularized by use in trading and military establishments.

Leaders of the Muslim elite came from western Uttar Pradesh, and their ideal was Persian. Hindu literary figures often came from the middle Gangā plains, and their ideal was Sanskrit; they did not accept the Persian and Arabic borrowings, nor did they relish Urdū script. They therefore invented a new literary style, using the Devanāgarī (Sanskrit) script, and grafted lexical borrowings from Sanskrit on the Hindustānī base.

These two literary forms, Hindī and Urdū, became recognized as standard by people speaking various geographical and social dialects. Grierson's survey grouped five "languages" under Hindī: Bihārī, Eastern Hindī, Western Hindī, Rājasthānī, and Pahāṛī, though these merge into neighboring languages such as Gujarātī and Nepālī. Other dialects include Chattīsgaṛhī in Madhya Pradesh, the Urdū of Deccan Muslims, bāzār Hindustānī, and

army Hindustānī. A villager in the North Indian heartland generally has two dialects superimposed above his own: the regional variety used in towns and by traders and servicing castes, and the modern standard Hindī or Urdū.

The use of language as an indicator of social identity is clearly seen in the distribution of certain phonemes in the Hindī area, as studied by Gumperz. Phonemes of Persian origin, such as *z*, *f*, *x*, *ḳ*, and *g*, are found only in certain Muslim homes. In Delhi and Lucknow, *z* and *f* are used but *x*, *ḳ*, and *g* are only heard on formal occasions. Farther east in Bihār *f* and *z* are rare while the other three are scarcely heard. There are none of these phonemes in the regional Hindī dialects. In Delhi both Urdū and Hindī speakers learn standard Hindī, but the former can differentiate *f–ph*, *z–j*, *k–ḳ*, *g–g*, and *x–kh*, whereas the Hindu ordinarily cannot. On the other hand, the Hindu will differentiate *n–ṇ*, which the Muslim may not. The Urdū speaker from Bihār will use phonemes close to those of the Hindī of Hindus.

During the years when the Congress Party sought independence, Gandhi worked for the idea of a common comprehensible language. He selected Hindustānī as a compromise and in 1942 founded an organization to promote it; he even set up centers for the propagation of this speech in the South. He rebuked both paṇḍits and maulvīs for exaggerating linguistic differences.

Considerable high quality literature, including poetry inspired by the Persian model, was produced in Urdū even before Independence. Now that Urdū is the chief unifying language of Pakistan, the highly Persianized form is falling into disuse in popular journalism, but some writers cater to it as a symbol of national identity. Not much quality literature was produced in Hindī before Independence; Bāngālī, Marāṭhī, and Tamil̲ were ahead of Hindī in this respect—a fact avidly noted by anti-Hindī zealots today who refer to Hindī as a neophyte language.

The development of Hindī since Independence accurately reflects both the rate of modernization and nationalism. The government has encouraged the creation of technical terms by establishing in 1950 a Board of Scientific Terminology. Official Hindī today is loaded with new words, mostly coined from Sanskrit bases, some 350,000 of which have been devised and incorporated into new dictionaries, glossaries for specialized subjects, and encyclopedias. It has Sanskrit features not used in colloquial speech, including final consonant clusters *-mr*, *-jy*, and *-sy*, and the short final vowels *i* and *u*. Even Nehru complained that he could not understand the Hindī translations of his own radio speeches.

Characteristic of the hierarchy of social dialects in South Asia, this highly Sanskritized Hindī is more symbolic of social and political features than a means of lucid communication. Yet it does to some extent serve as a model, and some of the coined words catch on. Colloquial-spoken Hindī is sprinkled with English words when spoken by English-educated people, but

journalistic Hindī has only a few words of English origin, such as *ilaktrikal enjiniyari* (electrical engineering) and *aprentis* (apprentice) while incorporating a large corpus of spontaneously evolved new words. It can be written in a variety of impersonal and personal styles which are an index of modernization and the drift of Indian intellectual life. After studying technical terms in journalistic Hindī, Di Bona concludes:

> We can say that Hindi is an adequate vehicle for the transmission of technical ideas in the field of education. It has developed and evolved a terminology that is not unduly dependent on an English heritage and is flexible enough to promise the same in the future. On the other hand government efforts at language standardization seem to be of limited consequence since the rapid changeover to the use of the vernaculars has far outstripped the ability of the government to provide leadership in this area.[6]

Language and Social Change: Tamiḻ

Tamiḻ is unique among Indian languages in the extent to which it resists Sanskrit borrowings; there is a conscious effort to move the language away from Indo-Āryan influence. Even the Tamiḻ of the Śangam literature nearly two millennia ago borrowed very few Sanskrit words. In medieval centuries the effect of Sanskrit was felt under increased Brāhmaṇ influence and for a time a script distinguishing aspirated stops was used. But the modern Tamiḻ script cannot represent the aspirated phonemes common to all other Indian literary languages. The rejection of Sanskrit became especially conscious around the turn of the century when the literary form began to be purged of words deemed to be of Sanskrit origin. Rejection of Sanskrit and Hindī has become a widely popular political issue, and expresses not only identity distinct from North India but also rejection of the historic Brāhmaṇ supremacy.

Regional dialects—whose roots are known from literature to extend back two millennia—are focused on a few major cities in Tamiḻ Nāḍu, and a dialect maintaining some old pronunciation forms is used in Sri Lanka. As for social dialects, Brāhmaṇ speech is clearly distinguishable, for it reproduces loan words from Sanskrit more faithfully and has a greater inventory of phonemic contrasts. Since Brāhmaṇs early went in for English education their speech also reproduces English more faithfully; for example, they may even pronounce the word "Brāhmaṇ" with a broad *a* as in "bran," as in colloquial English. Some aspects of Brāhmaṇ culture and rituals are expressed in their dialect. "Son-in-law" is differentiated from "younger sister's husband" in the Brāhmaṇ but not in the common colloquial dialect. Brāhmaṇs use separate words for drinking water, water in general, and nondrinkable water. It is clear that the Brāhmaṇ dialect serves as a social marker and is not just the result of greater literacy, for the Brāhmaṇ dialect of Tuḷu, a language not generally written, has the same effect, according to

Ramanujan. It may also be pointed out that Muslims of the South retain as many socially indicative dialect forms as do Brāhmaṇs.

Regional and social dialects aside, the formal or written dialect is quite different and requires some years of schooling to learn. Of course, this also serves as a social marker, for uneducated people cannot use it. A common oral standard is also just beginning to emerge. The word "it sees" has been cited by Ramanujan as an example:

Formal	pārkkiratu
Brāhmaṇ	pākk(a)radu
Standard colloquial, Madras to Madurai	pākkudu
Regional colloquial (Nāgarkōvil)	pākku

The standard colloquial is not readily recognized as standard yet and is just beginning to emerge. In effect, it is the speech of the agriculturalist dominant middle castes over the central part of the state. For the Tamil of the future the Brāhmaṇ dialect is not acceptable and the dialects of extreme regions such as Madras or Sri Lanka are also not acceptable. There are Harijan dialects, but these too do not qualify. Consequently the speech of the middle castes over the central part of the state is likely to become the standard.

Evolution of a standard dialect has been restrained by insistence that the formal Tamiḻ is the only pure Tamiḻ, and it is used in all writing and taught as the supposed standard in schools. On this point Bāngālī and Hindī, which are written in a form much closer to at least one spoken dialect than is Tamiḻ, have an advantage over the South Indian languages: the early development of widely read journalism in Calcutta, for instance, was due to the adoption of a written form very close to the spoken.

In common with other South Asian languages, Tamiḻ is being adapted to new uses, many of them modeled after English. Oral and written advertisements use abbreviated and innovative forms to produce a crispness not found in the traditional language. Single words or short phrases are used in new ways, such as "push"-"pull" on doors, "exit" in cinemas, "stop" on street signs, and "flush" on toilets. An impersonal scientific style has been developed for textbooks. Newspapers sometimes now carry short stories written in the informal standard colloquial, a practice likely to increase in use in the future with social leveling and more intense statewide communication.

Language and Social Change: Tribes

The 40 million tribal people of South Asia (see Chap. 15) are undergoing acculturation in greatly varying ways. While many can communicate

omewhat in a neighboring regional language, some also are bilingual in ther tribal languages. For example, in Pakistan most Brāhūīs speak Balūchī nd only a few know Sindhī or Urdū. In the Chittagong Hills of Bangladesh he smaller Buddhist tribes have made Marma their lingua franca because is closer to their own than Bāngālī and they resist Bāngālī acculturation. ut in the same area the Chākmās, numbering some 150,000, have forgotten heir own Burmese-type language and now speak an almost incomprehensible orm of Bāngālī. The Mīzos, being Christians, use the Roman script for their wn language and tend to favor English as a second language. The direction f acculturation each tribe is pursuing determines in what language extra-ribal communication will be conducted.

The tribes of central India and Assam are in some cases undergoing anskritization, in which case they adopt as second language the proximate egional one, especially Hindī, Bāngālī, Uṛiyā, and Assamese, while at the ame time their own languages are affected by borrowings from the regional anguages and from English. Robbins Burling gives the example of Gāro of Meghālaya as a language which has undergone extreme lexical borrowing. Untouched by the outside world until the 1860s, Gāro culture has since ad to ingest thousands of new named objects as well as new abstract deas.

> Garos sometimes eat a pastry known as *biskut*. Some of these *biskut* are nade in the shape of an "s" and are known as *esbiskut*. When a Garo drinks ea he calls it *cha*, the word used throughout most of Asia, and more rarely he rinks *kapi*. The beverages are flavored with *dut* (from the Bengali word for milk") and *chini* (Bengali for sugar) and are drunk from a *kap*. Garos have their wn numbers, but for telling clock time they have adopted Bengali numbers, hough they have modified them to suit their own tongues. Poinsettias are known s *krismas pul* from the time of year when they bloom and the Bengali word for flower." A Garo lights his house with a *lem* that he fills with *kerosin*. He writes vith a *pensil* or *pawnten* (from "fountain pen") on *leka* (Bengali for "paper") and eads from a *kitap* (Bengali for "book," ultimately of Arabic origin).[7]

A Gāro can hardly speak without using such borrowed terms. Burling ays it is utterly futile to try to draw limits around the "real" Gāro vocabu-ary, for the entire resources of the English dictionary are available, besides ll of Bāngālī. But while it is impossible to say whether a particular word s Gāro, one can almost always tell whether a sentence is. Though the Gāros are not particularly highly educated, some of the tribes in the Assam egion are more literate and fluid in their outlook than are most Indians nd Pakistanis. Ease of linguistic borrowing is symbolic of ease of cultural orrowing, and among Nāgas, Mīzos, and some other mountain groups, here is a real readiness to adapt and change, to bypass the old great raditions and move directly into modernization as they see it.

Linguistic Tensions

Language issues have evoked more emotion in South Asian countrie than any others since Independence; at least, language is more easil focused upon as a target for spontaneous demonstration than other mor subtle problems. The student of South Asian society will see reflected i language issues almost every area of social tension: rural-urban, religious secular, centrifugal-centripetal, Hindu-Muslim or Hindu-Buddhist, tradition modernization, north-south, east-west, and others.

In India before Independence, the Congress Party was committed t the principle of formation of linguistic states because it was believed tha democratic or representative government could not operate unless admin istration, at least at the state level, was in the languages of the people The Constitution of India makes Hindī the Official Language of the Centra Government and a link language among the states. Hindī was to replac English by 1965, but before the deadline the Constitution was amende to allow for the continued use of English for some time as an associat Official Language.

Upon the departure of the British, Hindī became a focal point fo nationalism, and likewise the regional languages became foci for regionalism Linguistic states were formed attended by violence. Āndhra came int being only after fastings and demonstrations. Gujarāt and Mahārāshtr were separated from the old Bombay Presidency (after some delay becaus people of both states wanted the city of Bombay). In 1966 Haryāṇā wa separated from Panjāb after a long period of public fastings and excitabl public demonstrations—though in this case Sikh religious identity was als an issue. The question of the status of Bāngālī as a minority language i Assam produced violence. One reason for the separation of Nāgaland an Meghālaya from Assam was that those tribal people did not wish to b governed in Assamese. In Tamil̲ Nāḍu the violence, demonstrations, fla burning, and train burning culminated in the election in 1967 of the DM party on an essentially anti-Hindī, pro-Tamil̲ plank: "Down with Hind imperialism." In Mahārāshṭra the Śiva Sena has arisen as a rightist pro Marāṭhī political party, while in Uttar Pradesh the Jana Sangh party ha a large following and is demanding the immediate replacement of Englis by Hindī in the Central Government. College students in Banares deface so many English signboards with threats of further violence that mos merchants advertise now only with Hindī signboards. For many Indians most noticeably for Bāngālīs and Tamil̲s, loyalty to the linguistic area i more meaningful than loyalty to an abstract united India. This is als symbolic of demands for state autonomy in economic affairs.

The states are now turning to the regional languages for administra tion, and in some of them colleges and universities are switching languag

media. English is also to be replaced in the state legal systems. Hindī speakers are impatient for the Central Government to switch completely from English, but this is delayed for the pragmatic reason that Delhi wants above all else to hold the country together. Speakers of regional languages feel that if Hindī only is used in the Central Government, Hindī speakers will be at an advantage in getting jobs, with the result that the Hindī area will dominate the rest of India. Practical problems of running railroads, postal and telegraph services, and airlines—all monopolies of the Central Government—loom large, for how can these be run in a dozen languages? If India hangs together in spite of these linguistic tensions, one wonders what kind of compromises can possibly be worked out. With the exception of population growth and the attendant economic crises, language issues have been the most volatile internal issues in the past quarter century.

In Pakistan Ayub Khan tried to gloss over the regional realities by abolishing the four provinces, but in 1970 after his overthrow they were again delineated, essentially coinciding with Panjābī, Sindhī, Pashto, and Balūchī. The latent linguistic loyalty appeared, attended by riots, with the designation of Sindhī as the official language of Sindh, and one could predict the same for Pashto in the North-West Frontier Province. It remains to be seen whether national unity and the Islamic ideal are powerful enough to enable Urdū to retain preeminence for formal purposes.

Meanwhile in Bangladesh Bāngālī came to be viewed as the single most important symbol of ethnic identity. Even before independence in 1971 almost all signboards on stores were in Bāngālī, the English having been removed or printed very small. Now the signs on university office doors are in Bāngālī. The "Bihārīs" (Muslims in the country of Indian origin) are afraid to speak Urdū. Exchange of Bāngālī literature with India, prohibited under the Pakistan government, is thriving.

In Sri Lanka since Independence the ethnic and linguistic patriotism of the Sinhalas has alienated the Tamil minority, who comprise 30% of the population. In 1958 legislation was passed to implement use of Sinhala only for official purposes and for education, but this precipitated violence. Tamils tarred Sinhala letters on bus and taxi license plates, which led to mutual defacement of Tamil and Sinhala signboards. The government ultimately conceded "reasonable use" of Tamil. Of course, the issue was not purely a language one; the attempt to eliminate Tamil for official purposes was a tool to eliminate the predominance of Tamils in many branches of the administration of government and business, providing jobs for Sinhalas. Sri Lanka has signed an agreement with India to repatriate half a million Tamils of Indian ancestry, mostly plantation laborers who were born in Sri Lanka but whose ancestors were brought over by the British. Few have been repatriated so far, but Sri Lanka keeps them as stateless persons for fear that the extra Tamil votes will challenge the progress of Sinhala nationalism.

In Nepal the government is trying to forge unity throughout the

culturally bespattered country by using Nepālī only. A Nepālī-speaking Hindu official told the writer, "We have no language problem here in Nepal. It is not like India and Pakistan. Everyone speaks Nepālī." Yet half the people do not have Nepālī or related dialects as mother tongue. Hindu Chetrīs never learn the languages of the Newārīs, Magars, or Limbūs, but these have to learn Nepālī or Pahāṛī dialects if there is to be communication. In recent years Newārī and other languages have acquiesced to weakening by a purposeful government policy of reduced use in schools and on the radio, but one can feel the tensions roiling underneath.

English as the Badge of the Elite

The power structure in most South Asian countries is comprised of an English-speaking elite. It is the college-educated minority who are eligible for important government offices, industrial executive appointments, or careers in law, medicine, science, or secondary education. Though not quite an "English-speaking caste," this minority of 2% has acquired most of the prerogatives of the Sanskrit-speaking and Persian-speaking elites of the past. It is they who attempt to engineer social and economic change and set norms which they hope the rest of society will emulate.

One who is "educated" is commonly understood to mean one who can handle English. Naturally, people in professions who attained their positions because they could move among the English-speaking urban elite are loath to give up this symbol of their status. Where the displacement of English by regional languages has been forced, as by Sinhala in Sri Lanka and Hindī in parts of North India, a clerk must still show evidence of having had an English education to maintain status among his peers. Government officials visiting villages will chatter in English simply for effect. Businessmen will print stationery and visiting cards in English for prestige.

But English education, like "Sanskritization," implies much more than dissemination of a language: it has molded the thinking patterns of South Asia's elite. There is little doubt that such ideals as democratic elections, an economically equalitarian society, technical and scientific creativity, constitutional government, membership in the Commonwealth, and in some countries secular government have been fired and refueled through the medium of English literature. College students know their Shakespeare better than do their American counterparts, while such writers as T. S. Eliot, Aldous Huxley, Ernest Hemingway, and Bertrand Russell have become prescribed, their works placed on the list of "set books" which students read to pass the B.A. examination.

At the same time the continued use of English is symptomatic of a wide cleavage in society. A thin crust at the top, 1% to 3%, benefit from the sophistication and scientific thought transmitted in English, and because

they use it largely to keep wide the gulf between themselves and the rest, there is little diffusion of these benefits to the three-fourths million villages. "Educated" people do not generally engage in physical work. No doubt many college graduates return to their villages, but they find what they learned so unrelated they keep it in cold storage, awaiting the day when they might land a respectable job.

Universities have recently shifted to regional languages, or are in the process of shifting, and the full effect of this will appear in a generation. Most college, and even graduate, instruction in the Hindī area is in Hindī, while Gujarātī, Telugu, and other languages are coming into their own in their respective regions. In Sri Lanka students have the option of studying in Sinhala or Tamiḻ even in the Medical School and Law School. Bangladesh intends to complete the change to Bangālī in the universities in five years. But in some Indian states, in Pakistan, and in cosmopolitan cities change is slower. In the established prestige institutions old professors who had their education when English was at the apex of its prestige do not wish to have their positions undercut, and students do not wish to be at a disadvantage in the job market.

Many excuses are given why large businesses, higher levels of government, and some universities are slow in shifting from English, such as lexical inadequacy of the regional languages, possible restrictions on mobility, and the need for English as a "window on the world." The underlying reasons, however, concern status. Products advertised in English have an aura of modernity and urbanity. Those who claim to be the new elite need something to set themselves apart from the rest, and English does this for them as well as Sanskrit did for the old Hindu elite and Persian for the old Muslim elite. Studies have shown that South Asian languages have lexical adequacy for almost all contemporary functions, and their use in all institutions would not restrict mobility any more than use of national languages does in Europe.

Even the reading matter available in English shows the concern readers have with status and urbanity. English newspapers have a considerable volume of international news, but it almost all pertains to the most prominent countries. And this is generally presented in such a way that it refers to the status of India or Pakistan among nations, or pertains to colonial questions in which these nations see reflected their own actual or potential status and influence. This is a projection into international affairs of the concern the individual feels over the place of his own social group in the larger society and is analogous to what Ruth Benedict documented for Japan during World War II when that country sought to establish its place among the hierarchy of nations.

In the long view there are but a few alternatives. One is to opt for English as the medium in all levels of education and government as has been done in many African countries, but this would be unacceptable in

South Asia because of the long literary traditions of important languages. Another alternative would be to retain the use of English among the elite, but the price of that would be retention of the existing social cleavage and prevention of the benefits of higher education diffusing below. The third alternative would be the use of major regional languages in all levels of education and government, as in Japan and European countries. This is the trend today, though progress is slow because the unity of existing nations is threatened and because English is so important as a social marker. But the development of standard colloquial forms of the regional languages suggests a trend that will intensify. From a sociological point of view, it seems certain that the prevailing trend to a more equalitarian society will eventually vaunt the standard urban dialects of the major languages as the media for all functions, and the political straws will be blown where they may.

REFERENCES AND NOTES

[1] W. Norman Brown, "Class and Cultural Traditions in India," in Singer (1959), p. 36.
[2] Burling, p. 115.
[3] Bright, p. 470; Burling, p. 195.
[4] Alan Beals, "Gopalpur, 1958–1960," in George Spindler (ed.), *Being an Anthropologist* (New York, 1970), p. 48.
[5] Munier Chowdhury, "The Language Problem in East Pakistan," in Ferguson and Gumperz, p. 75.
[6] Joseph di Bona, "Language Change and Modernization: The Development of a Hindi Technical Terminology in Education," in Robert Crane (ed.), *Transition in South Asia* (Durham, N.C., 1970), p. 96.
[7] Burling, pp. 177–178.

IMPORTANT SOURCES

Bright, William. "Social Dialects and Language History," in Dell Hymes (ed.), *Language in Culture and Society*. New York, 1964.

Burling, Robbins. *Man's Many Voices: Language in its Cultural Context*. New York, 1970. (Chap. 8 and other parts refer to South Asia; a readable book.)

Das Gupta, Jyotirindra, and John Gumperz, "Language Communication and Control in North India," in J. A. Fishman, C. A. Ferguson, and J. Das Gupta (eds.), *Language Problems of Developing Nations*. New York, 1968.

Ferguson, Charles, and John Gumperz (eds.). *Linguistic Diversity in South Asia, International J. American Linguistics* XXVI, No. 23 (July 1960). (Articles by William Bright, M. Shanmugam Pillai, Edward Dimock, Munier Chowdhury, William McCormack, and John Gumperz.)

Ghurye, G. S. *Social Tensions in India*. Bombay, 1968. (Note pp. 430–484 on "Linguistic Tensions.")

Grierson, G. A. *Linguistic Survey of India*. Calcutta, 1927.

Gumperz, John. "Hindi-Panjabi Code-Switching in Delhi," *Proceedings of the Ninth International Congress of Linguists*. The Hague, 1962.

———. "Speech Variation and the Study of Indian Civilization," in Dell Hymes (ed.), *Language in Culture and Society*. New York, 1964.

Kearney, Robert. *Communalism and Language in the Politics of Ceylon*. Durham, N.C., 1964.

Ramanujan, A. K. "Language and Social Change: The Tamil Example," in Robert Crane (ed.), *Transition in South Asia*. Durham, N.C., 1970.

Shills, Edward. *The Intellectual Between Tradition and Modernity: The Indian Situation*. The Hague, 1961.

Singer, Milton (ed.). *Traditional India: Structure and Change*. Philadelphia, 1959. (Articles by W. Norman Brown, Daniel Ingalls, A. M. Shah, and R. G. Shroff, M. B. Emeneau, and William McCormack.)

———, and Bernard Cohn (eds.). *Structure and Change in Indian Society*. Chicago, 1968. (Articles by William Bright, A. K. Ramanujan, and William McCormack.)

10

Survey of Northern and Western India

Now let us carve up South Asia into major culture zones to discuss settlement patterns, kinship, family, and other anthropological subjects about which it is difficult to generalize for the whole. Chapters 10 through 15 will deal with six such zones. Proceeding from the most distinctive, they are as follows: 1) The most unique in every aspect of culture are the "tribal" people in the hills around Assam. Somewhat less distinct but still separate from Hindu peasant populations are the tribal peoples of central India. 2) Next we would think of the whole Himālayan zone stretching from northernmost Pakistan through Bhutan. 3) Among the plains peasant populations linked with the wider civilization we can easily demarcate the four states of South India, especially in terms of language and kinship, and to this may be added Sri Lanka. 4) Next we would think of the relatively homogeneous Bānglā plains on the eastern side, together with several outlying plains areas. 5) Finally, we can visualize Pakistan as a separate zone, with a geographical focus in the Indus River but extending westward into the hills, to which may be added half of Afghanistan. 6) After lopping off these geographical appendages, like carving a turkey beginning with the wings and legs, what is left is the heartland—the Gangā plains, western India, and central India.

The companion volume, *South Asia: Seven Community Profiles*, has descriptions of life in villages or communities in each of these six zones (plus a separate one for Sri Lanka). The author of each community profile presents an intimate view of life as a coherent and rational pattern in a particular locality to balance the generalizations and abstractions to follow herein.

Zone 6 of the above, arbitrary as it is, forms the subject of this survey chapter. It includes the Gangā states of Uttar Pradesh and Bihār, the central Indian state of Madhya Pradesh, and a bank of western states: Mahārāshṭra, Gujarāt, Rājasthān, Haryāṇā, Panjāb, and part of Kashmīr. Across the center of this vast region the inhabitants speak Hindī or its dialects, to which Panjābī is similar. But Kashmīr, Gujarāt, and Mahārāshṭra have their own languages. We group these eight states together in this chapter, not because we wish to obscure the very real differences between Marāṭhīs and Sikhs or between villages in the desert of Rājasthān and the rice fields of Bihār, but because there is a limit to the length of this book.

Settlement Patterns and House Types

Settlement patterns in South Asia include 1) the isolated homestead, 2) the dispersed cluster, 3) the linear cluster, 4) the amorphous nucleated cluster, and 5) the rectangular nucleated village. Each is related to landscape, agriculture, water resources, caste configuration, and defense needs. All of these are found in northern and western India.

Isolated homesteads occur in the hill areas of Jammū and Kashmīr where isolated plots are farmed, and in the Bhīl tribal areas of Rājasthān and neighboring Madhya Pradesh, as well as in the dry parts of central and northern Rājasthān where fields are necessarily large. Often there are dispersed clusters of two to five, or perhaps 10 homesteads in Mewār and the Arāvalī upland region of Rājasthān, the Mahādeo Hills of Madhya Pradesh, and the northern hill regions of Uttar Pradesh. Linear villages are not so common in these parts of India, but may be seen in some of the valley areas of Madhya Pradesh where they tend to follow streams or roads.

A more complex form of linear settlement is houses in parallel lines often paired face to face and back to back. Especially interesting are the community streets that are dead-end and sometimes demarcated by a gate; these tend to be occupied by relatives living in separate but substantial houses. This type is preferred by merchants and other relatively prosperous groups in the larger villages and towns of Gujarāt, for instance. Such specialized streets are often found integrated into a larger grid plan, with main streets at right angles, which generally prevails in western India and the South. Such well-planned villages tend to be rectangular and suited to the needs of fortification, as in Mahārāshṭra where until recently each sub-

Rājasthānī women prepare supper in the courtyard. Wheat flour is flattened into capātīs and baked on fireplace.

stantial settlement was fortified and was crowded and compact. Some of the larger villages of Rājasthān are also rectangular.

Madhya Pradesh is a state of generally small hamlets dotting basins where agriculture is good, as in Chattīsgaṛh. In the western part of the state some of the settlements were fortified because this was an area of banditry. But the grid or rectangular pattern that apparently diffused down the Deccan to the South bypassed these areas.

In eastern Uttar Pradesh and northern Bihār the pattern is one of somewhat amorphous nucleated villages interspersed with many smaller homestead clusters which are sometimes satellites linked by jajmānī relations. Here, and even more so in Bānglā, the population is heavy, and higher pieces of ground such as will escape monsoon floods are particularly desirable for settlements. Caste complexity and hierarchy tend to be less in such areas than where villages are large and more highly organized.

The most important physical feature of most village homes is not the house but the courtyard. Cooking is done there in many areas, and most social activity takes place within its walls, which may be of mud, shrubbery, or mat fencing. The sun dries and disinfects whatever is laid out, ranging from pots to clothes; children play without wandering; animals can be tethered, and cow-dung cakes or hay are stacked. The one-room elementary rural hut which is entered from the courtyard may be of mud with a flat mud roof in the drier areas, or it may have a gabled thatched roof or a tile roof. Respectable families may plaster their huts with mud and whitewash

FIG 10–1 House types in Panjāb, Haryāṇā, and Himāchal Pradesh.[1]

1) Houses in Lāhaul and Spiti are of stone and mud mortar; ground floor is for animals and fodder; above are rooms for cooking, sleeping, guests; latrine is cubicle with hole in floor; old houses are windowless.
2) Houses in Kāngṛā are also of stone, but typically have only 2 rooms; charcoal is burned for heat.
3) Sikh Jāṭs have houses of 3 to 6 rooms, but Khatrīs, Brāhmans, and Rājpūts may have 5 to 10 rooms, mostly with compounds and large gates.
4) In this hot, dry, and sandy region over half the houses have only one room, with flat mud roofs; rooms are in rear of mud-walled compound.
5) In this hot and dry region a compound is flanked by houses with 4 rooms, or sometimes 6; they are single storeyed, with walls of mud clods and flat roofs.
6) In this rocky region most houses are kaccā, one storey, with two rooms behind a veranda; some have separate rooms for animals; roofs are of slate, reeds, tile, or iron sheets.
7) Soldiers who saved money during the war returned to build such pakkā houses of brick and mud plaster; arched door leads to hall flanked by several rooms, including one for animals.
8) Most pleasant houses are of mud, with either tile or thatched roofs.
9) Houses built before Independence, even in poor areas, may show influence of Muslim architecture; men socialize on veranda, and women in interior sun-well.

them, or may build brick or stone houses. Often two or three houses open onto the same courtyard, usually occupied by brothers or other relatives. Where women are kept secluded the courtyard will have high walls. Substantial brick houses in urban or rural areas may be built without courtyards, but will have instead a sunwell inside the house, which becomes the women's domain.

In northern Bihār where the population is dense and very poor most houses are of bamboo, reeds, and matting, with partial walls of mud, but here and there will be a pakkā brick and tile house of a landowning family. In Uttar Pradesh, as in much of India, more and more people are replacing thatch with tiles, but in Panjāb and Rājasthān where it is drier, flat roofs are often thought sufficient.

There is a range of very interesting designs of the more substantial houses, from the multistoried wood houses with ornate carving found in Kashmīr, to the three-story brick houses with wooden overhanging porches clustered around the private dead-end streets such as Gujarātī merchants prefer. There are spacious bungalows built after the Mughal pattern of architecture, flanked by verandas with arches and tiled floors, and the substantial but nondescript brick houses of the smaller landowner-cultivators. Fig. 10–1 depicts some of the house types in Panjāb and Haryāṇā.

Kinship

Irawati Karve in her *Kinship Organization in India* divides most of South Asia into four kinship zones: 1) This zone extends across the whole of both the Indus and Gangā plains. It is most characteristic in the North Indian heartland, where it evolved from the exogamous patrilineage or patriclan ideal of early Indo-Āryan speakers. On the western side, in Pakistan, this type has been modified by Islamic social norms which allow closer in-marrying, while on the eastern side it is mitigated to some extent by the dispersed settlement pattern of Bihār and Bānglā, and in Bangladesh again the Islamic norms have been superimposed. 2) This zone is the western one, comprised of Mahārāshṭra, Gujarāt, and parts of Rājasthān and Madhya Pradesh, where Indo-Āryan speech and kinship terminology prevail but the underlying patterns are characteristically South Indian. Zones 1 and 2 are discussed in this chapter. 3) This zone consists of South India and Sri Lanka, where kinship is characterized by preferential cross-cousin marriage. 4) The last zone consists of the motley of tribal people throughout eastern central India, many of whom use Muṇḍa kinship terminology.

The North Indian kinship system is not only expressed in Indo-Āryan terminology but is derived to a great extent from prehistoric tribal society in which lineages or clans formed the fundamental building blocks of the society before absorption into the stratified caste system of the settled

peasant and urban population. Its most striking feature is the exogamy of the lineage going back several generations, and in some cases the exogamy of large segments of the caste-group which are sometimes called clans. But the English terms family, lineage, clan, phratry, tribe, and caste are more or less used to refer to different degrees of the same thing, and are as confusing as the Indian terms they stand for. It is clear that caste and kinship are closely intertwined, particularly among the groups in this part of India that have knowledge of their lineages going back several generations. Lineage segments may serve as corporate groups, and these merge into exogamous clans in the case of prestigious landowning or ruling caste-groups, but the clans are not corporate groups. Lower castes have less knowledge of their lineages and simply prohibit marriage with anyone known to be a relative.

The patrilineal, patrilocal extended family is strongly idealized, and the politically dominant caste-groups also maintain an ideal of masculinity derived from a militaristic past. Hence male-female roles are quite differentiated. The people of a particular village may have agnatic (patrilateral "blood" relatives) and affinal (through marriage) links with several hundred other villages. The latter, called by Mandelbaum collectively as the feminal kin, include a man's relatives through his mother, married sisters, wife, and married daughter. This kinship pattern produces an exceedingly extensive network of kin over the plains.

But whatever kinship system is employed—whether it be the North Indian, the South Indian, or the Muslim—kinship ties are practically essential for a person to achieve much. The more kin a person has and the better he cultivates their relationship, the more he is likely to have opportunities presented to him. Naturally kinship and lineage tend to be more complex among the higher and more wealthy castes who have more to lose if their collective efforts should be dissipated. Political power, at the village level or on a wider scale, is heavily dependent upon kinship. But a person with many kin also has many obligations, and his pursuit of power and wealth are morally justified because he uses them for the benefit of his kin. Whereas nepotism is seen as an evil by those who believe in the Western ideal that the individual should have the maximum control over the course of his own life, the support of kin in whatever position a person finds himself is accepted as his moral duty in India.

Marriage Regulations

In the North Indian heartland, as everywhere in India, marriages are arranged by parents, for there are a large number of regulations to be observed in selecting a spouse. A fundamental rule here, as in all parts of India, is: 1) endogamy of caste and for practical purposes endogamy of

linguistic region are usually observed, as well as limitations on geographical distance. A fundamental rule pertaining to the North Indian heartland is: 2) exogamy of the lineage (variously defined) and two important extensions of this principle—exogamy of the mythical lineage called a *gotra* and exogamy of the village. Growing out of this is another principle, observed particularly by higher castes: 3) hypergamy, in which the bride marries a groom of status higher than herself, or at least not beneath her. When these principles are considered along with such factors as age, horoscope readings, dowry or bride-wealth as the case may be, and physical appearance, it can be seen that it is indeed a major achievement to find a spouse for one's progeny.

The Brāhmaṇical texts stressed the exogamous group known as *sapiṇḍa*. All the immediate descendants of an ancestor eligible to offer him *piṇḍa* (rice balls) at the śrāddha (funerary) ceremony are sapiṇḍa and are prohibited from intermarrying. At the funeral the eldest son of the deceased, or someone who stands in his place, offers up these piṇḍa and repeats the offering after a specified number of days and again on the anniversary of the death. Originally a son offered piṇḍa for his father, grandfather, great-grandfather, and their wives, and offered holy water to more distant ancestors. Later it became acceptable for a childless widow to offer piṇḍa for her husband, a daughter for her father, and a pupil for his gurū. Traditional law says that for some castes sapiṇḍa exogamy extends to the sixth or seventh generation on the father's side and the fourth or fifth on the mother's. So strong is this sentiment in the North that the Indian Parliament in 1955 considered making this a law applicable to all Hindus in India, which if implemented would have provoked an impossible situation in the South and among lower castes in the North and tribals. As passed, it allowed for variation as permitted by custom or region. But even in the North these rules are not observed, nor even known, to many castes.

In the North generally the minimal lineage, three to six generations, is the most important, and for common folk three or four generations of lineage depth is all they know. Among landed castes there may be several levels of agnatic kin, such as the birādarī (brotherhood) which may even include agnatic kin not acquainted with each other, but is exogamous (though it is preferentially endogamous among Muslims). Above that in some cases is the clan, perhaps even sanctified by a clan deity. The most complex agnatic kin structure is found among ruling and landowning groups, for it is an inherent part of their political system.

A similar category is known in some places as the *kula*, a lineage segment consisting of agnates descended from a single named ancestor which has a number of rituals unifying it. A bride is initiated into her husband's kula by a ritual described below.

A gotra (mythological lineage) is strictly exogamous; in the case of Brāhmaṇs and other orthodox castes gotras are traced back to some vener-

able sage. Other castes trace it to some plant, animal, or object—obviously this is a relic of clan totemism. Some gotras are actual lineages with names of town of origin or of occupation. One's gotra is derived from his father, but sometimes one's mother's gotra or all four grandparents' gotras are proscribed for marriage. In castes having such a four-gotra rule one's spouse has to have grandparents of yet four other gotras! Such a rule not only prevents a man from marrying into his patrilineage no matter how far back the link may be but generally prevents marriage with nearby people of the same general type. However, many castes prohibit marriage within only one or two gotras, or do not have any at all.

An example of the caste and regional variation in these matters may be cited from K. S. Mathur's study of a village in western Madhya Pradesh, in the region known as Mālwā. Here only the higher castes observed sapiṇḍa exogamy; Śūdras and untouchables had not heard the term and did not observe its principles. They generally avoid marrying within the minimal lineage segment, and they have rules to prohibit marriage within 1) one's own gotra, 2) one's mother's gotra, 3) one's father's sister's kula, and 4) one's mother's sister's kula. A further general rule is to avoid giving a daughter to a lineage from which a bride had been accepted, or taking a bride from a lineage to which a daughter had previously been given.

Village exogamy is a rule throughout the northern heartland from Haryāṇā to Bihār but is less rigid near Gujarāt and Bānglā. Even where there is no rule about it, there is a tendency to marry outside the village because chances are slight that enough members of one caste would reside in it for a girl of the right type to be found; moreover, it is seen as advantageous to a man if his wife's family is some distance removed. The main reason for the origin of village exogamy in the northern heartland is that a village was often founded by a particular lineage segment which continued to own the land and village, though the owners would bring into it enough other castes and specialists so that all needed functions would be performed. Karve points out that the members of a caste in a village behave, for purposes of marriage, as if they were descended from a common ancestor, but this is never stretched to all social functions. "The distinction between a joint family and a caste group in one village is very elastic depending on the history of the founding of the village."[2] In Uttar Pradesh, village exogamy is often extended to prohibit marriage into a village whose lands touch one's own village lands. On the other hand, brides are not usually brought from very far away; 20 or maybe 40 miles is as far as it is desirable to extend the search for an eligible girl.

In the North a girl upon marriage is expected to completely switch her allegiance from her father's family to her husband's. Mathur writes of his Mālwā village that the people believe: "If I take a wife from the same village, her affiliation to my household and lineage is never satisfactory, since her attachment to her natal kin is a barrier which a woman can

seldom overcome."[3] There was no rule there about village exogamy (which operates principally in the northern plains), but many people thought it generally undesirable to marry within the village and also thought a suitable selection of mates was seldom locally available. However, four couples in this village had married within it.

Because in the politically dominant groups the lineages or castes are hierarchically arranged within the caste-group or caste cluster, who can give a bride to whom is a fine indicator of the hierarchies of families, kulas, birādarīs, or clans. Among these people the bride-giving family is lower than the bride-taking family; the bride-giver also symbolizes his relative inferiority by providing a dowry. If he can afford a large one he can improve his status by marrying his daughter into a more desirable family. But many marriages, perhaps the majority, are arranged between equals, and in some castes, particularly the lower ones, bride-wealth is given by the groom's family.

Giving a Daughter in Marriage

When a father begins to think about his daughter's marriage, he contacts a matchmaker, perhaps a Brāhmaṇ astrologer, who will come with a list of eligible boys from suitable places. It is the responsibility of the father of the girl to initiate marriage arrangements. The matchmaker will want to know what dowry will come with the girl or the expected range of financial transaction. (Giving of money or gifts in consideration of marriage has been made illegal since 1961—but who is to say whether vessels or expensive sāṛīs or money are part of the bargain or simply wedding gifts?) The marriage is not an individual affair. A family tries to gain advantage by marrying its daughter into a prestigious family perhaps by offering a large dowry; it may be a matter of protracted negotiations. The whole village is concerned too, for the reputation of the village is symbolized by what kinds of girls it gets and to what families or places it gives girls. A young person generally has no idea of arranging his own marriage—except again among the lower castes—and recognizes that the family's prestige, and often political and economic factors, are involved.

A girl in the North may be married before puberty or even in infancy. Mathur in his Mālwā village collected 75 case histories of girls married in 1954–1955, and even as late as this date only 17 were married after the first menstruation; 9 said they were not sure, and the rest were married before puberty.[4] But the social dynamics are even more interesting. Of 56 unmarried girls in the village above the age of five, 9 had been menstruating for some time. Of these 9, 1 was a Brāhmaṇ, 3 Rājpūts, and 5 Khatis. But there was not even one unmarried girl past puberty among the artisan, Śūdra, or untouchable castes. This illustrates the principle that traditional

strictures which are being given up by the higher classes are meanwhile being copied by the lower classes.

Child betrothals and marriages have not been the unmitigated evil some missionaries and Indian reformers have imagined. Inasmuch as marriages are arranged, the younger a girl is when she becomes integrated into her husband's household the less will be the shock of transition. In any case such girls do not go to live permanently with their husbands until well after the first menstruation. Yet child marriages are fading out. The Hindu Marriage Act of 1955 set the minimum marriage age for girls at 15, later raised to 16, and over the course of decades this does have effect. There is a slowly increasing assertion of individualism at the expense of family and kin.

Then too, there is considerable emphasis in North India and among high castes everywhere on virginity of brides. T. N. Madan reports that among Kashmīrī Brāhmaṇs a pregnant unmarried girl would be expected to commit suicide; if she failed, her parents would poison her, and neighbors would approve. It became prestigious for a family to marry off a daughter before puberty because her virginity could not be questioned and her family could handle the arrangements with proper decorum. A paṇḍit in Mathur's Mālwā village told him that according to the Śāstras, a girl staying in her father's house three years after first menstruation becomes ritually low like a Śūdra, and the father of the girl commits the sin of killing the fetus every time the girl menstruates.

When the parents of a married girl feel she is mature enough to embark upon conjugal life, they may invite the groom to visit for a couple of days, during which time he does not speak to his bride in public. On such a visit, or when the girl visits his home, the marriage may be consummated. It may not be possible for the bride and groom to share a separate room. He will continue to sleep with the men but will visit her at night in the women's quarters. The other women will try to let them have some privacy.

Marriage is a terrible crisis in a girl's life, says Mrs. Iravati Karve. Early marriage to a total stranger and separation from parent's house have given a peculiar tone to all the northern folk songs. At the wedding the bride scarcely dares to look at the groom, and the groom too is supposed to be shy. While the family and village celebrate, marriage is not thought of as a joyful event for the central participants, and the girl particularly should look downcast at having to leave her parental home.

In Mathur's village in Mālwā a few days after a girl is brought to the groom's house, there is a ritual by which she is integrated into the new household and transferred to her husband's kula. She is taken out in procession to the village well where she draws up a pitcher of water which she then ceremonially offers to the household deities. Male elders of the house each take a sip of this water and give the girl a gift. She is thenceforth a member of her husband's kula, and if she dies within it she is

treated honorably. As with the death of a male, at the funeral the kula members will shave their heads and observe pollution for 10 or 13 days. But if a divorce should occur, a woman is no longer part of her husband's kula.

Termination of marriage is not common among upper castes, but among untouchables it is much more frequent, for not so many kin and financial transactions are involved. Perhaps 20% of marriages end in separation, but few go through formal divorce proceedings. It is common for a young bride who finds her new life intolerable simply to go home. Someone from her family, especially a brother, will try to patch up difficulties and persuade her to return. Caste or village panchāyats may consider cases involving marriage or separation or sexual offenses. This one was reported from a village in the western Gangā plains:

> The man did not want his wife and refused to bring her home [for the consummation]. Her family complained to the panchayat, which ordered him to go and get her. He still refused, and the panchayat therefore excommunicated the man and his family from caste. This meant that no more marriages could take place with this family. A year later the man went to the panchayat, begged for reinstatement, and promised to take back his wife.[5]

The Joint Family

When the young couple continues to live in the groom's household, a bride achieves status only by degrees. Immediately after marriage she may return home at intervals and stay even for weeks together, but such visits become less frequent after children come. The established women of the groom's household may resent the presence of the young girl, and in any case she is beholden to her mother-in-law and other seniors. A new wife may eat only after the other women; later she will eat with them but not facing them. Still later as she establishes her position in the household and bears sons, she may eat side by side with the other women and perhaps establish intimate friendships with them.

In Mahārāshṭra and Gujarāt, Karve's central kinship zone, a girl maintains closer links with her natal home than in the northern plains. She may, in some castes, be a cross-cousin of the groom, and she may come from the same or a nearby village. In those parts it is customary for a girl to return to her parent's home for the birth of the first child. But in the northern plains a child is clearly a member of the husband's family line and if at all possible should be born in his household.

In Uttar Pradesh a groom does not have much to do with the bride's family, and in some areas even the father or elder brother of a bride cannot visit the village into which she was married nor drink water from a well there. They are givers of the bride, and it would be deemed shameful for

the groom's family to give anything to the bride's natal family. Such restrictions have a function in encouraging a wife to fully ally herself with her husband's household and to treat him as master.

The newly married couple do not at first publicly acknowledge each other's existence, and are rarely together during the day. Mayer writes of the village he studied in Mālwā, that after several years, especially if the wife has borne a son, the couple may talk in front of the elder women of their generation, later before the younger brother and mother, and lastly if at all, before the elder brother and father. Four old men in this village were said to have never talked publicly to their wives, even in front of small children. A young wife has a much freer relationship, including joking repartee, with the husband's younger brother.

Many behavioral norms are directed at maintenance of the unity of the family and the authoritarianism of its head. A son should not appear to be more interested in his wife than in his agnatic family, and if the daughter-in-law speaks to the father or elder brother, she half-covers her face with her sārī, for they should not be attracted to her. A father shows affection toward his son when he is small, but when the boy is old enough to do a little work and during his pubescent years, the father is generally stern. Boys should not show any disrespect to their fathers by talking back, smoking before them, or in some cases even touching them. But a man's mother is always his friend and intercedes for him on occasion.

Among the landless, however, even when a married son lives in with his parents, which is seldom, paternal respect is much less, for the father has little political or economic clout. Indeed a young man can earn as much or more than his father at labor, and the women are also much more free to work in the fields and earn money.

In fact, most families are not joint families, even in North India where this ideal is strongest. The average number of persons per household in 1961 was 5.54 for Jammū and Kashmīr, 5.51 for Bihār, and 5.29 for Uttar Pradesh. Households in the North are slightly larger than for India as a whole, for which the average is 5.2 persons. In Mahārāshṭra, as would be expected, it is lower, 5.12.

Though Western sociologists distinguish between the nuclear and joint family types, Indian texts do not, for in fact there is a cyclic pattern. When the father dies, the married sons usually break apart. There may often be a widowed mother or other relative living with the nuclear family, who helps in child care and kitchen work. Even to define the joint family is difficult, though most commonly it is defined as two or more related conjugal couples who share a common hearth. But it frequently happens that married sons will live in separate rooms or houses around the sides of a common courtyard, cooking separately, but managing the land jointly. Who conducts family worship together is also a point to be considered.

The joint family exists chiefly among landowners or owner-cultivators

in rural areas, or among those who jointly own and manage stores or factories in urban areas. Owner-cultivator brothers often find it advantageous to work the land together, and any family will wish to enjoy the power and prestige of property ownership as long as possible before the assets are fragmented.

Inheritance laws have been spelled out in the *Mitākshara*, a work composed in the Deccan and followed in both North and South India, but not in Bānglā. According to it, all the male agnates in a family are co-parceners, entitled to a share of the land at birth, and they can demand their share at any time. If there is no son, a boy can be adopted (generally from some related family), as is frequently the practice. It is also possible for a father without a son to bring a groom for his daughter to take care of the property after him, but the groom in such a case has quite low status in the family. Since a bride in the North comes from an unrelated family, she receives no land from either her father or father-in-law, but the dowry she brings from her father is a form of female inheritance. Her jewels and valuables are hers personally, and she can pass them on to her daughter. Recent legislation in India has decreed that daughters have inheritance rights equal with sons, but up to the present they have not generally been claiming it.

Children raised in joint families tend to look back fondly on happy days when there was constant activity in the house, people coming and going, and always someone to laugh with or turn to in time of need. As they raise their own families, they come to realize the practical difficulties of joint family living—and also the economic and political benefits of maintaining a large and strong family.

Women

The foreign visitor to North India will not see many women on the streets in towns, and might think that he is in the midst of an all-male society. But in villages women do move about, work in the fields, and sell vegetables. In general they do not come out as much as in the South, where they emerge with bright sāṛīs and jewelry; in the Himālayan areas women are quite free to move about and earn. In Panjāb among the Sikhs relatively high status for women is an ideal; Rājasthānī women too, especially if they are of tribal origin, may be seen decked out in numerous bangles, anklets, noserings, and earrings. But in the northern settled peasant areas the principle of hierarchy is extended to include male-female relations.

It is sometimes asserted that the low ritual status of women in the North is due to six centuries of Muslim rule, but in fact classical Hindu literature makes it clear that a woman's husband is her lord and it is her dharma to serve him. She successively obeys her father, husband, and son.

Rājasthānī women at the village well cover their faces if a male stranger appears.

She is literally given away in marriage, and her pollutability is symbolized in birth and menstruation (though menstrual pollution is not really an important matter now except among orthodox castes). Some Hindu law texts say that if a woman by chance hears the Vedas, she should have hot lead poured into her ears! She eats after her menfolk and walks down the street a few paces after her husband—and these at least are universally practiced in villages.

Yet both the ancient texts and modern practices make it clear that a virtuous woman is worthy of considerable honor. Her personality may blossom in middle age, and she may dominate her husband in old age, for her sons confide in her more than in their father. Many women control their husbands at home, make crucial family decisions, and manage the budget.

It is among larger landowners and townspeople that women are most

protected, and a few Hindus even practice pardā. A family's reputation depends in part on its treatment of women, and the tendency to hypergamy demands that women be pure before marriage and protected after marriage. Also, high caste women should not have to go out to work. But lower caste women have to work in the fields, and may have no one to shop for them. While lower castes are increasingly secluding women and prohibiting widow remarriage as they rise in status, the higher castes and the educated and English-knowing elite are more and more encouraging their women to become educated and enter professions.

Traditional orthodox norms dictated that a woman should be so devoted to her husband and his family that she should remain in his household even as a widow, and she is legally entitled to support. Among the orthodox there was the well-known practice of a widow immolating herself on her husband's funeral pyre, becoming a *satī*. A woman who was a voluntary satī was highly honored—and sometimes such a decision was a practical one for she thus avoided years of miserable existence as a dependent of her husband's family, suffering not only from low status but from the implication that something she did caused his death. The practice of satī was never as widespread as is sometimes popularly believed. In 1829 the British forbade it, under pressure from Baptist missionaries. Once or twice a year reports of it still reach the press.

Prohibition of widow remarriage is an important criterion of high status according to Brāhmaṇical standards, and its adoption signifies considerable achievement to this end. But widows in lower castes do remarry. In fact, a sprightly widow may force herself onto a man by simply moving into his house. Karve reports such an instance:

> A servant in a family living in Simla started suddenly sending money to his "wife" in the plains. The lady of the family whose servant he was asked him in surprise as to how and when he had got married. He said that a woman X, a widow, had entered his house in his native village and started living in his house as his wife. He was informed of this, apparently accepted the situation, and started sending money to his new "wife." He said that this type of thing happened among his people and was accepted by all.[6]

The practice of a woman entering a man's house by force has been noted among Munda tribes and is mentioned in early Marāṭhī literature, so doubtless antedates the evolution of the complex Hindu social structure. Another practice found among lower castes especially in Panjāb is the levirate, whereby a widow is taken as wife by her deceased husband's younger brother. This also is an old practice, and in fact shades of it can be discerned in the common acceptance of a joking relationship between a woman and her husband's younger brother.

Across North India and also in Bānglā when men migrate for work to the cities, they leave their womenfolk in the village. The wife looks after

the property and tends the cows, maintains family connections, and raises the children in the ancestral village. She is under the care of the husband's brother or other relative. This practice has produced a severe shortage of women in North Indian cities.

But women's position is ambivalent because there are a great many women in prominent positions in India, in national and state legislatures, as ministers and governors, and in professions such as medicine, education, and welfare—but seldom in business, commerce, or law. While educated single women do serve as village teachers, family planning workers, or nurses, many North Indian women are reluctant to take jobs in unprotected places and South Indian women occupy many such positions in the North. Among the English-educated urban classes women now go to college as a matter of course, ride buses by themselves, and nowadays even ride bicycles and occasionally drive. Even in the North some women do stand in elections. And whereas men played female parts in traditional dramas, women today can dream of becoming cinema stars.

Attitudes toward Sex

What has been said here about the family and the interaction of family members obtains more or less throughout India, even where kinship patterns are different. Similarly, attitudes toward sex as discussed here are similar throughout India, except in tribal areas, though the sex roles are somewhat more dichotomized in the North and western India.

Extramarital sexual escapades are far more common than most visitors to India are led to believe. An informant in a village near Delhi told Lewis that he believed that 9 out of 10 women in his village had had extramarital experiences at one time or another.[7] Most common is that between a woman and her husband's younger brother. While virginity is expected in high class girls, among untouchables it is not. Untouchable women are often available in a village for a couple rupees, and in a way this fits in with the jajmānī relations, allows boys who can afford it to have premarital sexual experience, and provides the low caste women with some income. But upper class Indians are, on the surface, notably prudish and reticent to talk about sex publicly.

Men seem to be preoccupied with thoughts of sex more than what superficially appears, especially in North Indian towns where women are scarce. But in India there is an added dimension to sexuality in men. It is believed that a man is endowed with a specific quantity of life force which should not be wasted; he who controls his sexual urges and other appetites develops psychic power as an ascetic. Semen loss results in weakening of the body, while its retention not only stimulates mental and physical

development but is symbolic of self-control in general and may even lead to mind-over-matter control of one's environment. There are many indigenous medicines to prevent nocturnal emissions, and if masturbation is frowned on, it is for this reason and not as a sin.

At the same time the Kshatriya model of behavior, as opposed to the Brāhmaṇical, idealizes virility. Townsmen enjoyed their courtesans, and princes and warriors had sexual license, along with other un-Brāhmaṇical activities such as liquor drinking and meat eating. South Asia has been, and still is, characterized by an ambivalent attitude toward sex—a polarization of sensuality and asceticism.

Morris Carstairs elicited attitudes toward sex among several castes in Rājasthān. As for Brāhmaṇs, sex was never discussed directly between generations, but it could be talked about quite candidly by an older man while his son looked on. They all deplored all forms of extramarital relationships as inimical to godliness, but the younger men when alone would boast of their exploits. Brāhmaṇs insisted that a person should go regularly with his wife during the span of their reproductive years, but also stressed that it is the women who demand sexual intercourse. The Baniyas (merchants), overtly at least, make more noise about the value of continence, no doubt for the same reason that they give to charity; that is, to accumulate dharma in compensation for their accumulation of wealth and their interest in mundane matters. The Brāhmaṇs ridiculed this attitude of the Baniyās. One Brāhmaṇ commented on what he thought was the misguided piety of the Baniyās:

> There are many of them who avoid sex relations altogether—*shil-vrit*, that's called. They regard it as a sacrilege because so many small creatures must die every time the semen comes out, and they think that that will prevent their getting Release. Many of them take oaths—"I won't have sex for six months"; or twelve months, or for the rest of their lives. Brahmins are not like that; they copulate a great deal, all through the month—not like those Banias who say that one shouldn't copulate on certain days of the month. We copulate all the time, except when our wives are menstruating.[8]

Rājpūts are more ambivalent than Baniyās or Brāhmaṇs because their tradition is one of power and authority leading to a tolerance and even an admiration for drinking, meat eating, anger, and sexual indulgence. At the same time they feel a need for being exemplary according to Indian ethics, which abjures all of these. One of Carstair's informants, a former prince, recalled especially fine parties at princes' wedding feasts:

> "They will call the dancing-girl to sit on their lap, then they will get stirred and take her into a room and bar the doors—and the others will beat upon the door and say: 'Eh, Rao Sahib, we also want to see this girl'—but pay no attention! Poor girl, where can she go, all the doors are locked. Enjoy till morning, she must do what you want. Then give her rupees 100/–, she goes away happy. That is what Rajputs are like, Sahib; uneducated, uncivilized, lusty men."[9]

This informant was nagged by the idea that sexuality is an impediment to the progress of emotional maturity and that asceticism and continence enable one to rise above mundane matters and achieve psychic powers, "and he would for a time apply himself with extra zeal to his program of self-discipline."

A pattern of sexual response documented by Carstairs in Rājasthān is the sharp distinction between potency men have when they are with prostitutes or with girls of inferior caste, and with their wives. In the former, men take the initiative and are willing to describe their adventures, which must be done in secret but are nevertheless understandable. But in their own homes they believe it is their wives, ritually inferior, whose sexual appetites must be satisfied, draining strength and threatening the potency of the husband.

A young man's sex life is restricted by the partial segregation of mature females, by his wife being not of his own choice, by his living in his parents' house, by his being unable to show affection to his wife while in the presence of his parents, by the threat of his father's dominating position, and by the idea that preservation of semen is necessary for physical and spiritual attainments. These are the circumstances in which one would expect to encounter either homosexuality or impotence. Evidence can be cited for strong repressed homosexual urges, while impotence is also not uncommon, and many informants indicated preoccupation with fears of impotence.

The concept that control of sexual appetites—as of eating, drinking, and pleasure in general—is necessary for psychic and spiritual development is highlighted in the life of Gandhi. Along with his rejection of violence, the simplification of his dress, his refusal to own property, and his vegetarianism which he carried to the extent of living mostly from nuts and fruits, he aimed to develop his own sexual self-control. He was bedeviled all his life by the regret that when his father lay dying, he went away for a while to his room to join his wife. At the age of 37 he took a vow of celibacy for life, to which his wife did not demur. During the partition of Bānglā while working among riot-torn villages, he felt problems were almost beyond his mastery. He asked his 19-year-old grandniece to share his bed, a desperate attempt to control external events by putting his own self-control to the test. Later he discussed this lust control publicly, which created something of a scandal. Gandhi wrote, "It is my full conviction, that if only I had lived a life of unbroken *brahmacārya* (self-restraint) all through, my energy and enthusiasm would have been a thousand fold greater and I should have been able to devote them all to the furtherance of my country's cause as my own."[10]

Visitors to South Asia have often thought, and some have even written, that homosexuality is very common because they see men affectionately holding hands. No doubt homosexuality and exploitation of young boys occur, but it should be understood that physical contact between men is

Physical contact among men who are friends, in Mahārāshṭra. Americans should not interpret this or hand holding as homosexuality.

accepted because bonds of male friendship are strong, especially among students in the all-male schools and colleges, and in urban areas. It would be as wrong for an American to project the implications of his own culture on two Indian male college students holding hands as it would be for an Indian to project the implications of his culture on the scene of an American unmarried couple holding hands—for that is regarded as a symbol of marriage. A young man and woman in India would no sooner hold hands on the street than would two young men in America. Carstairs writes:

> It would be an act of blindness indeed to suggest that because relations between a Hindu son and his parents, between a man and his wife, lack that warmth and spontaneity which is expected in western society, they are necessarily inferior. Each patterning of human behavior has its positive as well as its limiting aspects.[11]

Jhelum River, Śrīnagar, Kashmīr. Wooden houses, Hindu temple, attached bathing ghāṭ, and wooden mosques flank the river.

The Kashmīr Brāhmaṇ Family

While agriculturalists and artisans in the Vale of Kashmīr are Muslims and call themselves Shaikhs, 5% of the population are Hindus, and in the Jammū part of the state half are Hindus. Hindus in Kashmīr are largely landowners who had nothing to gain by conversion to Islam, and include a caste-group of Brāhmaṇs called Paṇḍits. They are aristocratic and have produced prominent persons, including Jawaharlal Nehru. Many retain their land and traditional family structure, studied in detail by T. N. Madan.

The houses of the Kashmīr Paṇḍits are substantial, with two, three, or four stories and a god's room on the second story. The front steps are washed each morning and red marks put on the door as part of pūjā. The majority of households include members outside the nuclear family; the average household has 6 members, but some have 12 or 14, with each couple occupying a room.

Kashmīr Paṇḍits believe in the laws of Manu, which state that a man must marry and have sons to ensure heaven for himself and his ancestors. If there is no son, one may be adopted. It is also possible for a daughter to marry and bring her husband as sole heir of her father's property, but the line of descent will die. The father manages the property and has moral authority over the family, and though he and his sons are coparceners of the property, shares are not recognized as long as it is held jointly. The eldest son succeeds to the authority of the father. A son can claim his share and set up his own household any time after he marries, but in fact seldom does so before the death of his father and the marriage of his brothers. Reunion of the family is possible but rare.

When the property is divided, the debts as well as the assets are apportioned equally. But if one of the sons has been gone a long time, or has an unusually large personal income, or many dependents to support, it may be divided unequally. If a man has no son, his property is divided among his brothers. At the time of separation of the joint family people do bargain, but litigation is regarded as unseemly. As elsewhere, men tend to blame women's quarrels as the cause of separation, but in fact the men also have their disputes.

The father's widow has no right of inheritance, only of maintenance. However, she can keep the gifts and ornaments given to her personally at the time of her marriage, which only her daughters can inherit. A childless widow can adopt a son. Widow remarriage is now common among the urban Paṇḍits and even to some extent in rural areas because of the shortage of females.

A girl given in marriage is a ritual gift, and she is handed out of the window of her father's house when she leaves. As a ritual gift, she cannot

be taken back nor abandoned, neither can bride price or money be received for her. She should come from a family outside the sapiṇḍa relations, but if genealogies are not well kept, the rule is she should not be a known relative of the groom. When she joins her husband's family, she should avoid him in the presence of others. A son cannot take his wife's side openly in a quarrel at the expense of relationships between him and his agnatic kin. If he returns from a trip everybody will come out to greet him, but his wife will go into the kitchen. If a young wife wants to wash her husband's shirt, she must go and gather up all the clothes of the others that need washing, as a pretext. Sex is to be engaged in at night in their room.

When the new couple has a child, it is cared for by its grandparents, except for nursing and sleeping, and after weaning it also sleeps with its grandparents. A young father should not fondle his son nor show affection to him in the presence of his own father, lest his loyalty appear to be distracted, but many fondle the child in the presence of its grandmother. A rite is performed 12 days after birth, and at the age of about two the child is given his first ritual haircut; if it is a girl, her ears are pierced. A boy is initiated as a Brāhmaṇ with the sacred thread ceremony before he is 12. He may be taken on visits to his mother's family, but his father's parents dislike such visits if they are frequent, saying the boy is spoiled there. Kashmīr Paṇḍits have no formal associations other than kinship. A boy grows up in an active and lively household, realizing that kinship is the bedrock of his identity and social existence.

Rājpūts

Rājpūts ("sons of kings") have in recent centuries been the epitome of the Kshatriya model of behavior, as opposed to the Brāhmaṇical. They are a jāti-cluster that is widespread over northwestern India and extends into the Gangā plains, Madhya Pradesh, and the Himālayan valleys. While the majority today are landowning peasants their self-image is based on the historic Rājpūt princes who governed large areas by means of a hierarchical series of lineages or clans. During the Mughal period these clans ruled what is now Rājasthān, and the Mughals were required to seek their support. In the early 19th century the British made treaties with the Rājpūt states recognizing the legitimacy of the mahārājās but committing the states to alliance with British India. After Independence 23 Rājpūt states were consolidated to form the Indian state of Rājasthān, while those Rājpūts who were large zamīndārs in the Gangā region were dispossessed of their estates through land reform.

The history of ruling Rājpūt lineages in eastern Uttar Pradesh has been studied by Richard Fox, with the view of uncovering the relationships

between their complex lineage system and the political system of pre-industrial India. Fox has charted eight lineage levels for this region, which are briefly as follows: 1) Rājpūt, a behavioral and status category and a caste cluster; 2) Cauhān, a subcategory of Rājpūts denoting status rather than kinship, one of a few dozen such categories which were ranked and among which there was hypergamy; 3) Bachgotī, a "lineage of identification," for all Bachgotīs traced descent from a ruler in eastern Uttar Pradesh who established his power as the Mughals declined; 4) Rājkumār, a "stratified lineage," the exogamous category, which various writers call the major clan, phratry, or tribe, and which was the widest kin body recognized in the administrative and revenue organization; 5) the "lineage of maximal incorporation" whose jurisdiction coincided with the *parganā* administrative unit, 6) the "lineage of minimal incorporation" whose jurisdiction coincided with the *tālūkā* administrative unit, which was the smallest corporate kinship unit recognized in the administrative structure of the state and whose head served as tax collection agent for the tālūkā; 7) the minor lineage segment, usually equivalent to the *paṭṭī* revenue division, and of which there were likely to be several in a village; and 8) the minimal lineage of three to six generations.

When a central government was weak, these Rājpūt lineage levels coincided with, and were largely determined by, bureaucratic boundaries. One minimal lineage provided the rājā or other elite membership of the kin body. But when central government was stronger the kinship levels bore less relationship to the bureaucratic levels, as was increasingly the case during the British administration.

A caste would consist of a number of exogamous lineage segments of the type of the above-mentioned Rājkumār, within a geographical region, which intermarried hypergamously, and these would be commensally equivalent. Because of hypergamy there is sometimes a shortage of girls at the bottom and an excess of them at the top. Regions are also ranked, the Rājpūts toward the east in the Gangā region and toward the south or southeast in central India being lower than those toward the northwest. Therefore girls tend to move northwestward up the Gangā, and even some of the central Indian tribes who have become peasantized and adopted fictitious Rājpūt lineages refuse to give their daughters in marriage toward the south or east. The diffusion of the Rājpūt name and its ideals over such a large area in the late medieval centuries meant that diverse peasant groups were absorbed into it. Hypergamy is one mechanism for this, for a family of lower caste whose daughter was taken by a prestigious Rājpūt would have enhanced status. A second mechanism has been described by Mayer for Mālwā. In one village 13 out of the 27 castes had clans which had taken the names of Rājpūt clans such as Cauhān or Solānkī, and this was done by such castes as Barbers and Blacksmiths, who would in time claim closer connection

with the corresponding Rājpūt clans. And we have given already the example of the Noniyās, Saltmakers who produced a fictitious Cauhān genealogy and partially succeeded in their efforts.

Minturn and Hitchcock studied a predominantly Rājpūt village in Uttar Pradesh 90 miles north of Delhi in which Rājpūts, as the largest caste group, held 90% of the land. The researchers were impressed by the spirit, by the sometimes rough and raw vitality, with which Rājpūt living is diffused. Their greetings and laughter are loud and hearty, and their friendship demonstrative. Even farming Rājpūts think of themselves as bearing the qualities of martial princes. One Rājpūt father, upon hearing that his son was to participate in a school athletic event outside the village, remarked, "I am not going to let my son participate. Rājpūt boys do not have to participate in athletics. They are already stronger than other castes." On another occasion, when someone remarked that a highly placed official was a good administrator, a Rājpūt man remarked, "And why not? He is a Rājpūt. He belongs to a ruling race, and they have been doing this work since time immemorial." Village Rājpūts feel they should own land, preferably enough so they do not have to cultivate it with their own hands. They maintain jajmānī relationships with the occupational and serving castes with a paternal and benevolent air. But winds of change are blowing, and their pride is challenged by the new universal adult franchise: "These are critical times because now we have to fight (the members of other castes) with the vote. Formerly it meant something that we were bigger and stronger men."[12]

A Rājpūt ideal is that women should be protected, and some are kept in pardā. In the village studied by Minturn and Hitchcock an unmarried girl had a baby. The girl's father delivered the baby, then killed and buried it. The village women were highly critical of the parents for having raised their daughter so badly, but made no comment about killing the baby. Furthermore, the village officials took steps to see that the police would not investigate the incident. Rājpūts must maintain their honor, which women do by avoiding cause for gossip and which men do by reacting strongly against insults and by maintaining protective control over wives and daughters.

Typically, Rājpūt owner-cultivators have separate men's and women's houses. In the men's house there is an open platform leading to a roofed platform with rooms on either side. When not working the men and adolescent boys spend their time sitting on the platform and smoking the hukkā. There are fewer houses for men than women, for sometimes related men share a house, but each will have an establishment for his women and children. The women's lives go on within the confines of the courtyard which has rooms around it; windows open onto the courtyard but never onto the street. Women may be able to move to neighboring women's houses by going across the flat roofs. People who share a courtyard are generally

wives of brothers, their younger children, their unmarried daughters, married sons' wives, and their sons' children. The tensions generated by confined living often result in quarrels among the wives, which may cause separate family hearths to be set up within the courtyard. Brothers usually divide the land after their father's death. Within the courtyard the rank of women depends on the rank of their husbands. At night a husband has access to the courtyard where the women sleep, and he can share a cot there with his wife for a time, after which he returns to the men's house for the rest of the night.

Jāṭs and Other Groups

Jāṭs are the dominant agricultural caste group in Haryāṇā, southern Panjāb, northern and eastern Rājasthān, and the upper Doāb; they have traditionally produced wheat in this area, as well as cotton and sugar cane. They number 8 million or so and are more numerous than Rājpūts even in Rājasthān, while there are many Muslim Jāṭs, and most Sikhs are converted Jāṭs. The Vedas do not mention them, and the epics refer to other peoples living in this region. But like Rājpūts they seem to be essentially indigenous peoples consolidated into lineage groups as a result of or in response to the continual invasions from the west. They have patrilineal clans, the joint family ideal, and separate houses for males and females. Jāṭs are a steadfast and pragmatic people, and among them the Ārya Samāj has had some influence, while beliefs such as the evil eye and black magic are decreasing.

Jāṭs allow widow remarriage (which Rājpūts do not), and the levirate is often practiced. A younger brother may have access to his elder brother's wife, and the elder brother may even encourage this to forestall separation of the land. Here we see a remnant of fraternal polyandry such as is widely practiced in Himālayan regions today, and everywhere its function is preservation of the integrity of the landholding. In the *Mahābhārata* the five Pāṇḍava heroes, brothers, shared a common wife, but this practice did not find favor in the Brāhmaṇical system.

Many other caste groups in western India claim, correctly or not, that their lineages go back to once dominant militaristic clans. The Mers of Saurāshṭra in Gujarāt, who were studied by H. R. Trivedi, claim that their 14 exogamous clans descended from Rājpūt princes, and their bards have produced supporting genealogies. They maintain their position as landlords, keep their women honorable, and require the services of Brāhmaṇs. They practice cross-cousin marriage as South Indians do.

Other groups such as Ahīrs and Gūjars were earlier movements of this type, often traceable originally to Panjāb and Sindh. More recently the

various Muslim lineages and the Marāṭhās expanded by similar processes. Even tribal people in Madhya Pradesh have latched onto these movements as they became peasantized. But all these contests for power have been essentially irrelevant for the low castes, especially the untouchable groups called Ḍoms in the North.

Sikhs

The Sikhs, 11 million strong, have Panjāb as their home state, but they have diffused widely over India, and indeed to England, Canada, and California. The Sikhs began as an antiritual devotional sect and developed, by a strange process of transmutation, into a fierce army, and then into a hard-working and relatively prosperous ethnic group. The founder of the sect, Gurū Nānak (1468–1538) was born a Kshatriya Hindu, but renounced all to wander about and sit at the feet of bhakti and Sūfī teachers. Since eastern Panjāb is transitional between Islam and Hinduism he sought the best of both religions. But he rejected both ritual systems and sought for the essence of spirituality. Gurū Nānak found this essence as union with God, whom he called Sat Nām, True Name. He borrowed from Hinduism the idea that the ultimate goal is absorption into God, but thought it could be accomplished by the Muslim posture of submission to God. Rejecting the Qur'ān and the Vedas, he wrote another book, the *Ādi Granth.* Rejecting priesthood, he adopted the institution of the gurū. Most Sikh ceremonics and beliefs were derived from Hinduism, including belief in karma and sentiment against cow slaughter. Most converts came from Hinduism; hence most Panjābī castes have Hindu and Sikh branches.

As a heterodox sect, Sikhism, by the usual dialectic processes, became an established and formal religion. Each gurū came to be considered an incarnation of his predecessor, continuing the tradition of religious authority. The *Ādi Granth* came to be placed in the sanctum of temples, where it is worshiped with pūjā-like ceremonies. A Sikh must distinguish himself by five identifying marks: uncut hair, a comb, shorts or pants, an iron bangle, and a sword. Hence all Sikhs today should have a topknot (covered with a turban) and beard (sometimes enclosed in a hairnet), while the sword is worn symbolically. All Sikhs have the surname Singh (lion).

Sikhs were obliged to fight for their identity and their independence in the days of the Mughal empire. They developed a great hate for the Muslim rulers, which served to weld them into a cohesive ethnic group. The Golden Temple in Amritsar, the physical center of Sikhism, has an art gallery exhibiting large paintings of barbarous atrocities alleged to have been committed by the Muslim rulers against the Sikhs. A Sikh kingdom was set up in 1800, but its life was short, for in the mid-19th century the British, after

two important wars with the Sikhs, subdued Panjāb. As part of India, Sikhs fought the Muslims in 1948. Still, they did not feel territorially secure until in response to repeated demands and fastings, the Government of India in 1966 split the state of Panjāb into Haryāṇā, dominated by Hindī-speaking Hindus, and the smaller Panjāb, a predominantly Sikh state. A further symbol of the Sikh identity is use of the Panjābī language written in their Gurmukhī script, the writing form used in the *Ādi Granth.*

Golden Temple of the Sikhs in Amritsar, Panjāb. A man is prostrate in worship; women participate freely.

Kitchen of the Golden Temple. Volunteer men and women roll dough into capātīs for free mass feeding, which Sikhs believe helps ensure prosperity.

Sikhs are known as industrious people, and they have caused Panjāb to have an economic growth rate of 7% a year over many years, the result of hundreds of small-scale, individually-owned industries and also agricultural innovation. It is here that the "green revolution" in wheat production has been most spectacular. Sikhs believe their land will remain prosperous so long as people are charitably bounteous. The Golden Temple in Amritsar feeds thousands of people daily—devotees who come to worship, indigents, and travelers. Sikh women are not as ritually low as among Muslims or neighboring Hindus. Sikhs can be seen in cities all over India, engaged in business or trade or driving taxis. Others have emigrated overseas. Usually they retain their ethnic identity markers, but in Canada some have begun to shave their beards and cut their hair. Most people in India and abroad have favorable attitudes toward the Sikhs because they are achievement-oriented, while at the same time most have pleasant personalities.

Mahārāshṭra and Gujarāt

Mahārāshṭra and Gujarāt are characterized by a fairly high level of commercial and industrial activity for which they have to thank their location on the sea and centuries, indeed millennia, of access to wide-ranging trade. In Gujarāt there are many businessmen, and the state as a whole has a tone of financial success coupled with a business-like conservatism without ostentation. Gujarātīs have gone in numbers to Bombay, South Africa, and other distant places in pursuit of business. In addition, the black soil of the region is good for raising cotton and oil seeds, both commercial crops. In Gujarāt education in the regional language has been pushed more than in any other state, with the result that English is declining in importance while colleges are rapidly shifting over to Gujarātī. A considerable quality in journalistic literature has appeared, and most young adults are literate.

Servant of a Gujarātī business family eating on kitchen floor. This man worked all his life for the business and now in old age is kept as a trusted household helper.

Dour Baniyā merchant in a Mahārāshṭra town. Bulk foods and spices are weighed in balance scales.

Mahārāshṭra is blessed with Bombay, a city which yields more personal income tax than any other in India. In the city itself and in the hinterland there are a great many factories, and the dynamic quality of economic growth here has affected the whole state. In 1965 Mahārāshṭra produced 23.6% of India's gross industrial output. Agriculture has been affected, too,

and one can see tractors plowing the rich volcanic soil over the western part of the state.

Since the formation of linguistic states, both Mahārāshṭra and Gujarāt have experienced a resurgence of regional identity, but in the former it has taken more political overtones. The Śiva Sena, a right-wing party, demands increased use of Marāṭhī in Bombay and a reduction in the influence of South Indians, Gujarātīs, and Hindī people. This is the Marāṭhī counterpart of the pro-Hindī Jana Sangh party in the North and the pro-Tamiḻ DMK party in Tamiḻ Nāḍu.

In these states there is a variety of interesting ethnic groups. The largest agricultural caste-cluster in Mahārāshṭra is the Marāṭhās; in most villages the headman is a Marāṭhā. Originally an army which turned into a caste, it absorbed many other castes with less prestigious names, much as Rājpūts did farther north. All those who listed themselves as Kunbīs in Mahārāshṭra a generation ago now call themselves Marāṭhās; Marāṭhās and Kunbīs together make up 40% of the population of the state. The original prestige of the Marāṭhās derived from the short-lived 17th-century Marāṭhā empire of Śivājī. In those heroic days Śivājī led western India in a last, valiant stand against the Mughals of Delhi and is now regarded as a semideity of the Marāṭhās. The Marāṭhās have clans, and there is a tendency to hypergamy among them. Bride-wealth is given instead of dowry, and the South Indian custom of the bride returning to her mother's home for delivery of the first child is followed.

The Ahīrs are an important pastoral caste found in Gujarāt and throughout the North. The Ahīrs may have been derived from the Ābhīrs, who moved southwestward from Panjāb and Sindh in early historic times. The Rabārīs are an interesting gypsy-like group. Dressed in colorful clothes and jewelry, they can be seen on the roads moving all their baggage slung over camels and donkeys—even their rope cots are piled on the animals. Bhīls occupy a large section of northeastern Gujarāt and adjacent parts of Rājasthān and Madhya Pradesh, and are considered to be a tribe, but in fact most are settled agriculturalists. Bhīlī is a dialect of Gujarātī. The Mahār are a large untouchable caste ranging throughout Mahārāshṭra and into Madhya Pradesh. They have become largely neo-Buddhist to escape untouchable status. They will be discussed in Chapter 16.

There are a number of Baniyā, or merchant castes, many of whom are engaged in the textile industry, which is the largest in Gujarāt. Māṛwāṛī Baniyās are the best known mercantile caste, originally from western Rājasthān. They originated in a region where it is so dry there is little possibility of making a good profit locally, so one finds Māṛwāṛīs in business all over India. Gujarāt has since protohistoric times been a center for the lapidary industry, which also tends to be controlled by certain castes.

Jains, who number only 3 million, are centered in this part of India

and particularly in Gujarāt. They form an influential community and are well represented in commerce and in the professions. In recent decades they have come to conceive of themselves as more distinct from Hindus than they previously did. The most important geographical focus of this religion is the temple complex atop Mount Ābū, an abrupt 5600 foot peak in southern Rājasthān. The images of tīrthankaras (Jain saints) ensconced in the inner sanctums of Jain temples are revered in much the same way Hindu gods are, with similar pūjā ceremonies. Theologically, Jains today believe that man has two parts, the spiritual and the material, that imperfection is due to karma, and that perfection is to be strived for by subjection of matter and the avoidance of killing living things. Each individual can separate his own soul from the overwhelming encumbrance of matter by belief, knowledge, and conduct.

Jainism does not theologically or ritually recognize caste. But there are over 100 jātis or jāti-clusters, mostly Jain segments of Hindu occupational castes. Intermarriage between Hindu and Jain branches of the same caste is allowed if the wife changes religion. Brāhmaṇical distinctions of pakkā and kaccā food are not observed, but in fact lower caste people are not invited to feasts. There is no untouchability. Under Jain law widows may remarry. There is a different set of castes among Jains in Karṇāṭaka and in Madhya Pradesh. The texts say that cross-cousin marriage is no sin, and in fact Jain marriage patterns in each region follow local custom.

Pārsīs (literally Persians) are descendants of Zoroastrians who fled Persia upon the Muslim invasions during and after the 7th century A.D. They landed mostly in Gujarāt where they began to engage in business and acquired land, but after the development of Bombay as the primate city of the region, they have become centered there.

Pārsīs are Zoroastrians by religion, maintaining their ancient priesthood and the sacred book, the *Avesta*. It was from the Pārsīs of Bombay that a copy of the *Avesta* was secretly taken to Europe, translated, and given to the world. The chief object of worship is fire, and Bombay has a number of "fire temples." Some of them can be seen with cuneiform script, which no Pārsīs can read now, but which was preserved in Persia from the time of Darius who brought in Aramaic scribes from Mesopotamia. Pārsīs do not cremate their dead, but follow the Zoroastrian custom derived from prehistoric Persia of exposing the corpses to birds. For this purpose Pārsīs maintain "towers of silence" in Bombay. In the Pārsī temples priests officiate and tend the fires, but they are not learned and cannot expostulate on the *Avesta*. The most important ceremony in the life cycle is the tying of the sacred thread when adolescent boys are initiated; both this and the Brāhmaṇical sacred thread ceremony can be traced back to a common Āryan source. Since non-Pārsīs are excluded from the fire temples, not much is known of Pārsī ritual.

Pārsīs today are known as successful capitalists and businessmen, and

control a significant chunk of the economy of Bombay as well as its stock exchange. In proportion to their numbers, they are the most economically influential ethnic group in India. They are also envied for their light complexion.

Madhya Pradesh

Central India, largely occupied by Madhya Pradesh, has been a historic area of expansion of the Hindī-speaking peoples of the northern plains. Ancient kingdoms flourished in the major basins, but elsewhere there is something of a frontier flavor. Most important of the basins or plains are Mālwā on the west, Bundelkhaṇḍ on the north draining into the Gangā, Chattīsgaṛh on the east draining into the Mahānadī, and the long valley of the Narmadā which flows through Gujarāt. Interspersed among these are low plateaus with numerous tribes, peasantized tribes, detribalized castes, bandit castes, intrusive Hindī-speaking peasants, and elite castes. Some of the tribes are discussed in Chapter 15. This large and varied state with 42 million people is sometimes considered somewhat backward, but its literacy and urbanization rates are slightly higher than those of Uttar Pradesh, and there are mineral and fuel resources in its hills.

Stephen Fuchs has described the Nimār Balāhīs, a low caste-cluster numbering perhaps a million spread over the western half of the state. They are in some ways similar to the large and depressed Kolī group in Mahārāshṭra, and also to the Mahārs of that state. Balāhīs serve as weavers, village watchmen, and village servants. There are a number of endogamous castes, each having several clans which have little function except that they are theoretically exogamous. Some of them have become Christians, but they make poor quality Christians, says Fuchs, who spent 10 years among them. They thought baptism would entitle them to assistance from the missionaries whom they thought were rich and charitable, while the missionaries were deceived by their profession of faith. Balāhīs also have strong dependence on higher caste landowners and employers.

Uttar Pradesh and Bihār

The northern plains stretching 700 miles from Delhi to West Bengal consist of monotonous yellowish, stoneless soil. Its northern fringe is flanked by the tarāī, marshy lowlands under the Himālayan foothills. In this region live the Thārūs, described by S. K. Srivastava. They are a Hindī-speaking people who have a tinge of Mongoloid appearance but are really the northernmost of the central Indian aboriginals who have become peasantized. Traditionally cattle raisers who at times hunted, they are now farmers

and are caught up in the Hindu caste hierarchy. Upper class Thārūs are wont to call themselves Rāṇā Ṭhākurs and emulate a Kshatriya model, observing some of the Hindu commensality rules. Thārūs have gotras, but the lower level ones are not exogamous. Women have considerable freedom and influence, and may divorce their husbands. They have increased in numbers and in prosperity because malaria control has made it possible for more of the tarāī to be occupied.

In the heartland plains, the hearth of classical Indian civilization, tourists from Western countries commonly follow the route connecting the cities of renown: Delhī and Āgrā with their imperial Mughal architecture; Kānpur and Lucknow, industrial and administrative cities; Allāhābād at the confluence of the Gangā and the Yamunā where every few years the *khumbamelā* festival attracts literally millions of people to the sacred confluence; Vārāṇasī (Banaras), where retired Hindus try to go for their final years to bask in the sanctity of that spot, and for whom the cremation fires on platforms along the Gangā burn continuously; Paṭnā, Aśoka's capital, the nexus of Buddhist sacred spots, and now the capital of Bihār.

In this vast region there is no dominant caste. Whereas in Panjāb a large village of 400 families will have an average of 12 castes, in central Uttar Pradesh it will have 25 or even 30, according to Schwartzberg's survey. In Uttar Pradesh 21% of the population consists of Harijans called Ḍoms; except for Panjāb and parts of Madhya Pradesh, such a large percentage is not found in any other major region of India. Camārs are the most numerous Harijan caste group, and in some areas, Pāsīs, toddy-tappers and laborers. In eastern Uttar Pradesh the most numerous caste groups are Ahīrs, Brāhmaṇs, Kurmīs, Rājpūts, and Lodhs, each comprising 5% to 10% of the population, and most are engaged in managing or cultivating farms. In Uttar Pradesh 14.6% are Muslims, mostly urban Shaikhs; Baniyā merchant castes have settled where cash crops are grown. In northern Bihār the numerically dominant caste is Goālā, pastoralists and now mostly cultivators, who are part of the Ahīr jāti-cluster. Here other important castes are Brāhmaṇs, the cultivating Rājpūts, Kurmīs, and Lodhs, the laboring Duśādhs, Muslim Julāhā weavers, and the Camārs.

The population density of these vast plains boggles the imagination; Uttar Pradesh had 88.4 million people in 1971, and Bihār had 56.3 million. Western Uttar Pradesh is wheat-growing and its people are temperamentally more like those of the rest of northwestern India; urbanization is increasing significantly. But eastern Uttar Pradesh and the northern half of Bihār have few resources except rice agriculture, and there is a dispersed settlement pattern so that Bihār has only 10% of its people urbanized (as compared with 30% in Mahārāshṭra). Four districts have over 1500 people per square mile, and north Bihār and eastern Uttar Pradesh have an average of over 1000. People are closely tied to subsistence cultivation and not much given to change or to achievement in the modernizing sense.

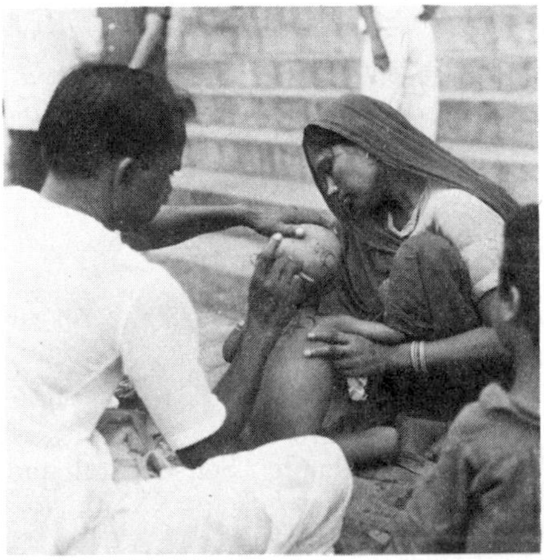

Ghāṭs of the Gangā at Banares. To bathe or hold the tonsure ceremony (required ritual in orthodox families) here is particularly sanctifying.

In spite of a brilliant role in the history of India, these two states today seem economically stagnant. Such indices of modernization as geographical density of market towns, electrification of villages, paving of roads, and intensity of bus traffic are less than in many other states. Literacy is also low, being 21.6% (of the total population) in Uttar Pradesh and 19.8% in Bihār; only in Rājasthān with its traditional avoidance of scholarship is it lower, at 18.8%. But in Haryāṇā it is 26.7%, Panjāb 33.4%, Gujarāt 35.7%, and Mahārāshṭra 39.1%, which is double that for the middle Gangā plains. The heavy population and lack of economic opportunity in Uttar Pradesh and Bihār produced a multiplicity of political parties and a succession of ineffective state governments in the 1960s.

Brāhmaṇ landowner in northern Bihār. He has little land and a house of stalks, but sweeps it respectably clean.

REFERENCES AND NOTES

[1] Adapted from *Census of India, 1961*, I, Part IV–V, (iii), pp. 165–176.
[2] Karve, p. 129.
[3] Mathur, p. 51.
[4] Mathur, p. 46.
[5] Lewis, p. 190.
[6] Karve, p. 134.
[7] Lewis, p. 189.
[8] Carstairs, p. 117.
[9] Carstairs, pp. 110–111.
[10] Susanne Rudolph, "Self-Control and Political Potency: Gandhi's Asceticism," *The American Scholar* XXXV, No. 1 (1965–1966).
[11] Carstairs, pp. 167–168.
[12] Minturn and Hitchcock, pp. 12, 14, 18.

IMPORTANT SOURCES *

Blunt, E. A. H. *The Caste System of Northern India.* Oxford, 1931.

Carstairs, G. Morris. *The Twice-born: A Study of a Community of High-Caste Hindus.* Bloomington, Ind., 1967. (A psychological study of Brāhmaṇs, Rājpūts, Baniyās, and Muslims in Rājasthān.)

Chauhan, Brij Raj. *A Rajasthan Village.* Delhi, 1967. (A rather complete village study in the Mewār area.)

Crooke, William. *Ethnographic Handbook for the North-West Province and Oudh.* Allahabad, 1890.

———. *Natives of Northern India.* London, 1907.

Fox, Richard. *Kin, Clan, Raja, and Rule.* Berkeley, Calif., 1971. (A theoretical study of the political aspects of Rājpūt lineages.)

Fuchs, Stephen. *The Children of Hari: A Study of the Nimar Balahis in the Central Provinces of India.* Vienna, 1950. (Study of an untouchable caste.)

Karve, Irawati. *Kinship Organization in India*, 3d ed. New York, 1968. (An important survey.)

Leaf, Murray. *Information and Behavior in a Sikh Village.* Berkeley, Calif., 1971.

Lewis, Oscar. *Village Life in Northern India.* New York, 1958. (A village near Delhi.)

Madan, T. N. *Family and Kinship among the Pandits of Rural Kashmir.* Bombay, 1965. (Kashmīr Brāhmaṇ landowners.)

Mandelbaum, David. *Society in India*, I and II. Berkeley, Calif., 1970.

Mathur, K. S. *Caste and Ritual in a Malwa Village.* Bombay, 1964.

Mayer, Adrian. *Caste and Kinship in Central India.* Berkeley, Calif., 1966. (A village in Mālwā, western Madhya Pradesh.)

Minturn, Leigh, and John Hitchcock. *The Rājpūts of Khalapur, India.* New York, 1966. (With special emphasis on child raising.)

Orenstein, Henry. *Gaon: Conflict and Cohesion in an Indian Village.* Princeton, N.J., 1965. (A village near Puṇe, Mahārāshṭra.)

Pradhan, M. C. *The Political System of the Jats in Northern India.* Oxford, 1966.

Schwartzberg, Joseph. "Caste Regions of the North Indian Plain," in Milton Singer

and Bernard Cohn (eds.), *Structure and Change in Indian Society*. Chicago, 1968.

Srivastava, S. K. *The Tharus*. Āgrā, 1958. (People of the plains under the Himālayas.)

Trivedi, Harshad. *The Mers of Saurashtra*. Baroda, 1961.

Wiser, William and Charlotte. *Behind Mud Walls*. Berkeley, Calif., 1963. (A study of a village near Āgrā which was revisited by the author after 30 years.)

* For serious work on any region of India the reader is advised to consult the *Census of India, 1961*, which can be found in a number of university libraries in the United States. It is a truly heroic undertaking, published in some 1500 tomes, with nearly 400 village studies (of varying quality) and many state volumes devoted to such subjects as fairs, festivals, handicrafts, tribes, and the like. It is a cultural as well as a statistical survey of India.

11

Survey of South India and the Islands

When a Hindī *wālā* (fellow) from near Allāhābād gets on the train for the three-day trip to the far South, he is prepared for an adventure, like going to another country. In the southern states—Āndhra, Karṇāṭaka, Tamiḻ Nāḍu, Kēraḷa—he will encounter customs strange to him, and some which are offensive. He will immediately see that the people dress differently; in southern Karṇāṭaka, Tamiḻ Nāḍu, and Kēraḷa the men wear their length of cloth, the *dhotī*, like a skirt, while in Sri Lanka many wear the *lungī*, a length of plaid cloth having the ends sewn together. In Kēraḷa and Sri Lanka most of the women do not wear the sāṛī, but a skirt-like length of cloth sometimes arranged with a fan-like pleat on the back, with a sort of blouse. Whereas our Hindī wālā values shoes as a status symbol (though even in his own village most will not be able to afford them), in the South few people care to wear them; some wear sandals, but most go barefoot, for this is a sunny clime. Southerners eat steamed rice cakes and strange pungent curries made with coconut, and do not like wheat. They drink coffee instead of tea. Their hand gestures are unfamiliar, and above all there are those polysyllabic languages which make our wālā feel more out of place than in Gujarāt or Bānglā. The speech reminds him of a bag of

pebbles rolling down a slope. And the farther south he goes the worse it gets.

Our northern wālā may feel he is among incestuous people when he finds out that they marry their cross-cousins, and he may note that there is no rule of village exogamy, while the gotra system and hypergamy are weak or absent. There are different attitudes towards women, who may be seen moving about in the streets more than he is accustomed to, and he will note few widows except Brāhmaṇs wearing the distinguishing mark of the white sāṛī. The joint family is not so common. The varṇa system is truncated so that Brāhmaṇs, non-Brāhmaṇs, and Harijans are the main blocs of castes, and the names of castes are mostly different. Many castes bury instead of cremating. Deities and festivals are largely different.

Yet our northern wālā will recognize a certain cultural unity in India and will consider with pride the pervasive Sanskrit tradition and what he believes to be Āryan values. He will be aware that all of India was emotionally drawn together in the struggle for Independence and in the subsequent wars with China and Pakistan. And he will find plenty of intellectual stimulation during his sojourn in the South.

Settlement Patterns and Households

In Āndhra, Karṇāṭaka and Tamil̲ Nāḍu villages are generally compact and fairly large. Compact villages made defense easy and enable a wide range of castes to interact in a complex manner. Blocs of castes generally occupy different sections of a village, but castes are not particularly segregated within the sections. Harijans live in satellite hamlets or in a particular section. Streets tend to intersect at right angles. In the vastly fertile alluvial soils of the Godāvarī, Krishṇā, and Kāvēri rivers where rice is grown, villages are located wherever there is a little high ground. Ancient kings considered it their duty to dig irrigation channels. Where river irrigation is not possible, as over the largest part of Tamil̲ Nāḍu and also much of southern Karṇāṭaka and northern Sri Lanka, there are "tanks" for irrigation. These consist of a few acres of water retained after the monsoon by a low mud embankment, below which are rice fields and on the side a village; thousands of these dot the landscape. But over much of western Āndhra and northern Karṇāṭaka irrigation is not possible at all, for the Deccan Plateau is largely dryish, and the chief crops are the various millets.

In the rice-growing deltas houses are often of mud thatched with palm leaves or millet stalks. But almost every village will have a fair number of brick or whitewashed mud houses with tile roofs, for the land has not generally been held by zamīndārs but divided up among many cultivators or small landowners. In the Deccan stone for building is readily available, and

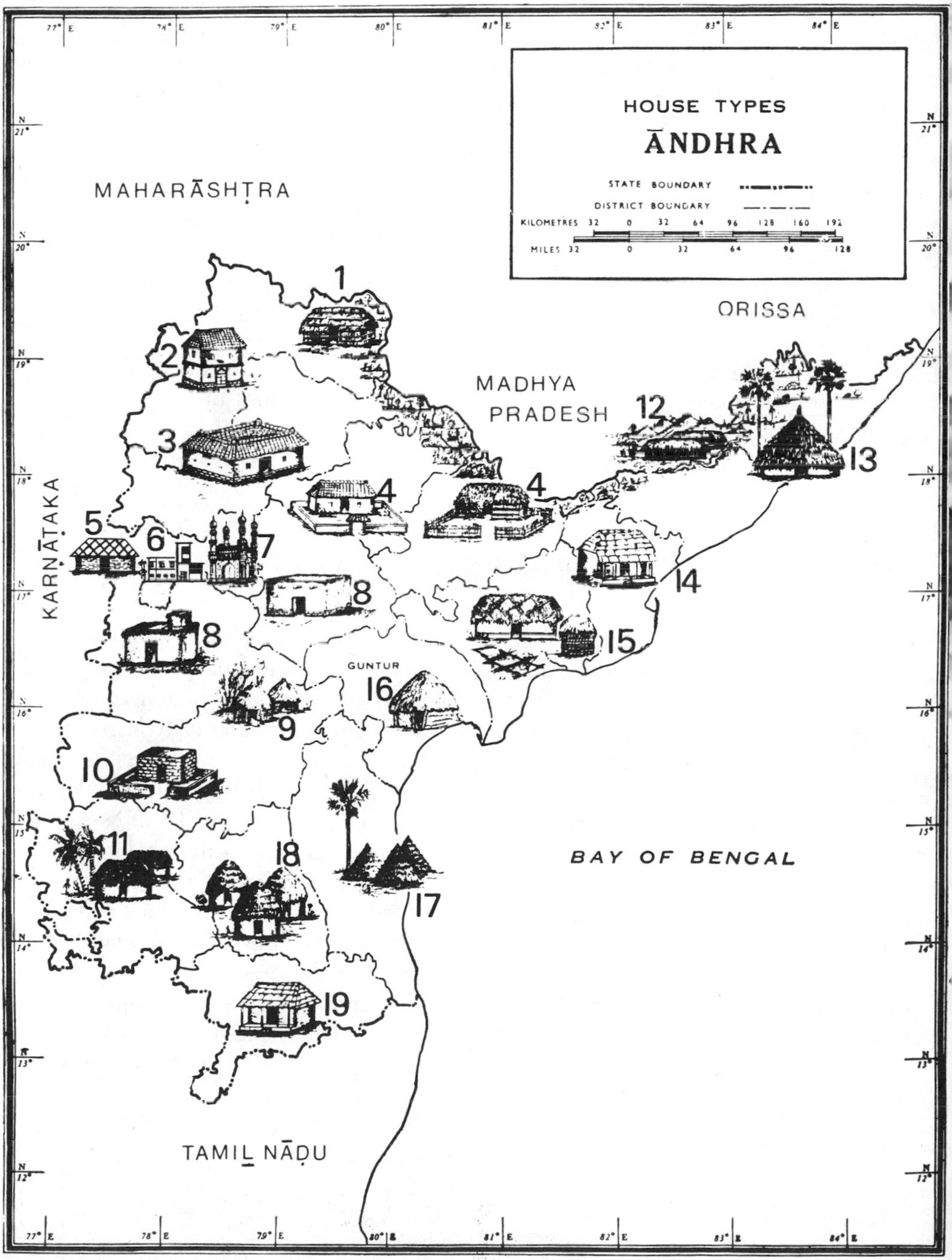
HOUSE TYPES
ĀNDHRA
STATE BOUNDARY
DISTRICT BOUNDARY
KILOMETRES 32 0 32 64 96 128 160 192
MILES 32 0 32 64 96 128
MAHARĀSHṬRA
ORISSA
MADHYA PRADESH
KARNĀṬAKA
GUNTUR
BAY OF BENGAL
TAMIL NĀḌU
1
2
3
4
4
5
6
7
8
8
9
10
11
12
13
14
15
16
17
18
19

FIG. 11–1 House types in Āndhra.[1]

1) Huts or houses of tribals are of wattle daubed with mud or dung, with thatch of forest material.
2) Most houses have mud walls and roofs of local tile common in all northwestern Āndhra; poor people use thatch.
3) Interior courtyards are a traditionally valued pattern; they afford protection and privacy.
4) Exterior courtyards may accommodate bullocks, cows, and buffaloes.
5) Houses here are of local limestone with roofs of slate shingles.
6) Hyderābād is dominated by modern Indian urban architecture; houses are of brick, with terraced tops of brick or cement, or tile roofs.
7) Mosques date from the days of independent Hyderābād State.
8) Flat-roofed mud houses prevail in these drier districts.
9) Huts of Cencus in the Nallamalai Hills are of bamboo mat with grass thatch.
10) Because it is dry, flat roofs of stones mixed with mud suffice; walls are of locally available stone.
11) This poor dry area has drab houses of mud or stone, with flat mud roofs or date-palm thatch.
12) Conical houses withstand monsoon cyclonic weather; thatch, beams, and rope are all made of palmyra palms.
13) Hill tribals' flimsy row huts are of daubed wattle and forest thatch.
14) Many houses have factory-tile roofs over mud or brick walls.
15) Mud houses prevail in densely populated delta districts, with cow-dung plastered floors and roofs of rice straw; cylindrical paddy bins of rice-straw rope daubed with dung stand near houses.
16) Houses are of mud or stone with roofs of rice straw or millet stalks.
17) Most houses are of laterite blocks or mud; Yanādi field laborers have tiny conical sheds of palmyra leaves, without walls.
18) Round mud huts are found in many villages of this poor region.
19) Neat tiled houses are common, but to the west poor people live in round huts with millet-stalk thatch.

stone slabs may even be used for roofing, or houses may have flat mud roofs in the drier areas.

But in Kēraḷa, as also in southwestern Sri Lanka and coastal Karṇāṭaka, rainfall is very heavy and the land is undulating. There are not many large compact villages here but separate houses scattered over the countryside surrounded by tapioca fields, coconut palms, and mango and jackfruit trees. They often form a linear pattern along roads, backwaters, or valleys. Because the population is heavy, houses will be seen everywhere, and a surprising number of them are quite respectable, whitewashed with tile roof and often built of laterite blocks which can be easily cut out of the ground in this belt.

The variety of house types found in Āndhra may be cited as an example of their adaptation to environmental and social features (Fig. 11–1). The rice-growing alluvial regions have mud or mud-brick houses, and space for building is scarce. In Telengāna (the northwestern part of the state, formerly part of the domains of the Nizām of Hyderābād) stone is available and courtyards are larger, for there is plenty of space. In the southwest (Rāyalasīma) the climate is dry and the villagers poor. In the tribal areas along the northern fringe of the state (occupied by Gōṇḍs such as Fürer-Haimendorf describes in the companion volume) houses may be made of forest materials. Villages in Āndhra are fairly large; 94% of the people of the state live in villages having over 100 houses and 500 people, while many villages have several thousand people (but generally a place is considered a town if there are over 5000 people).

The 1961 census showed the average number of persons per household in Āndhra to be 4.71 in rural areas and 4.76 in urban places (lower than the all-India average of 5.20 and 4.97). Thus rural households in the South are somewhat smaller than in the North, but urban households are perhaps a little larger, for southerners are more prone to bring their families when they migrate to cities.

Throughout Āndhra in 1961 65% of the houses or huts had only one room, 22% had two rooms, 7% three, 3.5% four, and 2.5% five or more rooms. But many houses have attached to the main room a shed for cooking, a front porch, and often an attic. In the South it is never cold enough to prevent people from spending time outdoors.

The household is as fundamental as it is in the North, but joint families are not as widely idealized except among certain higher castes and owner-cultivators in certain regions; seldom among lower or middle castes do two married brothers live together, except in crowded urban situations. Joint families range from 4% in a low Tamiḻ caste, to 11% in an untouchable group in Bangalore, 20% in a group of landowning Tanjāvūr Brāhmaṇs, 37% among all castes in a part of northern Karṇāṭaka, and over 50% among the matrilineal people of Malabar (northern and central Kēraḷa).

People perceive a hierarchy of social territories, according to Brenda

Beck's knowledgeable study of a region in western Tamiḻ Nāḍu. Most intimate is the individual household, the commensal group built around the hearth. Next is the village or hamlet, the cluster of houses. Above this is the revenue village, which may include several hamlets or satellite villages together with their lands. Then there is the subregion, important in the organization of the dominant agricultural caste, in this case the Kavuṇḍar. Finally there is the region, in this case Coimbatore District and parts of three adjacent districts, having a historical and cultural identity within the language region. The whole is like a set of Chinese boxes, says Beck, each fitting neatly into the next size box. And each of the five levels has its own sacred places.

Kinship

The two most fundamental areas of difference between North and South India are in language and kinship. Kinship terms are similar among all peninsular Dravidian languages, including the central Indian tribal ones, and suggest a basic similarity of kinship structure. This extends beyond the zone of Dravidian speech to Sri Lanka, and also partially to Mahārāshṭra and parts of Gujarāt, for in these regions Indo-Āryan languages were adopted without imposition of the entire North Indian kinship system.

The key features of this system is that marriage is preferentially with one's actual or classificatory cross-cousin (for a male, mother's brother's daughter, or father's sister's daughter), and such people comprise a group of *complementary* kin, while marriage is forbidden with *parallel* kin such as parallel cousins (having as parents siblings of the same sex). Therefore kin, and sometimes nonkin, are classified into two categories. The terminology also expresses a hierarchy according to relative age, and distinguishes sex.

In this system genealogical depth is not important. Few people know the names of distantly removed ancestors except a few who have had reason to employ genealogists. In some Kēraḷa lineages the founder's name is remembered and some tribes have mythical ancestors. But in general the word lineage as used in the South would refer only to agnatic kin of three or four generations. The important distinction is not venerable ancestry, but whom one should or should not marry.

Table 11–1 lists some of the important kinship categories of the Urali, a hill tribe numbering a few hundred in south-central Kēraḷa. They are isolated in the Western Ghāṭs, are little influenced by Brāhmaṇical Hinduism, and have now given up hunting for agriculture. They are matrilineal but tending to become patrilineal, and practice levirate, marriage by exchange, and some polygyny. The kinship categories and most of the terminology is common to other Dravidian-speaking peoples, most of whom are patrilineal. The fundamentals of this system no doubt originated in the dim

TABLE 11–1 Urali Kinship Terms[2]

Generation	*Term*	*Relationship*	*Relatively Elder*	*Relatively Younger*
Grandparents'	mūttan	FF, MF		
	mūttiyammā	FM, MM		
Parents'	appan	F, FB, MZH, step-F	pēr-appan FeB	citt-appan FyB, step-F
	ammā	M, MZ, MBW, step-M	pēr-ammā MeZ	kōcc-ammā MyZ, step-M
	ammāvi	FZ, MBW, WM, (HM)		
	ammāccan	MB, FZH, WF, (HF)	kāraṇavan MeB	
Ego's			cētan eB, FBS-e, MZS-e, WeZH	tambi, aṇiyan yB, FBS-y, MBS-y, WyZH
			(cētati) (eZ, FBD-e, MZD-e, HeBW)	(aṇiyatti) (yZ, FBD-y, MZD-y, HYBW)
	(āṇgaḷ)	(B, FBS, MZS, SWF, HZH)	valiya-āṇ	kuñjangaḷa-āṇ
	peṇgaḷ	Z, FBD, BZD, WBW, SWM	valiya-peṇ	kuñjangaḷa-peṇ
	(natūn)	(FZD, MBD, HZ, SWM, BW)	valiya-natūn	kuñjangaḷa-natūn
	aḷiyan	WB, ZH, SWF, FZS, MBS	valiya-aḷiyan	kuñjangaḷa-aḷiyan
	muṟṟapeṇṇu	FZD, MBD, WZ		
	(bhārtavu)	(H)		
	bhārya	W		
Son's	makan	S, BS, WZS, (ZS)		
	makaḷ	D, BD, WZD, (ZD)		
	marumakan	DH, WBS, ZS, (BS, HZS)		
	marumakaḷ	SW, WBD, ZD, (BD, HZD)		
Grandson's	pēran	SS, DS		
	pērati	SD, DD		

BFS = brother's father's son, etc. Z = sister; e = elder, y = younger. Terms are those used by male ego; those in parentheses are used by female ego only. Pēr-, valiya-, mean "big"; cit-, kōcc-, kuñju-, mean "little." Aṇiyan means "close one." Āṇgaḷ is "menfolk" or honorific "man"; peṇgaḷ is "womenfolk" or honorific "woman," and these terms are used for siblings of the sex opposite the speaker. Mūttan means "ripened one," "aged one"; pēran, pērati, mean "namesake." Maru, as in marumakan, means "opposite," "other." Muṟṟapeṇṇu means "mature girl" and is an eligible bride. Note especially the unique position of kāraṇavan (MeB), who is important in the marriage ceremony. The terms bhārtavu (H) and bhārya (W) are not Dravidian but are borrowed from Indo-Āryan via Malayāḷam.

tribal past, but it has been adapted to various economic and civilizational levels, and also to people speaking Indo-Āryan languages.

In Table 11–1, ego, a male, can marry a *murrapeṇṇu*, which means a girl of his own generation who is either a kind of cross-cousin or can be classified as such. This term is also used for his wife's sister. In the generation below his he can marry a *marumakaḷ*, his (elder) sister's daughter or anyone who can be so classified; the term is also used for his son's wife and wife's brother's daughter. All girls classified as *peṇgaḷ* in his generation are like sisters, and all girls classified as *makaḷ* in the generation below his are like daughters, and these are ineligible as brides for ego.

There are numerous caste and regional variations. Some Brāhmaṇ and other high castes prefer a man to marry his elder sister's daughter if one is available. Other castes prefer the cross-cousins on the father's side, and yet others, those on the mother's side, but for many castes it makes no difference, and the distinction seems not to be fundamental. The system works essentially the same for the few matrilineal groups as for the patrilineal ones, and a few seem to be bilateral. Brāhmaṇs in the South have taken the gotra system, but do not follow the sapiṇḍa exogamy rule which prohibits marriage with kin of the fifth or seventh degrees. But a goodly number of southern castes do have clan-like exogamous groups. Nambūtiri Brāhmaṇs of Kēraḷa place cross-cousins in the same terminological category as sisters and require marriage to unrelated people, but theirs is a special case. In most of the South lineage is traced through the male and people are patrilocal (a couple moving to the groom's locale upon marriage); yet almost everywhere there is some occurrence of "adoption" of a daughter's husband if there is no son. Mate selection is a complex procedure as in the North, and requires community approval. There are different preferences about age of marriage. It is accepted that a man should be older than his wife, but how much older varies—and can be important if a family does not wish the wife to take an important part in her husband's affairs. Physical appearance and astrological readings are also important. Some castes give dowry and some bride-wealth; dowry is more common among Brāhmaṇs, but the bride's father has heavy wedding expenses even among those castes that give bride-wealth.

But though many features of kinship and marriage are similar to those in the North, it is the ability of the terminology to clearly distinguish who may or may not be bride to ego that is crucial. This is so because, as Beals puts it, ego bears the seed of his father's line, as do his brothers and sisters, his father's brothers, and their children. They are all parallel people, like brothers and sisters. But his father's sister's children, and also his own sister's children, have received their seed from males of other lines, so they are all complementary people, and those females are referred to as eligible brides.

These principles are extended to the ascending generation, as can be

seen in Table 11–1. An Urali man, for example, will use the same term in referring to his father's sister, mother's brother's wife, and wife's mother. These may, indeed, all be the *same person*. There are few or no terms for affines or in-laws, which are terminologically reduced to "blood" relatives.

A South Indian can hardly use English in talking about his relatives, else communication breaks down. The English word "cousin" stands for eight different kinds of cousins: combinations of male and female, cross and parallel, patrilateral and matrilateral. Dravidian terminology invariably distinguishes male and female, and cross and parallel. A South Indian, in referring to his father's brother's son, may say, "My cousin-brother is coming today." The English-speaking foreigner will query, "Who, a cousin or a brother?" What is meant is a parallel cousin, referred to by Dravidian-speakers as a brother—and indeed he is treated as such. He is not a potential brother-in-law. But the "cousin" who is brother of a potential bride must be received with more formality than a "cousin-brother," and it was necessary for South Indians to coin this compound term if they wished to speak English. Even more troublesome is the extension of the terms "brother" and "cousin" to more distant kin or to nonkin. What relationship is incestuous and what is not is defined entirely differently than in North India or in Europe, and of course this is accurately expressed in the respective terminologies.

The generations above and below ego's are terminologically distinguished in accord with this because they are directly related to ego's marriage, or he may marry into them. The chief difficulty foreigners find here is that these terms are often used casually for nonkin.

A fundamental feature of Dravidian kinship terminology is hierarchy according to generation and age. Urali kinship terminology has no words for "brother" and "sister," only "elder brother," "younger brother," etc. If Dravidian languages have words for "brother" and "sister" they are generally borrowed from Indo-Āryan. In the ascending generation, father's elder brother is literally "great father" and the younger "little father." If father has several younger brothers (not shown on the Urali example) they will be distinguished by further adjectives indicating their exact chronological and hierarchical position. Moreover, a half-brother is referred to as "elder" if he is the son of the first mother or first union, and as "younger" if he is the son of a subsequent union. A concubine, perhaps from a lower caste, is referred to as "younger mother" even if she is older than the first wife.

In the Urali system ego's mother's elder brother is referred to by a specific term. This is because at the marriage ceremony he has a particular role to play, and in matrilineal societies in Kēraḷa he is the property manager, and is referred to by this same term. In most Dravidian languages he is called *māma* (referring to mother's elder or younger brother), and since the same person may also be wife's father the term can be used as an affinal one or as a cognate one.

Functions of Dravidian Kinship

A number of anthropologists have constructed models and theories for this system. S. J. Tambiah emphasizes for Sri Lanka the importance of land ownership and suggests that the kinship system tends to break down when land is not involved. This may be true in certain instances but it does not explain how the system has functioned in tribal or landless populations. Others have assumed, on analogy with cross-cousin marriage patterns in other parts of the world, that lineage and descent is the key, but this does not seem to be the case for South India. Kathleen Gough, studying Tanjāvūr Brāhmaṇs, stresses assimilation of a woman by her husband and his family, and notes the asymmetrical male-female relationship. These Brāhmaṇs prefer marriage with mother's brother's daughter because the prestige of the wife-taker is higher than that of the wife-giver, so they wish the wife-giver to be on the maternal side. Leach also stresses the status differentiation between wife-givers and wife-takers. But this asymmetrical relationship does not hold for most castes, and in the South generally this is less notable than in the North.

Dumont observes that there is considerable variation in marriage preferences among Tami̱l castes and has elaborated the theory that the common factor is the importance of the marriage *alliance*. The mother's brother has an important role in initiating the reciprocal exchanges attendant upon marriage, and his sons inherit some of these obligations, so that to some extent the role of mother's relatives is an affinal one. But it has been as strongly argued that their role is a cognate one. Karve has pointed out that in Mahārāshṭra cross-cousin marriage is spreading because some families who marry their daughters hypergamously send their daughters up to the same families in succeeding generations. But again this is not fundamental for most population groups in the South.

Nur Yalman in studying villages in several parts of Sri Lanka wrestled with the problem of finding a common thread through the diversity of variant Dravidian kinship practices. After studying a Kaṇḍyan hill village (of Sinhala-speaking Buddhists) which was patrilineal and patrilocal, he went to a Dry Zone village and found that dowry and hypergamy, mere tendencies in the Kaṇḍyan village, were much more common. Then in a Tami̱l Muslim village on the island he found the same basic structure but with matrilocal residence the norm. Finally he went to an east coast village where he found Hindu and Muslim Tami̱ls claiming to be matrilineal and matrilocal, though the kinship system was but a variant of the Sinhala system, and in fact Tami̱l and Sinhala kinship terms were used interchangeably. Yalman concludes, after comparing these with South Indian systems having cross-cousin marriage and classified variously as patrilineal patrilocal, patrilineal matrilocal, matrilineal, hypergamous, and bilateral,

that the general structural model may be connected to a great variety of descent patterns. The important feature is not lineage at all:

> Suffice it to recall that it is the systematic linguistic categories of kinship (the terms of reference) which structure the entire kin circle and specify in an orderly manner marriageable and unmarriageable persons in that universe. What we call cross-cousin marriage is simply a restatement of the rights and obligations inherent in certain categories. There is no lineal emphasis at all, but only rules regarding the interconnections between categories.[3]

He also suggests that though brother and sister must be separated, their offspring must be united—and he finds overtones to this concept in religion. The system is also fundamental to the principles of caste endogamy in South India and Sri Lanka.

Alan Beals believes that we should not construct models just on what people say is their ideal regarding marriage and kinship, but should instead observe their behavior. He compared the percentages of different kinds of marriage in eight villages in South India and Sri Lanka, including three that he studied in Karṇāṭaka. He found that stated preference for either matrilateral or patrilateral cross-cousin marriage had little bearing on actual marriages, but that both types were found in all these villages. Marriage of a man to his elder sister's daughter was also found in all these villages except the Sri Lanka example; this type comprised from 1% to 20% of marriages in these villages. The percentage of cross-cousin or uncle-niece marriages among all marriages in these villages ranged from a low of 4% and 5% up to a high of 50%. In his village of Gopālpur he found that these comprised 19% of 2757 marriages. Cross-cousin marriage, then, is not as frequent as kinship models suggest. He suggests that a distinctive system of Dravidian kinship and marriage does exist but that present theoretical approaches are unlikely to uncover it.

As for the origin of this system, it was suggested long ago that Dravidian people must have been in general matrilineal. There is some correlation on a worldwide scale between matriliny and horticultural subsistence. This generalization holds for the Khāsis of Meghālaya, for instance, but the matrilineal Nāyar of Kēraḷa were warriors. And numbers of the Kēraḷa tribes, as also the Väddās of Sri Lanka, are patrilineal. It is doubtful whether it could be proved that matriliny was ever more widespread among Dravidian-speaking people, and the ancient literature does not give evidence of it.

Karve suggests that the aboriginal Dravidian-speakers were organized as totemistic clans, which gave rise to lineage exogamy. In Āndhra, for instance, the most numerous caste-group is the Reḍḍis, who are divided into a large number of clan-like groups which bear the names of animals, trees, fruits, and other objects. A relationship may develop between two "clans" calling for successive exchange of brides. Even the Urali formerly had exogamous moieties, but these have now broken up. It is also reported that

some castes having such clans or gotras follow the principle that the people of one's group marry the people of a complementary group, and the people of a third group are not eligible for marriage, but are referred to with kinship terms used for agnates. What does appear likely historically is that this terminological system diffused from western South Asia southward through Gujarāt and Mahārāshṭra—whether with late hunters or in the aftermath of the Indus Civilization we don't know—and as it diffused from western India to the peninsula the terminological system was adapted to a variety of tribal structures, subsistence and civilizational levels, and descent modes.

The hierarchical classification implicit in distinguishing brothers, sisters, uncles, and other kin, often by age in relation to ego, has apparently been of fundamental importance in the development of wider society in India. This distinction is extended beyond kin to strangers. A lad in a Tamil̲ village might address a visitor as "elder brother" and treat him similarly. Two Americans visiting that village will be referred to with the usual title *durai*, but as soon as it is determined which of the two is in authority, he will be termed "big durai" and the other will be "little durai," even if the latter happens to have a larger body. An influential person or a landowner is a "big" man. Thus it will be seen that reference to elder brother or elder uncle as "big" is societal hierarchy in microcosm. This tendency to graded statuses might have been fundamental to the evolution of hierarchical caste in western South Asia in protohistoric times, and it certainly applies to interpersonal relations even in modern political or commercial organizations.

Marriage and Sex

Among many castes there is a celebration upon the first menstruation of a daughter. Guests are invited, perhaps with gaily printed announcements, and a feast is provided at which the girl is publicly presented arrayed in womanly finery. The girl is likely to receive a larger portion of good food in the two or three years preceding her marriage so she may look healthy and become a little plump. Betrothals are made by parents, but infant marriages have not been common among cultivating castes of the South.

Marriage rites for high castes are conducted by Brāhmaṇs, but among many of the middle agricultural groups and all Harijans, caste priests perform the ceremonies. At the wedding the bride and groom sit in a little booth in the courtyard of the bride's home while the priest pronounces certain formulae and conducts rituals symbolic of fertility. The ceremony culminates when the groom ties the wedding symbol, a gold pendant, around the bride's neck. Then there is a feast of rice and curry for all, including the women, who eat at the same time but sit together on one side of the courtyard. If the wedding is conducted in a farmer's house, his oxen

and buffaloes are likely to remain tethered along the sides of the courtyard, munching rice straw as they benignly observe the proceedings.

There is a series of reciprocal givings, which may be recorded in a notebook at the time of the wedding. Among Brāhmaṇs and other high castes dowries may be considerable. Among Christians also fabulous dowries may be given, worth one's income for a year or several years, in order to get a husband for one's daughter who is highly educated and well placed. Among such families woe be the father who has several daughters and no sons—such have been known to commit suicide. But probably more castes give bride-wealth than dowry, and in fact the two are not separable because giving is somewhat reciprocal over a period of months before the wedding.

Divorce or separation occurs with some frequency except among the more orthodox castes. If a young bride finds life intolerable she simply returns home to mother. In most cases reconciliation will be achieved in time, but if not, some or all of the value of wedding gifts will be returned. If someone makes an issue of adultery, the caste or village panchāyat will be obliged to take action and may levy a fine, or if they feel the caste or village has been publicly disgraced, they may outcaste or otherwise publicly punish the guilty party. Such decisions are not made by strict adherence to any rules, but by the need to settle quarrels, to appear to satisfy the aggrieved party, and to reconcile the personalities involved who are almost always well known to the panchāyat members.

Village youths have furtive sexual relations in fields, and those who can afford two or three rupees may have the company of low caste women.

Non-Brāhmaṇ priest (on low stool) performs wedding for Tamiḻ farming family. Wedding booth is built in courtyard of bride's home. She should not show joy at leaving home.

Musicians at elaborate wedding. Instruments are *mridangam* (drum), double-reed *nāgaśuram*, and harmonium for drone.

In a village the middle and lower caste young men may acknowledge that none of them are without premarital sexual experience, but in the same village the more prestigious landowners will deny knowledge of such activities and think their sons are innocent; among them brides are expected to be virgins, and generally are. In some areas apparently there are no known indigenous contraceptives but in Kēraḷa at least women may insert a half a lime. Abortions are available in most villages and may number 20 or 50 a year in a village of 2000. Theories of anatomy and folk psychology pertaining to sex such as are found in the North are also believed in the South, and men fear semen loss. But in general the relations between the sexes are less strained than in the Northwest where their roles are more polarized.

Women

Because a man and his bride may have known each other as children and may indeed have been playmates, a wife in the South is less likely to be a docile creature thrust as a youngster into an unknown family where she would be expected to revere her husband and defer to all in his household. On the whole women have more freedom to move about than in the North. Satī was rare, and emulation of Muslim social conventions was also not strong, except in capitals of Muslim states such as Hyderābād. When South Indians migrate to cities, they take their womenfolk, hence the sex ratio in southern cities is not very uneven.

But it should not be imagined that women have formal status equal to that of men. As in the North, a woman follows her husband by a few paces when they go down the street, never displays public affection, and in fact seldom talks to him unnecessarily in public. Women eat after their menfolk. A husband speaks to his wife using the form of the pronoun "you" otherwise reserved for servants and children, while she speaks to him using the honorific pronoun. At an all-night epic narrative or in a Christian church, women sit on one side and men on the other. Among Brāhmaṇs young women are strictly protected, and in regions affected by Rājpūt concepts of prestige such as the village in northern Karṇāṭaka described by Ishwaran in the companion volume, middle-rank farming men may even carry the household water and do all the shopping if they cannot afford servants to do it.

The percentage of literate women to literate men as of 1971 was much higher in Kēraḷa (83%) than in India as a whole (44%), and also higher in the other three southern states (50%). In the delta districts of Āndhra, for example, male literacy is about 45% and female literacy 30%; half the girls 5 to 14 are in school today. Even in Hyderābād city with its Muslim traditions, 42% of all females were literate in 1971. In the poorer western parts of Āndhra, however, rural female literacy drops as low as 5%.

The high female literacy rate in Kēraḷa is due to the high value Christians there have placed on education and also to the relative prestige women enjoy because of the matriliny of some castes. Malayāḷi nurses by the thousands are employed in North India because North Indian women of rural origin hesitate to do cleaning work such as nurses do for fear of pollution, and also because few of them take up professions. There is a great surplus of teachers, including female teachers, in Kēraḷa and Tamil̲ Nāḍu, so that it is customary to pay a year's salary as bribe to obtain an elementary school teaching position.

Another indication of the relatively equitable treatment of women in the South is that the sex ratio is not skewed; in the four southern states and in Orissa there are about as many women as men, but in northwestern India and Pakistan there are 10% fewer women than men. This is a phenomenon of some complexity which will be touched on later, but at least in part it is due to different attitudes toward women.

The institution of *dēvadāsis*, temple dancing girls, caught the imagination of a number of early observers of the South Indian scene. Missionaries thought it horrid that parents would give their girls to temples—and sometimes poor mothers sold or abandoned their small daughters to this livelihood. The British regime outlawed the institution, regarding it as an elaboration of prostitution, but it is reported that it still exists in some temples. Dēvadāsis were married to the temple deities and were trained in the arts of song and dance. It was they who perfected the Bharatanāṭyam dance form in the great temples of Tanjāvūr, Tamil̲ Nāḍu, and they played an important part in the daily routine. They were also trained in the arts of love to please patrons who paid for their ceremonies, and to please priests too. But they were not considered dishonorable like prostitutes; rather they were highly honored for they could never become widows. Their offspring tend to form a caste of courtesans. Prostitutes, however, are often sent as young girls by their desperate mothers to earn money, and many of those who fill the numerous brothels of Bombay come from the poorer districts of Karṇāṭaka.

Entertainment

Most of the forms of village entertainment cited here are not limited to South India but are widespread in South Asia. Some of them such as performances of traveling drama troupes are especially well developed in the South.

Children's toys may be made of local materials: a rattle of palm leaves or pottery, a little cart with wheels of palmyra palm nuts, an iron hoop made by the blacksmith which kids push with a long wire, very high stilts of bamboo, a kite made of paper and bamboo perhaps equipped to fight other

Stilt-walking in Āndhra.

Boys in Kēraḷa playing indigenous game with stone gamesmen on grid.

kites by having glass powder glued along the string. The children themselves produce ingenious toys: a clay cart with a stick axle, a cart of leaves pinned with twigs, a clay model kitchen complete with fireplace and firewood, a leaf whistle. Everywhere girls enjoy hopscotch and boys revel in games of marbles, which they shoot with great power by springing back the middle finger. A number of entertainment forms were clearly connected with religious rites at first; stilt walking and kite flying are even now done during particular festival seasons.

Musical epic narrative performed in temple festival in Tamil̲ village.

During the heat of early afternoon or in the dusk when the day's work is done, men sit on a platform under a giant tree and play various games moving gamesmen on a grid drawn on the ground, using dice or cowrie shells (parchisi is of Indian origin, as are elements of chess and checkers). Such games had early origins, for many gamesmen are found in Indus Civilization sites. Even the *Rig Veda* has a famous hymn, a spell, to dice nuts which may fate a man to lose his all in gambling, and in the *Mahābhārata* the Pāṇḍava brothers gambled away even their common wife. Now playing cards are very popular too.

Wrestling is an old tradition, and its methods are set down in numerous old manuals. There are wrestling contests in some villages. In the Karṇāṭaka village described by Ishwaran in the companion volume there is a semisubterranean pit in which men and boys work out and wrestle, which causes profuse sweating because it is completely enclosed. In the same village large round boulders line the streets and men compete in lifting the larger ones a few inches off the ground. These two practices stem from the medieval militaristic traditions of that region. Young people play a sort of tag called *kabbaḍi* in which opposing teams line up facing each other. This is so popular it has recently become a tournament sport with state teams competing against each other. The most popular organized sport today is football (soccer to Americans), played in villages everywhere and promoted by high schools. Other Western sports such as hockey, basketball, and cricket are played in towns.

Village dancing is performed more by tribals than by farmers, but there are some exhunting castes who have dances which are said to be relics of prehunting rituals. One ancient form of dance which does live on today, especially in Kēraḷa, is the "baton dance" in which young men or young women form a circle, each holding two batons which they alternately strike against the batons of their neighbors as they dance round and round to music. In Sri Lanka a fairly elaborate Kaṇḍyan form of folk dance has been preserved. Elsewhere, aside from those of the tribals of central India, the best known folk dances are from Rājasthān and Maṇipur.

Then there are transient entertainers of many kinds such as mendicants with dancing bears or performing monkeys, or groups of transvestite singers and dancers (regarded essentially as a caste). Paul Hiebert studied a village in Āndhra through which people of 41 transient castes passed over the course of a year and a half, including: masked beggars; beggars and acrobats who perform for Merchants; Harijan acrobats for Leatherworkers; Harijan courtesans and entertainers for Leatherworkers; bards and historians for Cowherds; historians and beggars for Barbers; dramatists for Cowherds; bards for Śūdras; leather puppeteers; a caste of magicians, snake charmers, and ropemakers; watchmen and minstrels; mendicants with performing bulls; entertainers of children and singers; palmists and storytellers;

a caste of jugglers, tumblers, tightrope dancers, and prostitutes; a caste of snake charmers and sleight-of-hand artists; and a semitribal caste of soothsayers and fortunetellers.

The epics are living traditions sung in villages throughout the land. In Tamiḻ Nāḍu at times of important temple festivals a troupe to perform "bow songs" will be called, and they will perform under a palm leaf shelter erected near the temple for the occasion. The chief singer will intone the epics accompanied by a huge bow with resonance pots attached, together with several other percussion instruments. Beginning with local legends and weaving them into regional and national epics, particularly the *Rāmāyaṇa*, the narrator will go on through the night. The narrator may be a man or a woman. In Kēraḷa the epics are intoned accompanied by a highly elaborate form of dance-drama called Kathākali. For this dancers are trained a minimum of eight years and drummers four years. The bodily movements are exceedingly deliberate and subtle, and by all accounts this is one of the most impressive art forms ever devised. Over the course of the whole night two or three scenes from the *Mahābhārata* may be enacted, accompanied by the intoned narrative and cymbals. Christians too have musical narrations of their stories. A singer may go on for four hours, accompanied by drums and a stringed instrument, expanding on the account of the Prodigal Son. He may sing in the yard of a church of the Church of South India (a union of Protestant denominations) while the crowd sits enthralled on an expanse of palm leaf mats and the children drop off to sleep.

In some areas there are expert traveling drama troupes, especially in Kēraḷa and Mahārāshṭra. Or dramas may be put on by local villagers. Hiebert describes such a performance in Āndhra, at which young men from the village have secured a donation from a sponsor in return for recognizing him at the performance, and have secured the help of a gurū to teach them songs. The performance is conducted on a makeshift stage of bamboo poles and blankets while the audience squats on the ground. All are ready about nine o'clock:

> The performance begins with music—a chorus accompanied by drums and a few assorted instruments. One by one, each character dresses in the cubicle; then he bursts from behind the curtain to the cheers of the chorus. The first is a king, but which king? He drops a hint here, a clue there, as the audience tries to guess his identity. A clown enters, ridiculing the king and uttering asides to the audience about some shady sides of the king's past life. Someone in the audience shouts a jibe at the king and the others laugh. No one loses the thread of the story in the confusion. Each line is sung and resung by the leader. Each line is echoed and reechoed by the chorus. A half hour passes, but only the first character has been introduced.
>
> The second character appears, a young man dressed as a queen. The queen dominates the scene for a quarter of an hour during which time the clown drops by to make passes at her. By two or three in the morning all the characters have

been introduced and the plot thickens. Those who have stretched out to sleep are awakened and kept informed by others. Kings and tyrants march back and forth across the stage. Right is about to triumph when suddenly the tyrant's aide turns out to be a demon who overpowers the hero. Now that all seems lost, the hero's charioteer reveals himself to be a god in disguise. The battle which began between men becomes a cosmic struggle between all the forces of good and evil, but right triumphs in the end. Dawn is breaking when the last blows are struck and gods, demons, kings, and queens march off the stage to trek around the village and collect a few gifts of grain or coins.[4]

Nowadays the most common form of public entertainment is the cinema, available in most towns and sometimes also in villages. India produces more films than the United States. More are produced in Hindī than any other language, followed by Tamiḻ and other languages such as Telugu. For a few coins people can enjoy three or four hours of escapist entertainment.

Syrian Christians

In Kēraḷa over 21% of the people are Christians, most of whom practice a faith they claim was introduced by the Apostle Thomas in the 1st century. The church was well established from at least the 4th century and there were in fact several Thomases in those early centuries. There were also Christian churches in Sri Lanka and around Cape Comorin, but they died out. The question remains, how did the Christians of Kēraḷa retain their distinctiveness for the better part of two millennia?

Europeans had heard of these Christians, who seem to have contributed to the European legends of Prester John. When Vasco da Gama landed in Calicut in 1598 (having been shown the way from South Africa to India by Arab pilots) he saw what he thought was an image of the Virgin in a place of worship, attended by flowers and lamps, and bowed down before it. He unwittingly worshiped an image of Kāḷi, Hindu goddess of death. The Christians, heretofore under the Patriarch of Syria and using Syriac in their liturgy, soon fell under Portuguese persuasion and acknowledged the supremacy of the Pope. Subsequently a large group of them split off and returned to their own rites; these are known as Marthomite Christians today. Another group retained many Catholic rites but do not recognize the Pope, and these are Jacobites. Syrian Christians can be recognized by their names derived from the Syriac of their liturgy: Chākko (Jacob), Cheriyan (Zecharaiah), Mathāi (Matthew), Verghese (George), Chandy (Alexander). They are found mostly in the heavily populated parts of central Kēraḷa, and distinguish themselves from more recent converts.

These Christians did not fight the caste system, but succeeded in fitting themselves into it, and therein lay the secret of their continued identity. From the ninth century the rāja made grants to them, inscribed on copper

plates, assigning villages and also some low caste people to be servants of the church. When the Portuguese found them they were living in the villages granted, collecting revenue for the rāja, and enjoying certain concessions of the pepper trade. They were roughly on the status plane of the Nāyar warriors, used Nāyar titles, sometimes patronized the Nāyar women who coveted alliances with prestigious men, and occasionally even worshiped in Nāyar temples. They avoided the polluting castes lest they indirectly pollute the Nāyar. They also tacitly acknowledged the position of Brāhmaṇs by borrowing many of their customs. They did not proselytize, but were accepted as a sectarian group within Kēraḷa and were divided up into a handful of endogamous castes.

The Syrian Christians maintained certain essential markers of Christianity but borrowed most of the local appurtenances of status, according to the historian William Brown. In church ceremonies they used umbrellas, drums, local musical instruments, and fly whisks. They borrowed elephants from Hindu temples for their processions and erected flagpoles before the churches such as are found before Hindu temples. They consulted horoscopes, used the gold pendant as a wedding symbol, observed pollution after birth and death, kept the ceremony of the first rice feeding for infants, never blew out a flame (to avoid insulting the fire deity), believed in omens, and practiced trial by ordeal. They slept with the head towards the east, and acknowledged Ōṇam, the most important Hindu festival in Kēraḷa, by making cloth presents. Under Brāhmaṇ influence they were marrying off their daughters before puberty, giving them dowry, and keeping their women generally secluded. They remained patrilineal but under the influence of the matrilineal Nāyar gave a son the name of the maternal grandfather and the second son the name of the maternal great-grandfather, while daughters were named from the paternal side.

When the Portuguese arrived, these Christians were not in highest favor with the rāja and therefore opted for the patronage of the new foreign merchants and the Pope. The Catholic clergy insisted that they give up, in addition to Nestorian ideas, three types of "error" locally acquired: the concept of rebirth, resignation to fate as with horoscopes and belief in karma, and the belief that each had to follow his own dharma. Thus Christianity in Kēraḷa was preserved because it did not fight the local ethos but functioned as a caste-cluster within the broader society.

Kēraḷa Christians today have a very high literacy rate and manage numerous educational institutions. They have contributed largely to the intellectual level of Kēraḷa. On the whole they have now been weaned from Hindu influences and the Marthomites are evangelizing. Now they do not function so much within the framework of Hindu society but prefer to identify with the wider Christian world. They do not intermarry with more recent converts to Christianity in Kēraḷa, however, who are generally of low caste origin.

The Matrilineal Nāyar and Māppiḷḷas

A number of matrilineal castes are found in Malabar (north and central Kērala) and Tuluva (the Tulu-speaking Karṇāṭaka coast). Only a quarter of the people of Kērala belong to these castes, and among them the full matrilineal structure has disintegrated, but it has been the subject of considerable anthropological investigation, especially by Kathleen Gough.

The Nāyar are a large caste-cluster who were a martial people and strictly disciplined their soldiers; they also worked as temple servants, noncultivating tenants (managing Brāhmaṇ's lands), village headmen, royal retainers, and petty kings. The Nāyar were ritually quite high, so that in the 18th century an untouchable was not supposed to approach one closer than 64 feet.

Nāyar matrilineages lived in a great house called a *taravāḍ*. A girl born there lived there all her life, and so did a son except when on military service or out for work. A girl was ceremonially married before puberty to a suitable relative of the complementary category according to the Dravidian system, and had the marriage pendant tied around her neck. She was then free to begin having sexual alliances in her room in the taravāḍ. A visiting man would maintain the alliance as long as he wished, while at the same time he and the girl were free to establish other alliances. A man could stay in his girl's room in the taravāḍ only at night, leaving some object of his outside the door so other suitors would know he was there. If children were born, he might bring them small gifts and play with them on occasion, but if he ended the alliance with their mother, he severed connections with them as well. The children were brought up within the taravāḍ, took its name as part of their personal name, and traced their lineage through its ancestress. Thus the unity of the matrilineal family was maintained at the expense of the conjugal family, though this ideal pattern did not prevent many of the Nāyar from setting up conjugal households.

Hypergamy was an integral part of the system; women of each Nāyar jāti married into, or had alliances with, men of their own or a higher jāti, ranging from low temple servants to the royal or chiefly lineages. In late medieval Kērala there was probably greater caste stratification than anywhere else in India. The lowest were of aboriginal origin while groups claiming partial descent from immigrants, such as Nambūtiri Brāhmaṇs, Muslims, and Baṇṭs, tended to acquire rank even higher than that of the Nāyar. The taravāḍ was an exogamous unit, and there were precautions to keep the sexes separate; or several taravāḍs might be linked as an exogamous clan-like group within the jāti. Each taravāḍ had 6 to 30 members or even well over 100.

There was a particularly interesting symbiosis between the Nāyar and Nambūtiri Brāhmaṇs. The Nambūtiris practiced primogeniture; only the

oldest son married and established a family, a practice which had the function of keeping the property intact and limiting the population of this exclusive and elite caste. If the eldest brother failed to continue the family line, a younger brother would do so, but otherwise the younger brothers arranged alliances with Nāyar women. The women coveted such hypergamous alliances. Nambūtiri Brāhmaṇs were not only priests but also landowners and officials. Often the Nāyar would manage the lands of their Brāhmaṇ patrons, but of course hired out the actual cultivation. Alliances of Brāhmaṇ men and Nāyar women were not legal marriages for Brāhmaṇs because they were not conducted with Vedic rites, nor were the children legitimized as Brāhmaṇs. But for the Nāyar, children of such alliances were legitimate and became part of the matrilineal taravāḍ.

The property of each taravāḍ was managed by the eldest brother of the mother. Since lower castes did the laboring work, the Nāyar had leisure, and most Nāyar men and women were literate in Malayāḷam. Agriculture was a fairly complex process, and the proceeds were distributed among the hierarchy of jātis by jajmānī economic reciprocity.

Nāyar matriliny was retained because conditions upon which it rested did not change much until the early 20th century. Brāhmaṇs and rājas continued to own most of the land, managed by the Nāyar or Tīyar and farmed by peasants who were more or less serfs. Villages were largely self-sufficient and their lands delimited, while there were no roads in Malabar itself until a century ago. Cash crops were not much grown until the British established plantations in the hills. The mahārājas of Travancore and Cochin ruled until India became independent, while Malabar was never heavily administered by the British. Until the British disbanded them, the rājas kept their own armies, manned by disciplined Nāyar soldiers. Wherever these soldiers went, they could establish temporary sexual alliances, and this served the state, too, for it prevented the soldiers from becoming attached to domestic affairs.

But in the 20th century the system began to disintegrate, and today probably fewer than 5% of the Nāyar live in matrilineal taravāḍs. Most live in conjugal families which may be matrilocal, avunculocal, patrilocal, or sometimes neolocal. As Kathleen Gough has pointed out, these changes are not the result of any culture contact or borrowing of social systems, but almost inevitably result with reliance on cash crops and wages from professional income, relaxation of the caste hierarchy upon which hypergamy depends, and the spatial mobility and urbanization trends of modern India. Now not only can Nāyar men earn their own living but by law children are eligible to inherit property acquired by their fathers.

Today the Nāyar are conscious of their matrilineal past, and still a man's full name will consist first of his mother's brother's (instead of his father's) name, his house name, and his given name, and finally his caste name. The Nāyar form a rather cohesive caste-cluster, go in for education,

and are active in the endlessly churning politics of Kēraḷa. Most are overtly Hindu, thus distinguishing themselves from the large Christian and Muslim minorities of the state.

Other matrilineal groups include the Tīyar, who are traditionally coconut tree climbers, though many engage in common labor. Even before the 20th century they frequently lived in conjugal households, and of course placed fewer restrictions on their women than did the Nāyar. Today most Tīyar live neolocally, while those toward the south are patrilineal. In politics the Tīyar have manifested a resurgent ethnicity.

The Māppiḷḷas, or Moplas, are Muslims who were, and to some extent still are, matrilineal. They are fairly numerous in northern Kēraḷa, and have part-Arab ancestry. It may appear surprising that Islam could be grafted onto such a family structure, but in fact it was quite convenient for visiting Arab merchants. In early medieval centuries Arabs came to the Malabar coast for wood and vegetable products not available in their arid homeland. They would stay every year for a few months awaiting winds to drive them home. In the meantime they would establish alliances with local women who were happy to have children fathered by such traders with relatively high prestige. In time a part-Arab, Malayāḷam-speaking community grew up. The Māppiḷḷas have been engaged largely in trade, and as a man would spend long periods away from home, he could establish temporary alliances, while a brother would manage the affairs of his sister's household. Probably the most entrenched matrilineal structure to be found today is among Muslims in the Lakshadvīp Islands off Kēraḷa; it is reported that in Minicoy the authority of women is equal to, or perhaps even exceeds, that of men.

Other Minority Groups

The western littoral of the South harbors a number of other unique peoples, only a few of which can be mentioned here. Jews are rumored to have come to Kēraḷa around 72 A.D. as part of the diaspora, and they well might have, for there was trade with the Roman empire at that time. They intermarried little by little and became known as "Black Jews" in contrast with "White Jews" who came fleeing from Spain in the 15th century. In the 18th century there were six clusters of Jews around the port city of Cochin, divided into castes with their separate synagogues; other colonies of Jews were in Gujarāt. Some of the Black Jews have by now lost their identity, and White Jews are so few they have trouble getting a quorum for worship in their synagogue in Cochin. Traditionally the Jews played a role in the society of Kēraḷa as an occupational caste-cluster as well as a sect, for they controlled certain trading and mercantile rights. They were never part of

the agricultural social hierarchy. The largest concentration of Indian Jews today is in Bombay.

The Tuḷus, living in the southern Karṇāṭaka coast and the northern tip of Kēraḷa, number over a million. In many ways this region is similar to traditional Kēraḷa: Brāhmaṇs controlled much of the land and some of the main castes such as Baṇṭs and Billavar have been matrilineal. Because of the isolation bred by geography and their distinctive language they have retained some customs now rare among other Dravidian-speaking peasant populations. Some of their wooden temples have hook-swinging posts set in front, regularly used until the 1930s. A devotee is swung around the post suspended on hooks in the flesh of his back, a practice still reported to occur in several other parts of the South, though rarely. Tuḷus have unique local deities, a distinctive style of temple car, and some old Jain practices, besides the sport of bull racing. As there is practically no literature in Tuḷu, they learn Kannaḍa in school.

Farther north on the Karṇāṭaka coast is a Negroid people called Sidhis, numbering only 3000. They are of interest because though so few, they are divided into Christians, Muslims, and Hindus. In pre-Portuguese times when Arab traders frequented these coasts, they brought slaves from Africa who have been absorbed elsewhere as in Kēraḷa and Sri Lanka, and only here have they formed a distinct community. They have frizzly hair, but retain no observed remnants of African culture.

Goā, now part of India after four and a half centuries of Portuguese rule, is topographically like the Karṇāṭaka coast. The fine harbor was an attraction long before the Portuguese arrived, and the language of Goā, Konkaṇī, is a distinctive Indo-Āryan one that may have been brought to this port from farther north many centuries ago. (One should not confuse this language with the region called Konkaṇ, the coast of Mahārāshṭra, where Marāṭhī is spoken.) Because Goā with its 900,000 people has a distinct cultural heritage it has so far resisted assimilation into any neighboring state. Some 5000 Goānese, mostly of mixed ancestry, speak Portuguese as mother tongue, and a third of them are Catholics.

There are various other distinctive peoples in and around the Western Ghāṭs, such as the tribal Toḍas and Koṭas well known to anthropologists. In southern Karṇāṭaka there is a region called Coorg where the people, Koḍagus, have retained consciousness of their pleasant little civilization. They have been made famous by Srinivas' study of them, on which he based his theory of Sanskritization. A major ethnic group in Karṇāṭaka is the Lingāyats, a sect which rejects Brāhmaṇism but in other respects are similar to Hindus. Spread throughout the state, they have their own caste hierarchy, and most are owner-cultivators. Ishwaran discusses them in his chapter in *South Asia: Seven Community Profiles.*

Anglo-Indians (Eurasians) are found in all major cities. In the South

they are concentrated in Bangalore and Madras, where numbers of Englishmen lived. Typically they are Christians, speak English at home, and have a negative attitude toward Indian languages. They prefer only Western dress and eat what they imagine to be English cooking, using English table manners. They generally refuse to do common labor, though some have skilled jobs. During the British period many supervisory jobs and professions were open to them, as well as well-paying skilled work such as engine

Anglo-Indian at station in Karṇāṭaka. He affects behavior of British elite, with coat, pipe, and dogs; he would not care to eat in the vegetarian restaurant behind him.

Washing steps of Buddhist *dāgäba* in highland Sri Lanka.

driving. But now they find it difficult to maintain their style of life and some are in difficult straits. They have no links with the countryside. Sometimes other Indians comment that they must be descended from untouchable women, as respectable caste women would not have made themselves available to English soldiers and officers. Numbers of Anglo-Indians have emigrated to Canada or Australia. Those who remain are slowly learning to take pride in being Indians rather than British, and are acquiring fluency in Indian languages. As they continue to do so, their distinctive contribution to Indian society will receive due appreciation.

Sri Lanka, Maldives, and Mauritius

Since Sri Lanka is discussed in Chapters 6 and 18 and elsewhere in this book, further description is not necessary here. The reader is referred to Obeyesekere's excellent study of a Sinhala village in *South Asia: Seven Community Profiles*. Among the anthropological studies made in the island, those by Yalman, Wijesekera, and Leach are especially notable.

The resemblances between Sri Lanka and Kēraḷa are fascinating, in spite of the great differences in language and religion. The two regions are similar in appearance: humid palm-studded lowlands intersected by many waterways, having a dispersed settlement pattern, backed up by 7000-foot hills. Not only does Sri Lanka have the Dravidian kinship pattern (expressed in Indo-Āryan terminology), but it also has matriliny in certain areas. Younger brother succession to the throne was historically found in both. Women's dress is similar, and so are foods: rice-flour string-hoppers eaten for breakfast, rice and coconut pressed in bamboo and cooked, fish curry preparations. Both were historically subject to the same influences coming by sea from North India and the Mediterranean, with settlements of Christians, numbers of converts to Islam, and the impact of the Portuguese.

The revival of Sinhala language and Buddhist culture since Independence is a corollary of the Dravidian movement. Some 30% of the people of the island, however, are Tamiḻs, centered in the town of Jaffna and other parts of the north, and Colombo. Among these are 1.2 million Tamiḻs of Indian origin, brought by the British to work the tea and rubber estates. Most of them are not Sri Lanka citizens and are listed in its census as "Indians" because their votes are not wanted by the Sinhalas, though they were born on the island and are now stateless persons. An agreement was worked out with India to send 500,000 of them back, but few have gone. The main tensions in the island since Independence have been those between the Sinhalas and Tamiḻs, but of late this has been superseded by political tensions arising out of the deteriorating economic situation in relation to rising economic expectations.

The Andaman and Nicobar Islands, lying south of Burma, are governed as a separate Indian Territory. While the Nicobars are populated by the Nicobarese, the original Andamanese have practically become extinct. The Andamans are now populated by Indians brought there when it was a British penal colony, plus a few Burmese, and by numbers of recent Hindī- and Bāngālī-speaking arrivals, together with some Uṛiyās, Telugus, and Tamiḻs. Because the Andamans are large islands and the population density is only 40 per square mile, the Indian government has been encouraging immigration and homesteading, creating something of a frontier atmosphere. The main source of income is export of lumber and the Indian naval station

at Port Blair (because of which the government does not allow foreign visitors to the islands).

The Lakshadvīp (formerly called Laccadive) Islands, off the coast of Kēraḷa, are peopled by Muslims speaking a dialect of Malayāḷam. These islands constitute a separate Indian Territory, and the chief problem is population, for the density is a devastating 2600 per square mile. Historic links are with Kēraḷa, and there are traditions of matriliny, described by Leela Dube. The main basis of the economy is fish, sold to Kēraḷa.

The Maldives are 400–500 miles southwest of Sri Lanka; they comprise about 1000 coral islands, 200 of which are populated, including 19 atolls. Maldivian is close to Sinhala, which shows the origin of most of the population, but in the 12th century the people were all converted to Sunnī Islam. Subsequently the Portuguese, the Dutch, and the English occupied the islands, and in 1965 they became independent.

Because of the eight centuries of Islam, the ideal of the social order is based on the Sharī'at, and the government was traditionally a sultanate. Fish and the coconut trees are about the only resources, and the latter provides not only food and material for housing, but coir (fiber) for ropes and mats, the production of which is women's work. The men go fishing in boats made of coconut wood fitted with sails and venture out as far as 20 miles. Export of fish to Sri Lanka provides the only income for these crowded islands, whose economic prospects are not optimistic. In spite of infrequent transportation connections, change is becoming apparent even here; for example, women in the capital, Malé, who were formerly secluded, have begun to walk in the streets.

Mauritius, lying 500 miles east of Madagascar, was uninhabited until modern times. Today 66% of the population is of Indian origin, with the rest Africans, Creoles, and a few French. The Indians came as indentured workers to labor in the sugar cane fields, and after paying off their indentures, established villages over the island. Here too, the main problem is population, since it is a tenth the size of New Jersey but has 830,000 people who have to be supported off the export of sugar plus whatever shipping and tourist income the government can generate.

Burton Benedict has studied the social structure of the Indian population of Mauritius. Indians came between 1836 and 1924, mostly from the ports of Calcutta and Madras; immigration records show that they belonged to a number of linguistic groups and that a full range of castes was represented. What has happened, briefly, is that endogamy has remained the most persistent feature of caste up to the present, and for a time women were imported to make this possible. The larger castes, especially of the numerically larger North Indian groups, have retained their identity better than the castes of smaller linguistic groups, which have decreased in number. There were originally so many castes that they were not organized structurally, but a hierarchy of status symbols especially denoting the Kshatriya

and Camār categories evolved. Occupational specialization according to caste inevitably disappeared because all worked on plantations at first. Caste is not defended now on a religious basis, nor are there commensality restrictions; to the extent that it persists, it is as a cultural category, not structural. It is possible for individuals to claim a new rank by moving to the capital, Port Louis.

The linguistic and religious categories are proving more significant. Muslims, Telugus, and Tamils in particular have resisted assimilation into the numerically dominant North Indian category, and marriage across these lines is rare. Marāṭhīs also have remained distinct, but now are tending to identify with the North Indians as they are few in number. Christian Indians may marry Christians of African or mixed African descent. In villages with a predominance of Hindus there will be a number of socioreligious organizations, but no caste panchāyats. The organizations focus on orthodox North Indian Hindus as against Ārya Samājīs, high as against low castes, or South Indians as against North Indians. In villages in which Hindus form a minority even some of these differences may be submerged, and North and South Indians may share a temple.

Formation of Linguistic States in South India

Because the Congress Party had been committed for decades to the principle of linguistic states, after Independence the Central Government broke up the odd-shaped administrative monster that was Madras Presidency and merged the princely states such as Mysore, Travancore, Cochin, and Dravidian-speaking parts of Hyderābād into four southern linguistic states. There was some delay in the separation of the Tamil and Telugu regions because both claimed the city of Madras.

Prominent Indians gave warnings that this might ultimately threaten the unity of India. These warnings came largely from politicians whose paramount aim for India was maintenance of a centralized political system as opposed to the cultural integrity of its parts, or else they had a commitment to Western values such as the maintenance of English and evolution of uniform mass-culture. They spoke darkly of "fissiparous tendencies." And it is indeed true that formation of linguistic states has fostered a set of regional loyalties which are often expressed in promotion of the state languages, and in the case of South India, involved resistance to further penetration by North Indian cultural values. There has also been considerable dissatisfaction with the centralized economic planning generated from Delhi, to the extent that some of the southern states have threatened to proceed with industrial enterprises not included in the Five-Year Plans.

The largest of the four southern states, Āndhra, had 43.4 million people in 1971, mostly speaking Telugu. This state selected Hyderābād as its

capital, and though it is a fair city, it had the disadvantage of having been the capital of the Muslim princely state of Hyderābād and was dominated by an Urdū-speaking Muslim elite. This factor retarded the full acceptance of Telugu at all levels of government, while the Muslims were slow to acknowledge that their erstwhile prerogatives and the status of Urdū could not continue in the new populism. However, the Telugus have experienced a resurgence of interest in their history, from the early Buddhist monuments and the Sātavāhana empire up to Vijayanagara; they are deeply attached to the soil of Āndhra and to its culture but have not expressed such animosity towards the North as have the Tamiḻs. Telugu literature is developing rapidly and the state government is implementing its commitment to the use of Telugu as the medium of instruction in colleges and universities, but without the purging of Sanskrit words such as occurs in Tamiḻ Naḍu. The chief political problem has been the persistent demand for the formation of a separate Telugu-speaking state by Telengāna, the northwestern lobe, which was part of Hyderābād and maintains certain prerogatives therefrom, whereas the delta districts are populous and central to Telugu culture. The demand for splitting the state reached a high pitch in 1973, with the Central Government holding out against it. Indices of economic growth are only moderate and literacy (24.6% of the total population) is below the all-India average (29.3%). But the economy remains stable because of the large surplus of rice produced in the riverine lowlands.

Karṇāṭaka was formed by the fusion of the princely state of Mysore with parts of Bombay Presidency and Hyderābād state. The old Mysore princely government was an enlightened one and promoted irrigation works and industry, while its people maintained a conscious distinctiveness from North India in food, dress, and linguistic purity. But the northern parts of Karṇāṭaka have been much influenced by Mahārāshṭra; men don their dhotis in the North Indian fashion, and Marāṭhī words have been borrowed even for numerals. Since the formation of Karṇāṭaka as a linguistic state a new regional pride has developed. Its history is available in tens of thousands of stone inscriptions. The princely architecture of old Mysore city is vaunted as symbolic of the past, while the architecture of the new state capital at Bangalore, highly decorated with Indian motifs, is symbolic of the larger linguistic area. Bangalore has developed aircraft, telephone, machine tool, and other industries. Official use of Kannaḍa is increasing, while literacy stands slightly above the all-India average.

Kēraḷa is a very interesting state because of its cultural heterogeneity. Its terrain provides a feast for tired eyes: verdant mountains, palm-strewn lowlands, miles of placid backwaters, and gleaming beach sands. Malayāḷis take a pragmatic view of Hindī and the North because so many of them have to migrate out for work, yet there is a fond attachment to symbols of regional identity. Malayāḷam literature shows more vitality than that of any

other Indian language in the genres of the novel and drama, while a surprising number of newspapers flourish. People love their local strains of rice, local foods made with lots of coconut or tapioca, and local dress. While Malayāḷis may take jobs in Panjāb, Iran, or Singapore, they always return to their homestead; one can see them on the train approaching the mountain border of the state, taking off their pants and shoes in favor of their loose-fitting dhoti and sandals. Literacy is over 60% (of the population, including infants), double the all-India rate, and colleges have sprouted like gas stations in America, yet the problems of this state seem beyond solution. Opportunities for employment are extremely scarce; industries are few and labor problems produce hostility. Over-qualified people fill routine jobs, frustrated and poor. The state has twice elected Communist governments, but any government here seems inherently unstable. In addition the state is the most densely populated in India.

Dravidian Cultural Revivalism

The movement to revive Dravidian cultural distinctiveness has found fullest expression since Independence in Tamiḻ Nāḍu, and also to some extent in Karṇāṭaka. Its roots go to the cleavage in medieval society between the small Brāhmaṇ minority, who remained more distinctive in the South than Brāhmaṇs in the North, and the non-Brāhmaṇ cultivating castes. Brāhmaṇs not only controlled temple wealth but held much land in the most fertile and populous regions, and preempted classical learning. When the British came they were the first to go in for English education, and consequently came to dominate the bureaucracy.

The gradual decline of the power of Brāhmaṇs at the village level occurred as they moved into professions and took up residence in urban places, and as the government implemented land reform laws and introduced panchāyat village government on a regular basis. In Béteille's description of a Tanjāvūr village (Chap. 8) we can see the shift of power from the Brāhmaṇ section of the village to the dominant agricultural castes. In 1917 the non-Brāhmaṇ movement became effective with the issuing of the Justice Party newspaper, which put pressure on the British government to end its patronage of the Brāhmaṇ elite. In the 1930s more newspapers appeared which dwelt on the alleged duplicity and bigotry of Brāhmaṇs. Popular Tamiḻ leaders initiated what came to be called the Self-Respect Movement, which urged people to shun the services of Brāhmaṇs and not to use their rites in wedding ceremonies. A similar movement got under way in Karṇāṭaka.

After Independence a Dravidian society was launched and from it evolved the DMK party (Tirāvita Munnēṟṟa Kaḻakam, Dravidian Advancement Society). Propaganda shifted from direct attacks on Brāhmaṇs as a

caste group to attacks on obscurantism and intellectual dishonesty, and broadened the sentiment to an anti-North stance. Brāhmaṇs were seen as symbols of the vast cultural pressure exerted from North India, and DMK leaders urged people to shun Hindī and purify Tamil̠ of Sanskrit loan words.

Until 1965 the DMK advocated secession from India and its leaders publicly burned the Indian flag. There were anti-Hindī, anti-North riots in 1964 in which a number of trains (Central Government property) were burned, and foreign visitors were harassed until they expressed pro-Tamil̠ sympathy. Any object symbolic of "Hindī imperialism" came under the attack of eager youths. But the secessionist demand was given up on urging from the Central Government, and the DMK was swept into office in Tamil̠ Nāḍu in 1967 on a pro-Tamil̠ platform—language was almost the only issue and the party said little of economic or other plans. The DMK was again elected in the 1971 elections, and Tamil̠ Nāḍu was the only state whose people gave a clear mandate to one party in opposition to Indira Gandhi's Congress Party.

This movement is a modern-day nativistic revival, which differs from the ones anthropologists have observed among smaller and less sophisticated population groups elsewhere in the world chiefly in its lack of a cult. The charismatic leader, Annadurai the golden-tongued, spellbound audiences of tens of thousands. He made unrealistic promises, such as rice at half the going rate. Instead of utilizing a cult, however, Annadurai stressed rejection of all Brāhmaṇical rites and the deities of Sanskrit literature, indeed of the whole formal Hindu structure. Leaders of the movement declared themselves atheists, and though they did not press this point while campaigning, after attaining power in 1967 the new state government ordered all pictures of Hindu deities (such as are ubiquitous on the walls of homes, stores, and offices) to be removed from government premises. The order received only partial compliance, and of late the state government has been patronizing statues of early indigenous Tamil̠ heroes and deities.

Though all the Indian arts suffered a precipitous decline during British rule, they now have a new lease on life, especially in such areas as Tamil̠ Nāḍu where they are conceived of as part of the expression of indigenous culture. Societies have been formed to stimulate the revitalization of the major dance forms, and South Indian music concerts are available in Madras almost nightly. In the 1960s temples began to repaint the multifarious figures on their towers which had suffered neglect for centuries. And South Indians are pushing export of their peculiar foods to North India and indeed overseas. School textbooks in Tamil̠ Nāḍu overplay the Indus Civilization, implying that it was created by Tamil̠s, and have reduced the content of North Indian history. There has been a growing feeling of unity with the millions of overseas Tamil̠s in Sri Lanka, Malaysia, Singapore, Burma, Fiji, and Africa. The DMK government is the only state government in India that does not require students in school to study at least a little

Hindī. The obstinancy of Tamil̲ Nāḍu and West Bengal on the Hindī issue has been the chief political impediment to switching to Hindī for all functions of the Central Government, and the southerners keep reiterating Nehru's promises that Hindī would not be "imposed."

Revival of religious art. Newly constructed facade with multicolored scenes of gods, heroes, and devotees, at Pal̲ani temple, Tamil̲ Nāḍu.

There is no doubt that this cultural revival has had effect in economics and other indices of modernization. Literacy in the state is a third higher than for India as a whole, the majority of villages are electrified, bus service is very frequent, and the annual economic growth rate has been relatively high. The formation of linguistic states, though a real threat to the unity of India in the 1960s, seems now to have passed that stage and its beneficial results are being seen in the use of the people's languages for government and education, in a renaissance of the arts, and in a regional self-confidence which in some states at least is generating economic growth.

REFERENCES AND NOTES

[1] Adapted from *Census of India, 1961*, II, Part ix, Map 143.

[2] Adapted from data in Bhabananda Mukherjee, "Marriage Customs and Kinship Organization of the Urali of Travancore," *Bull. Dept. Anthro.* I, No. 2 (1952), pp. 37–55.

[3] Yalman, p. 357.

[4] Hiebert, p. 41.

IMPORTANT SOURCES

Aiyappan, A. *Social Revolution in a Kerala Village.* London, 1965. (The author revisited the village 40 years after the first study.)

Beals, Alan. "Dravidian Kinship and Marriage," in Andrée Sjoberg (ed.), *Symposium on Dravidian Civilization.* Austin, Tex., 1971.

———. *Gopalpur, A South Indian Village.* New York, 1961. (A popular case study of a village in Karṇāṭaka.)

Beck, Brenda. *Peasant Society in Koṅku: A Study of Right and Left Subcastes in South India.* Vancouver, 1972. (A detailed study of society and religion in Tamil̲ Nāḍu.)

Benedict, Burton. *Indians in a Plural Society.* London, 1961. (Mauritius.)

Béteille, André. *Caste, Class, and Power.* Berkeley, Calif., 1965. (Excellent study of social relations in a Tanjāvūr village, Tamil̲ Nāḍu.)

Brown, William. *The Indian Christians of St. Thomas.* Cambridge, England, 1956.

Dube, Leela. *Matriliny and Islam: Religion and Society in the Laccadives.* Delhi, n.d.

Dube, S. C. *Indian Village.* London, 1955. (Pioneer study of a village near Hyderābād.)

Dumont, Louis. "Hierarchy and Marriage Alliance in South Indian Kinship," *Occasional Papers of the Royal Anthro. Inst.*, 1957.

———. "Marriage in India, the Present State of the Question," in *Contributions to Indian Sociology* V (1961), VII (1964), and IX (1966).

———. *Une Sous-Caste de l'Inde du Sud. Organisation sociale et religion des Pramalai Kallar.* Paris, 1957.

Epstein, T. S. *Economic Development and Social Change in South India.* New York, 1962. (Pioneer study of economics of a Karṇāṭaka village.)

Gough, K. E. "Brahman Kinship in a Tamil Village," in E. R. Leach (ed.), *Aspects of Caste in Southern India, Ceylon, and North-West Pakistan.* Cambridge, England, 1960.

———, in David Schneider and K. Gough (eds.), *Matrilineal Kinship.* Berkeley, Calif., 1961. (With chapters on the Nāyar, Tīyar, and Māppil̲las.)

Gover, Charles. *The Folk-Songs of Southern India.* Madras, 1959.

Hiebert, Paul. *Konduru.* Minneapolis, Minn., 1971. (A readable and balanced study of an Āndhra village.)

Irshick, Eugene. *Politics and Social Conflict in South India: The Non-Brahman Movement and Tamil Separatism, 1916–1929.* Berkeley, Calif., 1969.

Iyer, A. K. *The Mysore Tribes and Castes.* Mysore, 1935.

Karve, Irawati. *Kinship Organization in India*, 2d ed. New York, 1965.

Kutty, A. R. *Marriage and Kinship in an Island Society*. Delhi, 1972. (A Lakshadvīp island.)

Leach, E. R. *Pul Eliya, A Village in Ceylon*. Cambridge, England, 1961.

Mayer, Adrian. *Land and Society in Malabar*. Bombay, 1952.

McCormack, William. "Factionalism in a Mysore Village," in Richard Park (ed.), *Leadership and Political Institutions in India*. Princeton, N.J., 1959.

Mencher, Joan, and Helen Goldberg. "Kinship and Marriage Regulations among the Namboodiri Brahmans of Kerala," *Man* (New Series) II (1967).

Nanjundayya, H. V. *The Mysore Tribes and Castes*, 4 vols. Mysore, 1931.

Nilakanta Sastri, K. A. *A History of South India*. Madras, 1958. (The standard work, with some description of social institutions.)

Ryan, Bryce. *Caste in Modern Ceylon*. New Brunswick, N.J., 1953.

Srinivas, M. N. *Religion and Society among the Coorgs of South India*. London, 1952.

Subrahmaniam, N. *Sangam Polity*. New York, 1966. (Ancient Tamiḻ society from literary sources.)

Thurston, Edgar. *Tribes and Castes of Southern India*. Madras, 1909. (A vast compendium of data gathered by officials; an invaluable source.)

Wijesekera, N. D. *The People of Ceylon*, 2d ed. Colombo, 1965. (An inside view of most aspects of Sinhala life.)

Yalman, Nur. *Under the Bo Tree: Studies in Caste, Kinship, and Marriage in the Interior of Ceylon*. Berkeley, Calif., 1967.

12

Survey of Eastern Indian Plains and Bangladesh

Bānglā (referring to the whole region otherwise known as Bengal) is a vast alluvium over 250 miles wide containing 125 million people. There is no physical boundary separating the state of West Bengal from Bangladesh, only the political boundary which separates the part having a Hindu majority from that having a Muslim majority. In other respects the people of the Bānglā plain are quite homogeneous, speaking the same language. The geographical parameters of this plain produced by the confluence of the Gangā and Brahmaputra river systems have determined the bounds of Bāngālī and the culture it represents.

An extension of the Bānglā plain is the 400-mile-long, tail-like Assam Valley, a cul-de-sac in which an offshoot of Bāngālī culture has found root, albeit superimposed on people of tribal origin. Another extension of the Bānglā plain runs southwestward and incorporates the Mahānadī delta and the coastal plain of Orissa. This region is cut off from the Hindī-speakers of Madhya Pradesh by the high hills and tribal populations of western Orissa, and at its southern end one suddenly encounters Telugu-speakers and cultural patterns associated with Dravidian speech. But the Uṛiyā-speakers of Orissa, though considerably influenced by Bānglā, have had a history somewhat independent of it. A further extension of the Bānglā plain

is the long coast of Chittagong District, the southeastward projection of Bangladesh, where Bāngālīs have penetrated into Ārākānese culture such as predominates in southwestern Burma. Lesser extensions of the Bānglā plain include the valley of Kāchār, now part of Assam, and the lowlands of Tripurā, a former princely state which is now one of the eastern hill mini-states of the Indian Union and has a substantial tribal population. Along the whole eastern and northern flank of Bānglā as soon as the plains give way to hills, one encounters tribal people whose cultures have more affinity with Southeast Asia and the eastern Himālayas, and on the western edge of the plains too one encounters the tribes of the Choṭā Nāgpur hills of eastern central India. But the Bānglā plain and its extensions clearly comprise a regional variant of Indic culture and civilization.

The Land and Agriculture

A glance at a map will show how this plain is intersected with scores of rivers, with numbers of distributaries continually building up the delta and forming numerous islands in the Bay of Bengal. The problem here is a surfeit of water, although before the spring monsoon the soil may get dry and hard. The economy is naturally agricultural, mostly devoted to "wet land" crops—rice, jute, and sugar cane. Dependence upon these crops makes peasant life here quite different than in the western plains of South Asia. Most rural labor is devoted to production, processing, and distribution of rice.

Bāngālī Hindu peasants, especially women, know how rice first came there. Lakshmī herself, goddess of prosperity, brought it down to earth for cultivation. Indeed, Lakshmī is paddy (unhusked rice) personified. Once there was a very poor cowherd whose lamentations came to the ears of Lakshmī and Nārāyaṇa as they were making a journey overhead in the sky. Lakshmī asked Nārāyaṇa to help the poor boy, but Nārāyaṇa replied that it was Lakshmī who had the power to do so. Thus fortified with her consort's permission, Lakshmī came down to earth and handed some paddy seeds over to the boy and advised:

> Take these, and poverty and sorrow will remain away from you. When the rains set in, go and sow these seeds in your fields. The plants will grow up and bear numerous fruits. When they take on the color of gold like that of my body, and a sweet-smelling odor, as if of my person, comes out of them, you reap the fruits and bring them home.

When the seeds came up and the grain ripened, lo, it was indeed lit with the color of gold like Lakshmī herself, and had a heavenly fragrance, as if the presence of the goddess was manifest in it.[1] For this reason the harvest months are times when she is especially worshiped.

The traditional methods of cultivation are employed with little change today. During the summer months rainfall and floods produce enough standing water in the fields so channel irrigation is not necessary. There is a finely tuned symbiotic relationship between man, cattle, and the land. People fertilize the fields with manure, ashes, and leaves; they plow and level with oxen motive power; they sow the seedlings in plots and after sprouting they are transplanted individually by hand into all the fields; next the people weed and hoe; they cut the grain with sickles and thresh it by hand or with oxen. They store it in giant baskets in their houses or transport it by boat for sale. Now there are new strains of paddy, and water can be pumped for an extra crop in the dry season.

Sugar cane was once widely grown on lands of the landowning castes who could obtain sufficient labor for the tiresome process of planting and transplanting, cutting, and pressing. Sugar cane production fell off after Independence as more peasants, especially in eastern Bānglā, came to own their own land and found raising this crop too tiresome. But now production is on the increase because of high demand for sugar and easier methods of handling; whereas formerly the cane had to be crushed in rollers powered by huge wheels revolved by four men, now a type of toothed cylinder press can be powered by oxen, or the cane can be sent to mills.

Jute is grown over a considerable area in Bangladesh and has been increasing in importance in West Bengal. It yields a fiber which is made into gunny sacks. The Bānglā plains produce most of the world's jute, which is also locally processed into fabrics. Jute provides the main cash income for many peasants, and also is the chief earner of foreign exchange for Bangladesh.

Settlement Patterns

Bānglā today has a denser population than any other comparable area in the world. In 1961 West Bengal had 35 million people, and by 1971 it had increased 32% to 44.4 million; with a population of about 70 million for Bangladesh, this alluvial region has a density of about 1300 per square mile! Including the Bāngālīs in Assam and neighboring states, Bāngālī is numerically the sixth language of the world, with 130 million speakers.

The population is rural to a surprising degree. Assam and Orissa are both a little over 8% urban. West Bengal is 24% urban, but excluding the connurbation of Calcutta with its seven million people, the population of the state is only 7% urban. The figure for Bangladesh is really astonishing; in 1961 only 5.2% were living in towns and cities, though this is the most densely populated significant country in the world. It is not known to what extent this has altered since the 1971 war, but Dacca has bloated.

Small clusters of houses, or even single homesteads, are scattered

everywhere, wherever land can be found a little higher than the level of the water which annually inundates the fields. Land may be built up for house sites. But seen from the air there is a pattern to the location of settlements over this vast alluvium; the clusters of houses tend to form concentric crescents, built on soil raised two or three feet above the surrounding terrain. These are old river banks, which retain their rows and clusters of homesteads long after the river has moved away, while the former broad river beds become rice fields which naturally flood in the monsoon. But these configurations can scarcely be seen except from the air. In parts of West Bengal, Assam, and Tripurā where the drainage is slightly steeper and dendritic patterns may be seen, settlement patterns tend to be linear.

Bangladesh potter going to market. Path meanders through rice fields and banana trees. Most of what is consumed must be produced from the alluvial soil.

One of the most important features of settlement here, then, is the dispersed nature of the homesteads; these are divided into villages not in terms of geographical layout but as socially defined villages—a point carefully made by Peter Bertocci in his chapter on a Bangladesh village in the companion volume. Where nucleated villages do get established they tend to consist of houses amorphously clustered around a rectangular center. Each house or group of houses occupied by relatives generally is surrounded by a thicket of bamboo, trees, and banana plants, providing a cool atmosphere and some privacy—a beloved feature of rural Bāngālī life. It is easy to be deceived about the population when passing through the countryside. One might drive 30 miles in Bangladesh and see only two small market towns, but the number of homesteads is not apparent because of the vegetation surrounding them—and this in an area having 2000 per square mile.

But the Santāls construct their villages differently. Santāls are a large Muṇḍa-speaking tribal group that is centered in the central Indian plateau but has expanded here and there onto the Bānglā plains. They not only build their houses on high and dry places, but cut down the vegetation

around them. Houses are built in a row, with the headman's house in the middle and a place for a deity and entertainment.

In this part of South Asia houses are predominantly kaccā, with walls of mud or matting, and roofs of thatch. Where bamboo is available it is a favorite building material. In West Bengal where there are some larger villages and more status differential, there are here and there brick houses with tile roofs, but in Bangladesh one can go through many communities having no brick buildings. Sometimes corrugated iron is used for roofs. In the southern low-lying islands of both parts of Bānglā, houses are constructed especially simply because of the imminent danger of floods and winds; it is here that cyclones strike annually, taking many thousands of lives.

In spite of their simplicity, the homes are pleasant, each flanked by a courtyard and surrounded by vegetation; often several houses of brothers or other relatives are clustered together, each having a separate kitchen shed. There may be a cattle shed, granary, straw stack, and refuse pit, and preferably the homestead will be on the edge of a body of water, perhaps a rectangular tank storing water for use on the fields after the monsoon. People bathe and wash their crockery here. The premises of the houses are kept quite clean and the courtyard and floor smeared with cow-dung wash. A distinctive Bāngālī architectural feature is to have the roof ridge slightly arched so that the eave arches over the doorway in the middle of the long side, while the four corners droop. This feature is mostly seen now on older houses, but was replicated in small masonry temples over the eastern Indian plains.

Hindu Castes and Kinship

Bānglā is quite homogeneous in culture, except for the distinction between Muslims and Hindus. Ralph Nicholas has suggested that the region may be considered as a frontier with population spilling over into it from the middle Gangā. Even in the 19th century there were considerable areas of forest and pasturage, and Englishmen went out to shoot Bengal tigers (which are down to about 1500 today). Assam is an even more recent frontier. Hence some of the complexities of society found in the Indian heartland are attenuated in the peasant culture of Bānglā. Also because of the dispersed settlement pattern large villages and incipient urbanization have not been as common as in western India, and hence social stratification has not been as complex.

Nicholas describes a village in Midnapur District of West Bengal which is rather typical. It has 597 persons, and the 108 households are strung out over a mile. The village has only 6 castes; 77% are members of the

Māhishya caste, while there are 11 families of the Vaishṇava faith who are mostly descended from Māhishyas and are equal to them in rank. There are 11 Muslim Weaver households in a compact neighborhood and in addition 2 households each of Fishermen, Washermen, and special Brāhmaṇs serving Māhishyas and Vaishṇavas. Here 86% of villagers are equal in caste rank. There is no brick building in the village; all houses are kaccā. According to Schwartzberg's survey in this district, villages have fewer than 8 castes each. Artisan castes are concentrated in a few locations, but so thickly settled is the region that a group of artisans clustered in a single village will have a potential clientele of some 80,000 persons within a radius of 5 miles.

Most land is owned by small cultivators, but three caste-clusters have acquired wealth through landowning and have become prominent in Calcutta: Brāhmaṇs, Kāyasthas (scribes), and Baidyās (doctors). Brāhmaṇism appeared relatively late in Bānglā, and it is evident that some of the Brāhmaṇs of the region are local castes which have attained that grade. Kāyasthas acquired wealth through landowning, and this caste crystallized and became prestigious only about the 12th century. Kāyasthas were the most numerous clean caste-cluster in eastern Bānglā before partition in 1947, upon which most of them came over to India. Calcutta has a disproportionate number of them, and they have contributed significantly to the brilliant intellectual life of that city. Baidyās are not mentioned in old texts, but the caste model jelled in recent centuries under Brāhmaṇical aegis.

While Māhishyas are a numerous cultivating caste in the southern part of West Bengal, Goālās (Ahīrs, cowherds) are cultivators in the north; Namaśūdras are another large cultivating group. The Scheduled Castes all seem to be aboriginal or tribal people incorporated into the system: Bāgdīs, Harīs, Mucīs, Bhuiyās, and the Bhūmij are among the aboriginals now considered as low castes, in addition to the Santāls who are numerous and maintain their language so they are more or less outside the Hindu social system. These form a third of the population in the western lobe of West Bengal.

The kinship system idealized by Bāngālī Hindus is generally the same as in the rest of North India. An important distinguishing feature, however, is the Dayābhāgā system of inheritance, according to which ancestral property is held and controlled by the father until his death, and he can give it to whom he will whether it is self-earned or inherited. In contrast, the Mitāksharā system used in most of the rest of India specifies that a man and his sons hold the land in common and the latter can claim their shares at any time. The Dayābhāgā system also obtains in Bihār. British law courts in Calcutta and Paṭnā upheld it, and it became the basis for their Hindu law code. Karve suggests that the exaggerated reverence for the father which was institutionalized in Bāngālī literature was due to the fact that

he held all the property, and where the joint family operates it is because the members have a common kitchen and worship together, rather than because they hold the land in common.

Though caste hierarchy is less on the Bānglā plains than in any other major region of India, an extreme form of hypergamy developed in the urban areas, lasting in Calcutta until the last century. This system was known as Kulīnism after the Kulīn Brāhmaṇs who emerged as the elite in the region. There appeared a hierarchical chain having a surplus of unmarried girls at the top and a shortage at the bottom. To get its girl married a wife-giving family would give a large dowry. This made it attractive to Kulīn men to accumulate several brides, each with her dowry, and the practice became institutionalized to the extent that the women stayed in their natal homes and were occasionally visited by their Kulīn husbands, which was considered an honor for the girl's family. It is reported that there was an abnormally high suicide rate among high caste Bāngālī girls. In Calcutta now, however, caste distinctions are less than in most Indian cities, and one does not talk about caste in polite society, though people will generally marry children off within the caste.

Muslim Society and the Family

Muslims comprised 81% of the population of East Pakistan in 1961; in Bangladesh today the percentage might be slightly higher because throughout the 1960s Hindus emigrated to India. Islam came to Bānglā as early as the 9th and 10th centuries with Arab merchants who visited the coast and won converts; further conversions occurred as the effects of the Delhi Sultanate and the Mughal regime reached the eastern plains.

A great many Bangladesh Muslims call themselves Śekh (Shaikh), the category supposed to have genealogies going back to those Arabs who assisted Muhammad when he fled to Medina. But there is little noticeable foreign admixture in the population and obviously most converts to Islam came from middle and lower castes of Buddhists and Hindus. Nicholas thinks the claim to Śekh status came about because every village was touched by Sūfī preachers who were almost invariably called Śekh, and their converts modeled themselves after these holy men. Genealogies can be rearranged to accord with economic fortunes; a village leader might style himself Khān and claim Mughal or Paṭhān ancestry, or a landowner might discover that he is a Sayyid, a descendant of the Prophet. Caudhuris and Majumdārs claim descent from former officers and landowners, while there are also Muslim occupational castes such as Weavers and Writers. Of the Hindu population of Bangladesh, over half are Scheduled Castes who engage in occupations respectable Muslim agriculturalists shun.

The joint family is idealized by Muslims as well as by Hindus. A

married son may live in a separate house in the homestead, and if he quarrels with his parents or brothers, he and his wife can establish a separate shed for cooking, an act considered separation. Misunderstandings within the family are commonly attributed by men to women's quarrels. An important factor in retention of the joint family ideal is the small size of the farms, averaging 1.5 to 1.7 acres for a family of six in the more populous parts of the country. Muslims do not adopt sons as Hindus do.

Among Muslims marriage of both cross and parallel cousins is permitted, indeed often encouraged. Sister exchange is also favored as it saves on wedding expenses. Polygyny is permitted under Islamic law but is seldom practiced, though occasionally a man may take on his deceased brother's wife and provide for her. Girls are often married by the age of 14 to avert the possibility of any furtive romance developing between marriageable cousins.

There are three ceremonies performed in connection with Muslim marriage, as described by Hafeez Zaidi. The first is the engagement, arranged when the parents or guardians of the boy visit the home of the girl and present clothing and toilet articles for her, with sweets, betel leaves, and areca nuts for all. The date of the wedding is set and the terms of transaction recorded in a formal document. It is thought that a Muslim marriage should be simpler and less costly than a Hindu marriage but Muslims, as their Hindu neighbors, do give at least a nominal dowry. On the day of the marriage the groom is given a ceremonial bath, with water poured from a pitcher by his sister's husband. The pitcher is decorated with napkins which the younger brothers and cousins of the groom scramble for, and then there is a hilarious party as they throw colored water and soil on each other. Both bride and groom in their respective homes apply mashed henna leaves to their palms, which makes them red, while household members sing and make merry. The marriage is conducted under a *pandal* (leaf shelter) at the bride's house, where witnesses formally hear the consent of those to be married and the ceremony is performed by the maulvī or *qāzī* (Muslim judge), followed by a feast. The bride goes to her husband's house for two days, then both return to her natal house for a final ceremony. Divorce seems to be uncommon in rural Bangladesh.

An exceedingly pervasive feature of Bangladesh Muslim rural life is pardā, in contrast with Pakistan where seclusion of women is a symbol of status observed mostly by landowning and high class or urban Muslims. Zaidi reports that 98% of Muslim women in his village survey observe pardā and that all of his anthropological data came from men only. Bertocci labored under a similar handicap for his village study. A stranger cannot glimpse a girl above the age of 10 except furtively. However, women are not secluded behind high walls as among the landowning Muslims of western South Asia, but are seen by male relatives in the homestead or even by men of neighboring homesteads. But if a stranger comes, the host will

ask him to wait outside until he has cleared the courtyard of women—who may be spotted gazing at the stranger from an unobtrusive corner. Women may sometimes be seen moving through the vegetation surrounding the homestead to the adjacent tank for washing pots or bringing water, and old women have more freedom. But a younger woman cannot leave the homestead unless escorted or with other women, and then only if she is covered with a *burqā* or a scarf. Muslim women in Bangladesh do not do any field work (in contrast with Hindu women in West Bengal who do most of the field work except plowing), and few of them contribute to the economy except as they perform household tasks. But on the western side of Bangladesh Islamic conservatism is less pronounced, and women may engage openly in some types of work such as soaking jute for separation of the fibers, or gathering firewood.

Zaidi reports that almost everyone believes in the usefulness of pardā and women accept it as a necessity for they know no other values. It diffused throughout the population originally because of its connotation of status in ideal Islamic society, and is practically regarded as a religious practice. But different families have different lists of persons in whose presence women are to be veiled. A career woman such as a teacher has no place in the fabric of village society and indeed could be forbidden, like a man, from freely entering women's quarters. The Bangladesh government is promoting girls' education and the role of women in national reconstruction, but pardā, more deeply rooted here than in villages elsewhere in South Asia, will persist for some time. Because of this even Hindu women in Bangladesh do outside work and go shopping less than women in West Bengal, and when they do go out, they feel insecure.

Bāngālī Homogeneity and Hierarchy

Life in Bangladesh is not so colorful as in most parts of South Asia. The dispersed settlement pattern, the lack of many complex villages or towns, the absence of a complex caste or class structure, the scarcity of resources other than agriculture, and the symbiotic relationship with the soil have produced a stultifying uniformity in the countryside. There are few people interested in the arts or even in erecting substantial buildings. Villagers have been taught by mullās that music, dancing, and visual art are not edifying for Muslims—though there is a rich tradition of emotive music (but women do not sing publicly). In addition, the burdensome population and lack of diversified resources have produced an almost uniform level of subsistence that is among the lowest in the world.

In West Bengal these features have been mitigated to some extent by the presence of Calcutta; women are more apparent and music and literature among the arts are particularly well developed. But urbanization

and attendant institutions such as large temple complexes have historically been weaker than in other parts of India. Nicholas says as regards a village he studied that the most striking feature of its population is its sameness. He believes, however, that there is an ideology of social hierarchy greater than that which actually exists, an ideology derived in part from Brāhmaṇical and other influences from farther west.

In this village, for example, a group of young men and also some women become temporary *sannyāsīs* (holy ascetics) during the Gājan festival which occurs just before the new year in April when the monsoon winds shift. People here normally glorify deities of the Vaishṇava pantheon, especially Krishṇa, but at this festival Śiva and a consort Śītalā, who protects from smallpox, are honored. Some of the young married men, and also women who desire favors such as relief from barrenness, remain sexually continent for eight days and do not eat before sundown. Daily they slowly circle the village temple twice, prostrating themselves after each step, and on the seventh day they make a third circuit, rolling on branches of thorny trees. They dance ecstatically to drum beating. Then the chief temporary sannyāsī enters the sanctum of the temple (normally he would not be permitted even to enter the temple) and performs the role of a Brāhmaṇ. The temporary sannyāsīs take turns boosting each other up by one foot to dangle by a rope above a fire. People get drunk on palm wine or smoke hemp, and dance in abandon before the temple. Finally on the New Year's Day the temporary sannyāsīs swing from ropes hanging from a rotating wheel set on a pole; before the 19th century they were swung on hooks inserted through the muscles of the back. The swinging sannyāsīs throw fruit at the crowd, and people catch these because they confer fertility. Then the sannyāsīs take off and burn the sacred threads they temporarily donned. Having served as Brāhmaṇs in a sense, they edified the village through their temporary holy status.

Another way in which these villagers emulate more hierarchy-prone societies is in having adopted giving of dowry instead of bride-wealth, which occurred early in this century. The amount of money exchanged is only symbolic. This was part of an uplift movement among the Māhishyas, and once adopted the practice spread throughout the essentially equalitarian society. This is analogous to the spread of pardā among the Muslim Bāngālīs, also in imitation of high status behavior of western South Asia.

Nicholas cites a third way in which hierarchy, in a symbolic sense at least, seems essential to the functioning of the village. The informal village panchāyat (not the same as the statutory panchāyat) is composed of "big men" owning substantial amounts of land, often over five acres. In this village where status differential is slight, existing differences are magnified to legitimize the power of the "big men." When the panchāyat sits to judge an accused, it is on mats clustered around the village headman, facing the public. Litigants or the accused stand reverentially facing the panchāyat,

with an appropriate slight stoop and the upper body covered with a cloth, having the fingers of the left hand touching the right forearm and pointing toward the right hand—a posture also employed when making an offering to a Brāhmaṇ. The headman remains silent while panchāyat members make speeches whose weight coincides with their relative status, and when they have reached a consensus he enunciates it. He states the fine to be levied on the accused, who then jumps forward and symbolically takes some dust from the headman's feet and licks it from his fingers. The headman reduces the fine to show the mercy of the court. The hierarchical relationship is an exaggerated one which legitimizes the decision.

Buddhism persisted in Bānglā in some places until the wave of Muslim conversions, and it did not have a hierarchical ideology. The Vaishṇavism of Caitanya, still popular in West Bengal, as well as the earlier Tantric Buddhism, expressed human equality in a devotional context in ways now considered morally suspect. On this was superimposed Islam, also with an equalitarian ideology. Sūfī mystics and Vaishṇava gurūs have disciples who form undifferentiated congregations. But the worship of the bloodthirsty Śaivite goddess Kālī, for which Calcutta is known to tourists, is mostly a cult of the high class Brāhmaṇs and Kāyasthas, who have promoted Hindu caste ideology in Bānglā.

The real basis of status differentiation in Bāngālī villages is landowning. According to Zaidi's survey in a village, Muslims agreed that ranking of families is on the basis of land and wealth, but they did not mention family aristocracy. Hindus in Bangladesh have been more differentiated, ranging from a large bloc of Scheduled Castes to Brāhmaṇs and an elite class of Hindu zamīndārs who held much of the land before the creation of Pakistan in 1947, whereupon the zamīndārs fled to India and their lands were distributed among smallholders.

T. K. Basu studied a West Bengal village 26 years after an earlier survey and concluded that there had been growth in the landless working class, mostly untouchable castes, because of population growth. But the percentage of people dependent upon agriculture was higher in 1959 than in 1933, and the 20 families who formed a rent-receiving class in the earlier survey had disappeared by the later date. A problem facing both parts of Bānglā today is land fragmentation rather than landlordism. And it might be argued that one of the results of this is lack of entrepreneurship and capital in the rural sector.

Hindus, Muslims, and Non-Bāngālīs

One can usually distinguish a Muslim man from a Hindu because he wears the lungī, whereas a Hindu wears the dhotī, in this region tied around the hips then pulled back between the legs. A Muslim does not

wear a turban or head cloth but may wear a cap and may also have a beard. A Hindu home has pictures of Hindu deities, whereas a Muslim home will have pictures of the *kaaba* (the most sacred Muslim shrine containing a meteorite) in Mecca, mosques, or tombs of saints. Muslims prefer ceramic vessels, whereas Hindus regard copper and brass as more prestigious. There are some differences in food and in expected roles of women. But otherwise there are not many differences. The basic world view and personality patterns of Hindu and Muslim Bāngālīs are similar.

Reliance on education rather than on individual aggressive action was said to be a Bāngālī trait by British writers and Bāngālīs of Calcutta alike in the 18th and 19th centuries. Bāngālīs did not take financial risks and were apathetic about business. Calcutta was developed through Britishers' initiative, and since they departed, commercial leadership has been usurped by Gujarātīs, Māṛwāṛī traders from Rājasthān, Sikhs, and South Indians, who came to the city in the 1950s. Bāngālīs preferred to get educated and take government desk jobs, join well-established firms, or enter professions:

> The Bengali had hoodwinked himself into believing that a university degree would open the door to world success. While the Scotsman, the Marwari, the Gujarati, and the Parsi were exploiting Bengal's natural resources, accumulating capital, and building commercial and industrial firms, the Bengalis were satisfied with serving them as clerks and typists for a few rupees a month. Bright Bengali engineers were begging for jobs at the doors of the rich but uncouth Marwari capitalists.[2]

Though this pertained largely to the Calcutta area, in Bangladesh now also people rely on education rather than entrepreneurship; most who get an education hope some day to enter "service," meaning government employ-

Merchant in West Bengal begins day by doing pūjā at Ganeśa shrine in rear of store. Mat and money box are practically sacred, and only prestigious customers are invited to sit there.

ment or any salaried job. Villagers rank education first among factors which enable them to raise their family status, assuming that one is not from a landed family.

But Calcutta has produced more than its share of intellectuals. In the 19th century the city was far ahead of the rest of India in English education and had the richest opportunity for sophisticated living to be found in the subcontinent. Landowners from the countryside flocked to Calcutta. In 1931 Bānglā had only 6% Brāhmaṇs, Kāyasthas, and Baidyās combined, but these three caste groups comprised 29% of the population of Calcutta, and they brought with them a taste for intellectual life as well as their money. Bāngālīs successfully moved into administration to the extent that they came to control decision making in Bihār, Assam, and Orissa, which in fact were thought of as parts of Greater Bengal then. Ten of the first 30 presidents of the Congress Party were from Bānglā. Rabindranath Tagore's poetry, which to this day has power to bring tears of sentiment to Bāngālī eyes, paved the way for development of a popular literature and focused attention on the Bāngālī language as a symbol of regionalism. In those decades it was said, "What Bengal thinks today, the rest of India thinks tomorrow."

However, the superimposition of the Calcutta connurbium and an industrial economy has produced a discquilibrium in Bānglā greater than in other parts of South Asia. Bāngālī culture and modal personality evolved consonant with an inherently stable rice-producing peasant society, as opposed to western South Asia where there have been large nucleated villages that grew into cities, and where people have been more action-oriented. The industrial growth of Calcutta in the 1950s was sparked and controlled by non-Bāngālīs, while in Bangladesh, until it became independent, the jute mills and other businesses were owned and operated by West Pakistanis. In the countryside there is no work and no land available, and people do not see their situation improving. Population pressure on the land has doubled since Independence while resources have remained almost the same. Zaidi found in a Bangladesh village that 40% of the people thought themselves worse off than before Independence in 1947, 10% better off, and 50% no different.

A further factor in the high frustration level is the extent of education. The literacy rate among the total population of West Bengal in 1971 was 33%, higher than the all-India rate. It is lower in Bangladesh because not many women are literate. But in West Bengal young men by the hundreds of thousands, their B.A.'s and M.A.'s earned (or failed), with no place to go, sit and write poignant Bāngālī poetry for obscure journals, become active in a radical political party such as the Right or Left Communists, or join some *guṇḍā* gang which can be employed to do political dirty work. Blair Kling suggests that the preference of Bāngālīs for left-wing ideologies is associated with their ambivalent attitude toward business. Their failure to

succeed in competitive capitalism is rationalized by adopting the Marxist ideology and by promoting a multitude of demonstrations and strikes. Bāngālīs are by temperament peaceable rather than violent, but for many the threshold of frustration tolerance has long ago been reached.

The creation of Bangladesh has provided a temporary respite, at least psychologically. The roots of the 1971 war go back to Jinnah's unrealistic vision that two wings of Pakistan, joined only by the common factor that they both had a majority of Muslims, could somehow form a nation. What he did not see was that Panjābīs had traditionally looked down on Bāngālīs who were thought to lack the personality traits Panjābīs idealized such as honor, militarism, and personal forcefulness, while they also viewed the eastern direction low in prestige. Bāngālīs had their own values and deeply resented the political and economic domination of West Pakistan. Most of the foreign aid and the benefits of the government and military bureaucracies accrued to West Pakistan, while East Pakistan with its jute earned over half the foreign exchange of all Pakistan. The disparity in personal income between the two wings grew from 17% in 1950 to 31% in 1960. By the time of the 1971 war the average West Pakistani consumed 19 times as much electricity, 10 times as many cars, 8 times as much tea (grown for Pakistan in the eastern wing) and petrol, 7 times as many radios, 6 times as many cigarets, 3 times as much cloth and sugar, and twice as much paper and coal as an average East Pakistani.[3] Even more significantly as far as the average villager was concerned, Pakistan tried to impose Urdū at first, then accepted Bāngālī as an official language but continued to govern with an Urdū-speaking elite. And the Pakistan government through the press kept up a continual barrage of propaganda against India, as it suspected the two wings would not remain united unless they had India as a common enemy. Importation of Bāngālī books from India was halted and the poetry of Tagore silenced.

When the people of East Pakistan voted almost as a man for the Awāmī League headed by Mujibur Rahman, West Pakistan was stunned, for it meant that the national legislature would have been controlled by Bāngālīs. Since no compromise could be worked out, the Pakistan army cracked down in March 1971 and with the support of the Urdū-speaking Bihārīs who had come from India after 1947, burned literally millions of huts of overt supporters of the Awāmī League. Much was made of the rape of Bāngālī women, which has to be seen in view of the values especially prevalent on the western side of South Asia, wherein the supreme way to dishonor a man is to dishonor the women under his protection. Bāngālīs interpreted the behavior of the West Pakistan soldiers as further evidence of contempt for Bāngālīs. In December the Indian army moved in to liberate Bangladesh which was followed by rejoicing everywhere—people danced on the streets of Chittagong for three days.

The opposition of the United States to the creation of Bangladesh and

the continued supply of arms to West Pakistan in violation of pledges to the Indian Foreign Minister to cut off such shipments produced exceedingly deep resentment throughout India and Pakistan. Even peasants continually asked foreign visitors the reasons for this policy. The United States had for years sought to establish a balance of power between India and Pakistan, a concept now rejected by India, and had armed Pakistan in pursuit of cold war policies. More concerned in 1971 with developing relations with China, which Pakistan befriended as part of her anti-India diplomacy, the United States pursued great power politics while appearing insensitive to ethnic realities within South Asia.

Nearly every bridge in Bangladesh, a land of rivers, was destroyed in the 1971 war; temporary spans were erected by Indian army. Fishermen are having a placid meal of rice and fish.

Of the 10 million refugees who fled to India during the 1971 war about 8 million were Hindus. Even in the previous two decades many non-Muslims fled from what was East Pakistan to India, so that the population of Tripurā, for instance, increased from 646,000 to 1,142,000 between 1951 and 1961, reaching a million and a half by 1970. Many of these were Christian and Buddhist tribals, as well as Hindus, who fled because they were uncomfortable in the resurgent Muslim nationalism of Pakistan. But the ethnic identity of Bāngālīs in time proved stronger than the Hindu-Muslim division, and Bangladesh did not become a Muslims state but a secular state. When the refugees returned they all got their lands back, and found that their Muslim covillagers had tilled them, giving the returned refugees half the crops (the proportion given for leased lands).

The creation of Bangladesh brought political stability for a time to West Bengal also. After years of chaotic coalition governments alternating with President's Rule, the state rallied behind Mrs. Gandhi's Congress Party, showing support for her Bangladesh policy. But already by 1973 political disaffection was growing in West Bengal, while in Bangladesh assassinations and political extremism were increasing menacingly and the country

had a shortage of foodgrains of nearly 3 million tons. It remains to be seen if the political adjustments of 1971–1972 can be translated into economic improvements and a lid put on population growth. If not, there are some who predict that Bānglā will have the distinction of being the Malthusian spectre of the world.

Assam and Orissa

The long Brahmaputra Valley has been an outlet for the expansion of northern Bāngālī and Bihārī people who have infiltrated this frontier, absorbed to some extent the indigenous Mongoloid population, and established cultural patterns essentially derived from Bānglā. On all sides of the valley are tribal peoples in varying stages of acculturation, but with the formation of four mini-states and two Territories in the hill regions the expansion of Indic culture into the hills may slow down. Assamese is the language linking all these regions formerly part of the larger Assam, but it is a mother tongue only in the Assam Valley proper.

As in Bānglā castes are not highly differentiated. Next to Brāhmaṇs the Kalitā agriculturalists have prestige, though technically they are Śūdras. Hinduized tribes such as Lālung, Mikīr, and Kāchārī may be enfolded into the Koc caste category, cultivators who sometimes call themselves Rājbanśī ("kingly lineage"). The largest low caste group are the Kaibarttā.

The people, almost entirely dependent upon agriculture, live dispersed over the plain and there are few urban places. A major problem here is floods as in Bihār and Bānglā. The eastern hills catch a disproportionate amount of the monsoon rains. In 1970, for instance, a million people were affected by floods and 50,000 were rendered homeless, but such events recur so often in the plains below the eastern Himālayas that they are scarcely noticed outside India.

Assam is far from the centers of political and economic power, and its economic potential has not been fully utilized. The state has resources for development of the paper industry, while fruits, jute, and sugar cane can be processed, and hydroelectric power is available. But the state produced only 1.8% of India's gross national product in 1965. In literacy, however, Assam nearly equals the rest of India.

Orissa consists of a coastal plain peopled by Uṛiyā-speaking rice cultivators, while a quarter of the population of the state is tribal people living in the hills. The state has a focal point in the Mahānadī delta and its four coastal districts. But even in these coastal districts, tribals and Harijans (mostly detribalized people) comprise 50% of the population. An Uṛiyā village will have a fair spread of castes, some tribal families, probably a few Bāngālīs, and if it is toward the south, a few Telugus.

Although in some ways the culture of Orissa resembles that of Bānglā

and kinship terms are similar, the region has had in fact an old and distinctive history. It was the object of a famous war of King Aśoka, and it boasts the vast temple complexes of Bhubaneśwar, Konārak and Purī, reflecting the power of ancient kings. But with the florescence of Calcutta, Bāngālīs came to overshadow Orissa, and moved southward to occupy important positions in the administration and economy. Orissa is now firmly established as a state because of the distinctiveness of the Uṛiyā language.

Most Indians think of Orissa as relatively backward. Its 51,000 villages are in fact conservative, and the state has the lowest level of urbanization among the states excepting Himāchal Pradesh. But its literacy rate is considerably higher than that of the North Indian heartland, and there are rich mineral and coal resources in its hills to the west which are being exploited. The integration of the Uṛiyā-speaking villages into the modern state political system has been studied by F. G. Bailey, who found that the politicians formed an "elite arena" wherein most of their time is spent. They are like absentee landlords, making a descent every five years to collect rent in the form of votes. In 1972 the Congress Party embarked on a program to limit land holdings to 10 or 12 acres and to eliminate the "feudal" characteristics of the state.

REFERENCES AND NOTES

1 Basu, p. 21.
2 Paraphrase of Profulla Chandra Ray, in Kling, p. 79.
3 Mahbub-ul-Haq, paraphrased in K. L. Seth, *Economic Prospects of Bangla Desh* (New Delhi, 1972), p. 4.

IMPORTANT SOURCES

Ahmad, Kammnidin. *The Social History of East Pakistan.* Dacca, 1964.
Bailey, F. G. *Politics and Social Change: Orissa in 1959.* Berkeley, Calif., 1963.
Basu, Krishna. *The Bengal Peasant from Time to Time.* New York, 1962. (Based on a village studied in 1872 and 1933 and by Basu in 1959.)
Bertocci, Peter (ed.). *Prelude to Crisis: Bengal Studies in 1970.* East Lansing, Mich., 1972.
Bose, N. K. *Peasant Life in India: A Study in Indian Unity and Diversity.* Calcutta, 1961.
Dalton, E. T. *Descriptive Ethnology of Bengal.* Calcutta, 1960. (A surprisingly comprehensive work originally printed in 1872.)
Islam, A. K. M. Aminul. *A Bangladesh Village: Social and Political Change.* Cambridge, Mass., 1973. The perspective of a Bāngālī who also did fieldwork in Jāva.)
Khan, Fazlur Rashid. *Sociology of Pakistan.* Dacca, 1966.
Kling, Blair. "Entrepreneurship and Regional Identity in Bengal," in Kopf.

Kopf, David (ed.). *Bengal Regional Identity.* East Lansing, Mich., 1969. (An interdisciplinary symposium with contributions from eight scholars.)

Mitra, A. *The Tribes and Castes of West Bengal: Census of India.* Calcutta, 1957. (A discussion with historical depth of all important ethnic groups.)

Morehouse, Ward (ed.). *Bangladesh: The Birth of a Nation.* Madras, 1973. (Handbook.)

Nicholas, Ralph. "Ritual Hierarchy and Social Relations in Rural Bengal," in *Contributions to Indian Sociology,* Dec. 1967.

———. "Vaiṣṇavism and Islam in Rural Bengal," in Kopf.

Risley, H. H. *Tribes and Castes of Bengal,* 2 vols. Calcutta, 1892.

Sarma, Jyotirmoyee. "A Village in West Bengal," in M. N. Srinivas (ed.), *India's Villages,* 2d ed. London, 1960.

Schwartzberg, Joseph. "Caste Regions of the North Indian Plain," in Milton Singer and Bernard Cohn (eds.), *Structure and Change in Indian Society.* Chicago, 1968.

Zaidi, S. M. Hafeez. *The Village Culture in Transition: A Study of East Pakistan Rural Society.* Honolulu, 1970.

13

Survey of Indian Muslims and Pakistan

Pakistan ranks second among countries of the world in numbers of Muslims (after Indonesia) with 68 million in 1973; India follows close after with 65 million, then Bangladesh with about 62 million; Afghanistan has 17 million, while Sri Lanka and the Maldives together have another million. South Asian Muslims are nearly twice as numerous as those of all Arab countries combined.

Historians, sociologists, and other scholars have not paid as much attention to these people as their importance warrants. One cannot count half a dozen book-length studies of Muslim villages or communities, for instance, and historical interest has generally stressed either the Hindu or British periods rather than Islamic civilization. In Pakistan itself there is considerable scholarship in Islamic literary studies and philosophy, but the social studies have been neglected; it was only in the 1960s that two or three universities showed serious interest in sociology, and none yet offers anthropology.

The reader is referred to the brief discussion of the spread of Islamic traditions in South Asia in Chapter 6 and the discussion of caste in regard to Islam in Chapter 8.

Diversity of Muslims in South Asia

In central Afghanistan a dialect of Persian is spoken, and Persian civilization is the ideal. North of the Hindū Kash there are Uzbeks and Turkomāns speaking Turkish languages, and Tājiks; their cultural affinities are with Soviet Central Asia. The southern and eastern parts of the country are populated by Paṭhāns who comprise half the population and are divided into numerous tribes as are the Paṭhāns of northwestern Pakistan. The southern fringe of Afghanistan has Balūchīs, and the northeastern corner Kāfirs. The country is thus astride the junction of South Asian, Persian, and Central Asian civilizations.

There are five distinct ethnic zones in Pakistan: Panjāb which has two thirds of the population, Sindh in the south, the North-West Frontier Province with Paṭhāns, and the sparsely populated Balūchistān hills with its "tribes." The Himālayan zone was formerly divided into several princely states such as Chitrāl, Dīr, Kohistān, and Hunza, but these have been incorporated into Pakistan and their rulers retired. The boundaries of Pakistan cut through ethnic entities on all sides: the India-Pakistan border cuts in two Panjābīs and also Sindhīs; the Pakistan-Afghanistan border cuts in two Paṭhāns, Balūchīs, and Kāfirs; the Pakistan-Iran border cuts through nomadic territories of Balūchīs and Brāhūīs. Moreover the cease-fire line in Kashmīr is a geographical anomaly. Pakistan makes sense geographically in that it has a focus in the Indus River, but ethnically its boundaries do not make much sense.

There are certain differences between the Muslims of Pakistan and those of India, generally speaking. There are clines of cultural traits stretching from the Arab countries through Iran and Afghanistan, gradually diminishing in Panjāb, western and central India, and Bānglā. In Pakistan the lineage segment is the strongest reference group outside the family, whereas in India Muslim castes are more clear-cut. In Pakistan, especially among Paṭhāns and also to a lesser extent among Panjābīs, *izzat* or personal honor is reflected in assertion of independence in prescribed kinds of situations and in quick reaction to slight, while these traits give way to more mellow and introspective personality types in India. Hospitality is strongly felt as an obligation of the local elite in Pakistan, but among Muslims in eastern South Asia this is not so much a feature of high status. Most Muslims in Pakistan are peasants, though in India few are cultivators. Since they form 11.2% of the population in India they behave as a minority.

Then there are substantial differences between Muslims of North India and those of the South.[1] Though their concentration and influence has been greatest in the western Gangā plains, they are distributed throughout all states, forming 7% to 10% of the population even in the southern states, but are not found in the eastern hills. Muslims in the North claim partial

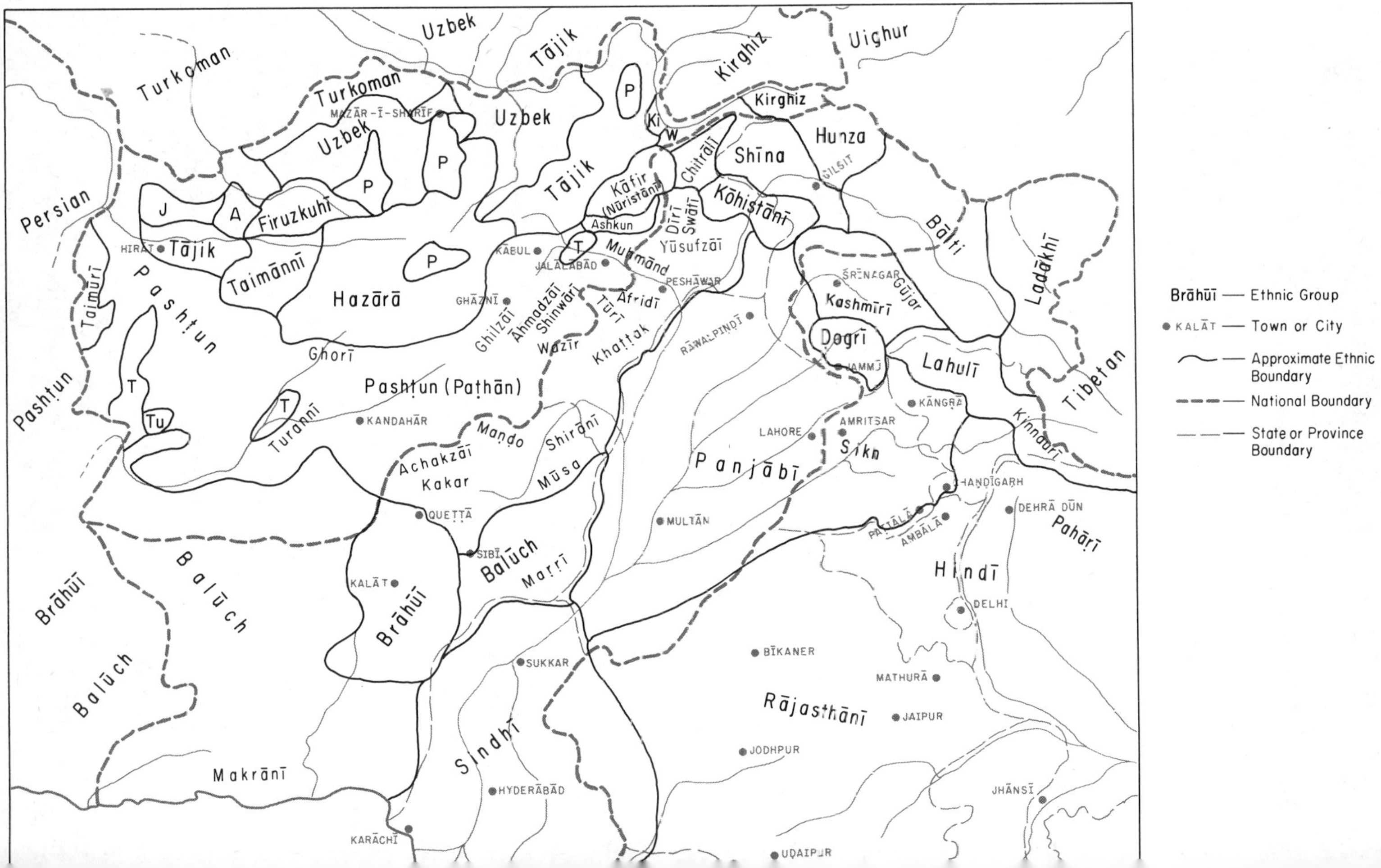
Uzbek
Turkoman
Tājik
Uighur
Kirghiz
Persian
Turkoman
MAZĀR-Ī-SHARĪF
Uzbek
Uzbek
P
Ki
W
Kirghiz
Hunza
Shīna
Chitrālī
GILGIT
J
A
Firuzkuhī
P
P
Tājik
Kāfir (Nūristānī)
Ashkun
Dīrī
Swātī
Kōhistānī
Bālti
Ladākhī
HIRĀT
Tājik
Taimānnī
P
KĀBUL
T
JALĀLĀBĀD
Muhmānd
Yūsufzāī
PESHĀWAR
ŚRĪNAGAR
Gūjar
Kashmīrī
Taimūrī
Pashtun
Hazārā
GHĀZNĪ
Ghilzāī
Āhmadzāī
Shinwārī
Tūrī
Afrīdī
Wazīr
Khattak
RĀWALPINDĪ
Dogrī
JAMMŪ
Lahulī
Tibetan
Ghorī
Pashtun
T
Tu
T
Turannī
Pashtun (Pathān)
KANDAHĀR
Mando
Shirānī
KĀNGRĀ
AMRITSAR
LAHORE
Sikh
Kinnaurī
Achakzāī
Kakar
Mūsa
Panjābī
CHANDĪGARH
DEHRĀ DŪN
Pahārī
QUETTĀ
MULTĀN
PATIĀLĀ
AMBĀLĀ
Baluch
Brāhūī
SIBĪ
Balūch
Marrī
KALĀT
Brāhūī
Hindī
DELHI
SUKKAR
BĪKANER
Balūch
MATHURĀ
Rājasthānī
JAIPUR
Sindhī
JODHPUR
Makrānī
HYDERĀBĀD
JHĀNSĪ
KARĀCHĪ
UDAIPUR
Brāhūī — Ethnic Group
KALĀT — Town or City
Approximate Ethnic Boundary
National Boundary
State or Province Boundary

FIG. 13–1 Ethnic groups of Western South Asia shown on map, Fig. 13–1.

- Balūch tribes
  - Makrānī
  - Marrī
- Brāhūī
- Dardic-speakers
  - Ashkun
  - Chitrālī
  - Kāfir
  - Kashmīrī
    - Gūjar
  - Kōhistānī
  - Nūristānī (Afgh. Kāfirs)
  - Shīna
- Dārī or Persian speakers
  - Chahār Aimak (Turkish origin)
    - Aimak Hazārā (A)
    - Firuzkuhī
    - Jamshedī (J)
    - Taimānnī
  - Hazārā (Turk-Mongol origin)
  - Kizalbash (Ki)
  - Taimūrī
  - Tājik (T)
  - Wākhnī (W)
    - Burusho (Hunza)
- Indic plains people
  - Ḍogrī
  - Hindī
  - Kacchī
  - Pahāṛī
  - Panjābī
    - Sikh
  - Rājasthānī
  - Sindhī
- Pashṭun tribes (also called Paṭhān, Pakhṭun, Afghān)
  - Āfrīdī
  - Ghilzaī group
    - Āhmadzaī
  - Ghorī
  - Kakar
  - Khaṭṭak
  - Manḍo
  - Muhmānd
  - Mūsa
  - Shinwāṛī
  - Shirānī
  - Turānnī group
    - Achakzaī
  - Tūrī
  - Wazīr
  - Yūsufzaī
    - Dīrī
    - Swātī
- Tibetan-related peoples
  - Bālti
  - Kinnauri
  - Ladākhi
  - Lāhauli
- Turkik peoples
  - Karakalpak
  - Kirghiz
  - Turkoman (Tu)
  - Uighur
  - Uzbek

descent from invaders, or were converted by invaders, such as Turks and Afghāns. But Muslims in the South—except in Hyderābād which was an offshoot of the Mughal empire—adopted their religion from Muslim traders for the most part. This is true especially of the west coast from Gujarāt to Kērala, and also of Sri Lanka. While the Islam that came to North India had been filtered through Iran and Afghanistan, the Islam of the peninsular coastal regions and also of coastal Bānglā was initially brought directly by Arab merchants who dominated the Indian Ocean until the arrival of the Portuguese.

Muslims in the North practice some hypergamy while those in the South marry equals. Those in the North have Urdū as mother tongue, and though this is true around Hyderābād and in some southern towns, many South Indian Muslims either have Urdū as a second language or do not know it at all. In the North and western India, Hindu-Muslim relations have been tense, but in the peninsula for the most part they have been relaxed.

The only Indian state having a majority of Muslims is Jammū and Kashmīr, and even in Jammū half the people are Hindus. The Mahārājā of Kashmīr, a Hindu, ceded his independent kingdom to India in 1948, which precipitated the Kashmīr war. Thus India's claim to Kashmīr is held to be a legal one, while Pakistan claims that on principle the state ought to belong to it because Partition was to separate the areas having a majority of Muslims. Since the cease-fire Pakistan has held the western fringe of Kashmīr and also a very large northern mountainous zone. India holds the areas having the largest part of the population—which in any case numbers fewer than 5 million—including the Vale of Kashmīr with Śrīnagar, the capital.

There are a number of Muslim castes in Kashmīr: Shaikhs who engage in trade, Rājpūts, Cultivators, Oil Pressers, Carpenters, Fishers, Potters, Barbers, and Bhangī sweepers. Then there are the Gūjars, of whom many are transhumant pastoralists, occupying villages on the fringes of the Vale or in other valleys in winter while driving their animals up as far as the glaciers in summer. While Śrīnagar itself is thought of as a resort, in the dusty villages over the plain most structures including mosques are mere huts, mullās are untrained, and the general level of literacy is low. Islam and Hinduism are not altogether mutually exclusive in Kashmīr; Muslims participate in Hindu festivals such as Holī and Śivarātrī and even may take vows at Hindu shrines and accompany the 50,000 Hindus who yearly come up from the plains to visit the shrine of Amarnāth in a high mountain. Like the Hindus their avowed purpose for the journey is "to worship God," but they will not participate in the pūjā ceremony at the shrine.

In his study of a market town in eastern Uttar Pradesh, Richard Fox lists 15 Muslim castes, including Vegetable Sellers, Weavers, Sweets Sellers, Banglemen, Barbers, Tailors, Goat Butchers, Dyers, Clerks, and Bhangī

Scavengers. Some Muslims in this town, when questioned, refused to give caste names at first because they said there is no caste in Islam. The processes of Muslim caste mobility are at work here, with Julāhās (Weavers), for instance, adopting the family name Ansārī and claiming Shaikh category.

Though retaining their separate identity, Hindus and Muslims have to some extent formed a synthesis. Yogendra Singh reports that in a village in northern Uttar Pradesh, Muslims participate in the Hindu festivals of Dasahrā, Holī, and Dīpāvalī. When there were zamīndārs, Muslims used to present gifts to their Hindu landowners during Dasahrā. They still help in organizing the Rāma Līlā dance-drama on this occasion and decorate their shops with paper effigies of the demon king Rāvaṇa which are burned at the conclusion of the festival. Muslims place lighted lamps around their shops during Dīpāvalī, and frolic with Hindus during Holī. Similarly, Hindus celebrate the Muslim festival of Muharram, making paper models of coffins ceremonially buried in memory of Hasan and Husain. Brāhmaṇs and Hindu Rājpūts also used to do this, but in 1943 there was a local conflict over land between Hindus and Muslims, whereupon they ceased to participate in this festival.[2]

In the South the most opulent traditionally Muslim city is Hyderābād, now capital of Āndhra. It was the seat of the vast kingdom of the Nizām of Hyderābād. Many features of Islamic civilization were introduced in Hyderābād, including the use of slaves from Africa, and Urdū was the language of the former elite. Today the Muslims of Hyderābād bemoan the fact that they are a minority among the 43 million Telugus.

In Tamiḻ Nāḍu most Muslims are townspeople; 55% live in urban areas and prefer to earn their living by trade. They do not engage in cultivation, and there are few occupational castes such as are found in the North. They also avoid taking up industrial labor. They are all Sunnī Muslims. Similarly, the Muslims of Sri Lanka, who are all Tamiḻs, live in towns or along the coast where they specialize in trade. In northern Kēraḷa there are the Māppiḷḷas, partially descended from very early Arab traders, who have adopted the local matrilineal mode of descent.

Marriage and the Family

Marriage patterns and jural codes of Muslims set them apart from Hindus, Christians, and Sikhs. These are thought to be based on the Sharī'at, the code of social rules derived from Qur'ānic principles. Muslims are expected to marry because the lineage must be perpetuated and also because marriage is the only legitimate outlet for sex. Except among a small urbanized minority, marriages are invariably arranged by the parents, though the young people may make their preferences known.

Marriage of a man to either kind of cousin is acceptable, and indeed

among Ashrāf Muslims is preferred. The North Indian Hindu calls his male parallel cousin *bhāī* (brother) and treats him as a brother. A Muslim also calls his male parallel cousin bhāī, while at the same time marrying the sister of the man he calls brother. This is viewed as incestuous by Hindus, and is one of the points on which Hindus and Muslims will never find a meeting ground. Therefore in India there are separate legal codes governing family and inheritance for Muslims, Hindus, and Christians. Another difference is that among Hindus the parents of the girl arrange the marriage, but in Pakistan it would be a shame for the father of a girl to have to seek out a husband for her, and arrangement of marriage is the responsibility of the father of the boy.

Marriages are preferentially within the birādarī, the lineage segment, a practice having its origin in Arab society where it functioned to reinforce bonds among brothers. The word birādarī literally and etymologically means brotherhood. Among Muslims in Pakistan it has the function of preventing property from being alienated from the family, and of course is practiced less commonly among tenant farmers who have no property. It is thought that a wife who is cousin or other kin to the husband will take more responsibility in the home. Among high status groups claiming Arab or other immigrant ancestry, preservation of lineage is considered quite important. But in marriages subsequent to the first a man traditionally makes his own arrangements based on his sentiment, and can take a bride from any source. The preference for lineage endogamy is not derived from Qur'ānic law, which states simply that a Muslim woman should marry a Muslim, while a man should marry a woman from among People of the Book (Muslims, Christians, Jews, or Zoroastrians, who have sacred scriptures). Lineage endogamy is not rigid. In the Swāt Valley, where lineage groups tend to be hierarchically arranged, Fredrik Barth reports that 60% of marriages are endogamous, 23% are hypergamous, and a surprising 17% hypogamous; the latter is often considered shameful in Pakistan. Among the tribes of the western frontier only four out of five marriages are within the tribe. It appears, then, that the concepts of birādarī, tribe, or caste apply more to men than to women in Pakistan.

While the Qur'ān allows a man to have up to four wives and any number of concubines, polygynous marriages in Pakistan are very few. Polygyny is not a symbol of wealth as in Africa, nor does it produce income. The Muslim Family Laws Ordinance of 1961 made it mandatory for a person seeking to take a second wife to get permission from an arbitration council, and the practice has effectively ceased. While traditional law regarded marriage as a contract, it was easy for a man to initiate divorce, but a woman could do it only with difficulty and with the help of the Sharī'at judge. Under the Muslim Family Laws Ordinance notice of intent of divorce has to be sent to the secular Reconciliation Council. In general,

divorces are less frequent among upper classes than among peasants, and the rate of divorce is low in Pakistan compared with other Muslim countries. The son of one of the landlords of the village Jalpānā (described in the companion volume) said in regard to divorce, "My father and family won't care. That's my business. But the parents of the girl will care, and I would have to give the dowry back and it would be a shame for the girl and her family, but not for me." Since one's wife's parents are often kin, divorce would mean breaking off relations with people of one's birādarī. Children are considered part of the father's lineage even though they might be raised while young by the mother.

Joint families occur, and as in India they primarily serve the function of maintaining land or a business intact. But it is usual for married brothers to break apart upon the death of the father, though they may live in separate houses in the same compound. Most houses are designed for nuclear families. According to Islamic law all the sons inherit equal portions of the property, and daughters each half a portion. In practice, females do not usually inherit land, and almost never among the Paṭhāns, even though according to secular law they are entitled to. It is the sons who are obliged to continue the family, which they cannot do without inheriting the land. A widow is traditionally entitled to one fourth of her deceased husband's property, but gets only one eighth if there are children, and even less if there are other wives. She is entitled to maintenance by her affinal kin. But if a widow is cast adrift, she can always expect maintenance from her brothers, and this is cited in justification of the division of inheritance among sons only. Also, in Panjāb daughters benefit from considerable expenditure on dowries and marriage ceremonies, and people got accustomed to Hindu laws of inheritance formerly in force which denied women the right to inherit property.

In western parts of South Asia masculine dominance is a notable characteristic, and among Muslims this is further reinforced by the brotherhood of the lineage segment and the emphasis on paternity. Marriage is not thought of as companionship. A husband can easily leave his home on business to be gone for months, or he may go abroad for education. He will not evince much sense of regret at leaving his wife and children if they can be looked after by his brother. In Pakistan, especially in tribal areas and among the traditional elite codes of sexual conduct are strict. Virginity of brides is highly valued. But in fact the great majority of Panjābī peasants engage in premarital sexual activity, a matter which the traditional elite and urban Pakistanis are wont to deny. Traditional law says that punishment for an adulterous woman is death and retribution must be taken against a known offending male. But generally no action on such matters is taken unless a husband is shamed or his ability to protect his wife publicly questioned.

Pardā (Purdah)

The seclusion of women in Pakistan and among Indian Muslims is more rigorously observed among townspeople and prosperous landowners than among peasants. Paṭhāns especially are noted for keeping women out of all public activities, for their concept is that izzat demands women be carefully protected. There are reports that some women in the North-West Frontier Province never leave the compound, while others venture out only at night. It is dangerous for tourists in or around Peshāwar to try to take pictures of a street in which a woman is walking, even though she be far away and covered with the burqā, the tent-like hooded gown with peep-holes. But among peasant Panjābīs, women work outside the home and can be freely seen. Sindhīs think Panjābīs are loose because their women are not so cloistered. Zekiya Eglar, a Muslim anthropologist, lived for five years among the women of a small Panjābī village in Pakistan while making her village study, and in her book she has almost nothing to say about pardā.

Muslim women in pardā in a Panjāb town, Pakistan.

Women of prosperous landowning household, Pakistani Panjāb. Walled courtyard and verandas are necessary for these women in pardā.

In India, because Islam is predominantly a religion found in towns, pardā is an important traditional criterion of status. Cora Vreede-de Stuers in her study of it in North Indian cities distinguishes four degrees of its practice. Those who observe it strictly are mostly Ashrāf women raised in the tradition of the old zamīndār class, as well as conservative non-Ashrāf

women of artisan or worker families brought up under the influence of the maulvī. These women seldom venture out, and if they do, preferably at night and always covered with their burqā which completely shrouds their body except for two embroidery-covered holes for seeing. Those who can afford it may go visiting in carts which can be curtained off front and back. There are women of poor but orthodox families who can afford to live only in dingy town apartments without sunwells, on whose faces the warmth of the sun hardly ever shines. Partial pardā is observed by women who stay at home in general but may receive a small circle of family friends; when they go out, it is in the company of other women, and they wear the burqā according to circumstances. Then there are those women who practice it occasionally but dislike the custom; some of these are educated women. Yet other women have given up the practice altogether.

The real function of pardā, both among Muslims and among Hindus to the extent that it is practiced, is clearly to distinguish the elite, whose women do not have to work in the fields, from peasants, and therefore it is a particularly important symbol for landowners and townspeople. It also functions as a symbol of avoidance of sexual impropriety and therefore of purity of lineage, which is also important for Muslims. A family coming into wealth may take a new name and claim a prestigious lineage, supporting its claim by stricter observance of pardā. Seclusion of women is not strictly enjoined in the Qur'ān, but it is firmly rooted in Muslim tradition.

But one should not suppose that this attitude toward women appeared in South Asia only because of Islam. In medieval Hindu town society, women had separate quarters within the houses. Rājpūts and other Hindus in western India who claim prestigious status generally keep their women indoors; in case women have to go out, as to the well for water, they drape their head with a sāṛī, and if they meet a strange man they are likely to pull it over the face. Even in the village in northern Karṇāṭaka described by Ishwaran, middle caste Hindu and Lingāyat men are willing to lug water home from the wells and do all the household shopping themselves, keeping their women indoors as a symbol that they are not very low nor very poor. Pardā among Muslims is the counterpart of prohibition of widow remarriage among high caste Hindus; both are symbolic of social class and of a woman's total devotion to her husband and his family. But this is not to say that woman's influence in the home is small; in middle or older age she might quite dominate the home.

Within the home pardā operates by segregating the sexes and by defining proper modes of interaction among them. However, it is not a device purely to prevent illicit sexual activity, for a young man is likely to have contact with his female cousin, who might indeed be an eligible bride. But it governs the behavior of every individual with his family members and acquaintances. Vreede-de Stuers points out that its rules, as they apply

to an individual, shift constantly with respect to age, social class, education, and context. It dominates the lives of high class women, and even in villages where women are not secluded, it is a pervasive ideal. In the houses of the traditional leisured classes, the women's quarters, called the *zanānā*, are alive with chattering and laughing, but if a man appears the women clam up. Men and women do not join in any public activities; if perchance they are together in public, the men either ignore their wives as if they did not exist, or else their attitude toward them is so stiff that the sexes appear to be segregated by an invisible curtain. Men eat separately. They have their own socializing rooms which women do not frequent; nor do men generally enter the zanānā. If the men and women of a family do happen to be together and a woman visitor appears, the men may arise and suddenly depart, returning only when the guest has left.

Pardā among the Muslim middle classes, artisans, and petty clerks in North India still remains an ideal, but many urbane women have given it up completely, or practice it intermittently. A woman may leave her house covered with a burqā, but once seated in a bus among people she does not know, she throws back the veil covering her face to look around and get a breath of air, to which her husband makes no objection. Or she may wear the burqā out of the house and then take it off and carry it over her arm, donning it again only when reentering her neighborhood. Vreede-de Stuers writes about girls studying in Alīgaṛh University, established in Uttar Pradesh to remedy the low level of higher education among Muslims:

> Those who lived off-campus sat unveiled in the classroom with their male teachers and fellow students, but returned home in *burqa.* Those living in the hostels strolled freely about the university grounds and passed unveiled from one building to another. Yet, as they showed me, they had a neatly folded *burqa* stowed in a suitcase or wardrobe, all ready to wear when the vacation came and they went back to their families. One girl left for her classes each day covered with her *burqa* and accompanied by her father, himself a professor at this institution. Near a bridge marking the entrance to the university campus, the girl took off her *burqa* and then walked on with her father until they reached the lecture hall, where they parted. At the end of the day they repeated the procedure on their way home.[3]

Older women have a real fear of venturing out into the world dominated by males, and a woman who decides to discard the burqā does not know how to act for lack of easy relationship between men and women. But a woman who observes pardā only because of family pressure and does so intermittently has to learn the social codes of two differing roles.

> This ambiguous solution, which she readily accepts for herself out of necessity, she rejects for her children. Among the young women I interviewed, in *parda* themselves and mothers of small daughters, not one told me that she would like to see her daughters in *parda* when they grew up.[4]

Birādarī and Caste

Beyond the family the most important link a man has is with his birādarī, the lineage segment. But the model of caste as it applies to India, even to Indian Muslims, does not fit so well when applied in Pakistan. In Pakistani Panjāb there is not the clear distinction of Ashrāf status (Sayyids, Qurayshīs, Shaikhs, Mughals, and Paṭhāns) as in North India. The middle ranks of Muslim lineages can scarcely be arranged in a hierarchy, ritual pollution is hardly a factor, and aside from claims of holy lineage the only readily available symbol of ritual status that can be adopted is pardā.

Opinions of anthropologists on Pakistani social order have not jelled, partly for lack of sufficient village studies. The only book-length report of a Muslim Panjābī village is that by Eglar, who divides all the people into two "castes": zamīndārs, who own land or whose ancestors did, and *kammīs*, the artisans. Kammīs include barbers, bakers, cobblers, carpenters, potters, blacksmiths, Musallīs (laborers), weavers, and tailors. These are found in most villages, while some also have Mirāsīs (bards), Kashmīrīs (goatherders), and Arāins (vegetable growers). In this region the term zamīndār is used for even a small landowner. Every zamīndār family has a set of traditional contracts with certain kammī families, giving grain in return for services—the jajmānī system. Kammīs also provide such services for each other.

Most Pakistanis, including social scientists, do not acknowledge that caste exists in Pakistan. It is true that no strong ritual or symbolic framework expresses the total ranking of endogamous groups as in the Hindu caste ideology. Everybody in Muslim Panjābī villages worships together in the mosque, and all can gather at the pīr's tomb. Ritual pollution, where it exists, is attached not so much to individuals as to occupations. People may not eat or smoke the hukkā with sweepers, but sweepers regularly engaged in some other occupation suffer no such disabilities.

Honigmann reports for a village in Shāhpur District that 95% of the people were Arāin and the rest were distributed among 10 endogamous castes. One of these was a caste of Christian Sweepers who lived at the end of the village, could not dine with Muslims, and did not share the hukkā when it was passed around. But in other villages younger people do smoke it with sweepers. In Pakistan most converts to Christianity have been sweepers who hoped to escape the disabilities attached to their status, and have formed a considerable Christian community around Lahore. In a village not far from the one Eglar studied, Inayatullah found 15 "castes" (endogamous lineages) of Zamīndārs, 11 of Kammīs, 2 others, and residual individuals not classifiable by caste.[5] If, as Alavi says, the central criterion of caste behavior is observance of ritual pollution and purificatory rites,[6] then caste is not the referrent for social action in Pakistan. These hereditary

categories are called *qaum* by the educated, a word of Arab origin meaning a people or a nation. But other villagers refer to them as zāt (jāti). The ideology of hierarchically arranged hereditary groups is strong in Pakistan.

Fredrik Barth delineated seven hierarchically ordered social classes in Swāt, a Paṭhān region in the far northwest. These are 1) persons of holy descent, 2) landowners or administrators, 3) priests, 4) craftsmen, 5) agricultural tenants and laborers, 6) herders, and 7) despised groups. The full range is found in nearly every Swātī village.

Whether or not these social classes, hierarchically arranged lineages, or hereditary artisan groups can be called castes is a matter of terminology. What is apparent is that the indigenous South Asian caste structure has had superimposed on it here tribal and lineage structure of peoples to the west of Pakistan, and for most purposes caste is residual and not as important among cultivators and upper classes as is the birādarī.

While the Hindu gotra is exogamous and is a ritual lineage, the birādarī is preferentially endogamous and is the pivotal institution. The transition from gotra and caste to birādarī can be observed in Muslim Rājpūts on the eastern border of Pakistan. They formerly maintained gotras and for them birādarī was weakly defined. Lately they also have begun to marry cousins, and this tendency has been speeded up since the new laws of Pakistan stipulate that daughters should inherit half a share each. These Muslim Rājpūts say, "Now we have to give out our land as well as our daughter—why should we not keep both in the family?"[7]

A person cannot afford to sever his links with his birādarī else he will be socially and economically adrift. If there is a rift in the birādarī, people will take pains to bridge it, unless a lineage fragment can form a viable new birādarī, which may occur if the old one gets too large or if a series of marriages is concluded outside it. The bounds of the lineage segment are defined by *vartan bhānjī*, a system of reciprocal gift giving, and by invitations to ceremonies at which such gifts are given. Gifts include money, sweets, fruit, cloth goods, and sometimes services and entertainment. At weddings invitees who accept bring gifts to the father of the bride and lesser gifts to the father of the bridegroom, and at circumcision ceremonies, to the father of the boy. At funerals they are given to the surviving male household head.

Records are kept of all gifts, both by the giver and the receiver. Alavi describes the recording process at a wedding. At an appropriate stage in the proceedings, a Mirāsī (bard) calls out to the gathering that the time for giving has come. Then he sits down in front of a large circular metal tray with the groom and another senior family member such as the groom's eldest uncle, and if the bard is illiterate, he has a priest record the names of donors and the amount given in a special account book. Each gift is handed to the bard who counts it and hands it to the family member sitting with him, who counts it also and puts it in the tray while the bard

announces, in ritual phraseology, the name of the donor, his household, and the amount. This is then recorded. At the end of the proceedings the account book is checked with the amount on the tray and discrepancies rectified. The record is preserved so that the gifts can be reciprocated on suitable occasions.[8]

Circumcision ceremony in Pakistani Panjāb village. Mirāsīs (bards) dance, then are given rupees by onlookers as vartan bhānjī.

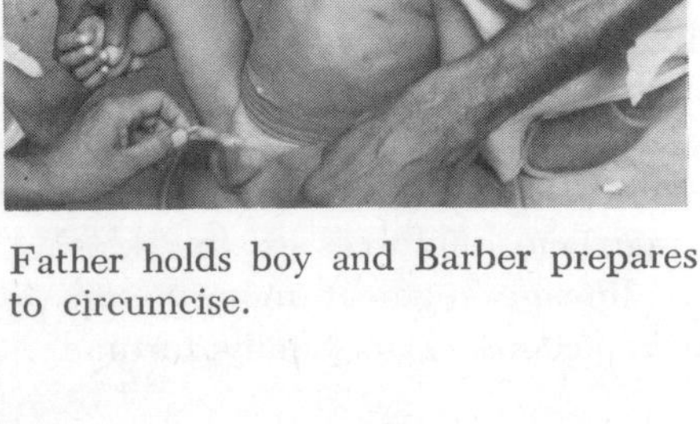

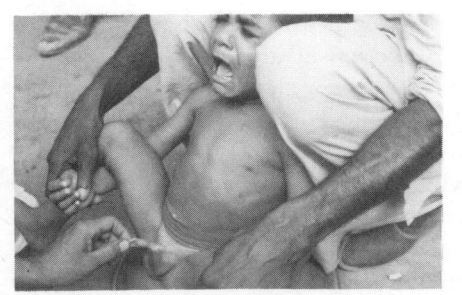

Father holds boy and Barber prepares to circumcise.

As boy lies on cot, Barber wipes his knife; neighbors give him wheat as vartan bhānjī to family of the boy.

Sometimes vartan bhānjī is given by guests to the functionaries rather than to the family having the ceremony. In the accompanying pictures of a circumcision ceremony (taken in the village of Jalpānā described in the companion volume), gifts of a rupee or two are given to the Mirāsī dancers, and gifts of grain are given to the barber, for their roles in the ceremony. These gifts are kept by the functionaries, but the household having the ceremony regards them as debts to be repaid on suitable occasions.

Each time vartan bhānjī is given, it abolishes the old debt and establishes a reciprocal one. On the occasion of a marriage, Eglar writes:

> The hostess weighs out the sweets or counts the number of pastries to be given in the presence of the recipient and says to her: "These five *seers* [a measure of about two pounds] are yours, and these two *seers* are mine." By this the hostess means that previously, on the occasion of a marriage in the household of the recipient, she had received five *seers* of sweets, which she was now returning; to these she added two more *seers* of sweets to keep the *vartan bhanji* going. On the next occasion, when she is a recipient, she will receive back her two *seers* plus one, two, or four *seers* more.[9]

On each such occasion the mutual roles of ritual creditor and ritual debtor are reversed. This ritual giving, plus invitations to ceremonies and acceptance or rejection of them, determine the boundaries of the kinship segment.

A poor family will not be expected to reciprocate as much as a richer family. And if a family suffers hard luck and cannot give anything, its head may offer an explanation and attend the ceremony. But a man's means and status are known. One can also embarrass the recipient by giving too much, or show dissatisfaction with the relationship by giving too little. One can terminate the relationship or remove himself from the system by giving exactly the amount he owes. But when people give approximately the right amount—and it is said that in vartan bhānjī people should count 19 as if it were 20—the spirit of the "brotherhood" is maintained.

Such exchanges can also take place between two birādarīs, two friendly landlords, or two old army friends. The function of giving as a ritual symbolizing relationship is fundamental to the hospitality visitors encounter. This is not limited to Muslim society, for among Hindus too it is commonly expected that a favor given demands a favor received. At Hindu weddings, too, records are kept and the host will reciprocate at a later ceremony, but in such cases giving is not so structurally important as in the birādarī.

Among Panjābī Hindus marriages form a network of links among unrelated families, but among Muslims marriage reinforces existing kinship ties. Because of this it is possible for a lineage segment to move up or down in status and adjust lineage claims according to family fortune.

Sindhīs

Sindh is a desert, receiving only four inches of rain yearly at Mohenjo-dāṛo, and agriculture is supported by the Indus. The province has considerable regional identity, symbolized in the adoption of Sindhī as the official language and its use in the educational system, while Urdū is used elsewhere in Pakistani schools. Sindhīs have a provincial attitude toward Panjābīs and Paṭhāns and also reject Muslim immigrants from India.

Many old cultural traits are preserved in this region, some of which presumably go back to pre-Āryan times or the Indus Civilization. Women use abundant jewelry, and there is emphasis on the actual and ritual cleansing functions of water and on having clothes clean. The 4000-year-old Indus ox cart having disc wheels firmly fixed to the revolving axle is still to be seen. Sindhīs have great appreciation of music and have preserved quaint musical forms. Islam came early to this region, Arabs having landed on the coast in the 8th century, and gradually extended their influence up the river. Yet Islam here is tainted with earlier cults, such as reverence for the Indus as a male fertilizing symbol, complementing the female elements in vegetation. Sindhīs practice the rituals of Islam in a more orthodox fashion than do many Panjābīs, and are proud of their stricter observance of pardā.

Social structure is more stratified than in Panjāb. The majority are landless tenants. Gentry, who style themselves Rājpūts, live lives of leisure. They may live in the same village as their tenants, but have a greater array of household furniture, go in for education and travel, and are active politically. Artisan castes are quite distinct, and until Independence trade was in the hands of Māṛwāṛī Hindus. In addition there are menial groups, nomadic Brāhūī tribesmen from the hills who set up their tents, and other remnant ethnic groups. Though Karāchī is in Sindh, it is predominantly an Urdū-speaking city filled with Panjābīs and immigrants from India, and is not focal to Sindhī culture. In the 1930s the British built vast irrigation facilities to utilize the Indus waters, and rice and cotton are the main crops. Schools have been built in every town.

But change in Sindh comes slowly. Relaxing in the cool of the evening in the courtyard of a farmer's mud-walled, flat-topped house, one senses it. Overhead the nīm tree rustles and undulates in the breeze, while the pleasing scent of freshly watered soil emanates from the fields and winged insects begin their evening escapades. One muses at the unreality of the machinations of distant Islāmābād and the irrelevance of what is reported in the Western press as supposedly important to Pakistan. And he doubts whether the modernized life envisioned for Sindhī farmers will endure for the coming four millennia as has Sindhī peasant culture over the last four millennia.

Brāhūīs and Balūchīs

Balūchistān is the largest of Pakistan's four provinces, comprising 134,000 square miles but with a population of only 2.5 million. Brāhūīs are a group of tribes numbering some 500,000, centered in eastern Balūchistān around Kalāt but extending into Iran and even up into the Soviet Union. During British times their confederacy, the Khānate of Kalāt, was the third largest of the Indian states. The Brāhūī language is Dravidian-based, but most of the vocabulary now is Balūchī, Persian, or Indo-Āryan. Most Brāhūīs speak Balūchī, and indeed many have been absorbed into the Balūchī population. Brāhūīs are slightly more swarthy than Balūchīs or Afghāns, and doubtless are remnants of a larger Dravidian-speaking population of the Indus region and also perhaps western Iran.

Brāhūīs are firmly nomadic and dislike agriculture, but constantly move about with their black tents, pitching them in villages even in Sindh wherever they can find grazing facilities for their animals. Like their neighbors, Balūchīs and Paṭhāns, their social structure is tribal with lineage heads aligned under a *sardār* (chief). They are quick to act but not given to innovation. They do not pay much attention to personal cleanliness, and are not fanatical. They retain shamanistic practices alongside Islam.

Brahuīs swaddle their babies for most of the first year, as do their neighboring tribes. They stretch a baby's legs out and bind them, stuffing in cotton so the legs will grow straight and not bow. The arms are also bound straight, the lips are rubbed to make them thin, and the nose frequently pinched and pressed upward. The swaddling is removed twice daily so the baby can kick. Brāhūīs covet the broad heads of Balūchīs but dislike the mortar-shaped heads of the Paṭhāns. To make a baby's head broader, they will shape it, laying it on a "soft pillow" of millet or peas. Brāhūīs say that "too many nurses make the child's head conical,"[10] which means the same as "too many cooks spoil the soup."

Balūchīs dominate Balūchistān, numbering nearly 1.5 million, while there are another half million in western Iran, 80,000 in southern Afghanistan especially around the Sīstān basin, 25,000 in Omān on the Persian Gulf, and even 10,000 around Merv in the Soviet Union. Their language is derived from Old Persian and has some resemblance to Kurdish. They diffused into Balūchistān in concentric ripples impelled by the disturbances of the Saljūqs and Mongols from Central Asia.

In Balūchistān there are a score of tribes and six Balūchī dialects, the speech of the eastern hills being distinct from that of the Makrān coast and the west. Traditionally a nomadic people keeping camels, cattle, sheep, and goats, they preferred to live in open country but now many live in little settlements and cultivate, while others have been drawn to the relatively

easy life of the plains or have gone to Karāchī. Balūchīs are an open-hearted people who laugh easily, are not fanatical about Islam, and narrate legends and ballads largely free from supernatural content.

The only recent ethnographic source on Balūchī life is the research of the Pehrsons, posthumously compiled by Fredrik Barth. This deals with the Marrī tribe of the Balūch, located east of Sibī, and provides a good description of formal tribal organization. The Marrī form a distinct political unit, a qaum whose members are interrelated by kinship and descent. Every Marrī can also identify himself as belonging to a particular section and subsection of the tribe. Many of the Balūch now cultivate, principally wheat, and landownership is important. A full member of a tribal section is entitled to a share in that section's estate whenever such lands are reallotted, say every 10 or 14 years, but only males receive a portion. Those males whose mothers are of low caste may be denied a share.

The central figure in the political organization of the Marrī tribe is the sardār, who now lives in the town of Queṭṭā. He is regarded with awe or even reverence and is succeeded by his eldest son by a mother of clean caste. The sardār's lineage has its own estate for income, and also gets half the money collected as fines by tribal courts in criminal cases. The sardār is invested by a tribal council presided over by a mullā, and at the ceremony part of his large turban is wound by the representative of each section of the tribe. Council members are acknowledged leaders of sections, and through them power flows from the sardār to all the tribe. Every council member has the loyalty of leaders of the subsections. For the Marrī, every group must have a formal leader, and because the lines of communication are vertical through the echelons, the different Marrī camps are mutually suspicious. Leaders are expected to be rapacious, which has a function of ensuring that communication to leaders is transmitted through their clients of lesser rank. Members of camps expect theft, deception, adulterous intrigue, and wrong information from neighboring camps; hence they tend to limit their contacts, avoid visitors, and build their camps so travelers will not see them. Barth suggests that this political pattern arose when nobles served as warrior leaders, but now that the Balūch engage in mixed farming and herding the only means of defense commoners have are withdrawal, dispersal, servility, and deceit.

Besides the two Marrī categories of nobles and commoners, there are other elements in the population: Hindu traders who speak Hindko (a dialect of Panjābī) and who maintain their dress and customs; Pashto-speaking tenants who are in effect serfs; Lorīs (gypsies, smiths); and Ḍoms (musicians), who are Balūchī-speaking but are regarded "like animals"; Jāṭ camel herders and peddlers; and finally exslaves (slavery was abolished in 1952).

A wife is taken preferably from within the section, and if possible from among agnatic cousins. Upon marriage she is legally totally separated from

her own family. Childbirth and menstruation are polluting and require cessation of cooking; intercourse is also polluting. As Muslims, pubic hair is removed every two to four weeks.

The marital relationship is one of subordination of the wife, who is the property of her husband to the extent that publicly known adultery is inadmissible. As a Marrī said, "Very few Marrī women are lovers with their husbands. It is not our way. Marrī women have other men as lovers. And not just one here and there, but everyone has a secret lover. Those few Marrī who are lovers with their husbands, they never let anyone see it."[11] Romantic secret love is a thing of beauty expressed in poetry, idealized in contrast with conjugal relations. But if it becomes known or threatens to damage the husband's honor, it becomes adultery. It is public knowledge of infidelity, not the act itself, that causes killings and feuds. And an illegitimate birth cannot be recognized because it would cause dishonor to the husband as well as to his lineage. Yet in their study of this tribe, the Pehrsons found lover relationships almost universal in the camps in which they could collect detailed information. They suggest that adultery denunciations may often begin by intriguing women informers and may serve in a fashion analogous to witchcraft accusations in other cultures. The researchers listed several instances of an accused woman being killed by her husband, or committing suicide; a son may also kill his mother. "A whole syndrome of cultural traits is elaborated around romantic love and adultery, which come to have the greatest importance for the members of the society."[12]

Pathāns

Paṭhāns are divided into a number of large tribes such as Durrānīs and Khaljīs on the Afghanistan side, and Yūsufzāīs, Khaṭṭaks, and Āfrīdīs on the Pakistan side. While Afghāns proper are the Paṭhāns, they comprise only half the population of Afghanistan, and in fact Pashto has given way to Darī, a dialect of Persian, for official purposes. The Durand Line, the political boundary, was delineated by the British who created Afghanistan as a buffer state to prevent expansion of Russia south of the Āmū Daryā (Oxus) River and to hinder any possibility of a united Paṭhān threat to their province of the Panjāb. The Durand Line cuts through two Paṭhān tribes, the Muhmands and the Wazīrs. In the 1950s there was considerable agitation for the union of Paṭhān peoples, a Pakhṭūnistān, or at least the formation of an independent state for Pakistan's Paṭhāns. Relations between the two countries were so strained that diplomatic contact and trade were suspended, forcing Afghanistan to find an outlet to the sea through Iran. It is doubtful that Paṭhāns can act in concert sufficient to achieve such

political readjustments, since their history has been one of intertribal disputes.

In Pakistan, Paṭhāns range from northern Balūchistān to the Hindū Kash and populate a number of administrative units called agencies, which from south to north are: South Wazīristān, North Wazīristān, Kurram, Khyber, Muhmand, and Malakand. In addition, Pashto is the language of two formerly independent states, Swāt and Dīr, and the region around Peshāwar on the plains.

In the tribal regions Paṭhāns retain their tribal structure, each segment occupying a specific territory. Those integrated into the sedentary village life of the Peshāwar plain or Swāt Valley maintain their lineage structure but function essentially as a landowning caste within the hierarchical village society. The Yūsufzāī is the largest tribe, numbering over 700,000, whose warriors came down from Afghanistan and spread through Peshāwar by 1604, and within a generation had penetrated the long Swāt Valley to the north. They claim descent from King Saul, supposing that his sons were captured by Nebuchadnezzar but escaped to Afghanistan and settled in Kandahār. The Yūsufzāī displaced the Swātī Paṭhāns, who had earlier displaced the millet-eating, Dardic-speaking people of Swāt who fled to Kohistān in the northern mountains. Dīrīs of Dīr are a segment of the Yūsufzāīs. The territory of the Muhmand tribe is so overpopulated that even drinking water is not available, so people tend to emigrate to the Peshāwar basin.

The Khaṭṭak, who live southward of Kohāt, look back to a 17th-century hero, Khushhāl Khān Khaṭṭak, a chief and a poet who died in battle with the Yūsufzāī. The following poem he composed illustrates the Paṭhān code of honor and attitude towards feuding:

He that finds fault with your rule,
Be quit of him, by gold, by treachery, or by arms.
Slay your son and your brother for the security of your state;
Closely guard your rivals in your jails. . . .
The tree of a chief's sovereignty, well watered
By the blood of his enemies, bears fair fruit.
It is better that bleeding heads should lie on the battlefield,
Than that live hearts should carry evil blood.
Either like a man enfold the turban on your head,
Or wear in its place a woman's veil.
Oh God! What use my writing? Who will heed me?
Yet have I said what must be said.

This chief also wrote about love and nature:

The thunder of heavens is in the waterfall
Wild birds dive above the placid pond;
The tulips are high as flashes from the Huntsmen's guns.
The roses stand, a warrior phalanx, spears by their sides.[13]

The inspiring values are war, women, nature, and religious devotion, and these have been the themes of many tribal poets. The same ideals were held by those of Central Asian, Persian, or Afghān origin who ensconced themselves as rulers of North India since the time of the Delhi Sultānate.

In the North-West Frontier Province many Paṭhāns are settled on the plains as landowners. Among them tribal political structure, in which allegiance is given to elected local chiefs who are under the protection of the *khān*, is vestigial. In the villages there are other respectable Muslim castes, such as Sayyids who claim descent from Muhammad, or Mīyāns who claim descent from some pīr. The Paṭhān disdains handiwork, but as a landowner, he acts the part of patron. If he loses his land or his means of income, he essentially loses caste status and becomes a client of somebody else, and may ultimately be assimilated into a caste of agriculturalists. Serving the patrons are a mullā, the tenants, Pirāchā businessmen, various artisans, Gujjars who herd cattle, Āhārs who herd sheep, and Kohistānīs from the northern mountains. Tenants get half the harvest but have to provide their own oxen, seeds, and manure. Barbers, washermen, and sweepers are not untouchable in the Hindu sense, but respectable people do not normally eat with them. Since caste status pertains more to men than to women, brides may be taken from other castes more frequently than in India, but middle and upper castes will not generally take brides from menial castes. Even for men, caste is not as rigidly prescribed by birth as in India, and it is possible for one to be accepted into a Paṭhān tribe for merit or bravery.

The Qur'ānic injunction that there are no genealogies in Islam and that all Muslims are members of a universal brotherhood is violated by Paṭhān emphasis on the descent group. Qur'ānic inheritance laws are violated in Paṭhān refusal to allow daughters to inherit property or women to manage it. These inconsistencies are scarcely recognized. Consonant with Paṭhān emphasis on patriliny and male bravado, women are regarded as weak, modesty being the most commendable quality they can exhibit. Any kind of kin or status endogamy, or sister exchange, is approved as an expression of male friendship, says Barth. In contrast with Panjāb where dowry is given, Paṭhāns give bride-price, and the respect a girl commands among her inlaws is directly proportionate to the amount paid in consideration of her marriage. One factor giving rise to bride-price may be the shortage of women in this part of Pakistan, suggested in that North Wazīr has the lowest proportion of females and the highest bride-price, ranging up to 50,000 rupees. The legal status of a woman is clear in that she must obtain permission to visit her parents, and there is no formal occasion when she is required to communicate with her agnates. Census takers in 1961 noted that fathers' memories tended to falter when questions about daughters were asked. In North Wazīr and Kalām Agencies, not a single woman had

emigrated unless married, and not a single woman in those two agencies was recorded as literate.[14]

Modal Personality

The British admired western tribal people because of their fervent independence and resistance to outside political and cultural pressures. Because so many incursions have emanated from these regions, tribal personality ideal has become diffused over the western parts of South Asia, but it is stronger in the North-West Frontier Province than in Panjāb or Sindh or the Gangā plains.

Hospitality is a trait commented on by most visitors. The origin of this lay in the necessity for the tribal chief to serve as host and protector of strangers in his territory, demonstrate his wealth, and personify a favorable image of the tribe. More important, hospitality has been a mechanism by which the host could reinforce his own leadership within the tribe. Today when a Pakistan landowner affords hospitality, the same functions are served. He acts the role of patron and offers hospitality to the stranger who

Landowning family hosting the author and his wife, Jalpānā village, Pakistan. This guest house and veranda is to entertain guests; other buildings in compound are residences where women stay. The landowner's sons have had higher education and only one will take over land management. The starched turban is out of favor with them.

Three leisured Pakistani Panjābīs in a tea shop. Their honor and self-esteem are symbolized by guns.

in accepting, acknowledges need. The guest is thereby beholden to, if not inferior to, the host. The guest must eat well and without hurrying. The higher the rank of the guest, the more the host enhances his own prestige in the village. As with the jajmānī system and vartan bhānjī, it is the ability to give that affords prestige. Tenants and artisans may also be hospitable and gracious, emulating the ideal behavior of their social superiors.

Paṭhāns are imbued with izzat, the ideal of honor. In tribal regions and to some extent on the plains too, violence against a close kinsman or openly known adultery of wife or sister requires revenge; an unfulfilled debt of honor may be inherited. Reaction to a slight is quick. Honigmann points out that for this reason Paṭhāns normally avoid degrading other people, and treat even menials with deference. Keeping one's word is a mark of honor. Paṭhāns, and Pakistanis in general, tend to act impulsively and from emotion predominantly, rather than after calculated reasoning or planning, concludes Honigmann. The individual is self-assertive, and a quiet discussion quickly turns into a highly emotional shouting session, though it would be wrong for a foreigner to interpret this as anger or hostility. Men have a low frustration threshold, and "a series of strong defenses exist to prevent recognition of ego weakness," such as concern with izzat, carrying of guns or weapons, concern with wealth, identification with Pakistan, and the symbol pool that is Islam. In certain situations maintenance of one's honor requires dishonor of another, and to dishonor an opponent's women in times of war is psychologically effective. This feature of Pakistani behavior was made into a political issue during the Bangladesh war in 1971.

It has been suggested that child-socialization practices instill these qualities, beginning with swaddling of babies which is practiced predominantly in Pakistan tribal areas. The child learns to respect authority and the uselessness of crying. A small child infringing parental authority is immediately punished and may be beaten or forced to sit with its head pulled down crying "shame, shame." Early circumcision, an arranged marriage, paternal obedience, and restraints on speaking with one's wife or fondling one's child in the presence of the father, all build up inner tensions. A man is expected to release these inner tensions outside the family circle or kindred. Hence killing in retribution is sanctioned.

Paṭhāns have not been much affected by the modernization process in spite of a century of contact with outsiders. While they are individually independent they are not creative, do not take much initiative, nor manifest a drive toward self-realization. This is part of the quality Honigmann calls leniency. They are

lenient when it comes to putting forward unaccustomed effort for the realization of future goals. They have little pioneer spirit. Ambitions are restricted to normal expectations; a son of the gentry works hard to finish college so that he may get a well-defined job. If the goal demands unfamiliar effort, exertion, or is not clearly familiar, then it will probably be abandoned.[15]

Tribal people are also not careful about personal cleanliness, though they may take pains to wear garments signifying rank.

The reader should beware that these personality stereotypes are only relatively valid. There are many urbane and sophisticated Paṭhāns living in Peshāwar and throughout Pakistan who are not much different from

Chief Justice swears in Tikka Khan of West Pakistan as Governor of East Pakistan after abortive 1971 elections. Pakistan elites still rely on symbolic trappings of authority instituted by the British.

Panjābīs and Sindhīs. On the other hand, these traits have to some extent diffused through Pakistan and are found in northern and western India, but without the feuding. The emphasis in the culture on izzat rather than on the intellectual life is reflected in the lower level of literacy in Pakistan than in South India or Bānglā, and in the success of the military establishment. It is not surprising that Pakistan's history since Independence has been characterized by a hard and defensive posture on international issues, adamancy about Islam, and a vituperative stance against India which has been evident in any daily newspaper up until the loss of Bangladesh and the resignation of Yahya Khan's government. For these reasons too, anthropology and sociology, which require a certain introspection, are not popular subjects. On the other hand, the action-orientation of Pakistanis and the absence of economic ideology such as pervades the Indian government has resulted in an economic growth rate in Pakistan well above that of India.

Pakistan and Islam

Because Pakistan was founded as an officially Muslim nation, few Hindus remained. But many Pakistanis are not religious-minded; indeed, Panjābī peasants are quite pragmatic. But verbal espousal of Islam and its symbols is universal. There are many injunctions in the Qur'ān and the Sharī'at that are out of keeping with contemporary values, such as the command to "stone an adulteress to death" and "cut off the hand of a thief." The proscription against taking interest can hardly be observed in a modernizing economy.

Pakistanis have tried various approaches to resolve these conflicts of values. Some wish to throw out the codes of European origin and return to pure Islamic law. Others suggest that the traditional guide books such as the *Hadīth* contain only a selection from Islamic tradition and new problems are to be solved by elaborating the basic principles and examples contained in them. Some scholars find ways of reconciling Islamic texts to contemporary needs by showing that each event in them had a particular local or temporal setting and that therefore Islam should not be regarded as a static religion, but as a dynamic one adjusting to new circumstances. Yet others play with philology to circumlocute passages of apparent difficulty. Even on the concept of the Muslim state there are different interpretations of scripture. Conservatives reject the Muslim state and wish only for a universal Muslim community. Others remember the grand history of the Caliphates. Democratically inclined people can rationalize their view by pointing out that the Muslim community was democratic for a generation after the Prophet's death. Yet others rationalize that there is nothing in the

Qur'ān about government, so democracy is all right as long as it is Islamic democracy.

Islamic scholars have been enjoined to elicit guidelines from the texts, though it seems that the government seldom turns to these for guidance in making decisions. As an example of the kind of writing that is encouraged, we cite the conclusions of the scholar Fazlur Rahman. Islam, he says, is progressive, a "social reform movement." Spiritual and moral welfare are not possible unless there is first a sound and just socioeconomic base. Islam is not other-worldly, but is a charter giving the government the right, indeed the duty, to interfere in, rectify, and mold social fabric. The ulamā (scholars of religious law) have a fundamental function in an enlightened society. Islam, says Rahman, gives equal rights to all creeds and colors, and castes are foreign to it. Islam forbids males to exploit females and also forbids polygamy "under normal circumstances," and in this religion women are equal partners with men. Muslim society degenerated in the middle ages, and now it is time to check wrong trends. The dignity of manual labor was demonstrated by the Prophet himself, but in the Middle Ages somehow labor came to be despised. When Ayub Khan was introducing his system of Basic Democrats (tiers of representative government), Rahman thought this could be supported by the Islamic injunction to "enlist each other's support for righteous causes," and this means social cooperation. The "feudal society" of the tribals must be broken. The one important area of conflict, says Rahman, is that between the universalistic Islamic community and the ideal of the modern nation.

The various Islamic sects have not offered a wide range of choice of practical theology. Most Afghāns and Pakistanis are Sunnīs, though the Shī'ās who managed to enter government have offered no new arguments. The urban sects cater to the needs of relatively conservative businessmen. When a few Islamic ideas were put in the form of legislation, peasants objected; they did not want their daughters, for instance, to get half an inheritance share each. Most social legislation has been essentially based on secular ideology.

Hindu-Muslim Tensions

When Islamic civilization in India lost its political prop and fell to the British *rāj* (rule), Muslims retaliated by developing a philosophy of separateness. They refused to be shaken from their confidence in Arab and Persian scholarship by the new English-educated, Brāhmaṇ-dominated elite. Muslims did not seriously compete in higher education nor go after administrative positions. Consequently in independent India they have been at a disadvantage, though the Government of India is making every

effort to show to the world that it is truly a secular state by placing Muslims in important positions and offering them educational incentives.

Richard Fox writes of the town he studied in eastern Uttar Pradesh, in which a quarter of the people were Muslims:

> I wish to note the quality and intensity of the mutual hatred, which so effectively divides Tezibazar town. . . . In the deeply felt distaste which characterizes Muslim-Hindu feelings, it is invariably the Hindus who pose the problem aggressively. They argue that the Muslim can never be a real citizen of India because he is loyal first to his religion and only secondarily to his country. The Muslim, they feel, is always capable and ready to perform traitorous acts if they will benefit Pakistan. As proof, various flamboyant stories about supposed Muslim betrayal of India to China in the Himalayas are brought forth. There is also a social distaste for the *musulman* which is evidenced in the statement that they are (physically) dirty. More sophisticated people in the town claim that their commensal avoidance of Muslims is based not on a wish to maintain caste rules but upon their displeasure in eating with someone dirty.[16]

There was a Hindu-Muslim riot here in 1925, and also agitation over Muslim cow slaughter. Yet, Muslims feel that relations with Hindus were better in prewar days. They attribute the present rancor to the democratic electoral system of independent India. The Jana Sangh, a right-wing Hindu party strong in Uttar Pradesh, is supported by Baniyās (merchants) and Brāhmaṇs, and most of the anti-Muslim feeling comes from these two groups. Conflict in this town is not just economic competition, for next to Baniyās, Muslims are the largest trading "community" and perform mostly services which complement Baniyā businesses. The root causes are Hindu antipathy to six centuries of Muslim rule, followed by strong Hindu cultural revivalism after the departure of the British, and communally-based electioneering. Muslims cannot afford to betray open resentment towards Hindus, neither can they openly espouse allegiance to Pakistan. They harbor some fear of the Hindu majority. Yet Muslims form the largest cohesive body of any communal group in this town simply because there are not many occasions for the various Hindu castes to unite. Muslims reflect this cohesion at their festivals more than do Hindus. But this Muslim cohesion is precisely one of the irritants to Hindus, who in general have been tolerant of diversity but not of exclusiveness.

Hindu-Muslim tension building up over the centuries came to a head after partition in 1947 and 1948. The story has often been told how within a few months 6 to 7 million Hindus fled from Pakistan and a like number of Muslims fled from India—the greatest mass migration known to history. The loss of lands, the privations as refugees, the atrocities, still rancor a generation later. Gandhi devoted his last months to ameliorating these differences, but lost his life to a Hindu extremist. Since the early years of Independence, Muslims in India have generally been peaceable, but riots do occur, such as in Ahmadābād in 1970 and Alīgaṛh in 1971. These are

embarrassing to India and blown up beyond recognition in the Pakistan press.

While it does not appear that the Indus drainage region, for reasons of geography and culture history and apart even from religious factors, will ever again become part of a wider India, it may be suggested that Hindu-Muslim polarization is likely to decrease in the future. With the creation of Bangladesh there is no question of any other country in South Asia achieving a balance of power with India. Pakistan has reduced the propaganda against "Hindu" India, and India has made concessions to Pakistan after the Bangladesh war. It is likely that these developments will further ameliorate Hindu-Muslim tensions, which in any case probably passed their apogee some years ago. Tensions of the future are likely to revolve around regionalisms within each country and economic issues, which are more substantive than religious ideology in the gradual secularization process.

REFERENCES AND NOTES

[1] Theodore Wright, "Islam in Modern South Asia," unpublished paper.
[2] Yogendra Singh, "Chanukhera: Cultural Change in Eastern Uttar Pradesh," in K. Ishwaran (ed.), *Change and Continuity in India's Villages* (New York, 1970), pp. 260–261.
[3] Vreede-de Stuers, p. 88.
[4] Vreede-de Stuers, p. 91.
[5] Inayatulla, "Caste, Patti and Faction in the Life of a Punjabi Village," in *Sociologus* VIII, No. 2 (1958).
[6] Alavi (1972).
[7] Hamza Alavi, "Vartan Bhanji—a Mechanism in Organisation of Patri-Clans in Villages of Panjab," manuscript, p. 2.
[8] Alavi, pp. 3–4.
[9] Eglar, p. 125.
[10] Bray, p. 46.
[11] Pehrson and Barth, p. 62.
[12] Pehrson and Barth, p. 70.
[13] James W. Spain, *The People of the Khyber* (New York, 1962), pp. 109, 113–114.
[14] Khalid Ashraf, pp. 25–26, 61, 102.
[15] John Honigmann, "Some Themes in Pakistan National Culture" (manuscript, Chapel Hill, N.C., 1957).
[16] Fox, p. 112.

IMPORTANT SOURCES

Abdoula, Ahmed. *The Historical Background of Pakistan and its People*. Karāchī, 1973. (Ethnohistoric survey of all the provinces.)

Ahmad, Aziz. *Studies in Islamic Culture in the Indian Environment*. Oxford, 1964.

Ahmad, Makhdum Tasadduq. *Systems of Social Stratification in India and Pakistan.* Lahore, 1972. (Includes a brief study of a Panjāb village.)

Alavi, Hamza. "The Politics of Dependence: A Village in West Punjab," in *South Asian Review* 4, No. 2 (1971).

Alavi, Hamza. "Kinship in West Punjab Villages," in *Contributions to Indian Sociology*, 1972.

Ansari, Ghans. *Muslim Caste in Uttar Pradesh.* Lucknow, 1960. (The most dependable work on this subject.)

Ashraf, Khalid. *Tribal People of West Pakistan.* Peshawar, 1962.

Barth, Fredrik. "The System of Social Stratification in Swat, North Pakistan," in E. R. Leach (ed.), *Aspects of Caste in South India, Ceylon, and North-West Pakistan.* Cambridge, England, 1962.

Bray, Sir Denys. *The Brahui Language*, 2 vols. Delhi, 1934. (Vol. II contains cultural data.)

Chand, Tara. *The Influence of Islam on Indian Culture.* Allahabad, 1952.

Dichter, David. *The North-West Frontier of West Pakistan.* Oxford, 1967. (A study in regional geography.)

Eberhard, Wolfram. *Settlement and Social Change in Asia.* Hong Kong, 1967. (Includes a 10 page bibliography on Islam and Pakistan.)

Eglar, Zekiye. *A Panjabi Village in Pakistan.* New York, 1960.

Fox, Richard. *From Zamindar to Ballot Box.* Ithaca, N.Y., 1969.

Gankovsky, Yu. V. *The Peoples of Pakistan: An Ethnic History*, trans. by Igor Gavrilov. Lahore, n.d. (Originally in Russian.)

Gardezi, Hassan Nawaz (ed.). *Sociology in Pakistan.* Lahore, 1966.

Government of Pakistan. *Census Report of Tribal Agencies.* Karachi, 1961.

Honigmann, John. *Three Pakistan Villages.* Chapel Hill, N.C., 1958. (Studies of villages in Panjāb, Sindh, and the North-West Frontier Province.)

Khan, Muhammad Sardar. *History of the Baluch Race.* Quetta, 1958.

Makhdum, Tasadduq Ahmad. *A Study of the Social Institutions of Swat*, thesis, Lahore, n.d.

Maron, Stanley (ed.). *Pakistan: Society and Culture.* New Haven, Conn., 1957.

Marriott, McKim. *Caste Ranking and Community Structure in Five Regions of India and Pakistan.* Puṇe, 1960. (Contains a brief study of caste in a middle Indus village.)

Mujeeb, M. *The Indian Muslims.* London, 1967. (An authoritative history.)

Pakistan Agricultural University, Lyallpur. *Punjabi Rural Social Institutions: An Exploratory Study.* Lyallpur, 1969.

Pehrson, Robert, and Fredrik Barth. *The Social Organization of the Marri Baluch.* Chicago, 1966. (A valuable study of tribal social structure.)

Quereshi, I. H. *The Muslim Community of the Indo-Pakistan Subcontinent.* The Hague, 1962.

Rahman, Fazlur. "Some Reflections on the Reconstruction of Muslim Society in Pakistan," *Islamic Culture* VI, No. 2 (1967).

Raza, Muhammad Rafique Raza. *Two Pakistani Villages: A Study in Social Stratification.* Lahore, 1969.

Vreede-de Stuers, Cora. *Pardā.* New York, 1968.

Wilbur, Donald (ed.). *Afghanistan.* New Haven, Conn., 1962. (The most useful work on the society and culture.)

Wilbur, Donald (ed.). *Pakistan: Its People, Its Society, Its Culture.* New Haven, Conn., 1964.

14

Survey of Himālayan Peoples

In this chapter we shall race through 1800 miles of territory, stretching from the Hindū Kash in northeastern Afghanistan and following the Himālayan slopes to Arunāchal Pradesh which touches the Burma border. Politically we are dealing with these entities: part of Afghanistan, the northern reaches of Pakistan, Āzād (Pakistani) Kashmīr, Indian Kashmīr and Ladākh (partly held by China), the state of Himāchal Pradesh, three Himālayan districts of Uttar Pradesh, Nepal, Sikkim, Darjeeling District in West Bengal, Bhutan, and part of the territory of Arunāchal Pradesh. Climate varies from the arid heights of Afghanistan to the rain forests north of the Brahmaputra River and from the steamy malarial plains of the tarāī to the highest mountains in the world. This Himālayan belt, with perhaps 25 million people, is of surpassing anthropological interest because its valleys and slopes harbor so very many isolated and refugee populations whose cultures throw light on the early stages of civilizational development in South Asia. Even more, it is in the nexus of four "great traditions" or classical civilizations: Persian, Central Asian, Tibetan, and Indian. It forms the Hindu-Buddhist contact zone and on the west has become Muslim. But underlying these religions are tribal cults and shamanistic practices.

Unfortunately today access to this region is difficult. The higher Himālayan regions of both Pakistan and India are closed to visitors for security reasons, and Tibet is inaccessible. Access to Bhutan and Sikkim is also controlled from India. Though in Nepal official permission must be obtained to travel, most of our recent Himālayan data comes from this interesting country.

Western Himālayas

In the upper reaches of the Hindū Kash, the lofty range extending from the western Himālayas into the heart of Afghanistan, are 70,000 Kāfirs, so called by the Muslims because they were formerly nonbelievers. When the British demarcated the Durand Line forming the eastern boundary of Afghanistan, these Kāfirs fell under the rulership of the Amīr. In 1895 he decided to put an end to idolatry within his domains and sent a force which massacred the Kāfirs, made slaves of some, and requisitioned others for his army. The remainder had to burn their wooden idols and build mosques. Having accomplished this, the Amīr renamed the territory Nūristān, Land of Light.

Kāfirs claim to be descended from Alexander's soldiers, and indeed the elite among them do have European features, with light-colored or brown hair and blue eyes. They abandoned the plains about the 9th century because of their unwillingness to embrace Islam and imposed their authority on the more swarthy indigenous inhabitants of the Hindū Kash. They live by herding and cultivation, and build grandiose wooden houses which contain no single item from the outside world. They speak Dardic languages.

The Kāfirs in Afghanistan are called Red Kāfirs, and today they are all nominally Muslims. But in Chitrāl, the northwestern extremity of Pakistan, there are about 3000 Black Kāfirs who retain their indigenous religion. They build wooden temples whose rites are conducted by priest-shamans. Imra (Indra?) is the supreme creator who heads the pantheon, while mother goddesses are also important. Early travelers recorded that cows were sacrificed to the dead; some corpses were buried in coffins and some were exposed. A year after burial a wooden statue, life-size or larger and representing the dead person, was erected over the grave. Such statues have been found all along the western Himālayas and suggest a former wide distribution of this religious practice. Kāfirs observe menstrual pollution (Chap. 8) and death pollution and make sacrifices. All these practices are significant in that they are not only pre-Muslim in origin but also the last extant relics of pre-Vedic religion of the Indus region and seem to have contributed to the formation of Hinduism in the Panjāb.

Chitrāl, formerly an independent kingdom, has 120,000 people who mostly speak Khuwār, a Dardic language, and they are considered by other

Pakistanis to be a different kind of people. They maintain a low level of subsistence on barley, wheat, millet, rice, and vegetables, and only 2% are literate (in Urdū). To the southeast are the two parts of Kohistān on the upper Indus and Swāt rivers. Kohistānīs are Dardic-speakers ousted from the Swāt Valley by the Paṭhāns who became landowners there and extended their hegemony to Kohistān. The people practice an extreme form of transhumance, a whole village sometimes moving from 2000 to 14,000 feet or higher. A family might maintain four or five houses at different altitudes, which they occupy in turn as they tend crops suitable to each level. Other Kohistānīs live permanently at 6000 or 8000 feet but daily trek several thousand feet higher for herding or cultivation.

In the part of Kashmīr governed by Pakistan, Āzād Kashmīr, is the former independent state of Chilās peoples by Shinas. Whereas the rest of the states of Dardistān were monarchical, Shinas evolved a republican form of government, with village assemblies and a state assembly of elders, who in fact could be replaced if they did not abide by majority opinion. Shinas have shamans who ritually avoid milk, and when they get spirit-possessed, they kill a goat and drink its blood. Islam is a cultural overlay. Among these and neighboring mountain people there is no pardā but premarital sexual activity is condoned. Illegitimate children may be killed, and there is a system of foster kin whereby children will be brought up by others for a time to promote social solidarity.

To the north on the Gilgit River which feeds into the upper Indus is the town of Gilgit, now a tourist resort connected by air with Rāwalpiṇḍī. Northward of Gilgit is the fabled 100-mile valley of Hunza, the subject of a number of popular publications because of the reputed longevity of the Burushos and their health food type of diet—fresh grains, fruits, nuts, and vegetables. The valley is very narrow and overcrowded, but the hillsides are carefully terraced. Though the people are Muslims, they retain their language, Burushaski, a relic of pre-Indo-European speech. To the southwest of Hunza is the large and high plateau of Baltistān, riven by the headwaters of the Indus. Balti is a Tibetan-type language spoken by 150,000 people who have adopted Islam. Racially they are a mixed Tibetan-Panjābī type.

The isolation of these frontier regions has ended because of troop movements in Āzād Kashmīr and the necessity for Pakistan to secure its administration. Pakistan has built a military road through Gilgit and Hunza which crosses the Pāmīrs over a 15,450-foot pass and descends to Kashgār in the Tārīm Basin of western China.

In the Indian state of Jammū and Kashmīr 68% of the population is Muslim and most of the Hindus live in the Jammū part in the foothills. Kashmīrīs accepted Islam only in the 14th century and the peoples toward the northern border only in the 16th. The Vale of Kashmīr consists of alluvial soil worked by Muslim peasants, though Hindus form an elite

Transhumant Gūjars of Kashmīr. These Muslims drive their animals up to the foot of the glaciers and camp for the summer.

minority and the Mahārājā who ceded the state to India was Hindu. The mountains around the Vale are occupied by Muslim pastoralists who call themselves Gūjars.

The Western Tibetan Frontier

The eastern part of Kashmīr consists of a high and somewhat arid plateau known as Ladākh where 50,000 Buddhists live. This is culturally a part of the Tibetan world, though sprinkled with a few Dardic-speaking settlements. Ladākh has historically been nominally linked with Lhāsa, capital of Tibet, under the Lāmaistic system of government by a hierarchy of monasteries, but in effect it was semi-independent and even expansionist. Monasteries own half the land, and the poor are perpetually indebted to them. There are as many monasteries as villages, and they contain up to a sixth of the population. Each family has a crematorium, but the poor are exposed instead of cremated, unless during their lifetime they have been able to accumulate a sufficient quantity of firewood—there is practically none to be had in these barren mountains.

As with neighboring Himālayan peoples, Ladākhīs build houses of two

or three stories, with the animals kept on the ground floor. Agriculture is dependent upon irrigation because the soil is very thin and precipitation infrequent. Fields must be carefully terraced. Barley, buckwheat, and wheat are the staple grains, while peas, turnips, and mustard supplement the diet. The men do the plowing with draft animals, though where it is steep they have to draw the plow themselves. Tibetans have a pastoral tradition, and Ladākhīs likewise rely heavily on the produce of animals. They keep oxen, yaks, sheep, goats, ponies, asses, and dogs, from which they obtain meat, milk and butter, and hides, while their ponies, yaks, and a kind of sheep transport bags of goods over the picturesque, precipitous trails of the Himālayas. Ladākhīs, as people all along the border of Tibet, formerly engaged in trading, bringing tea, shawls, wood, and borax into India, and carrying opium, saffron, and shawls to the Muslim populations of Sinkiang Province of China. But salt was the most essential commodity they disseminated. Since the occupation of Tibet by China, this trade has stopped.

Though there is no extended hierarchy of castes among Tibetan peoples, Lāmas form an elite group, while at the bottom there are groups of people whose position resembles that of untouchables in India, particularly sweepers and musicians. Ladākhīs, along with Tibetans and other Himālayan peoples, practice fraternal polyandry. The oldest son marries and shares his wife and property with his brothers, or a number of brothers may share two or more wives. The purpose of this is to prevent land from being fragmented, since cultivable land is very scarce in relation to the population relying upon it. Fraternal polyandry among the Ladākhīs is really an extension of the principle of primogeniture. A younger son has the alternative of the monastic life open to him, and a daughter can also serve in a monastery as a nun. If a family has a daughter but no son, she can marry by choice and inherit the property. As with other Himālayan people, there are not many rigid proscriptions regarding sexual relations, and in Ladākh the incidence of venereal diseases is reported to range up to 90%.

Ladākh has enjoyed relative isolation since it formed a kingdom in the 13th century, but in the early 1960s it flashed into international prominence with the China-India conflict. China, after her occupation of Tibet, built a 100-mile road across the eastern side of Ladākh which the Indian government was unaware of for a year. In the ensuing Himālayan war the Indian army was not prepared to fight at such altitudes. China still occupies the eastern bulge of the district, but India has since built a 205-mile road from Śrīnagar to Leh and jeepable roads beyond. India also is promoting cultivation of vegetables and animal husbandry to help feed the large army contingent now stationed in Leh and beyond. It has established a hospital and over 200 schools including five high schools, and is in general opening up these mountain reaches to the influence of the wider world, while connection with Tibetan civilization has been cut off.

Tibetan-like peoples along the upper Himālayas ranging across India,

Nepal, Sikkim, and Bhutan are called Bhoṭiyās, which literally mean Tibetans, and they have been influenced by Indian culture more than hav Ladākhīs. In northern Himāchal Pradesh the district of Lāhaul and Spitī i essentially Tibetan in culture. Most of the lāmas belong to the Yellow Ha sect, to which the Dalai Lāma of Tibet also belongs; his Tibetan govern ment in exile is located in nearby Dharmaśālā. This sect does not recogniz nuns, but some of the women do become nuns and remain in their ow houses. The people of Spitī do not practice fraternal polyandry, but onl the eldest son marries and inherits the property, while younger sons ma become monks. Each family is attached to a monastery, and a boy wi usually go there to study with his uncle. All the lāmas of one family ow the monastery property collectively and work for wages in the summe The region is poor and is considered to be the most "backward" district i the whole of the western Himālayas.

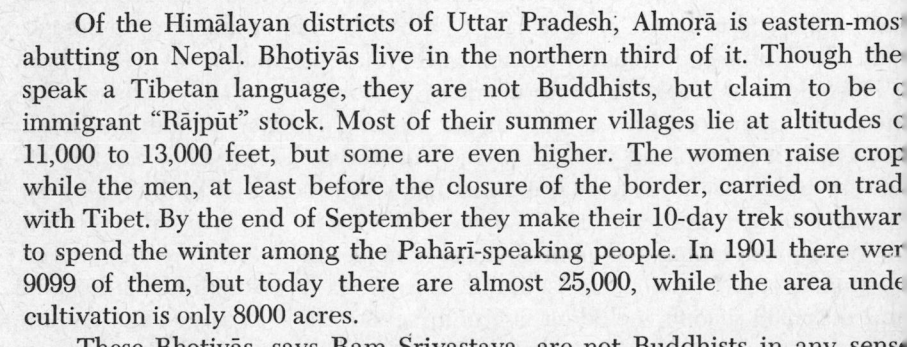

Tibetan women spinning and cardin

Of the Himālayan districts of Uttar Pradesh, Almoṛā is eastern-mos abutting on Nepal. Bhoṭiyās live in the northern third of it. Though the speak a Tibetan language, they are not Buddhists, but claim to be c immigrant "Rājpūt" stock. Most of their summer villages lie at altitudes c 11,000 to 13,000 feet, but some are even higher. The women raise crop while the men, at least before the closure of the border, carried on trad with Tibet. By the end of September they make their 10-day trek southwar to spend the winter among the Pahāṛī-speaking people. In 1901 there wer 9099 of them, but today there are almost 25,000, while the area unde cultivation is only 8000 acres.

These Bhoṭiyās, says Ram Srivastava, are not Buddhists in any sens The Kumāon region (Himālayan Uttar Pradesh) did profess Buddhism, mixture of Tantric ritual and local cults, but abolished it in the 11th centur

hough it probably lingered in northern pockets). Rājpūt kings ruled umāon and western Nepal for a millennium. Bhoṭiyās bid fair to be ac- epted as Rājpūts, and they could support this by their relative prosperity. ut they could not quite be accepted into the Hindu social framework ecause they were "beef eaters," "just like the Tibetans," and ate beef with he Tibetans. These Bhoṭiyās developed their own hierarchical caste system, ymbolized by rules of commensality. More recently they have been subject the impact of the wider society; they succeeded in getting themselves lassified as a "backward caste," which means they are entitled to special conomic, educational, and employment opportunities. Moreover, in 1962 he Tibetan trade came to a complete halt, with the result that they are eaving their valleys and drifting toward the towns in Kumāon. In such a ase as this, Srivastava points out, the tribe-caste dichotomy is not justified; hey are simply an ethnic group which has reacted in its own way to the uccessive acculturating forces in the Hindu-Buddhist contact zone.

lindu Himālayan Peoples of India

The main valleys of the Himālayas of Himāchal Pradesh and northern Jttar Pradesh, such as Kullū and Kāngṛā, harbor a number of refugee popu- ations which have been quite Hinduized because of the continual influx f Rājpūts, Brāhmaṇs, and Chetrīs from the plains. In addition the British opularized the use of hill towns as resorts, so in summer one finds flocks f people from the plains cities visiting Śimlā, Manālī, Dharmaśālā, and Maṇḍī in Himāchal Pradesh, or Missoorie, Nainī Tāl, and Almoṛā in Uttar Pradesh.

The bulk of the cultivating population along the lower Himālayan belt n India are Pahāṛīs, who merge into Nepālīs in western Nepal. Pahāṛīs umber over 6 million. They are quite Hindu and Indian in race and culture nd are also known as Khāsās or Chetrīs. Though marginal in terms of the ntrenched cultural values of the Gangā plains, these Pahāṛī people, Ber- eman points out, are certainly not marginal in terms of the internal con- istency of their own cultural patterns. Not only are they numerous, but heir culture area is rather sharply delineated from the Tibetans on the orth and the plains people on the south, though it is becoming less so. In he same way that Pahāṛī is related to Hindī but yet differs from it, most ultural features are part of the broader Indian civilizational region. Pahāṛī aste structure is less orthodox and less complex than that of the plains, hough outcaste Ḍoms are segregated. Instead of dowry, parents of the groom give money in consideration of marriage. Divorce and remarriage are asy. Houses are made of stone rather than of mud bricks and are roofed vith slate or wooden shakes. Agriculture is intensive and demands terracing

of the fields. Because of transportation difficulties, villages are often isolated and inward-looking.

Berreman reported for his village in Dehrā Dūn District that fraternal polyandry was not practiced. But it was the subject of a study in 1937 by the pioneer Indian anthropologist D. N. Majumdar in another part of that same district. In several villages around Jaunsār, 31% of women investigated had a single husband, 31.5% had two husbands, 15.5% three, 4.5% four and 5.5% five husbands each, while 12% had one living and one dead husband. Of 605 women examined, 285 had been divorced.[1]

In a household in these hills, says Majumdar, the services of several hands are required, and most families cannot afford to keep domestic servants; therefore, several brothers must work together on the land. Sometimes a wife prefers to have cowives to help with the household chores if there are several brothers, or to release her from the necessity of satisfying all the husbands if she is especially fond of one of them. By customary law the eldest brother owns the house and garden, marries the wife, and maintains and controls all the children. Conventionally the eldest born child is said to have been fathered by the eldest brother, the next by the second brother, and so on, but if a younger brother wishes to marry separately and leave, he cannot take any children with him. The number of children of polyandrous families is relatively small, and it is reported that old people remember that female infanticide was practiced. A daughter has unusual latitude in her sexual preferences, but when she becomes a wife, she is amenable to the control of her husband or husbands. A wife can periodically return home where she can again act as a daughter, so naturally she returns more often than is customary on the plains. Majumdar reports that when he asked a certain father why his daughter did not help much in the family, the father replied, "Oh, she is with us for a while. Let her play sing and dance, enjoy life as she must, for she may have no rest or leisure in her husband's house."

Nepal

Nepal was little known to anthropologists, nor to any outsiders, before it opened in 1951, but since that time a few researchers have proved the stamina of their walking legs and have published studies on some of its people. English anthropologists include the indefatigable Fürer-Haimendorf and Colin Rosser, joined by the American John Hitchcock, the Canadian Lionel Caplan, the Frenchman Bernard Pignède, and two Nepālī anthropologists, S. G. Nepali, and Dor Bahadur Bista who has written the first survey covering all important peoples of Nepal.

This country stretches 500 miles along the Himālayas and has 54,36 square miles. The population in 1961 was 9.4 million, and by 1973 was

12 million. It is naturally divided by altitude into four lengthwise zones. The tarāī, 50 miles wide but stretching the entire length of the country below the first range of mountains, is 1000 to 2500 feet high and contains 35% of the people. The middle valley and hill region ranges up to 7000 feet and has 60% of the population. Above these are the higher forested ranges which contain but 5% of the population, and the fourth zone is the treeless tundra-like fringe of the Tibetan plateau.

The tarāī has been increasingly settled within the last few decades, and there still remain some areas where there is land yet to be brought under the plow. The people are Hindu or Muslim, with Brāhmaṇs, Rājpūts, and occupational castes. The most important ethnic element is the Thārūs, who stretch clear along the tarāī belt. The crops produced here are rice, wheat, sugar cane, tobacco, jute, pulses, mustard, and forest products. Reduction of the incidence of malaria has been the most important factor in opening up the tarāī to the overflow population of both Nepal and the Gangā plains.

Behind the first range of mountains, a number of rivers have gouged out east-west courses which coalesce in three major riverine systems in the east, west, and center of the country. These and a number of lesser rivers spectacularly break through and drain into the Gangā system. Here and there are delightful valleys or alluvial basins, such as those which cup Kāṭhmāṇḍū and Pokhārā, and it is here that we find the people whom we think of as characteristically Nepālī. Communication among these valleys has been by foot path, with treks sometimes taking weeks. Nepal's projected east-west highway is not yet nearing completion, though a road from India to Kāṭhmāṇḍū has now been built with Indian aid and has been continued to Tibet with Chinese aid. Above these midmontane valleys and hills live Bhoṭiyās, while on the northeastern edge of the country there are the related Sherpas, Tāmāngs, and some Lepchas.

The Nepal valleys have not been completely cut off from the outside world. Gautama Buddha came from a royal Hindu line on the southern border of Nepal, and Buddhism of the Aśokan period seems to have reached the country. A Chinese mission came in 543. Tantric Buddhism from Bānglā made an impact and parts of Nepal at least were under Tibet until the 9th century. But Indian civilization from the plains gradually gathered momentum in the various valleys accessible from the tarāī, and upon the invasions of the Muslims in the middle Gangā region in the 14th century, Hindu Ṭhākurs moved in, followed by Brāhmaṇs and Rājpūts. Hindu kings of the Mallā line established an empire, but in general each valley remained more or less isolated, so it was said that there were 24 states in central Nepal and 22 in the west.

In 1736 a king of Gorkhā in central Nepal, a Ṭhākurī who claimed descent from Rājpūt princes of Udaipur in Rājasthān, invaded the Newār kingdom of the Kāṭhmāṇḍū Valley but was repulsed. In 1768 another king of that Gurkhā line, Prithvi Narayan Saha, took Kāṭhmāṇḍū and consoli-

dated rule over Nepal and Kumāon. His Gurkhā army incorporated indigenous tribesmen along with Ṭhākurī and Chetrī Hindus, and in this way Hinduism and the Hindu social order came to have official sanction over the indigenous Gurūng, Magar, Newār, and others whose languages belong to the Tibeto-Burmese phylum and whose religion was Buddhism or indigenous tribal cults.

With the establishment of this Hindu dynasty three caste groups gained ascendance. Ritually highest are the Brāhmaṇs, of which there are three castes. Below them ritually, but more important politically, are the Ṭhākurīs, to which the present royal family belongs, though in western Nepal Ṭhākurīs are hill farmers. Ṭhākurīs in their features betray Mongoloid admixture, and it is likely that they are racially of predominantly local origin. The third group, Chetrīs, have largely taken up cultivation. These three caste groups have been responsible for the dissemination of the Nepālī language, a Hindī-like speech which has become the lingua franca throughout the country. Two other ethnic elements of Indian origin are the Thārūs in the lowlands, and Pahāṛīs or Kumāonīs along the western part of the country.

From 1846 to 1951 the Rāṇā family ruled Nepal; they were almost fanatically Hindu and excluded visitors from the country so that it was isolated from the rest of the world. In 1951 King Tribhuvan of the Saha family ousted these Rāṇās, established good relations with India, and embarked on a program of modernization. Economic development has progressed with the implementation of three five-year plans, the third beginning in 1965 as part of a comprehensive 15-year program intended to double national income. A parliament was instituted in 1959, but the following year after only 18 months of operation King Mahendra abolished the first elected ministry, stating that parliamentary democracy had proved unsuitable to Nepal. Instead he instituted a four-tier panchāyat system whose foundation is 4000 village panchāyats and their capstone, the National Panchāyat.

The late King Mahendra realized the importance of Hindu ideology as a unifying factor because half the people are not of Nepālī-speaking Hindu origin. Hence he stated in a speech: "Today we can protect and advance our nation and national society only if all of us cease to have any shyness or scruples about calling ourselves Hindu, but march forward to protect, strengthen and develop Hindu society and revitalize Dharma." The traditional functions of the king include the power to raise and depose castes and the responsibility to protect Hindu orthodoxy. He is believed to be an incarnation of Vishṇu, but on this the late King said, "Personally speaking I don't believe in all those things. First of all, I am a human being. And whatever else I am, I must serve my country."[2] The new young King, Birendra Bir Bikram Saha Deva, continues royal tradition and has resisted

demands for electoral reform. In this ethnically diversified country Hindu symbols and veneration of the Hindu king are important unifying factors. In times past there was pressure on non-Hindu people to at least nominally accept Brāhmaṇs as priests, and even now laws favor settlement of lands by Nepālī-speaking Hindus over the indigenous ethnic groups. The Newārīs around Kāṭhmāṇḍū tend to call themselves Hindus rather than Buddhists if they achieve prestige, and cannot expect to get good jobs unless they can speak good Nepālī.

Limbūs in eastern Nepal.

Newār after an oil rubdown in preparation for Hindu festival. Nepal Hindus deem this to be cooling and purifying, as Indians do.

Hindu Chetrīs

The Chetrīs (Kshatriyas) have been described by Fürer-Haimendorf. In appearance they resemble North Indians, and they are quite numerous over central Nepal. One of their clans was the Rāṇās who ruled Nepal before 1951. Ṭhākurīs and Chetrīs have been the chief agents in the phenomenal spread of Nepālī. Both consider themselves as high caste Hindus, wear the sacred thread, employ Brāhmaṇs as priests, and hold high caste Hindu ideals of ritual purity and domestic life. The civilization of the Newārs, with its emphasis on architecture and the arts, centered in the Kāṭhmāṇḍū Valley, gave way to this intrusive ethnic element.

The replacement of Newar rule by the Thakuri-Chetri regime of the past two centuries involved not only a shift of political power from an urban ruling class indigenous to the Valley to a rustic aristocracy stemming from the hill-chiefs of the Gorkha region. It caused the decline of a pattern of life moulded by the

Newar's emphasis on the importance of aesthetic values and the commerce and crafts which provided the basis for their realization, and favored the growth of martial and nationalistic ideals. A liberal tradition under which Buddhism had thrived on equal terms with Hinduism, was set aside by the more puritanical outlook of the Thakuri and Chetri rulers, who lent the whole power of the governmental machinery to the enforcement of Brahmanical values and invested the Raj Guru, a Brahman heading an office of pandits, with the authority to regulate behavior in many spheres of life and to adjudicate caste disputes.[3]

Intercaste hypergamy is countenanced. Brāhmaṇs may marry Chetrī girls and may also live in unions unsanctified by marriage with Newār, Gurūng, Mȧgar, or Tāmāng women. Children of such unions are classified as Khatrīs and sometimes merge into the Chetrīs. Children of Brāhmaṇ fathers and Ṭhākurī mothers also form a special Khatrī caste. A child born to a Chetrī man and a woman of indigenous origin would bear the father's clan name but would not eat with members of his kin group. But over a number of generations, his descendants might work their way back to membership in the lineage. Khatrīs, too, after two or three generations, can begin marrying within the Chetrī caste-cluster.

Chetrīs maintain a clan structure, and a clan may be widely dispersed over the country. A Thapā Chetrī near Kāṭhmāṇḍū, for instance, will be aware of the existence of two or three other Thapā lineages, but may not be certain of their location or if there are even more farther away. What is important is the recognizable lineage, which is exogamous. Fürer-Haimendorf cites the example of an informant who knew of 200 families in his lineage, all but two of which lived in the Kāṭhmāṇḍū Valley. All in a lineage will worship the same lineage deity, and they should all observe death pollution if the deceased can be traced with a genealogical link within seven generations. But even if such a link cannot be traced, all the Chetrīs of a clan in one settlement will observe death pollution as a symbol of cohesion.

The Chetrīs of the Kāṭhmāṇḍū Valley are divided into a middle class and a peasant class. These two are distinguished not so much by wealth as by the refusal of the middle class one to work for wages, their feeling ashamed to carry loads, their reluctance to sell produce in small quantities instead of in bulk, and their maintenance of more formal relations within the household, as between father and son, or master and servant. Chetrīs have been settling in the overcrowded Kāṭhmāṇḍū Valley for the last two centuries. They do not invade Newār villages, but live in dispersed houses or house clusters, largely around the rim of the Valley, and pursue even today techniques of cultivation differing from those of the Newārs. A remarkable feature of the diffusion of the Chetrīs is that wherever they have settled they have refused to speak in local languages—Gurūng, Tāmāng, Rāī, or Newār—but instead these other people have had to learn Nepālī. This is one of the chief links unifying Nepal today.

Midmontane Nepal Peoples

The soldiers from Nepal who served with such distinction in the British army are known as Gurkhās, but they are not one people, since they come from various ethnic groups. Some are Hindu Ṭhākurīs or Chetrīs, but most are from the groups speaking Tibeto-Burmese languages such as Gurūng, Magar, Rāī, Limbū, Sunwār, and Tāmāng. Occasionally a soldier enlists from the Lepcha, Newār, Thakālī, Punyal, Sherpa, Manjhī, or Kumbal peoples. The Gurkhā regiments serving under the colonial government have now been divided between the English and Indian armed forces, and some still serve in Malaysia and Hong Kong. Returned soldiers are agents of change in their villages, and the pensions they bring are an important source of security. Many people from Nepal serve in India in other capacities, especially as watchmen since they benefit from the reputation of the Gurkhās, and are popularly sometimes called Gurkhās.

Gurkhā soldiers have a reputation for being self-confident, independent, and cheerful, and these qualities characterize Nepal people in general. There is none of the obsequiousness one finds in India, nor the dogmatism or seclusion of women typical of Pakistan. In the past decade tourists in increasing numbers have discovered Nepal's magnificent scenery and pleasant climate, the striking old architecture of the Kāṭhmāṇḍū Valley, and the cheerful self-reliant nature of its people.

The variety of midmontane peoples is great, and we can do no more than refer briefly to a few of them. The dominant ethnic group in the midwestern region is the Magars, who number a third of a million and provide more Gurkhā soldiers than any other ethnic group. They have been described by John Hitchcock, who has been interested in determining the interrelationship between altitude and culture. Those who live in lower altitudes are sedentary and cultivate millet, maize, and irrigated rice, whereas those who live high up are transhumant, but also engage in cultivation of maize and rice where possible, and more especially barley and potatoes which thrive at higher altitudes. Their language is an indigenous Tibeto-Burmese one. The transhumant Magars speak a form of Magar unintelligible to the sedentary ones; this bifurcation probably represents two historic migration phases. Aside from this, Magars are split up into a number of subtribes.

Magars all claim to be Hindus and perhaps never were Buddhists. Lower ones are more affected by Hinduism than are the transhumant ones. Even the lower sedentary ones retain a number of practices considered quite un-Brāhmaṇical in North India, such as marriage of a man to his maternal cross-cousin, sacrifice of a chicken at every marriage, and eating of the domestic pig. Mixed among the Magars, and to some extent interbred with them, are Brāhmaṇs, Ṭhākurīs, and artisans who have come up from the plains as refugees over the centuries. Magars are quite caste-conscious,

and have merged into the Hindu social structure as a fairly high clean caste. The untouchable castes here are Metalworkers, Leatherworkers, and Tailors. Hitchcock says that Magars will not accept any cooked food from untouchables and will accept only food cooked in ghī from clean castes beneath them. If rice is boiled in pure water drawn with and poured from vessels used only for cooking, they can accept it from any higher caste, but if rice is boiled in ritually impure water, they will take it only from the hands of Upadhyāya Brāhmaṇs.

Marriages are arranged by parents and performed with proper Hindu ceremonies. But Magars allow more contact between boys and girls than do plains Indians. For instance, there are many occasions during the year when groups sing and dance. Boys and girls in a group will alternately sing questions and responses, each following a leader who is informally chosen and who spontaneously composes the questions and responses. The subject matter is always love, marriage, and a bantering sexual antagonism between boys and girls. Later in the evening boys and girls will mix more freely; a girl who is fond of a boy may lie with her head in his lap. If premarital sexual relations are widely known or result in pregnancy, there will be community pressure for the couple to get married ceremonially, and there is much emphasis on the rituals of first marriage. Yet marriages frequently break apart, says Hitchcock; "in fact almost all Banyan Hill families at the time of the research were founded on marriages between spouses who had been married more than once." If a wife deserts, the husband may work through the headmen of his own village and the village where she went to get her back or seek redress, and pays the headmen a substantial gift for their help.

Portending changes include greater awareness of the outside world through education, greater response to the kinds of changes initiated through the government agencies, and less reliance upon the Brāhmaṇical model for emulation. The foreboding problems are largely economic, with an increasing proportion of farms too small to meet subsistence needs. Though the sedentary Magars still produce the food they require, land records indicate that the population of the administrative subdivision where this research was conducted has increased fivefold during the past century. As in all the main settled valleys of Nepal, population pressure is driving people to seek out nonagricultural means of support.

The Gurūng, who number a quarter of a million, live in several parts of midwestern Nepal and especially along the southern slopes of Annapurṇā. Their language is rather close to Tibetan, and though they are officially Hindus, they call lāmas more often than they call Brāhmaṇs. Death ceremonies are conducted by lāmas. Unlike Magars, Gurūngs consider the domestic pig defiling, but do favor buffalo flesh, which indeed is necessary for their ceremonies. They are a largely pastoral people who maintain sheep on the high mountains or bring them down to the fields to

fertilize the land with dung and urine. It is a measure of their isolation that 80% of their lambs die for lack of veterinary service.

The Thakālī, numbering fewer than 5000, are a different people discussed by Dor Bahadur Bista. They live in a high valley northwest of Pokhārā and formerly held a monopoly over the salt trade with Tibet. Marriage has traditionally been by capture. Their religion is a mixture of a shamanistic cult, ancestor worship, Buddhism, and Hindu rites. Lately they have increasingly been affected by Hinduism but retain a strong interest in their distinctive shamanistic cult. Another tribe is the Sunwār who live northeast of Kāṭhmāṇḍū. They claim to be Hindus, but are served by lāmas as well as Brāhmaṇs.

In eastern Nepal there are the Kirāntīs, numbering half a million, who, in fact, consist of two important tribes: Rāīs and Limbūs. These were not brought into the orbit of Nepālī culture until the Gurkhā invasions, and then it took 12 years of fighting to subdue them. Lionel Caplan has recently published an account of Limbūs' loss of lands and how they are preserving their identity, and has contributed a chapter on the Limbūs in the companion volume.

Among all these people the Newārs are best known. They number over half a million, 55% of whom live in the little Kāṭhmāṇḍū Valley in compact villages. But the Valley is now so crowded, with 2100 per square mile in 1961, that firewood has to be brought in from 80 miles, and the people are forced to relate to the urban economy even though they grow rice on every inch of land that can be terraced. They evolved a charming

Offering flowers at Buddhist temple in Pāṭan, the old Newār capital.

Newār village, Kāṭhmaṇḍū valley. Substantial brick houses have animal rooms on the ground floor, kitchen on the top. Women in the morning wash at the tap and do pūjā at Buddhist shrine.

little civilization, by far the most spectacular in Nepal, and had their own script. Most striking is the array of temples and palaces at the old capital of Pāṭan representing various schools of architecture inspired from India and Tibet. The civilization was predominantly Buddhist but has been Hinduized under the Gorkhās.

The Newār social system is of anthropological interest because there are parallel Buddhist and Hindu caste structures, described by Rosser. Newār lāmas ceased to be celibate and became a hereditary priestly caste approximating in status Newār Brāhmaṇs. At the bottom are Hindu untouchables and Buddhist untouchables. The castes are preferentially but not exclusively endogamous. A family will call either lāmas or Brāhmaṇs to perform ceremonies, depending on whether it claims to be Buddhist or Hindu, but because of the impetus to Hinduism given by the state as families rise in status and come to be called Śreshṭhas (moneylenders or merchants) for instance, they will switch from calling lāmas to Brāhmaṇs.

Annual ceremony to destroy evil spirits, outside Kāṭhmaṇḍū. Stalks are placed on path crossing to catch them, then cut down.

Newār villages look almost like towns, with three- or four-story brick houses contiguous along stone-paved streets. Elaborate carved balconies decorate the traditional homes. Houses of related people tend to be built around a little square containing an image of Buddha before which women do pūjā in the mornings whether they call themselves Buddhist or Hindu. Hindu concepts of ritual purity are strongly emphasized, especially among the higher castes, who do not touch cigarets or drinking vessels to their lips

and segregate women during menstruation. While animals are kept on the ground floor, the kitchen is generally on the top floor where it can be kept pure. No visitors are allowed in the kitchen, and an orthodox Hindu Newār will eat cooked rice only in his own home, Rosser reports, not even in the home of his brother.

Around the Kāṭhmāṇḍū Valley are the Tāmāngs, generally poor and exploited. They are nominally Buddhist but have an earth deity cult and a class of shamanistic priests. They also have lāmas who tend to marry daughters of lāmas, though they do not quite form an endogamous caste as do Newār lāmas.

Along the northern fringe of Nepal are Bhoṭiyās, meaning any of the Tibetan peoples. Most famous of these are the Sherpas, who have helped foreign climbers scale Everest and other high peaks with their mountaineering skills. A monograph about them has been written by Fürer-Haimendorf.

Sikkim

Sikkim is a tiny country of 2800 square miles and a population, assessed by the 1961 Census of India at 162,000. By treaty it has no dealing with any foreign power save India. Of the three ethnic elements in Sikkim the oldest are the Lepchas, who seem to have originally been shifting cultivators using the digging stick, and their cultural substratum is related to that of the hills south of Assam. Lepchas number only 30,000, of whom half live in Darjeeling District in India. Their language largely consists of old Tibetan, but seems to have elements relating it to Khāsi of Meghālaya, a language of the Muṇḍa group. Tibetans or Bhoṭs began moving southward by the 17th century, and three lāmas of the Red Hat sect are said to have made converts of the Lepchas. A Tibetan aristocracy became established in that century, with a king blessed by the Dalai Lāma of Tibet, and in time the Lepchas became a subordinate people. The Bhoṭs brought a dialect of Tibetan which became Sikkimese, spoken today by all Lepchas at least as a second language. Along the north are transhumant pastoral people similar to those of western Bhutan who profited from the trade with Tibet, but now they are having to take up cultivation.

The third ethnic troup is the Nepālīs, mostly of Rāī, Limbū, or Chetrī origin, who practice a simple frontier type of Hinduism and have extended Nepālī culture and language all over the lower parts of the country where they have settled as agricultural pioneers. They now comprise almost three quarters of the population of Sikkim and are threatening the distinctive Buddhist culture of the Bhoṭs and Lepchas. After elections in 1963 King Palden Thondup Namgyal requested the assistance of Indian forces to put down a revolt stemming from charges that the polling system favored the

Bhoṭ community, to which the King and the ruling elite belong. In 1973 even more serious riots broke out over the same issue, and the King was again forced to call in Indian forces and make some concessions. Should the Nepālīs achieve proportional voting rights the viability of the Bhoṭ government, and even of the Bhoṭ and Lepcha cultures, would be threatened. India wants to maintain Sikkim as a buffer state, and has a large military contingent stationed there to protect a strategic northern pass to Tibet.

The classic work on the Lepchas is that of Ceoffrey Gorer, though more recently they have been described by the Dane Halfden Siiger and the Japanese Chie Nakane. They cultivate terraced rice fields and plow with oxen, while on hillsides they grow dry rice, millets, buckwheat, and now much corn. They keep pigs and chickens such as the hill people around Assam do. Their houses are of bamboo and matting. Villages are not complex in layout but consist of a dozen or a score of houses clustered on a hillside. Nakane cites a typical village plan: a stream at an altitude of 3000 feet is bounded by cardamom plants which yield some cash income, above that to 4000 feet is rice, above that yet are the peasants' houses, and above all is the *gonpa*, the monastery. Bhoṭs and Lepchas mingle but seldom intermarry except among the aristocracy.

Lepchas are fully integrated into the state and religious system of Tibetan Buddhism, though they maintain a cult of their own with priest-shaman functionaries. The gonpa is the center of the local community, while at the same time it traditionally provided links with the outside world because it was a branch of some important monastery in Tibet. And while Tibet is now cut off, the monasteries are part of the fabric of the Sikkimese political system headed by the Bhoṭ king of the Namgyal line. It is expected that most families will have a member in the gonpa. Monks are arrayed in an elaborate hierarchy through which they are able to progress by a series of promotions; the most important criterion of piety seems to be the ability to meditate for days, weeks, or even years. Every family calls the lāmas at times of cremation and other rites of the high religion, while Lepchas call their priest-shamans, who can attain a state of trance and divine the future, on other occasions as when illness strikes. Both Bhoṭs and Lepchas can become monks, and though their Classical Tibetan is not as good as that found in Tibetan monasteries the Namgyal Institute of Tibetology in Gangtok, the capital, has lāmas learned in every aspect of Mahāyāna Buddhism.

Lepchas have patrilineal exogamous clans, and a person is greatly concerned to be known as a member of his clan. There is an interest in genealogical depth and proscription of marriage within the patrilineage, contrary to the practice of Bhoṭs who marry near relatives and have little interest in lineage. Both Lepchas and Bhoṭs practice some polyandry to prevent frequent division of the land. Though an elder brother shares his

wife with the younger, in practice polyandry usually involves one or more brothers who are away, trading or serving as lāmas or monks.

Gorer says of the Lepchas that they "are much occupied with sex; it is the subject of much of their conversation and nearly all their humor; it is regarded as almost as essential as food."[4] Men at monastery feasts talk about it, and people believe that the lāmas, if anything, need to be even more sexually active than other male Lepchas. Virginity at marriage is rare but adultery is not as common as may be supposed, which is not to deny the existence of furtive encounters in the woods or at feasts. "Sex is intended to be exclusively sensual and almost impersonal; the culture makes no allowance for deep personal relationships passionately adhered to between sexual partners. If sex becomes emotionally serious it is always a nuisance." Halfden Siiger, a Dane who more recently studied them, says the Lepchas themselves think Gorer's book is something of a sex thriller. Of the Lepchas who live in Darjeeling many have become Christians and the rest have been influenced by the attitudes of plains Hindus.

Bhutan

Bhutan was closed to the world until 1960, and less is known of it than of Yemen or New Guinea. Yet it is a country 200 miles long with a population approaching a million, and in 1971 was admitted to the United Nations under the sponsorship of India. Like Nepal, it has a belt of sultry foothills, above which are midmontane valleys containing the largest part of the population, while the border with Tibet runs along the Himālayan watershed. No ethnographic studies of this country are available, but a useful geography has been published by Pradyumna Karen.

In the 8th century Buddhist missionaries from the Nālandā monastery in Bihār came to Tibet, and in the 9th century that country became an expansionist Buddhist theocracy, consolidating the better part of the high plateau and sending troops into Bhutan. All 5000 monks in Bhutan are Red Hats, while in Tibet in the 14th century the reformist Yellow Hat sect assumed power. Bhutanese monks can be recognized by their dingy red robes and red caps; they practice tantric ritualism along with Mahāyāna Buddhism. Monastic recruits come from among excess sons of a family (since traditionally not more than three brothers would share a wife), and from illegitimate children of monks or nuns. Many monks are illiterate, while others are highly learned in esoteric philosophy and know foreign languages. The people of Bhutan are 75% Buddhist.

In the 17th century a Tibetan lāma established his authority in Bhutan and took the title Dharma Rājā. His successor Dharma Rājās were believed to be incarnations of him, and they ruled through governors of provinces.

Each province had a *dzong* such as can still be seen today—an imposing high fort with tapering walls of earth and stone, with richly carved windows across the top and surmounted by a pagoda-like roof sometimes gold-plated. Dzongs were centers of political life where the governor resided and people could come in time of danger. They were also centers of religious and intellectual life, with fine murals depicting scenes from Buddhist mythology. In 1907 the governors elected one of themselves as hereditary king and his great-grandson, Jigme Singhye Wangchuk, is the currently ruling young monarch. England recognized the independence of Bhutan but controlled its foreign affairs.

The Bhoṭs or Bhutanese in the dominant west-central parts call themselves Drukmi, and their language, which is the official one, is similar to that of the Khampas of eastern Tibet. Its script is also similar to that of Tibetan. People along the western edge are similar to the Bhoṭs of Sikkim and the southward-projecting Chumbi Valley of Tibet. Most people live in small hamlets and isolated homesteads. As farmers men and women are industrious and painstaking, cultivating rice in narrow valleys. But, says Karen, Bhutanese are of independent disposition and difficult to manage when taken into regular employment. Those who try to work in tea estates in Darjeeling or in road building soon give up such work.

In the southeastern part of Bhutan are people who speak other Tibeto-Burmese languages and have cultural patterns like those of the hill regions around Assam. They sacrifice pigs, goats, and mithāns, but are nevertheless Buddhists. These groups are closely related to the Sherdukpen of neighboring Arunāchal Pradesh. A quarter of the people of Bhutan are Nepālīs, deriving from Nepal's eastern tribes with admixture of a few Chetrīs, Thārūs, and Brāhmaṇs. By law these are restricted to the southeastern quadrant of the country, which they have opened to agriculture. These are frontier people, living in bamboo and thatch huts, in contrast with the substantial and comfortable stone houses of the Bhoṭs.

In 1959 when China occupied Tibet it also claimed part of Bhutan. Thereupon Bhutan began to look southward and took a decision to modernize. The first road to India was opened in 1961, and now there are several others, with an east-west road under construction. The king abolished slavery, banned polyandry, promised an end to compulsory labor, and opened free elementary and high schools. But Thimbu, the capital, has only 10,000 people, no radio, and only one weekly newspaper. When the king died in 1972 he was honored for two months with over 100 silver bowls filled with food offered to him twice daily, pending the state cremation. King Jimge Singhe Wangchuk, who assumed the throne at age 17, promised to open the door of the country a bit, but not so much as to threaten the essential cultural features of the Bhoṭ people.

REFERENCES AND NOTES

[1] Majumdar (1961), p. 202.
[2] *Sikkim Herald*, Dec. 13, 1967, p. 2.
[3] Fürer-Haimendorf (1966), p. 24.
[4] Gorer, p. 332.

IMPORTANT SOURCES

Berreman, Gerald. *Hindus of the Himalayas*. Berkeley, 1963. (An important work on the Pahāṛī-speaking people.)

———. "Peoples and Cultures of the Himalayas," *Asian Survey*, June, 1963. (A short survey of Himālayan culture areas.)

Bista, Dora Bahadur. *People of Nepal*. Kaṭhmāṇḍū, 1966. (A survey of all major ethnic groups.)

Caplan, Lionel. *Land and Social Change in East Nepal: A Study of Hindu-Tribal Relations*. Berkeley, 1970.

Crane, Robert (ed.). *Jammu and Kashmir State*. New Haven, Conn., 1956. (The only survey, but now out of date.)

Fürer-Haimendorf, C. (ed). *Caste and Kin in Nepal, India and Ceylon*. New York, 1966. (Includes chapters on Chetrīs and on Buddhist communities in western Nepal.)

———. "Caste in the Multi-ethnic Society of Nepal," *Contributions to Indian Sociology*, Vol. IV.

———. *The Sherpas of Nepal*. London, 1964.

Gorer, Geoffrey. *Himalayan Village: An Account of the Lepchas of Sikkim*. New York, 1967 (originally published 1938).

Government of Nepal. *Preliminary Report of the Population Census*. Kaṭhmāṇḍū, 1961.

Hitchcock, John. *The Magars of Banyan Hill*. New York, 1966. (A case study of the Magars of Nepal.)

Karen, Pradyumna. *Bhutan: A Physical and Cultural Geography*. Lexington, Ky., 1967.

———. *Nepal: A Cultural and Physical Geography*. Lexington, Ky., 1960. (A valuable atlas, produced from census data.)

———, and William Jenkins. *The Himalayan Kingdoms: Bhutan, Sikkim, and Nepal*. Princeton, N.J., 1963. (A useful little handbook.)

Majumdar, D. N. *Himalayan Polyandry: Structure, Functioning and Culture Change*. New York, 1962.

———. *Races and Cultures of India*. New York, 1961. (Chaps. 8 and 10 deal with the Pahāṛī-speaking Khasas.)

Maraini, Fosco. *Where Four Worlds Meet: Hindu Kush*. London, 1959. (A popularly written description of the Kāfirs and Nūristān.)

Nakane, Chie. "A Plural Society in Sikkim—A Study of the Interrelations of Lepchas, Bhotias and Nepalis," in Fürer-Haimendorf (1966).

Nepali, Gopal Singh. *The Newars*. Bombay, 1965. (A village study.)

Pignède, Bernard. *Les Gurungs, une Population Himalayenne du Népal*. The Hague, 1966.

Rosser, Colin. "A Hermit Village in Kulu," *Economic Weekly*, IV, Nos. 19 and 20.

———. "Social Mobility in the New Caste System," in Fürer-Haimendorf (1966).

Siiger, Halfden. *The Lepchas*, 2 vols. Copenhagen, 1967.

Srivastava, Ram. "The Tribe-Caste Mobility in India and the Case of Kumaon Bhotias," in Fürer-Haimendorf (1966).

15

Survey of Tribal Peoples

With nearly 40 million people today falling under the official category of Scheduled Tribes, India can be said to have more "tribal" people than any other country in the world. They are more numerous than the total populations of important countries such as Egypt or Spain, and their diversity is an anthropological ocean.

Table 15–1 shows the percentage of Scheduled Tribes and Scheduled Castes in the states of India. It is interesting to observe that tribal people are proliferating considerably faster than the population as a whole, while Scheduled Caste people have a growth rate slower than that of the population of India. This differential reflects the respective self-images of the two groups and confidence in their own cultural subsystems, as well as probable differences in economic subsistence. The low castes are becoming assimilated into the rest of the peasant population, but on the whole, the tribes maintain a confidence in themselves sufficient to resist assimilation.

It should not be thought that because a tribe is so listed that it is unsettled. In the last century these were sometimes called "wild tribes," a sentiment that still lingers among plains villagers who associate them with the wilds and dangers of mountains. Practically all today cultivate, some by shifting or hoe cultivation, but the majority in central India at least are

plow farmers, and many of the tribes are practically castes. Others, especially in parts of the eastern hills, have developed a relatively high level of education and sophistication; they are considered "tribal" because they are not part of the mainstream of Indian culture and have never been Hindu, Muslim, or Buddhist.

The tribal people of South Asia fall naturally into five groups: 1) Muslim tribals of nomadic origin in hilly western Pakistan and much of Afghanistan whom we discussed in Chapter 13; 2) Himālayan people whom we discussed in Chapter 14; 3) non-Indic peoples of the eastern hills of India and Bangladesh; 4) the vast tribal belt of central India centered in Madhya Pradesh, half of Bihār, half of Orissa, and extending into parts of West Bengal, Āndhra, Mahārāshṭra and Gujarāt; and 5) the small tribal groups in the Western Ghāṭs of the South and in Sri Lanka.

TABLE 15–1 Percentages of Scheduled Castes and Tribes in 1961

States	*% Scheduled Castes*	*% Scheduled Tribes*	*Territories*	*% Scheduled Castes*	*% Scheduled Tribes*
Āndhra	14	14	Andaman and Nicobar Islands	—	22
Assam (and Meghālaya)	6	17	Arunāchal Pradesh	—	89
Bihār	14	9	Delhī	13	—
Gujarāt	7	13	Lakshadvīp	—	97
Himāchal Pradesh	27	8	Maṇipur	2	32
Jammū and Kashmīr	8	—	Tripurā	10	32
Karṇāṭaka	13	1	Goā	—	—
Kēraḷa	8	1	Pondicherry	15	—
Madhya Pradesh	13	21			
Mahārāshṭra	6	6	All India: 1951	15.32	6.23
Nāgaland	.04	93	All India: 1961	14.67	6.80
Orissa	16	24			
Panjāb (undivided)	20	.07		*% Increase 1951–1961*	
Rājasthān	17	12			
Tamiḻ Nāḍu	18	.75	Scheduled castes	16.43	
Uttar Pradesh	21	—	Scheduled tribes	32.54	
West Bengal	20	6	Population of India	21.58	

In this chapter we will discuss categories 3, 4, and 5, briefly surveying the important tribes or especially interesting ones, beginning with category 3. The eastern hills were politically reorganized by the Government of India in 1972 into four small states and two Union Territories surrounding Assam. The states are Nāgaland (formed in 1963), Meghālaya, Maṇipur, and Tripurā, and the Territories are Arunāchal Pradesh (formerly known as North-East Frontier Agency) and Mīzorām. These all share Assam's governor and high court, though the mini-states have elected legislatures and the Territories elected advisory councils. The seven units will form a North-Eastern Council on which the Chief Ministers of these states will have seats, to discuss common problems and ensure India's territorial integrity.

Arunāchal Pradesh

Hugging the Assam Valley around the north and east, Arunāchal Pradesh stretches 350 miles from Bhutan to Burma. These eastern Himālayan slopes are lush and humid, and during the summer monsoon the runoff merges into the vast waters of the Brahmaputra which breaks through the range after a long sojourn in Tibet, often causing severe flooding on the plains. The Territory contained 445,000 people in 1971, divided into some 25 tribes. Parts of this Territory were not taken by the British until the beginning of this century, and indeed some areas were never explored by them. China invaded it in the 1962 war with India, claiming that it had formerly been part of Tibet. Since that time India has been keen to show that its people are not Tibetan in culture, and has actively wooed the population by sympathetic administration and infusion of technical assistance.

On the western edge of Arunāchal Pradesh are the Monpa and Sherdukpen, culturally close to the people of Bhutan, and along the northern fringe a few Tibetan Khampas. These are Buddhist peoples, having imposing monasteries with fluttering prayer flags and privileged priests. The rest of the tribes of Arunāchal Pradesh, however, belong to the Southeast Asian culture zone, which includes the hill regions south of the Assam Valley, northern Burma and Thailand, and Yunnan Province of China. Except for the few Tibetan groups, all the languages of Arunāchal Pradesh belong to the Himālayan group of Tibeto-Burmese languages. Sachin Roy points out contrasts between Tibetans who raise barley, buckwheat, and some wheat, with these people who practice shifting cultivation with hoes, grow hill rice and millets, and keep pigs, chickens, and mithāns. They have their own priest-shamans and do not employ lāmas. Whereas Tibetan craftsmen excel in manufacture of wooden articles, these people use bamboo; the Khampa or Monpa takes his tea from a wooden bowl but a man of these other tribes drinks his beer from a bamboo mug. Tibetans dress in elaborate woolen clothes, while these other tribals wear but a loincloth or perhaps a short coat; women wear a short skirt and mothers a distinguishing girdle. Cultural borrowings from Tibetan civilization have been few.

Cultural borrowing from Indic people have also been few, though the people of Arunāchal Pradesh are in many ways culturally similar to people of the range of hills south of the Assam Valley. In the 13th century the Thai-like Āhoms invaded from the east and drove a wedge between the northern and southern rims of the Valley, though their cultural impact was slight. In their wake, however, Hindu Assamese moved eastward, occupying all the Valley plains and incorporating those tribal peoples into Hindu

culture. But Hindus did not venture much into the hills of Arunāchal Pradesh or Nāgaland.

The Arunāchal Pradesh tribes, from west to east, are the Bagni, Aka, Dafla, Apa Tāni, Hill Mīri, Gallong, a group called Ādi (formerly Abor) including the Minyong, Pādām, Shimong, Tagin, Rāmo, and Pāsi, while on the eastern end of the territory are the Mishmi and Mīju. The Ādi group in 1961 numbered 72,000, the Dafla about 40,000, and the rest only a few thousands each. Two large groups in the process of merging into Assamese culture on the edge of the plains are the Mīri (137,000) and the Mīshing (over 40,000). Short monographs on some of these have recently been prepared by Indian anthropologists, while Frederick Simoons has made a special study of the role of the mithān, a stocky bovine, in the economy and rituals of these people as well as those south of the Brahmaputra.

Fürer-Haimendorf has compared the world view and social organization of the Daflas, who traditionally practiced primitive shifting cultivation, and the Apa Tānis. The latter, though a similar people, moved into Dafla territory, occupied seven large villages, and began growing rice on permanent irrigated fields. While the Daflas are organized in exogamous patrilineal clans, there is no mechanism for securing the cooperation of all the members of a clan, and it is not usual for clan members to oppose each other in raids and blood feuds. A number of nuclear families live in a longhouse, which may have 60 or 70 people led by the senior man who is regarded as owner and head of the house, and who may have more than one wife cultivating for him. There is no tribal organization or means for maintaining law and order other than the mutual protection of the members of a longhouse. Sometimes in a village one longhouse will be raided and burned, and the inhabitants carried captive, sold as slaves, or killed, while the people of neighboring longhouses may make no attempt to come to their aid. Feuding is mitigated by a well-established form of dialogue held on neutral ground, in which the principal opponents hold forth with skillful oratory; a speaker excitedly manipulates bamboo sticks to tally men and mithāns captured, persons killed, ransoms paid, or trade debts accumulated. Reconciliation may be possible. "Daflas look upon such negotiations as a national sport, and the display of oratory, the evaluation of cattle and valuables, and the recounting of deeds of valor serve as a kind of entertainment which gains in excitement as the values at stake increase." Sometimes feuds may continue for generations. Fürer-Haimendorf recounts:

Thus in 1945, when I toured the valley of the upper Kamla river, I met the kinsmen and descendants of men involved in hostilities with a British military expedition in 1912. Since then no European or other outsider had visited the area, and the feud had remained unresolved. As I wanted to establish friendly relations with the local tribesmen, and was taken for a kinsman of the only white man ever known to the people, I had no other choice but to pay compensation for their

> past losses. Subsequently I sealed our friendship by the performance of a *dapo* [peace] pact. The partners in that pact laid great stress on showing me their young sons. For the obligations of the pact would pass on to these children, who, as I was assured, would find themselves bound to extend their friendship also to my descendants.[1]

In this no-man's land between Indian and Tibetan civilizations, people have little attachment to specific localities, population has not been dense, and no organization traditionally held the society together—only the balance of power. Until the penetration of the Indian government in the 1950s and 1960s, an arrogant attitude and violence were not condemned, but were attributes admired in a strong man:

> In his approach to human relations the Dafla appears rather calculating. Commitments such as marriage alliances and ceremonial friendships are entered with a view to the political and material benefit which can be derived from them, and while a Dafla may be loyal to allies and close kinsmen, he lacks all feeling for the dignity of human beings in general. No Dafla has any scruples to capture and sell as slaves men and women born free and as members of families of good status, no one considers the feelings of a person kidnapped to serve as security for the unpaid debt of a kinsman, and no one expresses compassion for children torn from their parents. They are pawns in a game of raids and counter-raids, and their emotions and sufferings are not taken into account. In the hard world of these tribes there is no room for sentimentality, compassion and a spirit of forgiveness.[2]

Whereas Daflas had to rely until recently on personal retribution, Apa Tānis have a more organized society. They live in larger villages and are divided into exogamous clans which act with solidarity in nearly all circumstances. A thief is punished by being kept tied in a public place, or by public execution if his stealing is habitual. Whereas among Daflas slavery was a temporary condition not affected by one's birth, Apa Tāni society developed a hierarchy, with a class of patricians who could not intermarry with the class of slaves and freed slaves. The greater social organization of the Apa Tānis was apparently consonant with settled agriculture, denser population, and larger villages.

Change has come rapidly to Arunāchal Pradesh, especially since the Chinese invaded the territory. Raiding where it existed has been stopped, and tribal and clan patriotism has become less intense, though the government is encouraging tribal distinctiveness in such areas as the arts. Land rights for shifting cultivation have been given by the government, and in a few lowlands plow cultivation has been taken up. Money is accumulating and young people look outside for broader opportunities. Youth organizations and dormitories have rotted as people have developed new values in selecting marriage partners. There are a number of high schools, a college, and a polytechnic institute. Though the combination of extreme precipitation and steep hills prevents road building in many areas, the centuries of isolation have ended.

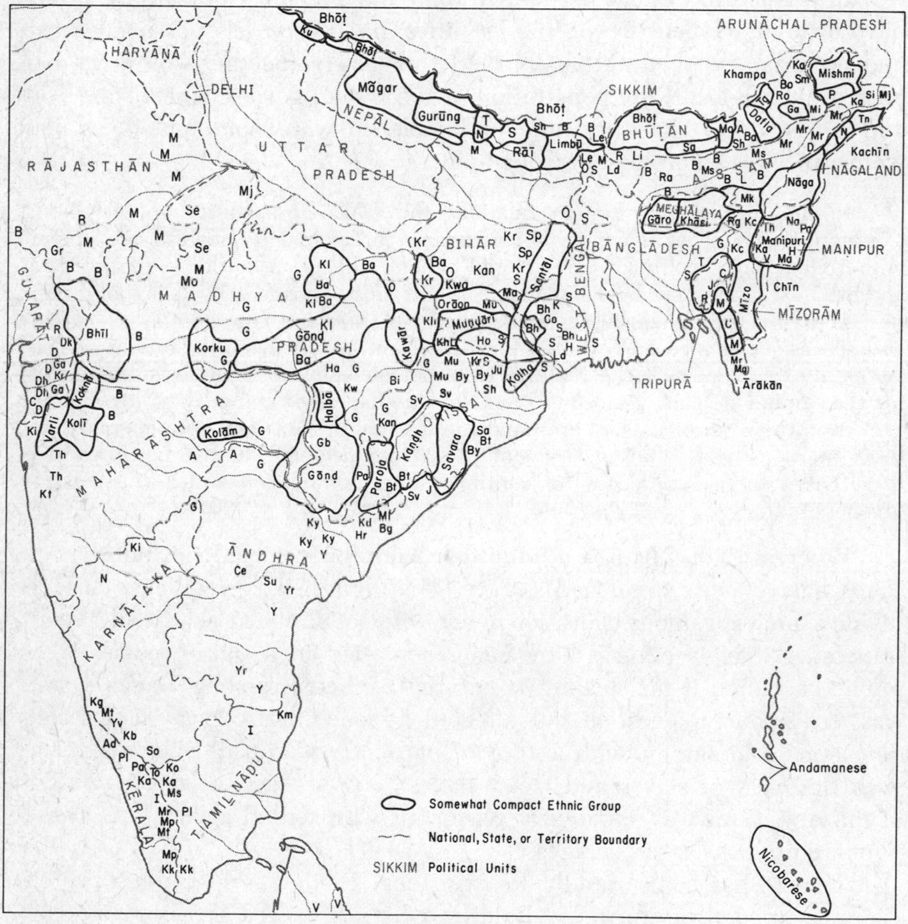

FIG. 15–1 Tribes of India and the Himālayas.

FIG. 15–1 Tribes of India and the Himālayas.

Central and South Indian Tribes

Adiyan	Ad	Kaṇḍh (Koṇḍh)	Kan	Māli	Ml
Āndh	An	Kanikkar	Kk	Marāṭī	Mt
Bagata	Bg	Kathodi	Kt	Mīna	M
Baigā	Ba	Kawār	Kw	Mogiā	Mo
Bhīl	B	Khāṛiā	Kh	Muṇḍārī	Mu
Bhottada	Bt	Khārwār	Kr	Mutuvan	Mt
Bhūmij	Bh	Khoṇḍā Dorā	Kd	Nāyakḍā	N
Birhor	Bi	Koknā	Kn	Orāon	O
Caudhrī	C	Kolha	Kl	Paḻaiyan	Pl
Cencu	Ce	Kolām	Km	Paṇiyan	Pa
Dhankā	Dk	Kolī	Ki	Paroja	
Dhodiyā	Dh	Koṛā	K	Rathawa	R
Dublā	D	Koṛagu	Kg	Sabar	Sa
Gabadā	Gb	Korku		Santāl	S
Gamit	Ga	Korwā	Kwa	Sauriā Pahāriā	Sp
Garosiyā	Gr	Koṭa	Ko	Savara (Saora)	Sv
Gōṇḍ	G	Koya	Ky	Sehariā	Se
Gorait	Go	Kuruba	Kb	Soligaru	So
Halbā		Lodhā	Ld	Sugali	Su
Hill Reḍḍi	Hr	Loharā	L	Ṭhākūr	Th
Ho	H	Mahlī	Ma	Toḍa	T
Iruḷar	I	Mājhī	Mj	Varli	
Jatapu	J	Malai Paṇḍāram	Mp	Yanādi	Y
Juāng	Ju	Malasar	Ms	Yerava	Yv
Kāḍar	Ka	Malayarāyar	Mr	Yerukala	Yr

Eastern Hill Tribes				*Himālayan Peoples*	
Aka	A	Minyong Ādi	Mi	Bhoṭ (Bhoṭiyā)	B
Ārākānese		Mīri	Mr	Gurūng	
Bangni	Ba	Mīshing	Ms	Khampa	
Bokar	Bo	Mishmi		Kumāonī	Ku
Boṛo, Boḍo	B	Mīzo (all)		Lepcha	Le
Cākma (Chakmā)	C	Monpa	Mo	Limbū	Li
Chīn		Mru	Mr	Māgar	M
Dafla		Mrung	Mg	Newār	N
Dimāsa	D	Nāga (all)	Na	Pahāṛī	
Gallong	Ga	Mokte	N	Rāī	R
Gāro	G	Padam Ādi	P	Sangla	Sa
Hill Mīri	Hm	Paite	Pa	Sḥerpa	Sh
Hmār	H	Rābhā	Ra	Sunwār	S
Jāmātia	J	Rāmo Ādi	Ro	Tāmāng	T
Kabui	Ka	Rangdānia	Rg	Thārū	
Kachīn		Riāng	R		
Kāchārī	Kc	Sherdukpen	Sh	*Island Tribals*	
Khāmti	Kh	Shimong Ādi	Sm	Andamanese	
Khāsi		Singpho	Si	Nicobarese	
Lālung	L	Tagin	Tg	Väddā	V
Maṇipurī		Tangsa	Tn		
Māo	Ma	Thādo	Th		
Marma	M	Tripurī	T		
Mīju	Mj	Vaipei	V		
Mikir	Mk				

Boḍo-speaking Tribes

The main speakers of languages which Grierson termed the Boṛo or Boḍo group of the Assam-Burmese branch of Tibeto-Burmese languages are shown in Table 15–2. These people seem to have once populated the Assam Valley and have ethnic links to its northern side with Bhutan and Sikkim, and also with southwest China. But Assamese Hindu culture has been, as it were, a 450-mile-long hypodermic needle injecting Indic cultural elements into the very heart of the eastern hill complex. The Boḍo proper are on the edges of the lowlands and have been partly assimilated by the Assamese.

TABLE 15–2 Speakers of Boḍo Languages in 1961

Gāro	307,000
Tripurī	300,000
Boḍo	280,000
Rangdānia	215,000
Mikir	154,000
Kāchārī	65,000
Riāng	65,000
Jāmātia	65,000
Rābha	44,000
Dimāsa	32,000
Lālung	11,000
Other	10,000
	1,554,000

Best known of these people are the Gāro, having been studied by Robbins Burling and Chie Nakane. Gāro identity has been preserved on the 4000-foot Shillong Plateau, which is also occupied by Khāsis and forms the new state of Meghālaya. The efforts of British administrators to identify and delineate tribes and the attention missionaries paid to tribal languages have been important factors in the development of self-identification of the tribe. Over a third of the Gāros have become either Baptist or Roman Catholic, while the rest practice a tribal cult slightly influenced by Hinduism. In 1964 roughly 100,000 Gāros fled into India from what was East Pakistan.

Gāros are matrilineal, a trait they share with their neighbors the Khāsis, but not with other Boḍo-speaking peoples. E. R. Leach has suggested that Gāros are at base a father-right society even though they have adopted matriliny and women own the land, for within their extended families the senior husband maintains his authority. A man controls his wife's property and disposes of his daughters, but has only marginal influence in the affairs of the married sisters' households.

Shifting cultivation, commonly called *jhūm* in India, has been the traditional basis of Gāro subsistence. An extensive forested area is selected for a whole village to clear with fire and broadcast seed. But whereas the jhūmming cycle was formerly 10 or 12 years, now with increased population the land is cleared again after 5 years, or only 3, with predictable erosion and reduction of fertility. The government is attempting to increase terraced land under permanent cultivation. Besides the hill rice, the other main crops are millets, corn, vegetables, ginger, and tapioca; Gāros also grow cotton from which they derive a cash income.

Gāros share with Nāgas the grand distinction of having once been famed headhunters. The British originally maintained a hands-off policy in regard to the tribal people of the eastern hills, but because of depredations entered Gāro country in 1874. By 1876 headhunting had been ended, and in that year the Gāros surrendered 200 skulls to the Deputy Commissioner at the District Headquarters. They have their own pantheon of deities and spirits, and believe in rebirth—the form of one's reincarnation is determined by his deeds in his previous life. Having a well developed ancestor cult, Gāros offer food to the departed while they are in the state of limbo, and erect memorial stones. Communal adhesion is fostered by important ceremonies, attended by animal sacrifices and formerly by human sacrifice. Most spectacular is the harvest festival at which people feast, drink, and dance for days.

The Mikirs are centered in the Mikir Hills south of the middle Brahmaputra. A little more swarthy than their Nāga neighbors on the east, they seem to be essentially indigenous. Their land has been notably malarious, consisting of low foothills, and leprosy is more common among them than elsewhere in Assam. Like their tribal neighbors they maintain youth dormitories, but unlike them there has been no tradition of feuding. Mikirs have not been as affected by Christianity as have the hill tribes, but are more easily absorbed into Hinduism; many have now become indistinguishable from the Assamese plains population. Most speak Assamese, though they may continue to use Mikir at home.

Kāchārīs, another numerous tribe, are also being attenuated by assimilation. They are closely related to the Boḍos, once numerous over the Assam plains. Another branch of them, Dimāsas, live in the North Kāchār Hills. In the 16th century when the Āhoms invaded from Burma, they shoved the Kāchārīs southward into what is now Kāchār District, which extends eastward from the Bānglā plains. Both the Kāchārīs in the plains of Kāchār District and the Dimāsas have long been in the process of Hinduization, and few have been attracted to Christianity. The mithān is not only a source of food but the chief symbol of wealth; Kāchārīs believe it was a gift to them from the God of Plenty. In this trait the Boḍo-speakers resemble the other linguistic groups of the eastern hill complex, according to Simoon's study.

Tripurā was a princely state which merged with India in 1948. The most important indigenous people are the Tripurī; other large tribes are the Riāng and Jāmātia, and their languages all belong to the Boḍo group. Tripurīs originally engaged in jhūm cultivation, but this method can no longer provide subsistence for the whole population; new colonies are being settled in the lowlands where permanent agriculture is feasible. Bāngālī culture has had considerable influence, and many of the people of Tripurā speak Bāngālī. In the 1960s the half million tribal people of Tripurā were outnumbered by an influx of nearly a million tribals and non-Muslim Bāngālīs fleeing from what was East Pakistan.

Khāsis

The new state of Meghālaya occupies the Shillong Plateau south of the Brahmaputra; it is a beautiful land undulating between 4000 and 6000 feet. The southern slopes catch the full force of the monsoon and receive over 400 inches of rain annually, measured at Cirapunji; the waters carve deep gorges as they make their way down to the Sylhet District of Bangladesh.

Of the 1 million people living in Meghālaya in 1971, Khāsis comprise half, and near them is a related tribe the Pnārs. These people are of considerable anthropological interest both ethnohistorically and because of their matriliny. Khāsi is the only Muṇḍa language remaining in the Assam region, and thus forms a link between the related languages of central India and the Mon-Khmer languages of Southeast Asia. Moreover, Khāsis have preserved a living megalithic tradition which in its origin is probably distinct from that of southern and western India but goes back to the eastern neolithic. When a corpse is cremated the remains are deposited in an individual cist, then removed to the family ossuary, and finally to the matriclan ossuary where huge upright menhirs and bench-like stone structures are erected. Funerary monuments of a related type have been noted among some of the central Indian Muṇḍa-speaking peoples. Another feature which links Khāsis with the early eastern neolithic is their use of iron hoes in the form of the stone shouldered hoes which were part of that neolithic complex. Khāsis learned to employ the iron ore found on the southern slopes of their plateau and produced iron goods formerly in demand by the neighboring tribes.

Khāsis grow hill crops such as sweet potatoes by hoe cultivation. They have a small-grain corn which is apparently indigenous to upland Southeast Asia or eastern India, which their tradition says they got from a Boḍo-speaking tribe. Nowadays white potatoes are an important crop.

Khāsis and Pnārs are divided into strictly exogamous matriclans, each of which consists of several lineages. They also practice female ultimogeni-

ture, in which the youngest daughter receives most or all of the inheritance including the house; she is ritual head of the family, serves as family priestess, and conducts funeral ceremonies for the parents. The land is managed by the elder brother. Elder sisters, when they get married, will have separate houses built for them by their husbands. A Khāsi husband goes to live in his wife's house until death, whereupon his bones are returned to his own clan for deposition in its ossuary. Among the Pnārs a husband may be a mere night visitor in his wife's house, may not be much attached to his children, and may divorce his wife with ease. The Pnārs also practice female ultimogeniture; almost all the land is recorded as held in the names of women.

Since 1914 when the Khāsis were studied by Gurdon, far-reaching changes have occurred, yet without causing the culture to disintegrate or to be assimilated. Over half the Khāsis have adopted Christianity, and as with the Nāgas, Mīzos, and Gāros, this was presumably a reaction against the tendency to Hinduization and the threat of absorption into the Indic cultural mainstream. In 1901 only 10% were Christians, but by midcentury 55% had taken to this religion. The changes that are ensuing have been analyzed by P. C. Biswas. The exogamous clan structure is still intact, even among Christians. When Christians marry non-Christians, the Khāsi ancestry ceremonies are performed, which shows the strength of the lineage structure.

But among Christian Khāsis a fundamental change is beginning to occur in the attenuation of the priestly function of the younger daughter. In earlier decades a younger daughter who became a Christian would lose all her property, but now that the new religion is respectable, she inherits it. However, since Christian daughters are not likely to continue performing the priestly functions, the pattern of younger daughter inheritance may disappear. Another portending change is that inheritance formerly consisted of the right to slash-and-burn, but now it consists of real property which has to be cultivated, for the government prohibits shifting cultivation on demarcated land. A third and even more potent agent for change is the increasing monetization of the economy. If a man can earn his own cash income without having any land, the economic root of the matrilineal succession and inheritance pattern will be cut. And if a man goes outside for employment, his marriage would no longer be matrilocal, but neolocal. Therefore Biswas is not sanguine about the preservation of the Khāsi kinship and inheritance pattern.

Khāsis have a literacy rate higher than that for all India. Education has been encouraged by Christianity, and they use Khāsi written in Roman script. Today many Khāsis serve outside as college professors, doctors, magistrates, administrators, and clerks in the government of Assam and in business. Women fully participate in the professions and maintain authority uncharacteristic of India.

Nāgas

Nāgas, so called because some of them formerly went naked, are not ethnically related to Nāgā kingdoms of epic tradition, nor related in mythology to Nāgā water spirits. In fact, they have been singularly unaffected by either Indian or Burmese civilization because prior to the end of the last century anyone who ventured into their hilly homeland risked the loss of his head. They occupy a plateau of about 4000 feet intersected by forested valleys, beyond which the land slopes toward the Kachīn states of Burma. Nāgaland was created as a state in 1963, and according to the 1971 census had a population of 515,000. But there are Nāgas in neighboring parts of Arunāchal Pradesh, Assam, and Maṇipur and if these were incorporated into the state of Nāgaland its size would be doubled. There are also Nāgas across the border in Burma.

Nāgas are divided up into some 20 tribes speaking as many languages or dialects. Most important are the Āos, Semas, Konyaks, Tanghkuls, Āngāmis, and Lhotas, while the Wanchus are in southern Arunāchal Pradesh. In some areas one can walk in a day through several linguistic regions. This extraordinary cultural diversity was bred not only by terrain but by the very real danger to one's personal safety if he walked to villages outside the circle of those in which he had relatives. Wider cultural contact became possible only after the British began to administer the area.

We are fortunate to have a series of excellent monographs on some of the Nāga tribes which describe a parochial way of life scarcely to be seen in the world today. The first was on the Nāgas of Maṇipur by T. C. Hodson in 1911, followed a decade later by monographs on the Āngāmi and Sema Nāgas by J. H. Hutton who was an administrator in the area (also known for his work on caste and the 1931 census). Works on the Lhotas, Āos, and Rengmas were written in the 1920s by J. P. Mills, another of the breed of well-educated British administrators, sympathetic and fair-minded. Fürer-Haimendorf came out in 1939 with his work on the Konyaks, recently revised and available in popular form as a case study.

It is not possible to summarize these works on the Nāgas here; they are replete with items of interest to the student of South or Southeast Asian anthropology and help us to understand some of the underlying cultural patterns of eastern India. But we cannot fail to mention headhunting. Fürer-Haimendorf says this practice was not inspired by vengeance or animosity, but by the desire to partake of the magical virtue attached to the severed head and by the need of the headhunter to acquire prestige. Feuds were pursued and the heads of enemy villagers taken until the score was evened, but aggression seldom benefited a warring tribe in any material way except in the acquisition of heads. These were thought to have power and bring fertility to the capturer and to the village where they were hung

as trophies. A head was fed rice beer and after a series of ceremonies was taken to the *morung* (youth dormitory) or clan house of the head-taker.

In common with many other tribal peoples of eastern India, the Nāgas maintained the morung as a central institution. Boys entered with initiation rites before adolescence, and the younger ones had to serve the older boys by cleaning, washing clothes, and running errands. The morung also provided the village guard and formed a cooperative task force which worked the boys' parents' fields in rotation. Girls had separate dormitories. Sexual relations were governed by fewer restraints than in most parts of South Asia. Among the Konyak Nāgas, for instance, sexual relations were considered a normal part of adolescence, though clan exogamy was observed in this as well as in marriage. A boy, after having become acquainted with a girl, would come to her dormitory or house at night and knock on the wall of the room where she was sleeping. He could have intercourse with her, either in the granary or on the veranda of her parents' house, and it was not considered shameful if the loving couple was detected by the girl's parents. Yet a betrothed girl was expected to reserve her favors for her fiance. It was not considered proper for a girl to change lovers too often nor to maintain affairs with two youths simultaneously. Even after marriage sexual relations with parties other than the spouse were not unusual as long as the couple lived in their respective dormitories, but once they established their own home, fidelity was generally expected.[3]

Protestant Christian missions made considerable impact among the Nāgas before the war, and now 55% of them are Christians, mostly Baptists. In 1961, 88,000 of them declared their religion to the census takers as "Nāga" or as the name of one of the Nāga tribes, and half that number claimed to be atheists. The implication of this is that Nāgas clearly reject Hinduization and pressure for assimilation into the caste structure, Assamese is widely understood, and there are many educated Nāgas who know English well and are quite Western in their thinking. Literacy in 1971 was 27%, up 53% in a decade.

The extent of cultural change in Nāgaland is not known because hardly any outsiders are permitted to visit the state. But the Zemi Nāgas and Konyak Nāgas who live in Maṇipur and Assam still maintain the institution of the morung together with their colorful dances. Only a few of the Zemi villages have become Christian, and in these the morungs are dying. Tribal cults are suffering because the people react against the economic demands of traditional sacrificial ceremonies, which require a continual supply of pigs, goats, and chickens. Fürer-Haimendorf reports of the Wanchus who live in Arunāchal Pradesh that hoe cultivation methods have not yet changed, but are being threatened by increasing population. Feuding has been ended. Both Christian and Hindu proselytization are banned, and Indian administrators go out of their way to respect tribal sensibilities.

The reason tourists and missionaries cannot enter Nāgaland is that the

Central Government fears further stirring up of secessionist tendencies. After Independence the Nāga region was incorporated into Assam, but educated Nāgas, who had gained an awareness of their ethnicity through missionary education, came to regard their incorporation into Assam and into India as an accident of history. Following a rebellion put down by the Indian army and a long series of talks between Nāga leaders and prime ministers, Nāgaland was created. But there is still an underground movement trained and armed by China in the late 1960s which keeps contact with a similar secessionist group among the Nāgas in Burma. Their cause has little hope but may have the latent support of a considerable segment of the population. Meanwhile Nāgaland wants to be enlarged to incorporate neighboring Nāga regions. The Indian government has answered by infusing economic aid many times more than that which can be raised within Nāgaland, apparently with some success.

Maṇipurīs, Mīzos, and Chīns

The people whose languages Grierson classified as the Kūki-Chīn group of the Assam-Burmese branch of the Tibeto-Burmese family live in the state

TABLE 15–3 Speakers of Kūki-Chīn Languages in 1961

Maṇipurī (Meithei)	621,000	
Mīzo group	221,000	(plus 350,000 in Burma as of 1943)
Hmār	26,000	
Thādo	24,000	
Kūki (unspecified)	29,000	
	921,000	

of Maṇipur, the Territory of Mīzorām, and adjacent parts of Assam and Burma. The term *Kūki* is used by plains people to refer to any of the nondescript tribes of this topographically tangled region and is not the name any tribes uses for itself.

Best known of these are Maṇipurīs proper, or Meitheis, living in the charming Maṇipur Valley surrounded by a medley of related hill people. Maṇipurīs are not "tribals"; they have been Hindus since at least the 15th century and later adopted the Caitanya school of Vaishṇavism. Their kings, claiming Kshatriya status, led them in wars in the 18th century with Burma and with the Chīns. Maṇipur is widely known for its unique genre of dance, its drama literature, music, and esthetic expression in textile design and embroidery. The language is written in a script similar to that of Assamese, and 33% of the total population is literate. Its population is over a million.

Most of the Chīn groups live south of the Maṇipur Valley, but some have moved westward into the Kāchār part of Assam projecting southward towards Mīzorām. The Baite and Rangkhol in the North Kāchār Hills are Chīns that got driven northward as Mīzos moved in from the Burma side, and are called by plains people Old Kūkis. In the 19th century under Mīzo pressure, Thādos, another Chīn tribe, were forced northward by the Mīzos and settled in western Maṇipur and the low hills around the Kāchār plain; they are called New Kūkis. In contrast with other Chīns, these have been somewhat affected by Hinduism and the little civilization of Maṇipur.

The numerous Chīn groups, Mongoloid peoples distantly related to the Nāgas, originated in southwest China in the early centuries A.D. and moved down the Chīndwin Valley of Burma to occupy the Chīn hills now bisected by the India-Burma border, and part of the Ārākān plains of Burma. The Chīn groups in British India in 1931 were enumerated as speaking some 44 related but distinct languages. They live mostly in the hills 4000 to 7000 feet, avoid the forested valleys, and practice shifting cultivation on the plateaus. They share with Nāgas and peoples north of the Assam Valley ritual use of the mithān, which they never yoke but use in paying bride-price and in sacrifices.

F. K. Lehman's study of the structure of Chīn society, though conducted on the Burma side, is useful for understanding the social structure of all the Chīn peoples. He writes:

> We may speak legitimately of a single over-all, Chin cultural and social system, despite the great diversity among the various Chin social types, precisely because the pattern of this diversity is ordered largely in response to a single major variable—the local mode of relationship to Burma.[4]

Chīn society is not, of course, peasant, nor is it purely "tribal." Lehman calls it subnuclear. Among the South Chīn, those in Burma, there are exogamous patrilineal clans and each village is mostly populated by one clan. The maximal lineage is the chief political unit and is also the basis of exogamy. There are no clan or village gods, headmen, nor inherited offices. Their lineages are not differentially ranked, but among the North Chīn, which includes the Mīzos and Lakhers of Assam, the clans are hierarchically ranked. Land is held by a few aristocratic families in each village and most people work on rented plots. This has led to the demand for imported goods, the accumulation of wealth, and the giving of feasts as evidence of status. Traditionally a prominent man had a major wife, for whom he paid full bride-price, and perhaps other wives, and among these aristocrats rules of inheritance were important. In contrast with some of their tribal neighbors, the Chīn people have always had an interest in outside civilization, and were affected by the rise of Burmese civilization from the 8th century. Their interest in the outside world has been continued by their mass conversion to Christianity.

Mīzo women.

Mīzo kitchen. Low dining table exemplifies eastern origin of cultural features.

Mīzos (formerly called Lushais) who occupy the finger-like Indian Territory of Mīzorām are a fairly homogeneous people, an offshoot of the northern Chīn, who have been assimilating their lesser neighbors such as the Pāwi. Mīzos formerly took heads, but in a more formal way than did Nāgas. Two competing village chiefs would personally fight on neutral ground, as in the middle of a bridge. The victor would take the head of the loser and also his village, which would then provide new subjects to work his land. But now the Mīzos are over 80% Christian, mostly Baptist, and in fact have Christianized half the Chīns on the Burmese side. It is important to Mīzos to be able to read their Bibles in Mīzo, and their new faith is so fervent that even insurrectionists will sit about for hours discussing such subjects as assurance of salvation. Practically all those in India can read, and many are multilingual. Like many hill people, they build large and airy houses of bamboo matting, with a separate kitchen and dining room. They eat seated around low tables, a habit derived from Burma and ultimately from China. Mīzos are an energetic and disciplined people who dislike being called "tribal."

Along with other eastern hill people, Mīzos have felt increasing alienation from India. They view as potentially threatening the Hindu revivalism in North India. The language policy adopted in Assam in 1960 made Assamese the Official Language of the state and though directed primarily against the Bāngālī minority, this had the effect of eliminating the advantages hill people had in knowing English, both in obtaining seats in colleges and in getting jobs with the government. The Mīzo National Front was formed which first captured all three Mīzo seats in the Assam legislature, then became a liberation movement and controlled almost all the Mīzo villages. The Government of India took a hard stand against it and in 1967 uprooted 50,000 Mīzo villagers and settled them in 18 fortified villages

Chākmā village. Women weave their own skirts.

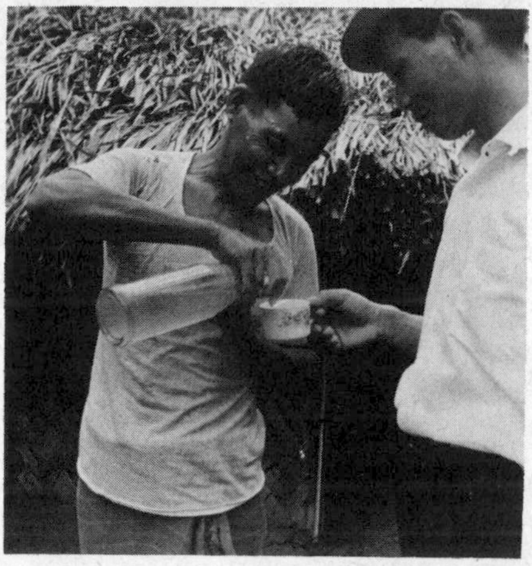

A guest must drink the Chākmā's home-made wine.

near roads. They were required to carry identification cards and hang pictures of every household resident on the house wall. A Mīzo "government" was set up in the Chittagong Hills of what was East Pakistan, financed by China and Pakistan, which conducted a guerilla war against the Indian army stationed in the Mīzo District. It claimed that if all the speakers of Kūki-Chīn languages in India, Burma, and East Pakistan would secede, they could form a country with a population of 2 million. But the emergence of Bangladesh and the formation of the new Territory of Mīzorām in 1972 have perhaps set the stage for direction of these energies towards Mīzo cultural and economic development.

Marma pastor of Baptist church of mixed Chittagong Hill people. The Bāngālī food is eaten with the hands; because of Christian influence wife eats with husband and son.

Chittagong Hill People

On the southwest corner of Bangladesh are the low Chittagong Hills which are populated by some 400,000 people who are mostly Buddhist tribals having some Mongoloid appearance and not at all Bāngālī. A few thousand Riāngs, Kūkis, and Mīzos spill over from India, but the rest of these people are ethnically related to the Ārākānese of southwestern Burma. In the north is a group of peoples called Marma, in the center the Chākmās, towards the south more Marmas, Mrus, Morungs, and Ārākānese—all Buddhists with historic links with Burma.

Chākmās are the largest tribe, and they have forgotten their language but have taken up an aberrant dialect of Bāngālī. Though traditionally living by hoe cultivation as the rest of these hill people, some have recently taken up plow cultivation, only to lose their best bottom lands to the large artificial Kaptai Lake. They retain some pre-Buddhist practices, such as sacrifice of a pig when a bride is brought to the groom's village. They live in peaceable little hamlets where women spend much of their time at looms producing distinctive fabrics.

The Marma language is related to Ārākānese and thus to Burmese and is written with the Burmese script. Marmas have several large monasteries, and monks come and go across the border at Burma. Some of the Marmas have studied Pāli in school as a sacred language. Outsiders sometimes call these people Mogh, a term they dislike for it means "pirate," stemming from the reputation Ārākānese had for centuries as sea pirates. Marmas do not have a fond attitude toward Bāngālī Muslims, and none have become Muslims. Plains people in turn fear to walk up a path in the Chittagong Hills lest a "pirate" jump forth. They ask, "Are there any bandits here? Tigers? Are people fierce like tigers?" These Buddhists, though participating in the economic life of Bangladesh, are not likely to become assimilated.

Muṇḍa-Speaking Peoples

The bulk of India's tribal population is not in the eastern hills but in the central Indian tribal belt stretching from eastern Rājasthān to western West Bengal and down to northern Āndhra. Over 8 million of these (roughly 30% of the central Indian tribals) are speakers of Muṇḍa type languages, divided into over 18 significant tribes. The number would be much larger if one were to add all those groups who have taken up Indo-Āryan speech. In West Bengal, for instance, only 78% of the Santāls claim Santālī as mother tongue, and only 7% of the Muṇḍārīs there claim Muṇḍārī. Other tribes, such as the Lodhās, have completely forgotten their original

tongue. When tribal people settle around industrial towns such as are sprouting in Choṭā Nāgpur, the eastern end of this tribal belt, sometimes their language is lost by the second or third generation.

TABLE 15–4 Speakers of Major Muṇḍa Languages in 1961

Santālī	3,131,000
Muṇḍārī	736,000
Ho	648,000
Kherwāṛī	647,000
Khāsi	364,000
Savara	266,000
Korku	220,000
Muṇḍa—unspecified	180,000
Khāṛiā	177,000
Karmalī	91,000
Kol	64,000
Gaḍaba	40,000
Bhūmij	23,000
Mahili	20,000
Korwā	16,000
Juāng	16,000
Other	40,000
Total	6,679,000

Though many of these tribes have territories where they predominate, there is much geographical admixture. The western corner of West Bengal, for instance, has 1.5 million Santāls and numbers of Muṇḍārī, Bhūmij, and Koḍa, while the Dravidian-speaking Orāons form the second largest tribe, all mixed among Bāngālīs. The southern half of Bihār, mostly Choṭā Nāgpur, has 6 million tribals, including half the Santāls, the majority of Muṇḍārīs and Orāons, and many thousands from the Loharā, Mahli, Ho, Chik Baraik, Koṛā, Khāṛiā, Khārwār, Sauriā Pahāriā, and Mal Pahāriā tribes, all mixed among Hindī-speakers. A quarter of Orissa's population is tribal and contains the majority of Savaras and Kols, half the Bhūmij, a third of the Hos, a tenth of the Santāls, some Boṇḍos, besides Dravidian-speaking Kaṇḍhs, Gōṇḍs, and Parjis. In Madhya Pradesh there are Korkus, Khāṛiās, and Korwās, and others, besides Indo-Āryan speaking tribes in the west and Dravidian-speaking tribes towards the south.

Though many of these tribes are now refugee populations, there is little doubt that in prehistoric times the eastern Gangā plain was occupied largely if not entirely by Muṇḍa peoples, whose linguistic, agricultural, and funerary traditions are related to the Khāsis and derive ultimately from Southeast Asia. On analogy with the assimilation of these peoples today, we may suppose that the menial castes of eastern India are largely such tribal peoples who have been incorporated into the caste structure. Many of the tribal villages have resident Hindu artisans who follow caste occupa-

tions, and now it is more common than not that a man from one of these tribes will understand Hindī, Bāngālī, or Uṛiyā.

People of the Muṇḍa tribes have a wide range of levels of cultural complexity. Perhaps the most primitive the British encountered while exploring the central Indian hill country were the Juāngs. Edward Dalton, who wrote his *Descriptive Ethnology of Bengal* in 1872 and was amazingly knowledgeable about the people on all sides of the Bānglā delta, visited the Juāngs in their homeland in the Orissa hills and referred to them as "the most primitive people I have met with or read of."

> Conasika, one of the largest of their villages, I found to contain twenty-five houses of Juangs. The huts are amongst the smallest that human beings ever deliberately constructed as dwellings. They measure about six feet by eight, and are very low, with doors so small as to preclude the idea of a corpulent householder. Scanty as are the above dimensions for a family dwelling, the interior is divided into two compartments, one of which is the store room, the other used for all domestic arrangements. The "Paterfamilias" and all his belongings of the female sex huddle together in this one stall not much larger than a dog kennel; for the boys there is a separate dormitory.[5]

Dalton was impressed with the garb of the Juāngs. For the women it "consisted in a girdle composed of several strings of beads from which depended before and behind small curtains of leaves. Adam and Eve sewed fig leaves together and made themselves aprons. The Juāngs are not so far advanced" but simply tuck in a few narrow leaves. The men formerly wore narrow bark strips, but by a century ago had adopted "the smallest quantity of cotton cloth that can be made to serve the purposes of decency." Dalton was also impressed with their dancing. Girls tucked in soft, fresh leaves lest the old ones scratch them, and proceeded to advance and retreat and wreathe in a line. They did a bear dance, with bodies inclined and hands touching the ground; "thus they move not unlike bears, and by a motion from the knees the bodies wriggle violently, and the broad tails of green leaves flap up and down in a most ludicrous manner." They performed a pigeon dance, a pig dance, a tortoise dance, and as a finale a vulture dance.[6] The Juāng practiced shifting cultivation by girdling and burning trees and scattering seeds of hill rice, corn, pulses, and chilies mixed in with sweet potatoes and ginger so that everything came up together. It is probable that they represent a pre-Muṇḍa stratum of population.

In 1912 the pioneer Indian anthropologist Sarat Chandra Roy wrote a work on the Muṇḍa (Muṇḍārī) tribe, and in 1937 another on the Khāṛiās, among whom he had lived 12 years. The word Muṇḍa means headman and the people under him are referred to as Muṇḍārī; this name has been applied to the whole linguistic group. Roy described practices typical of most Muṇḍa and many neighboring Dravidian tribes, such as use of ordeals and oaths, singing and dancing, and the institution of the youth dormitory. The Muṇḍārī count with 20 as a base number. Most Muṇḍa tribes cremate

the dead, a practice not necessarily borrowed from Hinduism. Early in this century their material equipment included the bow and arrow, shield, loom, and iron objects locally made. Even then they had taken on some of the characteristics of neighboring peasants, using oxen for pulling an iron-tipped plow, growing cotton, rice, and millets, and idealizing the joint family until the death of the father.

Most of the Muṇḍa tribes have exogamous clans, some of which are totemistic. D. N. Majumdar recounts in his study of the Ho of Singhbūm District in Bihār that in 1925 a 26-year-old man came home from working in the coal mines in order to participate in a festival which it was inauspicious to miss. He danced one night with a girl of his own clan and afterwards took her to a field and had intercourse with her. The matter was discovered and reported to the village elders, who did not take action immediately in order to allow time for the accused to expiate his crime of lying with a girl of his own clan. The accused could not decide how to atone for his wrong, and began to decline physically. When Majumdar saw him, he was prostrate with fever, the family standing around. He said, "I have earned my death and I am dying." Within two days he was gone.[7]

Rather than survey all the Muṇḍa tribes, we shall cite three differing examples of reaction to Hindu civilization about them. One became a low caste-like tribe with criminal tendencies, another evolved its own hierarchy after the Hindu model, and yet another began a nativistic revival.

A "Criminal Tribe": Lodhās

Lodhās are a tribe of over 40,000 who share the Midnapur District of West Bengal with over 1.5 million other tribals and also Bāngālī peasants. They called themselves Savaras in the census, and perhaps they were once a branch of that great tribe, which was mentioned by the classical Greek geographer Ptolemy as an independent people having two "cities."

This tribe has been described by P. K. Bhowmick. Lodhās have been affected by Bāngālī culture to the extent that they now are settled in farming villages. Whereas they formerly spoke a Muṇḍa language, they now use Bāngālī and retain only a few old folk songs in their own language. Only 3% of them are literate, which includes none of the women. Hardly any can recall the names of ancestors before grandparents. Most of them work as common laborers, or earn something by gathering fruits and nuts, and though they cherish their bows and arrows, there is no scope for using them today. They retain endogamous totemistic clans named after yam, shark, moon, or tiger. Whereas old people have the idea their totem is tabu, young people have little interest in totems. They have been Hindu for as long as they know, though they retain remnants of tribal cults such as marrying both bride and groom to a tree before the wedding so that if

Death visits, it will strike the tree instead of the spouse. They now bury their dead, and like Bāngālīs, they chaperone unmarried grown girls and arrange marriages.

As their own culture disintegrated, Lodhās reacted to the wider peasant society, not by becoming an untouchable or laboring group as so many tribals have, but by engaging in organized theft and banditry. In 1871 the Criminal Tribes Act was promulgated to identify and control those tribes so engaged, who were compelled to give fingerprints, were constantly watched, and had to notify the police of change of address even if for only a night. There were organized criminals called *ṭhagīs* (thugs) who were fanatical robbers and thought the ghosts of their ancestors would be pleased if they waylaid and ritually murdered their victims, or dug through the walls of houses to steal. In 1931 there were 4 million members of the so-called Criminal Tribes, mostly in Madhya Pradesh but including 26 active gangs in Midnapur District, two of which were large Lodhā gangs. While the Criminal Tribes Act was repealed in 1952, the tribes that had come under it numbered 6 million in 1961, and the government is still engaged in suppressing the activity of such "dacoits" in parts of Madhya Pradesh.

A "Rājpūt" Tribe: Bhūmij

Many of the settled tribal people of Choṭā Nāgpur and central India have long been associated with little state systems which evolved as migratory tribes, and jhūm cultivators came to live in larger villages and own their own land. In every case landowning and plow cultivation preceded the development of such state systems, though the Santāl and the Ho used the plow but had no such political systems.

The anthropologist Surajit Sinha has described how the Bhūmij, an offshoot of the Muṇḍārī tribe living in southeast Bihār developed such a state system and extended into West Bengal and Orissa. The Bhūmij in West Bengal have lost their language and refuse to be identified as Muṇḍas, while those in Choṭā Nāgpur may intermarry with the Muṇḍārī. Traditionally each of the many Bhūmij clans maintained an ossuary for deposition of the cremation remains of clan members. Over the ossuary they erected menhirs, horizontal stone slabs, or capstones—megaliths reminiscent of those of the Khāsis. The Bhūmij in West Bengal are probably an earlier population than the Santāl, Kurmī, or Ho who live among them, for they supply the village headmen and priests.

When the British arrived in 1770, they found an independent Bhūmij rājā of Barabhūm who spoke Bāngālī and claimed Rājpūt Kshatriya status. As the royal family gained ascendancy, it gave up use of its clan ossuary, forgot its creation myths, and began to employ high class Hindu officials.

It got Brāhmaṇs to develop Rājpūt genealogies, though there was no real Rājpūt invasion here. The rājā owned land in many villages. Every tenant had to provide quotas of labor and produce, while artisans also had to give their share. The king sponsored weekly markets. Foot soldiers were obtained from among the laborers who leased land from the king. The social classes that developed are listed by Sinha: 1) Rājpūt Kshatriyas, 2) inferior Rājpūts recognized as descending from the Bhūmij, 3) upper class Bhūmij who do not drink wine or eat chickens and who consult Brāhmaṇs in rites of passage, 4) ordinary Bhūmij who drink wine, eat chickens, allow widow remarriage, and can get the services only of "degraded Brāhmans," and 5) fallen Bhūmij who have breached the rules of clan exogamy or caste endogamy.

This social structure and emulation of the Rājpūt model helped the Bhūmij to withstand the pull of Christianity which affected so many of the less hierarchically organized tribes of central India. But now changes are in the air. The traditional aristocracy has become decadent, and at their meetings the Bhūmij now give only lip service to Rājpūt standards. They were shocked to find themselves in 1951 labeled as "Scheduled Wild Tribes" in electoral rolls, though now they are beginning to see the practical advantages of being listed as a Scheduled Tribe.

They are too far on the road to assimilation to readily revive a cohesive non-Hindu complex of traits. Most now speak Hindī, Bāngālī or Uṛiyā; some have become occupational specialists, such as iron smelters or blacksmiths, no longer call themselves as Bhūmij, and regard as essential the employment of Hindu castes such as Brāhmaṇs, Barbers, and Washermen. Clan exogamy is fading. Sinha thinks that such people are now at a disadvantage as compared with the Ho and Santāl or sections of the Muṇḍa and Gōṇḍ tribes who are undergoing nativistic revivals, and have a renewed self-confidence to move ahead. The Bhūmij have become locked into the Hindu social structure.

A Tribe Rejecting Hinduization: Santāls

The Santāls, our third example of Muṇḍa tribes' reactions to acculturating forces, now number 3.5 million. Santāls occupy the Santāl Parganās and the Rānchī and Singhbhūm Districts in Bihār as well as neighboring parts of Orissa, Madhya Pradesh, and West Bengal; they occupy, here and there, a territory 350 miles long. Their numerical strength alone draws attention.

Dalton, in his ethnological survey of 1872, observed that Santāls had antipathy to Brāhmaṇs and to Hinduism in general. Though not particular about food, nothing would induce them to eat rice cooked by Brāhmaṇs or any Hindus. "Unfortunately during the famine of 1866 this was not

known to us. The cooks who prepared the food distributed at the relief centers were all Brāhmaṇs, and it was supposed that this would suit all classes, but the Santāls kept aloof, and died rather than eat from hands so hateful to them."[8]

The encroachment of Hindus in their hill areas led to the Santāl Rebellion of 1855–1857. Though both their clans and their tribe are acephalous, the necessary organization spontaneously developed so that 30,000 of them, together with women and children, began marching toward Calcutta. With their arrows and axes they scattered the oppressive money-lenders and the conniving police and even defeated a crack British-led unit. But after a year they were inevitably defeated, about 10,000 were killed, and their leaders were executed or sent to prison. The grievances of the Santāls were that they were losing their lands to rapacious Hindu money-lenders, that they were bound by hereditary debts and were becoming tenants and even slaves of the Hindus who could bribe the police and manipulate the law, and that they could not get redress at the courts.

The reason the Santāls were so exploited is that their culture emphasizes redistribution of wealth and camaraderie rather than acquisition of power and hard bargaining. Also they had, and still have, what Martin Orans calls the "Santāl pleasure complex." Dalton noted in his time that Santāls were distinguished in playing the flute, a bamboo instrument two feet long which produced fine deep tones. Youths and maidens sang and danced after an evening meal, and marriages were usually love matches. Other aspects of "pleasure," as the Santāls view it, are camaraderie and exchanges of cigarettes and rice beer while moving about from house to house. On such occasions any Santāls present may join, and also people from other Muṇḍa tribes. Plains people regard Santāl dancing as leading to undue erotic behavior, and it is true that the Brāhmaṇical contemplative ideal has its antithesis in the epicurean behavior of the Santāls. But the practice most repugnant to Hindus is beef eating. Eclectic though Hindu society is, these customs made assimilation of the Santāls as a group impossible. After the Santāl Rebellion the Santāls experienced increasing difficulty in resolving their dilemma, for the very cultural features which most promoted tribal solidarity were at the same time viewed by Hindus as most demeaning. Over the decades ceremonies decayed and myths were half-forgotten. Orans thinks that, in spite of their tradition of parochialism, they would have gone the way of the Bhūmij had not new winds blown across Choṭā Nāgpur in this century.

Choṭā Nāgpur is the source of most of India's coal, and also has iron ore. For a century tribals have worked with other Indian laborers in the coal mines to fuel the railroads. In 1908 the Tata Company founded Jamshedpur, an industrial town in the southeast corner of Bihār in Ho country. This town has attracted workers from many tribes as well as plains

people who all communicate in Hindī. It has developed a class structure in which employment position, income, house, motor vehicles, and education are determinants of status, while caste persists as an ethnic distinction and as a criterion for marriage. It may happen that high caste Hindus who perform appropriate rituals at home are employed under the authority of men of tribal origin. But most tribal employees live in clusters of huts outside the town or in company housing. Santāls working there come from within 50 miles or so of Jamshedpur, and go home for festivals. Along with opportunity for advancement according to ability, such factors as the politicization of labor unions and the formation of an Ādivāsī Cooperative Society have halted the slow Santāl trend to Hinduization. The term *ādivāsī* (original inhabitant) has gained respect.

Santāls are now, as Orans says, a tribe in search of a "great tradition." Practices which Hindus pointed to in denigrating the Santāls are being revived. Santāl children were told in school that beef eating was bad for health, but in the 1950s some Santāls read and disseminated reasons why it was good for the health. Cow sacrifice has been revived, and where this is contrary to state law, has been done secretly. The focus of the religious revival is the worship of the traditional gods at sacred groves. A propaganda movement among Santāls caused 530,000 of them in 1961 to return in the census that their religion was "Sarṇā," signifying Sacred Grove, or that it was "Santāl." A unique script invented by missionaries gained some currency for a time. Drama clubs have sprung up to perform traditional epic and heroic dramas, even though the tribal origin myth had been partly forgotten by most people. An attempt has been made to induce all Santāls to celebrate their festivals simultaneously and to set dates for them not coinciding with Hindu ceremonies. Traditional dances, drinking, and offering rice beer have a new respectability.

But schools are not operated in Santālī. Moreover, educated Santāls are in an awkward position because they may not spontaneously drink or dance or develop an abiding attachment to the Sacred Grove, while at the same time they may wish to see Santāl solidarity enhanced. Common Santāls are uneasy when educated tribal members are in their midst, for it disrupts their easy conviviality and sharing. As more Santāls become educated and contemplative, it remains to be seen whether these elements of cultural revivalism will continue to provide the solidarity Santāls seek.

Bhīls and Neighboring Tribes

A tribal belt running through eastern Rājasthān and western Madhya Pradesh and extending into the Western Ghats of Gujarāt and Mahārāshṭra consists of a number of large tribes, all speaking Indo-Āryan languages,

who are much less distinct from the majority peasant population than the tribes of east-central India. Chief among these are the Bhīls, India's third largest tribe, numbering 3 million.

Bhīls speak Bhīlī, a dialect of Gujarātī. The name is derived from the Dravidian word *vil*, a bow. It has been suggested, though without firm evidence, that they were once a Dravidian-speaking people; Bhīls have no traditions of migration into their country. Hunting is now hardly possible since forest is so scarce (covering only 5% of Gujarāt, for instance), but in living memory some Bhīls practiced shifting cultivation. They also have a pastoral tradition, with legends of cowgirls like Rādhā. But now most of them live in villages and cultivate with the plow. They formerly had a clan structure, but now this is hardly important in marriage, and totemism has disappeared. Kinship terminology is based on cross-cousin marriage, and the family is generally nuclear. As with most tribes of western India, there are old claims of genealogical links with ruling Rājpūt families. They are known throughout India for their colorful dances.

Gujarātī Bhīls who have come to Baṛodā as temporary laborers. Unless tribal lands are sufficient, they can turn only to unskilled labor.

Neighboring populations regard Bhīls as "superstitious." They revere tiger, serpent, and boundary deities, and greatly fear the evil eye. If a person or cow falls sick, they call a shaman to cast off the power of the evil eye. Members of the same family may even sit in different corners of the house to eat in order to avoid the evil eye. The dead are cremated and the ashes collected after 20 days. It is of great importance that each tribe or caste has its own cremation ground. Filial piety is strong and ancestors are revered; there is a feeling of continuity of the living with the dead.

Bhīls worship Hindu deities, among whom Hanuman is important, in addition to some Muslim and Christian saints.

There have been several sectarian movements among the Bhīls. R. B. Naik describes one known as Bhagat (*bhaktā*, devotee), the adherents of which now form a Bhīl caste in western Madhya Pradesh. One bhaktā, Govindagiri, claimed to be an incarnation of a deity sent to reform degenerate Bhīls, and he was worshiped as such. He preached devotion to Rāma and abstention from falsehood, theft, adultery, meat, and wine, while enjoining cleanliness and bathing. He made disciples and established sacred fires at various centers. He promised a Bhīl kingdom and gathered a force in the hills in 1911, which was finally subdued by British artillery. Govindagiri was captured and transported for life, but the government let him go after only eight years. Depending excessively on *gānjā* (hemp), he soon died, but his sect lived on. Bhagats now form the top of a three-caste tier, with ordinary Bhīls in the middle and Christian Bhīls on the bottom. Bhagats and Christians are endogamous, and there are the usual commensality proscriptions among them. Bhagats are still puritanical, having given up gaiety at festivals, dance, drama, and music. The sect is now growing, since the Ādivāsī movement has provided a broader basis for tribal self-identification.

In eastern Rājasthān there is a large group called Mīnas, who are also classified as a tribe, though they are less distinct from the surrounding population even than are Bhīls and can hardly be distinguished at sight. In Gujarāt there are several tribes, chief of which are the Dublās, some 200,000 of whom live in the southeast corner of the state. Dublās do not relish living in the hills, but are mixed among other villagers, occupying separate streets. They have their own gods and priests, but are nonetheless quite Hinduized and require the services of Brāhmaṇs. They visit Hindu temples, are vegetarians, and refuse to take water from the hands of Harijans. Other similar tribes in eastern Gujarāt include the Gamits (numbering some 130,000), Dankās, Dodhiās, Nāyakās, Kukaṇos, and Codhrās, all of which are merging into Gujarātī culture.

In northwest Mahārāshṭra there are other tribes such as Ṭhākurs, who number over 100,000 and occupy the tableland behind Bombay, and the Kolīs, who are even more numerous. These people function within society essentially as separate low castes. The Ṭhākurs, for instance, live in little hamlets and hire out as laborers, gather firewood, and make rope. Their women wear their sāṛīs in a curious manner, wrapped high on the hips and pulled tightly between the legs. L. N. Chapekar, while observing them, noted that in the summer when food was gone, both adults and children had almost nothing to eat except a few berries and raw mangoes, and were just waiting for the rains to bring out the wild onions on which they could subsist for a season.

In Madhya Pradesh there are a number of other tribes who have lost

their original languages and speak some form of Hindī. Among these are the Baigā, made famous by Verrier Elwin's study. Elwin came out from England as a missionary but became a follower of Gandhi and then devoted the rest of his life to the sympathetic study of tribal people. He lived among Baigās and other groups, and married a Gōṇḍ for his first wife and a Pardhān for his second. He wrote 18 books on the tribes of central India and also the Assam region. He loved to recount the songs and folktales of his tribal friends, such as this Gaṇḍā story from Raipur District:

An old woman had a daughter. She would never let the girl go anywhere, and at night she slept beside her holding her hand over her part for fear some man would come to the house.

One night a man covered himself with a blanket, tied a bell around his neck, and went to the garden near the house. Presently he shook a tree and his bell tinkled. "Here is a cow eating the brinjals [eggplants]." So thought the woman. "Go, daughter, and drive it away." She removed her hand, and the girl went out and shouted at the cow. The man whispered to her. She came back and lay down by her mother.

After a little while, the man shook the tree again and his bell tinkled. "That dirty cow's back again. Tomorrow I will abuse the neighbors." So thought the woman. "Go, daughter and drive it away." She removed her hand and the daughter went out again and chased the cow round the garden. The man whispered again. The girl came back and lay down by her mother.

A third time the man shook the tree and his bell tinkled. "Go daughter and drive it away, drive it right away this time, out of our field into the neighbor's tobacco patch." She removed her hand and the girl chased the cow out of the garden and did not come back for a long time.

When she came back, she lay down by her mother and when the old woman put her hand, "Ah, mother, it is perspiration," so said her daughter.[9]

Central Indian Dravidian Tribes

Dravidian-speaking tribal people of India are listed in Table 15–5. The northernmost Dravidian languages are spoken by the Sauriā Pahāriās, whose language is Mālto and who live in the Santāl Parganās of Bihār. The Mal Pahāriās are a smaller related group in Bānglā who are forgetting their own language. These tribes have brought Dravidian speech almost to the eastern Gangā. The largest of all the tribes in India is the Gōṇḍs, though fewer than half now speak Gōṇḍi. They had a substantial kingdom in Madhya Pradesh before the days of the Marāṭhā raids. One of the Gōṇḍ groups is described at length by Fürer-Haimendorf in *South Asia: Seven Community Profiles.*

Kaṇḍhs (Khoṇḍs) are found over southern Orissa, except for the coastal plains. They gained notoriety in the middle of the last century for their human sacrifice, which the British suppressed. The sacrifice, made publicly,

was to the earth god to bring forth crops. The victim was feasted for a month and adorned, and on the day of sacrifice was made very drunk. He would be suffocated in a pit mired in hog's blood, or on occasion squeezed to death between two boards, or cut up alive. A piece of flesh

TABLE 15–5 Speakers of Dravidian Tribal Languages in 1961

North Dravidian	
Orāon (Kurukh)	1,133,000
Mālto	87,000
Central Dravidian	
Gōṇḍi	1,501,000
Kui	510,000
Kaṇḍh	168,000
Kōya	141,000
Parji	84,000
Kolāmi	46,000
Koṇḍa	12,000
South Dravidian	
Baḍaga	85,000
Koḍagu	78,000
Kōṭa	862
Toḍa	760
Total	3,846,622

would be cut off and buried in the earth by the priest as an offering. Afterwards a buffalo calf would be brought and its four feet cut off.[10] Kaṇḍhs believed they could not grow nice red turmeric without blood sacrifice.

A Kolām village in northern Āndhra. Shed in center of village is for holding ceremonies and for sitting and talking. Such neck rings are not worn by plains women.

Ceremonial dancing in Kolām and Gōṇḍ village. Headdresses are peacock feathers; musicians play drums and flutes.

The Orāons, who speak Kurukh, are India's fourth largest tribe, after Gōṇḍs, Santāls, and Bhīls. They are found in south Bihār and north Orissa and have a legend—probably correct—that they migrated northward. They have several features in common with some of their Muṇḍa neighbors, for they live mixed with other tribals, and in almost every Orāon village there are Hindu occupational groups such as potters, blacksmiths, and cattle tenders, and also Muslim weavers. Nowadays Orāons also go out for work to factories, brick kilns, roads, or tea estates in the Himālayas.

The Orāon youth dormitories have a system of age grades. An initiate serves the older boys for three years, then stays in the second grade for three years, and in the third grade until marriage. There is mixed singing and dancing at night, which is thought to have some increase function, and boys receive sex training in these institutions. An important function of the dormitories is that they weld the village together, tending to a leveling of the status of different clans. But many Orāons have given up this institution, for missionaries and caste Hindus disfavored them, and now there are other mechanisms for the education of youth. Some villages have not so much as heard that such dormitories existed.

Orāon village worship is centered around a sacred grove, in which two tall trees are called male and female chief spirits. Orāons revere a composite pantheon of tribal and Hindu deities, while some also follow Bhagat sects. A fire-walking ceremony (not an exclusively tribal practice) in an Orāon-Muṇḍa village near Rānchī has been described by Victor Rosner. If Śiva had granted a fortuitous marriage or recovery from sickness to a young man, he might vow to fire-walk for five consecutive years. Some days before the ceremony he would have his temples shaved and would abstain from meat, turmeric, salt, oil, and certain other foods.

Coming to the Śaivite shrine, the devotee scoops up glowing coals in his hands, holds them for two minutes, and takes them to the altar; the fire is rendered powerless by five twigs he obtains from a mango tree. Meanwhile a woman gets spirit-possessed and lies on the altar. Then the devotee walks 10 to 15 seconds, at least five steps, over the bed of coals, without hurrying, sinking in the embers up to his ankles. Then he plays with them with his feet. Another man stands in the fire 70 seconds and scoops up coals with his hands. Women wash the fire-walkers' feet, and all partake of a feast and put on a dance of the life of Śiva.

On this occasion none of the onlookers showed fear, and even after much inquiry none had heard of anyone burned. A medical doctor examined the devotees' feet as they lay flat, but there was no blistering or singeing. Hook-swinging used to accompany the ceremony, in which the devotees were swung around with huge hooks piercing the loins. Old men said this ought to still be done, as no ill effects were produced on the body. They still use 18-inch skewers to pierce the tongue while fire-walking, apparently without ill effects.[11]

Tribes of the Southern Peninsula

We turn now to the last of the five tribal categories of South Asia, those located in the South. There are a few tribe-like castes on the plains, especially in southern Āndhra and northern Tamil̲ Nāḍu where we find the Yerava, Varli, and Iruḷar. These diffuse groups are essentially laborers. Better known are the Cencus (Chenchus), a small tribe in the Eastern Ghāṭs of Āndhra. They are divided into the Forest Cencus, one of the very few peoples of South Asia who still have a culture adapted to hunting and gathering, and Village Cencus. Each of these two considers itself superior to the other. In Sri Lanka there are the Väddās whom we have described in Chapter 4. Now they are essentially absorbed.

A number of interesting tribes inhabit the Western Ghāṭs running southward from Karṇāṭaka and dividing Kēraḷa from Tamil̲ Nāḍu. The largest are the Baḍaga who keep cattle and do some cultivation in the northern Nīlagiri Hills, while the Koḍagu of Coorg, Karṇāṭaka, are really peasant people. Aside from these two and the Toḍa and Koṭa, all the tribes of the southwestern Ghāṭs speak Tamil̲ or Malayāḷam dialects. In Kēraḷa the largest tribes are the Puliyar (61,000) and the Paṇiyar (37,000); the rest have numerical strength ranging from 15,000 down to a few hundreds. Though Kēraḷa has 40 such tribes they comprise only 1.2% of its population, while the tribes of Tamil̲ Nāḍu and Karṇāṭaka make up less than half a percent of the whole.

Most famous of all are the Toḍas of the Nīlagiri Hills, known through W. H. R. Rivers' study of them published in 1907 which has become something of an anthropological classic. Recently Emeneau has published a lengthy annotated volume of Toḍa songs. Toḍas numbered only 765 in 1961, but that figure marked the end of a population decline. They live on a grassy plateau 6000 to 8000 feet high on which they graze buffaloes, while on a lower altitude are the Koṭas, who in 1961 numbered 956. Toḍa economy and religion is centered on the buffalo and dairying. A death is followed by an elaborate two-day ceremony which formerly involved slaughter of buffaloes. Toḍas practice fraternal polyandry, and women also have intercourse with other categories of men. A baby's paternity is established through a ritual in which one of its putative fathers gives a toy bow. Today Toḍas have income from the nearby resort city of Ootacamund, where tourists come in the hill season to escape the heat of the plains, often making visits to see Toḍa settlements which consist of large half-barrel-shaped, windowless houses, with tiny doorways, built just as Rivers saw them.

Of the tribes of Kēraḷa, the Kāḍar are best known because of Ehrenfels' monograph on them and also because of widely circulated pictures of a few of them having frizzly hair. They and their neighbors, the Mala Malāssars, used to file their incisor teeth to a point, said to hint at ethnic

links with Southeast Asian Negritos. Kāḍar culture is now disintegrating as more and more plains people encroach upon the forests, while the government, trying to preserve the remaining forests, has restricted its inhabitants from making clearings.

There are also tribes of honey gatherers which according to literary sources are of ancient origin. One such is the Allar, who number only 350 and live south of the Nīlagiris. They speak Malayāḷam with a peculiar intonation, wear no clothing but a strap over the genitalia, and live by selling honey, bees wax, firewood, and bamboo. They have never cultivated and do not even hunt with spears or bows, but use traps and nets. Plains people consider them polluting because they eat carrion and do not observe menstrual pollution. They are said not to be very solicitous of one another; a man eats food he collects regardless of the presence of wife and child, and a woman in childbirth looks after herself. Allar are now beginning to know a few Hindu deities and have necessarily become integrated into the money economy.

Plains people speak disparagingly of the sexual life of these tribes, saying that among the Allar a girl whose breasts have developed is given to any man who demands her. They report intercourse between prepubescent children and various kinds of relations considered incestuous. The Malapaṇḍārams, a fair-skinned tribe in the central Kēraḷa hills who today have trouble making a living because of forest conservancy rules, are said to tolerate some sibling incest, while marriage is to cross-cousins. Individual monogamous families are informally grouped together without a clan structure. Information about these tribes comes mostly from brief visits made years ago, and it is doubtful that the population growth of Kēraḷa will allow their continued existence as isolated ethnic entities.

The Kanikkar are an example of a tribe that has preserved many traits seemingly underlying the culture of Kēraḷa today. They are divided into exogamous matrilineal clans, and a man can marry into his father's clan. Divorce is not common and adultery is reported as rare, but sororal polygyny is practiced. Until recently they were shifting cultivators, and like most of these tribes, they place much emphasis on truthfulness and honesty as symbols of tribal status. In religion the Kanikkar call themselves Hindus, and they know the Hindu pantheon. Every settlement also has its own Śāstā deity—a form of the popular Kēraḷa god of the hills, Aiyappan. Each temple has a priest, and there are also shamans who perform rites for health, agriculture, or hunting while standing facing the sun which they call Bhagavan. They formerly sacrificed a boy once every 12 years and purified the village by sprinkling his blood, but now they make do with a goat. They observe ritual purity and pollution, and death pollution lasts 10 days. Everything connected with a corpse is thrown into its grave, and a coin is put in its mouth for the ferry fee.[12]

Such tribal cults as those of the Kanikkar gave rise to the Aiyappan

cult of Kēraḷa. For a month before the annual pilgrimage, devotees observe strict vows including celibacy, not shaving, and diet restrictions. They trek from villages and cities over the state, walking all night calling out "Aiyappā, Aiyappā," and ascend a forested hill where they imagine they have to brave all sorts of spooky forest dangers and fierce animals. This cult, of prehistoric tribal origin, has coalesced with Hinduism, and non-Hindus are not allowed on the pilgrimage. Kēraḷa was affected by Indian Civilization late because it was so heavily forested, but now the remaining tiny tribes decline from census to census.

Andaman and Nicobar Islands

The Nicobar Islands are on the shipping route between South India and the Straits of Malacca, and are mentioned in Greek, Arab, and Chinese travel accounts. A Cōḻa inscription of 1050 refers to Nakkavarman, "land of the naked," from whence we get the name Nicobar. Nicobarese, of which there are six dialects, is a Mon-Khmer language ultimately related to Khāsi and the Muṇḍa group, and has retroflex consonants. The language, as well as the complex of culture traits, came from the Malaysia side, and this is also betrayed in the physical features of the Nicobarese. They traditionally lived by shifting cultivation, depending upon the coconut, areca nut, yam, banana, and pig. Car Nicobar is well populated and has experienced great change since the Japanese occupation and Indian Independence; all are Christians and many speak Hindī. In Great Nicobar there is a tribe of 300, the Shompens, whose physical features and culture betray an earlier stratum of population like that of the Andamanese.

The Andamanese are well known among anthropologists from Radcliffe-Brown's study; more recently several Indians and the Italian Lidio Cipriani have written about them. The Arioto, who peopled the Great Andamans, once numbered 6000 or 8000, but at a recent count there were only 23 left, living in huts provided by the Forest Department and wearing clothes. All had syphilis. On Little Andaman the naked Jarawras have so far been successful in dispelling all outsiders. A related people, the Sentinelese, live on Sentinel Island.

Better known are the Onges (see Chap. 2) who number something over a hundred. Of the people of the world encountered in the days of European exploration, these were among the most primitive. Earlier writers stated, and Cipriani has confirmed, that they did not know how to produce fire, though they used it. They practiced no cultivation but dug for roots with digging sticks, and had no traps but fished with crude nets. They had no stone tools except for fire-shattered quartz flakes which they used for shaving and tatooing (which were later replaced by bottle glass), and did not have the domesticated dog. They hunted with bows and arrows, and had

Nicobarese village.

the harpoon with detachable head. Kitchen middens are scattered over the island with shards of well-fired thin pottery, but Onges did not make any ware except coarse sun-dried vessels, so it has been suggested they experienced cultural regression. Onges had no sacrificial ritual or marriage ceremony, and could not count above three or four. Visitors have noted a high frequency of sexual activity, but they are inbred, fertility is low, and their numbers are decreasing.

The Andaman Islands were a convenient place for Burmese and Indian convicts to be cast during colonial days. Now the Government of India is encouraging settlement, offering inducements to mainlanders, and exploiting the forest products of the islands. Hindī is gaining ground as the common language. Today Port Blair is being developed as a naval station, so the Government of India does not permit foreigners to visit the islands.

Administrative Policies

The British generally administered tribal regions with tolerance, having once put an end to violence, and sometimes protected tribal areas from incursions by plains people. They did allow Christian missionary activity, however. The British gathered vast quantities of ethnographic data, compiled in the hefty tomes of the "tribes and castes" series of different parts of India, and in the District Gazetteers.

Since Independence much more ethnographic data on the tribes has been published, most of it by Indians. Articles have long been appearing in *Man in India*, in the *Bulletin of the Department of Anthropology* (now

called the Anthropological Survey of India), and in newer journals such as *The Anthropologist* and *The Eastern Anthropologist.* Anthropology has become a subject for graduate research in 13 universities. Tribal research institutes have been established in Rānchī for south Bihār, in Chindwārā for Madhya Pradesh, and in Shillong for the Assam region. The list of really good ethnographers is a long one. N. K. Bose has been influential as Commissioner for Scheduled Castes and Scheduled Tribes; Surajit Sinha has been perceptive, and G. S. Ghurye has been prolific. L. P. Vidhyarthi and Sachchindananda have written about tribal Bihār, and a host of others have written about tribes around Assam. D. K. Sen is Director of the Anthropological Survey of India. Among foreign ethnographers one thinks first of Verrier Elwin (though he became a citizen of India), Fürer-Haimendorf, and Stephen Fuchs who was long a missionary in Madhya Pradesh; each of these has made a number of ethnographic studies.

Thus there is no dearth of data on the tribes. But the attitudes of the central and state governments have been ambivalent. After Independence there was a general feeling that India should be emotionally integrated. Some politicians accused the British of secluding the tribals as if they were an anthropological zoo, and suspected them of conniving to retain the loyalty of tribal people at the expense of independent India. On the other hand, the Constitution of India guarantees protection of the "weaker sections of the population," and Nehru himself enunciated the principles that tribal people should develop along the lines of their own genius, should have land and forest rights, should not be overadministered, and should be administered by tribal people whenever possible.

On the whole, the Central Government has shown a sympathetic understanding of the needs of tribal people, and the Commissioner for Scheduled Castes and Scheduled Tribes is entrusted with making the government aware of their problems. Governments of the newly formed linguistic states, however, have been much quicker to assume that the tribals would be assimilated soon. Lower-level officers have often manifested an overweening or condescending attitude toward tribals, or considered them polluting, or viewed their own appointment to tribal posts as a demotion or perhaps as an opportunity for personal profit. The vast Block Development Program launched in tribal areas often benefits primarily the nontribals, since tribals do not always have the mental set to change, nor do they view any government agency as altruistic.

Administration of tribals in the eastern hills is much more tolerant of cultural diversity than is the attitude toward tribals in central and southern India. Most striking has been the administration of Arunāchal Pradesh, which is a Central Government Territory. The tone for liberal and sympathetic administration was set by Verrier Elwin in *A Philosophy for N.E.F.A.* (Arunāchal Pradesh), for he was Tribal Advisor for that Territory until his death in 1964. Since the area never had been much affected by

plains land-grabbers or moneylenders, missionaries, or any administration, great efforts were made to develop a positive relationship with the tribes, to respect each as a cultural entity, and to encourage modernization without destroying their self-confidence. An important means to achieve this has been the use of tribal languages in the educational system, a considerable accomplishment since they were unwritten a generation ago. As of 1967, there were 247 schools operating in tribal languages, 191 in Assamese, and 16 in Hindī.[13] The administration of this region has been notably successful in implementing modernization without causing cultural disintegration or resentment against outsiders.

As for the tribes south of the Brahmaputra, the government wrongly assumed after Independence that they would willingly be part of Assam since Assamese was lingua franca over wide areas. The tendency for plains Indians to betray a superior attitude and Hindu ethnocentricity was not firmly dealt with at first, and when the tribes began to demand statehood or independence the government tended to blame missionaries, expelled them from the region, and put almost all of it out of bounds for tourists and scholars too. After conceding the formation of Nāgaland the government waited eight years before conceding political realignment of the whole hill region, but now perhaps the greatest of these problems are past. It remains to be seen if the infusion of large sums for development will produce a negative reaction in time. Education in Maṇipurī, Khāsi, Gāro, and Mīzo is quite well developed, but in other areas linguistic fragmentation and pride in English have delayed this. But as long as these states can implement their own policies on land tenure, language, education, and agriculture, it is likely that their people will remain as distinct cultural entities and will be in a position to make important contributions to civilizational development in South Asia.

The tribes in central and southern India are closer to assimilation, though this is not happening as fast as some people suppose. At a Tribal Symposium held in Hyderābād in 1964 there was a general feeling that special provisions would have to be made for tribals for 10 years or so, after which they would be integrated and there would be no more need for Scheduled Areas and protection of Scheduled Tribes.[14] Even professionals take this view sometimes, as exemplified by one sociologist who spent a long enough time among the Bhīls of Rājasthān to write a book-length ethnography of them and discuss their nativistic Bhagat sects: "The rise of Bhilism is a dangerous trend, the product of dirty politics adopted during elections." He thinks we should see how they should be integrated with lower castes.

> If cultural synthesis leads to our cherished goal of social integration, it should be accelerated. It is in the fitness of things that the tribals should be persuaded to modify their values, legal or social, so as to conform to those of the non-tribals.

. . . They will learn manners of speech and conversation. They will imbibe true social values.[15]

Hindu peasants expect the tribals to gradually conform in matters such as not eating beef, clothes, rituals, kinship, and acquisition of manufactured goods.

Obviously tribals are not going to be assimilated so fast; they are at present increasing faster than the population as a whole. They are being threatened, however, by the laying of new roads through tribal territories, along which squatters set up stores and eventually towns. Tribals deprived of their lands, being left with no saleable skills, can only become common laborers. Protection of forests also causes them hardship. The states have varying policies about protection of tribal lands. State legislators are often more concerned with indices of economic development and matters bearing on their electoral constituencies. But tribal affairs officers trained in special institutions set up in Madhya Pradesh, Bihār, and Āndhra do in many cases have grounding in the principles of applied anthropology.

State governments in central India refuse to allow education in tribal languages—even though this has proved successful in Arunāchal Pradesh and other eastern hill areas and even though Santālī has 3 million speakers and several other languages have over a million. Of course the children do not attend school regularly when it is not in their language, and the literacy rate is low. Teachers are usually plains people who manage to impart to the children a well-developed sense of tribal inferiority.

Some of the smaller tribes will probably cease to be viable cultural entities within a generation or will become nontribal cultural entities. Some of the larger ones may undergo further revitalization movements, either religious or linguistic, or may bypass the local plains hierarchy by unique accomplishments, as people of the eastern hills have done through education. The chapter on Gōṇḍs in the companion volume is an example of the effects of modernization and population growth on the tribes of central India.

REFERENCES AND NOTES

1 Fürer-Haimendorf (1967a), pp. 63–64.
2 Fürer-Haimendorf (1967a), pp. 72–73.
3 Fürer-Haimendorf (1969), pp. 81–84.
4 Lehman, p. 28.
5 Dalton, p. 151.
6 Dalton, p. 153.
7 Quoted in Sourindranath Sarkar, *Psycho-dynamics of Tribal Behavior* (Calcutta, 1964), pp. 76–77.
8 Dalton, p. 213.
9 Elwin (1944), p. 321.

[10] John Campbell, *A Personal Narrative of Thirteen Years Service among the Wild Tribes of Khondistan for the Suppression of Human Sacrifice* (London, 1864).

[11] Victor Rosner, "Fire-Walking the Tribal Way," *Anthropos* 61 (1966).

[12] K. Gnanamban, "The Kanikkars of Travancore—Their Religion and Magical Practices," *Bull. Dept. Anthro* III (1954); also B. Mukherjee, "Marriage among the Kanikkars of Travancore," *Bull. Dept. Anthro* V (1956).

[13] Government of India, *Report of the Commissioner for Scheduled Castes and Scheduled Tribes*, 1966–1967. New Delhi, 1968.

[14] Fürer-Haimendorf (1967b), p. 212.

[15] S. L. Doshi, *Bhils: Between Societal Self-awareness and Cultural Synthesis* (New Delhi, 1971), pp. 246–250.

IMPORTANT SOURCES

General

Bose, N. K. "Change in Tribal Cultures before and after Independence," *Man in India* X, No. 4 (1964).

Elwin, Verrier. *The Tribal World of Verrier Elwin*. Bombay, 1965. (Published posthumously.)

Fürer-Haimendorf, C. von. *Morals and Merit: A Study of Values and Social Controls in South Asian Societies*. Chicago, 1967a.

———. "The Position of the Tribal Populations in Modern India," in Philip Mason (ed.), *India and Ceylon: Unity and Diversity*. New York, 1967b. (An excellent review of government relations with tribal groups.)

Ghurye, G. S. *The Scheduled Tribes*, 2d ed. Bombay, 1959.

Government of India. *Census of India, 1961*. Vol. I, Part II-C (ii), *Language Tables*. New Delhi.

Government of India. *Census of India, 1961*. Vol. I, Part II-C (i), *Cultural Tables*. New Delhi.

Government of India. *Census of India, 1961. Census Atlas*. New Delhi, 1970.

Government of India, Ministry of Home Affairs. *Report of the Committee on Special Multipurpose Tribal Blocks*. New Delhi, 1960.

Government of India. Publications Division. *The Adavasis*. New Delhi, 1960.

Government of India. *Report of the Commissioner for Scheduled Castes and Scheduled Tribes*. New Delhi, annually.

Grierson, G. A. *Linguistic Survey of India*. Delhi, 1967 (originally published 1927).

Risley, Herbert. *The People of India*. Delhi, 1969 (originally published 1915).

Roy, P. C. "The Effect of Culture-Contact on the Personality Structure of Two Indian Tribes," *Bull. Dept. Anthro.* IV, Part 2 (1957). (On the Riāng and the Baigā.)

Sinha, Surajit. "State Formation and Rajput Myth in Tribal Central India," *Man in India* 42, Part 1 (1962).

Eastern Hill Tribes

Anand, V. K. *Nagaland in Transition*. Delhi, 1967.

Bareh, Hamlet. *The History and Culture of the Khasi People*. Calcutta, 1967.

Barkataki, S. (ed.). *Tribes of Assam*. Delhi, 1969.

Bernot, Lucien. *Les Paysans Arakanais du Pakistan Oriental*. Paris, 1967.

———, and Denise Bernot. "Chittagong Hill Tribes," in Stanley Maron (ed.), *Pakistan: Society and Culture*. New Haven, Conn., 1957.
Bhandari, J. S. "Land and Social Structure: An Economic Study of a Mishing Village," *Eastern Anthropologist* XXI, Part 1 (1968).
Biswas, P. C., and B. R. Ghosh. "The Khasis Today," *The Anthropologist* XIV, Part 2 (1967).
Burling, Robbins. *Rengsanggri: Family and Kinship in a Garo Village*. Philadelphia, 1963.
Das, Bhuban. *Ethnic Affinities of the Rabha*. Gauhati, 1964.
Dommen, Arthur. "Separatist Tendencies in Eastern India," *Asian Survey* VII, Part 10 (1967).
Dutta, Parul. *The Tangsas of the Namchik and Tirap Valleys*. Shillong, 1959.
Elwin, Verrier. *The Art of the North-East Frontier of India*. Shillong, 1959.
———. *Myths of the North-East Frontier of India*. Shillong, 1958.
———. *A Philosophy for N.E.F.A.* Shillong, 1959.
Endle, Sidney. *The Kacháris*. London, 1911.
Fürer-Haimendorf, C. von. *The Apa Tanis and their Neighbours*. London, 1962.
———. *The Konyak Nagas: An Indian Frontier Tribe*. New York, 1969.
———. *The Naked Nagas*, rev. ed. Calcutta, 1963 (originally published 1939).
Goswami, M. C., and D. N. Majumdar. "Clan Organization among the Garo of Assam," *Man in India*, Fall 1957.
Gurdon, P. R. T. *The Khasis*. London, 1914.
Hutton, J. H. *The Angami Nagas*. London, 1921.
———. *The Sema Nagas*. London, 1921.
Leach, E. R. "Aspects of Bridewealth and Marriage Stability among the Kachin and Lakher," *Man*, April 1957.
———. *Political Systems of Highland Burma*. Boston, 1965. (On the Kachīn.)
Lehman, F. K. *The Structure of Chin Society*. Urbana, Ill., 1963. (Based on fieldwork in Burma.)
Mills, J. P. *The Ao Nagas*. London, 1962.
———. *The Lhota Nagas*. London, 1922.
Mitra, A. K. *The Riang of Tripura*. Bull. Dept. Anthro., Calcutta, 1956.
Nakane, Chie. *Garo and Khasi: A Comparative Study in Matriarchal Systems*. Paris, 1967.
Parry, N. E. *The Lakhers*. London, 1932.
Playfair, Archibald. *The Garos*. London, 1909.
Roy, Sachin. *Aspects of Padam-Minyong Culture*. Shillong, 1960.
Shakespear, Lt. Col. J. *The Lushai-Kuki Clans*. London, 1912.
Sharma, R. R. P. *The Sherdukpens*. Shillong, 1961.
Shukla, B. K. *The Daflas of the Subansiri Region*. Shillong, 1959.
Simoons, Frederick, and Elizabeth Simoons. *A Ceremonial Ox of India: The Mithan in Nature, Culture, and History*. Madison, Wis., 1968.
Sinha, Raghuvir. *The Akas*. Shillong, 1962.
Srivastava, L. R. N. *The Gallongs*. Shillong, 1962.

Central and South Indian Tribes

Bhowmick, P. K. *The Lodhas of West Bengal*. Calcutta, 1963.
Biswas, P. C. *The Santals*. Delhi, 1956.
Bruce, George. *The Stranglers: the Cult of the Thuggee and its Overthrow in British India*. London, 1968.

Chapekar, L. N. *Thakurs of the Sahyadri*. Oxford, 1960. (In Mahārāshṭra.)
Cipriani, Lidio. *The Andaman Islanders*. London, 1966.
Crooke, W. *Tribes and Castes of the North-West Provinces and Oudh*, 4 vols. Calcutta, 1896.
Dalton, E. T. *Descriptive Ethnology of Bengal*. Calcutta, 1960 (originally published 1872).
Das, A. K., B. Roychowdhury, and M. K. Raha. *The Malpaharias of West Bengal*. Calcutta, 1966.
Dave, P. C. *The Grasias*. Delhi, 1960. (A tribe in Rājasthān and Gujarāt.)
Doshi, Shambhu. *Bhils: Between Societal Self-Awareness and Cultural Synthesis*. New Delhi, 1971.
Dube, B. D., and F. Bahadur. *A Study of the Tribal People and Tribal Areas of Madhya Pradesh*. Bhopal, 1966.
Dutta, Parul. *The Tangsas*. Shillong, 1959.
Ehrenfels, U. R. *The Kadar of Cochin*. Madras, 1952.
Elwin, Verrier. *The Agaria*. Oxford, 1942.
———. *The Baiga*. London, 1939.
———. *Bondo Highlanders*. Bombay, 1950.
———. *Folk Songs of Chhattisgarh*. Oxford, 1946.
———. *Folk Tales of Mahakoshal*. Madras, 1944.
———. *Leaves from the Jungle*. London, 1936. (A diary from 1932–1933.)
———. *Maria Murder and Suicide*. Bombay, 1943.
———. *The Muria and their Ghotul*. Oxford, 1947.
———. *The Religion of an Indian Tribe*. Oxford, 1955. (On Savaras.)
———. *The Tribal Art of Middle India*. Oxford, 1951.
———. *Tribal Myths of Orissa*. Oxford, 1954.
Emeneau, M. B. *Toda Songs*. Oxford, 1971.
Enthoven, R. E. *The Tribes and Castes of Bombay*, 3 vols. Bombay, 1920.
Fuchs, Stephen. *The Children of Hari*. Vienna, 1950. (On Nimar Balāhīs.)
———. *The Gond and Bhumia of Eastern Mandla*. Bombay, 1960.
———. *Rebellious Prophets*. Bombay, 1965. (On revitalization movements.)
Fürer-Haimendorf, C. von. *The Chenchus: Jungle Folk of the Deccan (The Aboriginal Tribes of Hyderabad*, Vol. I). London, 1943.
———. *The Reddis of the Bison Hills (The Aboriginal Tribes of Hyderabad*, Vol. II). London, 1945.
———. *The Raj Gonds of Adilabad (The Aboriginal Tribes of Hyderabad*, Vol. III). London, 1948.
Ghurye, G. S. *The Mahadev Kolis*. Bombay, 1957.
Gnanambal, K. "The Magical Rites of the Urali," *Bull. Dept. Anthro.* III, Part 2 (1954).
Government of Madhya Pradesh. *The Tribes of Madhya Pradesh*. Bhopal, 1964.
Government of West Bengal. *Hand Book on Scheduled Castes and Scheduled Tribes in West Bengal*. Calcutta, 1966.
Griffiths, Walter. *The Kol Tribe of Central India*. Calcutta, 1946.
Grigson, M. V. *The Maria Gonds of Bastar*. London, 1938.
Hivale, Shamrao. *The Pardhans of the Upper Narbada Valley*. Oxford, 1946.
Iyer, A. K. *The Cochin Tribes and Castes*. Madras, 1909.
———. *The Mysore Tribes and Castes*. Mysore, 1935.
Joshi, Madan. *Bastar, India's Sleeping Giant*. Delhi, 1967.
Karve, Irawati. *The Bhils of West Khandesh: a Social and Economic Survey*. Bombay, 1961.
Krishna Iyer, L. K. Anantha. *The Cochin Tribes and Castes*. Cochin, 1909.

Luiz, A. A. D. *Tribes of Kerala*. New Delhi, 1962.
Lwuva, K. K. *The Asur*. New Delhi, 1963.
Majumdar, D. N. *The Affairs of a Tribe*. Lucknow, 1950. (On Hos.)
Mathur, Kaushal Kumar. *Nicobar Islands*. New Delhi, 1967.
Mukherjea, Charulal. *The Santals*. Calcutta, n.d.
Nag, D. S. *Tribal Economy: An Economic Study of the Baigas*. Delhi, 1958.
Nag, M. K. "A Demographic Study of the Kanikkars of Travancore," *Bull. Dept. Anthro.* III, Part 2 (1954).
Naik, T. B. (ed.). *The Abujhmarhias*. Chindwara, 1963. (On Maria Gōṇḍs.)
———. *The Bhils: A Study*. Delhi, 1956.
———. (ed.). *The Changing Tribes of Madhya Pradesh*. Indore, 1961.
Nanjundayya, H. V. *The Mysore Tribes and Castes*, 4 vols. Mysore, 1931.
Nath, Y. V. S. *Bhils of Ratanmal*. Baroda, 1960.
Orans, Martin. *The Santal: A Tribe in Search of a Great Tradition*. Detroit, 1965.
Radcliffe-Brown, A. R. *The Andaman Islanders*. New York, 1964 (originally published 1922).
Raghavan, M. D. *Handsome Beggars: The Story of the Ceylon Roḍiyā*. Colombo, 1957.
Raghaviah, V. *The Yanadis*. Delhi, 1962.
Ramdas, G. "The Gadabas," *Man in India* XI (1931).
Risley, Herbert. *The Tribes and Castes of Bengal*, 2 vols. Calcutta, 1891.
Rivers, W. H. R. *The Todas*. Oosterhout, Netherlands, 1969 (originally published 1907).
Roy, Sarat-Chandra. *The Khāṛiās*. Ranchi, 1937.
———. *The Mundas and Their Country*. Calcutta, 1912.
Russell, R. V. and R. B. Hirlal. *The Tribes and Castes of the Central Provinces of India*. London, 1916.
Sachchidananda. *Culture Change in Tribal Bihar: Munda and Oraon*. Patna, 1964.
———. *Profiles of Tribal Culture in Bihar*. Calcutta, 1965.
Sankalia, H. D. "Prehistoric Men and Primitives in South Gujarat and Kondan," *J. Asiatic Society of Bombay* XII, Part 1 (1966).
Seligman, C. G., and B. Z. Seligman. *The Veddas*. Oosterhout, Netherlands, 1969 (originally published 1911).
Shah, P. G. *The Dublas of Gujarat*. Delhi, 1958.
———. *Tribal Life in Gujarat*. Bombay, 1964. (A survey of all Gujarāt tribes.)
Thurston, E. *Castes and Tribes of Southern India*, 7 vols. Madras, 1909. (A valuable and comprehensive compilation.)
Vidyarthi, L. P. *The Maler*. Calcutta, 1963. (On Mālto-speaking Pahāṛiās.)
Wijesekere, Nandeva. *Veddas in Transition*. Colombo, 1964.

16

Rural Change and Development

Anthropologists are caught in dual roles—as a Malayāḷi expression goes, they have their feet in two boats, and the greater the pressure the farther the boats drift apart. Should the goal of anthropology be objective understanding, or should it be the applied anthropology approach? Should one's efforts be devoted to abstracting universally valid models, or should they be devoted to devising methods to meet felt needs and problems? This bifurcation is particularly acute in the case of South Asia which is so rich as a hearth of human culture and has been called the social science laboratory of the world, while at the same time apparently insuperable crises are looming and "modernization" is perceived as lagging.

Though the pre-World War II generation of anthropologists steered quite clear of South Asian peasant society while they expended their efforts on tribal peoples, once they embarked on village studies in the 1950s they discovered it was necessary to obtain something of a broad humanistic background in the formal culture and civilization of the peasant regions, in addition to training in the concepts and methodology of anthropology as a discipline. Such training in humanities and area studies—Indian arts, religions, South Asian literature, the traditional ideal social order—all these stimulate emotional identification with the culture. One comes to admire

the civilization and appreciate cultural variegation for its own sake. Such an outlook has been considered "liberal" and has been bred by the liberal arts. The contrary opinion is that anthropologists should jump into the fray of applied social sciences for they are responsible to use their expertise to help mitigate problems; proponents of this view also consider it as "liberal." The dilemma is between personal identification with the cultural system and the need for making value judgments about it if one is to engage in applied anthropology. And most of the value judgments acceptable today in the applied social sciences are of Euro-American origin, which is not to deny that they may also be held by some Western-oriented educated South Asians.

In the United States, South Asian area studies have been heavily laden with a social science emphasis. Whereas the disciplines of economics and politics clearly identify with "development" goals, anthropology stands at the end of the social science spectrum and links it with humanities. While every year more books appear on South Asian village change, agriculture, economic development, village politics, caste, family, population, or rural health, how much of this is anthropology or applied anthropology?

All the major governments of South Asia hold the philosophy that induced change is desirable and necessary. The severe problems faced in 1947–1948 demanded quick answers. India had 7 million refugees from Pakistan to settle somehow, and Pakistan had almost as many from India. In India over 600 princely states ranging from miniscule fiefs to giant Hyderābād had to be enticed into the fold, while Pakistan had to incorporate nine significant princely states and unify the two wings of the country. Governments had to be formed and constitutions written. In 1948 Gandhi was shot, Jinnah died, and war broke out over Kashmīr. Still, by the early 1950s ambitious social legislation, land reform, and economic development programs were under way. Today India channels 15% of its national income through the government—a high proportion for a country with a per capita annual income of $110.

Is There a Tradition-Modernity Dichotomy?

The changes that are occurring in South Asian countries have sometimes been called Westernization, but the majority of social scientists today express preference for the term *modernization*. Modernization has less connotation of imitation, which is very important to nations seeking self-identity, and moreover there is no one culture complex representative of the West. Srinivas points out, however, that modernization inevitably implies value judgments while the term Westernization is ethically neutral; "its use does not carry the implication that it is good or bad, whereas modernization is normally used in the sense that it is good."[1] Some an-

thropologists have been casting about for a new term. It is clear that today there is little sentiment for the kind of Westernization such as existed among the English-educated Bāngālī anglophiles of the mid-19th century, of whom Trevelyan wrote:

> Fimiliarly acquainted with us by means of our literature the Indian youth almost cease to regard us as foreigners. They speak of our great men with the same enthusiasm as we do. Educated in the same way, interested in the same subjects, engaged in the same pursuits with ourselves, they become more English than Hindus.[2]

There are but a few such xenophiles in South Asia today, notably some Anglo-Indians and perhaps a handful of company officials replacing British tea estate managers.

The prevailing mental set among planners and politicians is that modernization is an indigenous process, uniquely building on the genius of the country, but that there is a great gulf between what is modern and what is tradition; this gulf had better be bridged as quickly as possible, for there is a moral obligation. Indeed, we may say that the "white man's burden" has devolved upon the English-educated power structure, and we may call it the "urban-elite burden." We have to view this attitude as a function of elite status and not just altruism. Most of the urban elite are as removed from village life as are the graduates of American private eastern colleges from the rural Midwest or Harlem. And if any of these elite in Delhi or Karāchī or Colombo had rural origins, they have usually handled the matter by developing a certain level of amnesia.

Yet there is probably more of Westernization embedded in modernization than most South Asians wish to admit. The compulsion to believe that what is modern is good is itself derived from the West, for it was Euro-American civilization which for the first time in the world's history openly philosophized that change in the whole cultural system is good for its own sake and that change equals progress. The list of particular goals of these countries as stated by their governments is mostly comprised of ideals historically traceable to the West: democracy, secularism (for India and Bangladesh), equality under law, socialism, abolition of class and caste, industrialization, formal secular education, government involvement in such areas as public health and cattle breeding, and numerous others. It is notable that as soon as the South Asian countries became independent, they enacted a flood of legislation molded by these Western ideals which the British colonial administration did not dare to enact: new laws on marriage (inhibition of polygyny in Pakistan and of dowry in India), regulation of temple finances, family planning programs, and limitations on landholding. On some of these, governments pronounce that the true antecedents are dormant features of traditional culture. Pakistan says its laws on women's welfare are inspired from the Qur'ān, while India and

Nepal claim that the panchāyat system is a resurrection of ancient village democracy. India and Sri Lanka claim that the ideals of peace and neutrality are derived from Buddhism and King Aśoka. Then there is conscious rejection of certain features believed to be characteristic of Western cultures, notably proselytizing Christianity, "materialism," and the supposedly decadent family structure—though Westerners would argue that South Asians' views of the West on these points are ill-founded.

Modernization seems to be something more complex than the diffusion of any of the classical "great traditions." From the broad view of world culture history, there is no doubt that the communications revolution has produced at least a halting tendency to evolution of world mass culture; most of the specifically advertised features to the contrary will be seen as symbols of political or ethnic identity. Thus modernization in South Asia has been viewed by some as not unique but as consisting of the same general type of changes that occurred in Europe and America and more recently in Japan. Such an approach is necessary if the applied social sciences are to work out theories of "development" applicable transculturally. Economists tend to abstract certain kinds of internationally comparable data, implying that this is something real unto itself while the jajmānī exchange system will inevitably melt into it. Agronomists stress that certain techniques will cause food production to increase anywhere, an argument supported by the history of the "green revolution." Political scientists trained in the West tend to see a unilineal evolution to broad-based democratic or representative government—and the arguments of the Americans in this field are reinforced in that they usually read only the English press which expresses similar opinions and interests. But while most anthropologists dealing with South Asia have described change, only some have claimed to know what kind of change is best.

The bifurcation between "traditional" and "modern" in classical theory has left an increasing number of anthropologists disaffected, beginning about midcentury. They saw that some qualities ascribed to "tradition" in South Asia are derived from ancient texts and not verifiable in the field, while most "modern" institutions function in such a way that they incorporate much of "tradition." Caste, joint family, priesthood, and religion have been excessively polarized against modernization. Among those disaffected with this polarization has been Milton Singer, who inveighs against the equation of the traditional with the indigenous and the modern with the foreign. Indian culture is not "traditional" in that it is unchanging, nor even in that characteristic institutions and beliefs persist alongside the new:

> The traditionalism of Indian civilization lies elsewhere—in its capacity to incorporate innovations into an expanding and changing structure of culture and society. This capacity is reflected in a series of adaptive mechanisms and processes for dealing with the novel, the foreign, the strange.[3]

(*Left*) Bus station in Mahārāshṭra town. Such aspects of modernization have not altered the jovial and animated conversation characteristic of India nor brought the Western stigma against sitting on the ground. (*Right*) Carpenter in Pakistan village. He formerly made farming implements for payment by jajmānī system. Now he makes modern products for cash and has installed mechanized sawing and flour milling equipment.

Singer supports this view with extensive data from such aspects of Indian civilization as Rādhā-Krishṇa *bhajanas* (devotional songfests), urbanization, and industrial leadership.

Harold Gould, however, cautions against throwing out the tradition-modernity opposition altogether, saying this would be like dumping out the baby with the bathwater. Though it is true that the broad structure features of modernization can be articulated with an amazing variety of indigenous non-Western traditional social institutions, the very fact that they operate latently gives them a different structural relevance than they had before:

> We must, therefore, distinguish between traditional social structures which *qua* structures are patently incapable of assimilation to modern social structures and the mobilization of traditional values, skills or artifacts in behalf of modernization and nation-building. Social systems cannot be mutually reinforcing when they rest on different, mutually exclusive levels of social evolution, *but idea systems can*. . . . Ultimately the new purposes for which traditional material is mobilized helps promote the new society with the new complex of social relationships which progressively negate the contents upon which the traditional consciousness rests.[4]

Singer would agree with Gould, however, that a group wishing to change its position in the structure must change not only behavior but thought as well. This may mean relinquishing the Sanskritizing model in favor of the Dravidian movement model, or the Panjābī, or even a religiopolitical movement like the Jana Sangh, which seem to be not incompatible with other contemporary directions of change.

Caste in India since Independence

There is no doubt that society in India is undergoing fundamental changes. Most ethnographers concur that caste is not disappearing, but whether they think it is weakening depends upon their philosophical outlook and region of research. Generally it seems clear that the traditional caste *structure* is weakening, while castes may retain considerable strength as subethnic entities.

In villages this writer has been familiar with since Independence, castes remain about as distinct from each other as ever. There may be shifts in the bases of power and new kinds of opportunities for individuals through education or salaried employment. The old elite classes were supported on the twin pillars of landowning and religious authority, both of which are undergoing modification. The observation of ritual purity and pollution is anachronistic in buses, post offices, and public restaurants where strangers eat together, but in villages where people know each other, there is only slight weakening of this symbolic system.

Joan Mencher reports for a village in Tamiḻ Nāḍu how various occupational specialists have found new forms of income and how they have developed links with towns. The dominant agricultural caste proportionately increases while Brāhmaṇs and other specialists tend to leave, seeking nonagricultural jobs. The Paraiyar caste of Harijans, which owned 2.3% of the land in 1912, now own only 1.5%, but they are bold to act corporately, having successfully staged a boycott against the owner-cultivators for six months. The farming castes then had to act in a corporate manner in reaction. Rules relating to ritual pollution here are as strong as ever but some penalties are not as strictly applied, while ritual ranking is giving way to economic status. Caste solidarity here is, if anything, stronger than in earlier times.[5]

What is happening to the jajmānī system is shown by a report from Joseph Elder on a village in Uttar Pradesh, comparing it in 1927 and 1957. In this village of 11 castes, Jāṭs, comprising 16% of the people, owned 33% of the land; they functioned as jajmāns at the time of both surveys, dispensing grain, cloth, cooked food, and money for traditional services. The Vegetable Growers also commanded a few jajmānī services. Water Carriers have all had to find other work—farming, working in the sugar mill, carrying water at the train station—because Jāṭs have installed hand pumps in their backyards. Potters have suffered because of the popularity of metal vessels, though some have gone into large-scale production of disposable clay cups. Cotton Carders probably never lived entirely by their traditional work, and by 1957 only two of eight did this work and then just part-time for cash payment. Camārs, the largest caste, had mostly worked as farmers or field laborers even in 1927, and by 1957 land reform had improved their

lot. Most had given up leatherwork, for galvanized buckets had replaced leather bags used for irrigation, and Muslim entrepreneurs handled animal carcasses, helped by the Sweepers. Carpenters were working more for cash, and two had set up shops to repair carts and make benches and desks. The one Blacksmith was a farmer and had given up smithy; people got their implements repaired in town. Of the Muslim Oil Presser caste, only two of the 41 men did any oil pressing because of the popularity of kerosine for lamps and commercial vegetable cooking oils; half were farmers, and some had jobs in the sugar mill, with the railroad, or as laborers. The Muslim Barbers continued to work for their jajmāns as before, receiving a grain allotment. Most, however, had supplementary income as sugar mill worker, servant, or truck cleaner. The jajmāns preferred getting a haircut and shave in their own yard rather than going to the town barber shop. The Bhangīs (Sweepers) kept the village clean, and whereas they formerly received an allotment of grain from the jajmāns, by 1957 they received sacks of it from the village panchāyat, plus special donations at times of ceremonies. As for Brāhmaṇs, they had for long been too numerous to all live off the priesthood, but those who did continued to receive a double armload of grain from each farmer, or cash, and sugar-cane juice at crushing time. In addition they received clothing, sweets, or fruits for performing special services to jajmāns. The village had no Dhobīs (Washermen), and while most people washed their own clothes in both periods, Dhobīs from nearby villages were sometimes compensated in kind.

The conclusion Elder makes is that Brāhmaṇs, Nāī Barbers, and Bhangī Sweepers retained their core jajmānī relations because they provide services unaffected by either population growth or technology. Carpenters and Blacksmiths became too numerous for the land and the resources; Leatherworkers gave up their jajmānī relations to escape the stigma of leatherworking, and the rest were affected by technological change and population growth. Elder thinks that if the sugar mill were to employ 500 more persons, the system would disappear.[6] Orenstein reports that by the early 1960s it had practically died in a village he studied in Mahārāshṭra, though this does not mean that either the social or religious structure of the village had disintegrated.[7]

Caste endogamy is hardly relaxing at all in villages, and only to a very slight extent among "mod" college students. On the other hand, there is a tendency for fusion of castes, especially within the caste-cluster, producing more formidable political and economic entities while also widening the bounds of the endogamous unit. Though it is true that even within a village, people may talk together in a cooperative meeting or in a school without any recognition of caste, the modernization process has provided new avenues for expression of caste solidarity. The politicization of caste since the introduction of elections has been an India-wide feature—though it cannot be assumed that a caste delivers a bloc vote. Rather, there is a tend-

ency for blocs of votes to support personalities and patrons, and factions in a caste may surface at election time. In most villages caste and attendant economic considerations dominate panchāyat elections. Caste has also emerged a new metamorphosis in that it has taken on some of the functions of labor unions, while the growth of caste associations (see accounts of the Noniyās in Chap. 8 and the Umar in Chap. 17) provide social services and exert various kinds of pressures.

For the Indian leaders who foresaw the evolution of a "casteless society" all this has been a disappointment. Aside from caste, religious and regional entities have been able to delineate and press for their interests. Government rhetoric frequently condemns "casteism," and "communalism" which in India refers to ethnic rather than to geographical entities. "Communal conflict" sometimes should be read as a euphemism for Hindu-Muslim antagonism, while "fissiparous tendencies" refers to regional loyalties. The cultural diversity of India has surfaced in the political system. Democratization has produced, at least in this generation, increased particularization.

In sum, castes are tending to become *cultural* entities while the intercaste traditional structure is weakening. Leighton Hazelhurst suggests on the basis of his study of merchant castes in Panjāb that we must make a distinction between the cultural and structural dimensions of caste.[8] Castes might appear to be autonomous, endogamous jātis having an ascribed status and practicing prescribed rituals, but "what we observe among merchants in structural terms is a wide range of relationships elicited not by caste principles but by the demands of certain political and economic situations." Gould says that "castes have become ascriptive structures not radically different in appearance from ethnic minorities elsewhere in the world." They grow more and more remote from the socioreligious hierarchical castes and act as subcultural communities. "They are not old forms which persisted; they are new forms which recruited their members from the old by using sufficient quanta of cognitive material to sustain them in a sense of cultural continuity."[9] The relevance of this opinion, for urban areas at least, will be apparent in the following chapter. As Mencher points out, even in a village where orthodox intercaste relations largely remain, they need not be regarded as inhibiting change, but as channeling it, and the detailed study of this channeling has important implications for any attempt at economic development.

Untouchability

The crusade to eliminate public discrimination against Harijans has many parallels with the Negro movement in the United States. Members of Scheduled Castes, or Harijans, comprise 15% of India's population, numbering over 80 million in 1971. The movement for their uplift, going

back to the 1930s, has posed the problem of identifying them. Hutton, the Census Commissioner for 1931, determined they could not be identified on an all-India basis, but in some regions, such as what is now Madhya Pradesh, they had to be listed district by district. He suggested the following tests to identify an "exterior caste": 1) if it cannot be served by Brāhmaṇs, 2) if it cannot be served by barbers, water carriers, and others who serve high caste Hindus, 3) if contact or proximity pollutes high caste Hindus, 4) if high caste Hindus cannot take water from its members' hands, 5) if it is debarred from using public conveniences such as roads, ferries, wells, or schools, 6) if it is debarred from entering temples, 7) if in social intercourse high caste persons of the same educational qualifications do not treat its members as equals, 8) if its depressed condition is due not only to poverty or ignorance, and 9) if its depressed condition is due not only to occupation.[10]

For example, the Census Superintendent of British-administered Balūchistān found that members of the Cūḍā caste called themselves variously as Hindus, Muslims, Sikhs, and Cūḍās by religion, but "these persons without exception are not allowed to drink from wells belonging to real Hindus, Muslims or Sikhs, and are not permitted to enter their places of worship."[11] These comprised 14% of the Hindu population and 1% of the total. But in Assam the picture was very different. "Exterior castes" formed 37% of the Hindu population and the Census Commissioner reported that "caste in the Assam Valley is not as elsewhere, chiefly a functional division; it is really a racial division and functional castes are very few." Some of the untouchable castes of the Assam Valley and Sylhet (now Bangladesh) raised themselves and became "superior exterior castes." One officer remarked, "All the Assamese castes have a chance of rising in the social scale except the Ḍoms and Harīs whose case is hopeless."[12]

Change came fastest in the South where the caste hierarchy and distance pollution discriminated against untouchables the most. German, Danish, and English missionaries reaped an unexpected harvest of souls of untouchables who hoped that by becoming Christian they could evade their ascribed status. Many more worked in the tea estates of Sri Lanka and others such as the Nāḍar developed business interests. By 1930 there were a quarter million untouchables in school in Madras Presidency, and in the same decade the government moved to insist on the right of "exterior caste" pupils to be admitted to all publicly managed schools, provided amenities such as house sites, wells, and burial grounds for them, and legislated on temple entry. Untouchables and ex-untouchable Christians paraded down Brāhmaṇ streets in many towns to end forever their exclusion therefrom.

In Bombay Presidency there was less legislation but a mass movement began among the Mahār, a large untouchable caste-cluster spread throughout the Marāṭhī region and parts of central India. The Mahār traditionally

work as village servants—watchmen, messengers, and sweepers. They were inspired by Gandhi's crusade in the 1920s for Harijans, as he called them; he fasted for temple entry rights for them. Already by 1920 there were Mahār newspapers in Marāṭhī published from Bombay, Puṇe, and Nāgpur, and they began to learn the benefits of group solidarity:

> Some 2000 untouchables collected outside the Kala Ram temple at Nasik on 3 March 1930, and a meeting which attempted to bring about a settlement was stoned by the orthodox. Ultimately some 150,000 Mahars and Chamars were reported to have collected at Nasik and the temple had to be closed for about a month to keep them from entering it. The admission of caste Hindus by a private passage ended in violence in which the orthodox were the aggressors, and which was extended to Mahar villages in the neighborhood, where the exterior castes were violently attacked by caste Hindus, their wells polluted and in some cases their houses burned.[13]

The Mahār acknowledged as their leader Dr. Ambedkar, one of their sons who had studied in England and America. In 1935 he renounced Hinduism, led many Mahār verbally to do the same, and founded a new political party. Ambedkar became Law Minister in India's first cabinet and served as chairman of the Drafting Committee which produced the Constitution of India, completed in 1949. Though Ambedkar succeeded in enshrining in the Constitution provisions for the elimination of untouchability, he felt that the Mahār had to be further weaned from the Hindu fold, and in the mid-1950s he began a crusade to convert them to Buddhism. He led a mass conversion in a field outside Nāgpur, and the movement spread. The 1951 census recorded only 181,000 Buddhists in India, but in 1961 the figure was a surprising 3.3 million, and of these Buddhists, 2.8 million were Mahār converts in Mahārāshṭra.

The credo of the Buddhist converts included affirmations such as these: I believe in the principle that all are equal; I will not lie; I will not commit theft; I will not indulge in lust or sexual transgression; I will not take any liquor. Eleanor Zelliot thinks from her study of this movement that "there is little doubt that conversion to Buddhism on the part of Ambedkar himself, in spite of the admixture of politics to the history of the movement, was a matter of complete sincerity." Buddhist inspiration was courted from Sri Lanka while monks were imported from Japan. Though this movement "has not automatically lifted the Mahār from untouchability, it has added a dimension of self-respect and an inner sense of being removed from the constraints of the caste hierarchy."[14]

The Constitution of India, in Part III which deals with Fundamental Rights, abolishes untouchability and makes its enforcement an offense, along with public discrimination on grounds of religion, race, caste, sex, or birthplace, and no citizen shall be subject to restriction in shops, public restaurants, hostels, or place of public entertainment, or in use of wells, tanks,

bathing ghāṭs, or roads. The Untouchability Offenses Act of 1955 provides for fines or imprisonment for such discrimination except in home life, private religious ceremonies, or private employment.

In general, these laws can be applied only where such disabilities are not enforced by the majority. In urban areas, trains, buses, schools, and markets, people have been mixing together for decades. Even in a tea shop on a crossroad where buses stop there may be no distinction. In parts of India there is change within villages; Orenstein reports for his Mahārāshṭra village that many higher caste people will enter Harijan houses, and about 15% have taken water from the hands of Harijans. They may not be regarded as literally untouchable. But in villages in most areas the low castes have their own wells and will not think of using water from high caste wells. In tea and coffee shops they will have their own cups kept in some corner, and rather than sit on the bench they will squat on the floor or use a low stool. This writer has seen these practices in the early 1970s in North, Central, and South India, Nepal, Buddhist Srī Lanka, and Muslim Bangladesh, while in Pakistan also sweepers suffer some disabilities in villages.

Where people know each other and generally accept caste strictures, it is virtually impossible to enforce prohibition of untouchability in public. Marc Galanter, one of the few American students of Indian law, believes that "undoubtedly the total effect of the Act as propaganda, as threat and as leverage for securing the intervention of political and executive figures outweighs the effect it has as an instrument for prosecution of offenders." Untouchables are often not aware of their "rights," do not engage lawyers, and do not often question the equitability of the old social order. Moreover, "the effectiveness of the Act depends upon the initiative of the local police and the sympathy of local magistrates, both of whom have obvious reasons to be disinclined to antagonize the dominant elements in the community."[15]

The Constitution provided for reserved seats in Parliament and in State Legislatures (but not separate electorates) for Scheduled Castes and Scheduled Tribes, as a temporary measure. In addition, there are reserved seats for them in all categories of government employment. The states extend further benefits to these groups and also to other disadvantaged castes lumped together as Backward Classes. They can go to school by paying reduced fees or no fees, have reserved seats in industrial schools and colleges, and benefit from many welfare schemes ranging from housing and pure water supply to cooperative societies. These are so beneficial that numbers of ex-untouchables have been reconverted to Hinduism. At one time some 10,000 Christians in southern Tamil̲ Nāḍu declared themselves as Hindus.

All are agreed that these benefits accruing to Harijans are temporary. The Constitution stipulates that they are temporary, but the provisions were

extended in 1960 and again in 1971. The Indian intelligentsia are now demanding an end to the listing of Scheduled Castes because they feel that in so listing them, their distinction is perpetuated—it is the battle of the quota system. Probably this demand is based not only on the belief that village social patterns will change within a generation but as much so on the desire to end international attention to untouchability.

Law and Social Legislation

Hindu law is so vast the *Dharmaśāstras* can scarcely be mastered in a lifetime, and in addition there is the customary non-Brahmāṇical law of a multitude of regions and castes. The British early made an effort to develop a substantive body of civil law applicable to all Hindus of British India, and employed Brāhmaṇs to search the *Dharmaśāstras* to come up with a suggested code having the authority of tradition. But by the 1820s the British learned, as Bernard Cohn points out, that there was no fixed Hindu law, only a vast mosaic. For a century and a half the history of law in South Asia was one of attempted reconciliation of differing cultural values: the British penchant for equality and uniformity, the variegated pattern of Brāhmaṇical, caste, and customary law, and the legal codes of other ethnic groups such as Muslims, Christians, Jains, and tribal peoples.

The British generally avoided legislation and legal decisions on personal law, caste, or subjects having religious sanction, but were not able to entirely exclude these. They acquiesced to demands for legislation abolishing satī and infanticide (which had been occurring at temple festivals), and made marriage into a legal ceremony instead of a purely religious one. Legislation dealing with "Criminal Tribes," untouchability, land inheritance, tenancy rights, and such produced complex clashes of cultural values.

> Every time new regulations, interpretations, or legislative enactments came into force, the structure of social relations for the bulk of the population was affected, usually in ways not anticipated by the law-makers. Landed property became a commodity; new groups—urban-based landlords, bankers, merchants, moneylenders—who previously had had minor roles in the rural society, came to prominence. Rights previously had been based on kinship, physical force, custom, and political obligation to superordinate chiefs and rulers. They were now based on the accident of who was entered in what register by local officials who were corruptible or by British officers who were often ill-equipped to understand either the intricacies of lineage-based or corporate holdings or the obligations and rights of intermediaries between landholders and the state.[16]

Having established a hierarchy of courts and made legal justice available to the villagers at the *tahsīl* (a governing unit of a few score villages) level, the legal profession built up a repertoire of precedents which sta-

Delhi high court, outside which attorneys and typists have set up shop. The legal system at all levels is difficult for villagers to utilize unless they can afford professional assistance.

bilized customary law and made it less flexible. Rama Rao points out that "Indian lawyers and intelligentsia took a liking for the common law and the methods of legal reasoning embodied in it, as they were in tune with the hoary dialectal traditions of Indian philosophy."[17] Since dialogue and argumentation were not new to Brāhmaṇs, it is not surprising that Brāhmaṇs came to dominate the bar throughout British India, in which they found a pleasurable and prestigious profession. Litigation is rather common now in India and Pakistan. Courts are always humming with activity. Outside the high courts are dozens or hundreds of sheds where attorneys, legal counselors, and typists set up shop and manage to get a piece of the action.

One of the most important effects of the new legal system was to reduce the legal prerogatives of caste councils and the importance of customary caste laws. Factionalism in a village in former times would be expressed in violence or would be settled in the informal village panchāyat according to customary law, but now such animosity can be expressed in litigation which may be pursued for years. And every new piece of legislation can cause a clash of cultural values bringing on a flood of new court cases. Cohn reports from Purī District in Orissa:

> A Tahsildar, a revenue office responsible for a sub-division of a district, told me in 1958 that after the Zamindari Abolition Act (a land reform act) of 1952, he had more than 20,000 petitions and cases under one provision of the Act from his Tahsil, which had a population of about 300,000 people.[18]

The Government of India, having incorporated a series of personal rights into the Constitution in 1950, proceeded to adopt legislation to make

the civil code far more specific than the British dared to. Some of the important acts are as follows:

The Special Marriage Act of 1954 enables people to marry even if they disown personal religion, and also enables divorce if certain conditions obtain.

The Hindu Marriage Act of 1955 prohibits marriage of girls under 15 (later raised to 16) and prohibits polygamy among Hindus.

The Hindu Succession Act of 1956 sets the precedence of inheritance. Daughters have rights to receive shares equal with sons.

The Hindu Minority and Guardian Act of 1956 defines power and responsibilities of legal guardians.

The Hindu Adoption and Maintenance Act of 1956 legalizes the Hindu practice of adoption of a son to continue the family, and also allows women to adopt. It makes a man liable for maintenance of his wife, children, aged parents, and widowed daughter-in-law.

The Suppression of Immoral Traffic in Women and Girls Act of 1956 decrees that procurers, pimps, and brothel keepers are liable to stand trial.

The Women's and Children's Institutions Licensing Act of 1956 prevents exploitation at orphanages and other institutions.

The Children Act of 1960 provides that Child Welfare Boards can entrust neglected children to institutions.

The Dowry Prohibition Act of 1961 forbids giving or accepting by either party to a marriage, or their families, of valuables in consideration of marriage. It does not forbid gifts given not in consideration of marriage, so that jewels and money may still be given at weddings.

The Special Marriage (Amendment) Act of 1970 makes divorce easier for couples not living together or having no conjugal relations.

The Medical Termination of Pregnancy Act of 1972 legalizes abortion on grounds of "mental agony" of the mother.

It must be admitted that so far these provisions have had little impact on village family life—less than land reform legislation. But the ideals embodied herein do slowly diffuse through the countryside so that even though people give dowry, tolerate brothels, and inhibit women from adopting, they are often aware of the law code.

The cultural plurality of India demands a plurality of personal legal codes. Therefore there are separate codes for Hindus, Muslims, Christians, and Pārsīs. For instance, a Christian marriage must be performed by a clergyman licensed to perform the ritual. Muslims may practice polygyny and inherit according to Islamic laws, and they are not bound by the Dowry Prohibition Act. The Government has refrained from amending the Muslim Civil Code to contradict the Sharī'at so there might be no grounds for criticism of its treatment of the Muslim minority.

Islamic and Tribal Law in Pakistan

Muslims in South Asia have been guided in their beliefs, rituals, practices, public and personal laws, and even dress and behavior in social intercourse, by the Sharī'at. Based on the Qur'ān, it assumed the indivisibility of religious, moral, and personal law. It is interpreted by the ulamā who have generally regarded it as a whole, not subject to selection of bits and pieces. It incorporates such features as the permissible level of taxation, but says higher taxes can be levied if the king has power to do so. It specifies punishment for criminal acts, such as cutting off the hand for theft, and allows a person to make personal retribution for certain kinds of wrongs suffered. It decrees the giving of charity. It allows polygyny, permits a husband to divorce his wife but not the wife her husband, and specifies that a daughter receives half the inheritance of a son. It does not, however, provide much support for pardā as it has been practiced in South Asia.

Though the superimposition of British law did not much affect Muslim norms regarding the family and inheritance, the Government of Pakistan has promulgated a personal law code which in some respects goes beyond the Muslim Civil Code in India. For instance, Pakistan has inhibited polygyny, and this provision apparently will remain in Bangladesh too. The 1956 Constitution guaranteed equal protection under law together with due process, and again the 1962 Constitution specified fundamental rights. Doubtless the new constitution of Bhutto's regime will incorporate the same.

Both the British administration and the Government of Pakistan have found difficulty in applying modern legal systems to the Paṭhāns and Balūchīs of the western frontier. Feuding in these areas has been governed by local customary law. Whereas the Sharī'at allows retribution in the form of murder only if a man finds his wife having an adulterous relationship with another man or if killing cannot be averted in defense of one's person or property, these tribal people have a commitment to honor which enjoins retributive murder.

The British found that crimes (as they defined them) were difficult to detect. If police arrived on the scene of a murder, they would be at the mercy of the villagers who would "treat the matter in what may be called a professional manner," as Willard Berry says. One would resort to false accusation to ruin his rival. Ignorance of courtroom proceedings was conducive to perjury, wherein a witness might think it impossible that the court would believe a true account so he would exaggerate until the court discounted his credibility. Motives for "crimes" were very complex and difficult to establish, and punishment was generally ineffective in halting the level of crimes. Moreover, Paṭhāns had for centuries borne firearms, even

producing them by hand, and they were quick to use them if they felt any threat, before considering the implications of shooting.

Therefore the British in 1901 instituted a system of local tribunals. The Assistant Commissioner could refer any case to a local body of elders who would meet in secret and after "such inquiry as may be necessary" and without due process of British law, could make recommendations according to tribal juridical norms. This system resulted in the conviction of numerous accused persons against whom sufficient evidence could not have been adduced in regular courts.

Within Pakistan some legal practitioners think that this system is conducive to administration rather than to justice, that it holds back social and economic development in such areas as Balūchistān, and that it is unconstitutional for different systems of rights to be applied to different segments of the country's population. Others think that this system combined with Islamic juridical norms would provide justice as equitable as that of the British system. In 1962 the tribunal system was extended to apply to cases of feuding in all parts of Pakistan, for this type of behavior operates according to principles recognized in neither Sharī'at nor British-derived law. Men acting on such local tribunals must be men of integrity and social status; they have to take oaths, and serve on a rotating basis. Here three legal systems intersect. Berry stresses that:

> The Western legal system is often unsuitable for the needs of the people of Asia and Africa and appears distant and alien to most of them. . . . The basic legal problem in many of these countries issued from this disparity between indigenous values and transplanted institutions, for it is only with the cloture of this gap that law can be meaningful and effective. . . . The way it can be accomplished under pressure of political development and accelerated social change, is an area of study deserving more serious attention.[19]

Land Reform in India and Bangladesh

Among the first priorities of India and Pakistan after Independence was land reform. But the interrelationship between land tenure systems, kinship, and social structure is an intricate one, complicated by diverse inheritance rules and a succession of Hindu, Buddhist, Mughal, British, and independent governments. In 1892 Baden-Powell produced an extensive survey of land tenure systems encountered by the British in their administration, in which he distinguished several types of villages. In one type, called *raiyatwāṛī*, many peasants or a few larger landholders owned property independently and paid their own property taxes. The *raiyat* (farmer) formerly paid a sixth or so of the produce to the king or his appointee, and under the British paid at a more modest rate. Such villages often had a headman, and were the most common type. In contrast, other villages were

joint and formed something like unit estates; these were concentrated in the zone from Panjāb to Uttar Pradesh. All the landholders were members of a clan or lineage assumed to have first settled there, or were descendants of an assumed founder, and the village paid taxes jointly. The land and village was owned by either an aristocratic family or a few related families, or it was governed by a panchāyat of heads of landowning families.

In parts of the North and especially in Bānglā the zamīndārī system was inherited by the British from the Mughals. In the 16th century the Mughals instituted a system of taxing the land, not the crop. And though they made an assessment of the land in Bānglā, Bihār, and Orissa, the Mughal center of power was so far removed that the government did not measure all the fields but relied on reports of village accountants. During the latter days of Mughal rule, as central authority waned, local governors or zamīndārs discovered they could keep the land revenue. The British took the area in 1761, and Lord Cornwallis under the Company Government enacted the Permanent Settlement Act of 1793 which declared zamīndārs hereditary proprietors of the land and also fixed the dues they were to pay to the government. Correction of abuses was sought by further legislation in 1859, 1885, 1926, and 1938, prohibiting eviction of tenants who paid their share and slowing down rent increases. Yet this system

> permitted the creation of a number of intermediate interests between the zamindar and the actual cultivator which in some districts had reached fantastic proportions. In some cases as many as fifty or more intermediaries had been created between the zamindar at the top and the actual cultivator at the bottom.[20]

The British ruled large parts of South Asia for two centuries through the zamīndār system. It provided for the colonial government a class of loyal persons with considerable local authority. The government could also assure a constant supply of grain to such cities as Calcutta. It was assumed that the zamīndārs would develop their lands because they would stand to benefit by increased production; in fact, however, most of them took their money from the countryside and invested it in places such as Calcutta. Since the zamīndārs could tax their peasants as they wished, provided they passed on fixed dues to the government, it became exploitative. The zamīndārs were sometimes called rājās.

Until Independence peasants were passive. During the great Bānglā famine of 1943 when transportation was dislocated by war and rice was commandeered to support the army, starvation took the lives of 2 or 3 million people—who perished almost passively. But by 1946 a peasant movement with some Marxist leadership developed in Bānglā, demanding that tenants pay landlords and zamīndārs only a third of the crop instead of the customary half. But at harvest time the managers of the zamīndārs' lands (who in fact had been taking the largest cut) obtained police support and through

Muslim League and Congress Party politicians prevented passage of the bill specifying a third of the crop as the rate of tenancy rental.

The government in East Pakistan therefore recognized the urgent necessity of land reform and in the early 1950s abolished zamīndārī, paid some compensation in the form of bonds to those zamīndārs who did not flee to India (most were Hindus), and began to directly assess the 6 million independent peasant proprietors. The problem in Bangladesh is not landlordism—for 80% of owners are cultivators—but land shortage.

In India the individual states enacted land reform legislation during the First Five-Year Plan (1951–1956), for according to the Constitution agriculture is a subject allocated to state governments. The maximum holding varied but was generally set at about 30 acres of irrigated land or two or three times that amount of dry land. As a result, in the northern and eastern plains some of the ex-zamīndārs became a decadent aristocracy living off past memories, but in general many large landowners were able to apportion most of their holdings among family members or trusted front men. Land reform legislation seldom produced as much land for redistribution as was anticipated.

It turned out to be a mixed bag for the peasants too, at least at first. In some areas tenants with hereditary tenancy rights were evicted, only to be hired back as coolies for daily wages. In a village in Uttar Pradesh low caste villagers said, "It has not helped us in any way."[21] They were too poor to buy the land and could not afford the taxes. But as tenants they could borrow seeds or oxen from the zamīndār, or get a loan for a wedding, and enjoyed a certain security they now lacked as day laborers or even as marginal landowning farmers. The states have since abolished or reduced the land tax.

Where the raiyatwāṛī system prevailed, as in much of western and southern India, land reform legislation had little effect, for many peasants were owners and only a few holdings were very large. Some state governments have felt that the limits were still too high, for the legislation affected only a minute percentage of those millions of people, including numbers of families in most villages, who were able to lead lives of leisure and do no work because they had 5 to 30 acres. Some states reduced the maximum acreage to 15 or even less per household. In 1972 the Central Government, following the ideological lead of the Congress Party, asked all the states to set the maximum at 10 to 18 acres of wet land and 54 acres of dry land per nuclear family (orchards and such enterprises as tea estates being exempt). Prosperous farmers in Panjāb, Haryāṇā, and elsewhere who had invested in tractors and other equipment now found their investments uneconomical, and land reform in India has not generally resulted in increased production. Against these factors must be weighed the millstone around India's neck—the growing sea of landless and jobless people.

Land Reform in Pakistan, Nepal, and Sri Lanka

In Pakistan land tenure patterns range from villages comprised mostly of smallholders, such as are found in much of the older settled parts of Panjāb, to huge landholdings of thousands of acres. Large holdings are more common in the southern parts of Panjāb where irrigation canals were constructed in past decades and a privileged elite was permitted by the British to bring in whole villages to populate the new farmlands. There are also some large landholdings in the Northwest and in Sindh, for according to traditional values only a large landholder is considered a person of substance. In the 1960s there was some show of land reform, with maximum holdings set at 500 acres of wet land or 1000 of dry land, but even these high limits were often evaded. Farmers did not generally clamor loudly for land reform, and indeed in some of the settlements opened by the government on reclaimed lands the farmers expressed malcontent at having to live in villages consisting entirely of small farmers without the edifying presence of a "big man" capable of playing the role of a patron. Then too the vastly increased wheat production of the late 1960s brought a new prosperity even to tenants. But after the loss of East Pakistan and the formation of the new democratic government a more serious attempt was made at land reform. Now a family can own a maximum of about 200 to 300 acres, depending upon the quality, and 40 more if it owns either a tractor or a tube well. Water cess (for canal waters) was formerly payable by both owners and cultivators, but now owners have to pay it all. Tenants have first rights to lands declared to be excess. But the impact of this reform has been less than expected because owners transferred titles to relatives and retainers in anticipation of it. The maximum limits are still 15 or so times what is allowable in most states in India. The power structure of Pakistan has largely derived from the old landed families, who have provided the administrative and military leadership of the country and also much of the capital and entrepreneurship. While the old elite had no mind to legislate themselves into poverty, it is probable that the populism reflected in the Constitution given by President Bhutto will further stimulate economic democratization.

In Nepal land reform acts in 1958 and 1968 abolished large estates, fixed rent at 50% of the crop, and set a 10% ceiling on interest. More legislation in 1964 and 1968 set limits on holdings: 17 hectares in the tarāī and 4.1 hectares in the midmontane valleys. This is tacit recognition that the population of the country doubled since 1911. A persistent tendency has been the settlement of Nepālī-speaking Hindus on lands formerly held by the indigenous Himālayan ethnic groups, sometimes serving as moneylender and then foreclosing to acquire the lands. The government at Kāṭhmāṇḍū has generally had a long-term policy of encouraging the Nepālī-

speaking Hindus to gain legal titles to the lands they cultivate, thus weakening the economic base of the Newārs, Magars, Rāīs, and Limbūs. Lionel Caplan has recently described how the Limbūs had a special position as regards land tenure and the effect of the erosion of their resource base on the cultural system; a summary of this appears in *South Asia: Seven Community Profiles.*

As for Sri Lanka, Obeyesekere has shown through the study of Dutch and British records the effect of legislation, such as that requiring inheritance to be bilateral. He showed that as population increased and outsiders came to acquire land in hill villages, there appeared strains in the culture, changes in the strategy of marriage arranging, and in fact a radical reorganization of the traditional hamlet structure in part of the island; a summary of this also appears in the companion volume. The maximum holding has been set at 25 acres of rice land, but in the populous southwest zone farms are tiny.

Community Development and Panchāyats in India

India's Community Development Program was launched in 1952. It was conceived as part of the First Five-Year Plan, begun in 1951, which was modest in scope and essentially an assemblage of existing programs. It aimed for self-sufficiency in food, which appeared to be a reasonable goal at that time. Economists in those days were ill-prepared to offer theories about an economic structure such as India's. But in the government there was a prevailing romantic view about villages which was part of the heritage of Gandhi. The village was conceived of as a happy and integrated community in a pristine state which only needed a little infusion of outside assistance to help itself. It was Gandhi's view that if the government promoted cottage industries such as handspun and handwoven textiles, the economic level of a village could be raised and its people would be spared the worst evils of Western capitalist and industrialist societies. As a personal example Gandhi handspun thread daily till the end of his life. Nehru's government was more pragmatic on industrialization, but nevertheless set the goal of a "socialistic pattern of society" which the Congress Party has espoused ever since.

The Community Development Program was implemented by means of the Block Development Program, a vast plan carving out Blocks of about 100 villages and 60 or 70 thousand people each. In each Block there was to be concerted action on many fronts: irrigation, wells and pumps, improved seeds and breeds, poultry, cultivation techniques, cooperative credit societies, "basic education" in the schools involving time devoted to crafts, community centers, youth clubs, public health, assistance for Harijans, cottage

industries, roads, tanks, small savings, and even propaganda on international issues—all these and more were to be attacked simultaneously.

The agent to accomplish this was to be a dedicated village-level worker called a *grām sevak*. Of him, John Mellor says, "His function was to set up field demonstrations, to initiate talks and group discussions, to find out what the villagers needed, to awaken their concern, to interest them in change, and to carry out the programs of all eight assistant development officers [within the Block]. It is difficult to visualize such a paragon: India did not find him."[22] Supervising the grām sevaks were the desk men, officers with specialized training in agriculture, rural industries, cooperatives, and such, and above these was the prestigious Block Development Officer, known to villagers as the BDO. The usual grām sevak was a high school graduate who thought he should have a better desk job somewhere, while now he found himself walking dusty lanes in villages where he could not even buy a noon meal, and conversing with little-educated men and illiterate women. He was transferred every other year to prevent bribery, and as an officer without broad background, he could scarcely expect promotion. He was evaluated on written reports, which he naturally padded as much as possible, while within the village he sought to bolster his status and maintain his image as a middle-level government official by associating with prominent villagers and landowners.

By the end of the First Five-Year Plan, the Block Development Program had encompassed 123,000 villages and by the end of the Second Plan had reached most of India's 564,258 villages. Though the program did not have the anticipated impact, it did produce a little change in attitudes and practices. Even more important, as Mellor points out, was its function as a focus for idealism in the Government of India; it drew national attention to rural problems and produced a sense of confidence that the new government was really doing something.

In the Second Plan (1956–1961) the main thrust was development of the infrastructure of the economy—steel, railroads, electric power, and heavy industry—after the Russian model for national economic development. On these goals the Plan was overambitious. The Block Development Program focused attention on two points: rural credit and village governance. The All-India Rural Credit Survey highlighted the extent and causes of rural indebtedness—a problem which had pricked the conscience of the British too. Indebted peasants, who in many places formed the majority, were paying interest averaging about 25% a year to moneylenders. The government set about encouraging cooperative credit societies to compete with the rural moneylenders, and by 1957 it was reported there were 200,000 such societies. But such figures may "attest to the success of the Indian game of setting a target for number of cooperatives and seeing that it is met—a method which provides more cooperatives than substance."[23]

It was a cherished hope that initiative for village development would

Bank in a Mahārāshṭra market town, opened with government encouragement to assist farmers and small industries. Officials distinguish themselves from villagers by use of English, writing English name above Marāṭhī.

Sikh machine shop in Panjāb market town. In the parts of India that are prosperous, individuals have taken initiative to open many such establishments.

be taken over by the villages themselves 10 years after the launching of the Community Development Program, but as it developed, villages came to look on the government as benefactor. And it became apparent that lack of an organized pattern of village leadership was a real impediment, since peasants were viewing all improvements as dictated by government officials,

and indeed felt that the whole plan was foisted on them. The government then launched a program to develop village councils—panchāyats—in all villages and link them to two higher tiers of panchāyats. Panchāyat officials were to be elected and were to represent different classes of the population.

The writer observed the first meeting of the panchāyat in a Tamil̲ Nāḍu village. The elected president was a doddering old fellow who exerted no control over the meeting, and in fact scarcely spoke. He sat on the bench with great aplomb during the "function." But he was the second largest landowner in the village. (The largest was of the Nāḍar caste, an aggressive caste of semi-Harijan origin which was not considered quite indigenous to this village.) The first decision of this panchāyat was to fell two immense tamarind trees on a village street and sell them for firewood to raise money for the panchāyat. This decision was most shortsighted, for the trees were a century or two old and provided the only shade on the street. Worse, tamarind is in very short supply because population has grown faster than the production of the slow-growing trees, though tamarind is an essential ingredient of South Indian curry.

Now after 10 or 15 years of Panchāyatī Rāj there are signs the system is beginning to produce the intended effects. More competent people are elected; they levy more local taxes and provide more local amenities. In the above-mentioned village a competent Nāḍar was recently elected panchāyat president, signifying some progress in the democratization process. This panchāyat has installed piped water and provided half a dozen spigots on main streets, cemented drains, built a bridge, obtained a branch post office for the village (housed in the premises of the most prestigious landowning family), and donated land for the government to build a new middle school. In most villages, however, the panchāyat is controlled by the main landowning castes. Where customary panchāyats exist, they are partly superseded by the new statutory ones, but may still function to settle local disputes, while caste panchāyats continue to enforce caste behavior norms.

A number of changes have occurred in this village as a result of individual initiative, apart from official incentives. A farmer set up a small rice mill, which is a success; it employs three village youths from time to time. Another set up a shop to repair and rent out bicycles, and hired an underemployed Blacksmith. Since the two Potters in the neighboring village did not have enough work, one began mass-producing clay stoves to sell at the weekly market 10 miles away. A young farming man set up tailoring in a little booth, with a sewing machine (making most of his money at festival time when clothes are ordered for children). A number of people have taken outside jobs. Two men commute seven miles by bicycle to work in a textile mill; others work in a nearby cashew nut processing shed and in a small plastics factory. The non-Brāhmaṇ priest turned responsibilities over to his younger brother and took work as a stonemason in a distant town. One son of the largest landowner became trained as a teacher and got a job

through family contacts. Bus service increased in the 1960s from 5 a day to about 12, houses subscribing to the electric service increased from 10% to over 25%, and a few houses installed Indian-type porcelain latrines with underground pits.

In other villages other kinds of changes occur. Orenstein reports for a village in Mahārāshṭra that the panchāyat remained inactive to avoid tensions but that the cooperative movement had become an important fact of village life, especially cooperatives for giving loans and for establishing sugar processing factories. People also had a noticeably more favorable attitude toward the government—whereas old people remembered that they used to go home and bolt their doors when government officials came. In tens of thousands of other hamlets and small villages, however, the years since Independence have brought almost no change in the economic picture.

The Third Five-Year Plan

The Third Plan (1961–1966) was a model of tight national planning, and though the high goals were not achieved, gains were many. By its conclusion most villages in Kēraḷa, Tamiḻ Nāḍu, Panjāb, and Haryāṇā had electric supply, while parts of Mahārāshṭra, the Calcutta environs, western Uttar Pradesh, and southern Karṇāṭaka were also fairly well supplied. Irrigation pumps by the thousands were installed—the major reason for electrification of villages. In some states almost all villages were provided with access to roads, though in "backward" areas this was not true. Most important roads were paved with single-lane asphalt, supposed to be "dustless," and in the "advanced" states bus service became surprisingly frequent. The British legacy of the largest railway system in the world was improved, with indigenous manufacture of locomotives and railroad cars (400,000 of them in service!). Government-sector factories successfully produced tanks and sophisticated military hardware, small jet planes, and freight ships. Though assembly plants for three kinds of automobiles were set up in the private sector, production was severely limited in conformity with socialist ideology, for automobiles are considered "luxury" items. Meanwhile villages fully entered the bicycle age, and watches, radios, fountain pens, and artificial textiles became ubiquitous.

In fact, however, economic growth during the Third Plan only kept a little ahead of the annual 2.4% population increase, and though villagers bought small manufactured items and handled more money, many felt less well off than in the past when most homes stored up large quantities of grain, and when the land and the gold was divided up among fewer people.

By the end of the Third Plan it was recognized that the chief problem was agricultural production, which fell far short of the goal. Whereas there was a sense of euphoria at the end of the Second Plan because of an excep-

tionally good harvest resulting from favorable weather, by 1966–1967 the shortfall in grain production had reached disaster levels, so that in a single year India received nearly 12 million tons of wheat from the United States—three shiploads a day! The culprit was again said to be unfavorable weather. Many who knew India well predicted imminent and uncontrollable famine. This food deficit plus the failure of exports to meet expectations made the whole economy sluggish so that by the end of the decade the gross national product was increasing at only 2.6% a year, just keeping up with population growth. The rupee was devalued, and the late sixties were marked by disturbances in labor, the universities, and state governments. In the nationwide elections of 1967 Mrs. Gandhi's party failed to carry many of the states and later suffered a split, while both leftist and rightist parties held forth new promises.

Two Views on Agricultural Development

Should rural economic development be tackled by the community development approach or by stress on agricultural technology? The former has generally been espoused by psychologists, sociologists, and applied anthropologists, while economists and agronomists have tended to assume that peasant attitudes and rural society in general can scarcely be "modernized" without an improved economic base. It is generally agreed within India, however, that some of the cherished programs developed within the framework of Gandhian ideology have been fiascos. The government subsidy of millions of weavers has resulted in production of huge quantities of coarse handloom textiles that nobody wants even when offered for sale at subsidized prices. And the "basic education" program has not been favored by parents, who send their children to school to learn to read and not to learn bookbinding, basket weaving, or banana cultivation.

Kusum Nair, a lady journalist turned social scientist, traveled all over India and in 1961 produced a little book called *Blossoms in the Dust.* A simple record in villagers' own words of their attitudes, hopes, and gripes, in developing as well as economically backward regions, it made something of a stir in New Delhi. Planners had all along been thinking that peasants *wanted* all these benefits. Kusum Nair recorded the farmers' aspirations. One in Tamiḻ Nāḍu with a family of five calculates, and is sure: he wants just one and a half acres. Another with a family of four wants just two acres and will share the crop on a 50/50 basis, while yet another will settle for two acres shared on a 40/60 basis. In one village in Karṇāṭaka not a single villager had yet deigned to avail himself of the irrigation waters of the Tungabhadra project, though water was being offered free for the first three years. In Uttar Pradesh a peasant says corruption is eight times more than it had been in the zamīndār's time. Another says that he gets no con-

sideration from the government such as the zamīndār used to give, and besides now he pays more taxes. One farmer uses improved agricultural implements provided by the Pilot Project, but "they give us implements, and when we go for spare parts to the Cooperative Union in Mahewa it charges one rupee for a bolt. In Barthena I can get three bolts of the same kind for one rupee." The farmers give to the Small Savings Plan pushed by the government because "these officials come and ask for it. We do not give because we want to." In Bihār certain villagers are working on a fine masonry community center, half financed by the government. When asked its use, they are silent, then they are confused. One man concludes that since so many government officials are coming and going nowadays, they need a place to sit and to hold meetings! Nair concludes of such peasants that most "do not share in this concept of an ever-rising standard of living," and "the peasant does not consider it moral to want more." This lends some support to George Foster's concept of the limited good, said to be an attribute of traditional peasant societies in general.

In the states where there is economic growth Nair attributed it to attitudes. Panjāb and Haryāṇā, for instance, have numerous small-scale machine tool and equipment repair establishments to service the tractors and other equipment farmers have invested in, and grain production has soared. This region was injected with new life by the opening of vast canal projects both before and after Independence. The population was jarred by the massive migrations of 1947–1948. Sikhs travel widely and thus are open to new ideas, while they are also thought of as persistent workers; pride in Sikh identity is no doubt a factor. In Gujarāt too there is prosperity in parts, the result of generations of entrepreneurship and overseas trading, while western Mahārāshṭra is stimulated by Bombay. In Tamiḻ Nāḍu there is notable progress especially where the land is managed by Veḷḷāḷas or other cultivating castes proud of their agricultural expertise. And in Arunāchal Pradesh there is astounding change among the tribal Minyong, who are hard-working, self-reliant, and cooperative—to the extent that the Hindu officers working there have fallen under this spell of optimism and ideology favoring change.

In 1969 Kusum Nair was still not optimistic about the Fourth Plan emphasis on specific agricultural inputs expected to yield specific outputs; the human factor is too variable. A Tamiḻ farmer has an ambition to own only 1.3 acres; if he has more he has to hire help and he does not want the management responsibility. "It would be sufficient. But I think I could raise another 1000 pounds more rice per acre." "How would you do it?" "Well, I would apply more farmyard manure. I would plow better. I would plow two times more." But this farmer did not weed his field this year because the landlord did not ask him to do it. "I do what he tells me. He did not ask me to weed this year so I didn't." In this region rice production varies from 1600 to 5500 pounds per acre; the Pilot Project has a yield half

again the district average. The difference depends upon timeliness of operations and precision, not just on measurable inputs as seeds and fertilizers.

Nair thinks that stress should not be on production goals, but on social expectations, changes in farmers' attitudes, values, and practices, and a heightened floor of subsistence feasibility. Farmers will adopt new techniques in many different ways and in ratio to the range of alternatives open to them, not in line with a planned unilineal procedure for increasing production. And the price efficiency model of the Fourth Plan will produce uneven development and "the resulting disequilibria would not be in the nature of residual problems of growth, mere lags in adjustment. They could overwhelm and destroy the total fabric of society."[24] The Swede Gunnar Myrdal and some American observers also see a problem here. The "green revolution" has indeed widened the rift between successful and marginal farmers and raised aspirations that cannot be met. The farmers with tiny plots do not have the resources to innovate, nor can they afford any risk, and many may be forced off the land to swell the ranks of the landless and unemployed. As the Fourth Plan was launched, the *Indian Express*, a widely-read English daily, complained that there was erosion of the basic concept of community development in favor of emphasis on community production, and blamed "the hierarchical and authoritarian set-up in the countryside," the attitude of civil servants, and the partial failure of land reforms: "most of the defects in the working of the panchayati raj institutions are also traceable to the gross inequalities in rural society."[25]

A sharply different view is held by those who see insoluble economic crises looming and who feel that the prerequisite to other rural change is generation of increased agricultural productivity by increased inputs. The Swiss economist Gilbert Etienne made a study of agriculture in Uttar Pradesh, Mahārāshṭra, and Tamiḻ Nāḍu and concluded that rural development projects have been driving down some blind alleys. One is the supposed panacea of land reform. Further land redistribution, he says, would benefit only a few of the poorest peasants but production would decline, and in any case sharecropping is not an unmitigated evil. A second blind alley he finds is confidence in panchāyatī rāj; since panchāyats have not yet fulfilled their originally expected role, how can they be given more? A third blind alley is cooperative farming. "In every region that I visited I got the same impressions . . . the peasants do not want it and the experiments that have been made have failed with the exception of an extremely well-managed cooperative farm that I visited in the Coimbatore district . . . one can hardly agree with the proposal to set up 10,000 cooperative farms during the Fourth Plan." Etienne also debunks faith in community development as deviation from realistic planning. Finally, he disparages the faith in primary and compulsory education; the penchant of politicians to promise schools and electrification of villages does not meet the economic problems

head-on. Etienne pleads for specific hard-nosed projects to improve agricultural organization and services—pragmatic programs for fertilizers, minor irrigation, high-yield seed varieties, pesticides, rural credit, and agricultural research.

John Mellor also thinks the problem does not rest in the peasant's apathy or attitudes, but in lack of opportunities. He feels the Community Development Program was necessary for India, but it is too bad that the need for an organized and efficient approach to agricultural productivity did not receive due attention until the end of the Third Plan, far too late. A major error, says Mellor, was the assumption that agricultural research was not a high priority item, and its crucial importance was recognized 15 years too late. It is also unfortunate that grām sevaks have been sent out as generalists rather than as specialists trained in agronomy and innovative techniques. But he is cautiously optimistic about the Fourth Five-Year Plan: "the agricultural development process is about to be mastered in India."

The Green Revolution and the Fourth and Fifth Plans

After the food crisis at the end of the Third Plan, the economic slump, and the 1967 elections, the Government of India felt it needed a rest from planning; the Fourth Plan was shelved until 1970 while unfinished projects were completed and gains consolidated.

Meanwhile efforts were being made to intensify agricultural inputs. A series of pilot projects in seven districts in as many states, later augmented to include nine more districts, was financed by the Ford Foundation and the Government jointly. This was popularly called the Package Program and required considerable outlay as the districts had an average population of 1.75 million each and were distributed over diverse ecological zones from Panjāb to Tamiḻ Nāḍu. The Package Program experimented with many agricultural techniques but especially emphasized application of inorganic fertilizers, and achieved measurable, but spotty success.

The development of new strains of wheat in Mexico, financed by the Rockefeller Foundation, began in 1968 to revolutionize wheat production. Combined with the application of the most successful innovations of the Pilot Projects, these new wheat strains were responsible largely for the "green revolution" which doubled wheat production in seven years. The success of the new wheat varieties stimulated the government to work on new varieties of other grains; experimental stations produced a variety of *jvār* (a millet) that could yield 50% more, *bajṛā* (another millet) 70%, and corn 80%. These grains, though grown on the largest part of the farmed surface, are generally not irrigated and environmental factors are more difficult to control. Rice is the most important grain, but in spite of creation

of nearly a thousand new varieties, only a 10% increase in yield could be achieved by this means. People are quite conscious of the differences among varieties of rice, and many of the new varieties, especially those developed outside South Asia, are too glutinous or too tasteless, while nutritional value has also not been enhanced. Rice yields per acre in India are among the lowest in the world, and such gains as have been made are largely the result of agricultural planning, fertilizers, and pesticides. But agronomists have concluded that the plains of India will never produce the abundant rice yields of Japan nor even of Kashmīr, for in the high temperature too much of the plant energy is expended on respiration, while maintenance of soil fertility is also much more difficult.

Between 1966–1967 (the low year) and 1970–1971, wheat increased from 11.4 to 23.2 million tons, rice from 30.4 to 42.4 million tons, and other grains from 24.1 to 30.6 million tons (jvār 8.2, bajṛā 8, corn 7.4, grāms or pulses 5.3, barley 2.7, and rāgi 2.2 million tons). Foodgrain production in 1971 was 107 million tons, double that of 1951. India stopped importing American wheat and began building up a buffer stock. For the time being, at least, it appeared as if the viewpoint of the agronomists on how to achieve rural development had been proved correct.

But in spite of these gains and the general achievements of the first three Five-Year Plans (Table 16–1), the Government realized that only a

TABLE 16–1 Indian Rural Development 1950–1971[26]

	1950–1951	*1970–1971*	
Population	363.4	564.2	million
Life expectancy	35.3	53	years
Literacy	17	29	percent
School students	13.5	83.2	million
Children 6–11 in school	43	75	percent
Doctors	51	116	thousand
Post offices	36	100	thousand
Villages electrified	3.7	105.4	thousand
Power output	2.5	16.8	million kw.
Foodgrains	50.8	107.8	million tonnes
Bicycles produced	99	1954	thousand
Automobiles	165	800	thousand
Radios	54	1456	thousand

reprieve of a few years had been achieved, for the 1971 census showed population growth in the decade of the sixties to have been 24.8%, even higher than in the fifties, and it was predicted that by 1980 there would again be a foodgrains deficit of 10 million tons. Could an agricultural miracle be expected each decade, and each more intense than the preceding one?

Planning was removed from its exalted pedestal in the Government and the Fourth Plan was recast and published in 1970. It set a target of 5.5% annual economic growth (still very optimistic, since annual growth

since Independence only averaged 3.5%) and realigned priorities. The Planning Commission acknowledged that in the previous plans it had been incorrectly assumed that providing a certain rate of economic growth would take care of social problems such as unemployment and maldistribution of wealth. The new Plan incorporated specific proposals to tackle unemployment, but even if the goal of 19 million new jobs were achieved, unemployment would go on increasing! Family planning was finally given more serious attention. In addition it was acknowledged that since agriculture provided nearly half the national wealth and 70% of the employment, this was the only sector where a large number of jobs could be created. The Fourth Plan also set out to produce items needed by farmers in quantity, such as fertilizers and pumps, to economize on giant prestige industrial projects, increase exports, check inflation, and end deficit financing.

But the government prognostications of 1971 that India would soon be able to export food were challenged by less sanguine economists, and their views were vindicated in 1972 and 1973, when food production actually declined because of monsoon failure in large parts of northern and western India (Gujarāt received only 10 instead of 30 inches of rain, for instance). The government depleted its buffer stocks and negotiated importation of 6 million tons of grains. A draft of the Fifth Five-Year Plan had already been promulgated, drawn up when the food situation was not so tight and the euphoria of the successful Bangladesh involvement still lasted. The Fifth Plan draft was widely publicized as an attempt to "abolish poverty," since it was discovered that 40% of the people lived below the "poverty line," low as that was set, and was generally to help India achieve a "socialist pattern of society." But as it turned out 1973 was the most difficult year since Independence, as acknowledged by several government ministers. There were chronic food shortages of many kinds, deep hydroelectric power cuts, a dip in industrial production, shortages of coal for the railways because the mines had been taken over by the government, poor procurement of wheat even though the government took over the wholesale wheat trade, and rampant inflation. High officials suggested that maybe the Fifth Plan should be postponed pending economic recovery; finally the Planning Minister said he would try to save the core of it, though inflation had skewed all the projections. Given the population growth of 14 million a year, unemployment approximating 35%, and the per capita income of $110 (1971), the long-range picture for India and all South Asia looks grim indeed.

Community Development and Planning in Other South Asian Countries

The Government of Pakistan, unlike Nehru's government, did not inherit Gandhi's mantle. While the two wings of the country remained together, the government was dominated by West Pakistanis who were

inclined to pragmatic economic and military development. Their ideology was one of nationalism rather than socialism, and while the Indian government tried to regulate the economy by a veritable jungle of licenses, permits, and controls, Pakistan did it by price incentives and taxation. Under Ayub there was marked economic growth, 5.9% annually in 1960–1969, most of which accrued to West Pakistan. The country suffered the same reverses India did after middecade, and likewise benefited from the revolution in wheat production, which exceeded the Third Five-Year Plan (1965–1970) target by 26%. Nevertheless the 1971 per capita annual income of undivided Pakistan was the same as that for India—$110, while its population growth rate was even higher.

In 1957 two Academies for Rural Development were set up, with technical assistance and finance provided by Michigan State University and the Ford Foundation in cooperation with the government. These academies intended to develop pilot projects whose successes could be fed into wider "nation-building" policies. One academy was at Peshāwar for the western wing, and the other at Comilla for the eastern wing.

The academy at Peshāwar, in addition to development of agricultural techniques, has been experimenting with other rural development programs. It established youth clubs to "break through any resistance to rural development by working with youth." It hoped to make youth labor available for "cleaning village streets and levelling approach roads" and for establishing "an agricultural museum containing improved varieties of seeds, fertilizers, and insecticides," and such, and the club "should stage a flag parade" in the village streets each fortnight to attract attention. Most such projects have had little impact and have been limited to the environs of the Academy. A more successful program, piloted in the eastern wing, was partial integration of mosque schools into the public school system. Advantages included securing the weight of mosques and imāms behind the rural development programs, and capitalizing on the ability of the mosque schools to draw girl students. The pilot program was successful enough so that in the Fourth Five-Year Plan (1970–1975) the government intended to integrate the mosque schools as "one of the streams of the national education system with a statutory board of administrators in each province for laying down curricula, conducting examinations, and preparing textbooks."[27]

As applied anthropologists are aware, the introduction of almost any innovation has wide and often unexpected ramifications in the culture and the economy. After an intensive effort to get members of cooperative societies around Comilla, now in Bangladesh, to hire tractors instead of keeping oxen for plowing, the farmers were asked to cite advantages and disadvantages of both. Table 16–2 lists the most frequent replies. An accounting of both direct and indirect costs of renting tractors as against keeping oxen concluded that "there is a clear indication that the tractor operation is going to be a losing concern within the present level of earnings" for the

cooperative society. Yet "the costs of the maintenance of the tractors and bullocks exceed their monetary earnings, with the relative difference perhaps greater for the bullock than for the tractor."[29] This is partly because the average farm is less than two acres.

TABLE 16–2 Farmers' Opinions on Oxen versus Rented Tractors[28]

Advantages of Oxen	*Disadvantages of Oxen*
Dung available for fertilizer, fuel, house flooring	High cost of maintenance
Eat rice straw, oilseed waste, fruit skins, rice water	Pasture land unavailable
Working hours flexible	Stray oxen damage crops
No difficulty plowing small plots	Disease a great problem, especially at plowing time
Selective plowing possible	Insecticide poisoning common
Used for sugar cane pressing	Oxen may suddenly die
Used to thresh harvest	Ox carts too slow and damage roads
Used to press oilseeds	
Used to prepare earth for brickmaking	
Ox carts very useful, and travel where power vehicles cannot	
Can be rented out	
Can be offered as loan security	
Carcasses used for meat, hides	
Urine used for treatments	
Advantages of Tractors	*Disadvantages of Tractors*
Plowing possible after harvest when soil too hard for oxen	Damages surrounding plots gaining access
Can sow land earlier at more optimum time	Costly for fragmented plots because time wasted in moving about
Can plow any hard or dry land	Seed germination not uniform because moisture quickly lost after disc harrowing
Soil turned over better	Cannot be used for threshing
Plows 6–8 acres a day as against ½ acre for pair of oxen	Cannot be used for "laddering," an essential process
Plows 4–6″ as against 3″ for oxen	Cannot be used for puddling
Cost of weeding reduced by half	Raking not possible where seeds broadcast
Many small farmers cannot afford to keep oxen	Gives no dung
Yield increase by 20% in some cases	Immediate cash required for rental

Since 1960 the Academy at Comilla has piloted a number of projects in the surrounding administrative unit, the *thānā*. A key goal has been establishment of a system of primary cooperative societies linked to a central cooperative having specialized equipment and trained personnel. Primary cooperatives have 20 to 70 members who conduct weekly meetings and have elected chairmen and managers. As of 1968 a third of the farmers in the thānā had joined. The central cooperative maintains 25 tractors which it hires out to members, and has a hundred irrigation pumps and sundry other equipment. It provides demonstrations and training classes. Farmers

are expected to bank savings with their cooperative and borrow from it rather than from local moneylenders. A team of Japanese experts in rice cultivation was brought in, and many farmers have been constrained to plant their rice in rows and have installed tube wells to facilitate double-cropping. It is estimated that crop yields of cooperative members are 24% higher than yields of nonmembers in the thānā,[30] though of course these are likely to have been the most aggressive farmers in any case.

Sikkim began its First Five-Year Plan in 1956, and Bhutan initiated its first in 1961. Both have been financed entirely by India and aim to achieve modest gains in such fundamental economic areas as road construction, power production, and fruit cultivation. Bhutan's per capita annual income in 1971 was about $70 but its people are not thought of as leading a dismal existence. Sri Lanka had a Ten-Year Plan, but changes in the government and decline of exports have combined to vitiate hopes for rapid economic growth. But its per capita annual income is the highest in South Asia, $190.

Nepal initiated a four-tier panchāyat system in 1961. Village panchāyat members can be elected to district panchāyats, whose members are thence eligible for election to zonal panchāyats and thence to the National Panchāyat. Though the primary aim of this system is political integration, it does provide a channel for induced change. Whereas Nepal was near the bottom among all countries in the indices of "development" before it opened to the outside world in 1951, foreign aid offered by India and many other countries has resulted in the establishment of a few roads, power plants, small-scale industries, and handicrafts. Half a million children are in school. But in this country only 10% of the land is cultivable, much of it consisting of steep hillsides and only a fifth irrigated. For lack of roads it takes a year to distribute even a shipment of school supplies over the country. Nepal's per capita annual income in 1971 was $80.

Afghanistan initiated a Five-Year Plan in 1956. Only 15%–17% of the population are nomads, even though the country is known for its nomadic traditions and export of sheepskins. Development plans have concentrated on production of wheat, barley, corn, olives, and silk, as well as new kinds of fruits and vegetables. Irrigation dams have been built in three river systems. But much of this arid country is not tied into the wider economy for lack of roads, even though a few good highways span it, and there are no railroads whatever. The famine of 1971 and 1972 highlighted the inability of the government to move gift wheat to stricken areas, and news reports asserted that while some people starved and half the sheep died, local officials held up relief trucks, demanding bribes. Afghanistan's per capita annual income is estimated to be $90.

The lesson seems to be that community development or agricultural development can be modestly successful in a pilot project if there is really generous financing and if there are a large number of dedicated and specialized personnel involved. The Package Programs in selected districts in

India as well as the Academies established by Pakistan bear this out. But extension of such comprehensive programs to 700,000 villages on the subcontinent would require an unthinkable level of funding and a legion of trained people, who would likely be less dedicated than those serving pilot projects. And India's vast Community Development Program is an example of how well-conceived plans can get bogged down in bureaucratic rigidity.

Education

The fond hopes that rapid increase in educational opportunities at all levels would improve the economic outlook have not been realized. Nevertheless gains in this area have been spectacular. In India in 1951 only 17% were literate and there were 13.5 million pupils. By 1971 literacy had touched 30% (of the total population, including infants) and there were 83.2 million students! India has over 700,000 schools, nearly 2000 teachers' training and technical institutes, and 1600 colleges.

In states such as Kēraḷa, Mahārāshṭra, Tamiḻ Nāḍu, and Panjāb most working men can read, except sometimes Harijans, but in Uttar Pradesh and Bihār the literacy rate is low. Most villagers now wish their children, or at least their boys, to go to school, and this is true of low castes too. Parents wish their children to have some chance of getting salaried employment. In all states schools through high school are conducted in the state or mother languages (though a small minority, often government officials, send their children to private English-speaking schools as a symbol of status, apparently unconcerned that this is likely to be regarded as a detriment within a decade or two). Universities are in principle shifting to regional languages, and in Gujarāt, Āndhra, Uttar Pradesh, and some other states, have largely made the shift. All this tends to promote cultural revitalization. In India in 1966 there were 5279 newspapers and periodicals in Indian languages, and though the majority may be classed as pulp journals, their cumulative effect is substantial. A newspaper in a village tea shop may be read by a dozen men, or it may be read aloud. Schools and literacy are indeed vital to "nation building," to political participation, and in terms of attitudes to the wider world, tolerance, and change. But the effect of the massive investment in education on India's economy is moot.

Until recently a peasant's son educated through high school would rarely touch a plow. He might get some job in a store or as a clerk, or he may sit at home awaiting admittance to college or hoping some job would befall him. Since competition for seats in colleges is very keen, he may not be able to get in unless he got high marks in high school, has some pull with the college principal, or applied to a college catering to his particular ethnic group. Half of college students do not get the degree even after completing three of four years of work because they fail the B.A. or B.Sc.

final exam. They then come around to houses of people who appear relatively prosperous and plead, "I have studied in X college; I am B.A. fail. Can you give me some job?"

College graduates who return to their villages may wait for years in their parents' houses, hoping for some respectable job. The present writer has visited most of the villages portrayed in the companion volume, as well as others in many parts of South Asia, and has found educated people in almost all of them, waiting at home while their geology or economics or literature becomes rusty. It is a noted phenomenon that these people seldom contribute much to the intellectual or economic life of their villages, for what they studied is far removed, especially heretofore when their college work was in English. The national unemployment rolls have 2 million college and high school graduates, and many more don't bother to register. And it is not a matter of their having studied arts instead of technology, for of the country's 300,000 engineers 70,000 are jobless and 40,000 more are underemployed. One can sense, however, some change of attitude both as regards the reluctance of educated people to do farming or labor and as regards faith in education to open doors automatically to salaried employment. For the low castes, however, there is still hardly any other route.

The two states of Kēraḷa and West Bengal have had long traditions of higher education; Kēraḷa is highest in literacy today and West Bengal is also high. The history of these two states in recent years epitomized the plight of the educated unemployed and underemployed. It is these two states that have the longest record of political instability and labor problems, and both have had elected Communist state governments. In Kēraḷa it almost seems as if every bus driver and clerk has a college degree, while in West Bengal the educated unemployed in Calcutta have a penchant for whiling away their time writing poignant Bāngālī poetry for obscure journals.

In Sri Lanka literacy was 76% in 1970, and is nearly universal among Lowland Sinhalas. But studies have shown that over 50% still have not found work 5 years after leaving school. The "insurrection" of 1971 which convulsed the whole country and came within a hair's breadth of toppling the government of Mrs. Bandaranaike, was widely reported to have been staged by the educated unemployed young men; this writer has met a number of these in rural areas who feel that some sort of radical shift in policy holds out the only hope. Along with a high literacy rate the island has achieved the highest life expectancy in South Asia, and is known for a pleasant standard of living and clean respectable houses. But it can hardly be said that the high level of education has caused economic growth, for there is little indigenous industry and a stagnant or declining economy.

In Bangladesh the majority of working men can read, but the rate of literacy among females in 1961 was only 9.6%. Scores of colleges sprouted in the 1960s, and the sons, and daughters, of many poor peasants attend them. Few of these graduates have found jobs since there is little scope in this country for regular employment outside the government. Pakistan has

paid less attention to education. In 1961 only 12.1% in West Pakistan were literate—half the rate in India for that year (one reason is that Urdū rather than the regional languages is used in schools, except in Sindh). Yet through much of the 1960s West Pakistan had the highest economic growth rate in South Asia—the inverse of what might have been predicted two decades ago. Literacy in Pakistan may now be about 20%.

Literacy in Mauritius is 62%, in Sikkim 16%, in Nepal 9%, and in Bhutan negligible. But by 1970 Nepal had opened 36 colleges and had high expectations for the role of education in the modernization process.

The South Asian village school functions within the context of the culture and it would be difficult for an American teacher or pupil to adjust to it. In primary schools (the first five grades) boys and girls generally sit on the floor or on very low benches. One classroom is separated from the next one by a matting except in the newest buildings. One can hear the children chanting the alphabet two blocks away, the same chant week after week. When they read they generally develop the habit of vocalizing, which helps the teacher ascertain the progress of the pupil but in later years becomes a drag. Students stand to recite and expect the teacher to be authoritarian. Most learning is by rote, the object being to learn the contents of textbooks to pass the examinations. The state sets examinations at the end of each year, and crucial ones at the end of the primary, middle school, and high school stages, which may weed out half the students. Students often stay home to tend the buffalo, help with weeding, or babysit, and one of the criteria on which teachers are ranked is how well they can round up students. The main thing parents expect of teachers is somehow to get a

Primary school in Bangladesh. Only the newest schools have pakkā buildings. Headmaster (left) stands with teachers; few villages here accept women teachers.

Primary school in Tamil̤ Nāḍu. Girl stands up to recite.

fair percentage of the students to pass the annual examinations; some achieve zero or 10% success, while a good teacher will get half his class through. Many children drop out after two or three years after achieving basic literacy, and some also revert to illiteracy. While many larger villages have high schools, it is not uncommon to see students walking four miles each way, and most of those who pass the middle school go on to high school. If the village has no electricity, or if the house does not have it, students will study in the evenings by the light of a tiny kerosine lamp. The school system does not jar village life but it does slowly create wider awareness and instill a sense of patriotism.

Aspirations and Attitudes

To discover what appears important to villagers themselves, we will turn to a study of peasant responses and attitudes in villages in Uttar Pradesh, recognizing that some of these might not appear typical of other parts of South Asia. The research was published by Durganand Sinha. The researchers divided the responses into those from more developed and those from less developed villages, as one objective was to provide information on the effectiveness of the Community Development Program. The research methodology involved informal discussion and oral questioning to which respondents replied in their own words with as many details as they desired; responses were then tabulated.

One question was about what constitutes a happy life (Table 16–3).

TABLE 16–3 Percentage of Persons Volunteering Each Item in Response to the Question, "What does a person possess who is said to have a happy life?"[31]

More Developed Villages		*Less Developed Villages*	
Food	78	Food	75
Cattle	68	Cattle	63
House	63	Money	63
Money	55	Land	60
Clothing	49	Transportation and communication	50
Irrigation	49	House	49
Desire for family	39	Clothing	48
Implements	35	Desire for family	39
Transportation and communication	34	Education	29
Education	31	Implements	28
. . .		. . .	
Health and sanitation	10	Health and sanitation	12
Village peace and progress	6	Happy family relations	10
Happy family relations	4	Village peace and progress	6
National peace, progress	3	National peace, progress	4
Social service	.3	Social service	3

Assurance of food supply heads the list of responses. This bears out Gandhi's opinion: "To the millions who have to go without two meals a day, the only acceptable form in which God dare appear is food." Cattle is second on the list, symbolic of peasant self-sufficiency and success as a farmer as well as essential for cultivation and a multitude of other functions. On the whole there was little difference in responses between the two sets of villages, though peasants in the less developed ones are a little more concerned with money and with transportation (carts, bus fare, bicycles), while those in the more developed ones think more frequently of housing, clothing, irrigation, and implements.

It is striking that 9 of the 11 top responses deal with immediate materialistic needs. The social needs which the idealistic urban elite frequently project on villagers are mentioned by only a small percentage of respondents. The following three responses are typical of those from the more developed villages:[32]

One will get proper food and clothes. There will be facilities for drinking water. The number of cows, buffaloes, and bullocks will increase. One will have money. The country will become prosperous. One will possess bicycles, motor cars, bullocks and bullock carts. Roads will be constructed and all the lanes will be paved. The house will have electricity. He will have guns, spears, sword, motor cars, machines, and Persian wheel [for irrigation]. He would have plenty of money and lend out his money to others. He would not think ill of any one. . . . I have two bullocks. This number could go up to four. My family would grow. I should not be jealous or think ill of any one.

One has horses and elephants. One has tractor; a furnished guest room, gun, pakkā house, and possesses ten flour mills. . . . He has motor car, elephant, horse, agriculture, well, pond, house, children, cows, and buffaloes. He would always be entertaining some guests.

One is not in debts and after work, eats and rests well. Children live happily, and have plenty to eat, and are employed. One is happy only when one is not in debts.

These are representative of responses from the less developed villages:

One will have cushions, cots, and beds, will get plenty of milk and ghī to consume. Someone would help in work. He will have machines in his house, so that he will not have to exert. He would have nice house to live in and good clothes to wear. No one will be harassed. . . . enough to eat and dress, has a house, servant, gun, elephant, horse, wristwatch and a cycle. He would have plenty of milk and ghī for happy living.

I should have all happiness. Physically I should be sound. To be happy, one will have ten rupees in one's pocket. If I am able then, I shall go on a pilgrimage to Gayā and Jagannāth. . . . I should be able to pay off my debts. I would have enough food, clothes, linen and other things. God has blessed me with children. I would need only food.

It depends on his fate. One gets in this world what he had done in the past birth. . . . A happy life is when one has enough to eat, has no fear from the

king [government]. To people who are happy, God gives what they possess. Some have guns, spears, pistols, and so on, and many have got hatchet and axes.

In a good life, one has no fears. The Government would give all kinds of help. There would be no need for flattering anyone. People would not be afraid of anyone's threat in the realization of land dues. He would have buffaloes, children, garden, the riches and everything, educated children. I need a buffalo, facilities for not paying land dues, new plows and seeds, fertilizers, radio set, all kinds of riches. I should be able to earn sufficient to live.

In a happy life one is satisfied with one's food, clothes, and everything. One will also have good house, and cultivation, cows and buffaloes, and a school. . . . There are facilities for drinking water, and a house which, if not pakkā, should at least be earthen; and I would need foodgrains, money for purchasing oil and salt and household necessities. I do not think that I would be able to get any of these things.

Sinha observes that many of the respondents had difficulty expressing specific goals or wishes. Many were vague or mentioned unattainable and unrealistic wishes. Elephants, horses, guns, knives, and cushions were status symbols of the zamīndārs and Rājpūts of a bygone day. He concludes that "wants are there in a general and diffused form. What is required is the conversion of general wants into *specific needs*" if the objectives of the Fourth Plan are to be realized.

To the question on what is the main thing for getting ahead these days (Table 16–4) respondents from the less developed villages saw less use in

TABLE 16–4 Percentage of Persons Volunteering Each Item in Responses to the Question, "What is the main thing for getting ahead these days?"[33]

	More Developed Villages	*Less Developed Villages*
Work and effort	62	49
Education	62	22
Fate or divine grace	44	53
Wealth	28	37
Friend's help	7	6
"Undue influence"	6	4
Approach to minister and officials	3	5
Don't know	1	4

working hard or getting educated but were more fatalistic and attributed more efficacy to wealth. These responses are reasonable, given the life experiences of such villagers. Almost half the respondents in both sets of villages wished their children to go in for "service" (government or any salaried employment), 40% wished them to go into farming, and 7% into business. As for themselves, "there was absence of much dissatisfaction with the past, or frustration with the existing conditions."

On tests designed to rate actual behavior, most adults displayed "extreme caution and lack of enterprise. There was absence of risk-taking and fear of failure. These constituted the most important feature of their behavior on the test." People from the more developed villages indicated higher accomplishment and reflected stronger motivation, but

> in comparison to what they had already accomplished, the families from the developed areas were not optimistic concerning what they expected in the next five to seven years. The future was perceived with uncertainty and doubt, and they did not anticipate that the present level of achievement would be maintained in years to come.[34]

Whatever changes are engineered in South Asian society, it will be done by South Asians, not foreign "experts." For some years now the Government of India has been chary of social scientists peering as through a microscope at minute details of caste, subsistence, fertility, regional political loyalties, and the like, and feels that much that is written abroad is uncomplimentary and that many studies are useless as regards the broad goals set for development. Since the United States "tilt" to Pakistan during the Bangladesh war, India has hesitated to issue visas for foreigners to study many anthropological topics: tribes, border peoples, caste, villages, regional loyalties, and population. Pakistan has never cared for social scientists' probings, while Sri Lanka and Nepal are looking more closely at what foreigners do. Clearly it is in the fitness of things that "academic imperialism" should end and that Western social scientists should refine their standards of professional ethics. While the dilemma of objective as opposed to applied anthropology is still with us, a clearly satisfying aim would be for Westerners to develop the intense personal relations with individual South Asians that the latter expect from their own people. Many American young people who have gone to South Asia have succeeded in doing this better than their elders.

REFERENCES AND NOTES

1 Srinivas, p. 52.
2 Srinivas, p. 85.
3 Singer (1972), p. 385.
4 Harold Gould, p. 3.
5 Mencher, pp. 208–213.
6 Joseph Elder, "Rājpur: Change in the Jajmāni System of an Uttar Pradesh Village," in Rowe.
7 Orenstein, pp. 86–87.
8 Hazelhurst, p. 286.
9 Gould, p. 11.
10 Hutton, p. 195.
11 Hutton, p. 219.
12 Hutton, p. 215.
13 Hutton, p. 203.

[14] Eleanor Zelliot, "Background of the Mahar Buddhist Conversion," in Robert Sakai (ed.), *Studies on Asia* (Lincoln, Neb., 1966).
[15] Galanter (1963), p. 553.
[16] Cohn (1965), p. 109.
[17] T. S. Rama Rao, "The Study of the History of Law and Courts in South India" (manuscript, 1969).
[18] Cohn (1965), p. 106.
[19] Berry, pp. 3–4.
[20] Qadir, pp. 28–29.
[21] Mildred Luschinsky, "Problems of Culture Change in the Indian Village," in Rowe, p. 70.
[22] Mellor and others, pp. 36–37.
[23] Mellor and others, p. 62.
[24] Nair (1969), pp. 225, 231.
[25] Editorial, *The Indian Express*, July 10, 1970, p. 6.
[26] *India News*, June 30, 1972, p. 3; Aug. 11, 1972, p. 3.
[27] F. A. M. Tirmizi, "Ulema Project" (Peshawar, 1968); Ali A. Bhuiyan, "Imams as Teachers" (Comilla, 1968); Ministry of Education and Scientific Research, Government of Pakistan, *The New Education Policy of the Government of Pakistan* (Islamabad, 1970).
[28] Anwaruzzaman Khan, *Introduction of Tractors in a Subsistence Farm Economy* (Comilla, 1962).
[29] Anwaruzzaman Khan, p. 62.
[30] Syed Rahim, "The Comilla Program in East Pakistan," in Clifton Wharton (ed.), *Subsistence Agriculture and Economic Development* (Chicago, 1969).
[31] Sinha, p. 69.
[32] Sinha, p. 61–66.
[33] Sinha, p. 200.
[34] Sinha, pp. 150–153.

IMPORTANT SOURCES

Aiyappan, A. *Social Revolution in a Kerala Village: A Study in Culture Change.* New York, 1965. (A restudy of a village after three decades.)

Appadorai, A. *India: Studies in Social and Political Development, 1947–1967.* New York, 1968.

Baden-Powell, B. H. *Land Systems of British India*, 3 vols. Oxford, 1892.

Bailey, F. G. *Politics and Social Change: Orissa in 1959.* Berkeley, Calif., 1963.

Berry, Willard. *Aspects of the Frontier Crimes Regulation in Pakistan.* Durham, N.C., 1966.

Béteille, André. *Caste, Class, and Power: Changing Patterns of Stratification in a Tanjore Village.* Berkeley, Calif., 1965.

———. *Castes Old and New: Essays in Social Structure and Social Stratification.* Bombay, 1969.

Caplan, Lionel. *Land and Social Change in East Nepal: A Study of Hindu-Tribal Relations.* Berkeley, Calif., 1970.

Cohn, Bernard. "Anthropological Notes on Disputes and Law in India," *American Anthropologist*, Dec. 1965.

Crane, Robert (ed.). *Transition in South Asia: Problems of Modernization.* Durham, N.C., 1970. (Includes article on the Brahmo Samaj, language change, and political modernization.)

Etienne, Gilbert. *Studies in Indian Agriculture: The Art of the Possible.* Berkeley, Calif., 1968.

Galanter, Marc. "Changing Legal Conceptions of Caste," in Singer and Cohn.

———. "Law and Caste in Modern India," *Asian Survey,* Nov. 1963.

Ghurye, G. S. *Social Tensions in India.* Bombay, 1968.

Gould, Harold. "Is the Modernity–Tradition Model All Bad?" *Economic and Political Weekly* V, Nos. 29–31 (1970).

Government of India, Ministry of Irrigation and Power. *Report of the Irrigation Commission.* New Delhi, 1972. (An Important state by state survey showing agricultural potential.)

Haq, M. Nurul. *Village Development in Bangladesh.* Comilla, 1973. (A study of one village.)

Hardgrave, Robert. *The Nadars of Tamilnad: The Political Culture of a Community in Change.* Berkeley, Calif., 1969.

Hazelhurst, Leighton. "Caste and Merchant Communities," in Singer and Cohn.

Hutton, J. H. *Caste in India,* 4th ed. Oxford, 1963 (originally published 1956).

Inayatullah (ed.). *Bureaucracy and Development in Pakistan.* Peshawar, 1963.

Ishwaran, K. (ed.). *Change and Continuity in India's Villages.* New York, 1970. (Analyses of change in particular villages by Beals, Berreman, Elder, Gough, Mencher, and others.)

Kapadia, K. M., and S. Devadas Pillai. *Industrialization and Rural Society.* Bombay, 1972.

Khan, Akhter Hameed. *Community and Agricultural Development in Pakistan.* East Lansing, Mich., 1969. (Describes experiments in East and West Pakistan.)

Laska, John. *Planning and Educational Development in India.* New York, 1968.

Mahar, Michael (ed.). *The Untouchables in Contemporary India.* Tucson, Ariz., 1972. (Essays by 17 authors.)

Mason, Philip (ed.). *India and Ceylon: Unity and Diversity.* New York, 1967. (13 essays by well-known South Asian specialists.)

Mathur, S. C. (ed.). *Agricultural Policy and Food Self-Sufficiency.* New Delhi, 1970.

Mellor, John, and others. *Developing Rural India: Plan and Practice.* Ithaca, N.Y., 1968.

Mencher, Joan. "A Tamil Village: Changing Socioeconomic Structure in Madras State," in Ishwaran.

Morehouse, Ward (ed.). *Science and the Human Condition in India and Pakistan.* New York, 1963.

Mukherjee, Radhakamal (ed.). *Social Sciences and Planning in India.* New York, 1972.

Nair, Kusum. *Blossoms in the Dust.* New York, 1962. (A survey of villagers' views and hopes from many Indian states.)

———. *The Lonely Furrow.* Ann Arbor, Mich., 1969. (Farmers' attitudes in United States, Japan, and India.)

Orenstein, Henry. "Village, Caste, and the Welfare State," in Rowe.

Pakistan Agricultural University, Lyallpur. *Law at the Grass-Roots: A Study of Muslim Family Laws and Conciliation Courts.* Lyallpur, 1968.

Pakistan Agricultural University, Lyallpur. *Man, Water, and Economy: A Socio-Economic Analysis of Fourteen Rural Communities in Mona Project.* Lyallpur, 1970.

Qadir, S. A. *Village Dhanishwar: Three Generations of Man-Land Adjustments in an East Pakistan Village.* Comilla, 1964.

Reed, Horace, and Mary Reed. *Nepal in Transition: Educational Innovation.* Pittsburgh, 1968.

Rogers, Everett. *Modernization among Peasants: The Impact of Communication.* New York, 1968. (Mass media in India and other peasant countries.)

Rowe, William (ed.). *Contours of Culture Change in South Asia. Human Organization*, Monograph No. 9, 1966. (Articles by 12 South Asian specialists.)

Sarkar, P. C. *The Planning of Agriculture in India.* New York, 1966. (Specific recommendations for agricultural policy.)

Singer, Milton. *When a Great Tradition Modernizes.* New York, 1972. (Modernization of Indian civilization; the latest synthesis.)

———, and Bernard Cohn (eds.). *Structure and Change in Indian Society.* Chicago, 1968. (A symposium of recognized importance.)

Singh, Balajit, and S. Mitra. *A Study of Land Reforms in Uttar Pradesh.* Honolulu, 1964.

Sinha, Durganand. *Indian Villages in Transition: A Motivational Analysis.* New Delhi, 1969. (Psychological testing in Uttar Pradesh villages.)

Srinivas, M. N. *Social Change in Modern India.* Berkeley, Calif., 1967.

United States Department of Agriculture. *Agricultural Development and Farm Employment in India.* Washington, D.C., 1973.

17

Urban Change

Because this chapter has a different title than the preceding one, it should not be assumed that it is always possible to demarcate rural from urban life. The two form a continuum in South Asia, for the market town is not really removed from the rural scene. Sociologists have suggested that urbanization everywhere is to be defined in terms of life style rather than in purely demographic terms. In concluding this chapter we shall see to what extent this is possible for South Asia. Census takers, however, have to work with quantitative data. In India an urban place is defined as one having at least 5000 people and a density of at least 1000 per square mile with at least three fourths of the people working outside agriculture. If there are up to 100,000, it is a town, and above that, a city. For Pakistan also an urban place is one with 5000 or more people and having urban conditions. But in Nepal an urban place is one with 10,000 or more people.

There is a fair congruence between urbanization as statistically defined (Table 17–1) and the level of economic development in the various parts of South Asia. In general, the states or countries having a fourth or more of the population urbanized are the same ones that lead in industry and have a notably increasing level of economic activity. Among the states of India there is also fair correlation between the rate of urbanization and rural

development such as agricultural productivity and electrification of villages, but the literacy level does not always correlate with the urbanization level. It is interesting to note that the regions that have historically had large nucleated villages and have a tradition of entrepreneurship and commercialism—western India, parts of Pakistan, parts of the South—are the same ones that today lead in urbanization and its accruing benefits. The picture looks dismal for eastern Uttar Pradesh, Bihār, northern West Bengal, Orissa, Assam, and Bangladesh, not only because urbanization rates are low but also because the population is so suffocatingly heavy that the existing urban regions cannot provide sufficient outlets for it. Kēraḷa and Sri Lanka are special cases, for the heavy population and rather low urbanization rates are mitigated in that people tend to be rather urban in attitude and literacy rates are very high, while houses are pleasantly dispersed among coconut groves and rice fields.

TABLE 17–1 Percentage of Population Urbanized in 1971

Indian States		*Indian Territories*	
Mahārāshṭra	31.2	Chaṇḍigaṛh	90.7
Tamil̲ Nāḍu	30.3	Delhī	89.8
Gujarāt	28.1	Pondicherry	42.1
West Bengal	24.6	Goā	26.3
Karṇāṭaka	24.3	Andaman and Nicobar Is.	22.8
Panjāb	23.8	Arunāchal Pradesh	3.1
Āndhra Pradesh	19.4	Lakshadvīp	—
Jammū and Kashmīr	18.3		
Haryāṇā	17.8	*Countries*	
Rājasthān	17.6	Mauritius	34.9
Kēraḷa	16.3	Pākistān	22.5 (1961)
Madhya Pradesh	16.3	India	19.9
Uttar Pradesh	14.0	Śrī Lankā	19.1 (1963)
Maṇipur	13.3	Maldives	11.5
Meghālaya	12.0	Afghānistān	7.0 (?)
Bihār	10.0	Bānglādesh	5.2 (1961)
Nāgaland	9.9	Sikkim	5.2
Assam	8.4	Nepāl	2.8
Orissa	8.3	Bhūṭān	—
Tripurā	7.8		
Himāchal Pradesh	7.1		

Urbanization in Pakistan must be nearly 25%, while in Bangladesh one may guess that it is double that shown for 1961. The figure for Sri Lanka is also an old one, and Nepal's definition of an urban place depresses the figure for that country. The Maldives have only one town, Malé, which has a tenth of the people. Mauritius, the most urbanized of these countries, is a special case because of its very dense population of immigrant origin relying on sugar cane as an exportable cash crop.

The Preindustrial City

The preindustrial city of traditional South Asian civilization originated within the context of the civilization and was fundamentally different from the industrial or cosmopolitan city such as was established after the Europeans came. The former has been called orthogenetic, in contrast with the heterogenetic city such as grew up in coastal regions where European presence was significant.

The preindustrial city as defined by Gideon Sjoberg in his world survey of such cities, was generally girdled by a wall. It had a central area focusing on a governmental, religious, or marketing structure, and the upper classes clung to their residences near these foci of power. In such "feudal" cities, as Sjoberg calls them, class distinctions were marked, and the elite distinguished themselves by certain manners, patterns of conduct, and sometimes also by speech and by cult. Ethnic groups were segregated in different parts of the city, while the lowest classes had to live outside the walls. There were highly developed religious, governmental, or educational institutions, and "knowledge" and literacy were the prerogative of the elite. The idealized family structure also applied to the upper classes. There was little standardization in commerce and few fixed prices, but much adulteration of produce. Businessmen did not have as high status as the political, religious, or learned elite because they mixed with all manner of people and constantly manipulated for profit. Moreover, in accumulating wealth, they challenged the status of the established power structure. From such towns there was a complex network of communication linking the surrounding towns and countryside.

Most of the above generalized description is applicable to South Asian preindustrial cities, such as existed from the time of the Mauryas, whose capital of Pāṭaliputra was described glowingly by Megasthenes. Anurādhapura in Sri Lanka was carefully laid out to accommodate all classes of people, was a royal city, and also a sacred center. In the northwest of Panjāb, Takshaśilā was a vast commercial and university center. The last of the great Hindu royal cities, Vijayanagara of the 14th century, is said to have had a wall 60 miles around. Numerous gates and towers, moats, palaces connected by underground tunnels, formal gardens, and busy merchant streets were features of such cities.

Whereas these cities and many others of Hindu kings have vanished, a few have been maintained by Hindu princes, while Hindu sacred cities such as Vārāṇasī (Banaras), Madurai, and Purī have remained to the present orthogenetic cities in close symbiotic relationship with the countryside. A wave of new cities appeared with the Muslim rulers, while some old ones such as Allāhābād and Paṭnā were given new functions. Most of the great orthogenetic cities in South Asia, such as Lahore, Delhi, Āgrā, Peshāwar,

Main street of Khushāb, an old fortified trade town on the bank of the Jhelum in Pakistan. Merchants and craftsmen live above or behind their places of business. Towns selected by the British as district headquarters outpaced this one.

General store in a town in northwestern Pakistan.

Hyderābād, capital of Āndhra. As capital of a great princely state with a Muslim ruler, it developed as a spacious city in pre-British times.

Lucknow, Hyderābād, and Dacca grew to be so important because they were Muslim administrative centers while they also carried on commercial functions.

With the Europeans came a third wave of cities, this time along the coasts. New ports appeared such as Karāchī, Bombay, Cochin, Tuticorin, Madras, and Calcutta, while a few old ports such as Goā, Colombo, and Chittagong were Europeanized. These were heterogenetic cities which did not grow up supported by a network of links to the countryside. Indeed the three biggest ones, Bombay, Calcutta and Madras, had singularly little local support when they were established, so they were able to become all the more European. The previously existing ports were eclipsed by these. The main trend was a flow of power *outward* from the heartland of the subcontinent to the coasts.

Only since Independence have the interior cities, for the most part, been rejuvenated to the point where they can supersede the foreign-established coastal cities: Delhi has displaced Madras as India's third city, Dacca has superseded Chittagong, and the Pakistan capital has been moved to the Panjāb from Karāchī. Most production is now carried on in interior industrial cities instead of on the coasts.

Most of the market towns which dot South Asia are still essentially preindustrial in character, but a few have made the transition to a partly industrialized economy while yet retaining regional primacy and intimate links with the countryside. Here we will take a glimpse of Ahmadābād as a city that has made such a transition, then shift to Calcutta as an example of a coastal city founded under British stimulus.

An Old City: Ahmadābād

Ahmadābād, the temporary capital of Gujarāt, is India's seventh largest city, having 1.6 million people in 1971 and growth of 38% in a decade. Its economic mainstay is the textile mills which feed off the cotton produced on the coastal plains of Gujarāt. Its primacy is due to the entrepreneuring tradition of Gujarātīs, which probably goes back to the Indus Civilization, and certainly in the earliest Buddhist and Hindu texts we find thriving mercantilism centered in the several Gujarāt ports. As a result of this trade, Indian civilization was exported to Sri Lanka and Southeast Asia, and in this century Gujarātīs have taken over much of the trade of East Africa. As Bombay came to primacy, the coastal cities of Gujarāt, especially Surāt, faded, while Gujarātī businessmen migrated to Bombay where they comprise 10% of the population. But Ahmadābād grew to be the urban focus of Gujarāt.

A study of the development of this city has been recently published by Kenneth Gillion. He finds that Ahmadābād has had a tradition of corporate spirit and a hereditary bourgeois elite. During the British days it had no Western-educated middle class, no Hindu intellectual renaissance. It has been a conservative city, and until 1850 it had the qualities of a preindustrial city as enumerated by Sjoberg. It was a medieval Indian city whose prosperity rested on ancient crafts. Guilds in Gujarāt lasted longer than in the rest of South Asia, elsewhere squeezed out by royalty and the British. By the turn of the century guilds were still strong, but declining. Ahmadābād was encompassed by walls outside of which were suburbs, seats of Mughal officers, and outcaste hamlets. Inside there were unpaved lanes with unpainted wooden houses clustered around cul-de-sac streets closed off by gates. Each of these dead-end streets, or *pols*, usually was occupied by one caste and often by related families, providing privacy and coziness.

Ahmadābād was probably a worse place to live after the coming of the textile mills than it was in 1550. There arose vast lines of single-room tenements near the mills, and not one building of architectural quality was erected during the century and a quarter of British rule. Under British aegis the Town Wall Committee evolved into a Municipal Commission, but this was a conservative body which disliked levying taxes for improvements. In 1874 the death rate was 46 per 1000, and by 1916 it was still 39. One reason was that all the surface runoff drained into the river above the point where the city water supply was taken. Piped water was opposed by Brāhmaṇs while businessmen thought drains an extravagance. When purer piped water was finally supplied, incidence of cholera decreased, but malaria increased because there were more pools of standing water. By 1872 the density within the walls was 53,400 per square mile (double that of London) and by 1902 it was 60,000 and in some wards 120,000. But by 1960 the city had expanded in area so that the density was down to 24,300, and it was the hub of 52 cities and towns within 60 miles, many of them on the main transportation routes southward to Baroḍā and Bombay. It had begun to pay some attention to the arts, and some good architecture was appearing.

Gillion suggests that the economic development of this city belies the claim that modern infrastructure and Western contact are preconditions for industrialization. There was no important British presence in the city, few people knew English, and there was no Western law. The banking system was indigenous, as were bookkeeping methods. There was an indigenous market economy with a high level of commercial responsibility and a reputation for honesty. There was little technological innovation except the introduction of British textile machinery, and the establishment of the mills did not disrupt the old social ways. Firms were owned and managed by family trusts, which meant that there were administrative continuity and care of equipment. The mill owners did not compete with each other, but cooperated, most of them being related by marriage. There was sufficient local capital at reasonable interest rates.

The dominant ethic has been one of hard work, frugality, and money-making. Unlike in other parts of South Asia, businessmen have not been stigmatized nor considered antisocial. There is a staid religious conservatism, Hindu and Jain; parallels with the Calvinistic entrepreneuring Dutch are obvious. These traits are still characteristic of Gujarāt, which has made more progress in use of the regional language for higher education and business than any other Indian state. Ahmadābād has successfully made the transition from a preindustrial to an industrial city without British assistance or liberal ideology, without Brāhmaṇ leadership, and without relying on rural land revenues. Gillion calls this a study in continuity, not change.

A City of Colonial Origin: Calcutta

Greater Calcutta has over 7 million people; it includes Calcutta proper with 3.1 million, Howrah across the river, and seven other major cities. It is at the hub of India's largest urban agglomeration, with an industrial belt extending northward and also westward into the Dāmodar Valley with its iron and steel industries. The Calcutta Metropolitan District has within it 97 urban centers and 472 villages, all within a 30 mile radius of the city and mostly ranging along the Hooghly River. Of the male population of Calcutta proper, 26% are engaged in manufacturing, 24% in trade and commerce, and 12% in transportation and storage. Calcutta also probably has the greatest expanse of abject slums in the world.

Bānglā had wide-ranging sea trade from Mauryan times, and was noted for such ancient ports as Tāmraliptī which traded with Southeast Asia and Sri Lanka, while ships holding hundreds of persons plied the Gangā. But all that faded, first with the usurpation of the Indian Ocean trade by the Arabs, then by the Portuguese and other Europeans. The site of Calcutta (Kālīghāṭ) consisted of swamps and peasant hamlets, the most exciting event being an annual fair for the sale of cotton yarn. The Portuguese built a mud fort nearby on the bank of the Hooghly and four Bāngālī families moved there as trading agents. In 1690 the British East India Company chose Kālīghāṭ as its headquarters and laid the foundations of that city that was to serve as the capital of British India until the inauguration of Delhi by the great *darbār* ceremony of 1911. The city prospered not only from the presence of the government and the military, and the export of jute and tea, but also from the investments of the zamīndārs in the countryside. In 1802 an Englishman remarked:

> So pleasing is that Capital now, that those who are absent, sigh for the sprightly joys and gentle ease of Calcutta . . . its founders must have been a race of virtuous, industrious, and honorable men; and pious and beautiful women, who enlivened society in general and afforded every domestic social comfort to husbands far distant from the house of early consanguinity and the joys of England . . . with what sensations would the father of Calcutta glow to look down this day upon his city![1]

It was in Calcutta that the clash of British and Indian value systems first moved toward resolution. David Kopf has made a study of the 19th-century intelligentsia of the city in order to understand the two-way process of acculturation: "We have somehow been led to believe that the true modernizers before the twentieth century were those who rejected their own heritage and readily accepted the only path to modernity—rapid Westernization."[2] Kopf finds that Englishmen in Calcutta tended to react to

Indian culture either as Hinduphiles or as Hinduphobes. Among the former were William Jones whose investigation of Sanskrit opened the door to comparative linguistics for Europeans, and to some extent also Warren Hastings, Governor-General of Bengal from 1773. The Baptist missionary William Carey in 1792 settled outside Calcutta at Serampore, and though he did not make a convert for seven years, he mastered a dozen Indian languages and set up a press which printed scripture and other works in 36 languages. The ex-Baptist missionary William Adam helped Rammohun Roy found the Brāhmo Samāj, while a group of orientalists such as H. H. Wilson promoted careful study of the Indian classics and supported the Asiatic Society.

Among the Hinduphobes, most of whom never learned an Indian language, were Alexander Duff, a missionary who thought the only remedy for the decadence of Hinduism was acceptance of the West through Christianity. Governor-General Bentinck and the lawyer Thomas Macaulay were responsible for making English the medium of education "for the promotion of European literature and science" and for the development of an elite Indian class amenable to the English and their culture. Macaulay thought the Indian "dialects" were "poor and rude" and that even Sanskrit and Arabic "are languages, the knowledge of which does not compensate for the trouble of acquiring them." He thought that "we must at present do our best to form a class who may be interpreters between us and the millions whom we govern; a class of persons, Indian in blood and color, but English in taste, in opinions, in morals, and in intellect."[3]

As for the reaction of Indians to British culture, the emergence of the Bāngālī English-educated middle class in Calcutta is well known. Kopf writes, "Each of the dozen or more intellectuals I have studied for the Orientalist period, 1772–1830, acquired his new linguistic competence, professionalism and fresh mental outlook from some Englishman and generally within an institutional setting." Bāngālī intellectuals indeed did shine in many fields: literature, history, law, journalism, education, and after the 1870s in natural sciences as well. In 1895 the physicist Jagadischandra Bose won a Nobel Prize for work on the polarization of electric waves, and in 1913 Rabindranath Tagore won it in literature. Indians were elated at their success in the intellectual sphere.

But there were seeds of an intellectual nativistic revival, too. Rammohun Roy tried to recover and rationalize the spiritual and ethical essence of Hinduism in the Brāhmo Samāj movement, founded in 1830. Debendranath Tagore, father of the poet, carried it forward to halt the tide of conversion to Christianity. A different reaction to the West was evinced by Ramakrishna, a "God-intoxicated" man who disliked the "single note" of the Brāhmo Samāj but saw Hinduism as "several notes producing a sweet and melodious harmony."[4] The Ramakrishna Mission defended and sought to revive traditional Hinduism. Another expression of cultural synthesis became known to the West in the person of Swami Vivekananda, who lec-

tured in America and England in the 1890s. He rationalized caste and idol-worship and spread the message, "We must conquer the world through our spirituality and our philosophy."

> On the one side New India is saying: "If we only adopt Western ideas, Western language, Western food, Western dress and Western manners, we shall be as strong and powerful as the Western nations"; on the other, Old India is saying: "Fools! By imitation, other's ideas never become one's own—nothing, unless earned, is your own. Does the ass in the lion's skin become the lion?"[5]

Bāngālī cultural revivalism was most personified in Tagore, the father of modern Bāngālī literature, who spoke to China in 1924 warning her of India's experience with Western culture:

> It will never do for the Orient to trail behind the West like an overgrown appendix. . . . The West has no doubt overwhelmed us with its flood of commodities, tourists, machine guns, school masters, and religion which is great, but whose followers are intent upon lengthening the list of its recruits, and not upon following it in details that bring no profit, or in practices that are inconvenient. But one great service the West has done us by bringing the force of its living mind to bear upon our life; it has stirred our thoughts into activity. For its mind is great; its intellectual life has in its center intellectual probity, the standard of truth. . . . We are finding our own mind, because the mind of the West claims our attention.[6]

Kopf concludes that the cultural response and modernizing role of the intelligentsia in Calcutta is a universal process, similar to what happened in urban centers in Turkey, China, or Japan, and asks:

> Should we characterize them more as marginal men or as an intellectual elite? If we choose to view them as an elite, we must also keep in mind that they were an artificially-created class that emerged in response to Western intrusion. Education, sophistication, and often wealth separated them from the mass of their own people, whereas color, religion, and nationality separated them from the foreign overlord. How does one perform as a modernizer under such conditions?[7]

The Disequilibrium of the Heterogenetic City: Calcutta

In spite of the contributions of Calcutta in the 19th century and its leadership in accommodating European and Indian values, it has sunk farther into an economic quagmire with every passing decade of this century. Census figures from 1901 to 1951 show the percentage of people who could support themselves by agriculture in Bānglā declined; at the same time the percentage of nonagricultural people who had to depend on agriculture for a secondary source of livelihood increased 13 times, while in that period the population of West Bengal doubled.

Calcutta grew so large not because of the needs of the Bānglā hinterland but because of outside forces. The British established their colonial capital there because they did not yet have access to the Indian heartland, and they developed the indigo and jute industries for the benefit of England.

In the 20th century it has become an industrial center because of the iron and coal available in Choṭā Nāgpur not far to the west and because of the port and convenient river and rail transportation. As the urban agglomeration expanded and commercial jute cultivation became profitable, rice farmers were displaced. Tanners suffered because the hides were exported. Boatmen lost their jobs as power vessels took over. These people came to Calcutta as unskilled laborers, but had to compete with immigrants flocking there from other parts of India. By 1950 only 50.7% of the families in Calcutta were Bāngālī-speaking, while 34.7% were from the overcrowded villages of north Bihār and eastern Uttar Pradesh, and others came from Orissa and South India. Bāngālīs in Calcutta found themselves competing not only with willing labor from depressed areas but also with people from western states who had a long tradition of entrepreneurship: Gujarātīs, Māṛwāṛīs, Pārsīs, and Sikhs. The history and social organization of Bānglā had not prepared it for the imposition of such a huge metropolis.

Caste came to mean less here than in any other great Indian city. N. K. Bose comments than when the Hindī-speaking migrant comes to Calcutta, he is shocked by the apparent castelessness of the Bāngālī working man and by his lack of vegetarianism and other orthodox Hindu practices:

> It is not merely a matter of urbanization, or a question of the quantity of Western ideas incorporated. It is also a matter of internal change, whereby the character of Bengali culture has been altered to a large extent, which makes the North Indian or the Tamil rightly suspect that Bengali culture is not quite Indian, as he knows his India.[8]

Caste hierarchy, as we have seen, is less complex in rural Bānglā than in most other parts of India, and the jajmānī system of slight consequence. This may have been a factor in the Bāngālī reluctance or inability to become successful entrepreneurs, while because of English education anti-caste ideology took root here earliest.

The unsolvable problems of Calcutta today are well known. From 1951 to 1961 West Bengal increased in population 32.8%, and by 1971 had increased another 28%, to a total of 44.4 million. Already by 1943 it was apparent the region was overpopulated, with the famine that drove starving people to the streets of Calcutta, where they perished. Then came Partition, with an influx of 3 million from East Pakistan, and a continual stream of them until formation of Bangladesh. By 1961 the density in Calcutta proper was 73,182 per square mile, triple that of Ahmadābād and quadruple that of Delhi, and in that year 72% of the families lived in one room. Roughly a quarter live in *bastīs*, settlements with village-like mud and matting houses, or even flattened cans or tarpaulins, while perhaps 300,000 live on the streets. One survey showed that in Howrah across the river the average bastī tenant lived in 22.7 square feet of space, while the tenant in Calcutta bastīs enjoyed 24.8 square feet of "housing"[9]—enough to spread out a sleeping mat 4 by 6. A dismal fact is that there are 141 men for every 100 women

in the city. All public services are overextended—it is a heroic exercise to manage to get into a bus. The inability of the city to provide a satisfying way of life is seen in the slow growth rate: only 8.5% in the decade preceding 1971, while the whole of Greater Calcutta grew by only 22%, which is less than the state's population growth rate.

The proliferation of educational institutions in Calcutta has produced rising expectations which cannot be met, as well as an enormous number of unemployed and underemployed high school and college graduates. Yet 29% of the unemployed, mostly educated to high school at least, express unwillingness to do manual work.[9] The economy of the city's industrial belt ceased to grow in the late 1960s, while strikes, hartals, *gherāos* (in which managers are shut up in their offices until demands are met), and the violence of radical political groups increased until the 1972 elections, which brought at least a temporary respite.

Perhaps the ground swell of urban modernization is taking place in regions where there was a preindustrial tradition of urbanization. The pragmatic traditionalism and puritanical industriousness of Ahmadābād has contributed to India more quietly, but perhaps as effectively, as Calcutta, and certainly such cities have a greater sense of cultural continuity and better equilibrium with the regional social pattern and economic network.

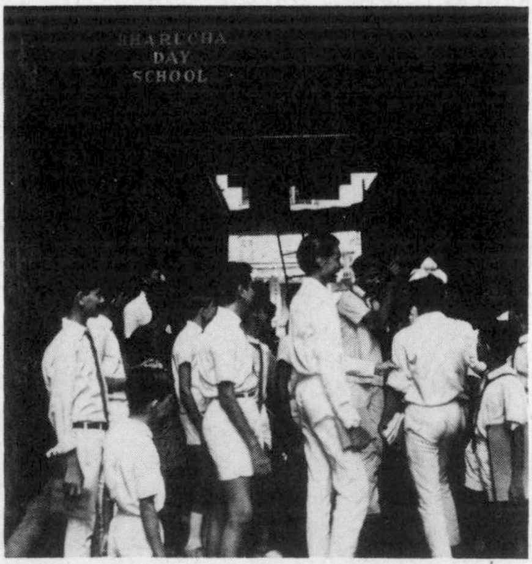

English-medium school in Calcutta. Many of the elite send their children to private schools that teach in English hoping it will help them get respectable jobs. English is still utilized as the chief symbol of urban elite status.

New Towns in Pakistan and India

The difficulties of regenerating the old metropolitan centers are so stupendous that they have been bypassed in a number of instances by the establishment of new towns and cities. During British days a number of well-planned park-like cities were created adjacent to old cities upon which they depended for labor and traditional services. New Delhi and Bangalore

Cantonment are examples of these. The old cities are bustling and crowded while the new ones have strict zoning laws. Such new cities have become havens for upper classes, and many of their residents eat partially Westernized food and speak English in their jobs. In such areas foreigners rent bungalows and Anglo-Indians live, even though their income may not be high. The proximity of the old city is essential to the survival of such a new town, which cannot provide its own services or labor.

An early attempt by Pakistan to create new towns was carried out on the fringes of the Thal Desert which was being reclaimed by the introduction of irrigation canals. The government made the new lands available to landowners. To encourage investment and population expansion into the desert fringes, the government erected three new towns, each complete with schools, a college, a hospital, roads, and electricity, with large brick houses in rows on paved streets. Today the houses are turning into shambles and the government took a large loss on their construction. The new towns are sterile and ghost-like.

What went wrong? First, the houses were not designed according to felt needs of Pakistanis, but were drawn up by people sitting in Karāchī whose architectural training was oriented to Western countries. The yards are not surrounded by walls such as bungalows usually have; neither are they built with a sunny interior courtyard. These two features are particularly important in upper middle class Muslim homes where women like to socialize in the interior courtyard and the adjacent kitchen. These new houses were not built with verandas such as men use to relax in the evenings with their friends. Nor do they have proper facilities for housing servants because they are constructed in a compact two-story design; anyone able to buy such a bungalow would need nearby servant quarters. Consequently people did not come forward to buy the houses. Local peasants could

Housing project in new town in Pakistan. Houses were not designed for local living patterns and had to be sold at a loss. The new town is not flourishing.

Bombay bastīs house hundreds of thousands. The man in the center is taking his morning bath.

certainly not afford them, and big landlords who might invest in the new lands did not wish to come to this remote region to live. The new town was designed with a modern suburban life style in view, apparently oblivious to the need for such a life style to be supported by a far larger number of ordinary skilled and unskilled people. The government eventually dumped the houses at considerable loss, such buyers as there were have not kept them up, and the new towns are not flourishing.

A better planned effort is Islāmābād, Pakistan's new capital to replace Karāchī, situated against a backdrop of hills on the northern edge of the Panjāb plain. With its graceful white buildings tinged with Muslim architectural motifs and its beautiful setting, Islāmābād promises to be one of the most impressive new capitals in the world. It is within commuting distance of Rāwalpiṇḍī, a bustling old commercial city which can provide the new administrative center some support. But it is not near enough, and the job shortage and class structure of the society has imposed itself on the urban planning of the elite. In 1970, even before completion of the civic, commerce, and business zones in Islāmābād, the government was forced to lower the standard allotment of space per person from 47 to 35 square feet.

The hierarchy of the bureaucracy as well as the general class structure compels modification of architectural dreams. When Le Corbusier designed Chaṇḍīgaṛh as the new capital of Panjāb, he was required to plan the housing to accord with the bureaucratic hierarchy; employees in each particular grade of officers and clerks were allotted a certain square footage. The same has been true of industrial towns, such as Neyvēli in Tamiḻ Nāḍu, a lignite mining and power generating town. Separate streets have houses designed for separate grades of officers and workers, while essential supportive services are provided by people who have inevitably put up hutments along the edge. The industrial city of Durgāpur in West Bengal, though reasonably well planned, has around it hovels which in sordidness match any to be found in the "industrial black spots" of the Calcutta area.

New Delhi was laid out by the British early in the century, and the government attempts to keep it spacious and park-like, especially around high government offices and foreign embassies, while Old Delhi is a vibrant and crowded city. But not far from the elite areas are squatters' hutments. In 1967 some 10,000 squatters were shifted by the Delhi Development Authority to a new site, but as of 1970 they still were not connected with the government-owned bus service, only four water taps had been provided (having water a few hours a day), and though 20 hand pumps had been installed, half did not work. Another Delhi bastī, Nāgloi, is the largest with 20,000 residents; it is dependent upon 25 hand pumps and 40 latrines. Commented a newspaper reporter: "About the sanitary conditions the less said the better. The lanes lie littered with garbage and nightsoil, which makes the whole place stink."[10]

The apparent impossibility of providing an ideal standard of amenities

for all India's urban dwellers has caused planners to give priority to other problems. Where public housing has been built, it did not solve the problem, for invariably any pakkā housing would cost more to rent than most bastī dwellers could possibly pay, and would have to be located where the cost of bus transportation would be beyond their means. The government has taken a sudden interest in Calcutta because of political unrest, and has increased the Fourth Five-Year Plan allotment for the city from 400 million to 1.5 billion rupees. But the lesson to be learned is that as long as great disparity of income and a hierarchical urban society exists in South Asia, the moneyed classes will continue to require the services of a preponderance of people who cannot afford expensive amenities. Officials dealing with urban matters are quick to point out that urban crowding is not much worse than in rural areas: in 1961 49% of rural and 54% of urban families lived in one main room. Only 3% of rural houses had built-up latrines, but 19% of urban families had this facility and 37% shared it with other households. As for individual bathrooms, 7% of rural and 28% of urban families had them. Proportionately more families in urban areas had pukka houses, and electricity. No doubt *felt poverty* is greater in urban than in rural areas, as it is in the United States, but presumably even bastī dwellers came to the cities because it was of some advantage to them.

Migrants to Cities: Bombay

Greater Bombay had 5.97 million people in 1971. The general health of the city, as compared with Calcutta, may be seen in that it increased 43.8% in the decade, double the rate for Calcutta. Industrial production is more profitable, and 41% of employed people are in manufacturing. Literacy is 63%. Still, the city faces the same kinds of problems Calcutta does, and moreover is confined to a peninsula until such time as a causeway is built connecting it to the mainland.

Though Indian cities now grow more by natural increase than by immigration, people have migrated to Bombay from many linguistic regions rather steadily. In the decade up to 1961 a million came from Mahārāshṭra, 450,000 from Gujarāt, 326,000 from Uttar Pradesh, 171,000 from Karṇāṭaka, 111,000 from Pakistan, and others from South India, and the Northwest. Most got jobs either as laborers or in textile mills, while some found work as domestics, in stores, or in trades.[11]

Why did all these people come to Bombay? Is it the "push" of the village or the "pull" of the city? K. C. Zachariah's study of Bombay migrants shows that some 30% of male and 20% of female migrants leave the city within three or four years after arrival. People come to earn money for specific projects, such as a dowry or a pair of bullocks, or to earn income in a bad year. The rate of reverse migration for those over 55 years of age

is 76%, which means that people return to villages for retirement. N. V. Sovani cites a number of studies to show that it is not the economically marginal persons who generally leave for the cities; in Karṇāṭaka Brāhmaṇs are the most migratory, "backward" and Scheduled Castes the least. Moreover, studies from several cities show that unemployment is greater among local residents than among in-migrants (who usually have the option of going home, however).[12] Harijan laborers may come to Bombay, but sometimes they are rounded up by a manager who provides them with tickets (which they may not be able to read) in order to work on some particular project such as pounding stones into gravel. Sovani concludes that urban migration is caused more by "pull" than "push" and that the poorest people are hesitant to leave what little security they know, though they may utilize the city to improve their situation in the village.

People do not come to Bombay individually or without connections. Most have reason to expect jobs when they come, which are usually obtained through kin and personal contacts. People tend to come from villages where there is a tradition of migration to Bombay, with new arrivals sometimes taking the jobs of those who return. Even the housing in bastīs is obtained this way. Lambert found for factory workers in Puṇe (Poona), inland from Bombay, that two thirds of all employees already knew someone in the factory before they were first hired and that in almost all cases the employed person gave a recommendation or helped in some way. Lambert found that bribery has become less important than formerly, but that workers believe that "influence" is the prime determinant affecting career enhancement.[13]

Zachariah found that for Bombay certain immigrants tend to get employment in certain kinds of jobs. Gujarātīs tend to go into commerce, Panjābīs into transportation, Christians and Pārsīs into services, Jains into trade and commerce, Malayāḷis into clerical work, Telugus into construction, and Buddhist ex-untouchables into manufacturing. Prostitutes are often girls sent or sold from the poorer sections of Karṇāṭaka. Nepotism in a particular company or government department need not be an unmitigated evil—it can lead to conscientiousness and a stable set of social relations.

In Bombay, as in India generally, people accept that society should be plural. There is no thinking that because Malayāḷis, Gujarātī Jains, Panjābīs, or Tamiḻs occupy a particular section of the city that it forms a "ghetto." Each major linguistic group maintains its own schools for instruction in the mother tongue, which are government-financed, and often has its own cinemas, restaurants, and newspapers. Laboring immigrants commonly know only their own language, but one can get around with Marāṭhī, Hindī, or English. The ethnic divisions are developing increasing political significance, and in the 1960s a pro-Marāṭhī right-wing party, the Śiva Sena, won considerable support as a countervailing force to South Indian and other ethnic loyalties.

The sex ratio in Greater Bombay in 1971 was 140 males to 100 females. A decade earlier it was 151 and the sex ratio (number of males per 100 females) of immigrants from different states was quite variable: Uttar Pradesh and Bihār 560, Kēraḷa 271, Rājasthān and Panjāb 218, and Gujarāt the lowest with 133. Generally the North Indian migrant, especially from the Gangā and eastern plains, leaves his wife in the village in care of a relative and is free to find work to boost the family fortune; there is also the feeling that women should not be exposed to the city. But most Gujarātī migrants to Bombay bring their wives because they are businessmen who get established. The South Indian migrant, however, also takes his wife to the city (though men from Kēraḷa may come without women because of the three-day train trip). Among India's first 42 cities, 13 are in the South and all but one of these has a sex ratio of under 111 per 100 women, whereas all the other 29 have a sex ratio over 111.

The shortage of women in Bombay, as in all cities in North India and Pakistan, produces a peculiar color to the society and may be a factor in some of the volatile behavior. Certainly an effect of this is the flourishing prostitution business, protected by bribing the police. In Bombay prospective customers are beckoned to from crowded balconies without embarrassment, while in the bastīs girls are available for a couple rupees. Homosexuality also flourishes (though this is to be distinguished from male affectionate hand holding), and in Bombay not only are there rows of boy prostitutes, but one hears of men fighting over them as they might over a woman. But with the decreasing proportion of migrants in the population and with the improvement of the sex ratio, these aspects of Bombay life may decrease in quantity.

Social Organizations

Various kinds of voluntary associations and mutual aid societies flourish in South Asian cities, based on caste, language, district, village, occupation, and residence—there are even associations of bastī dwellers who pressure the city to provide piped water and other amenities. These associations are vital to living in urban regions, providing some of the security people are accustomed to in villages. They maintain revolving loan funds, provide news of home village or region, and sometimes act as marriage agent. They also provide avenues for the politically ambitious to gain a following.

Of the social organizations, or *sabhās*, found in cities, caste sabhās are among the most important. We cite here recent studies of four contrasting ones. First is R. P. Khare's study of the Brāhmaṇ Kānya-Kubja caste-cluster. From their home in towns around Lucknow, these Brāhmaṇs have spread out between Bombay and Vārāṇasī and between Hyderābād and Delhi, where they have established sabhās in all important cities. Each sabhā is

autonomous, but all are held together by the caste journal published in Lucknow. Kānya-Kubja sabhās began to be organized about 1880, and numbered 200 by 1930, declined to 100 by 1950, and since have increased to about 150.

These sabhās, as Khare reports, have the function of preserving traditional identity in the face of increasing occupational diversity and geographical dispersal, and enhancing the secular achievements of the members. They are not the same as caste panchāyats, as one old Kānya-Kubja man said, which:

> . . . are prevalent in lower castes and are meant only for the management of individual breaches of conduct in these castes. We never had any need for such an organization in the past, and we certainly did not want to imitate lower caste groups in organizing ourselves.[14]

The sabhās are registered organizations which must meet state requirements in having a governing body of elected representatives with clearly defined duties, and their monies are considered to be public funds. They all have an elected president, vice-president, secretary, treasurer, and executive committee members. Members pay dues of 10 rupees or so a year. The journal carries biographic items of notable personalities, which the editor thinks will induce less prestigious members to better themselves, some discussion of social and welfare issues, and matrimonial advertisements.

Among the specific aim of the sabhās stated in the journal are the education and marriage of orphans, provisions for widows, employment for the jobless, improvement of the social condition of the low-ranked Kānya-Kubjas, promotion of religious education and commensality among the pure and pious families, and preparation of a roster of horoscopes for prospective marriage mates. The sabhās and the caste elites have founded and patronize quite a few high schools and several colleges, among them Kānya-Kubja College in Lucknow. Khare says that the college is paternalistically cared for by its patrons, who visit it every day, though there are some non-Kānya-Kubjas, even Muslims and Sikhs, on the faculty and on the management committee of the college and there are students from all castes, including Harijans. Some of the faculty wear traditional dress, while others wear Western dress and leather shoes, but both groups are likely to keep betel leaf and nuts in a box in the pocket and avoid free interdining. The effect of the sabhās and the educational institutions may be seen in the professions of the "titled" members who have substantially contributed to the caste journal: in order, there are advocates, successful businessmen, physicians, government administrators, judges, professors, bankers, non-government executives, engineers, and contractors. The majority of Kānya-Kubjas, of course, are in less prestigious occupations.

Close to half the "urban" people in India live in towns of under 100,000. Richard Fox made a study of one such market town in eastern

Uttar Pradesh, and particularly of the Umar caste-cluster of merchants who dominate it. The Umar belong to the Baniyā or Vaiśya category, and they formed an "all-India" sabhā in 1929. The aim of this has been to induce cohesion among the various Umar jātis by eating together and to raise the relative prestige of the membership by encouraging education of boys, but more recently it has become involved in politics.

The effect of this sabhā, says Fox, is that the individual Umar's reference group has expanded from the jāti to the jāti-cluster. Until 40 years ago the Umar on the western side of Uttar Pradesh considered themselves higher than those to the east, whom they accused of having once engaged in the low occupation of oil pressing. Even now the ones to the west are more urbanized and wealthy, but do interdine with those from the east at sabhā functions. The old caste panchāyats had judicial functions, but these have been taken over by the civil courts, especially since the Umar live in towns and have access to the courts. Therefore there is now no effective agency to enforce limits on the permitted range of behavior of individual caste members.

The difference between the old Umar castes and the organized caste-cluster, says Fox, is a fundamental one. Instead of being based on commensality and endogamy, the new organization "succeeds only to the extent that it is intellectually subsidized by forward-looking, generally rich and urbanized Umar." The goal of politicians now is not control of the caste panchāyat, but control of the town.

The new organization has helped the Umar achieve the latter goal. In the town council:

> the listing of castes shows a similarity of appointment over many years, with the Umar holding a consistent and a preponderant plurality. There is also often a continuity of family and individual membership. Since 1943, sixty-six individual seats, counting the Chairman's place, have been open on the town council. Only twenty-eight different individuals or families have filled these posts. Every year since 1948 has seen at least one place occupied by each of the two leading Umar lineages, and sometimes they have been joined by a third. For the same length of time, one or the other or even both of the factions within the leading Umar lineage of the town have gained a voice in the council. Every year since 1948 has seen a Kalvar [wine-merchant] Baniya on the committee, and each time it has been a different member of the same joint family. On a different plane, a Muslim elected on the basis of communal backing has held office in the town every year since 1953.[15]

Effective leadership, then, accrues to those families or factions which can muster the support of their respective caste groups or religous communities. A Harijan may be elected to the council as a symbol of the new India, but he neither has much personal force, nor are many Harijans linked with the power structure of the town.

As a third example here we cite Robert Hardgrave's study of the Nāḍar of Tamiḻ Nāḍu. The Nāḍar were a "half-polluting" caste which could

not enter temples nor draw water from public wells, but they were not untouchable. Their traditional work was said to be tapping the sap of palmyra palms, and they were concentrated in the poor and dry southeastern part of the Tamiḻ area. In the 19th century a number of them became Christians and began to flout the symbols of low caste status. In what is now southern Kēraḷa they were supposed to work for Nāyar landowners, and the women were not to wear blouses, for to bare one's breast in the presence of a superior was a sign of deference. A long "breast-cloth controversy" ensued, detailed by Hardgrave, in which the Mahārājā of Travancore (part of Kēraḷa) and British officials issued contradictory edicts as to whether Nāḍar women could or could not cover their breasts. Missionaries held that they should since they were Christians, while the Nāyar landlords felt threatened; meanwhile the hierarchy weakened.

Briefly, many Nāḍar earned money on the Sri Lanka tea estates or in towns and began to invest their capital. They moved in numbers from the palm-strewn sandy coasts to the towns of Tamiḻ Nāḍu and the Christians among them became educated and entered professions. A caste association was formed which "provided the critical link between tradition and modernity," and today they control the largest private bus company in the state, trucking concerns, automobile sales agencies and repair shops, petrol pumps (gas stations), printing presses, and match factories. Many have become landowners also, while others continue to climb palmyra trees. In the towns there are Nāḍar clerks, teachers, factory workers, and coolies. What has happened is that within the Nāḍar caste there has developed a class structure, and marriage generally takes place within the class. The differences between the town entrepreneurs and the rural laborers are greater than the differences between the Nāḍar and other castes at comparable class levels, though even the poor Nāḍar are proud to use the caste name. Judicious exploitation of links with urban areas for over a century, in addition to education and the caste association, have provided new referrents for emulation and proved the adaptive functions of caste in the modernization process.

As a final example, we cite Owen Lynch's study of a Camār caste in Āgrā, called Jāṭavs, who have given the city a reputation as a shoe production center. In the past Jāṭavs tried to raise their status by Sanskritization, but failed. Since Independence they have become Buddhist, an experiment which has at least raised their own self-esteem, and they do not wish to be called Harijans. Most Jāṭavs are engaged to some extent in shoe manufacture, either in homes or in large factories where they are paid by piecework, and though the wages are not high there is little competition from others in this work. They fear, however, that Panjābīs will increasingly take over the shoe factories, and that mechanization will eliminate need for their skilled work.

Caste solidarity has increased, says Lynch, along with economic mo-

bility. This was because the "big men" who had prospered economically could not raise their caste rank without pulling their caste mates along with them, so they started a caste association. These big men are also the ones who are able to take advantage of the various government schemes to help Scheduled Castes—bank loans, marketing facilities, and aid to small industries. The shoe-making business has not been the only means whereby Jāṭavs acquired clout, however. Since they are numerous and live in compact areas, their votes must be solicited. Lynch details how they have increased their influence in the Āgrā Municipal Corporation, and he predicts that political participation is the path that mobility movements will increasingly follow in India. Moreover, "what is happening in villages can be analyzed with the same theory used for cities and can be seen as identical in process."[16]

The Urban Family

Most studies of urban family life have concentrated on upper or upper middle classes and castes, and for good reason: these groups have more complex family structures, while at the same time they are becoming urbane at a rate faster than the urban population as a whole. Most sociologists studying the subject also have interest in what is happening to the joint or extended family.

The primacy of the family is cherished, not only for ideological reasons but also because of the difficulty of subsisting in a South Asian city without such support. True, there is a tiny minority of highly Westernized or radicalized young people in Bombay, Delhi, Lahore, Bangalore, and Colombo in particular and in other cities to a less extent, who rebel on the issue of arranged marriages. But most of these have been educated on their parents' money and will eventually take up careers in the family line or with family influence. An estimated 90% of urban people marry within the caste, generally in arranged marriages, and in smaller cities even among college students arranged marriages are the norm. A survey of college students in Tiruppati, Tamiḻ Nāḍu, showed that the most important factors in choice of marriage partner (which boys and girls ranked the same) were caste, character, education, health, and family position. Arranged marriages (within the caste) were wanted by 85% of the boys and 100% of the girls.[17] Among college girls in a survey at Panjāb University in Chaṇḍīgaṛh (all of whose fathers were literate), 68% would obey their parents and marry the mate selected for them even if they objected to the choice.[18]

Pakistanis and Indians have a tendency to moralize about the stability of their families, in contrast with their jaundiced view of the American family derived mostly from the cinema: "Divorce shouldn't be a farce as it is in America. If it is, sex will become the major consideration and this will affect family life."[19] Among Muslims and in Pakistan preferential marriage

within the birādarī remains strong, particularly because it is the upper classes, often landowners, who have the most wealth to keep within the family and the most to benefit by purity of lineage. The writer was conversing with an educated bank manager in Panjāb in Pakistan. This gentleman expressed the opinion that all Americans leave home as young adults and are forever lost to their parents. He was indeed incredulous to hear that almost all Americans maintain contact with their parents as long as they live and that many have warm relations with them.

M. S. Gore's study of Aggarwāl merchants in and outside of Delhi helps us understand the mixed bag of changes in process. The Aggarwāls are conservative, live in a part of India where the joint family and the inferior position of women are idealized, and have traditionally viewed prohibition of women working and widow remarriage as status criteria, which should be kept in mind in evaluating the following figures. There is almost no urban-rural difference in observation of pardā (90% among the urban and 91% among the rural), opposition to widow remarriage (20% and 19%), and men expressing a closer feeling for the mother than for the wife (55% and 50%).

But urban people are less conservative than rural people in their responses to questions on a number of other subjects: toleration of marriage outside of caste (17% and 5%), arranging of marriages only after consultation with the boy or girl (71% and 56%, with a low of 26% in the urban fringe), acceptance of youth deciding their own marriages (4% and 0%), preference of nuclear family over joint family (23% and 9%), men in favor of divorce under some conditions (23% and 12%), women in favor of divorce under some conditions (8% and 4%), wives feeling closer to husbands than to children (29% and 12%), and women eating after the menfolk (permanent urban residents 67%, urban immigrants 81%, and agriculturalists 100%). Aggarwāls in the rural fringe around Delhi are more firmly traditionalist than either urban or rural people on three subjects: women's status, the family bond as opposed to the conjugal bond, and attitudes toward choice of marriage partner. This exemplifies the well-known tendency for certain traditionalist status criteria to be held by rural and lower middle classes while those same criteria are being given up by more modernized or urbane classes.

Sometimes urban people express romantic sentiments about the joint family and decry its decay. But it is not certain that it is decaying. Sociologists have defined it in a variety of ways, and it exists with diverse kinship systems. There might be a slight shift from the joint family, in the sense of a land or property-owning unit, to the extended family, and if so the change would be qualitative rather than quantitative. But statistically there is little rural-urban difference in family size, averaging five to six persons in most regions.

Among the Aggarwāls studied by Gore in and around Delhi, there is

no real urban-rural difference in family size, membership composition, or acceptance of familial obligations. In fact, the urban joint family turns out to be larger than the rural (8.8 and 8.2 members), but the urban nuclear family is smaller than the rural. Neither age nor educational level is very significant in the percentage of people expressing approval of it, and though more rural than urban people are favorable toward it, type of family background of the respondents is more significant than residence. Surprisingly, fewer urban than rural Aggarwāls (53% and 64%) think that life in joint families causes difficulties—which is probably to be explained by the romantic idealization of this social feature. But more urban than rural families enunciate pragmatic functions of the joint family—social security such as care of the aged and other dependents, and also reduced household expenses. There is a tendency for immigrant families to function as extensions of the original joint families, with more frequent visits home and more fulfillment of family obligations.

An idea previously held, that there is a unilinear tendency for the extended family to give way to the smaller nuclear family in the urban or industrial situation, is belied by the census figures. For most South Asian countries the urban household is not smaller than the rural household:[20]

	India	*Pakistan*	*Nepal*	*Mauritius*	*Sikkim*
Urban household	5.2	5.5	5.4	4.9	4.3
Rural household	5.2	5.4	5.3	4.8	5.6

It is as important for shopkeepers or manufacturers to keep the business within the family and jointly operate it as it is for landowners to keep their land within the joint family. Sovani shows that in the town of Navsārī there is a higher percentage of families living jointly than in the surrounding countryside, but that nuclear families are increasing among Brāhmaṇs. An important reason for relatives to live as extended families in urban areas is the housing shortage. Lambert has shown, too, for Puṇe (Poona) factory workers that those who earn higher salaries or have better jobs have larger families or more dependents. The mean number of household members for workers is 5.1, for supervisors 5.5, and for clerks 5.9. Larger incomes attract more dependent kin.[21]

Singer studied the family histories of 19 top industrial leaders of Madras, all of whom were born in a village or small town. Of the 19, 12 lived in small nuclear households with their families, and in this class of people there is a marked trend toward smaller number of children and practice of birth control. But Singer asks why the joint family persists among seven of these families, four of which are very large. He shows that "for

every item of evidence indicating structural change, there is a complementary item of evidence indicating structural continuity and persistence."

> When the married sons are "kicked out" they may not be kicked very far. They may be given a bungalow in a family compound or a house nearby. Contact is also maintained with relatives in village and town through visits to them on the occasion of weddings, births, deaths, etc., and through philanthropies in the form of a school, a college, a clinic or hospital, or renovation of a local temple. Relatives also come to the city for life cycle rites or to ask for help, and they send children to be raised and educated in the city. . . . Even those one or two exceptional families who self-consciously subscribe to the norms of a Western-style nuclear family have not abandoned their joint family obligations and many features of that system, such as arranged marriages, separation of the sexes in eating and visiting, and doing domestic worship.[22]

And when the children grow up the modified joint household may reappear. He concludes that "structural change and structural persistence are not mutually exclusive phenomena, and that both are occurring simultaneously." Indeed, it may be advantageous for a large family to manage a business or industry. Raising capital may be easier, and there is a "well-structured pattern of authority, succession, and inheritance" and it also "meets many of the requirements of industrial organization for direction, management, diversification, and continuity. Decisions can be taken by mutual consultations and consensus."

Adjustments of Values among the Elite

It is possible to find in major metropolitan centers a tiny fraction of people who appear quite "mod." Though it may appear to the tourist that there are many such people, in fact they comprise only a small percentage of the 2% in South Asia who speak English. Generally they are modern young couples from the upper middle classes, or students in "deluxe" colleges and universities. Some of them consider themselves part of the international permissive society; in Bombay and Delhi at least there are evening parties at which couples throw apartment keys into a pot and draw them to determine who spends the night with whom. Cabaret and striptease has gained in popularity so that the Delhi Municipality announced in 1971 that it would prosecute nude and seminude performances. In a few universities "pot" is used, even by girls; LSD is available at five rupees a trip, and some students take "speed" before examinations. This small minority of students verbally condemns traditional high caste separation of the sexes, expresses no opposition to nudity, and deplores censorship of Western films.

Yet even among these few urbanites attitudes might not have shifted as radically as might superficially appear. Products of the cannabis plant

from which marijuana is made have been used probably for 3000 years, from the time of the soma ritual of the *Rig Veda*; gānjā and the stronger hashish have been smoked for centuries by large numbers of people, and a related drink, *bhāng*, is consumed today at social gatherings and as medicine. As for apparently modern attitudes toward sex, one should keep in mind the enormous range of tolerated practices found in South Asia. Sly love affairs have always been common in peasant villages, while among the upper classes, those who traditionally emulated the Rājpūt model have idealized sexual virility. But the Western custom of dating is scarcely to be found. Writes one Delhi observer, "sex is still sin; drugs are preferred to sex as an expression of dissent adventure," and in the universities "the demand is for jobs, not changing values; modernism is only a pseudo covering for traditional vices."[23]

Most students cherish their family connections, but some can no longer abide the authoritarianism, career planning, and orthodox tabus of their parents, and react as this man in Bangalore:

> It is no exaggeration to say that Father completely dominated us when we were children. We never used to discuss things at home, and he never reasoned with us. I wanted to go in for a professional course, but he wanted me to remain at home and teach: so I decided to leave home, and went to Bombay. I got a job there and cut off all contact with my home. Father was very annoyed at this. He sent one of my cousins to fetch me, and this man finally persuaded me to return. Father tried to persuade me again to go into teaching, which I hated. Mother was very worried because she thought that the situation would develop into a real fight between us; so she persuaded him to give me some money and I returned again to Bombay. I have not gone home since then.[24]

One father could not reconcile his diminishing authority:

> I have serious disagreements with my daughter and son. My daughter is in her last year at college. She is a wild girl with modern ideas of the day. I don't like my daughter singing in a public auditorium or dashing about like a tomboy.
>
> My quarrels with my son are about his spending more time on college activities, such as sports and cadet corps, than on his studies. He smokes, sees many movies, never is home early, and seldom studies hard.[25]

In millions of urban Hindu homes, particularly among Brāhmaṇs and other traditionally pure castes, religious rites are observed and family worship conducted every morning, even though the altar may be a simple one, or even just a picture of a deity in the corner of a one-room apartment. Businessmen do pūjā before their patron deity before opening shop in the morning. But participation in family ceremonies—weddings, funerals, sacred thread ceremonies, or annual religious celebrations—becomes attenuated in proportion both to the length of residence in major urban centers and to dispersal of relatives. Most of the young men Eileen Ross interviewed in Bombay who had moved from the South were no longer interested in

attending family ceremonies, or found it too difficult to attend many of them. Respondents in Bangalore said family ceremonies are not as important as in the past, nor as strictly attended:

> In the past, weddings and other celebrations were shared with relatives. The whole family went and stayed at the wedding house for weeks. In these days of food and housing shortages, it isn't convenient to be either the host or the guest. In those days, too, the parents weren't very particular about their children's education, and didn't mind their losing school to go to the weddings; nowadays children have strict schooling and music, dancing, and painting classes as well; so now it has become the habit to have one member represent the family at weddings and ceremonies.[26]

Most of these interviewees were Brāhmaṇs or other high caste people whose forebears were leisured landed folk who could take the time for lengthy ceremonies. Their children now have salaried jobs. An interesting conclusion was that those who had been brought up in joint families or in orthodox homes felt that they had changed less from the customs learned as children than did those who had grown up in "modern" homes. "They tend to feel happy and secure in the old ways and the support of their parents and relatives. On the other hand, so-called 'progressive' parents help to pave the way for change in their children."[27]

The minority who insist on selecting their own mates do have to face conflict with their parents in most cases and also with other relatives, for marriage traditionally is an affair of the wider family, not just the engaged couple:

> I have told my parents that I will absolutely not have an arranged marriage. They told our relatives and they came to see me, not in anger, but to reason with me. They told me to think of the family name, and how my decision would affect my brothers and sisters. I'm still more of a family member than an individual to them. Finally, they decided that they would let me marry into any caste, but not into any religion.[28]

In spite of such tensions in some cases, Ross concludes from her study that high caste students in Bangalore mostly still had some, if not complete faith in the wisdom of their parents. Not many wanted to part from their parents' moral precepts. The family is still the chief enforcer of discipline.

Salaried employment produces shifts of behavior within the immediate family, whether it be a son or a wife. As one woman said:

> We working wives have no time now to show our reverence for our husbands. My husband is a headmaster, but I am a headmistress, and I have a lot of work to get through before school. So in the mornings all I have time to do is to stand at the bottom of his bed and say: "Utha-Utha" (up you get!) and after that I am far too busy cooking for him to have any time to waste in worshipping him.[29]

Some urban people find they can easily indulge in behavior switching, analogous to linguistic code-switching. A Muslim woman may keep pardā

in the company of one set of people and not with another, or a Brāhmaṇ may be a vegetarian at home but not when he goes away. A college lecturer in Bangalore said:

> I have often seen students hide their smokes and drinks, and even change romantic novels and detective stories for serious books when their fathers are coming to visit them at college. College men don't tell their fathers anything about what they are doing. They *won't* discuss their problems with them because, first of all, it would hurt their fathers to know, secondly, they want to avoid their displeasure, and thirdly, they know their parents simply won't understand them.
>
> Students who change into European clothes at the college often return to their native dress when they go home because they feel they would meet a lot of opposition from friends and relatives; so when the boy goes home for a visit, he conforms to the old ways of the family. I once went home with one of my students to his village. The boy was thoroughly westernized at college, but when he got back home, he sat on the floor for his meals, said early morning prayers, etc.[30]

Most people seem able to integrate new behavior into their upbringing without much stress or troubled conscience; it should not be supposed that an orthodox Hindu, Muslim, or Buddhist background gives way in a sudden conversion experience, or that there is an irreconcilable dichotomy.

In his study of the family relations of 19 top industrialists of Madras city, Singer found several adaptive processes at work. One is compartmentalization of life into two spheres—work and residence. In professional urban work one may wear Western dress, speak English, eat foods and take drinks not acceptable at home, eat with other caste people, and concentrate thinking on practical and mundane matters. But at home the same man is likely to doff his pants and shoes in favor of lighter indigenous clothing, speak his own language, eat ritually pure foods, use little furniture, and perhaps give time to ritual activities or meditation.

Another such adaptive process, enabling a person to retain his religious moorings while forging a secular urban career, is referred to by Singer as vicarious ritualization:

> Although most of the Hindu industrialists are convinced they are good Hindus, this belief is based not on a personal conformity to ritual observances but on a "vicarious ritualization." They contract their daily ablutions and prayers from four hours to fifteen minutes, done while shaving or washing, but maintain that symbolically "the worship is no less." Similarly, weddings, birth ceremonies, sacred thread ceremonies, and other life cycle rites have all been contracted, and some have been consolidated. Weddings which took at least a week in the village are now done in a single day. . . . [The successful businessman] does not assume personal responsibility for carrying out the ritual observances. He delegates that responsibility to professional domestic priests whom he employs for the purpose and to his wife and children, who have the time. He also increases his personal religious merit by making gifts to priests, to temples and maṭhs [monasteries], and by supporting charitable endowments of all kinds.[31]

Urbanization in Pakistan

Pakistan is urbanized to a slightly greater degree than India, but about the same as India's western states. Cities grew greatly after Partition, with the influx of 6 or 7 million refugees and the need to develop a new bureaucratic apparatus and a national economy. Figures for these four cities are exemplary:

	Karāchī	*Lahore*	*Hyderābād (Sindh)*	*Lyāllpur*
1901	136,000	203,000	69,000	9,000
1951	1,068,000	849,000	242,000	197,000
1961	1,912,000	1,296,000	434,000	425,000
1972	3,469,000	2,148,000	624,000	820,000

Several social classes in urban Pakistan have been distinguished by Donald Wilbur. The old elite families have hereditary landholdings. They live in large bungalows surrounded by substantial walls, with cars in driveways and numerous servants. In general they are educated, read the English press, and often send their daughters as well as their sons to college. House furnishings betray a high degree of Westernization of material culture. Most marriages are arranged by parents, and spouses are obtained from within the lineage segment with the exception of a few moddish youth who rebel against this. Because of their landed wealth, this class has maintained control of political and military establishments in Pakistan, and the indirect electoral system instituted by Ayub Khan's government did not serve to broaden the power base. It remains to be seen whether the new constitution prepared by Bhutto's government will enable this class to retain its position unchallenged.

A new elite class of entrepreneurs has developed since Independence. The large industrial houses of Pakistan are each managed by a family; in 1960, 7 of these families controlled 25% of all private industrial assets, and 16 families controlled 40%. Most of these families belong to Muslim trading castes and came from India after 1947; of the 12 largest houses, 2 were in Lahore before Partition, and the rest all came from Bombay, Calcutta, or other Indian cities. They felt, correctly, that Pakistan would allow more private enterprise than India, and in addition the whole economic structure of what became Pakistan had to be reorganized and many new products indigenously produced. Each of these families belongs to a different community (caste) which is endogamous, and with two exceptions, each was from a traditional business community. The Memons came from Gujarāt, while the Khojā Isma'īlīs, Khojā Isnāsherīs, and Dawood Bohrās came from Bombay. The last three belong to different sects of Shī'ās, for whom religious observances and internal religious organizations are signifi-

cant bonds of solidarity.[32] Then there are the middle class small businessmen in marketing, importing, banking, and small-scale industries, besides a host of middlemen. These may be organized into trade associations, each having men of a single trade, often belonging to the same caste; for instance, there is an association of dealers in foodgrains and spices, most of whom also happen to be Memons.[33]

The artisans form another class—shoemakers, goldsmiths, weavers, rope makers, furniture makers. Such traditional occupations tend to be hereditary and caste-bound. Some artisans, especially weavers, have been displaced by large-scale production and have had to take up factory work or casual labor.

The urban industrial laboring class has rapidly grown since Independence as one of the dimensions of urbanization, but their contribution to the economy is not publicly recognized, nor is the pay scale commensurate with industrial profits. Wilbur suggests they need more recognition to function in industrial development, while skilled foremen and supervisors are in short supply because of the bias in favor of desk jobs. There are also a large number of unskilled laborers and the unemployed, who form a class below the skilled workers.

Then there are specialized occupations such as prostitution. There is a hereditary caste of prostitutes who are also trained to sing and dance after the manner of the Mughal court. These girls are in demand because of the traditionally all-male public society of Pakistan's towns. Other people are permanently engaged as beggars; Karāchī has 30,000 of them and Lahore 15,000, whose ranks are augmented by the temporarily impoverished. Giving of alms and engaging in public charities is a requisite of the prosperous, both according to the Muslim code of personal behavior and public expectations.

Lahore has been Pakistan's most urbane city. A Catholic missionary said in 1581 that it was "not second to any city in Europe or Asia."[34] To its Indo-Muslim architecture and formal gardens, the British added a cantonment. It also became the center for the Christian missionary effort in Panjāb, which was successful among the low castes, and Lahore became a city of many schools and colleges. It also publishes sundry journals in Urdū and English and functions as the intellectual center of Pakistan. One can even see large numbers of girls going to high school and college on bicycles. Probably half the people in Lahore and other Panjāb cities settled there as refugees from India. Karāchī, a larger city, is a heterogenetic one that did not grow up out of the soil of Sindh—and in fact the chief language spoken there is Urdū, the only city in Pakistan where this is the case. Karāchī has a mixed population of Sindhīs, Panjābīs, Balūchī and Brāhūī tribals, Indian refugees, and a few Pārsī businessmen. The difference between the elite here and in the traditional towns of Pakistan can be seen in that of the 5000 students at Karāchī University 54% are women, but only 20% of

those who graduate get jobs, for here also men are reluctant to employ women.

Urban living conditions in these cities are not better than in Indian cities, at least for the poor. In Lahore 80% of the families live on less than $10 a week, with never fewer than two to a room and sometimes as many as 12. A medical study showed that 87% of babies born in its slums get insufficient food during the first year and are consequently physically and mentally stunted even before they learn to talk. A third of the infants remain ill with diarrhea through the first year of life, and a fifth of them are reported to never reach the age of one.[35]

Ideologically, there is some polarization in Pakistan cities between the orthodox Muslims and those who vaunt Western ways. In general, orthodox Islam is strongest in the cities, not in peasant villages. Orthodox ideology and behavior is a function of traditional elite status, while peasants are more pragmatic and do not worry much about ideology. It is in the towns that one finds the majority of women in pardā, the theological debates, and the political parties that demand a return to the law of the Sharī'at. Most middle class merchants observe the prescribed Muslim rituals and prayers. There is suspicion of public education, at least higher education, and as a result Pakistan has spent much less on education than India has, and its literacy rate is lower.

On the other hand, material symbols of Westernization are slightly more in evidence than in many Indian cities. Raised toilets of Western type and toilet paper are more common in public places. Western furniture is considered necessary in homes of the educated elite, and educated people ordering breakfast on a train are likely to order fried eggs, toast, and tea, which they consume using Western table implements, napkins, and tea cozies. As a young man from a Panjāb town who was searching for a path to success said, "There are two careers open—to join the civil service or the army." Both of these maintain anachronistic features of the old English elite; the symbol-pool of Islamic orthodoxy, which is the distinguishing feature of the old landowning aristocracy and the shopkeepers, is not sufficient for the bureaucrats and the military officers. But at the same time the government has been markedly reluctant to speak out on issues which might offend the traditionalist elite and the religious functionaries, and sticks to a rigid view of Islamic nationalism.

> A person who reads, for example, an English daily and an Urdu daily in West Pakistan will immediately recognize what we are trying to say. English dailies will carry articles, for example, about family planning, about reforms in the 'ulamā education, etc. but an Urdu daily will hardly dare to do that. This is a manifestation, in the final analysis, of the educational dichotomy.[36]

Pakistani urbanites have not been able to find a set of high class cultural symbols which are not part of the image of India and at the same time are of indigenous origin.

A bazar street in Rāwalpiṇḍī, Pakistan. Edibles are sold on sidewalk. Automobiles reinforce status claims of the elite who can afford them, for frequent horn blowing forces pedestrians to move over.

Bank office in Karāchī. No symbol of Pakistan culture or traditional urban elite status is apparent. In this desert city such men even wear coats.

The Role of Urbanization

By European standards it may appear that a 20% level of urbanization is low. But the scale of this urbanization in absolute numbers is something else—in 1971 it was 109 million, equivalent to two Englands. What are the changes to be wrought by this in the South Asia part of the world? A few trends are apparent.

Is India overurbanized? Sovani replies in economic terms: urban employment is found to be more productive than rural employment. In any case, urbanization seems to find its own level in relation to economic conditions; in the decade preceding 1971 Calcutta grew very slowly and many other cities in the Gangā and eastern plains ended the decade with a lower percentage of the regional population than they began it. But obviously

cities in states such as Mahārāshṭra and Tamil̠ Nāḍu have by no means reached the saturation point.

Are the cities too large? The urban scholar Ashish Bose evaluated the towns listed in the Census on the basis of population, density, and economic activity, and concluded that only 49% of towns having less than 20,000 people are really urban, and he calls towns of this size quasiurban. He also states that a government committee found that a large number of towns having urban-type governing bodies, mostly with populations under 50,000, would be disenfranchised if the criteria of urbanization were local amenities; such governing bodies did not have adequate financial resources.[37] But the larger cities are not stagnant in most areas; in the decade preceding 1971 the cities of over 100,000 accounted for 63% of urban growth and now contain 53% of all urban population. The 9 cities with million-plus populations in India (Calcutta, Bombay, Delhi, Madras, Hyderābād, Bangalore, Ahmadābād, Kānpur, and Puṇe) are said to not be able to generate enough income to spend on social overheads,[38] but in fact the percentage of income tax collected outside these largest cities is insignificant; all except Calcutta are growing much faster than the population.

Do cities have characteristics of villages? Here the answers are not all alike. Quantitatively we have shown that there is little difference in the family. The age of marriage in cities is slightly higher than in villages, and the fertility rate is slightly lower. Crowding is worse, and literacy is notably higher. Qualitatively the question is more difficult to answer. Caste is found in both, though with some differences in function. Secularism, sophistication, wider reference groups, recognition of achieved as against ascribed qualities in persons—it would be difficult to prove that these and similar qualities thought of as urban are found among city laboring people more than among village laborers or farmers. Such qualities are to some extent idealized among the English-speaking elite, and certainly these have more options open to them as regards life style; they can frequent the mosque or they can frequent the Rotary Club. But even among them the pattern of interpersonal relations seems to be almost a constant, and caste hierarchy has been replaced by new kinds of hierarchy. Sovani concludes that Indian cities are neither preindustrial nor industrial, but stand in between.

Are the cities being peasantized? This question has been asked on analogy with cities in other countries which attract a flock of rural poor people. It may be reiterated that in South Asia cities grow more by natural increase than by in-migration, and in any case the life style of laboring people born in cities is not much different from that of in-migrant laborers. Gould has shown by his study of rickshawālās in Lucknow that urban laborers indeed have many "peasant" characteristics, but Muslim ricksha pullers, 70% of whom had no rural kin connections, also have the same characteristics.[39]

Are cities having the dynamic role in culture change that European

cities had? The ability of cities to radiate change seems to be slight. Many anthropologists have stayed in cities while they studied villages just outside, which were scarcely different from villages far away except that a few people had found urban employment. The situation was typical in the village 15 miles outside Delhi studied by Oscar Lewis; the majority of the villagers gave little or no importance to the germ theory of disease in their explanation of disease causation,[40] and this writer has talked with many people living in cities who agree that germs exist but think they are not the cause of disease, only the means. On the other hand, the power elite who set the ideological tone for change in the various South Asian countries almost all live in sizable cities; these people control the direction of change through government, industry, the educational structure, and the communications media. Economically the impact of large cities on the economy is increasing and agriculture has now fallen below 50% of the gross national product. The urban elite are maintaining or increasing the proportion of wealth they control, to the point where the government is actively considering a ceiling on urban wealth similar to that on landholding. While tax rates are confiscatory, the actual tax collected has not succeeded in reducing wealth disparity.

A cogent argument has been made by E. A. Johnson to plotting a denser pattern of rural market towns, rather evenly spaced, with a hierarchical series of towns and cities. A rural market town, with a regulated market, would presumably have a salutory developmental effect on the villages within a few miles' radius, and this has been a crucial factor of economic development in some countries. Coordination of location of diverse government facilities could stimulate the evolution of thousands of new market towns. Johnson cites east-central Uttar Pradesh as having 468 villages to each town, whereas other parts of India have 50 to one, still more than in many agricultural countries. While such towns may provide an outlet for part of the population growth and stimulate farmers to grow cash crops, it is interesting to observe that according to the 1971 Census of India, towns under 20,000 actually declined in average population in eight of India's states. Cities above 100,000 grew 49% in the decade, and the percentage of urban population to the total population grew by 2% in the same time.

Will cities be able to handle the geometric increase in the coming years? Even the best projections of the Fourth Plan admit an increase in urban unemployment through 1975. The proposed Fifth Plan has a lofty aim, to "fight poverty and inequality." The problems of Calcutta, at least, are being strenuously tackled, and family planning is being boosted. Optimists will say that indescribably bad conditions, such as some predict for South Asia's major metropolises a decade hence, have a way of ameliorating themselves in unexpected trends.

REFERENCES AND NOTES

[1] From "The East Indian Chronologist," in Edward Dimock, "The City in Pre-British Bengal," in Park, p. 17. The founder of Calcutta was Job Charnock, the Company's chief.

[2] Kopf, p. 31.

[3] Thomas Macaulay, *Prose and Poetry*, selections in William de Bary (ed.), *Sources of Indian Tradition* (New York, 1958), pp. 596–601.

[4] Ramakrishna. *The Gospel of Ramakrishna*, in de Bary, p. 645.

[5] *The Complete Works of the Swami Vivekananda*, in de Bary, p. 657.

[6] Rabindranath Tagore. *Talks in China*, in de Bary, pp. 798–799.

[7] Kopf, p. 49.

[8] N. K. Bose, p. 248.

[9] N. K. Bose, p. 229.

[10] *Indian Express*, July 9, 1970.

[11] Zachariah, pp. 32, 52.

[12] Sovani, pp. 71–72, 147–155.

[13] Lambert, pp. 179, 217.

[14] Khare, p. 51.

[15] Fox (1969), pp. 190–191.

[16] Lynch, p. 215.

[17] Anna Mathew, "Expectations of College Students Regarding Their Marriage Partner," *J. Family Welfare*, March 1966.

[18] Amarjit Mahajan, "A Study of Attitudes of Women Students toward Mate-Selection," *J. Family Welfare*, Sept. 1965.

[19] Ross, p. 275.

[20] United Nations, *Statistical Yearbook, 1968.*

[21] Lambert, pp. 52–57.

[22] Singer (1968), p. 437.

[23] "Delhi's Permissive Society," *The Hindustan Times Weekly*, July 12, 1970, p. iv.

[24] Ross, pp. 99–100.

[25] Ross, p. 101.

[26] Ross, p. 85.

[27] Ross, p. 281.

[28] Ross, p. 254.

[29] Ross, p. 204.

[30] Ross, pp. 126–127.

[31] Singer (1968), p. 439.

[32] Hanna Papanek, "Pakistan's Big Businessmen: Separatism, Entrepreneurship and Partial Modernization" (manuscript, 1971), pp. 22, 26, 28.

[33] *Ibid.*, p. 11.

[34] S. M. Ikram, *Muslim Civilization in India* (New York, 1964), p. 225; this was stated by Fr. Monserrate.

[35] *The New York Times*, Oct. 25, 1970.

[36] Fazlur Rahman, "The Ideological Experience in Pakistan" (manuscript, 1971), pp. 20–21.

[37] Ashish Bose, pp. 8, 18, 19.

[38] P. B. Desai, quoted in Ashish Bose, p. 9.

[39] Gould, p. 62; see also his "Lucknow Rickshawallas: The Social Organization of

an Occupational Category," in K. Ishwaran and Ralph Piddington (eds.), *Kinship and Geographical Mobility* (Leiden, 1965).

[40] Oscar Lewis, *Village Life in Northern India* (New York, 1958), Chap. 8.

IMPORTANT SOURCES

Bose, Ashish. "The Process of Urbanization in India: Some Emerging Issues," in Fox (1970).

Bose, N. K. "Calcutta: The Economic Background," in *Introduction to the Civilization of India.* Chicago, 1964.

Braibranti, Ralph. *Research on the Bureaucracy of Pakistan.* Chapel Hill, N.C., 1966.

Di Bona, Joseph. *Change and Conflict in the Indian University.* Duke University monograph, Durham, N.C., 1969.

Fox, Richard. *From Zamindar to Ballot Box.* Ithaca, N.Y., 1969. (Social and political change in a market town in eastern Uttar Pradesh.)

Fox, Richard (ed.). *Urban India: Society, Space and Image.* Durham, N.C., 1970. (A symposium with 12 papers.)

Ghosh, Murari, *et al. Calcutta: A Study in Urban Dynamics.* Calcutta, 1972.

Gillion, Kenneth. *Ahmedabad: A Study in Indian Urban History.* Berkeley, Calif., 1968.

Gore, M. S. *Urbanization and Family Change.* New York, 1968. (A study of the Aggarwāls of Delhi.)

Gould, Harold. "Occupational Categories and Stratification in the Achievement of Urban Society," in Fox (1970).

Hardgrave, Robert. *The Nadars of Tamilnad: The Political Culture of a Community in Change.* Berkeley, Calif., 1969.

Hazelhurst, Leighton. *Entrepreneurship and the Merchant Castes in a Panjabi City.* Durham, N.C., 1966.

Johnson, A. E. J. *The Organization of Space in Developing Countries.* Cambridge, Mass., 1970.

Kapadia, K. M. *Marriage and the Family in India.* Madras, 1958.

———, and S. Devadas Pillai. *Young Runaways.* Bombay, 1971. (Based on records of the Bombay Juvenile Court.)

Kearney, Robert. *Communalism and Language in the Politics of Ceylon.* Durham, N.C., 1967.

Khare, R. P. *The Changing Brahmans: Associations and Elites among the Kanya-Kubjas of North India.* Chicago, 1970.

Kopf, David. "The Urbanized Intelligentsia of Calcutta and their Asian Counterparts in the Nineteenth Century," in Park.

Kurian, George. *The Indian Family in Transition.* The Hague, 1961.

Lambert, Richard. *Workers, Factories, and Social Change in India.* Princeton, N.J., 1963. (A sociological study of Puṇe factory workers.)

Leach, Edmund, and S. N. Mukherjee. *Elites in South Asia.* Cambridge, England, 1971. (11 contributed papers, mostly historical, but containing one by E. Shills on the contemporary academic profession.)

Lynch, Owen. *The Politics of Untouchability.* New York, 1969. (A study of the Leatherworkers of Āgrā.)

Misra, Vishwa. *Communication and Modernization in Urban Slums.* New York, 1972.

Mutatkar, R. K., and A. Ansari. "Muslim Caste in an Indian Town: A Caste Study," in *Bull. Deccan College and Research Inst.*, Puṇe, 1966.

Nazeer, Mian. "Urban Growth in Pakistan," *Asian Survey*, June 1966.

Palmer, Norman. *The Indian Political System*, 2d ed. New York, 1971.

Park, Richard (ed.). *Urban Bengal*. East Lansing, Mich., 1969. (Papers from seven contributors to the Conference on Bengal Studies, 1967.)

Prakash, Ved. *New Towns in India*. Durham, N.C., 1969.

Punekar, S. D., and Kamala Rao. *A Study of Prostitutes in Bombay*, rev. ed. Bombay, 1967.

Ross, Eileen. *The Hindu Family in Its Urban Setting*. Toronto, 1961.

Rudolph, Lloyd, and Susanne Rudolph. *The Modernity of Tradition: Political Development in India*. Chicago, 1967. (A culturally perceptive view of the political process.)

Singer, Milton. "The Indian Joint Family in Modern Industry," in Milton Singer and Bernard Cohn (eds.), *Structure and Change in Indian Society*. Chicago, 1968.

———. *When A Great Tradition Modernizes*. New York, 1972. (See especially the sections on urbanization, industrial leadership, and modernity in Madras.)

Sovani, N. V. *Urbanization and Urban India*. New York, 1966.

———, and others. *Poona: A Resurvey*. Puṇe, 1956. (Comparison with prewar statistical data.)

Turner, Roy (ed.). *India's Urban Future*. Berkeley, Calif., 1962. (A useful symposium, but based mostly on the 1951 census.)

Vatuk, Sylvia. *Kinship and Urbanization*. Berkeley, Calif., 1973. (White collar migrants in North India.)

Wilber, Donald. *Some Aspects of Contemporary Pakistani Society*. New Haven, Conn., 1964.

Zachariah, K. C. *Migrants in Greater Bombay*. New York, 1968. (Based on demographic data.)

18

Population

It may be argued that the most successful way of life yet devised by man—in a purely biological and ecological sense—is intensive peasant cultivation, especially of irrigated rice. The magic of this crop can be seen if one compares the population supported in the Gangā plains with that supported in the Congo or Amazon basins where people do not have the habit of plodding in puddled fields. Whole districts in north Bihār, West Bengal, and Kēraḷa have densities of over 1500 per square mile, while eastern Uttar Pradesh and southwestern Sri Lanka have densities almost as great. Large parts of Bangladesh have densities over 2000 per square mile—and the people live off the land. But for the magic of rice to work there must be standing water, and for such populations the land should be double- or triple-cropped and be in symbiotic relationship with the cattle. Recently irrigated wheat has proved to be equally productive.

While the density for India as a whole is about 450 per square mile (including hill areas, the Thār desert, and the dryish Deccan), Kēraḷa and West Bengal have over 1300 per square mile, and Bangladesh as a whole has an equal density. Among industrialized countries the most dense are Belgium and Holland with 830, Japan with 730, and West Germany with 630; moreover, it is questionable whether these countries will be able to

maintain an industrial economy beyond the present generation because of rapid depletion of resources. Presumably the existing peasant populations in South Asia could be supported indefinitely.

However stable peasant economy may seem, though, it is marred by one factor: population growth. Today in South Asian countries growth is 2.3% to 3.1% a year, which means population doubles in 23 to 32 years.

Criticism has been leveled against anthropologists, and justly, that though there have been scores of village studies, few have paid much attention to demographic factors, in spite of the statistical data available in many areas for a century. While some anthropologists recently have considered the general implications of population, we still await book-length studies of villages or limited regions exploring analytically demographic tendencies over several generations and their relationship to ecological factors, land tenure, land use, local resource depletion, livestock population, and such cultural factors as the family, inheritance, and social and religious institutions. Here we summarize brief studies of demographic factors in the cultural history of two villages.

The reader may note the population figures for South Asian countries and states in Table 0–1 on page xix.

A Village in Bangladesh

The village of Dhanīshwar, near Comilla in the densely populated east-central part of Bangladesh was selected by S. A. Qadir for a three-generation study of man-land relations. Population here increased from 140 to 426 in a little over 60 years; it doubled in the last generation alone, and doubtless has been increasing at the same rate from 1960 when the study was made to the present. What has been the effect of this on the economy and social structure of the village?

As late as 1800 there was an occasional tiger or wild boar to be seen in the vicinity of Dhanīshwar, and immigration continued until the 1870s. Throughout the 19th century, in spite of the zamīndārī system, prosperity and amenities increased and "the cultivator had more opportunity for indulgence in his favorite form of gambling, namely, litigation."[1] Around the turn of the century emigration began, which continues up to the present. In contrast with the 1800s, within the last generation there has been little or no evidence of increase of prosperity; any increase of goods or services above the rate of population increase is scarcely noticed because of rising expectations attendant upon education and travel.

Table 18–1 shows how land use has been affected by population growth over three generations. Population has *tripled* while acreage available for cultivation has slightly *decreased* because more land has been required for house sites and tanks. In addition, the number of plots has doubled, reducing

the size of the average plot to less than a third of an acre. Because of this an additional 3% of the land is taken up for boundaries and though these produce a little green grass for cattle, they produce no rice. It is doubtful if production of rice has tripled in the last three generations, even with increase in double-cropping from 15% to 83% of the land. The average farm today is less than half the size it was three generations ago. In this area a family can exist modestly on 2.5 acres of double-cropped land, and though the average farm family has 2.3 acres, some nonfarming families also have to be supported. In Dhanīshwar the average family is in want for two months before harvest. (This village is better off than its neighbors. In the thānā as a whole, consisting of 246 villages, the average farm is 1.7 acres and supports *six* persons, and in 1961 the population density of the thānā was 2031 per square mile in addition to about 600 bulls or cows per square mile.)

TABLE 18–1 Population and Land in a Bangladesh Village after 61 Years[2]

	1899		*1960*	
Number of families	26	(in 1894)	77	
Population	140	(approx.)	426	
Kaccā (mud) houses	68		162	(17 with sheet-iron roof)
Pakkā (masonry) houses	0		1	
Village lands	158.8 acres		158.8 acres	
Cultivated land	85.9%		83.3%	
Homesteads and associated land use	2.0%	(est.)	6.0%	
Tanks and embankments			8.8%	
Roads, stream			1.6%	
Cultivated land per family	4.5 acres		1.95 acres	
Land per cultivating family			2.32 acres	
Land per person			.35 acres	
Number of plots	242		453	
Average plot size			.31 acres	
Plowing oxen	45	(plus 11 non-plowing)	80	
Plows	26		41	

What changes in culture or social structure have occurred because of population growth? In the past there was public grazing ground but now there is none at all; since Partition from India, cattle have not been driven into the uplands to the east because that area is in India. Therefore cowherds have been reduced to few and the pattern of cooperative herding has practically ceased. The actual number of cows has decreased in recent years, resulting in decreased consumption of dairy products. In 61 years the number of plowing oxen has doubled, however, though they work the same amount of land. Each brother inheriting land wants to have his own plowing oxen, so now the land has to support these, as well as the

increased human population. Now the plots are so small that many brothers who wish to separate cannot afford a new pair of oxen, and even if they could, there might not be enough rice straw for them; thus, the tendency to more nuclear families which sociologists have thought of as part of the modernizing process is not in evidence here. Homesteads were formerly fenced with easily available bamboo matting to ensure privacy for the women. Now such fences are harder to obtain because there are few bamboo stands; consequently women are not so well secluded as formerly. The most common subject of litigation originating in the village is land. Hunting as a sport has long since ended; the famous Bengal tiger is not found in the vicinity now, and in fact is threatened with extinction.

Perhaps the most telling feature of this survey of Dhanīshwar is that the number of pakkā (masonry) houses increased in 60 years from zero to one, in spite of growth of a town nearby, rail and road accessibility, "modernizing" influences, and government planning. By contrast, in many parts of India and Pakistan where economic growth has advanced over population growth, tile roofs are very common, and most villages have numerous houses made of brick or stone. But in the densely populated Indian eastern plains and Bangladesh there are very few. Nevertheless literacy and aspirations are rising. Very little of the excess rural population has found an outlet in cities because as of 1961 the country was only 5% urbanized (though there are signs that in the 1970s urbanization increased, with Dacca growing to a million and a half). Six families did manage, however, to leave Dhanīshwar in this generation.

This study was made in 1960, and since Bangladesh's population increased perhaps 25% in the following decade, Dhanīshwar might have grown from 426 to well above 500 people, reducing per capita land by an equal percentage. Population growth ate up two thirds of the increase in productivity in East Pakistan during the Third Five-Year Plan. Whatever efforts have been expended in the last decade on land reforms, community development, agricultural extension, education, elections, or social change, probably the doubling of population within a generation has had more effect than any of them, both in inciting certain kinds of change and in inhibiting others.

A Village in Uttar Pradesh

Let us glance at the records of a village in eastern Uttar Pradesh, compiled by Etienne, to see what has been wrought by a century of unabated population growth (Table 18–2). Population has tripled in a century. In 1861 there was 1¼ acres of cultivated land per inhabitant, but by 1961 this was reduced to less than half an acre. In 1861 there were 93 acres of sandy but usable village lands lying fallow, but by 1890 this had all been

brought under cultivation, there was no more forest, and no more pasture land. While population has tripled, the land required for housing and domestic purposes has quadrupled. But the irrigated area rose from 25% to 84% of cultivated land, thanks to electric pump sets.

One feature which has not changed much in the last 50 years is the pattern of caste-based differential land ownership. Of the 10 major caste groups in the village today, Jāṭs hold 1 acre per person, Ṭhākurs and Brāhmaṇs .75, Muslims .3, and a Harijan caste .24. The proportion was almost the same two generations ago, though the absolute holdings were larger. The Jāṭ zamīndārs have had their estates limited by land reform, but this has provided very few people with more land. Of the 182 families in the village, 21 have holdings larger than 7 acres, 65 have modest holdings of 3 to 7 acres, 30 have absolutely uneconomical holdings, and 40 families are landless laborers. In this area 5 acres represents the dividing line between a reasonable if frugal standard of living, and precarious existence, but if all the land were divided equally, each family would have only 3 acres, or half an acre per person. Further fragmentation of the land is not desirable. In 1916 there were 47 holdings in the village, but 40 years later these had been fragmented into 116, divided into 613 plots! A state program to consolidate such fragmented holdings, initiated in 1964 and concluded after two years of complicated evaluations and negotiations, succeeded in reducing the number of plots to 135.

TABLE 18–2 Population and Land in an Uttar Pradesh Village after 100 Years[3]

	Population		*Acres Cultivated*	*No. of Holdings*	*Irrigated*	*Acres Built Up*
1861	451	1862	565 (+93 fallow)		25%	6.3
1891	506					
1921	731	1916	658	47	50%	8.8
1941	865					
1951	1041					
1961	1227	1963	690	116	84%	27.5
(density 1200 per square mile)						

The increasing pressure on the land has induced some cultural changes and has been accompanied by some improvement in agricultural technology: switching from cotton to more profitable sugar cane as a cash crop, attaching an iron point to the simple ancient type of plow so that it scratches the field surface slightly deeper, use of a hand-powered chaff-cutter, and the seed drill. The ex-zamīndār today has a dozen cattle, whereas his grandfather had 100—but there was pasture land in those days. Here too the number of oxen has increased because of the greater number of farm families. The land has to be used for cereal production or for cane rather

than for crops to produce a varied diet, and crop rotation is scarcely feasible.

Twenty years ago a certain Brāhmaṇ and his brother managed 25 acres. Now this is divided into three parts, but the owners still manage to live fairly well off 8 acres each. One of these three has four sons, of whom one has a job with the district administration and another is going in for higher education and dislikes farming. The two remaining sons will get 4 acres each. Such higher caste people can more easily move to salaried jobs and professions because they are more likely to get educated. But a certain man of low agricultural caste lives with his three married sons and their families. They must keep peace within the joint family out of economic necessity, for if the family split up, each son would inherit 1.8 acres. There are already several grandchildren in the family, and what will they do? There is no need for more landless laborers in the village, and because such low caste people often lack education and outside experience, it is more difficult for them to find alternate means of subsistence. Yet a pattern has developed in this village (and in this part of India) of men leaving their families and going outside to work, either as laborers on roads and construction projects, or if they can get employment, to cities for factory work. From this village 47 men had left their wives and children to earn outside income.

Sex Ratio

Whereas in most parts of the world the sex ratio (number of males per hundred females) is about 97, in South Asian countries it is remarkably high; 107.2 in India and even higher for the other countries, except Nepal. What is the reason for this apparent shortage of women?

First, let us see which areas have the greatest preponderance of males as of 1971. Highest is Pakistan (with a sex ratio of 113), and certain North Indian states: Haryāṇā (114), Kashmīr (113), Panjāb (113), West Bengal (112), Uttar Pradesh (111), and Rājasthān (110). Also having an excess of males are Sikkim (111), Bangladesh (108), and Sri Lanka (106). The central and South Indian states and eastern hills have lower sex ratios; lowest are Maṇipur (102), Āndhra (102), and Orissa (101). Only in Kēraḷa (97) and Nepal (97) are there fewer males than females.

Though this disparity is difficult to explain entirely, several of the factors that cause it can be pointed out. Kēraḷa and Nepal, though having sex ratios approaching the world average, are aberrant for South Asia, probably because of the out-migration of men for work. But this would not explain why Āndhra and Orissa have sex ratios well below the average for India. Rather, it is the seeming preponderance of males in western South Asia and in both parts of Bānglā that calls for explanations.

Could this be a racial trait? Sex ratio at birth seems to average about

103, close to the world average. Could the preponderance of males be due to the selective neglect of girl babies? This indeed might be a factor, especially in regions where girls do not add as much prestige to the family as boys, require large dowries, and are given quite away in marriage—and these features are generally found where the sex ratio is most skewed. It is easy to imagine that in very poor homes boys will likely get better food than girls. However, it is most unlikely that a family living in a village would kill or badly neglect a baby without the matter being known and strongly disapproved throughout the village, and inquiries on this point lead one to believe it doesn't happen very often except perhaps among the poorest of slum dwellers or migrants. In India sex ratio for ages 1–4 is 101; for ages 5–14 it rises to 108, and for ages 35–39 it is as high as 115. In Pakistan and Sri Lanka also the sex ratio increases with each age bracket. Could childbirth deaths be a major factor? No doubt this is a factor in the lower percentage of women among people in their 20s and 30s, but it does not provide the whole answer, for childbirth is not notably safer in Orissa and Āndhra than in other states, and it does not explain why Bihār has a lower sex ratio than Panjāb which presumably has better medical facilities.

Probably much of the disparity in sex ratio can be accounted for as underenumeration of females. Clearly there is a general correlation between areas of high sex ratio and pardā or at least the ideal of careful protection of women. The census takers in these areas must be men, and they must get their information from men. In Lahore Division the census showed the sex ratio to be 113.5, but a resurvey taken by female enumerators in Lahore Tehsīl showed it to be 108.[4] We thus might suspect that half the apparent deficit of females—which is great in the middle married years—is due to underenumeration.

But the sex ratio in India has *increased* from 106 in 1961 to 107.2 in 1971, and this at a time when infant and childbirth mortality has been presumably decreasing, and when longevity has been rapidly increasing, which would normally mean that the population would have more females. Moreover a deficiency of women is reported in states where seclusion of women is not idealized. Even more of a puzzle is Sri Lanka, where women come out freely, and the life expectancy of females in 1967 was as high as 66.9. A population estimate for 1973 shows a deficit of 450,000 females out of a population of 14 million. The sex ratio in Pakistan and Sri Lanka is, however, decreasing slightly.

Whatever other explanations there may be for this phenomenon, it has produced certain effects on the cultural patterns. Dowry, for instance, though it may be given by upwardly mobile castes, seems not to be given as much as bride-wealth in most of the areas having a great shortage of women. Also the difference in age of spouses at marriage is greater; it is 7.6 years in Pakistan. Here one out of 15 or so men does not marry, whereas girls even with physical defects are not left single. Madan says of Kashmīr

Brāhmaṇs that a middle-aged man who has not been able to find a wife is pitied. And doubtless prostitution and homosexuality are at a higher level than they would be if the sex ratio were more equal; this is particularly true in urban areas across northern South Asia where the sex ratio is very much higher because women are left in the villages. And finally, a factor of population growth is the percentage of fertile women in the population.

Population in Sri Lanka and Lesser Islands

Sri Lanka is an example frequently cited by demographers of dramatic population growth due to modernization. The country had perhaps 1 million people in 1800 and has grown to over 13 million (Table 18–3). The population grew about 1% a year in the first half of this century. In the 1950s the World Health Organization spearheaded a comprehensive program of spraying houses and mosquito breeding places all over the island with DDT in an attempt to eradicate malaria. This was the greatest single factor in causing the death rate per thousand to plummet from 46 in 1946 to 25 in 1958 and 18 in 1961 (partly a reflection of a more youthful population). So successful was malaria eradication and other health measures, combined with what was then the highest standard of living in any South Asian country, that in a decade the population growth *rate* shot up from 1.4% annually to 2.5%. Life expectancy *doubled* in a generation; this had the effect not only of doubling population, but of producing a very young population which continued to breed very fast. The life expectancy at birth is 66, the highest in South Asia.

TABLE 18–3 Population in Sri Lanka 1871–1973[5]

Census Year	*Population in Millions*	*Life Expectancy*		*Percentage of Annual Increase*
		Males	*Females*	
1800	1.0 (est.)			
1871	2.4			
1881	2.8			
1891	3.0			
1901	3.6			
1911	4.1			
1921	4.5	32.7	30.7	
1931	5.3			
1946	6.7	43.9	41.6	1.44
1953	8.1	58.8	57.5	2.65 (1955)
1963	10.6	61.9	61.4	2.56
1967	11.7	64.8	66.9	2.41
1973	13.4			2.30 (1970)

Now Sri Lanka cannot feed itself. Though the island is verdant in the southeast, all land suitable for conversion into rice fields has long ago been

terraced; the central hills must be given over to production of tea and rubber for export so that rice can be imported, while the northern part of the island is rather arid. Forests covered 44% of the island as recently as 1956, but this had been reduced to 35% by 1966 after the government settled 50,000 people in the interior hills and allowed squatters on other government lands. Much of the "forest" is in the dry zone and is not productive, so that the country can produce only 75% of the teak it needs for its 800 miles of rail lines, importing the rest from Thailand at thrice the price. In recent years Sri Lanka has exported rubber to China for rice, while it gets vegetables from India.

Sri Lanka was long known as having the highest wage scale in South Asia, and all manner of imported goods considered "luxuries" in India were available there. Many Indian Tamil laborers went there to pick tea and stayed on. Now the gap between the prosperity of Sri Lanka and that of India has narrowed. While the world market for its exports has declined, foreign exchange has to be used to import food. Congestion on buses increases yearly, and unemployment soars. According to the 1953 census 36.9% of the people were "gainfully employed," but by 1963 this had gone down to 30.2%. Meanwhile expectations have increased as literacy has jumped to 76%, though this has not had much effect in stimulating individual initiative in industrialization. The growth rate has come down to 2.3% yearly because of family planning efforts and economic hardship, but people still need children for future security, and the growth rate may not soon come down to a tolerable level because abortion is not acceptable to Buddhists who value all life.

The Marxist government of Mrs. Bandaranaike won the election of 1970 after promising to double the daily rice dole to every person on the island, but the success of its economic efforts may be judged in the spontaneity of the "insurgency" of 1971 which demanded more radical experiments and convulsed the whole island. The Government imposed night curfew for months. And two years later there were dark rumors of more uprisings. This delightful island, though still the pearl of the Indian Ocean, has little time to alter the course which has caused population to increase 14-fold since the appearance of the British on its shores.

Even more precarious is the situation of the three island groups in the Arabian Sea. Of these the Lakshadvīp group is the most crowded, with 2600 per square mile. But the total population is only 32,000, and the islands are part of the economy of India.

Mauritius now has 830,000 people with a density of 1110 per square mile. The volcanic soil is no doubt rich, but the foreign exchange earned from sugar does not grow fast enough to meet the increasing demands of the population, which is mostly literate. The problem is that only half the people are needed for work in the countryside, and the slight tourist and port activities cannot support the rest. The main cause of recent population

growth has been malaria eradication. Slight encouragement may lie in the reduction of the birth rate from 39.7 per thousand in 1964 to 31 in 1968, but the annual population increase is still over 2%.

The Maldives have less than 100 square miles, with over 1100 people for each of those miles. The country can export only fish and a few coconut products. It is connected by infrequent ship service with Colombo, the only city in which it maintains a legation. The Maldives were admitted to the United Nations, but could not afford to keep a representative in New York. The meager resources of these coral islands and the subsistence fishing do not provide any grounds for optimism about the future state of the economy, and meanwhile the birth rate continues at above 40 per thousand.

Population in Nepal, Pakistan, and Bangladesh

Since Nepal opened to wider world contact, its population has grown strikingly. It was 5.6 million in 1911 and grew slowly to 9.3 million in 1960, then to 10.3 million in 1965, and to well over 11 million in 1970. The density is much less than in India, 175 per square mile, but the main midmontane valleys are very densely settled. In this country food can generally be obtained, but many men find it necessary or desirable to go to India for work. The tarāī has been a zone of rapid population increase in the last two decades, again because the region has become habitable by virtue of malaria eradication, and expansion will continue to take place there, along with increased food production. Nepal has various minerals and water for power, and could be industrially productive, but with the subsistence economy that now obtains the country is probably overpopulated. As life expectancy, now 32, rises to above 50 as it has elsewhere in South Asia, and as infant mortality, now 24%, goes down, we can expect rapid population increase for at least the coming generation.

Pakistan has come to recognize the effect of growing population because of its implications for national economic planning. The First Five-Year Plan (1955–1960) was predicated on the assumption that population was growing at 1.4% a year, but the Plan had to be revised when it was discovered that the rate was 1.8%, and before completion of the Plan the government acknowledged that it was 2%. In the early 1960s a growth rate of 2.6% was acknowledged, and the population grew 24% in a decade. At the end of the Second Plan it was claimed that population was growing annually by 3.4% in the western wing and 3.5% in the eastern, and though these figures are not accurate, they stimulated the government to invest more in family planning programs.

A modest family planning program was initiated in the First Plan, but little was done besides establish some administrative structure and popularize the intrauterine device as the proposed method. By 1968, however,

family planning assistance became available over almost the whole country. Village midwives were employed at 15 rupees a month, and they were further paid for each person they brought to the clinics for IUD insertion. Sterilization was also stressed. Impressive figures were compiled for the Third Plan (1965–1970): 3.1 million IUD insertions, 1.1 million sterilizations, and 65 million contraceptive units distributed (condoms, foaming tablets, diaphragms, liquids).

An interesting contrast in the cultural patterns between what were the two wings of Pakistan may be seen in the contraceptive techniques preferred. In the western wing where masculine dominance is more idealized, it is the coils, foam, and diaphragms which women use that have had the best response. In the eastern wing men were more willing to use condoms, while vasectomies were four times the rate obtaining in the western wing.

The Pakistan Family Planning Division reported that these efforts had been effective, claiming that between 1965 and 1970 the crude birth rate dropped from 50 per thousand per year (close to the highest in the world) to 41, that the death rate declined from 20 to 17.5 because of improved health measures, and that the annual population growth rate had significantly dropped. But inaccurate census figures cast doubt on these claims, for both the 1951 and 1961 censuses were underenumerated by 6% to 9%, and the 1972 census by about 3%. Some of the problems of census-taking in Pakistan are: children who die shortly after birth may not be reported; very young children also may not be reported; young females in the house may not be publicly acknowledged to exist, while beggars, migrants, nomads, and others may be missed. The continuous recording of vital statistics on births and deaths is not any more accurate, and sample surveys, while they may be methodologically sound, may not portray the demographic picture of the whole country with sufficient accuracy. The population of Pakistan was in doubt until the census of 1972, a summary one which nevertheless showed that the country had as many as 64.9 million. And apparently the family planning program had made no measurable impact, for the annual growth rate, after adjustments for previous underenumeration, was shown to be a runaway 3.1%!

In 1970 a new program of family planning was devised, based on experimental centers. There was to be a shift from goals such as certain numbers of IUD insertions or vasectomies to continuous prevention or postponement of pregnancies. Male and female full-time workers were to replace the village midwives, and they were to identify all eligible couples in their territory, with financial incentives for the number of couples they brought into the program and induced to remain without pregnancy. Four layers of verification and inspection were to ensure accuracy of reporting, and oral pills were to be introduced.[7] Though this assumes that desire for family size is sufficient to motivate use of family planning assistance, the plan is otherwise sound. Demographers claim that the notion that con-

Match factory in Bangladesh. Employees here are privileged to have even this job; women do not contribute to labor force. Industry must be labor-intensive.

troling family size is desirable has been widely disseminated among villagers, but that teachers and others who might normally be expected to exert leadership are silent on this subject because of the expectations of middle and upper-middle class behavior. Not many of Pakistan's bureaucrats really perceive the enormous consequences of geometric population growth of over 3% annually. Abortion is illegal and will remain so because of the commitment to Islamic ideals. The only grounds for optimism lies in the decision of the Population Planning Council to make contraceptive pills widely available at a cost of a quarter rupee per month, but so far women have not found it so easy to obtain them.

In what is now Bangladesh there is some evidence fertility has been declining a little. But no 1971 census was taken there, and the exact population is unknown; in 1961 it was 50.8 million. In 1971 it was probably well above 65 million, but the claim of the Bangladesh government that it was 75 million was probably too high.

In any case, it has been pointed out often enough that this country has all the qualifications to make it the world's first Malthusian test case, with a density of 1300 per square mile, urbanization at about 8% so that there are few alternate means of livelihood, no mineral resources nor even stones, and no fuels available now. It has only cheap labor and water resources. Over 51% of farms are smaller than 2.5 acres, the per capita annual income is roughly $55, and only about 10 million people are really employed; even the farmers are occupied for only two thirds of their time.[8] No doubt agricultural productivity could be raised by a quarter, industries such as paper and prawns could be developed, and the determination of the new country to succeed economically is a powerful psychological factor. But the population is young and is likely to go on increasing, and even if the birth rate can be brought down somewhat, the number of people is likely to double in a generation. The prospect of the economy being able to support them looks bleak indeed.

Population Growth in India

It can be seen from the accompanying table (Table 18–4) that from 1881 to 1931 the population of British India increased by a third, a rate of growth far higher than that prevailing before the British arrived. Then between 1931 to 1971 it doubled. The decennial growth rate throughout the 1960s, if it persists, will cause doubling in 30 years.

The reasons for the growth in the rate of increase are primarily improved health measures and food distribution; the Pax Britannica was also a lesser factor. Railroads were built in the 1860s, and by the 1880s had extended to all parts of the subcontinent. This alleviated local famines. But in the 1890s a spate of famines was again responsible for lowering the

decennial increase to only 1%. The low growth rate during the teen years may be attributed largely to the vast influenza epidemic which took an estimated 20 million lives in India. Control of communicable diseases and reduction of infant mortality have been uneven, but generally persistent, and have contributed most to the spurt in the population growth rate. Malaria has been reduced to the extent that 1 or 2 million lives a year are saved. Cholera and typhoid, two fearsome epidemic diseases spread by human waste entering the water supply, have had a slowly reducing incidence, due largely to protection of water supplies and improved sanitation facilities. Smallpox has long been a dread disease and in many regions is personified as a goddess; it is still rampant in some years, but vaccination is reducing its incidence. Plague was a killer in the decade after the turn of the century, taking maybe 6.5 million lives, but now it has practically vanished from the land.

TABLE 18–4 Population in India, Pakistan, and Bangladesh 1881–1971[9]

Decade End	*Births per 1000 per Year*	*Deaths per 1000 per Year*	*% Decennial Increase*	*Population (millions)*	*Population India Only*
1891	49	41	9.4	277	
1901	46	44	1.0	281	238
1911	49	43	6.1	300	252
1921	48	47	0.9	302	251
1931	46	36	10.6	334	279
1941	45	31	15.0	378	318
1951	39.9	27.4	13.3	431	360
1961	40.0 (India)	18.0 (India)	21.5 (India)	529	439
1971	37.6 (India)	17.6 (India)	24.8 (India)	673	547.9

Because of this there has been a shift in the causes of mortality. In certain hospitals in western India, the main causes of adult mortality are in order of frequency: pneumonia, tuberculosis, accidents, intestinal diseases, and parasites.[10] The old bugaboos of smallpox, cholera, typhoid, and malaria have lost their primacy to more subtle causes of death, and in urban areas heart disease is about as common as in Western countries. Yet the epidemics still break out; cholera came with the refugees from Bangladesh, smallpox breaks out yearly in one place or another, and in the early 1970s health officials in both India and Sri Lanka became concerned about an apparent resurgence of malaria, due to growing genetic resistance of mosquitos to DDT and also to a relaxation of vigilance against a disease thought to have been largely conquered. Fertility is also inhibited by the millions of persons suffering from nondescript stomach ailments, and the 2 million blind. Leprosy is known to affect 2.5 million persons in India, and probably double that number if all could be counted.

A number of traditional cultural factors have also continued to operate

Leper in Bihār, one of 4 or 5 million in India. Incidence of the disease is greatest where subsistence is poorest.

in checking fertility. Among these are prohibition of widow remarriage among higher castes and in certain regions, avoidance of sexual relations at times of vows or on certain religious days, the impossibility of a young couple living with parents to have sexual relations except at night, migration of males for work, and the high sex ratio. Careful protection of women by high caste Hindus and their seclusion by town Muslims are also factors. The fear of weakening due to semen loss and the valuation of continence as conducive to psychical and spiritual strength may have had some effect on fertility. The lactation period is relatively long, often about three years, and though intercourse is not prohibited during that time, the interpregnancy interval is relatively long. As for indigenous contraceptive devices, some are used in particular regions: half a lime or other acid substance may be inserted, or aspirins, rock salt, or tampons. Abortions are performed with locally available herbs, and old women experienced in midwifery can

tell pregnant girls whom to visit for the treatment, which may cause complications. Certain groups, such as a particular Kavuṇḍar caste of landowners around Coimbatore, have traditionally kept their population down by means of abortion so that their economic strength will not be dissipated.

In spite of these factors tending to depress the fertility rate, married Indian women who as of now have completed their child-bearing years have borne an average of over six babies, of which nearly half died before reaching maturity—though these averages will go down rapidly now. Traditionally if one wanted security in old age, he would need two sons, which meant four children alive, which required perhaps seven births. The need for support in old age is a compelling reason to have children, and as long as there is no social security program it can be questioned whether utilization of even the best family planning aids will, on a voluntary basis, ever bring the birth rate down to the desired level.

Family Planning in India

In the First Five-Year Plan the Government of India embarked on the first officially supported family planning program in the world, albeit timidly, and allotted $1.3 million for the five years. In the Second Plan this was increased to $10 million, with a goal of establishing 4200 clinics under the auspices of state governments. But during the Third Plan the government was shocked to learn from the 1961 census that India had 439 million people—far in excess of even the highest projected estimates. The family planning program was now organized in earnest, and the Ministry of Health was redesignated the Ministry of Health and Family Planning. The goal was to reduce the crude birth rate from 40 to 25 per thousand per year—and it is still the goal. Early propaganda consisted of pictures of model four-member families, with captions in English—so strongly did officialdom feel the need to be elevated above the plane of the common people! But by the end of the 1960s there were huge yellow and red family planning advertisements painted on walls and buildings all over India, with captions in local languages. Soon villagers even in remote parts came to know that the government was advocating smaller families.

There is surprisingly little objection to birth control on ideological or religious grounds, except among Catholics as in Kēraḷa and to some extent among conservative Muslims who believe implicitly in the will of Allah. Most Hindu women seem eager to know more about contraceptives, though their husbands might be less quick to opt for smaller families. The main problems, therefore, are communication and the reliability of the contraceptive devices.

As for the success of the most massive family planning program in the

world during the 1960s, room for encouragement was slight. Different methods were tried one after another. In the midsixties there was great hope for the IUD, and though the goal of distributing it by the millions was reached, the rate of removal was 70% or more that of insertion. Women complained of discomfort or bleeding, and newspapers published suggestions that it might cause cancer. With the appointment of Dr. S. Chandrasekhar, an internationally known demographer, as Minister of Family Planning, emphasis shifted to vasectomies, and this method was then hailed as certain to bring success. For voluntary vasectomies state governments gave small sums ranging from 7 to 30 rupees, or even small transistor radios. Though by 1970, 9 million men had undergone the operation, it was apparent that most of them had already procreated large families, while newspapers carried stories of pathological individuals who had been operated on to fill the quotas, or even operations recorded but never performed. Numbers of men complained that improper operations were performed, and others said they had children in spite of the operation. Condoms were made easily available. Village level workers distributed them by the millions, but a fair percentage ended up being used as children's balloons (and this is reported from Bangladesh villages also). Consequently the men who asked for condoms were given only a limited number every month. In the 1960s pills were not used much, both because of women's illiteracy and because the recurring cost is prohibitive. Other methods such as jellies and diaphragms have been utilized to a limited extent. After 1972 doctors were authorized to perform abortions, and while this method of population control has a potential greater than most contraceptives, according to experience in some countries, it takes a few years for public acceptance of it to reach a plateau. Demographers are still searching for the mix of methods best suited to India.

But whereas the 1961 census showed a 21.5% decennial increase, the 1971 census showed it to be 24.8%! The average annual increase from 1961–1971 was 2.23%. The two most crowded states were still increasing faster than India: West Bengal at 27.2% for the decade and Kēraḷa at 25.9%. Other rapidly increasing populations were in Nāgaland (39.6%), all the eastern hills and Assam, Kashmīr (29.6%), Gujarāt (29%), and Rājasthān (27.6%). States growing the slowest were Tamiḻ Nāḍu (22%), Bihār (21.3%), and Uttar Pradesh (19.8%) during the decade. The states where family planning did apparently have some effect now complained that reduced representation in Parliament was a disincentive.

Many criticisms have been leveled at this vast program, aside from the fact that the *rate* of population growth kept on increasing. Family planning information was disseminated through clinics staffed by doctors, until recently, while villagers tended to avoid hospital-like establishments. Emphasis is on numbers of devices distributed rather than on long-term pregnancy avoidance. Abortion was illegal until 1972. Mrs. Gandhi, while

Main streets of Vārāṇasī (Banares). Streets are always full of people and bicycle rickshas. Wages in this densely populated area are among the most depressed in India. Sign atop building exhorts family planning.

Labor union procession in Calcutta. Such demonstrations occur here daily.

Political demonstration in Comilla, Bangladesh.

advocating many socialist programs, never through the sixties publicly stressed family planning as an imperative. Another criticism is that not sufficient empirical research on specific contraceptive devices suitable for India has been done. This shortcoming is being mitigated by special research centers funded by the Ford Foundation, but it will take some time for results to have widespread effect.

Another criticism is that the family planning program has neglected to work through the media of practitioners of indigenous medical systems: Āyurveda (a Hindu system using herbs and stressing total mental and physical health), Unānī (a Muslim system derived from ancient Greek medicine), and Siddha (a South Indian system using powdered medicaments). Practitioners of these systems far outnumber doctors trained in Western medicine and hold the confidence of villagers more than do doctors in government hospitals. There are many Āyurveda colleges supported by the government, but so far the family planning program has ignored them, as have doctors of Western medicine. But local practitioners of these systems do express willingness to cooperate in the family planning program.

Urbanization of itself did not seem to lead to decreasing fertility throughout most of the 1960s. In 1964 the birth rate per thousand in some cities was lower than the all-India average of 39 for that year: Calcutta (22), Bombay (29), Delhi (32), Ahmadābād (37), but these are all cities having a distorted sex ratio. Other cities at the same time had birth rates higher than the population as a whole: Madras (40), Bangalore (45), New Delhi (45).[11]

But there were signs that by 1971 the high point in Indian fertility had been passed, even though the decennial census showed a growth of 24.8%. The urban birth rate per thousand that year was 32.8, probably because of the greater availability of contraceptive devices. The birth rate for all India had come down from 40 per thousand in 1961 to 37.6—still far from the goal of 25. Meanwhile the death rate has been falling rapidly, from 27.5 per thousand per year to 17.6. The average child born in India today can expect to live to be 52.5 years, up from 30 in 1947. Surely this is one of the most significant achievements of India since Independence, duly noted in the Silver Jubilee celebrations in 1972.

In the 1970s under the Fourth and Fifth Plans family planning is receiving serious attention. The aim is still to bring the death rate down to 25 per thousand, and to do this a health center will be built for each 10,000 inhabitants. Over 5000 primary centers and 26,000 subcenters have already been set up. The pill will be more widely used, and research will soon make other techniques available. Up to 1972, 10.6 million sterilization operations had been performed, a quarter of them on women. Vasectomy "fairs" are being set up in which men are given 100 rupees and their wives sārīs; 63,000 men were sterilized in one such fair in Kēraḷa. Mahārāshṭra was the first state to legislate economic disincentives in certain public programs for

couples with more than three children. It is estimated that so far 10 million births have been averted. But meanwhile the population continues to increase at an unacceptable rate, 2.2% yearly.

Population and the Future

Notwithstanding the progress on all fronts, it appears to this author that the 1970s will lead to a population crunch, unless demographic factors can be stabilized. But the population has a young median age so will continue to be highly fertile for some years. Mrs. Gandhi has stated unwillingness to go beyond voluntary controls. After the agricultural miracle of 1968–1971 can another miracle be expected to provide 25% more food by 1981? And the following decade?

The overoptimistic statements by the Government of India in 1971 that self-sufficiency in food had been attained and that exports might be possible, were cast under the pall of widespread and severe drought already by 1972–1973, with loss of grain and cattle across western India and a decline of industrial production because of hydroelectric power shortages. And aside from the question of food, what about other aspirations? Shanti Tangri has calculated that if urban growth is 4% annually (less than in many other Asian countries), the provision of a minimum acceptable standard of housing will require 8.3% of the national income, and there would then still be a shortage of 16 million urban housing units in 1981. Square footage of urban housing available per capita declined from 113 in 1921 to 91 in 1951 and to 70 in 1966, not just because of the population growth rate, but because new housing units have not been built, while bastīs have proliferated. Shortages of all kinds continue to plague the consumer, from newsprint to synthetic textiles, as any resident of India knows.

The question of unemployment is even more serious. By the end of the Fourth Plan in 1975 India will require 22.1 million more *urban* jobs and 56.4 million *rural* jobs. But more cultivators are not needed, while urbanization and employment in the organized sector can scarcely proceed faster than at present. The Indian unemployment registers, with the names of nearly 2 million educated people, are being augmented by 200,000 yearly, and few of these are placed commensurate with training and expectations. The initial Fourth Plan proposals acknowledged an expected 28 million unemployed by the end of the plan,[12] and whether revisions to provide for more employment will be successful remains to be seen. In its 25th anniversary celebrations India cited its accomplishments: striking rises in longevity, near doubling of literacy, doubling of food production, tripling of industrial production, declining reliance on foreign aid by two thirds, and nearly doubling exports. Still, in 1970 the Gross National Product increased at only 2.6%, while population increased over 2.2%.

It is easy for outsiders to blame the socialist policies of the government: emphasis on distribution of wealth rather than on production, limitations on expansion of large successful private concerns, requirements that new plants be built in less developed areas, rigid limitations and licensing of imported components and raw materials, a cumbersome procedure for obtaining industrial licenses, bureaucratic delays, and a taxation rate on both corporate and personal income that ranks among the highest in the world and invites widespread evasion. But the idealism of the Government has been genuine, and it is ready to make an all-out assault on "poverty" in the Fifth Plan. It is now acknowledged that nearly 40% of the people of India live below the "poverty line," set at 40 rupees, or $5, a month.

The social scientist can no longer ignore the relationship between demographic factors, unmet aspirations, and the kind of political disorganization or violent rending of the social fabric that one can observe in several parts of the world. Both within India and in other countries it seems that a pattern is discernible that regions having very dense populations with rising and unmet expectations break out with spontaneous violence: Java in 1966, Egypt in 1967, southern Nigeria in 1969, Sri Lanka in 1971, Bangladesh in 1971, the Philippines in 1972, Burundi in 1973. In such situations social and political trends may veer sharply in unexpected directions.

The pattern is consistent within India also. The two states with densest populations are Kēraḷa and West Bengal, and both have high literacy rates. These are the two chronic problem states of India, with the longest records of political instability. Kēraḷa twice elected communist governments, and both times the state had to be taken over by the Central Government. The election of 1967 brought to power in West Bengal a coalition government of 14 parties, and the state became notorious for daily political murders in Calcutta and expropriation of land by rural gangs through 1972; industries began moving out. The two states having the next densest populations are Bihār and Uttar Pradesh. Both have a very low level of subsistence, and the governments of both states have at times ceased to function and have been taken over by the Central Government. As disaffection with government and hard economic conditions increased in the 1970s there were riots in both states.

After the Bangladesh war Indians everywhere rallied to the Government, and the food situation was good. But within two years violence again began breaking out. The specific causes were said to be demands for a separate state in part of Āndhra, food shortages in Mahārāshṭra, maladministration in Orissa, a police revolt in Uttar Pradesh, and kidnapping of children in Bihār. These are all symptoms of a deeper pessimism. Per capita income actually declined in India in 1972, due to the drought and famine across the bank of western states, but it is seldom publicly acknowledged that an increase of 14 million in the population of the nation during that year was partly responsible. Disaffection with government in general

was reported by newspapers with such headlines as "India's Problems Growing Worse," and 1973 saw a decline in the level of employment, in the industrial growth rate, and in confidence in government in general, though a timely monsoon brought assurance of food supplies for the following year. But in the same year there were rumors of impending disturbances in Sri Lanka, which suffered a decline of 1.1% in Gross National Product and a high suicide rate. In Bangadesh political murders numbered some 2000 in 18 months and an array of radical parties was sprouting. Two years after achieving independence the economy seemed to be deteriorating, with few exports to buy imports, continuing food shortages, and unprecedented burglaries by gangs of armed youths. It seems highly doubtful to this author that the *compounded* population growth which is still nearly 25% in a decade can be peaceably accommodated, given the sluggish rate of economic growth and the conclusion of the green revolution. Surely this generation will be the generation of the population crunch, accompanied by abrupt and unpredictable shifts in the political structure and in social values; some predict that this will occur, beginning in Bangladesh and eastern India, by the latter half of the 1970s.

It has been said of Indian history that one of the qualities in the subcontinent is a timelessness that enables it to somehow muddle along and ride out what appear to be imminent crises. But the looming shadow is not a cultural intrusion such as precipitated previous crises, but is essentially biological in nature. Whether the discussions in this book of South Asian village life will remain valid after a decade may be judged by the reader. But there is no doubt that among all major world regions South Asia is, in statistical terms, by far the most precarious. This alone makes it worthy of our attention, and we can surely expect an increasing level of newsworthy reports from this segment of the world in the next few years.

REFERENCES AND NOTES

[1] Qadir, p. 37.

[2] Qadir, pp. 38–89.

[3] Etienne, pp. 52–69.

[4] M. S. Anwar, "A Study of the Relative Completeness of Quarterly and Annual Surveys for the Collection of Demographic Data," in *Pakistan Sociological Studies* (Lahore, 1965).

[5] *Census of Population, Ceylon, 1963 and 1971; United Nations Demographic Yearbook*, 1970.

[6] Lee Bean, "Pakistan's Population in the 1970s: Certainties and Uncertainties" (manuscript, The Population Council, New York).

[7] Bean, p. 15.

[8] K. L. Seth, *Economic Prospects of Bangla Desh* (New Delhi, 1972), p. 85.

[9] See Freymann, p. 156; *Census of India 1971, Provisional Population Totals,* p. 35. Birth and death rates 1951–1971 are for final year only.

[10] *United Nations Demographic Yearbook*, 1968.
[11] Government of India, *Vital Statistics of India for 1963 and 1964* (New Delhi, 1968).
[12] Nair, pp. 221–225.

IMPORTANT SOURCES

Agarwala, S. N. *Population*. Delhi, 1967.

Bhatia, B. M. *Famines in India 1860–1965*, 2d ed. New York, 1967.

Chandrasekhar, S. *Asia's Population Problems*. New York, 1967.

———. *Infant Mortality, Population Growth and Family Planning in India*. Chapel Hill, N.C., 1972. (By the best-known authority on this subject.)

Dandekar, Kumudini. *Demographic Survey of Six Rural Communities*. Bombay, 1959. (A study of contrasting diets and modes of subsistence in Mahārāshṭra villages.)

Davis, Kingsley. *The Population of India and Pakistan*. Princeton, N.J., 1957. (Outdated, but a pioneer study.)

Driver, Edwin. *Differential Fertility in Central India*. Princeton, N.J., 1963.

Etienne, Gilbert. *Studies in Indian Agriculture: The Art of the Possible*, trans. Megan Mothersole. Berkeley, Calif., 1968.

Europa Year Book, The. London, 1972.

Freymann, Moye. "India's Population Program," in Robert Crane (ed.), *Transition in South Asia*. Durham, N.C., 1970.

Government of Ceylon. *Census of Population, Ceylon, 1963* and *1971*, Colombo.

Government of Ceylon, *Statistical Abstract of Ceylon, 1966*. Colombo.

Government of India. *Census of India, 1961*. New Delhi. (Published throughout the 1960s and comprising some 1500 volumes.)

Government of India. *Census of India, 1971: Changes in Sex Ratio*. New Delhi, 1972.

Government of India. *Census of India, 1971: Housing Reports and Tables*. New Delhi, 1972. (A volume for each state.)

Government of India. *Census of India, 1971: Intercensal Growth of Population*. (Population trends in 100 years of census taking.)

Government of India. *Census of India, 1971: Provisional Population Totals*. New Delhi, 1971. (This census is being published throughout the 1970s.)

Government of Pakistan. *Census of Pakistan Population, 1961*, Karachi; and *1972*, Islāmābād.

Jones, Gavin, and S. Selvaratnam. *Population and Economic Development in Ceylon*. Colombo, 1972.

Krishnamurthy, K. G. *Research in Family Planning in India*. Delhi, 1961.

Mankekar, Kamla. *Abortion: A Social Dilemma*. Delhi, 1973.

Mehta, Balraj. *Crisis of Indian Economy*. New Delhi, 1973.

Nair, Kusum. *The Lonely Furrow: Farming in the U.S., Japan, and India*. Ann Arbor, Mich., 1969. (The last part discusses economic and demographic tendencies.)

Nawaz, Mohammad. *Unemployment in Pakistan*. Lahore, 1973. (A Progressive Series pamphlet.)

Pakistan Sociological Association. *Pakistan Sociological Studies*. Lahore, 1965. (Includes some papers on population.)

Qadir, S. A. *Village Dhanishwar: Three Generations of Man-Land Adjustments in an East Pakistan Village*. Comilla, 1964.

Schultz, T. Paul, and Julie DaVanzo. *Analysis of Demographic Change in East Pakistan: A Study of Retrospective Survey Data*. Santa Monica, Calif., 1970.

Tangri, Shanti. "Urban Growth, Housing, and Economic Development: The Case of India," *Asian Survey*, July 1968.

United Nations Demographic Yearbook, 1970.

Weiner, Myron. *The Politics of Scarcity: Public Pressure and Political Response in India*. Chicago, 1962. (Statistically outdated, but a useful approach.)

Index

abbreviations

Afgh.	Afghanistan	h.	history
anc.	ancient	lang.	language or language group
arch.	archeological site or period	lin.	lineage
Bang.	Bangladesh	Pak.	Pakistan
c.	caste or caste cluster	R.	river
d.	deity	tr.	tribe
dy.	dynasty		

Spindler, John Hitchcock, and Alan Beals also made helpful suggestions about the work in general. Particular chapters in draft form were read by the following: Lionel Caplan, C. von Fürer-Haimendorf, A. M. K. Aminul Islam, Jerome Jacobson, Hafeez Malik, Marcha Tatkon, Helen Ullrich, and Baidya Varma. Dhanesh Jain and Zahid Sharif made notes on diacritical marks, and A. Chandrasekhar helped gather samples of scripts. And, above all, thanks are due to the countless people in South Asian villages and towns, ever hospitable and always ready to sit down and talk with the inquiring anthropologist. It is the deeply satisfying interpersonal relations one has with the people of South Asia that draw one back time after time.

C. M.

sistent local cultural systems. Thus this volume represents a diachronic approach, the companion volume a synchronic one.

It is suggested that each chapter in the companion volume be read as follows after the appropriate chapter in this volume:*

Chapter in This Volume	*Chapter in* South Asia: Seven Community Profiles	*Author*
11	1. A Village in Karṇāṭaka: Mapping Everyday Life in Śivapur	K. Ishwaran
11	2. A Village in Sri Lanka: Mädagama	G. Obeyesekere
12	3. Rural Communities in Bangladesh: Hājipur and Tinpāṛā	Peter Bertocci
13	4. A Village in Pakistani Panjāb: Jalpānā	Saghir Ahmad and Hamza Alavi
14	5. A Himālayan People: Limbūs of Nepal	Lionel Caplan
15	6. A Central Indian Tribal People: Rāj Gōṇḍs	C. von Fürer-Haimendorf
10 or 17	7. Cities on the North Indian Plain: Contrasting Lucknow and Kānpur	Harold Gould

Although the names of a large number of social scientists appear in the text, together with summaries or references to their works, there are others too numerous to incorporate. Generally, however, their works are listed in the bibliographies following each chapter. I was raised in India, lived there many years, and have been to almost all parts of South Asia, but most of the scientific observations in this book have been drawn from the works of other scholars. And I can only hope that their ideas are represented with a minimum of distortion. I have tried to draw from the works of South Asians as well as Westerners, for their research, in India at least, is equal in quality and now supersedes in quantity the work of Western observers. For some parts of South Asia, such as Pakistan and Bhutan, there are almost no anthropological studies, so that what is said about such regions is based on personal knowledge and must be regarded as tentative.

It is strongly recommended that readers become familiar with the names of the states in India and the provinces of Pakistan before *proceeding with the text. Use the map (Fig. 0–1) and table (Table 0–1), on pages xviii and xix respectively, designed for this purpose.*

I wish to thank those who have helped in the progress of this work. Paul Hiebert read the whole manuscript and made useful notes. George

* Color filmstrips of the communities described in *South Asia: Seven Community Profiles* are available. Each was taken in the particular village, tribe, or city described, and consists of 50 to 70 frames accompanied by a commentary. The cost is nominal. Orders, or requests for quotations, may be sent to the author, in care of College Department, Holt, Rinehart and Winston, Inc., 383 Madison Ave., New York, N.Y., 10017.

existing works on the anthropology of South Asia to deal only with parts of it or with particular topics. The study of Hindu society has been a hardy favorite with social scientists, often to the neglect of Muslims, who comprise a quarter of the population of the subcontinent. Similarly, many observers have concentrated on the Indian geographical heartland to the neglect of the South and the Himālayas.

The approach of this volume is not that of highly structured social anthropology; it is cultural anthropology in its broadest sense. One cannot appreciate South Asian society by looking at it only as it is today; hence Chapters 2 through 6 incorporate a large element of prehistory and history, viewed in anthropological perspective. There are no existing books that blend this analysis of contemporary society with a review of South Asian prehistoric archeology, history, linguistics, and human physical variation.

In view of the escalating crises in the subcontinent, one is not justified in studying South Asian society only in its classical form or as an ideal system. Urbanization is increasing, new elites are being formed, government planning is playing a larger role, and demographic factors keep intruding into every facet of social science research. However, since 80% of South Asians live and work in villages, the largest part of the book deals directly with village life. Four studies in the companion volume describe particular villages.

Several theoretical insights have been generated by the anthropological data garnered from South Asia, particularly in the areas of caste and social hierarchy, interaction of formal and informal levels of religion, the role of villages in a complex society, peasant subsistence economy, civilizational development, and evolution of linguistic patterns in a civilizational area. I have not thought this book the place to distill any grand universal theories of my own, but have attempted to introduce the main points of a large number of scholars, often juxtaposing contrastive views. One aspect likely to draw criticism, especially from South Asians, is the tone of pessimism regarding population and the economy which prevails in the latter part of the book, but my conscience would not allow any alternative treatment.

While this book and the companion volume, *South Asia: Seven Community Profiles,* may each be used independently, they are designed to complement each other. Seven well-known anthropologists wrote the community profiles especially for the companion volume, and the studies represent seven geographical zones of the subcontinent as delineated in this volume. Of the seven studies, four are of villages, two of "tribes," and one of an urban area. This volume treats such topics as religion, family structure, and subsistence as discrete anthropological topics (political anthropology is treated more fully in some of the community profiles); in general the companion volume presents profiles of living, functioning, and internally con-

Preface

This volume aims to present as completely as possible an anthropology of the South Asian subcontinent. It may be used as a college textbook, either alone or with the companion volume, *South Asia: Seven Community Profiles*, edited by Clarence Maloney (New York: Holt, Rinehart and Winston, Inc., 1974).

The countries that comprise South Asia are:

India	Nepal
Pakistan	Bhutan
Bangladesh	Sikkim
Sri Lanka (Ceylon)	Mauritius
Afghanistan (in part)	Maldive Islands

The vast area of South Asia is comparable to the subcontinent of Europe in size, population, number of major languages, geographical and ethnic variation, while actually surpassing it in diversity of peripheral peoples. One of the marked features of traditional Indian society is the evolution of mechanisms to accommodate the most heterogeneous ethnic and cultural groups within the broad framework of its civilization. Despite the incredible variation, however, there has been an unfortunate trend for

ILLUSTRATION CREDITS

All the photographs were taken by the author, with the exception of those illustrations found on the following pages and which are gratefully acknowledged: Archaeological Survey of India: pp. 64, 68, 69, 73, 87, 88, 108, 126, 170; Cambridge University Press: pp. 76, 94, 132, 180; Lionel Caplan: p. 403; Pakistan Consulate, New York: pp. 185, 223, 262, 528, 545; Vales, Madras: pp. 100, 141.

Library of Congress Cataloging in Publication Data

Maloney, Clarence
Peoples of South Asia.

1. South Asia—Civilization. 2. Ethnology—South Asia.
3. Villages—South Asia. I. Title.
DS335.M32 301.29'54 73–17484
ISBN 0–03–084969–1

Printed in the United States of America.
3 4 5 6 7 038 9 8 7 6 5 4 3 2 1

Peoples of South Asia

CLARENCE MALONEY
Seton Hall University

HOLT, RINEHART AND WINSTON, INC.
New York Chicago San Francisco Atlanta
Dallas Montreal Toronto London Sydney

Peoples of South Asia